ORGANIZATIONAL
PSYCHOLOGY
& BEHAVIOR

AN INTEGRATED APPROACH TO
UNDERSTANDING THE WORKPLACE

SECOND EDITION

ZINTA S. BYRNE

Kendall Hunt
publishing company

www.kendallhunt.com
Send all inquiries to:
4050 Westmark Drive
Dubuque, IA 52004-1840

BRIEF CONTENTS

CONTENTS

PREFACE

What Is the Vision for the Book?

After having taught courses in organizational psychology for over 20 years, worked in industry for over 13 years, and consulted to organizations for over 20 years, I struggled to find a textbook for teaching organizational psychology that incorporated both theory and practice for upper-level undergraduates and first-year graduate students. Nothing captured the integration of Organizational Psychology and Organizational Behavior (OB), which seemed so natural to me.

Textbooks providing both depth and breadth on organizational psychology are nearly impossible to find. Most publishers want an Industrial/Organizational (IO) Psychology textbook, which honors the discipline, but fails to meet the needs of the client—the student. Not all students take both industrial psychology and organizational psychology courses and not all schools offer a single integrated course for which the single IO psych textbook would suffice. Thus, with only half a book devoted to each discipline, the students are left with only broad and fundamental coverage of both topics, and an inadequate coverage of each topic if taught alone. I wasn't satisfied!

Traditional organizational behavior books provide case studies of organizations relevant at the time of book's printing, but many become outdated fast and the inclusion of these case studies results in a very pricey textbook. The applied focus of these books is definitely a strength, but renders the review of theory non-existent or cursory at best. Although the application is great, without the scaffolding of theory to make sense of why or how the application works, students are unable to develop new approaches and solutions when confronted with a different situation than that described in the text. But isn't that the "real world"? The situation you face at work is rarely the same as what you read in your textbook.

Because I wanted a theory and research strong book and also like the colorful practice-oriented organizational behavior books, I aimed for something that could leverage the strengths of each: provide theory, research evidence (to promote more evidence-based practice), and application to make the material understandable in the classroom and also useful on the job. To incorporate the value of case studies without increasing the cost of the book or adding the case study outside of the concepts to which it provides clarity, I incorporated many case study-like examples embedded in the text itself. Thus, every chapter includes examples of companies from around the world and how they have or are implementing and using the principles in the textbook. In addition, several chapters include a "Company Example" enclosed in a graphic box to highlight a particular setting or situation that showcases a concept

from that chapter. Hopefully this book captured my desire to integrate organizational psychology and organizational behavior into a rich and comprehensive textbook that is useful in either course, and most valuable to students of either and/or both disciplines.

What Is My Approach?

My approach to the book is heavily influenced by my background and vision for the book. I wanted the book to be enjoyable and easy to read and represent a conversation-like style that could appeal to anyone. Some concepts give students' grief every year and so in those sections, I offer a variety of simplified analogies for understanding the material—analogies that have worked with students and that they noted I absolutely must include in the book. Thus, the book had to make complex and hard to understand concepts easy to grasp, while also sharing why the concepts were helpful to learn.

History and research methods are incorporated in the chapters throughout the book. There is no history chapter and no methods chapters, although the first chapter provides an initial time line and overview of how organizational psychology and organizational behavior started. The textbook, therefore, assumes students have a basic understanding in research methods and statistics. In terms of history, when it occupies its own chapter, I found students learn the history for that chapter but it is disassociated with the content to which it belongs. It's no surprise then that connecting history to its content simply doesn't happen. Learning about history just for the sake of history means you're just learning it to check a box; to say you had it in a course. Chapter one provides a historical map for the evolution of Organizational Psychology and Organizational Behavior, clearly showing how the two disciplines should be integrated in this textbook, but when history is necessary for understanding the evolution of a specific topic, like leadership for example, that history is provided in that chapter. Therefore, the history of the development of our theories and models of leadership are in Chapter 9. Likewise, the historical development of strategy is in Chapter 13—the chapter on strategy.

Another aspect of my approach to the book is the directional flow—that is, the book tells a basic story about how you enter an organization, work in it, and experience it, challenges you face in the organization, how you understand what to do and why, and where you fit into the organization. Ultimately, the story ends with where the organization itself is going—that is, the strategy.

It was a challenge to decide which direction to write the story flow—top to bottom (start with strategy and end with socialization) or bottom to top, as it is currently written? I chose to start with how you enter the organization (recruitment/socialization) because from an individual's perspective, this is the first way you experience an organization and work in that organization. Though you might read about the company strategy while considering the recruitment material an organization produces, it did not make logical sense to me to tell you about strategy without explaining why you would care in the first place—that is, because you want a job there. So I start from the individual and work my way up to the highest concept in the organization, strategy.

The chapters can be thought of as one big revolving story from the employee's experience. You want a job and so you look at advertising material from an organization and once you apply and get hired, you are socialized into the company. Once hired, there are a variety of aspects of the organization and job that can affect your motivation level. As you work, what you do on the job and in the organization affects your attitude about your boss, your coworkers, the job, and the organization. Your motivation and attitude affect your job performance, which can result in experiencing stress at work. And of course, employees' motivation reciprocally affects their performance, attitudes, and stress. So far, this story focuses on your experience at work from the individual view, but being a part of an organization of more than a handful of people often means being part of a team. How you are managed in that team falls under a manager's responsibility, though you can self-manage. The leader determines what managers' focus on and why. Underlying these concepts is communication; importantly, how your boss communicates with you, how you communicate with others (like those on your team) in the organization, and how the leader communicates the vision. To ensure that everyone is working toward achieving the organization's goals, leaders must establish an effective organizational structure, which is determined by the strategy of the organization and its supporting culture.

If starting from a 50,000 foot view instead of starting with the individual's view, ideally the organizational strategy is developed first as it determines the structure and culture of the organization. Leaders communicate that strategy to managers, who based on the vision manage employees' performance, which is affected by employees' attitudes, stress, and motivation. Socializing employees properly helps them learn and understand the culture and strategy.

How Is This Book Different from Other Organizational Psychology or OB Textbooks?

Unique features of this textbook include its integration of Organizational Psychology and Organizational Behavior, its explanation of theory, how managers use theory, and case examples of how theory and research actually come to life in familiar organizations. Chapter 1 provides a table summarizing the various topics covered in both organizational behavior and organizational psychology, showing where they are the same or overlap, and where they differ. For example, OB includes topics such as human resource management and corporate social responsibility, whereas Organizational Psychology typically does not. Organizational Psychology includes socialization and occupational stress, whereas OB typically does not. Both include topics of motivation, attitudes, culture, and leadership, but their approaches to these topics tend to differ. Thus, this book attempts to integrate across the common areas and incorporate one or two topic areas unique to each discipline, but that make practice and professional sense to include when teaching a course in either discipline (e.g., stress, structure).

A key and exclusive feature of this book is that neither a book on Organizational Psychology nor one on OB includes a chapter on strategy. After much discussion with colleagues about what to include in this book, I couldn't determine how best to finish the book. It didn't seem comprehensive to end the book on organizational transformation. I owe special thanks to Dr. Joan F. Brett and Dr. Karen Golden-Biddle for steering me away from the macro topic of organizational theory, which was too macro to include in this textbook, and steering me toward the inclusion of a chapter on strategy. The sentiment was that so many graduates of organizational psychology and organizational behavior programs lack perspective on strategy, yet in practice leadership and culture go along with strategy. No organization is without all three, regardless of how small, and all three topics reciprocally affect each other.

Instead of costly purchased case studies that can drive up the cost of the textbook, I include many examples of organizations throughout the book and Kendall Hunt does a great job of keeping the book affordable. No doubt some of my examples refer to start-ups that may fail before this edition is 5 years old. A difference between this book and other Organizational Psychology books is that this book includes many sections on how managers use the theories described in the chapters, how students can apply the material to their current part-time jobs, and a broader reference to business tools and practices.

What Are the Features of This Book?

Consistent with all chapters, they first asks key questions and then answer them as units or sections. Each chapter reviews the theoretical bases or foundation for the concept and then offers practical applications and explanations for how managers use the theories in organizations. Leveraging principles of reflection and metacognition, each chapter includes planning, monitoring, and evaluating (Schraw, 1998) self-learning. Each chapter starts with questions to help students plan their learning strategy for that chapter. Throughout the chapter, sidebars provide self-testing and activities to help students increase comprehension. At the end of each chapter, students can evaluate their own learning through small assessments (new discussion questions appear at the end of every chapter) and application activities. To avoid gendered language, this second edition removes nearly all references to "his" or "her" and instead uses "their"—even though grammatically, "their" is plural, or where possible shifts to a plural focus overall.

© GaudiLab/Shutterstock.com

Questions for Headings

As you can tell, I like to ask questions in this book. I find that students learn and retain material better when they have asked a question and sought an answer. Every chapter is designed with questions as its major headings and then the answers to each question fall within that section. My classroom and, therefore, this book is student-centered. There are many names for this approach to teaching, such as flipped-classroom, peer instruction, or just-in-time teaching. The general idea here is that the emphasis is on students actively participating in learning rather than being lectured to—thus, students drive the questions and answers, and learning comes from the discussion, elaboration, and sharing of thought. I was inspired by Dr. Eric Mazur, a Harvard University professor of physics, who has talked extensively about peer instruction, a style of teaching that focuses on students learning from students. This approach is driven by students asking questions and interacting in class to obtain and master the material through answering those questions. As part of my classroom environment and using the Mazur method, my students asked numerous questions about the topics covered in this book. It is from that approach and their questions that this book came about.

Leveraging Learning Principles

I used the principles described by Ambrose, Bridges, DiPietro, Lovett, and Norman's (2010) in "*How Learning Works: 7 Research-Based Principles for Smart Teaching*" (published by Jossey-Bass) and Schank's (2011) "*Teaching Minds: How Cognitive Science Can Save Our Schools*" (published by Teachers College Press) to structure some of the aspects of the book. Specifically, I wanted to get at students' prior knowledge and motivation to learn by giving mini-diagnostic tests at the beginning of each chapter (called a mini-quiz). These mini-quizzes give the students an initial exposure to the chapter content, hinting at what they are expected to know by the time they finish reading the chapter. In this second edition, I incorporated the science of learning by leveraging concepts shared in Kaplan, Silver, Lavaque-Manty, and Meizlish's (2013) edited book called "*Using Reflection and Metacognition to Improve Student Learning*," and "*A Guide to Effective Studying and Learning: Practical Strategies from the Science of Learning*" by Matthew Rhodes, Anne Cleary, and Edward DeLosh published in 2019. I also leveraged the work of Carol Dweck on mindset, which is a way of thinking about one's abilities - either we think they are fixed or they are flexible and capable of advancing. Our mindset can either stifle or facilitate our learning.

Why Should We Learn This or How Does This Apply

Students frequently ask "why" they need to know a topic or why is it important to learn a theory unsupported by empirical research if they can't apply it? Therefore, I made sure each chapter answers the question of why a particular topic or theory is important to learn and what relevance it has for application. I leveraged Wiggins and McTighe's (2005) book "*Understanding by Design*" to write the chapters such that course instructors could rely on the book to provide the essential content, connections, and applications necessary to support a good course design. Additionally, keeping in mind the focus of management courses, most chapters explicitly include a section on "How do managers use this theory in practice" or a heading similar to this one. Thus, each chapter provides a specific section on how to use the content.

Organizing Framework

A big complaint many of my colleagues have about the textbooks they use is that the book fails to provide an organizing structure, a way to help students understand how everything fits together. Learning scholars, such as Susan Ambrose,

Michael Bridges, Michele DiPietro, Marsh Lovett, and Marie Norman, and many others, recommend that instructors provide students with an organizational structure—a view of the big picture—so they can start with a framework upon which to connect ideas. I, therefore, encourage instructors to share with students the directional flow of this textbook and the story I offer above about my approach in writing the book. This gives students a high-level simple organizing framework about what they will learn across the 13 chapters and how they chapters connect. Throughout the chapters, tables and illustrations are provided for how the content of the chapter fits together. Each chapter is given an organizing framework of its own, usually beginning with an explanation of what the topic is, and why we care about it in organizations. These sections typically follow with what we know about the topic, how do we use it, change it, and how to get more use out of the concept.

Side-Bars

Here's an example of a side-bar:
Visit Dr. Carol Dweck's 10 minute Ted Talk on "The Power of Believing that You Can Improve." After watching the video, what are you going to do more of and differently to learn as much as possible from this book?

I incorporated side-bar discussions, activities, or questions to engage students in reflecting on their own experiences throughout each chapter. Some side-bars reiterate key points, whereas others ask students to relate the previous section to their work or personal experience. A few side-bars offer tips for tough student situations that may be relevant to the organizational topic. Additionally, many side-bar activities and questions are designed to encourage reflection, monitoring, and self-assessment; key dimensions of metacognition and engagement.

What are the Resources for Instructors?

To facilitate the use of this book, I developed several aids for instructors. Resources include a test bank, a study guide/outline for each chapter, powerpoint slides for each chapter, and a glossary of key terms to the book. Included with this second edition, I have provided several reflection questions that I assign students the week BEFORE I will cover that chapter in lecture. Students are expected to complete them about 2–3 days before that class. I review their answers and then use the lecture time to correct their understanding of the material, clarify confusing points from the reading, and engage students in discussing their responses and diving deeper into the topics of the chapter. The reflection questions prompt and require students to read the chapter before class, which I have found makes the lecture time more student-focused; it's not me lecturing on the chapter they could have read on their own. My job in the classroom, therefore, is to provide examples, enrich and deepen their understanding, and challenge them to think more about the theories and applications.

Who Am I?

I am Zinta S. Byrne, a full professor of psychology at Colorado State University in Fort Collins, Colorado. I earned my masters and doctorate degrees in psychology, with a focus on Industrial and Organizational Psychology, from Colorado State University in 1999 and 2001. Prior to studying psychology, I earned a double major bachelors of science degree in computer science with a second major in mathematics, in 1986 from California State University, Hayward. I transferred to California State University, Hayward from Temple University in Philadelphia, Pennsylvania, in 1984. Prior to getting my degree in psychology, I worked for Hewlett-Packard Company in the Silicon Valley (Cupertino, California) from 1986 to 1997, in various roles including software engineer, program manager, project manager, and technical marketing manager. Before settling down as a professor at Colorado State University but just after completing my PhD, I worked for Personnel Decisions International, a management consulting firm that has since been acquired by Korn Ferry, a large management consulting firm. I was based in Minneapolis with reporting relationships in San Francisco, Los Angeles, Houstin, and Dallas. My regional role had me traveling from Minneapolis to Denver to San Francisco, to Dallas and Houston on a regular basis.

When my Ph.D. advisor left Colorado State University in 2002, I was encouraged to apply for the assistant professor opening. I competed against several other applicants and to my surprise the university hired me. I've since graduated 15 PhD and 16 MS degree students. I've supervised over 50 undergraduates on research projects and taught organizational psychology for over 10 years. Other teaching assignments have included introduction to psychology, psychological measurement and testing, and graduate seminars in attitudes, justice, organizational culture, social psychology, and psychology of work. I've been nominated for the Best Teacher Award many times, received the first Psi Chi Distinguished Teacher Award at CSU, and received the Jacob E. Hautaluoma Distinguished Alumni Award for my work as a scientist-practitioner. Consistent with the scientist-practitioner model, I run my own consulting practice, Atniz Consulting, LLC, where I collaborate with organizations on employee engagement, culture change, and leadership development. I frequently incorporate practice into my teaching and teaching into my practice, and use Action Research as a model for my work. The Society for Industrial and Organizational Psychology honored me in 2019 with the Scientist-Practitioner Presidential Recognition, an award created to recognize members who engage in both science and practice, bridging the gap.

My recent research efforts have been focused on studying employee engagement and organizational culture and culture change. My book *"Understanding Employee Engagement: Theory, Research, and Practice"* published in July 2014. This book reviews the latest progress in both practice and research on employee engagement, includes chapters on the future of employee engagement research, as well as incorporates reflections and learning moments from my international talks on engagement in Russia, Africa, the United Kingdom, and France. Another related book which I coedited, *"Purpose and Meaning in the Workplace"* was published in 2013, and provides a wonderful review of research focused on workplace concerns related to increasing meaningfulness at work. I mention these two books because of their relevancy to organizational psychology, and how they both offer specific research findings and practical application to creating thriving and meaningful workplaces—an ultimate goal for both the organizational psychologist and organizational behavior practitioner. Consequently, I incorporate research findings and practical applications to improving and enhancing meaning at work.

As an industrial/organizational psychologist, I research a variety of topics—nearly all covered within this textbook (except I don't research socialization or strategy). As a consequence, I've published articles and book chapters, and serve on a variety of journal's editorial boards, as well as serving as an associate editor, and then Editor-in-Chief for the *Journal of Managerial Psychology*. My content knowledge, experience, and research as an organizational psychologist makes me an asset on interdisciplinary grants that involve organizational change, and as a result I have been CO-PI on research grants from organizations such as the National Science Foundation, a federal funding agency of the United States government. Over the last few years, I have been heavily involved in organizational change efforts at Colorado State University—efforts aimed at improving the student experience, faculty development, and the organizational culture. Specifically, one of my NSF grants led me to measuring and studying the organizational culture of STEM (science, technology, engineering, and math) and non-STEM departments. I've been working with two departments to instigate organizational culture change efforts. Additionally, I served on the President's Commission for Women and Gender Equity as a member, vice-chair, and interim chair—a group focused on improving the entire university culture. My work with the President led to the formation of the President's Council on Culture, a group dedicated to improving the university culture. I recently overhauled the university course evaluation survey—renaming it the CSU LENS (Learning Environment Survey)—designing it to focus on obtaining students' perceptions of their experience of the learning environment rather than their evaluation of faculty (a task for which they are not qualified, nor for which they should be responsible). I mention these various efforts because I have not only had many opportunities to study and practice organizational psychology in private, non-profit, and government organizations, but in higher education as well. Thus, I draw on these diverse experiences to share with students how dynamic and useful organizational psychology truly is. I hope you enjoy reading this book as much as I have enjoyed writing it.

ACKNOWLEDGEMENTS

This book would not have happened if Paul Carty at Kendall Hunt Publishing hadn't taken the time to listen to me complaining about the lack of books on organizational psychology—books that addressed my needs: education, practice, fun, easy to read, and yet loaded with resources and attention to accuracy of science. Thank You Paul for your never ending support and encouragement! It is such a pleasure to offer a very special thank you to Jennifer Betzmer, my writing coach for the first edition of this textbook. She helped me find and cultivate my writing voice, provided critical writing feedback, asked me tough questions within each chapter, and supported me on a very tight schedule. The first edition of this book was a vast improvement from the first draft, thanks to her coaching!

I appreciate the assistance of Kyla Dvorak (now Dr. Kyla Holcombe), a previous doctoral student, who provided helpful literature reviews to get me started and who wrote the initial mini-quizzes in the first edition of the book and that appear at the beginning of each chapter. Her concept models gave me insight into what I wanted to diagram as the visual for the end of each chapter.

I'm grateful to the following people who provided direct and indirect support with the book. Their help ranged from proof reading chapters, pointing me in the right direction, acting as a sounding board for ideas, and providing much needed support and encouragement:

Name	Affiliation
Devi Akella	Albany State University
Asad Aziz	Colorado State University
Michèle Boonzaier	Stellenbosch University
Kris Boesch	Choose People
Joan F. Brett	Arizona State University
Callie Burley	California State Polytechnic University, Pomona
Paul B. Carty	Kendall Hunt Publishing
Rebecca Clancey	Colorado State University
Todd Conkright	Midland University
Tori Crain	Colorado State University
Bryan L. Dawson	University of North Georgia
Gwenith Fisher	Colorado State University
Lyric Fortson	Colorado State University
Alisha Francis	Northwest Missouri State University
Karen Golden-Biddle	Boston University

(Continued)

(Continued)

Name	Affiliation
Christine Good	Metropolitan State University of Denver
Sheri Grotrian	Peru State College
Christa Kiersch	University of Wisconsin, La Crosse
Manu Mahbubani	Ivy Business School Western University
Linda McMullen	LaGrange College
David G. Myers	Hope College
Janet Peters	Washington State University
Isabelle Ponce-Pore	Colorado State University
Hong Ren	University of Wisconsin, Milwaukee
David Rentler	Western Connecticut State University
Kathryn Rickard	Colorado State University
Yolanda Sarason	Colorado State University
Victoria Stansberry	Colorado State University
Tammi Vacha-Haase	Boise State University
Wayne Viney	Colorado State University
Carla Zimmerman	Colorado State University-Pueblo

Many others provided indirect support along the way, including my current and former doctoral students and industry colleagues like Jennifer Anderson and Elaine LeMay. My mom, Anna Stofberg, provided needed phone call breaks from hours of focused attention during the editing process. She bragged about me to whomever would listen—Go Mom!! I owe a very special thanks to my husband Jon Byrne—he encouraged me during the many hours where my writing consumed my attention and time. Jon's mom, Betty Byrne, also provided indirect support through her ongoing interest in what I was doing, asking how the writing was coming along, and supporting my husband.

Lastly, I dedicate the book to my undergraduate and graduate students who all inspired me to write this book for them and to develop the second edition. Their questions and frustrations while trying to learn what should be easy to digest material gave me tremendous insight into what I needed to do in my book. I thank them for engaging in the class material with me and telling me what they needed from the book that they weren't getting. My students kept asking how the material they read applied in actual organizations—they couldn't make sense of theory after theory without some idea of how to use them, whether they were used in organizations, and how they could use them in their own work lives. Hence, their hunger for rich depth in understanding why people do what they do and also how they apply the theories and course content led to this integrated text. I thank all those hundreds of students for helping me believe I could write a book that would be more helpful than the ones they have now and that they wanted!

Zinta Byrne, Ph.D.

ABOUT THE BOOK

Preface

Within many, if not most, of the chapters of the book, I introduce and review various theories and models that have been and often still are used to explain why people do what they do in organizations. However, many times the theories and models I review, especially those introduced decades ago, have little to no empirical support. So you might ask—why am I reviewing theories that have little or no empirical support? Should not we just learn about theories that we know work? My answer to this is "no." The reason for learning about the various theories including those with little to no empirical support is that the general idea behind the theory may still be referred to or used because of its conceptual value—not its empirical value. That is, the theory may be very helpful in understanding a complex situation in more simplistic terms—something we can wrap our heads around and discuss without losing track of the idea. For example, Maslow's Hierarchy of Needs has received little supportive evidence for people linearly ascending the pyramid of needs from the lowest level—basic food and shelter needs—to the highest level of self-actualization. Yet, the theory makes some common sense when trying to understand why someone might be more motivated to pay the bills than to be recognized with awards. The awards do not pay the rent, buy food, or keep the utilities running. In other cases, theories or models that have empirical support make more sense when understanding which came before and when studied were found lacking, and then modified. Their progression from a starting point, to continued modification, to the current version can show the path by which researchers build on previous attempts to understand complex human behavior. As we learn, we discard parts of the explanation that do not work and add parts that do. Why the current theory has the components it does, may only make sense if you know where it started.

Chapter 1: Issues and Challenges Organizations Face: Introduction

Chapter 1 introduces the disciplines of Organizational Psychology and Organizational Behavior, and why an integration of the two disciplines makes sense. Because Organizational Psychology and Industrial Psychology are most often intertwined, a brief comparison to industrial psychology is offered. The chapter includes a historical review of how organizational psychology developed. The chapter ends with a brief review of the sequence or linear progression of chapters in the textbook, and a story of life in an organization.

Part I: Individuals in Organizations

Chapter 2: Joining the Organization: Socialization

Chapter 2 provides our entry into the organization—our first exposure to what it means to work in an organization. "How do we get in" and "how do we learn about the organization" are the key questions asked and answered in this chapter.

Chapter 3: Intentions and Drivers at Work: Motivation

As soon as we are inside the organization and initially socialized, motivation drives our behavior at work. Therefore, motivation is the focus of Chapter 3. The chapter first clarifies what motivation is, and provides several theories and approaches for understanding why employees might be motivated to perform at work, and then how to increase their motivation. Because our motivation to perform (or not) may be influenced by our attitudes at work, and vice versa, it makes sense for Chapter 4 on attitudes to follow the chapter on motivation.

Chapter 4: Predicting Feelings and Behaviors at Work: Attitudes

Chapter 4 focuses on attitudes at work. In addition, to explain how attitudes form and can be changed, the chapter reviews the most relevant attitudes at work, attitudes that organizations want to measure and change. As with other chapters, this one includes not only the practical approach to attitudes, but what theoretical explanations are available to understand why employees respond the way they do and how to use those theories to make meaningful changes at work. Both motivation and attitudes combine to direct or manifest themselves in job performance; therefore, the next logical chapter to follow is on performance at work.

Chapter 5: Doing the Job and Then Some: Performance

Perhaps the only real topic of interest to business leaders is performance. Chapter 5 reviews job performance in organizations, what constitutes performance and what doesn't (counterproductive work behavior), and how to encourage high performance at work. The chapter includes several approaches to managing and evaluating performance. Performing our jobs well can lead to stress at work and stress at work can affect our ability to perform. Hence, Chapter 6 on stress follows this chapter on performance.

Chapter 6: The Toll Work Takes: Occupational Stress

Chapter 6 is about stress at work, though a little background about stress in other domains and how those spillover into work are included. This chapter is very hands-on and very approachable for students. Because everyone experiences stress, and being a student can, at times, be likened to working in an organization, this chapter allows students to instantly grasp how the material not only applies to organizations, but to themselves. The chapter includes a section on what organizations can do to help employees develop appropriate stress-management plans. Managing stress can be enhanced or worsened by working on a team. Thus, the next chapter moves us from a focus on the individual into a focus on how we function within groups.

Part II: Running the Organization Using Teams and Leaders

Chapter 7: Being Part of a Group: Teams

Teams are ubiquitous and so no Organizational Psychology and Behavior book would be complete without a chapter on how groups or teams function. The chapter reviews the various types of teams that exist in organizations, how they form, and what key factors influence effective teams. Because organizations tend to implement teams even when it might not be a good idea, the chapter includes a section on when teams are not effective and when you should not form a team. Group norms and dynamics are incorporated into this chapter. Teams may be directed by a manager, thus the next chapter is on management.

Chapter 8: Running the Organization: Management

Although many books combine management and leadership into one chapter, treating them synonymously, this textbook does not—instead, each topic area receives its own chapter. In Chapter 8, an introduction to what differentiates a manager from a leader is followed by an emphasis on what managers do, how they manage employees, and how to become a manager. A key role for managers is giving feedback, thus a section of the chapter provides tips on how to give negative feedback and coach for performance. The chapter ends with a discussion of how to transition from being a manager into being a leader.

Chapter 9: Taking the Organization into the Future: Leadership

Chapter 9 picks up from chapter 8 by explaining what it means to be a leader and what we know from accumulated research and practice about leaders. Several theories of leadership are reviewed along with examples of how they are used in practice. A special section on culture is included because country culture norms influence what type of leaders is appropriate for which type of organization. Additionally, a section on gender reviews misperceptions about female and male leaders. The chapter includes best practices for developing leaders and what to do if you have an ineffective leader.

Chapter 10: Disseminating Information: Communication

Poor communication in organizations creates so many problems, yet little attention is paid to fully explaining what organizational communication includes and how to do it well. This chapter is especially critical because we all believe we already know how to communicate, both face-to-face and electronically. The chapter will provide tips for good communication and examples of where it's easy to assume you know it all and yet still make these common mistakes. Good communication is responsible communication and this chapter reviews effective, ineffective, and crisis communication. How to handle conflict is also included, as is a section on communication across cultures—sensitivity to culture cannot be understated, especially with so many organizations operating globally. This chapter includes a section on ethical and timely/private communication, and discusses the role of the leader in disseminating information throughout the organization.

Part III: Designing and Changing the Organization Itself

Chapter 11: Organizing the Organization: Structure

Chapter 11 gets into how organizations are configured or how responsibility is distributed (or not) throughout the organization. A variety of structures are provided and reviewed, as well as dissected for understanding of the elements that make up structure. Many examples of organizations with different structural elements are provided to clarify what exactly structure is and refers to. One section of the chapter reviews what leaders should consider when developing or designing an organizational structure. The chapter wraps up with a discussion of how structure impacts employees, driving home the understanding that structure is not just a wooden frame or scaffolding for name plates.

Chapter 12: Organizational Culture and Climate: Transformation

Chapter 12 discusses organizational culture and climate, their differences, and to what each specifically refers. This chapter offers a variety of images and illustrations, perhaps more so than a few other chapters, to help solidify an otherwise vague and "hard to get your head around" topic. A variety of approaches for assessing, understanding, and changing culture are reviewed. Because most organizations seek to change their culture, an entire section is devoted to change models and how managers apply the theories of culture and transformation. Change in organizations is often driven by the organizational strategy, which turns us to the last chapter of the book—strategy.

Chapter 13: The Future and How to Get There: Strategy

The last chapter of the book is fittingly about organizational strategy. Chapter 13 reviews organizational strategy by offering many examples from companies around the world. Different factors, both external and internal, that shape strategy are included in this chapter. Because of the leader's critical role in shaping, driving, and communicating strategy, this chapter ends with a section on the role of the leader in strategy.

CHAPTER 1

Issues and Challenges Organizations Face: Introduction

Learning Outcomes

Before reading the chapter, jot down what you know about organizational psychology and about organizational behavior, and a few notes on what you understand are the similarities and differences between the topic areas. Based on what you were able to jot down, make a quick list of what you you think you still need to learn to be able to effectively describe the fields, compare and contrast them, and integrate them.

After studying this chapter, you should be able to explain:

1. Why and how understanding organizational psychology and organizational behavior can positively influence your success at work.

2. The historical underpinnings that drove the development of the fields of organizational psychology and organizational behavior.

3. Top challenges facing organizations today and in the future.

Overview

An "organization" can refer to many types of structures or configurations including single institutions, such as Walmart, Amazon, AT&T, Boeing, and Gilead Sciences. They might be units within a larger category, such as police stations within a district within a state, or stores within a franchise, such as McDonald's, The UPS Store, Culver's, or Hampton by Hilton. The institutions can be for profit, such as Micron Technology, Bristol-Myers Squibb, or Penske Automotive Group, or not-for-profit, such as the United Way, Ocean Conservancy, and the National Defense Council. If you are not employed by an organization but instead work as an independent contractor, you might do what is called gig work, such as driving for Uber or Lyft, renting out your room or apartment via Airbnb, or rent your plane with OpenAirplane. Even though you are not employee of Airbnb, it is a private company with policies and terms that you agree to follow. For example, a list of requirements for postings, hosting, and cancellations can be found on their website. Thus, if you wish to use their online resources to list your apartment for rent, you must agree to their terms. In essence, you are indirectly experiencing aspects of their organization.

Most of our adult lives are consumed with working for an organization of some kind. Our ability to afford a home or apartment, connect with people in a productive way, and reach personal and professional goals all depend on organizations. Organizations provide community—the opportunity for people to connect with others who have common values and beliefs, and help to create an environment of well-being and health.

Agreements and disagreements between organizations, struggles with management within organizations, and the day-to-day challenges you face at work, all fall within the scope of organizational psychology and organizational behavior. Your awareness of this information can dramatically alter your **attitudes** and approach to work situations. Organizations and the overall effect of work affect your health, your personal relationships, and your long-term ability to find meaning and purpose in life. You will spend the majority of your waking hours working in, with, and around organizations, absorbing these effects. Thus, developing a clear understanding and mastery of the principles of organizational psychology and behavior is imperative for your successful functioning as a working adult.

This chapter introduces you to the integration of organizational psychology and organizational behavior and how they combine to address the major challenges both leaders and employees face while working in organizations.

Why Study Organizational Psychology and Organizational Behavior?

Organizational psychology and **organizational behavior** focus on dynamics and factors in the workplace, and as such, understanding them can positively influence your success at work. Work dynamics or factors include leadership, teamwork, individual **motivation**, stress at work, communication, and change. The strategic goals of the organization establish the focus of leadership, but the combined efforts of leaders and employees together move the organization in the direction of achieving the strategic goals. Many challenges pop up along the way for both you as an employee and your organization overall, sometimes causing either you or your organization to derail from achieving success. For example, internal challenges include your own motivation level, personality, and beliefs that cause you to act in one way or another, not always to your own benefit. External challenges, such as environmental conditions, regulations, and political dynamics serve to disrupt, challenge, or accelerate success or failure. Thus, understanding internal and external challenges at work, essentially the principles of organizational psychology and behavior, can lead to a higher likelihood for you and your organization staying on track.

We spend a majority of our waking hours in and around organizations; therefore, developing a clear understanding and mastery of the principles of organizational psychology and behavior are critical for successful functioning as working adults. **Organizations** are organized or coordinated bodies of people, people who come together to achieve a common goal. Thus, organizations may include clubs, churches, or community associations. Organizations are a major part of our lives, even if we do not think about their centrality on a daily basis.

Hence, the value of understanding organizations and work within organizations comes to life when the knowledge gained from theories and research is applied to the work setting. Theories and research provide the expertise for developing new solutions in novel situations. You can learn how to solve a problem for a specific situation, but if you cannot develop a new solution when encountering a new or different situation, then knowing that solution to that specific problem is of little value. Therefore, this book shares theories

Write down the number of hours you spend per day: sleeping, eating, preparing for school or work in the morning, preparing for bed at night, completing essential chores, and any other life activity you do on a daily basis. Now jot down how many hours per day you spend as a student and, if you work another job in addition to your job as a student include those hours here too. How many hours do you "work" per day relative to the hours you take care of yourself and/or others?

and research, as well as provides the explanation for how those theories and research findings apply to the workplace, so that you can solve new problems in novel situations.

What Comprises the Fields of Organizational Psychology and Organizational Behavior?

Organizational psychology and organizational behavior both focus on organizations and the human behavior therein. Though both fields focus on similar topics resulting in overlap, several fundamental differences between the fields explain their unique contributions to the study of organizations and organizational members.

Organizational Behavior

Organizational behavior is a multidisciplinary field of study, extracting knowledge from areas such as economics, sociology, anthropology, and political science, as well as psychology. In brief, economics includes decision-making, negotiation, and power. Sociology incorporates group dynamics, socialization, and communication. Culture and leadership derive from anthropology, whereas interpersonal conflict and individual power come from political science. Lastly, psychology provides theories of learning, personality, attitudes, relations, and motivation.

Organizational behavior traditionally focuses on macro-level (broad, large-scale, overall) issues in organizations such as organizational structure and *how* groups within organizations interact (Moorhead & Griffin, 1995). Organizational behavior, in general, does not necessarily focus on psychological explanations for *why* people behave as they do in organizations. Organizational behavior instead focuses on the application of research results to determine how organizations and their members can be most effective. Although theory is important, the primary orientation is toward business success and efficiency; hence, application takes a front seat in its orientation. In sum, organizational behavior tends to orient toward management and enhancing organizational effectiveness, relying heavily on theories and research findings from other fields (i.e., sociology, economics, psychology) as well as its own.

Organizational Psychology

In contrast to organizational behavior's multidisciplinary and eclectic aggregation of content, organizational psychology is a distinct subfield of psychology that draws from other subfields of psychology, such as social psychology and cognitive psychology, and uses scientific methods to understand individuals within organizations. In brief, social psychology includes the study of interactions of people in groups and cognitive psychology focuses on how people think, remember, and learn. The lens of organizational psychology incorporates the individual and group, and can include the study of many organizations, groups/teams, and individuals.

Consequently, most researchers consider organizational psychology more micro (small, specific) focused than organizational behavior. In addition, organizational psychology is oriented toward the development and use of psychological theories and research in organizations, with the application of research results

Visit the Academy of Management website, find the Division of Organizational Behavior, click on the Domain Statement. You'll find a description of what organizational behavior is according to this association. Now do a general Internet search on organizational behavior—what are some of the definitions you find there? After reading a few different definitions and explanations, what do you think organizational behavior is?

Search the Internet for descriptions of organizational psychology and look at the Society for Industrial and Organizational Psychology for their description. After reading a few different definitions and explanations, can you explain what organizational psychology is and how it differs from organizational behavior?

that solve organizational problems. Emphasis tends to be placed on explaining why people behave the way they do in organizations, as opposed to how they need to behave to satisfy corporate investors.

Thus, although there is substantial overlap between organizational psychology and organizational behavior, there are several distinct differences in how organizational psychology and organizational behavior approach the study of the workplace.

Distinguishing Differences

One distinguishing difference in how organizational behaviorists versus psychologists approach studying organizations is that organizational behavior researchers tend to focus on *how* organizations and their members behave, whereas organizational psychologists focus on explaining what makes employees' hold specific attitudes, act in specific ways, and predicting from their personal characteristics (e.g., attitude, personality, motivation) what they might do next. As a consequence, the unit of analysis or focus of attention often forms a second distinguishing difference between organizational behavior and organizational psychology. Specifically, organizational behavior traditionally emphasizes the organization itself, whereas organizational psychology concentrates on the individuals within the organization. Hence, at the risk of over generalizing, the **paradigm** of organizational behavior is top-down from leader to follower, whereas the paradigm direction is bottom-up from the individual to leader within organizational psychology.

Their theoretical foundations may characterize another distinguishing difference between the two fields. Organizational behavior researchers depend more heavily on their eclectic theoretical base, drawing from theories of political science, economics, and sociology, as well as management and organizational theory. In comparison, organizational psychologists generally draw from and rely heavily on psychological theory and subfields of psychology, such as social and cognitive psychology, as well as industrial psychology. Over time, the fields have increased their overlap, such that many could argue that the distinctions provided above are no longer accurate.

What do *you* think is the most distinguishing difference between the two fields? What do the two fields have the most in common? How might knowing the similarities and differences between these fields help you in future assignments? In your current or next job?

Industrial Psychology

Industrial psychology, another subfield of psychology, complements the study of organizational psychology, with its intense focus on the individual in organizations. In contrast to both organizational psychology and organizational behavior, industrial psychology focuses on the design and practice of determining how individuals differ from one another, to facilitate creating a workplace that distinguishes where and how they fit. For example, industrial psychology focuses on **performance appraisal**, the design of jobs, how one's personality may affect performance, and how individual employees are evaluated or assessed for selection. Rather than attempt to explain how groups of people work together to achieve an organizational goal, industrial psychology cares more about how each individual uniquely contributes and what makes him or her different from others in the group.

One way to view the relationships between organizational behavior, organizational psychology, and industrial psychology with their various foundational fields may be by concentrating on their focus, from broad to narrow (Figure 1.1).

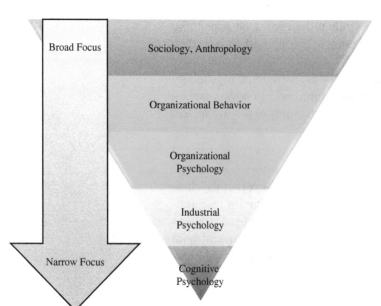

FIGURE 1.1 Focus of Study in Various Fields

Courtesy Zinta Byrne.

What role do you think industrial psychology can play in helping you to understand organizational psychology and organizational behavior?

Another helpful way to understand the similarities and differences between the fields of study may be through glances at the types of topics studied within each. Table 1.1 provides a quick view of a few topics of organizational psychology and organizational behavior, with a comparison column showing topics of industrial psychology. Although the topics often overlap and researchers across the three fields may study any one or more of the topics in the various columns of the table, the delineation is pedagogical and used to help provide an understanding of the focus that each discipline has within and about organizations.

The understanding of topics within organizational psychology and organizational behavior, as well as industrial psychology, is not just an academic exercise. Even if you are not a researcher or academician, having knowledge of the theories and research findings from the fields can provide you with immediate application and benefit, every day at work. For more information about Industrial Psychology, see resources such as Levy's (2012) "Industrial Organizational Psychology," Aamodt's (2012) "Industrial/Organizational Psychology: An Applied Approach" or Riggio's (2012) "Introduction to Industrial and Organizational Psychology."

TABLE 1.1 Quick View of Topics within Industrial Psychology, Organizational Psychology, and Organizational Behavior

Orientation on Individual Differences	Orientation on Groups and the Organization	Orientation on Leadership and Broad Organizational Impact
Industrial Psychology	**Organizational Psychology**	**Organizational Behavior**
Single discipline drawing from other subfields of psychology (cognitive, experimental). Focus is on the individual worker.	Single discipline drawing from other subfields of psychology (cognitive, social, counseling). Focus is on the worker in social and organizational contexts.	Multidiscipline (sociology, psychology, anthropology, economics, political science). Focus is on the organization and leadership.
Individual assessment	Teams	Organizational structure
Job analysis (task delineation)	Jobs and job factors as part of the contextual environment	Divisions within organizational structure
Performance ratings	Group performance, citizenship behaviors	Organizational performance

(Continued)

TABLE 1.1 Quick View of Topics within Industrial Psychology, Organizational Psychology, and Organizational Behavior (*Continued*)

Orientation on Individual Differences	Orientation on Groups and the Organization	Orientation on Leadership and Broad Organizational Impact
Industrial Psychology	**Organizational Psychology**	**Organizational Behavior**
Selection, recruitment	Socialization	Onboarding
Training for individual improvement	Leadership development	Leadership, corporate governance, board of directors
Motivation	Motivation	Management
	Job attitudes (commitment, turnover, fairness, job satisfaction)	Organizational attitudes (support, employee satisfaction)
Logic of decision-making	Leadership, interpersonal relations	Organizational politics and power
	Organizational climate	Organizational culture
Individual change	Organizational change and transformation	Organizational change and transformation
Individual differences, personality	Group creativity	Organizational innovation
Psychometrics	Uses results of psychometrics	Uses results of psychometrics
Person–situation fit	Person–organization fit	Organization–environment fit
Human attributes (cognitive ability, physical, and psychomotor abilities)	Health issues at work (work-life balance, safety, stress)	Human resource management
Individual differences within virtual workplace	Group differences within virtual workplace	E-commerce versus brick-and-mortar institutions
	Coaching	
Employment law	Fair policies and procedures	Organizational and leader ethics
Solutions for measurement invariance	Cross-cultural psychology	Cross-cultural leadership

Courtesy Zinta Byrne.

How Did Organizational Behavior and Psychology Develop?

Many times, the understanding of theories and solutions partially comes from seeing how the knowledge came to be. Hence, history can be more than just "history."

Writings and drawings reveal that organizations and practices within organizations have been around for thousands of years. For example, Chinese multiple-hurdle selection systems were documented over 3000 years ago (Katzell & Austin, 1992), and Egyptian hieroglyphics depicted leaders and workers constructing pyramids. Yet, the scientific study and molding of human behavior at work did not "officially" begin until the 1800s, and the majority of progress occurred in the 1900s and through to today.

Illustration of Taylorism applied—assembly line factor workers building cars in the 1930s.

© Vyntage Visuals/Shutterstock.com

1800s: Scientific Management

In the late 1800s, Frederick Taylor systematically analyzed human behavior at work with the goal of making it more efficient and safe. His approach was called **scientific management** and emphasized economic and safety gains achieved through making physical activity at work more effective. As an industrial engineer in the iron and steel industry, he saw the efficiency of machines and decided to model human work after the machine. Specifically, he attempted to dissect work in organizations such that he could assign individuals specific and unique tasks at the smallest unit of work, thereby enabling employees to master their specific task and complete it as efficiently as possible. Thus, like each part of the machine performs a specific function that collectively contributes to the functioning of the whole, Taylor felt humans could be assigned to unique parts of work that contribute to the whole. He studied the social environment, tasks within the environment, and the physical environment, as well as human capacity, speed, durability, and cost of work to determine how to remove human error. He also examined how long each physical motion took to complete a task, with the goal of determining how to shorten that cycle by removing unnecessary movements.

As an outcome of his studies of exact physical motions and the time each motion took, Taylor's research was referred to as Time and Motion studies, and his approach of systematizing work is often referred to as **Taylorism** (Katzell & Austin, 1992). Under Taylorism, productivity increased, and new departments such as industrial engineering, personnel management, and quality control were created. A surge in middle management developed and incorporated a separate planning function, which marked the formalization of management.

Although Taylorism generated much efficiency, it was not without criticism for the oversimplification of work that drove many to boredom. The success and criticism of Taylor's work encouraged others, in particular Max Weber, to attempt the scientific study of organizations.

1900s: Bureaucracy

Weber proposed that organizations should be structured as bureaucracies, where employees know what to do and from whom to take direction (a clear chain of command). Managers in the **bureaucracy** have narrow spans of control (i.e., manage few people), and clear rules for promotion and achievement. Bureaucracy specifically refers to a type of organizational structure that Weber proposed would make the organization more efficient. Similar to Taylor's drive for efficiency was Weber's in focusing on improving the structure of the organization. Like Taylorism, however, bureaucracy has its share of criticisms, as well.

Today, bureaucracy is considered a negative concept because of the typical slow decision-making attributed to the many layers of approval. The positive aspects of bureaucracies, however, include formal rules and guidelines (ensuring fairness), enforced impersonal treatment (eliminating favoritism), duties divided by skill and performed by people with the prerequisite skills (maximizing expertise), a clear hierarchical structure (clarifying authority and responsibility), long-term employment expectations (providing job security), and rationality (organizational goals and plans to achieve profitability; Weber, 1921/1947).

In some situations, a bureaucratic design may be ideal, such as with the military, but in many others, the somewhat rigid structure prevents accommodating a fast-paced market or quick competition. As you will read in Chapter 11, an organizational structure must take on different forms depending on the demands of the situation, a necessity that was not part of Weber's design. As is typical in research, criticisms of previous studies create the fuel for new ones, which launches us into the **Hawthorne studies**.

1930s: Hawthorne Studies

In a reaction to the mechanistic perspective of scientific management and the rigidity of bureaucracy, researchers from Harvard University Business School attempted to relieve morale issues and thought the way to do so was by examining the relationship between lighting, efficiency, and wage incentives (Mayo, 1933; Whitehead, 1935, 1938). The researchers conducted a series of experiments between 1924 and 1933 at Western Electrical Company's Hawthorne Works Plant near Chicago, Illinois. Their initial results showed that increased lighting was followed by an increase in efficiency. However, to the researchers' surprise, efficiency continued to improve even after the lighting was significantly dimmed below original levels.

The researchers hypothesized that these steady performance results must have originated from the employees' desires to please and impress the distinguished investigators from Harvard University. Yet, as soon as the employees became accustomed to the researchers watching them, their work levels returned to normal (see Chapter 4 on Performance). In some cases, workers even restricted each other's performance (see Chapter 7 on Teams) to keep the overall group's performance at a steady, but slower pace.

After several attempts to pinpoint when employees did and did not change their performance, the researchers concluded the change in productivity was due to the social environment. The workers increased their performance with the introduction of novel treatment, after which their performance returned to normal. This change in behavior following the onset of novel treatment (in this case, being a part of an important study) was termed the *Hawthorne Effect*.

There were many studies of the Hawthorne effects and not just increases in performance. Thus, the group of studies at the Hawthorne Plant were named the "Hawthorne studies" (also discussed in Chapter 12). These efforts marked the beginning of studies in organizational psychology and organizational behavior. Other studies were launched creating a movement toward studying group relations and how work environments affect worker motivation.

1940s and 1950s: Human Relations Movement

The **human relations movement**, characterized by researchers interested in motivation theories and the emotional world of workers, followed shortly after

Why do you think the
Hawthorne studies
are so important to
the advancement
of organizational
psychology?

the Hawthorne studies. Rather than treating employees as cogs in a machine, the human relations movement emphasized people as individuals with specific and unique needs, and as people with desires for creativity (Herzberg, Mausner, & Snyderman, 1959). Attitude surveys and interviews became popular and effective methods for understanding employees' opinions and behavior in organizations (Katzell & Austin, 1992).

Around the same time, Kurt Lewin initiated **Action Research** (also discussed in Chapter 12), an approach to research where organizations and researchers collaborate on studying specific problems within the organization and then apply the results to solve those organizational problems. Lewin studied the effects of leadership on worker productivity and job attitudes (see Chapter 5) such as satisfaction, group dynamics, group structure, communication, and theories of motivation on worker performance (Lewin, 1947, 1951; Lewin, Dembo, Festinger, & Sears, 1944; Lewin, Lippitt, & White, 1939). Collectively, his research on organizational constructs and attention to applying research findings to solving organizational problems launched the study of organizational change (Chapter 12), which continues today.

In addition to the insight provided by Action Research, the human relations movement shed light on examining the discrepancy between how an organization is supposed to work and how workers within the organization behave (Argyris, 1957; McGregor, 1960). The dominant themes in research included group dynamics, job attitudes such as satisfaction and withdrawal, organizational communication, and organization factors, such as how leadership contributed to driving employee performance (Katzell & Austin, 1992). The Tavistock Institute of Human Relations established in 1947 in London still dedicates itself to the study of improving working conditions and organizational practices leading to the growth and development of employees. Moreover, these early efforts in job motivation and **job redesign** (Chapter 3) paved the way for current research in work–life balance (Chapter 6), which focuses on the constant juggle between the demands from home and demands from work.

With increasing interest and growth in research, and growing attention on the improvement of organizations and employee welfare, the organizational behavior and psychology disciplines blossomed.

1960s and 1970s: Naming the Fields

In the 1960s, after decades of accumulated research and application in organizations, organizational behavior finally received its name (Porter & Schneider, 2014). The 1960s also marks the time when research focus increased on problems of marketing, economics, labor relations, leadership, and decision-making (Chapter 9). Interest in communication within organizations (Chapter 10), management (Chapter 8), and **organizational culture** (Chapter 12) also grew dramatically during that time (Bass, 1965; Porter, Lawler, & Hackman, 1975).

Pressure on business schools to conduct rigorous research drew many organizational psychologists to affiliate with business schools (Katzell & Austin, 1991), leading to the conjecture that it was during this time that organizational behavior as a separate field began seriously taking shape (Porter & Schneider,

2014). Several visible economic reports on business school education pointed out the need for business schools to emphasize behavioral science and promote behavior research agendas; however, the schools did not have trained faculty to execute such training and research programs. Consequently, they hired industrial and organizational psychologists into management departments to solve the problem (Porter & Schneider, 2014). The large influx of industrial and organizational psychologists into business schools during this time might also explain some of the overlap between organizational psychology and organizational behavior. Over the years, as more graduate programs offered degrees in organizational behavior, the tendency to hire industrial and organizational psychologists declined.

Even though the upsurge in research was promoting organizational psychology as a discipline, it took until 1970 before organizational psychology was officially recognized in the name of Division 14, Society for Industrial and Organizational Psychology (SIOP), of the **American Psychological Association** (APA). The APA is an association dedicated to the scientific and professional study and practice of psychology, and represents psychologists in the United States. Similarly, although the **Academy of Management**, a professional association dedicated to the study of management and represents management and organizational scholars worldwide, was formed in the late 1930s, it also wasn't until about 1970 that the Academy grew its membership and created a unique division for those focusing exclusively on organizational behavior (Porter & Schneider, 2014).

Nearly a decade later, the **European Association of Work and Organizational Psychology** (EAWOP) emerged from the European Congress of Work and Organizational Psychology, a conference held in 1983 in the Netherlands. EAWOP is an association dedicated to the development and application of work and organizational psychology in Europe. EAWOP became an official organization in 1991 and has grown in membership ever since.

Hence, the study of organizational psychology and organizational behavior existed in research and activity long before being officially named. With such late naming, many believe the two disciplines are "young" and have yet to establish their identity within the psychological and management fields. However, a glance at what is studied within these disciplines today shows they carry-over concepts from decades of efforts in improving organizations and the fates of their members.

Watch the following YouTube video from SIOP: httpps://youtube/ 1fLCmoxCdRc Why might you want to be an IO psychologist?

1980s to Today

Topics researched in organizational psychology and organizational behavior today include, but are not limited to, those noted in Table 1.2. Many of these topics are discussed in later chapters of this book.

Many of the challenges in organizational behavior and psychology that existed decades ago, such as motivation and conflict resolution still remain today. Many new challenges have also emerged, brought about by revolutionary technology, the environment, and internal growth of organizations from small, local-only businesses to large multinational conglomerates.

Organizational psychology and behavior are products of society—the problems solved and studied within organizations are created and driven by societal influences.

TABLE 1.2 Currently Researched Topics in Organizational Psychology and Organizational Behavior

Employee–Organization Relationship	Organizational and Occupational Identity	Corporate Social Responsibility	Corporate Reputation
Changes in work due to society and environmental forces	Training (online, cognitive models, team, leadership)	Effects of technology	Organizational climate and culture
Teams, including virtual teams	Motivation	Organizational change	Conflict resolution
Cross-culture	Employment law	Power and leadership	Management
Entrepreneurship	Human resource management	Strategy	Work and family
Large and small organizations	Family-run, not-for-profit organizations	Occupational health and safety	Well-being and meaningfulness
Cognitive perspectives on decision-making	Gaming	Advancements in psychometrics in the study of organizations	Diversity
Unemployment	Ethics and ethical behavior	Corporate boards	Human capital
Decision-making	Relational pluralism	Knowledge networks	Innovation
Shareholders and stakeholders	Organizational structure	Support	Workplace harassment
Job attitudes (satisfaction, commitment, turnover)	Employee engagement	Political skill	Emotions
Motivation	Psychological contracts	Workplace bullying and abusive supervision	Aging workforce

Courtesy Zinta Byrne.

Look up the following terms on the Internet to see what they refer to: entrepreneurship, organizational climate, occupational health, gaming, relational pluralism, shareholders and stakeholders, political skill, and psychological contracts.

What Are the Top Challenges Organizations Face?

Organizational psychology and organizational behavior grew out of a need to resolve various problems that organizations confront. One challenge that is consistent across all organizations is how to deal with constant change.

Additionally, challenges for organizations are frequently those instigated or pushed onto them externally by society or the environment, or internally caused by people dynamics, systems, and logistics of managing space and equipment.

Constant Change

Constant change is normal! Most organizations experience constant change in response to environmental pressures to change, efforts to satisfy shareholders, and stay competitive. Evolving technology, employment law, healthcare requirements, values of workers, and customer expectations all force organizations to be flexible and adapt frequently to survive. Not all organizations are required to make every change or adopt every innovation, yet most find themselves behind the competition if they do not at least appear to be constantly innovating, upgrading, and advancing.

Even small coffee shops (Figure 1.2) have to keep up with new technology as customers expect to pay with their mobile phone or tablet device rather than with a credit card or cash. The impact of constant change in rural, less well-developed nations may be less visible in the news, but none-

FIGURE 1.2 Keeping Up With Changes

© ChickenStock Images/Shutterstock.com

the-less still has the same effect on organizations in those regions—change requires attention. Frequently, in a falling domino-like effect, change creates yet more change and sometimes not in the intended direction.

The continuous cycle of change results from the push of external influences that force corresponding internal changes and the constant adjustments needed internally to accommodate both external and internal pressures. Organizations can sometimes influence changes in the external environment to facilitate internal goals. For example, Walmart joined business lobbyists in pushing the U.S. government for universal health care, with some speculating that the changes in health care resulted from the mammoth retailer's involvement (Foley, 2008).

External Challenges

Many of the external challenges that face organizations may be categorized based on financial pressures, resources, and the environment. Financial pressures typically include the need to make a profit while cutting costs and dealing with rising market prices of raw materials. Resources include workers, market share, and raw materials. Lastly, environmental initiatives, such as globalization and **environmental sustainability**, are top challenges organizations face.

FIGURE 1.3   Tracking Stock Prices and Investments

© MicroWorks/Shutterstock, Inc.

Financial

Shareholders

The demands of **shareholders** serve as an external challenge for organizations. Shareholders include people or groups with a financial investment in the organization, whose focus rests entirely on the financial value of the organization. These groups typically demand that companies perform so they get the benefit of the higher-priced stock offering (Figure 1.3) or other financial returns the organization gives in exchange for part ownership.

In addition to financial gains, shareholders also mandate that organizations maintain an ethical and successful reputation, and exceed customer needs—efforts that bring about increased value of the company. Shareholders sometimes possess **voting power**, which when used to vote in a particular direction or approach may force an organization to take actions it might otherwise have passed over. In some cases, the actions are taken to compete directly with other organizations that shareholders foresee may be a threat.

Although financial pressures on the organization often come from the shareholders, they also come about because of the need to balance costs against profit. That is, profit can only be achieved if costs are maintained or reduced.

Costs Versus Profitability

The need to keep costs low and profitability high forms a related challenge for organizations in hiring and retaining the best workers. Recent economic reports show the average salary across the globe has not kept up with the rate of increase in worker productivity (SHRM, 2014). Frankly, while productivity is steadily increasing, pay is remaining about the same. The lack of increase in wages may be attributed to the changes in technological advances—organizations achieve more with fewer skilled employees. Furthermore, as technology improves, organizations reduce the number of full-time workers on the payroll and cap workers at part-time employment, thereby saving costs in both salary and pay out of benefits (SHRM, 2014). In addition, global hiring opportunities enable organizations to find the cheapest labor, further reducing costs while increasing profitability.

The pressures to save money and do more with less are often driven by market pressures, but also environmental pressures as accumulated concerns about harm to the planet and consumption of nonreplaceable and nonsustainable resources grows.

Resources

Competition for Resources and Market Share

Organizations compete with one another for resources and profits, trying to outproduce one another. They strive to pay the cheapest rate for materials and labor.

This competition can drive prices up or down, and affects the world market place. Finding the cheapest resources may also include enticing and recruiting workers from other industries or companies and hiring cheap labor from economically downturned economies.

Competition for resources also refers to the need to innovate faster with more profitable and exciting innovations than the competition ensuring a higher market share. To innovate quickly requires recruiting, selecting, and retaining the best workers. Selecting and retaining the best people can consume tremendous organizational resources, in particular finding and retaining those with unique skills and/or experience not readily learned or available (sometimes referred to as "critical to hire"). Yet, expending financial resources to gain those who can innovate may be a worthwhile tradeoff.

With every purchase or acquisition of resource, an organization must make a cost/profit tradeoff—determining whether the cost of the resource will be returned in the profitability the resource should deliver. Consequently, resources as an external challenge is inherently tied to financial challenges, in particularly balancing costs versus profitability. In addition, resources and costs are intricately connected to an organization's **carbon footprint**: emissions caused by the use of environmental resources, such as coal, trees, or minerals expressed in terms of amount of carbon dioxide. The extent to which the organization uses up natural resources and produces toxins falls under environmental pressures to preserve or sustain the planet.

Environment

Environmental Sustainability

In many countries, environmental protection agencies limit the amount of carbon production from manufacturing (Figure 1.4) and number of trees that can be forested at any one time or in any single location. These protection agencies also enact shipping restrictions to limit gas and oil deposits in critical fishing areas, ban or limit chemical testing on animals, and in some cases penalize organizations for their use of **fossil fuels**. Such restrictions are frequently the result of activist groups (e.g., Green Peace) putting pressure on governments to regulate air and water quality. Similar groups put pressure on organizations to take ownership in the greening of the planet, by petitioning and lobbying against them and invoking the media to attack the organization's image and reputation. Consequently, many organizations seek to establish a reputation of being "green and clean," protecting the environment and using only sustainable, reproducible fuel sources.

FIGURE 1.4   Carbon Emissions from Manufacturing Plant Glows in the Evening Sky

© Calin Tatu/Shutterstock, Inc.

FIGURE 1.5 Bamboo Forest in Japan

© meanep/Shutterstock, Inc.

The need to manage environmental impact and find **renewable resources** can lead organizations to collaborate with manufacturers and suppliers in other countries, where there may be an abundance of a renewable resource. For example, bamboo (Figure 1.5), one of the fastest growing plants in the world, is considered a renewable resource because of how fast it grows, and like grass, when it is cut it grows back. Bamboo is native in Asia, Africa, Australia, and South America. **Globalization** has made it possible for manufacturers around the world to purchase and trade for bamboo.

Accordingly, another external change is globalization. Competition is no longer limited to the local organizations or those in the same continent—many organizations now face the challenge of competition across the globe, where labor markets may be cheaper and resources, like bamboo, may be more abundant.

Globalization

Globalization, the interconnectivity of the world's cultures, economies, and political systems (Lodge, 1995), can cause the economy of one nation to dramatically affect the economy of others. No longer is it sufficient for leaders to know and focus on their own industry and local market—they must now keep up with global and political trends. Nevertheless, political and economic trends are not the only aspects to track.

The gender, age, and ethnic diversity (Figure 1.6) in organizations today far surpass that of yesterday's businesses, partly to keep up with globalization. For example, the **Society for Human Resource Management, SHRM** (2014), reports that roughly 865 million women will enter the workforce by 2020. Populations are ageing and the number of workers over 64 years of age is rising, with some countries like Japan and China (because of restrictions on number of children per family) experiencing the most significant increases. The advancing age of workers also creates a large discrepancy between the youngest and oldest worker, which can create communication challenges within the workforce, and put pressure on retirement systems, opportunities for promotion, and staffing practices.

Many organizations, especially those in the technology industry where innovations occur regularly and fast, rely on older or more senior workers retiring and creating the space for hiring new people straight out of school who possess the newest knowledge of the industry. Without the natural attrition of senior workers from the workforce, organizations must alter their practices for obtaining new employees, such as hiring temporary workers.

Fitting with globalization, SHRM (2014) also reports that annual migration rates are rising causing increases in ethnic diversity in the workforce. Consequently, there are now expectations for managers and leaders to know how to handle the mix of culture, values, and languages that globalization brings

FIGURE 1.6 Workers Over 65 Years of Age

Left: © Air Images/Shutterstock, Inc.; Right: © Blend Images/Shutterstock, Inc.

(Steers, Sanchez-Runde, & Nardon, 2010). Steers and colleagues provide a comprehensive review of how management across cultures varies, even when the main concept can be similarly defined. For example, at its most basic level, management may be defined as getting things done through coordinating the efforts of others. However, how one coordinates varies by culture. Steers and colleagues reviewed four different typologies of national culture as defined by Hall and colleagues (Hall & Hall, 1990), Hofstede (1980), Trompenaars (1993), and House, Hanges, Javidan, Dorfman, and Gupta's (2004) GLOBE study (Global Leadership and Organizational Behavior Effectiveness). The review provides similarities and differences between national cultures on a number of dimensions with suggestions for how managers can develop the appropriate skills using the dimensions as guideposts for coordinating efforts across cultures.

What other external pressures do you think organizations face that aren't identified here?

Though the number of external challenges exceed those reviewed here, organizations must also handle internal problems that threaten their effectiveness and that serve as current topics of study for organizational behavior and organizational psychology researchers.

Internal Challenges

Internal challenges for organizations may arise from the handling of external challenges. For instance, new technology adoption requires training and adjustments within the workforce. New technology may be acquired in response to an external pressure, such as regulatory agencies demanding compliance with new reporting policies. If the organization is expected to comply with new regulations for which it has no internal expertise, new people may have to be hired specifically for that role, resulting in new job creation and new personnel management. With new people comes new policies to manage their work and control, to some extent, their actions (e.g., ensuring safety). In addition, as organizations grow and people are added to teams, the organizational structure changes. As the structure changes so too does the **strategy**, which in turn requires that employees change jobs within the organization to achieve the new strategy and fit into the new structure. Thus, internal challenges, like external challenges, are interconnected with one another.

Growing Pains

As an organization grows and takes on new business, personnel changes may become necessary. For example, reorganization often follows rapid growth. Groups that become too large for proper managing may be divided, with another new manager hired to supervise the newly formed group.

Political disagreements between executives sometimes causes changes internally within the organization. Although not necessarily business driven, such accommodations are made to keep the peace and retain key executives. As employees are promoted, new ones must be hired to take their place or shifted from other units causing a ripple effect of personnel changes. As new employees are hired, changes in business and the practices that maintain the business occur.

Changing Jobs

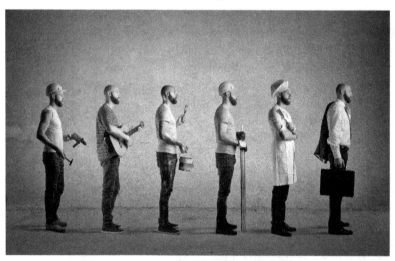

© Ollyy/Shutterstock.com

Job changes may come about as a direct consequence of restructuring the organization and hiring new employees, or job changes made to increase motivation levels of current employees. Chapter 3 focuses on motivation and some of the strategies for increasing motivation that may lead to new internal challenges for the organization. For example, several approaches to increasing employee motivation involve temporary **job swapping** to increase novelty, rotating employees into different jobs for temporary assignments that build new skills, and adding or changing responsibility to increase **autonomy** and sense of contribution. These changes affect multiple people, sometimes in multiple groups within the organization. Although these changes described here at the individual level—focused on the employee—many efforts to ignite motivation across the organization require bigger change, such as changes in policies or even changes in the **organizational strategy** (Chapter 13).

Changing Policies

Policy changes can occur for a variety of reasons including improvements or dealing with problems. Policy changes may be a consequence of finding flaws in the old ones. New policies may arise out of a realization that a policy could help clarify job roles and responsibilities, thereby reducing role ambiguity.

Internal problems also create the need for policy changes that affect all employees; not just those associated with the immediate internal problem. For example, employee theft, drug use, or other inappropriate and sometimes illegal activity must be handled for that event, but also policies must be developed to prevent repeat occurrences.

New and changing policies can happen frequently within organizations as a function of identifying where consistency is necessary to achieve safety, security, and productivity. Policy changes also occur in direct response to changes in the organizational strategy that are triggered by some of the external challenges noted previously.

Changing Strategy

Changes in the organization's strategy can create significant internal challenges within an organization. For example, the Poudre School District in Northern Colorado decided to change its strategy to construct high performance buildings for their schools rather than continue following the same school building plans that were clearly ineffective at saving energy, providing natural light for learning, using replaceable building materials, or becoming learning tools themselves. Old building models were simply not acceptable anymore according to the school district, which was attempting to respond to environmental pressures, as well as societal pressures, to do more. However, no one besides the superintendent knew what a high performance building was, nor that it incorporated sustainable building principles. This change in strategy, therefore, required employees to relearn their disciplines within construction, revisit how teachers teach and how students learn best, revisit how to calculate costs of materials and labor for a 50-year horizon, and much more. While many of these changes were for the better, many caused arguments and disagreements among key **stakeholders**, and challenges with the internal changes in the organization, putting pressure on external partners such as community partners and leaders.

Dealing with challenges is tough, but organizations can do so effectively, using the findings from research in organizational behavior and psychology, and leveraging the applied experience of practitioners in these two disciplines.

What other internal factors do you think organizations face that aren't identified here?

What Is the Design of This Book?

The chapters in this book were written specifically for you, to introduce the concepts of organizational psychology and organizational behavior in a sequential order from a micro to macro perspective. Though the chapters can effectively stand alone, and thus be taken in any order, they are best understood when taken in the order provided. Here and there, a concept or two is introduced in one chapter and subsequently referred to in another chapter. The book, therefore, was written as a single text, as opposed to independent, stand-alone modules.

To understand how the content relates and applies to the workplace, each chapter begins with a brief overview. Read this overview first, before reading the entire chapter, to orient yourself as to what comes next. Besides Chapter 1, each chapter also contains a mini-quiz that you can take before and after reading the

FIGURE 1.7 Chapters of the Book Build on Each Other

Courtesy Zinta Byrne.

Why is constant change a challenge for organizaitons?

chapter to assess your overall comprehension of the key topics (answers are in the back of the book). At the end of every chapter is a figure, a visual summary of the key concepts reviewed in that chapter. The visual summary can be examined before, during, and after you read the chapter as a means of helping you organize the content for understanding.

Chapter Sequence

As noted, the chapters fall in sequential order from micro concepts to macro. Effectively, each chapter builds on its predecessor (Figure 1.7).

In Chapter 2, we learn how **socialization** occurs within the organization and teams. In Chapter 3, we discuss what motivates employees. Chapter 4 gets into the **attitudes** employees hold and how these attitudes may drive motivation, in addition to leading to other attitudes and behaviors. As we work, we perform and our performance is evaluated (Chapter 5), and we experience stress (Chapter 6) because of our work and how we are evaluated. In Chapter 7, we move to a slightly more macro-level focus on employees by looking at teams, their structure, and team dynamics. In Chapter 8, we learn about **management**, a central concern of organizations as management drives projects, oversees the actions of teams, and directs employees to achieve organizational goals. In both Chapters 8 and 9, we learn the difference between management and **leadership**, but Chapter 9 explains leadership principles. We learn how leaders guide their organization on its path to achieving its purpose (**mission**). Employees, managers, and leaders must communicate to accomplish work (Chapter 10), and what is and is not communicated affects teams, stress, performance, and motivation. Leaders design and influence the organizational structure (Chapter 11), such as how reporting relationships are established, to better align with meeting organizational goals. As organizations expand and adapt to meet global challenges, employees experience organizational change and **transformation** (Chapter 12). Lastly, in Chapter 13, organizational strategy—the outlook and goals for the organization—takes center stage, giving us the most-macro perspective of organizaitons reflected in this book.

Chapter Summary

Working consumes our waking lives, and as such, we should know as much as we can about work to ensure our time is well spent and that we can derive as much satisfaction and meaning from our work. Researchers have been systematically studying work and organizations for over 200 years (longer if you include the Egyptians and ancient Chinese philosophers); attempting to understand and solve the challenges that organizational members face in dealing with external and internal pressures. Organizational psychology and organizational behavior are two fields of study that focus on human behavior in the workplace, and on the organizations in which we work. By integrating the approaches the two fields take to understanding the workplace, as well as providing theory and research with application, this book provides a unique and comprehensive review of organizational psychology and behavior.

Figure 1.8 provides a visual summary of the key concepts from Chapter 1. The visual summary of Chapter 1 (shown in Figure 1.8) provides a quick perspective on how the fields of organizational psychology and organizational behavior come together, what they focus on, and what within society corresponds with

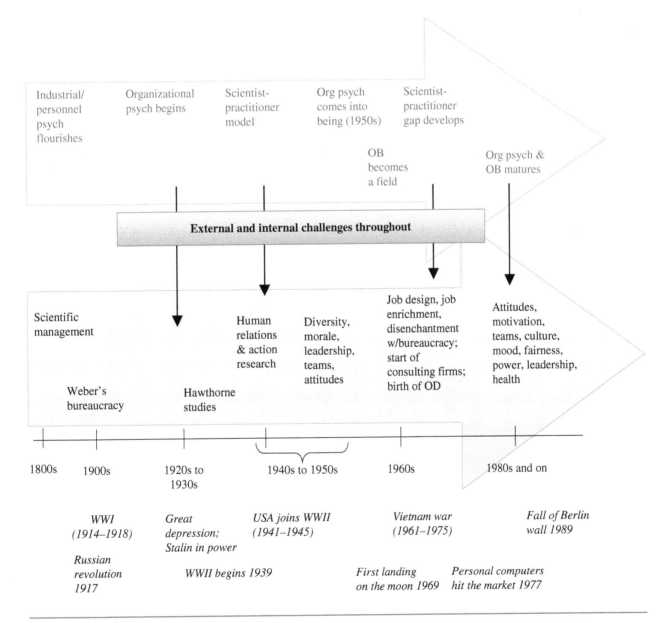

FIGURE 1.8   Visual Summary of Chapter 1.

Courtesy Zinta Byrne.

the different topics of study. Because organizational psychology and behavior often respond to what happens in society, the timeline of major world events helps provide perspective on why different topics were studied at those times. For example, different wars at different times instigated studies and findings to facilitate those wars.

Discussion Questions

1. Table 1.1 shows a number of topics in industrial psychology, organizational psychology, and organizational behavior, many of which overlap. With so much overlap and all three areas focusing on essentially the same field of study, do you think they will eventually combine into a single field? Why or why not? What is the value in keeping them separate—if any value? If you think they should remain separate, how do you think they can be differentiated even more?

2. Recognizing how societal events have played such a strong role in shaping the fields of organizational psychology and organizational behavior, what current events do you believe will affect the field(s) and in what ways? What do you think will be studied in the scientific arena? How will practitioners respond/change what they are doing in organizations?

3. Why do you think bureaucracy has survived so long even though there is so much criticism about it?

4. Why have wars had such an impact on the development of the field? If countries stop warring, what other kind of major events could help move the fields forward?

References

Aamodt, M. G. (2012). *Industrial/organizational psychology: An applied approach.* Belmont, CA: Wadsworth.

Argyris, C. (1957). *Personality and organization.* New York, NY: Harper.

Bass, B. M. (1965). *Organizational psychology.* Boston, MA: Allyn & Bacon.

Foley, S. (June 6, 2008). From Zero to Hero? For years, Wal-Mart was attacked for exploiting its staff and suppliers. But now the world's biggest retailer has stopped fighting its critics and started listening. *The Independent* (London), p. 46. Retrieved from www.lexisnexis.com/hottopics/lnacademic

Hall, E. T., & Hall, M. R. (1990). *Understanding cultural differences.* Yarmouth, ME: Intercultural Press.

Herzberg, F., Mausner, B., & Snyderman, B. B. (1959). *Motivation to work.* Oxford, England: John Wiley.

Hofstede, G. (1980). *Culture's consequences: International differences in work-related values.* Beverly Hills, CA: Sage.

House, R. J., Hanges, P. J., Javidan, M., Dorfman, P. W., & Gupta, V. (2004). *Culture, leadership and organizations: The GLOBE study of 62 societies.* Thousand Oaks, CA: Sage.

Katzell, R. A., & Austin, J. T. (1992). From then to now: The development of industrial-organizational psychology in the United States. *Journal of Applied Psychology, 77*(6), 803–835.

Levy, P. (2012). *Industrial organizational psychology*. New York, NY: Worth Publishers.

Lewin, K. (1947). Group decision and social change. In T. M. Newcomb & E. L. Hartley (Eds.), *Readings in social psychology* (pp. 340–344). New York, NY: Holt, Rinehart, & Winston.

Lewin, K. (1951). *Field theory in social science: Selected theoretical papers*. Oxford England: Harpers.

Lewin, K., Dembo, T., Festinger, L., & Sears, P. S. (1944). Level of aspiration. In J. McV. Hunt (Ed.), *Personality and the behavior disorders* (pp. 333–378). New York, NY: Ronald.

Lewin, K., Lippitt, R., & White, R. K. (1939). Patterns of aggressive behavior in experimentally created "social climates." *The Journal of Social Psychology, 10*, 271–299.

Lodge, G. C. (1995). *Managing globalization in the age of interdependence*. San Francisco, CA: Pfeifer.

Mayo, E. (1933). *The human problems of an industrial civilization*. New York, NY: The Macmillan Company.

McGregor, D. (1960). *The human side of enterprise*. New York, NY: McGraw-Hill.

Moorhead, G., & Griffin, R. W. (1995). *Organizational behavior: Managing people and organizations* (4th ed.). Boston, MA: Houghton Mifflin Company.

Porter, L. W., Lawler, E. E. III., & Hackman, J. R. (1975). *Behavior in organizations*. New York, NY: McGraw-Hill.

Porter, L. W., & Schneider, B. (2014). What was, what is, and what may be in OP/OB. *Annual Review of Organizational Psychology and Organizational Behavior, 1*, 1–21. doi:10.1146/annurev-orgpsych-031413-091302

Riggio, R. E. (2012). *Introduction to industrial and organizational psychology*. Upper Saddle River, NJ: Pearson.

SHRM (2014). *What's next: Future global trends affecting your organization. Evolution of work and the worker*. London, England: The Economist Intelligence Unit.

Steers, R. M., Sanchez-Runde, C. J., & Nardon, L. (2010). *Management across cultures: Challenges and strategies*. Cambridge, UK: University Press.

Trompenaars, F. (1993). *Riding the waves of culture: Understanding cultural diversity in business*. London, England: Economist Books.

Weber, M. (1947). *Theory of social and economic organization* (Translation by A. M. Henderson & T. Parsons). London, England: Oxford University Press.

Whitehead, T. N. (1935). Social relationships in the factory: A study of an industrial group. *Human Factors (London), 9*, 381–382.

Whitehead, T. N. (1938). *The industrial worker*. Cambridge, MA: Harvard University Press.

PART I

Individuals in Organizations

CHAPTER 2

Joining the Organization: Socialization

Learning Outcomes

After studying this chapter, you should be able to explain:

1. What it means to be socialized into an organization and why that's important.

2. How socialization contributes to the maintenance of the organization by fostering and maintaining norms and promoting employee retention.

3. How to use the process of socialization to your advantage when entering an organization of your choice.

Mini-Quiz: Organizational Socialization

As an introduction to this chapter, please take the following mini-quiz (answers are in the back of the book). As you read the questions and consider the answers *before* diving into the chapter, you'll challenge yourself before you master the content, a process that helps facilitate learning for long-term retention. Some questions may have more than one correct answer. Don't worry if you cannot answer all questions correctly on your first try. By the time you read through the chapter and spend some of your own time thinking about these concepts, you should be able to determine the best answers. Try the quiz again after you finish reading the chapter.

1. When first becoming part of an organization, socialization involves:
   a. Picking up social cues from other employees
   b. Attending after work parties
   c. Reading company materials or exploring internal databases and employee profiles
   d. Individualized processes, such as being assigned a mentor

2. True or False: Socialization happens only once, when an employee joins the organization.

3. If a manager elected to "onboard" a new employee, they are most likely:
   a. Picking up an employee from the airport
   b. Securing the employee's agreement in regards to standard policies and procedures
   c. Introducing the employee to their new team
   d. Facilitating a team building exercise for the group of new hires

4. If an organization doesn't adequately socialize its employees:
   a. New hires may be more likely to quit
   b. Employees may feel less attached to the company
   c. New employees may experience less stress because they can dive right into their work and not have to mingle
   d. It may not recruit the right kinds of employees

5. Which of the following is/are true about socialization methods?
   a. When recruiting employees, more information is better
   b. People who are socialized with both formal and informal organizational socialization methods tend to stay at the organization longer than employees who receive only formal socialization

c. Having current employees help socialize the new employees is not very beneficial

d. Processes that focus on employees' first experiences (e.g., first mistake in the new role) do not work because first impressions don't stick with employees very long

Overview

Your first days on the job with an organization affect your short-term and long-term view of what it means to be a member of that organization, as well as your desire to remain with the organization over the long run. Joining an organization is like making a new friend or finding a new club and deciding from the first meeting whether you like the group and fit in with the group. When you first join a new group, are you introduced to everyone by someone else (Figure 2.1) or do you have to introduce yourself? Are you invited to a social function right away or do you first have to attend several group meetings before you are invited out socially? Are people willing to teach you how the group works, such as who talks or makes decisions, or are you left figuring it out for yourself? Being hired by an organization is not

FIGURE 2.1   First Day on the Job.

© fizkes/Shutterstock.com

exactly the same as joining a social group or club, but there are similarities in that those first few introductions in both cases make a difference in how close you feel to the group.

An organization is an entity made up of many people, with policies and rules for interaction, and with policies and rules for how to socialize newcomers into the organization. Thus, the socialization process is not as simple as meeting someone and deciding yes or no on the friendship; rather the socialization process is about joining an established group of many people who have a common purpose and rules for membership.

This chapter reviews the socialization process—the process of joining an organization as a new employee or joining a new group within the same organization. The chapter also reviews why socialization matters to organizations and what *you* can do to ensure your socialization process into the organization of your choice is a successful one.

What Does Socialization Mean?

Socialization, synonymous with organizational socialization, refers to the process of sharing the values, beliefs, and **norms** of the organization with new employees. Existing members of the organization ensure the permanence of how the organization operates by how they welcome newcomers and share with them "how things work around here." Van Maanen and Schein (1979) define socialization as "the process by which an individual acquires the social knowledge and skills necessary to assume an organizational role" (p. 211). It is how a newcomer (whether new to the organization or just new to a different group or unit within the same organization) learns what is expected of him or her and what is not allowed in the group.

Feldman (1981) concluded from a year-long study that organizational socialization is a continuous process that includes change and learning, and involves both the employee and the organization. However, socialization does not guide people to a single accepted set of standards, but rather relaxes any extreme attitudes and behaviors newcomers may have, bringing them closer to the norm, to what is acceptable within the organization. Socialization doesn't necessarily change people but rather encourages them to fit in with the organization as it is, while also allowing the organization to adapt to incorporate the new employee. Organizations typically change very little to bring on newcomers, unless that newcomer is at a high level in the organization and the purpose of bringing that person in is to change the organization. Socialization is much more about getting a person to fit into the organization than vice-versa, though new people joining an organization can have a changing effect.

The simplest way of describing the socialization process may have been offered by Bauer and Erdogan (2011), who defined socialization as the process by which outsiders become insiders. It is how employees gain the knowledge, skills, and understanding of expected behaviors necessary for performing effectively in the organization. Some researchers separate organizational socialization from task socialization (Haueter, Hoff-Macan, & Winter, 2003). Organizational socialization is as described here in this chapter, whereas task socialization refers to how employees learn the job, what tasks they must perform, and how to get information about their job. Does the difference matter? A little. Madlock and Chory (2013) found that organizational socialization was more strongly related to organizational commitment, job involvement, and work alienation than was task socialization.

Notice that the definitions of socialization refer to it as a *process* that is *ongoing*. Socialization does not happen as a single, finite event. As an employee, you are constantly and continuously socialized into an organization. As the organization changes, you change, and as you change, the organization slowly changes. A good visual example of how an efficient socialization process works may be to imagine a well-established river with another feeding into it (see Figure 2.2).

The current of the larger river is strong and as additional rivers or streams join the larger river, they blend in and become part of the larger stream (see Figure 2.2).

Like a small river entering into a larger one, Jablin (2001) suggested that communication affects how employees enter into the organization and consequently, influences the probability that they will assimilate and stay. Like other researchers before him, he labeled the step just before entering the organization as **anticipatory socialization**, to reflect that employees collect information as they anticipate entering the organization, and this information has long-lasting effects on their expectations and perceptions of the organization. Newcomers obtain information through the organization's advertisements,

Remember a time when you joined a new group. What was it like learning about the group, how they worked together, what they liked, and how you'd fit in?

FIGURE 2.2   Confluence of Two Rivers Illustrating Socialization.

© Iri_sha/Shutterstock, Inc.

reports, and brochures, or through interaction with members of the organization during interviews or casual contact with current employees (such as via common acquaintances). These first introductions to the organization, through either the written material or interactions with others, serve as the anticipatory socialization. Jablin additionally suggested that as employees begin their first days on the job, their exposure to written communication within the organization can be more effective in the socialization process than their exposure to oral communication, such as during a new-hire orientation. This is because new employees can become overwhelmed by the amount of information received and reading written material over a period of time (as opposed to in a single sitting) can ease their cognitive load. Jablin emphasized the importance of clear and well-documented orientation materials to facilitate the socialization process because poor communication ultimately contributes to employees' quitting.

Organizational socialization is not quite the same as ***onboarding***, a term used in many organizations to describe introducing newly hired employees into the organization. The difference lies in that socialization generally refers to the process of psychological investment; of transmitting norms, sharing the culture, and providing employees with information concerning expectations for behavior on the job and in the organization. Socialization has not typically included the human resource management tasks associated with hiring an employee such as completing necessary forms like insurance, tax, and personnel records. Socialization has also not included equipment allocation, desk location and phone service installation, or other physical aspects of working.

Onboarding, in contrast, refers to the process of form completion, equipment assignment, personnel records, issues regarding regulatory compliance, and the physical aspect of introducing new employees to the organization. Onboarding may also include sending the employee documents that share the company history, but the primary focus of onboarding is the form completion, equipment allocation, and other human resource functions (see Robb, 2012 for an example of electronic onboarding).

So, we get that socialization is a process, but what are employees getting socialized about? Chao and her colleagues (Chao, O'Leary-Kelly, Wolf, Klein, & Gardner, 1994) determined organizations socialize employees in six different areas: History, Language, Organizational goals and values, People, Performance proficiency, and Politics.

Chao and colleagues found that socialization on Performance Proficiency, People, History, and Language increased over time, providing evidence that socialization is, indeed, an ongoing process. Similarly, Klein and Weaver (2000) conducted a **quasi-experimental study** wherein some newcomers underwent orientation training, whereas others did not. After comparing the two groups, the researchers determined that newcomers who underwent orientation training across the six categories in Table 2.1 showed higher levels of understanding and socialization with goals, history, and people, and they reported higher levels of commitment to the organization 2 months after training, in comparison to those who did not experience the new-hire orientation.

TABLE 2.1 Six Areas in Which Newcomers Are Socialized

Area of Socialization	What Is Included
History	Traditions, rituals, and customs about the company that are important to maintaining the history and company culture.
Language	Learning the technical language of the organization, including acronyms, the group jargon, and informal conversation styles.
Organizational goals and values	Learning the formally documented values and goals, as well as the undocumented, informal values and goals that guide behavior. These include the unwritten, unspoken rules that are sometimes only learned when they are violated.
People	Developing interpersonal relationships with others in the organization, and in particular on one's team.
Performance proficiency	Learning the tasks that are required of the job.
Politics	Gaining formal and informal information about the organization, how the chain of command really works as opposed to what the organizational structure says.

Courtesy Zinta Byrne.

Why Do We Care So Much About the Socialization Process?

How you're socialized into an organization affects your view of membership in that organization for many years to come, and possibly for the entire time you're with that organization. Socialization determines your relationship with the organization until some event or other socialization process wipes the previous one away. Researchers have found the highest rates of **turnover** (quitting) are among new employees, as opposed to established employees (Farber, 1994; Griffith & Hom, 2001). For organizations, turnover of new employees means their investment in hiring and training the new employee is lost before the organization sees a return on that investment. Though numerous reasons exist for employees quitting, one reason may be inadequate socialization (Feldman, 1988; Klein & Weaver, 2000).

As a hew hire, you should care about the socialization process because it affects how you view the organization, how you feel connected to or aligned with the organization, and to what degree you develop attachment to the organization and its members. Some researchers summarize the socialization process as an expectation-setting or uncertainty-reducing process (Bauer, Bodner, Erdogan, Truxillo, & Tucker, 2007; Saks & Gruman, 2011). When you're hired into the organization, you may not know what to expect or you may have different expectations of entry than what the organization had in mind. The more different your expectations are from the organization's, the more the socialization process must do to get you aligned with the organization's goals and **vision** (Saks & Gruman, 2011). People dislike the unknown and seek to reduce anxiety and the uncertainty experienced upon entry. Hence, your efforts in the socialization process revolve around gaining as much information as you can to increase your understanding and ability to predict what is expected. The socialization process reduces the uncertainty (uncertainty reduction theory; Falcione & Wilson, 1988; Lester, 1987). As uncertainty is reduced, you as a newcomer can focus on learning the job, performing the job, and developing feelings of job satisfaction and commitment to the organization (Morrison, 1993). Thus, socialization serves an important role in anxiety and uncertainty reduction for newcomers.

When you think of starting a new job, what are you most concerned about?

Additionally, organizations want newcomers to be effective; to learn quickly how to perform the expected jobs accurately, and to become productive in the shortest amount of time possible. By observing others in the organization, such as supervisors and colleagues, newcomers learn to mimic or model the behavior of appropriate role models (i.e., vicarious learning). Through mimicking the behaviors they see (i.e., mastery modeling), newcomers achieve a sense of mastery that then translates into higher levels of self-efficacy. Higher **self-efficacy** leads to reduced anxiety. Thus, socialization can be explained using Bandura's (1986a, 1986b) **social cognitive theory** and self-efficacy theory. That is, socialization is important because it promotes vicarious learning and the development of self-efficacy in the job, both of which help newcomers master their new roles and tasks.

Successful socialization can be indicated by high **job performance**, positive job attitudes like satisfaction, commitment, and intentions to remain with the organization, role clarity (i.e., know what is expected of your job role), and interest in recruiting and socializing others into the organization. Thus, the organization gains from a successful socialization and so does the employee.

Socialization Contributes to the Organization

When is socialization not good for the organization? When might it backfire?

By molding newcomers to match existing employees' attitudes and behaviors, the organization maintains its brand, look and feel, and way of operating. Thus, the socialization process helps keep the organization as it is, whether good or bad. When change is desired, the socialization process makes it hard to accomplish that change because it reinforces the way the organization does things now, rather than the way the organization may want to do things in the future. Organizations can and do purposefully change their socialization processes, but those formal and collective processes do not affect the informal and individualized socialization that still occurs within teams. In this way, the socialization process can be both helpful and hurtful to an organization. Similarly, if those doing the socializing disagree with the goals of the organization, they may subject the newcomer to potentially conflicting attitudes and behaviors. If the socialization process is good, however, and properly brings new people into the system, the process helps to maintain order. Thus, choosing the right people to do the socialization is important.

In addition, organizations benefit from socializing newcomers in that an effective process leads to new employees' job satisfaction, performance, commitment to the organization, and intentions to stay with the organization (Bauer et al., 2007).

Exercise 2.1

In your own words, write a paragraph explaining what socialization is and why organizations socialize their employees.

What Does a Socialization Process Look Like?

Both employees and organizations play an active role in the socialization process. That is, employees seek information to acquaint themselves with "how things work around here" and organizations have procedures to acclimate new people to the norms of the organization. Employees first have to be recruited, however, before they can be socialized. Because socialization starts with **recruitment**, some knowledge of what is involved in recruiting employees is helpful. Therefore, we begin with recruitment (Figure 2.3).

The recruitment process from the organization's perspective, as shown in Figure 2.3, involves developing a clear objective for recruitment efforts, designing and developing a strategy and plan for how to achieve that objective, implementing the plan, and then evaluating whether the recruitment efforts were successful. As Breaugh (2009) explains, *objectives for recruitment* may include number and types of positions to be filled, how many applicants the recruitment efforts should obtain, diversity of the applicant pool, and whether specific criteria exist for performance or knowledge levels that recruits should meet.

The *recruitment strategy* should include details of proposed methods for recruitment such as sources (e.g., advertisement, employee referrals), messaging (i.e., what should be said about the organization, the position), and where to recruit (e.g., universities, conferences).

Implementing the recruitment strategy is relatively straightforward—advertisements get distributed, employees incentivized to recruit family and friends, communication specialists craft careful messages that convey the nature of the job and organizational culture, and recruiters are trained and sent to the locations identified in the recruitment plan (e.g., high school or university career fair day, attending conferences for recruiting experienced applicants).

Lastly, the *evaluation process* involves gathering information that indicates the quality of applicants, which source produced the most applicants, how long the process took, the costs associated with the recruitment efforts and filling the desired position(s), the hiring manager's satisfaction with the process, and the applicant's retention rate and perceptions of the process. Unless a plan for obtaining this evaluative information exists, the organization will be hard pressed to gather it later to justify the return on investment of recruitment.

The recruitment process applicants follow is more simplistic in comparison to that of the organization (Breaugh, 2012), and may look more like Figure 2.4.

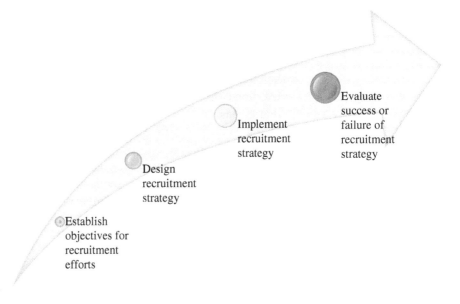

FIGURE 2.3   Model of the Employer's Recruitment Process.

Courtesy Zinta Byrne. Source: Breaugh (2009).

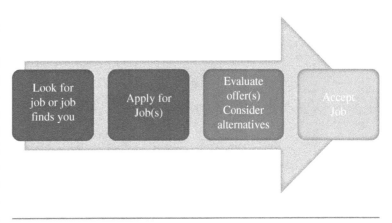

FIGURE 2.4   Recruit Process Applicants Follow.

Courtesy Zinta Byrne. Source: Breaugh (2012).

Attracting New Employees Through Recruitment

The recruitment literature is vast and therefore the coverage here is limited to a general overview for the sake of understanding the socialization process as it relates to organizational psychology and behavior. There are many different methods, sources of recruitment, locations, and processes organizations use for recruiting new employees and for socializing them.

How Are You Recruited—Methods

Think about what it means to look for a job with a particular organization. You have to be interested in the job the organization is advertising and you have to be interested in the organization that has the job opening. Organizations work to maximize the number of job seekers interested in them and in their jobs, in hopes that at least some, if not most, of the applicants are qualified.

A number of different methods for recruiting job applicants have been used, including: employee referrals (i.e., asking employees to refer people they know), college campus recruiting such as job fairs on campus, organization's web site, **job boards** (e.g., Monster.com), job fairs at local conference centers, advertisements at job placement agencies, and social networking (See Breaugh, 2012 for an explanation of each).

How Do You Hear about Jobs—Sources

People are recruited to join organizations through a variety of sources, including online and paper marketing materials, employment agencies, existing employees, friends, and family members. Think about how you heard about your first job—from which source did the information come? (Figure 2.5).

The *War for Talent* (Chambers, Handfield-Jones, Hankin, & Michaels, 1998) focuses on recruiting because simply hiring whoever is conveniently

Job Ads, Agencies, Job Fairs   **Coworkers, Friends, Family**

FIGURE 2.5   Sources Where You Find Out About Jobs.

Top left: ©Pixsooz/Shutterstock, Inc.; Top right: ©Dragon Images/Shutterstock, Inc.; Middle left: ©PureSolution/Shutterstock, Inc.; Middle: © wavebreakmedia/Shutterstock, Inc.; Middle right top: ©Pressmaster/Shutterstock, Inc.: Middle right bottom: ©CREATISTA/Shutterstock, Inc.; Bottom left: ©1000 Words/Shutterstock,Inc.; Bottom middle: ©dboystudio/Shutterstock, Inc.; Bottom right: ©Monkey Business Images/Shutterstock, Inc.

available does not guarantee the best and the brightest employee. In the global market, recruitment through one source (e.g., family) may have greater impact than others (e.g., job ad) because of cultural values and organizational norms, or your access to one source versus another may differ. For example, the Internet is widely used for advertising jobs and organizations, but not every country or city is wired for access to the Internet. There may be very qualified applicants in remote locations where Internet access is spotty, expensive, or not available because of geography.

Researchers have shown that when organizations adapt their online advertisement to fit each culture (e.g., photos of people and places from those regions, content that fits cultural values) and incorporate greater diversity, while still projecting their global brand, they do far better than just presenting a single and identical advertisement in every market (Avery & McKay, 2006; Baack & Singh, 2007; Brandel, 2006). Thus, attending to local norms and access is essential for effective recruiting.

Recruitment Approaches and Types of Information

Recruitment can be divided into formal and informal recruitment approaches. Recruitment information comes in the form of word-of-mouth, advertisements, Internet websites, and job boards.

Where do you look for job openings?

Formal Recruitment

Formal recruitment sources include those involving a person or agency who clarifies and explains the job and the organization (Saks & Ashforth, 1997). These may be college placement officers, recruiters, search or placement firms, and advertisements.

Advertisement can be a powerful tool for prospective employees and the recruiting organization alike. Vivid recruitment messages with credible information attract the most attention (Breaugh & Starke, 2000). Enhancing the credibility of the message involves incorporating some criticism about the organization, which it turns out has little negative effect on the attractiveness of the job (Maio & Haddock, 2007; Van Hoye & Lievens, 2009). Lots of applicants and in particular those of high quality (e.g., potentially good fit and have highly developed skills) tend to be attracted to organizations with positive reputations (Collins & Han, 2004; Turban & Cable, 2003), and reputation can be conveyed through advertising.

Informal Recruitment

Informal recruiting sources do not include intermediaries, such as advertisement or hiring agencies. Informal sources include friends or family, employee referrals, and direct applicants or walk-ins (Saks & Ashforth, 1997).

Which Is Better—Formal or Informal?

In general, people recruited through informal sources (e.g., employee referrals) stay with the organization longer than those recruited through formal job ads or agencies (Decker & Cornelius, 1979; Saks, 1994; Wanous & Colella, 1989). A possible explanation for findings indicating informal sources may be better than formal sources is that people most likely stay after hiring because they have received more accurate and realistic information during the recruitment process; they have more appropriate expectations for the job (Breaugh, 1992; Caldwell & O'Reilly, 1985). Thus, rather than receiving the "only positive and glowing" view of the organization that advertisements may share, people recruited through informal sources can ask about the positives and negatives allowing them to form a more accurate picture of employment at the organization. Another possible explanation is that the informal source of information is a friend, and thus the friendship retains the new hire. However, in contrast to the earlier studies, several researchers have found there is no difference in turnover rates between employees who were recruited informally versus formally (Werbel & Landau, 1996; Williams, Labig, & Stone, 1993), suggesting there may be other unknown factors that explain when formal versus informal sources are best.

Which type of recruitment approach do you think you would trust more—formal or informal? Why is that?

In terms of effectiveness for the organizations, recruitment via employee referrals (informal) appears to result in better employees than those recruited through formal methods; however, employee referrals result in a small number of applicants who tend to be mostly men (few women or minorities are recruited; Breaugh, 2012). Referrals do seem to result in hired applicants, though. Breaugh, Greising, Taggart, and Chen (2003) demonstrated that 11.2% of employee-referred applicants received job offers, whereas only 1.3% of college placement referred and recruiter obtained applicants received offers. Overall, Breaugh et al. (2003) found that when comparing recruiting sources such as advertisements, job fairs, and college placement offices with employee referrals and applicants off the street, employee referrals and direct applicants produced the highest quality of applicants and the highest perception of those actually hired.

So far, it would seem informal approaches to recruitment are better than formal ones. That argument can be countered, however, by suggesting that formal recruitment is better than informal because formal advertisements can also help narrow the applicant pool by allowing applicants to appropriately self-select into (or out of) the possible applicant pool. For example, socially and environmentally responsible organizations that advertise about such values attract applicants seeking positions where they can have a significant impact on society through their work (Gully, Phillips, Castellano, Han, & Kim, 2013). Thus, they seek fit.

Research has demonstrated that applicants are attracted to organizations with whom they perceive they will fit, such as those that seem to have similar or compatible national cultural perspectives or characteristics that mimic personality traits similar to those of the applicant (e.g., Judge & Cable, 1997; Parkes, Bochner, & Schneider, 2001). For example, research has shown that applicants scoring high on conscientiousness (i.e., personality trait characterized by attention to detail, structure, planning, and follow through) tend to prefer working for large rather than small firms because large firms tend to have more policies, long-term goals, and structure than smaller firms, which fits their personality. Those scoring high on openness to experience (i.e., a personality trait characterized by an appreciation for beauty, imagination, flexibility, and interest in novelty) tend to prefer working for global or multinational organizations (e.g., Lievens, Decaesteker, & Coetsier, & Geirnaert, 2001) where they can be exposed to many new situations, since this fits with their preference for novelty and flexibility.

Fit in the organization, called **person-organization fit** (P-O fit), affects employees' success in the organization, where those sensing a fit report higher attraction to the organization and once employed, demonstrate longer commitment to the organization (e.g., Judge & Cable, 1997; Kristof, 1996; Lievens, Decaesteker, Coetsier, & Geirnaert, 2001). Perceived fit can be enhanced for minorities by including pictures of minorities in the ads, especially in supervisory positions (Avery, 2003). However, a company's reputation for supporting and valuing diversity carries more weight than recruitment literature (Avery & McKay, 2006). Attracting applicants who might best fit the organization has been attempted using social media websites such as LinkedIn or Facebook, where people are connected to others like themselves or can provide friendly recommendations (Breaugh, 2009). However, employers should be careful in how they use social networking for recruitment for fear of discrimination lawsuits (Hansen, 2009).

Types of Information

Researchers have studied what kind of information about the organization (e.g., specific versus vague) catches job seekers' attention and which sources of information (e.g., friends or media) are most effective at reaching prospective job seekers. Realistic information, which can be negative, is sometimes discounted relative to positive (more glowing) information about the organization, though the effects of negative information differ by experience level of the job seeker, job itself, industry, labor market, and the information itself (Ryan & Delany, 2010). Information is helpful, though. Relevant job information, such as scarcity of the job or time to apply within job advertisements, is associated with applicants' attraction to the job more so than when no information is provided (Ryan & Delany, 2010). Job ads that include explicit statements regarding termination policies and diversity statements, such as being a firm with a termination policy that follows due process and/or being an LGBT(lesbian, gay, bisexual, transgender)-supportive firm discourages job pursuant intentions in job seekers with strong heterosexist attitudes (Lambert, 2015). The implications of Lambert's research are that to encourage an inclusive work environment, one must start at the recruitment stage.

Boosting job seekers' familiarity with an organization, similar to the approach television advertisements use to get you to buy their product on your next trip to the market, does not necessarily result in positive outcomes. Greater familiarity tends to result in more questions or ambivalence (Brooks & Highhouse, 2006). Balancing how much exposure people get to the organization while ensuring the exposure conveys positive prestige and increases job applicants' attraction (Ryan & Delany, 2010). One way to boost prestige is to use publicity and endorsements from sources outside of the organization (Collins & Stevens, 2002).

Where the Organization Recruits

Recruitment on college campuses involving advanced publicity in the form of employer sponsored news stories, faculty endorsements, and specific job ads on campus all contribute to students' attitudes about the potential employer, and intentions to apply (Collins & Stevens, 2002). College recruiters who were personable, perceived as trustworthy, informative, and competent were well received by potential job applicants; recruiters' gender did not matter (Chapman, Uggerslev, Carroll, Piasentin, & Jones, 2005).

However, recruiters do not need to go to campuses to recruit. The organization's website serves as excellent recruiting, in particular if the site is easy to navigate, attractive, and readable. This is especially true for companies with name recognition or an already well-known reputation (Cober, Brown, & Levy, 2004; Rynes & Cable, 2003). Common recruitment web sites that serve as job boards include Monster.com and HotJobs.com. In particular, these sites allow potential applicants to search for jobs based on location, industry, occupation, experience, salary levels, and much more. Because of the ease of finding the job and applying, the number of potential applicants can be unmanageable, creating a disadvantage for the organization posting to these job boards. Job boards such as Ladder.com provide organizations a mechanism for charging job seekers who apply, creating a method for reducing the number of unqualified applicants. The idea is that only qualified applicants will be willing to pay for applying for a job.

Very little research to date has been conducted to determine the effectiveness of electronic recruitment methods (see Breaugh, 2012). However, research has shown that recruiters have a positive effect on job seekers' intentions to apply because recruiters help job seekers determine their fit (or lack of fit) with the organization (Rynes, Bretz, & Gerhart, 1991). Therefore, the disadvantage of relying on electronic recruitment only is that recruiters are not part of the recruitment process. Thus, Internet applicants do not interact with recruiters, resulting in loss of fit information. Given the findings of the importance of P-O fit, organizations would do well to require that after perusing their website or using other Internet resources such as job boards, applicants meet with a trained recruiter (Barber, Hollenbeck, Tower, & Phillips, 1994; Stevens, 1998).

> Where else do you think organizations should recruit? Why—what do those recruitment sources or mechanisms offer that the ones listed here do not?

Positive consequences of the use of technology in recruitment include increased numbers of job applicants due to availability of information and ease of applying, increased scope of reaching potential applicants, and cheaper cost and more efficient process than previous nontechnologically oriented methods of recruiting (Lievens & Harris, 2003). Whether the increase in applicants results in higher quality applicants than with nonelectronic recruitment is still questionable (Chapman & Webster, 2003).

Exercise 2.2

List the various recruitment sources and approaches organizations use. In one sentence, for each approach define or explain what the approach is and why it is effective, and/or not effective.

Processes and Strategies Organizations Use to Socialize

From the organization's perspective, recruitment serves as an important first step in the socialization process. The next steps include a variety of methods that socialize new employees on the norms and overall culture of the organization.

As an employee, you may be exposed early on to the employee manual, which usually documents practices and policies. You may participate in orientations where people share policies and practices as well as tips for how to get physically oriented within the buildings and offices. Similarly, you may participate in meetings with groups of existing employees and managers to discuss roles, responsibilities, and general duties. Below are several (but not all) models of socialization, organized by date of introduction and prominence in the literature.

Van Maanen and Schein's Model

Van Maanen and Schein (1979) offer six bipolar dimensions of **socialization tactics** (actions taken to bring people into the organization and influence their behavior) that are best understood as contrasts between endpoints on a continuum, with a wide range of tactics in between. This is just one way to look at socialization.

More than one tactic from Figure 2.6 can be used at a time, and not necessarily in the exact form as described here. Additionally, hundreds of other tactics may exist—these are the six Van Maanen and Schein found most visible across a variety of organizations, and the tactics that seemed to have a notable impact on the newly hired employee.

Walking through Each of Van Maanen and Schein's Dimensions:

Collective vs. Individual   The advantage of collective socialization processes over individual processes is that group members socialize each other in ways the organization can't. For example, in military facilities the cohort of recruits often set a standard for behavior keeping each other in line outside of the scrutiny of the drill sergeant. The disadvantage of this process is that the recruits' standards for behavior may not be the same as what the organization wants. The United States Air Force Academy in Colorado Springs, Colorado, takes advantage of collective socialization—the cadets want to fit in, excel, and demonstrate they have leader capability. The first way to do this is to demonstrate how to be an excellent follower. Such socialization simply cannot be done by the instructors alone; learning to be a good follower means doing so everywhere, not just under the watchful eye of the instructor.

Another excellent example of collective socialization is with Chinese military academies. In 2011, over 20,000 high school graduates and over 8,000 national defense students from universities in China were recruited into the People's Liberation Army and the Chinese People's Armed Police Force (see *People's Daily*, online newspaper). With such numbers, individualized socialization is not an option.

There is no set tipping point in terms of how many new hires warrants collective versus individualized socialization; the key is whether an isolated, unique, and individually tailored experience of socialization can be achieved with the number of recruits on hand. Individualized socialization is often used at top levels of the organization, where the goal is to "groom" one's successor, or in graduate school where the advisor mentors one or two new students at a time, with the eventual goal of them furthering the advisor's work or even taking over his or her lab one day.

An example survey item measuring collective vs individual socialization is: "In the last six months, I have been extensively involved with other new recruits in common, job related training activities" (Jones, 1986, p.277).

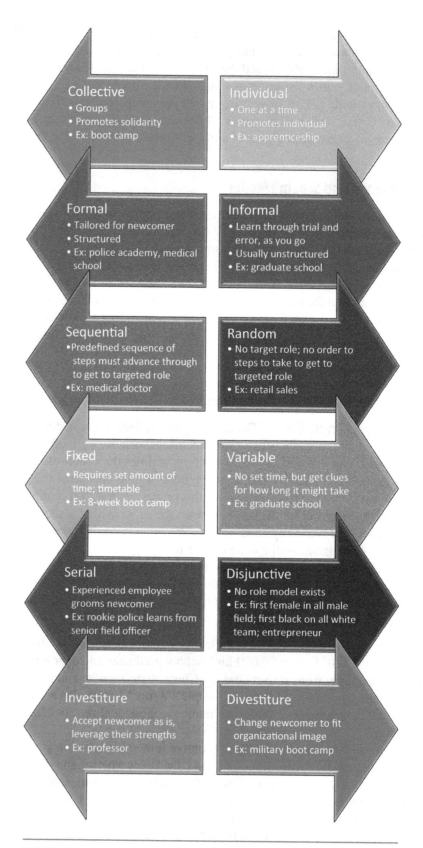

FIGURE 2.6 Dimensions of Socialization Tactics.

Formal vs. Informal   The biggest difference between formal and informal socialization is that formal socialization distinguishes the newcomers as separate from all others in the organization and engages the newcomers in prescribed ways. This form of socialization is preferred when the organization is particular about the attitudes, values, and behavior that employees' display (e.g., customer service organizations). The formal process allows for judgment of the newcomer by existing members of the organization, thus incorporating another layer of scrutiny and socialization (that from existing employees). Again, military academies such as the United States Air Force Academy or the South African Military Academy provide good examples because the goal with the new cadets is to teach them to embrace and embody the attitudes and values, and adopt the behaviors befitting a military officer. Socialization into the system is regulated, prescribed, and organized.

Starbucks Coffee Company and Apple, Incorporated provide examples of nonmilitary organizations that have reportedly used formal socialization processes. At Starbucks, all new hires follow a set plan for training and development, told how to greet customers, and everyone new to Starbucks goes through the same orientation and training process. At Apple, all employees are taught the value of creating and marketing innovative, user-friendly and life-enhancing electronics. Employees working at Starbucks or Apple stores wear uniforms, taught that customers come first, and are shown how to greet and interact with customers.

The informal process, in contrast to the formal process, involves no clear distinction between the newcomer and existing members of the organization. Newcomers learn through trial and error, sometimes costing the organization and/or to the newcomer time and/or money. The process is dependent on whatever event occurs and what learning opportunity comes from that situation. This means that some things have to be learned "out of order," in which the newcomer hasn't yet acquired the right skills or knowledge of the organization to handle the situation effectively. Small- to medium-sized consulting firms and university departments often have informal socialization processes. There are no preset rules or processes for bringing the new person on board—he or she is encouraged to ask questions as needed.

Not all organizations believe in the "sink or swim" mentality, and instead provide a mentor. With large consulting firms, the new person is often placed with a more senior consultant who teaches him or her how to do the job, how to approach clients, the best way to represent the organization, and the right way to present the organization at sales meetings. In smaller firms, the luxury of a mentor is not there and the expectation is that the new consultant will be able to jump into the job and be immediately productive. In an academic setting, the hope is that the new faculty member will infuse new ideas from his or her own training into the hiring department, bringing up new ideas at meetings and opposing old and possibly no longer effective behaviors. The hope, in this case, is that the socialization process changes the organization to a degree to fit the person, rather than just changing the person to fit the organization.

Some organizations use a combination of formal and informal socialization. For example, Apple Inc. has a structured formal process for training new hires, but also provides informal socialization through mentoring or having senior managers acting as role models.

A sample item assessing formal vs informal socialization is: "I have been very aware that I am seen as "learning the ropes" in this organization" (Jones, 1986, p.278).

Sequential vs. Random

Sequential vs. random refers to order of events, not the timing of events. Sequential socialization tends to be quite formal, where the order of steps in the process is known. For example, becoming a doctor, advancing to mastery levels in craft or trade fields with a journeyman process (e.g., carpentry, electrician, plumbing), or becoming a pilot (e.g., you have to advance through sizes of planes, length of flights, and rank), and ranks in the military are all prescribed and sequential. You cannot get to more advanced-level stages in the process without having first gone through and successfully passed criteria established in the previous steps. Though the ranks or stages of professorship in the United States differ from Europe, they both follow a sequential order. For example, in the United States for a tenure track position the standard progression from lowest rank to highest: assistant professor, associate professor, and full professor. In London or the Netherlands, this order follows: lecturer, senior lecturer or reader, and professor, though you sometimes see "Professor Dr." as the title indicating both an advanced degree (a lecturer does not always have a doctorate of philosophy degree) and rank. In Bulgaria, the order from lowest rank to highest is assistant professor, chief assistant professor, docent, and full professor. In addition, in the People's Republic of China, the rank follows from assistant lecturer or associate lecturer, lecturer, associate professor, up to professor. Regardless of country, the order is sequential from lowest rank to highest rank; only the labels differ. The socialization for journeyman in trades such as carpentry or plumbing also follows a sequential order: one must first serve as an apprentice for a fixed term before becoming a master. Random socialization follows no developmental sequence or delineated process. Incidentally, socialization occurs whenever and opportunity presents itself.

A sample item assessing sequential vs random socialization is: "There is a clear pattern in the way one role leads to another or one job assignment leads to another in this organization" (Jones, 1986, p.278)

Fixed vs. Variable

Fixed socialization refers to the process following a preset timeline where the beginning and end dates are known. Thus, fixed vs. variable refers to timing, not order. For example, boot camp in many military institutions tends to last about 2–3 months. The timeline is fixed, and all recruits go through this process at the same time. In contrast, graduate training for an advanced degree in the sciences (e.g., chemistry, psychology, engineering) tends to be variable, where there is some idea of how long the process takes but it varies by person, by field, by specific study, and by country.

A sample item assessing fixed vs variable socialization is: "I have a good knowledge of the time it will take me to go through the various stages of the training process in this organization" (Jones, 1986, p.278)

Serial vs. Disjunctive

With serial socialization, an experienced employee serves as a role model or mentor for newcomers. Advantages and strengths of the serial socialization process include that newcomers can learn from an experienced member of the organization, get help understanding the rules and policies, and not feel alone in trying to make sense of what happens in the organization. This model is powerful when the organization has experienced members whose behaviors, values, and attitudes are consistent with what the organization wants of its employees. The downside of this model, however, is that the experienced members can perpetuate bad habits and negative attitudes that the newcomers may adopt.

Disjunctive socialization occurs when there is no person available who previously occupied the role and could therefore serve as a mentor, such as when a woman firefighter is entering a district that has male firefighters only or if the role is one that did not previously exist. Disjunctive socialization may occur in growing organizations in which new positions are created, new industries or markets

A sample item assessing serial vs disjunctive socialization is: "Experienced organizational members see advising or training newcomers as one of their main job responsibilities in this organization" (Jones, 1986, p.278)

where established organizations simply don't exist (e.g., renewable energy companies such as those in wind or solar power), in the midst of mergers and acquisitions, or when a company's organizational structure (i.e., reporting chain) is overhauled for survival or other purposes (e.g., consent decree).

Investiture vs. Divestiture This socialization approach involves reinforcing or changing the qualities of a person that he or she brings into the organization. Investiture encourages using and emphasizing what a person already knows and can do; there is no desire to change the newcomer. Investiture is most common when hiring people with specific skills and experience desired in the organization; such as hiring a new chief executive officer or specialized engineer who comes from a highly respected organization. Divestiture socialization aims to strip personal characteristics from a newcomer, such as with new cadets at military academies and institutions. The idea is to remove or eliminate all characteristics of the newcomer that could potentially get in the way or prevent the employee from fitting in, and replace them with desirable characteristics that help the employee fit in and espouse company values. Another aim of divestiture socialization is to help newcomers shed their old identity with previous employers and take on a new identity tied to their new place of employment. Divestiture, however, is not always associated with helping newcomers adjust, but instead makes them feel they cannot be themselves or express their unique talents and skills (Cable, Gino, & Staats, 2013; Levine, Choi, & Moreland, 2003).

Research has shown positive relationships between collective, fixed, and investiture tactics with on-the-job-embeddedness for new employees (Allen, 2006). On-the-job-embeddedness refers to the extent to which employees become enmeshed in or are fully entwined within the network of relations and influences that connect or tie the employee to the organization. Since on-the-job-embeddedness has also been shown to relate negatively to turnover and mediates between the socialization tactics and turnover, this study demonstrated that socialization tactics affect the long-term attitudes of newcomers by determining to what extent they become connected to others within the organization.

Allen and Meyer (1990) examined tactics from Van Maanen and Schein's dimensions to see which might have an effect on new hires' commitment to the organization 6 and 12 months after socialization. The researchers found that after 6 months, those who received institutionalized tactics, represented by a combination of collective, formal, sequential, fixed, and investiture tactics, reported higher levels of commitment. In contrast, those who received individualized tactics, a combination of tactics representing individual, informal, random, variable, disjunctive, and divestiture dimensions combined reported lower commitment to the organization.

Others have also tested Van Maanen and Schein's (1979) model. For example, Saks, Uggerslev, and Fassina (2007) showed that institutionalized tactics were associated with less anxiety over roles and expectations (i.e., lower role ambiguity and role conflict), and higher intentions to remain with the organization. Substantial research evidence demonstrates support for Van Maanen and Schein's model, though more so for tactics all used together rather than for the individual tactics as distinct actions.

Van Maanen and Schein's model is distinguished from other socialization models in that it focuses on the tactics organizations can use to socialize employees as opposed to the process or stages of socialization, like Feldman's model reviewed next.

A sample item assessing investiture vs divestiture socialization is: "My organization accepts newcomers for who they are" (Ashforth & Saks, 1997, p.455).

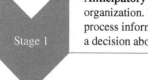

- **Anticipatory socialization:** occurs *before* the employee is hired by the organization. Prospective recruits form expectations, gather and process information about the organization, and eventually make a decision about employment.

Stage 1

- **Accommodation:** occurs when the employee actually becomes a part of the organization. These new hires learn their job tasks, establish trusting relationships with coworkers, define personal roles within the work group, and evaluate their own progress.

Stage 2

- **Role management:** occurs as employees balance the demands from their work group with demands from other work groups. An employee successfully completes this stage after developing effective rules for dealing with conflict arising from the balancing of demands.

Stage 3

FIGURE 2.7   Dimensions of Socialization Tactics.

Courtesy Zinta Byrne. Source: Feldman (1976).

Feldman's Model

Feldman (1976) proposed that socialization occurs across three developmental stages: anticipatory, accommodation, and role management. According to this model, newcomers must progress through and successfully complete each stage before moving to the next (Figure 2.7).

The assumption of the model, that newcomers proceed through one stage before moving to the next, has not held up to empirical scrutiny. That is, the theory suggests stages are independent, yet research shows that mechanisms in earlier stages affect later stages (Dubinsky, Howell, Ingram, & Bellenger, 1986). Thus, later models, such as Jablin's (2001), incorporated the idea of continuous and overlapping processes.

Jablin's Model of Socialization

Jablin (2001) challenged previously defined models of socialization, suggesting that instead of having what seemed to be finite stages of socialization (i.e., you're either in a stage or not), the socialization process comprises communication-related processes: Orienting, Strategies or Tactics, Training, Informal & Formal Mentoring, Information Seeking & Giving, Relationship Development, and Role Negotiation (Figure 2.8). He suggested that people become assimilated into the organization through the communication culture, where they attempt to change the environment while the environment attempts to change them.

Why would you use collective vs. individual socialization approach? Why serial vs. disjunctive?

- Orienting
  Newcomers use oral and written communications to get acquainted with the organization and/or the job. The length of the orientation process ranges from a few hours to a few months, depending on the job and organization.

■ Strategies or Tactics
Van Maanen and Schein's (1979) typology can be collapsed into two ways of socializing people: institutional/structured or individualized/unstructured. According to Jablin, a disadvantage of typologies like these tends to be their one-sidedness (the organization does something to the newcomer). Rather than rely on typologies, he recommended that more research focus on identifying memorable messages, turning points, and critical incidents in the socialization process. For example, studies like Barge and Schlueter's (2004) on memorable messages suggest newcomers understand the messages as encouraging them to fit in while also establishing their uniqueness.

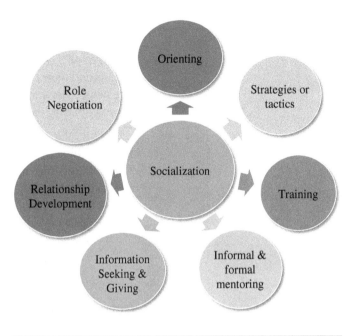

FIGURE 2.8   Communication-Assimilation Processes.

Courtesy Zinta Byrne. Source: Jablin (2001).

■ Training
Training transmits the culture to the newhires and plays an important part in the socialization process. Training programs can be formal, informal, and may take place across a period of time as opposed to a single event only.

■ Informal & Formal Mentoring
Formal mentoring involves an assigned pairing of a newcomer with an experienced employee; in contrast, informal mentoring refers to a spontaneous relationship that naturally develops between individuals (not assigned to each other). Formal mentoring provides newcomers with career-related support, coaching for advancement in the organization, and an understanding of organizational issues. Informal mentoring provides newcomers with information about their jobs and the organization and career support.

Why do Millennials need a mentor?
Watch www.youtube.com/watch?v=4klHR-tkf_g&t=

What are the reasons Lauren gives for why Millennials need a mentor?

■ Information Seeking & Giving
Newcomers participate in the socialization process by proactively seeking out information. Miller and Jablin (1991) suggested that newcomers may seek information through:
❑ Overtly, asking directly
❑ Indirectly hinting rather than asking directly
❑ Asking a third party, someone other than the intended person
❑ Testing, breaking a rule and seeing what happens
❑ Disguising the intent, such as joking or using self-disclosure to get information
❑ Observation, such as watching others' actions or attending to the environment
❑ Surveillance, which includes monitoring conversations
Newcomers tend to seek information about the job itself, as opposed to the organization overall, and ask questions of their colleagues or bosses, or

may find information through reading organizational material like a handbook or policy manual.

Information giving refers to the exchange of information between newcomers and their current employers and employees (if they are managers). The newcomer can provide valuable information and insight about his or her role, clarity (or lack thereof) concerning processes and expectations, or offer ideas for improvements.

▪ Relationship Development

The relationships that develop between newcomers and their supervisors and colleagues serve to facilitate the assimilation process. Recent research shows that a supportive supervisor can offset negative consequences associated with divestiture approaches to socialization, such as making employees feel they cannot be their authentic selves (Montani, Maoret, & Dufour, 2019). Relationships tend toward acquaintances as opposed to best friends, though research has explored the factors that encourage conversion of acquaintances into best friends (e.g., physical proximity, shared tasks, similar life events, socializing outside of work). The more conflict associated with developing relationships at work, the harder and longer the socialization process for newcomers. Organizations like Google offer free beer and wine every Friday to encourage employees to develop friendships at work.

▪ Role Negotiation

Newcomers negotiate the expectations of their jobs and their roles (e.g., manager or not a manager). The success of the negotiation relies on the newcomer's ability to convince the person who has the authority to make changes to the job (e.g., boss or human resources manager). Most often, the negotiations focus on job tasks, scheduling, and benefits.

Jablin's model has inspired the development of new theories of socialization (Scott & Myers, 2010), as well as triggered empirical examinations of the various components of his model. For example, Fonner and Timmerman (2009) found that the primary methods of gathering information included overt questioning, observation, and surveillance. Jablin's scholarship was grounded in organizational communication, and thus it is no surprise that his model of socialization is framed from the communication perspective. However, not everyone sees socialization as revolving around communication, as we see in Saks and Gruman's model (2011).

Saks and Gruman's Model

Saks and Gruman (2011) have argued that the nature of work is very fast-paced, competitive, and requires preparing the newcomer so he or she can tackle organizational challenges rather than inundating the newcomer with a lot of information about the organization. They suggest, instead, an effective organizational socialization process should include a focus on creating positive behavior, which is done by improving newcomers' self-efficacy, hope, optimism, and resilience (collectively known as **psychological capital**; Luthans, Youssef, & Avolio, 2007). Psychological capital is positively related to several valuable employee behaviors and attitudes, such as job performance, satisfaction, and commitment (Luthans, Avolio, Avey, & Norman, 2007).

Saks and Gruman noted the way organizations build psychological capital is by offering four different resources (see Figure 2.9):

1. *Orientation training*, which includes practice, feedback, role modeling, and coping skills.

2. *Task characteristics* that make for an interesting job by including a variety of key characteristics, namely skill variety, autonomy, and information on how the job contributes to the overall organization (i.e., task significance—see Chapter 3, Job Characteristics Model), and performance feedback.

3. *Social support* in the form of mentoring and interacting with others who can provide emotional support.

4. *Leadership* in goal setting can help employees by creating a self-fulfilling prophecy in employees in which employers' actions change employees' actions based on belief. Through conveying to employees that they should expect and believe in their capacity to demonstrate high performance in the organization, the Pygmalion style leader boosts employees' psychological capital.

What do you think you need from an organization to help you feel hopeful, optimistic, and confident you can do the job?

According to Saks and Gruman, the four socialization resources (i.e., leadership, social support, training, task characteristics) foster the four components of psychological capital (i.e., self-efficacy, hope, optimism, resiliency), which result in outcomes associated with socialization, including commitment and retention. Though the full model has yet to be empirically tested, it offers a different view of socialization—away from the focus of information sharing on building capacity within the newcomer. Different aspects of the model have been empirically

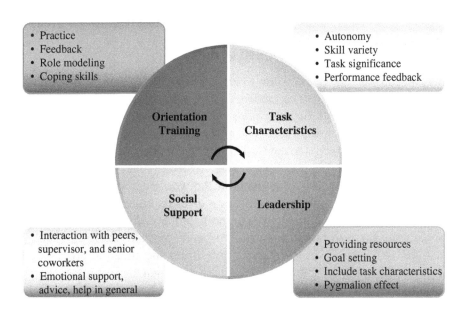

FIGURE 2.9 Model of Socialization.

Courtesy Zinta Byrne. Source: Saks and Gruman (2011).

supported, such as social support facilitating the development of psychological capital (e.g., Wang, Zheng, & Cao, 2014).

The socialization models may all seem quite unique, yet they do build on each other and can be combined.

Making Sense of All the Models

As you've now read from the section above, many socialization models and strategies exist that organizations can use to convert newcomers into insiders (i.e., employees committed to the organization). The models were organized by year of publication because later models make more sense after understanding how the earlier models were developed. For example, the earlier models implied that stages were necessary, suggesting socialization is a linear process. However, additional research exposed that stages were not finite or linear and that employees worked through the socialization processes and mechanisms at varying times, sometimes simultaneously, and as needed. Additionally, early models viewed socialization as what the organization does to the employee. In contrast, later more recently introduced models, such as Saks and Gruman's, view socialization as an interdependent process between the organization and newcomer. This latest view acknowledges the role and capacity of the newcomer in his or her socialization, and the efforts of the organization to not just convey policy but also build psychological connection.

> So which model is best? None—they are equally valuable and each contributes to our understanding of how organizations socialize newcomers.

Exercise 2.4

Compare and contrast Feldman's model, Jablin's model, and Saks and Gruman's model. What components are distinctive of each model?

How Do Managers Use these Models in the Workplace?

Managers can use the socialization models either independently, by combining some together, or using parts of models that seem to apply best to their organizations. The models are not meant to be exclusive of one another—as noted above, later models build on earlier models as researchers' understanding of the socialization process developed. However, that said, the models do not have to be used sequentially by the year in which they were created.

One approach to using the models in the workplace may be to start with Feldman's model. This framework makes it clear that the socialization process has already started before employees enter the organization, and therefore, part of socializing them to the norms of the organization may be to dislodge pre-conceived assumptions. In this case, a divestiture socialization process, taken from Van Maanen and Schein's dimensions may make the most sense since your aim is to help the newcomer separate from any previously held identities tied to another company or institution, or from characteristics and habits that will prevent good fit in the new organization. An example of a company that capitalizes on several models of socialization is the anticipatory socialization stage (Feldman), as well as information seeking and relationship development

(Jablin) is Reaktor—a digital company headquartered in Finland, which offers business design and high performance engineering solution services in New York, Helsinki, Amsterdam, and Tokyo. During the initial interview, applicants are required to meet with as many people as they can in the company to find out about the company, whether they will fit, and also learn about the working context and norms. This is done BEFORE they are hired. If they are hired, on the first day of the job the new hire is treated to coffee and a *korvapuusti*—a Finnish cinnamon bun, and *hygge*—a Danish term meaning warmth and well-being. The idea here is to build relationships (Jablin) and establish a network for social support (Saks & Gruman). Reaktor's model of socialization employs individual and informal tactics (Van Maanen & Schein).

Managers can use any of the dimensions of Van Maanen and Schein's model to choose the type of socialization that fits best with the organization's structure and culture. For example, not all organizations can accommodate individualized socialization; therefore, collective may be the way to go. Batistic (2018) recently proposed an integration of Van Maanen and Schein's socialization dimensions and human resource management systems. Figure 2 in the study shows which dimension might be most effective for which type of Human Resource system. Such an integration can offer a guide for managers or human resource professionals in applying the dimensions within their organizational structure.

Jablin's and Saks & Gruman's models can be used together, as they both suggest that different aspects of the work environment must be introduced and taught to the newcomer as stand-alone parts, though recognizing they interact or overlap. Accordingly, through mentoring, training, and information giving, employees can be introduced to social support and task characteristics of the job. In addition, through boosting self-efficacy in newcomers, managers can encourage them to use their own strategies, such as information seeking, to help work through the organizational socialization process.

Company Example 2.1   What Does Socialization Look Like at the Ritz-Carlton?

In his 2002 Harvard Business Review article, Paul Hemp talked about his experience being oriented (i.e., socialized) into the Ritz-Carlton as a room-service waiter. To avoid plagiarism or fully repeating the article here, just a brief explanation of the process with a connection to the topics in the chapter is provided here [noted in brackets like this]. You are encouraged to read the full article—it's very well-written and rather entertaining.

Day 1 of orientation involved a formal greeting between Paul and a few others being oriented at the same time [collective]. Though everyone received some of the same orientation-training, Paul received specific instruction from others in the same role as him [serial]. Presentations by different Ritz-Carlton employees, including hotel executives, were made to share the vision of what the Ritz-Carlton stands for and represents. Part of these presentations included the legendary story of how Cesar Ritz opened the first hotel in 1898. Stories, coin phrases, key events, and other legendary leaders of the Ritz-Carlton Hotel Company were shared thereafter [history]. After reviewing the Ritz-Carlton 3-paragraph credo line-by-line [language, Jablin's orienting], orientation involved getting a uniform, which differed depending on the job. Norms were then shared, such as what language was okay and what was not okay [language], what level of performance is expected and how to demonstrate that level of performance, and how to think of and view customers [organizational goals and values]. On the second day of orientation, Paul was shown by experienced role models [serial, Jablin's mentoring and training] how to tackle all the aspects of his role. It was not until the 6th day before Paul was ready to go solo as a room-service waiter. Thus, orientation was a 6-day packaged event [fixed, formal, sequential].

Strategies Newcomers Themselves Might Use

Which model of socialization do you think is most useful and why?

Newcomers recognize they need to find out how an organization works so they can fit in and be productive. Newcomers have roles they need to take on, such as task leader, manager, or just new employee, and tasks to perform that might require first knowing something about the organization. To learn about how new employees get information, Ostroff and Kozlowski (1992) conducted a longitudinal study in which they surveyed newcomers within the first couple of months on the job and then again 5 months later, about how they obtained information about their tasks, roles, and the organization. They found that to get information newcomers relied most on observation, and then secondarily on asking interpersonal sources such supervisors and colleagues for information. To learn about tasks and roles, new employees: asked supervisors and colleagues, used experimentation to see what worked and did not work, observed others to see what they did and did not do, and asked questions. When trying to learn about the group or organization, newcomers mostly observed to gain such information. When learning about roles, supervisors provided more information than did colleagues; however, colleagues gave more information about the group itself. As far as amount of information gained, newcomers received the most information about tasks, then about roles, then about groups, and least about organizations. It turns out that Ostroff and Kozlowski's findings were similar to those reported earlier by Miller and Jablin (1991).

As noted above under Jablin's (2001) model, newcomers obtain information about their organization and job through a variety of communication processes. Experienced new hires use their own strategies to facilitate their own socialization. Experienced new hires are employees who may be new to a group within the organization for whom they have already been working or they could be experts in their field but new to that specific organization (such as a professor who switches universities or a senior consultant who switches consulting firms). In conjunction with what the organization does, experienced new hires use their own strategies to facilitate the socialization process.

Cooper-Thomas, Anderson, and Cash (2012) used semistructured interviews to explore newcomer socialization strategies, feeling some may have been overlooked in past theories and research. After interviewing 86 new hires in a professional services organization in London that provides infrastructure services in the energy (oil) industry (thus the professionals the organization places into these various jobs are experienced professionals new to these organizations), Cooper-Thomas and her colleagues found quite a few strategies that experienced new hires used to facilitate their own socialization (see Table 2.2).

TABLE 2.2   Socialization Strategies of Experienced New Hires

Strategy	Explanation
Asking	Directly request information
Attending	Choosing to attend training, orientation, and induction events
Befriending	Establishing social relationships, both in and outside the team
Exchanging	Trading resources with colleagues
Flattering	Trying to make other feel good about themselves
Following	Rely on guidance by experienced workers
Gathering	Seek information and reflect on it to improve understanding
Giving	Give information or advice to other employees
Minimizing	Reduce the amount of new learning needed by taking on tasks and demonstrating current skill set
Negotiating	Discussing and agreeing to role expectations
Networking	Gaining relationships with key people in the organization
Proving	Demonstrate abilities to gain credibility, typically by choosing to work with a specific boss or team
Reading	Using manuals or other available documents
Role modeling	Copy others' behaviors
Socializing	Attending social events outside of work
Talking	Picking up information in passing through casual conversations
Teaming	Putting effort into the team and showing commitment to the group
Waiting	Wait for information and resources to come to them

An interesting contribution of Cooper-Thomas and colleagues' work is that they studied what new hires actually do, versus what they should do. Recently, Tang, Liu, Oh, and Weitz (2014) studied 239 retail employees in a large U.S. retail store and found employees' goal orientation and proactivity (i.e., taking initiative) were significantly related to their gathering and asking, observing others (role modeling), and networking—socialization tactics identified by Cooper-Thomas et al. Additionally, those tactics were positively related to the newcomers' commitment and retention. Researchers have also been focusing on what affects newcomers' ability to socialize, in an effort to identify stumbling blocks within the socialization process.

What strategies have you used to help yourself fit or figure out what behavior is desired or expected and what isn't? Do your strategies fit nicely into any one of the tactics or models discussed in this chapter?

What Affects Newcomers' Socialization?

Bauer and Erdogan (2011) proposed a model of socialization describing how the personality characteristics of newcomers determine, to some degree, how well they adjust. For example, the more extraverted the newcomer, the better his or her adjustment to the organization. **Extraversion** refers to being outgoing and social, and needing or thriving on interactions with others. Additionally, those with adjustment experience, such as employees who have changed jobs a number of times, tend to show faster and easier adjustments than those who have changed jobs few times, if any. New hires with prior knowledge of the organization before joining tend to master their roles and tasks quickly, as do those with a **proactive personality** (Kammeyer-Mueller & Wanberg, 2003).

There are many ways to socialize employees and few would argue that any of the models presented thus far are no longer useful—all provide a slightly different take on the process, a perspective that is still valuable.

What Are the Best Kinds of Socialization Processes?

Researchers studying orientation programs have found that although developing and implementing orientation programs costs more than simply providing employees with the company handbook, such programs retain employees, ultimately reduce costs in selection and training, and lead to more dedicated, knowledgeable, and experienced workers. Gustafson (2005) demonstrated that online instruction integrated with traditional classroom-type learning and personal conversations with newcomers' facilitated socialization and led to reductions in cost and high employee retention. Gustafson offered ten guiding principles for orientation (Figure 2.10),

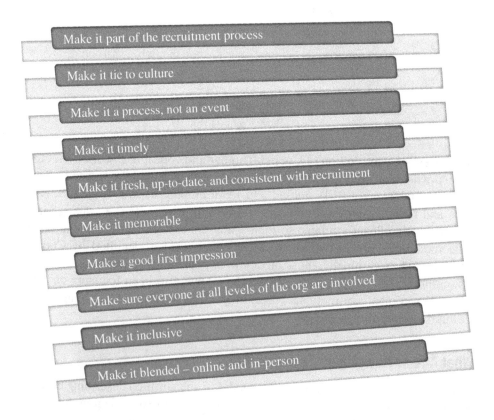

Make it part of the recruitment process

Make it tie to culture

Make it a process, not an event

Make it timely

Make it fresh, up-to-date, and consistent with recruitment

Make it memorable

Make a good first impression

Make sure everyone at all levels of the org are involved

Make it inclusive

Make it blended – online and in-person

FIGURE 2.10 Guiding Principles for Orientations.

Courtesy Zinta Byrne. Source: Gustafson (2005).

though these principles have not been subjected to empirical testing—rather, they were derived from Gustafson's review of a few different organizations that have developed socialization programs, including Applied Materials, a semiconductor equipment supplier, and Randstad North America, a staffing company.

Others have found that involving current employees in the socialization of new employees reduces newcomers' anxiety and increases their desire to contribute to the organization later after they have been on board for a while (Slaughter & Zickar, 2006). The personal contact with insiders in the organization played a strong role in making new hires feel connected with the organization, which related to their later performance in the organization.

Socialization processes designed to keep the newcomer's first experiences in mind can create a better overall process for the newcomer. Specifically, Bennington (2012) suggests that socialization processes should address how the newcomer handles his or her first experience with:

An administrative problem	A client visit
An on the job mistake	A company-sponsored social event
Personality conflicts	Speaking up at a meeting
A real win or success	Presenting at a meeting
Receiving negative or critical feedback	Public recognition (or failure to be recognized)

First experiences, such as first meeting or first conflict, can dramatically affect the socialization process by either helping the newcomer adjust or making him or her feel like an outsider. Pay attention to newcomer's first experiences.

By providing help to the newcomer on how to handle his or her first interactions or experiences with many aspects of organizations such as those noted in the chart above, organizations can ensure that new employees feel supported in learning their roles, learning the organizational norms, and developing appropriate skills to handle the challenges that arise with simply being new.

Dan Cable suggests a novel approach to socialization—instead of making the first day of work stressful, why not activate them to be their best from day one? Watch Daniel Cable talk about self-activation in the following Ted Talk at https://www.youtube.com/watch?v=q-vp8cuRxxU

Chapter Summary

If you consider the processes of socialization, the best ones connect the employee to the organization and its people, and use as many appropriate methods and technologies as might be beneficial to convey large amounts of information in an organized and interactive manner. The socialization process provides opportunities for employees to interact with members of the organization across divisions or groups in both formal and informal settings. Sometimes new employees are assigned mentors who coach them through moments of uncertainty and on how to interpret feedback, providing mechanisms for clarifying uncertainty or understanding norms. People are recruited via a number of mechanisms including job ads, online websites, friends, and family. The Chapter provided several processes for socialization including six dimensions from Van Maanen and Schein, Feldman's developmental stage model, Jablin's model of communication-assimilation, and Saks and Gruman's 4-quadrant model.

Figure 2.11 provides a visual summary of the key concepts from Chapter 2.

The visual summary (color coded) shows how sources of socialization can include family and friends, the organization, and from the new hire him

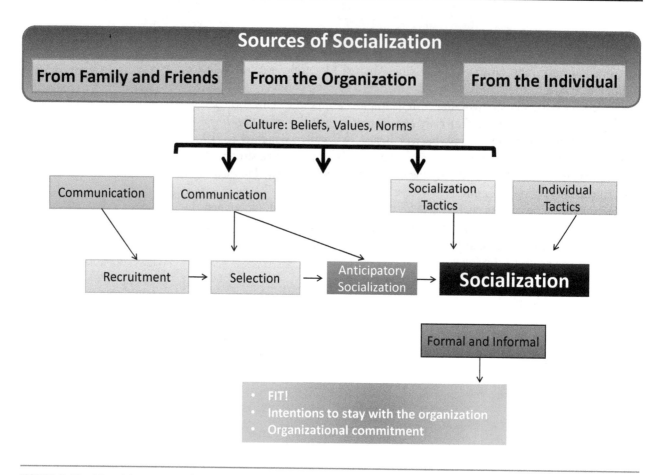

FIGURE 2.11   Visual Summary of Chapter 2.

Courtesy Zinta Byrne.

or herself. Those sources carry with them beliefs, values, and norms that are inherent in their originating cultures. Thus, family and friends may have strong cultural beliefs that affect how new hires view businesses and/or expected behavior in the workplace, which may or may not align with those of the organization. Similarly, individuals may adopt their own beliefs, values, and norms based on their unique experiences. The sources of socialization communicate the norms, beliefs, and values of the organization using various mechanisms such as straight dialogue (e.g., your mom or dad tells you to always do what the company tells you), or socialization tactics (e.g., Van Maanen and Schein's model). Methods of recruitment, selection, and anticipatory socialization affect the overall socialization process, which can be informal or formal. Ultimately, all these effects come together to determine whether new hires feel they fit or belong with the organization, and in the long run, determine hew hires' commitment and intentions to stay with the organization. Hence, socialization may seem like it is only important at the start of a job, but in fact, the socialization process is not just what happens to you at work, but also how other experiences/influences come together and continue to influence you overtime, and how you influence the organization.

Discussion Questions

1. Why are some recruitment sources so much more effective at getting people to apply and stay at an organization than others? If you could develop another form of recruitment, other than what was provided in this Chapter already, what would it be? Why would it be effective?

2. With so many jobs moving to a Gig economy and/or small entrepreneurships, what role does socialization play anymore, if any? Why would it still be valuable to have socialization for the Gig economy?

3. Why should we pay more attention to anticipatory socialization?

4. Given the focus on inclusivity and recognizing that a variety and number of identities can exist and do not necessarily view the world in the same way (e.g., lesbian, bisexual, gay, transgender, queer, nonbinary), how should organizational socialization change—or should not it?

References

Allen, D. G. (2006). Do organizational socialization tactics influence newcomer embeddedness and turnover? *Journal of Management, 32*(2), 237–256. doi:10.1177/0149206305280103

Allen, N. J., & Meyer, J. P. (1990). Organizational socialization tactics: A longitudinal analysis of links to newcomers' commitment and role orientation. *Academy of Management Journal, 33,* 847–858.

Avery, D. R. (2003). Reactions to diversity in recruitment advertising—are differences black and white? *Journal of Applied Psychology*, *88*(4), 672–679. doi:10.1037/0021-9010.88.4.672

Avery, D. R., & McKay, P. F. (2006). Target practice: An organizational impression management approach to attracting minority and female job applicants. *Personnel Psychology*, *59*(1), 157–187. doi:10.1111/j.1744-6570.2006.00807.x

Baack, D. W., & Singh, N. (2007). Culture and web communications. *Journal of Business Research*, *60*(3), 181–188. doi:10.1016/j.jbusres.2006.11.002

Bandura, A. (1986a). *Social foundations of thought and action: A social cognitive theory.* Englewood Cliffs, NJ: Prentice-Hall.

Bandura, A. (1986b). The explanatory and predictive scope of self-efficacy theory. *Journal of Social and Clinical Psychology*, *4*(3), 359–373. doi:10.1521/jscp.1986.4.3.359

Barber, A. E., Hollenbeck, J. R., Tower, S. L., & Phillips, J. M. (1994). The effects of interview focus on recruitment effectiveness: A field experiment. *Journal of Applied Psychology*, *79*(6), 886–896. doi:10.1037/0021-9010.79.6.886

Barge, J. K., & Schlueter, D. W. (2004). Memorable messages and newcomer socialization. *Western Journal of Communication*, *68*(3), 233–256.

Batistič, S. (2018). Looking beyond - socialization tactics: The role of human resource systems in the socialization process. *Human Resource Management Review*, *28*(2), 220–233.

Bauer, T. N., Bodner, T., Erdogan, B., Truxillo, D. M., & Tucker, J. S. (2007). Newcomer adjustment during organizational socialization: A meta-analytic review of antecedents, outcomes, and methods. *Journal of Applied Psychology, 92,* 707–721.

Bauer, T.N., & Erdogan, B. (2011). Organizational socialization: The effective onboarding of new employees. In S. Zedeck (Ed.), *APA handbook of industrial and organizational psychology: Maintaining, expanding and contracting the organization* (Vol. 3, pp. 51–64). Washington, DC: American Psychological Association. doi:10.1037/12171-002

Bennington, E. (2012). All aboard! *NACE Journal, 72*(4), 21–25.

Brandel, M. (2006). Fishing in the global talent pool. *Computerworld, 40*(47), 33–35.

Breaugh, J. A. (1992). *Recruitment: Science and practice.* Boston, MA: PWS-Kent.

Breaugh, J. A. (2009). *Recruiting and attracting talent: A guide to understanding and managing the recruitment process.* Alexandria, VA: SHRM Foundation.

Breaugh, J. A. (2012). Employee recruitment: Current knowledge and suggestions for future research. In N. Schmitt (Ed.), *The Oxford handbook of personnel assessment and selection* (pp. 68–87). New York, NY: Oxford University Press. doi:10.1093/oxfordhb/9780199732579.013.0005

Breaugh, J. A., Greising, L. A., Taggart, J. W., & Chen, H. (2003). The relationship of recruiting sources and pre-hire outcomes: Examination of yield ratios and applicant quality. *Journal of Applied Social Psychology, 33*(11), 2267–2287. doi:10.1111/j.1559-1816.2003.tb01884.x

Breaugh, J. A., & Starke, M. (2000). Research on employee recruitment: So many studies, so many remaining questions. *Journal of Management, 26*(3), 405–434. doi:10.1177/014920630002600303

Brooks, M., & Highhouse, S. (2006). Familiarity breeds ambivalence. *Corporate Reputation Review, 9*(2), 105–113. doi:10.1057/palgrave.crr.1550016

Cable, D. M., Gino, F., & Staats, B. R. (2013). Breaking them in or eliciting their best? Reframing socialization around newcomers' authentic self-expression. *Administrative Science Quarterly, 58*, 1–36. doi: 10.1177/0001839213477098

Caldwell, D. F., & O'Reilly, C. A. (1985). The impact of information on job choices and turn over. *Academy of Management Journal, 28*(4), 934–943. doi:10.2307/256246

Chambers, E. G., Handfield-Jones, H., Hankin, S., & Michaels III, E. G. (1998). Win the war for top talent. *Workforce, 77*(12), 50–56.

Chao, G. T., O'Leary-Kelly, A. M., Wolf, S., Klein, H. J., & Gardner, P. D. (1994). Organizational socialization: Its content and consequences. *Journal of Applied Psychology, 79*(5), 730–743. doi:10.1037/0021-9010.79.5.730.

Chapman, D. S., Uggerslev, K. L., Carroll, S. A., Piasentin, K. A., & Jones, D. A. (2005). Applicant attraction to organizations and job choice: A meta-analytic review of the correlates of recruiting outcomes. *Journal of Applied Psychology, 90*(5), 928–944. doi:10.1037/0021-9010.90.5.928

Chapman, D. S., & Webster, J. (2003). The use of technologies in the recruiting, screening, and selection processes for job candidates. *International Journal of Selection and Assessment, 11*(2–3), 113–120. doi:10.1111/1468-2389.00234

Cober, R. T., Brown, D. J., & Levy, P. E. (2004). Form, content, and function: An evaluative methodology for corporate employment web sites. *Human Resource Management, 43*(2–3), 201–218. doi:10.1002/hrm.20015

Collins, C. J., & Han, J. (2004). Exploring applicant pool quantity and quality: The effects of early recruitment practice strategies, corporate advertising, and firm reputation. *Personnel Psychology, 57*(3), 685–717. doi:10.1111/j.1744-6570.2004.00004.x

Collins, C. J., & Stevens, C. (2002). The relationship between early recruitment-related activities and the application decisions of new labor-market entrants: A brand equity approach to recruitment. *Journal of Applied Psychology, 87*(6), 1121–1133. doi:10.1037/0021-9010.87.6.1121

Cooper-Thomas, H., Anderson, N., & Cash, M. (2012). Investigating organizational socialization: A fresh look at newcomer adjustment strategies. *Personnel Review, 41*(1), 41–55. doi:10.1108/00483481211189993

Decker, P. J., & Cornelius, E. T. (1979). A note on recruiting sources and job survival rates. *Journal of Applied Psychology, 64*(4), 463–464. doi:10.1037/0021-9010.64.4.463

Dubinsky, A. J., Howell, R. D., Ingram, T. N., & Bellenger, D. N. (1986). Salesforce socialization. *Journal of Marketing, 50,* 192–207.

Falcione, R. L., & Wilson, C. E. (1988). Socialization processes in organizations. In G. M. Goldhaber, & G. A. Barnett (Eds.), *Handbook of organizational communication* (pp. 151–169). Norwood, NJ: Ablex.

Farber, H. S. (1994). The analysis of interfirm worker mobility. *Journal of Labor Economics, 12*(4), 554–594.

Feldman, D. C. (1976). A contingency theory of socialization. *Administrative Science Quarterly, 21*(3), 433–452.

Feldman, D. (1981). The multiple socialization of organization members: A longitudinal study. *Academy of Management Proceedings (00650668),* 380–384. doi:10.5465/AMBPP.1981.4977138

Feldman, D. (1988). *Managing careers in organizations.* Glenview, IL: Scott Foresman.

Fonner, K. L., & Timmerman, C. E. (2009). Organizational newc(ust)omers: Applying organizational newcomer assimilation concepts to customer information seeking and service outcomes. *Management Communication Quarterly, 23,* 244–271.

Griffith, R.W., & Hom, P.W. (2001). *Retaining valued employees.* Thousand Oaks, CA: Sage.

Gully, S. M., Phillips, J. M., Castellano, W. G., Han, K., & Kim, A. (2013). A mediated moderation model of recruiting socially and environmentally responsible job applicants. *Personnel Psychology, 66*(4), 935–973. doi:10.1111/peps.12033

Gustafson, K. (2005). A better welcome mat. *Training, 42*(6), 34–41.

Hansen, F. (September, 2009). Discriminatory twist in networking sites puts recruiters in peril. Retrieved from http://www.workforce.com/articles/discriminatory-twist-in-networking-sites-puts-recruiters-in-peril

Haueter, J. A., Hoff-Macan, T., & Winter, J. (2003). Measurement of newcomer socialization: Construct validation of a multidimensional scale. *Journal of Vocational Behavior, 63,* 20–39.

Hemp, P. (2002). My Week at the Ritz as a Room-Service Waiter. *Harvard Business Review, 80*(6), 50–62.

Jablin, F. M. (2001). Organizational entry, assimilation, and disengagement/exit. In F. M. Jablin, & L. L. Putnam (Eds.), *The new handbook of organizational communication: Advances in theory, research, and methods* (pp. 732–818). Newbury Park, CA: Sage.

Judge, T. A., & Cable, D. M. (1997). Applicant personality, organizational culture, and organization attraction. *Personnel Psychology, 50*(2), 359–394. doi:10.1111/j.1744-6570.1997.tb00912.x

Kammeyer-Mueller, J. D., & Wanberg, C. R. (2003). Unwrapping the organizational entry process: Disentangling multiple antecedents and their pathways to adjustment. *Journal of Applied Psychology, 88*(5), 779–794. doi:10.1037/0021-9010.88.5.779

Klein, H. J., & Weaver, N. A. (2000). The effectiveness of an organizational-level orientation training program in the socialization of new hires. *Personnel Psychology, 53*(1), 47–66.

Kristof, A. L. (1996). Person-organization fit: An integrative review of its conceptualizations, measurement, and implications. *Personnel Psychology, 49*(1), 1–49. doi:10.1111/j.1744-6570.1996.tb01790.x

Lambert, J. R. (2015). The impact of gay-friendly recruitment statements and due process employment on a firm's attractiveness as an employer. *Equality, Diversity & Inclusion, 34*(6), 510–526. doi:10.1108/EDI-03-2013-0012

Lester, R. E. (1987). Organizational culture, uncertainty reduction, and the socialization of new organizational members. In S. Thomas (Ed.), *Culture and communication: Methodology, behavior, artifacts, and institutions* (pp. 105–113). Norwood, NJ: Ablex.

Levine, J. M., Chaoi, H.-S., & Moreland, R. L. (2003). Newcomer innovation in work teams. In P. Paulus & B. Nijstad (Eds.), *Group creativity: Innovation through collaboration* (pp. 202–224). New York, NY: Oxford University Press.

Lievens, F., Decaesteker, C., Coetsier, P., & Geirnaert, J. (2001). Organizational attractiveness for prospective applicants: A person-organisation fit perspective. *Applied Psychology: An International Review, 50*(1), 30–51. doi:10.1111/1464-0597.00047

Lievens, E., & Harris, M. M. (2003). Research on internet recruiting and testing: Current status and future directions. In C. Cooper, & I. Robertson (Eds.), *International review of industrial and organizational psychology* (Vol. 18, pp.131–165). Chichester, England: Wiley.

Luthans, F., Avolio, B. J., Avey, J. B., & Norman, S. M. (2007). Positive psychological capital: Measurement and relationship with performance and satisfaction. *Personnel Psychology, 60*, 541–572.

Luthans, F., Youssef, C. M., & Avolio, B. J. (2007). *Psychological capital: Developing the human competitive edge.* New York, NY: Oxford University Press.

Madlock, P. E., & Chory, R. M. (2013). Socialization as a Predictor of Employee Outcomes. *Communication Studies, 65*(1), 56–71. doi:10.1080/1

Maio, G. R., & Haddock, G. (2007). Attitude change. In A. W. Kruglanski, & E. Higgins (Eds.), *Social psychology: Handbook of basic principles* (2nd ed., pp. 565–586). New York, NY: Guilford Press.

Miller, V. D., & Jablin, F. M. (1991). Information seeking during organizational entry: Influences, tactics, and a model of the process. *Academy of Management Review, 16*(1), 92–120. doi:10.5465/AMR.1991.4278997

Montani, F., Maoret, M., & Dufour, L. (2019). The dark side of socialization: How and when divestiture socialization undermines newcomer outcomes. *Journal of Organizational Behavior*, 1–16, doi: 10.1002/job.2351

Morrison, E. W. (1993). Longitudinal study of the effects of information seeking on newcomer socialization. *Journal of Applied Psychology, 78*(2), 173–183. doi:10.1037/0021-9010.78.2.173

Ostroff, C., & Kozlowski, S.W. (1992). Organizational socialization as a learning process: The role of information acquisition. *Personnel Psychology, 45*(4), 849–874. doi:10.1111/j.1744-6570.1992.tb00971.x

Parkes, L. P., Bochner, S., & Schneider, S. K. (2001). Person-organisation fit across cultures: An empirical investigation of individualism and collectivism. *Applied Psychology: An International Review, 50*(1), 81.

People's Daily Online (May 18, 2011). Retrieved July 9, 2014 from http://english.peopledaily.com.cn/90001/90781/7384173.html

Robb, D. (2012). Welcome onboard. *HR Magazine, 57*(5), 61–64.

Ryan, A., & Delany, T. (2010). Attracting job candidates to organizations. In J. L. Farr, & N. T. Tippins (Eds.), *Handbook of employee selection* (pp. 127–150). New York, NY: Routledge/Taylor & Francis Group.

Rynes, S. L., Bretz, R. D., & Gerhart, B. (1991). The importance of recruitment in job choice: A different way of looking. *Personnel Psychology, 44*(3), 487–521. doi:10.1111/j.1744-6570.1991.tb02402.x

Rynes, S. L., & Cable, D. M. (2003). Recruitment research in the twenty-first century. In W. C. Borman, D. R. Ilgen, & R. J. Klimoski (Eds.), *Handbook of psychology: Industrial and organizational psychology,* (Vol. 12, pp. 55–76). Hoboken, NJ: Wiley.

Saks, A. M. (1994). A psychological process investigation for the effects of recruitment source and organization information on job survival. *Journal of Organizational Behavior, 15*(3), 225–244. doi:10.1002/job.4030150305

Saks, A. M., & Ashforth, B. E. (1997). A longitudinal investigation of the relationships between job information sources, applicant perceptions of fit, and work outcomes. *Personnel Psychology, 50*(2), 395–426. doi:10.1111/j.1744-6570.1997.tb00913.x

Saks, A. M., & Gruman, J. A. (2011). Organizational socialization and positive organizational behaviour: Implications for theory, research, and practice. *Canadian Journal of Administrative Sciences, 28*(1), 14–26. doi:10.1002/cjas.169

Saks, A. M., Uggerslev, K. L., & Fassina, N. E. (2007). Socialization tactics and newcomer adjustment: A meta-analytic review and test of a model. *Journal of Vocational Behavior, 70*(3), 413-446. doi:10.1016/j.jvb.2006.12.00

Scott, C., & Myers, K. (2010). Toward an integrative theoretical perspective on organizational membership negotiations: Socialization, assimilation, and the duality of structure. *Communication Theory, 20,* 79–105.

Slaughter, J. E., & Zickar, M. J. (2006). A new look at the role of insiders in the newcomer socialization process. *Group & Organization Management, 31*(2), 264–290. doi:10.1177/1059601104273065

Stevens, C. (1998). Antecedents of interview interactions, interviewers' ratings, and applicants' reactions. *Personnel Psychology, 51*(1), 55–85. doi:10.1111/j.1744-6570.1998. tb00716.x

Tang, C., Liu, Y., Oh, H., & Weitz, B. (2014). Socialization Tactics of New Retail Employees: A Pathway to Organizational Commitment. *Journal of Retailing, 90*(1), 62–73. doi:10.1016/j.jretai.2013.11.002

Turban, D. B., & Cable, D. M. (2003). Firm reputation and applicant pool characteristics. *Journal of Organizational Behavior, 24*(6), 733–751. doi:10.1002/job.215

Van Hoye, G., & Lievens, F. (2009). Tapping the grapevine: A closer look at word-of-mouth as a recruitment source. *Journal of Applied Psychology, 94*(2), 341–352. doi:10.1037/a0014066

Van Maanen, J., & Schein, E. H. (1979). Toward a theory of organizational socialization. *Research in Organizational Behavior, 1,* 209–264.

Wang, X., Zheng, Q., & Cao, X. (2014). Psychological capital: A new perspective for psychological health education management of public schools. *Public Personnel Management, 43*(4), 371–383. doi: 10.1177/0091026014535182

Wanous, J. P., & Colella, A. (1989). Organizational entry research: Current status and future directions. In K. M. Rowland, & G. R. Ferris (Eds.), *Research in personnel and human resources management* (pp. 215–232). Greenwich, CT: JAI Press.

Werbel, J. D., & Landau, J. (1996). The effectiveness of different recruitment sources: A mediating variable analysis. *Journal of Applied Social Psychology, 26*(15), 1337–1350. doi:10.1111/j.1559–1816.1996.tb00074.x

Williams, C. R., Labig, C. E., & Stone, T. H. (1993). Recruitment sources and posthire outcomes for job applicants and new hires: A test of two hypotheses. *Journal of Applied Psychology, 78*(2), 163–172. doi:10.1037/0021-9010.78.2.163

CHAPTER 3

Intentions and Drivers at Work: Motivation

Learning Outcomes

After studying this chapter, you should be able to explain:

1. In your own words, the different theories used to understand why people act as they do in organizations.

2. How to apply each theory to various work-related situations.

3. Different theories of motivation, comparing and contrasting them to develop a critique of strengths and weakness for each theory.

Mini-Quiz: Motivation

As an introduction to this chapter, please take the following mini-quiz (answers are in the back of the book). As you read the questions and consider the answers *before* diving into the chapter, you'll challenge yourself before you master the content, a process that helps facilitate learning for long-term retention. Some questions may have more than one correct answer. Don't worry if you cannot answer all questions correctly on your first try. By the time you read through the chapter and spend some of your own time thinking about these concepts, you should be able to determine the best answers. Try the quiz again after you finish reading the chapter.

1. Which of the following factors has the longest impact on employee motivation?
   a. Providing more challenging work
   b. Presenting an "employee of the month" award
   c. Offering the possibility of a promotion
   d. A raise
   e. Purchasing new, updated equipment
   f. Better benefits
   g. Providing an opportunity for employee feedback
   h. Dedicate a time for employees to socialize

2. You were brought into an organization to improve employee motivation by redesigning jobs. You began by assessing core dimensions of several jobs, which helped identify areas for improvement. Now, a year later, you surveyed employees and found that your efforts were wildly successful. Not only are employees more motivated, they also reported higher job satisfaction and fewer intentions to quit. What explains why changing core dimensions of the job increases satisfaction and reduces intentions to quit?
   a. Extrinsic motivation
   b. Felt responsibility
   c. Meaningfulness
   d. Knowledge of results

3. How do organizations typically measure their employees' level of motivation?
   a. Observation
   b. Employee Performance
   c. Asking employees
   d. Organizations only care about performance and don't typically assess motivation

4. Does goal setting actually help employees achieve better performance?
    a. YES! Employees can take ownership of goals, which makes them personal
    b. NO! Goals are just assigned by managers because they have to
    c. Yes, because setting goals helps employees think through the strategies which may lead to successful performance
    d. Yes, because working toward a goal presents the opportunity to receive feedback
5. According to some theories in psychology, people are driven by certain needs. True or False: People cannot be motivated by higher level needs (e.g., belonging) until their basic needs (e.g., having food or shelter) are met.

Overview

Why do we complete unpleasant job tasks or pursue promotions at work? Something inside of us drives or moves us to take action—to do something, or in some cases to hold back from doing something that we think will result in a negative consequence. That internal voice that tells us to take action or hold back, called *motivation*, is an essential concept in organizational psychology.

Our motivation level can make the difference between success and failure on the job; when high, it propels us to action to achieve, but when low, it leaves us neglecting tasks. Motivation is a key construct in organizational psychology, and in the workplace, understanding and creating motivation consumes a substantial amount of time for human resource managers, leaders, employees themselves, and consultants alike.

This chapter introduces you to the topic of Motivation and offers a number of different theories that have been proposed to explain our motivation at work. Each section provides a description of how the theory can be applied, thus arming you with tools for making use of the material, on the job, starting today.

What is Motivation?

Motivation is defined as a psychological concept developed to explain why people get involved in, engage in, take action toward, do, or get excited about things (Figure 3.1). Probably the most frequently used simple definition of motivation is that it explains or describes *why* people do what they do in organizations. Motivation is also defined as variability in behavior (i.e., differences in behavior between people) that is not explained by individual difference characteristics (such as ability or personality), skill, or environmental conditions (Vroom, 1964).

Motivation itself is not unique to each person like finger prints are (i.e., we can experience the same level of motivation), it is not

FIGURE 3.1   What is Motivation?

© bleakstar/Shutterstock.com

learned, and it is not a **trait**—that is, people cannot be classified as either moti-vated (i.e., great worker) and not-motivated (i.e., lazy worker) as a consistent way of being. Motivation is a state - a temporary (although not necessary short) state.

Motivation is discretionary (Pinder, 1998)—the energy, arousal, or effort a person chooses to devote to a particular action or task, in a particular direction, with a particular intensity, for a specific amount of time (Kanfer, 1990; Pinder, 1998) at a specific moment or time frame. Motivation results from within a person and in accordance with what the situation demands or requires of a per-son. Motivation is not static. It changes with feedback and information, as an activity progresses, and therefore, may not necessarily be the same from one moment to the next (Frese & Zapf, 1994). Thus, you may be more motivated in one situation but not another, even when the situations seem very similar. Motivation **manifests** as emotional expression, **neurological** and/or **physiolog-ical arousal**, or physical activity. Personal factors (e.g., ability) and work set-ting (including task interdependencies, support, and resources) influence levels of motivation.

Since motivation is a construct that describes something we cannot see, but whose results are observable and measureable, we identify motivation by the following results, consequences, or outcomes (i.e., indicators) of motivation. Indicators of motivation include constructs discussed throughout this book and include job performance, **counterproductive work behaviors**, helpful work behaviors (e.g., **citizenship behaviors** or **contextual performance**), commit-ment, satisfaction, and enjoyment at work.

Organizational leaders want to know what motivates their employees, so they can provide whatever employees want, need, and care about to inspire them to work hard for the organization, day in and day out. Good managers want to influ-ence employees' desired level of performance and to predict when those levels will increase, stabilize, or taper off.

Motivation alone does not explain all behavior. Factors other than motivation also influence work behavior, factors such as technology or the social environment (Mitchell & Daniels, 2003). Thus, behavior cannot be attributed entirely to moti-vation (Ford, 1992). Motivation explains a portion of work behavior, and other aspects of people and their interaction with the environment explains another portion. As of yet, researchers cannot explain all variability in work behavior, but they can explain quite a bit using existing theories of motivation.

Exercise 3.1

Now that you have read this section on what motivation is, in your own words describe what you think motivation is and why it is important to define.

What Are the Theories of Motivation?

A theory is an idea or statement that explains why a concept works in a partic-ular way. For example, the theory of relativity explains how space and time are linked together, such that your observation/measurement of an object's motion depends on your position and speed of motion relative to the object you're observing. A theory of motivation, like Maslow's Hierarchy, says that what you're motivated to do depends on what needs you have or haven't satisfied, and that needs are ordered in a hierarchical fashion from basic to complex. Different theories of motivation explain why people are driven or propelled to involve themselves in different activities and display various emotions or job attitudes. By relying on theories explaining the triggers for, and results of motivation, organizational leaders have a starting place for creating the right conditions for employees to choose to direct their energy and persistence toward supporting the organization's goals and vision. Thus, the theories provide a mental **framework** for understanding the drivers or triggers of motivation and how to increase and/or sustain it in employees (this includes everyone at all levels of the organization).

Researchers use theories of motivation to hypothesize relationships between different constructs, and create new models for explaining behavior under various working conditions and in situations not previously studied or understood. Thus, like their use in organizations, theories in research provide a mental framework for understanding motivation and how it explains the relationships between constructs. The difference between research and practice lies in how researchers and practitioners use theory. Researchers are typically attempting to improve the theory by finding situations where behavior cannot be explained using the existing theory as it is currently expressed, and then by developing extensions to the theory or modify the theory. The objective is to explain not only the original viewpoint on motivation, but also to incorporate an explanation for why people behave as they do in this new or different situation. In practice, theories are applied to improve work behavior.

Why Should We Learn Theories of Motivation?

Theories are helpful for handling new situations at work, situations where it is unknown if previous approaches will work. If you only learn what specific behavior was displayed in one type of situation, like a **case study**, you won't know how to create motivation in a substantially new and different situation. Without understanding why or how motivation comes about, we can only apply the same approach over and over because we do not know what to change and still keep high levels of motivation. Therefore, learning theory that explains *why* motivation is encouraged or discouraged, and how, you as an employee or manager are prepared to create a new method for boosting motivation in a new situation. Understanding how theories of motivation work and not just how they are practiced or applied, empowers you to combine new or existing techniques in novel ways because you have the theory to tell you that this new approach should work.

Organizing Theories

Theories of motivation have been organized using many different taxonomies or categorization systems (See Table 3.1). Some text authors group the theories by their focus (e.g., need-based versus cognitive-based), others chronologically, and others by their approach (e.g., content versus process). Table 3.1 shows three ways of categorizing the theories of motivation. That is, broad vs. narrow, need-based vs. job-based vs. cognitive-based vs. behavioral-based, or internal vs. external to the person. The sole purpose of categorizing theories is to help you make sense of them.

The organization illustrated in Table 3.1 Broad versus Narrow provides ways of grouping theories to simplify learning them and initially recognizing their

TABLE 3.1 Organizing Theories of Motivation

Concept	Category	Category	Category	Focus
Maslow's Hierarchy	Broad	Need-based Dispositional-based	Distal from immediate cause of action	Satisfying increasing levels of needs or wants
ERG	Broad	Need-based Dispositional-based	Distal from immediate cause of action	Satisfying groups of needs or wants
Expectancy (VIE)	Broad	Cognitive-based	Internal to person	Explains under what conditions (when) motivation occurs
Motivation-Hygiene	Broad	Job-based	External to person	Satisfying types of needs or wants
Job Characteristic (JCT)	Broad	Job-based	External to person	Explains how job/work promotes intrinsic motivation and job attitudes
Control	Narrow	Cognitive-based	Internal to person	Self-regulation; often used with goal-setting
Equity	Narrow	Cognitive-based	Internal to person	Self-regulation
Social Cognitive	Narrow	Cognitive-based	Internal to person	Self-regulation; learning theory that ties behavior to desired outcomes
Self-determination	Narrow	Cognitive-based	Internal to person	Difference between intrinsic and extrinsic motivation
Need for Achievement	Moderator	Need-based Dispositional-based	Distal from immediate cause of action	An individual difference characteristic that explains why some are more motivated than others
Goal-setting	Narrow	Cognitive-based	Internal to person Proximal to cause of action	Relationship between intention and endpoint
Multidisciplinary Approach	Technique	Job-based	External to person	Approach to job design/redesign
Reinforcement Schedules	Technique	Behavioral-based	External to person	Shaping behavior

Courtesy Zinta Byrne

focus or contribution toward understanding why people behave the way they do in organizations. I chose a Broad versus Narrow categorization scheme because the theories in the Table explain a broad set of behaviors, or they are narrowly focused on a specific situation or action. For example, the job characteristics theory is considered a broad theory because it describes a variety of factors in one's job or work environment that can lead to motivation, job attitudes, and performance. In contrast, equity theory is considered a narrow theory because it is about perceptions of balance—did we get adequately compensated for what we gave? The result of that perception is either an emotion or an action solely focused on achieving balance. Thus, equity theory best explains a narrow set of situations and responses. No single approach for categorizing theories is right or wrong— you can develop your own categorization scheme to help learn and appreciate which theory is useful for which condition or situation. Note, the chapter doesn't discuss all these theories listed in Table 3.1 in depth.

Broad-based Theories of Motivation

Maslow's Hierarchy of Needs

Abraham Maslow's **hierarchy** of needs (1948) is well-known and one of the first theories typically introduced in chapters on motivation. Maslow proposed that people are motivated by a drive to satisfy particular needs, and these needs can be ordered in a hierarchy from the most basic human need to the most philosophical need (see Figure 3.2). Furthermore, he stipulated that people seek to fulfill or satisfy the lowest, most basic needs first before they are interested in or driven to satisfy a higher-order need. People do not advance up the hierarchy until they have fulfilled the lower-order needs.

Maslow argued that higher-order needs developed over time through evolution—simple organisms have physiological needs, but more developed

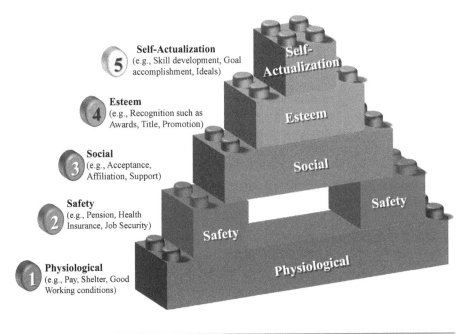

FIGURE 3.2   Maslow's Hierarchy of Needs.

organisms, such as humans, display needs of love and sense of self. The lower-order needs develop mainly out of fear and desperation, whereas higher-order needs lead to increased physical and mental well-being. Lastly, as people move up the hierarchy toward **self-actualization**, not only do they benefit by achieving happiness and satisfaction, but society and the greater population also benefit, according to Maslow.

In general, the levels are understood in the following way:

The linear progression from basic physiological needs to higher-order self-actualization needs is the Hierarchy's distinguishing characteristic—what separates it from all other theories of motivation

- *Physiological needs* include the basic needs for food, shelter, water (thirst), sex, and other bodily/biological functions. The most fundamental physiological needs such as air, water, and food for sustaining life form the base of the pyramid. Many physiological needs are **self-regulatory** in the human system, such as balancing sugar levels and body temperature, and we are driven to satisfy these balancing systems by grabbing a blanket when we are cold and seeking foods that provide us the desired nutrients. Basic needs are not always positive—for example, drugs that are addictive can end up becoming a physiological need.

- *Safety needs* include security for oneself and family, protection from physical or emotional harm, and stability such as financial or economic security. Focusing on safety needs promotes the purchase of guns, house alarm systems, airbags and anti-lock brakes in cars, and the many restrictions at airports and other mass-transit systems. People seek forms of protection and regulation to secure personal safety.

- *Social needs* include **affiliation** or belonging needs, such as acceptance, friendship, interactions with others, and feeling loved and giving love. Social needs drive us to join groups (e.g., church, sports, reading club) or attend social gatherings such as sports games, theatre, and parties.

- *Esteem needs* refer to the need or drive for respect, autonomy, achievement, and feelings of worthiness or value. Esteem needs are both from others and the self. Thus, we desire self-confidence and self-respect, to feel capable and competent at work, but also seek recognition from others that tell us our worth, value, and importance.

- *Self-actualization needs* refer to the desires for fulfilling one's maximum potential. Maslow suggested that few people ever achieve this level of the hierarchy, though later applications of the theory suggest that people can and do advance to the level they envision as their ultimate success, completing their life dreams, or winning all the awards possible in their field. What "maximum potential" means varies by individual.

The hierarchy of needs is appealing because of its simplicity, making it easy to use in the workplace. However, some empirical research has not supported the sequential nature of the theory (e.g., Hall & Nougaim, 1968) finding that people do not necessary move up the hierarchy in the way Maslow envisioned (they can jump levels). A recent study, however, in 2013 found support for correlations between the levels of need and regression analyses indicating that one can predict the satisfaction of higher-level needs by how much an immediate lower level need was satisfied (Taormina & Gao, 2013). The findings should be interpreted with some caution, though, as the study was not experimental or longitudinal, which would lend greater confidence to the order of prediction and satisfaction up or down the hierarchy. The hierarchy says that people have needs they are driven to fulfill and their needs vary according to their current situation or ideals; that fundamental message provides value for managers trying to figure out how to motivate their employees.

Figure 3.2 provides workplace examples of what may be considered a representative need at each level. For example, safety needs at work appear in the form of a secure pension or retirement plan, job security, and health insurance. When employees worry about dealing with health concerns or fear of losing their job, they cannot think about acceptance by their peers at work, their chances for the next promotion, or about developing new and exciting skills. According to Maslow, they are driven to fulfill these lower-order needs first, and once their concerns about the permanence of their job are relieved, they can then focus on fulfilling their needs at the next level up the hierarchy.

A recent study in China (Taormina & Gao, 2013) suggests that Maslow's Hierarchy is not limited to the western culture, as some have claimed. The hierarchy was supported in their study of 386 people between the ages of 18 and 67.

How Do Managers Use Maslow's Hierarchy in the Workplace?

Employees have varying needs, and they seek to fulfill or satisfy those needs in whatever ways they can. This means that people are motivated at work for various reasons and some may include a combination of the different levels of the hierarchy. For example, during major change at work when job security becomes questionable, it may be prudent to recognize that people worry about their job security more in that moment than whether they have been nominated for the next "employee of the year" award—especially if the award does not come with a job guarantee. An example of where the sequential nature of the hierarchy does not fit is when considering the motivations of athletes, artists, musicians, or entrepreneurs. Many individuals in these professions, especially those professions that pay very little unless you become famous, choose to sacrifice or ignore lower-order need fulfillment for the satisfaction of fulfilling a higher-order need such as goal attainment or recognition.

Learning what needs an employee seeks to satisfy can provide a manager with options for assigning tasks or projects, or providing rewards and assistance or support that will satisfy the specific needs and encourage the employee toward the work and behavior desired on the job. By tailoring the relationship and responding to employee needs, the manager can help employees move toward work that fulfills higher-order needs and ultimately greater levels of performance. Even though individuals can differ on what they consider a hygiene versus motivator factor, Herzberg found that across the many people he studied, there was enough similarity in responses to form these two general categories. Employees can put forth more energy to satisfying needs that also support the organization (e.g., seeking greater responsibility, collaborating with colleagues, seeking opportunities for creativity) when their concerns over basic needs are resolved. Basic needs tend to become major distractions at work (e.g., it is very hard to focus on work when your home was just flooded by a broken water pipe).

Draw Maslow's Hierarchy, and label each level.

Company Example 3.1   Intuit Motivates Top-Performers in Small but Powerful Ways

Founded in 1983, Intuit is a financial company that makes software such as TurboTax, QuickBooks, and Mint. TurboTax, for example, is a software program that thousands of Americans use to complete their annual tax returns and QuickBooks provides accounting support for many individuals and small to medium sized businesses. Intuit employs about 9,000 people worldwide and can be found in nine countries around the world. Intuit learned that regularly recognizing high performing employees using the basics, such as thank you and a small token of appreciation, could often go further than recognizing high performers with new titles, quarterly giveaways, or big bonuses. Being surprised with recognition apparently feels better than getting a big reward but one that is expected.

ERG—Existence, Relatedness, Growth Theory

Alderfer (1969) revised Maslow's theory based on the lack of research findings supporting individual levels of the hierarchy. He suggested, instead, that people have three fundamental classes or groups of needs: existence, relatedness, and growth (Figure 3.3). Furthermore, given the lack of evidence in support for the linear progression from lower to higher-order need fulfillment, Alderfer suggested that needs can be satisfied in any order. The three needs of ERG theory can be shown in terms of Maslow's needs, essentially clustering Safety and

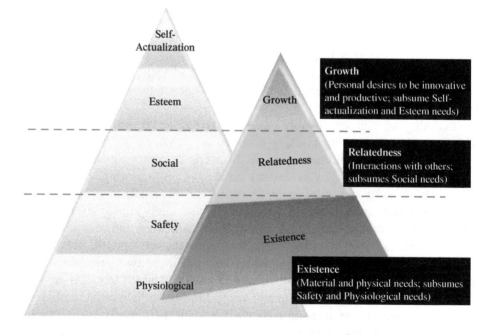

FIGURE 3.3   Alderfer's ERG Theory Mapped onto Maslow's Hierarchy.

Courtesy Zinta Byrne

Physiological needs into Existence, Social into Relatedness, and Esteem and Self-Actualization needs into Growth.

Alderfer, however, proposed a more complex model than just a clustering or regrouping of Maslow's needs. He suggested that Existence needs are limited such that when one person attains a specific need (e.g., pay), someone else receives less. The concrete nature of the Existence needs makes them consumable; hence, there's a limited supply. Unlike Existence needs, Relatedness needs are limitless; thus people are free to exchange as many thoughts, expressions of acceptance, and trust as desired. Likewise, Growth needs are limitless. Alderfer also referred to compound needs, which is when multiple needs are fulfilled by one event. For example, a promotion can fulfill growth and relatedness needs at the same time.

Furthermore, Alderfer suggested that needs are related to one another. The fewer Existence needs are satisfied, the more they are desired. The more they are satisfied, the more we desire to fill Relatedness needs. The fewer Relatedness needs are satisfied, the more they and Existence needs are desired. The more Relatedness needs are satisfied, the more Growth needs are desired. Both Existence and Relatedness needs become less important as they are satisfied, and Growth goals take their place. The more Growth needs are satisfied, the more they are desired; thus, they become increasingly important as they are satisfied. Although these relationships suggest a type of order in terms of advancing desires given the lack of or fulfillment of a particular need cluster, the order is not necessarily linear and not restrictive like Maslow's Hierarchy. Thus, we can seek to satisfy all three need groups at the same time (Alderfer, 1969).

Like Maslow's Hierarchy of Needs, ERG theory has received little empirical support (Wanous & Zwany, 1977). However, the support it has received suggests the theory explains more than Maslow's for motivation derived from need satisfaction (Luthans, 1998; Robbins, 1998).

> The distinguishing characteristic of ERG Theory is its three clusters of needs that are pursued simultaneously, where pursuit of the top needs (Growth) tends to function differently than pursuit of the lower-order needs—satisfaction of Growth is never fully achieved.

How Do Managers Use ERG Theory in the Workplace?

Alderfer (1969) suggested people become frustrated when they are unable to satisfactorily fulfill less concrete needs such as Growth, causing them to focus on satisfying more concrete needs such as Existence. He called this movement back down the pyramid to focus on more concrete needs as **frustration regression**. Managers use this theory by providing support for moving between levels. For example, when employees' efforts to be creative, attain promotions, or additional responsibilities are unsuccessful, employees will become frustrated and seek other ways to meet their needs, such as sharing their frustrations with colleagues or spending more time away from work. In this case, managers can provide opportunities for social gatherings among teams. This action not only supports individual Relatedness needs but also builds stronger connections between team members that can support future negotiations or innovations, and help employees who are experiencing frustration regression.

> Where do you see yourself in terms of these needs? How would you like ERG theory applied to you at work?

Allowing employees the flexibility to focus their energy toward fulfilling Relatedness or Existence needs when Growth needs are thwarted can help keep employees motivated at work. Likewise, supporting Growth needs when employees seek opportunities for job enrichment or upward promotion, might keep employees' motivation levels high.

Possibly, the most helpful aspect of ERG theory, like Maslow's Hierarchy, is recognizing that employees have varying needs that they seek to fulfill, and different triggers or events cause them to seek different needs at different times.

Empirical research shows that managers are primarily motivated by Growth needs (Arnolds & Boshoff, 2002). They are likely to perform better and at higher levels if they see potential for advancement opportunities. In contrast, these managers' employees are more motivated by satisfying Relatedness and Existence needs, as well as needs that reinforce self-esteem and increase relatedness among peers (Arnolds & Boshoff, 2002). Furthermore, as one would expect, employees' vary in their value of different types of rewards that satisfy their needs, suggesting managers need to get to know their employees to understand what they value.

Exercise 3.2

Compare and contrast Maslow's Hierarchy to ERG theory.

Herzberg's Two-Factor Model (Motivation-Hygiene Theory)

Herzberg, Mausner, and Snyderman (1959) found that factors producing job satisfaction at work were distinctly different from those producing dissatisfaction, and that the factors for satisfaction were not necessarily the simple opposites of those that resulted in dissatisfaction. At the most basic level, the researchers were interested in what people want out of their work. They conducted a study asking employees about work events in their daily lives in an effort to understand what made them happy and what made them unhappy at work (one approach to using the qualitative method of research involves conducting interviews to understand how people experience a phenomenon). The authors conducted roughly 200 interviews of people at nine different companies, extracting what events (e.g., promotion, salary decision) were related to general job attitudes (e.g., satisfaction). They asked participants what about the event sparked their corresponding attitude, such as which event and what about the event created feelings of guilt, status, or positive recognition.

Herzberg and colleagues determined that the central theme for satisfiers on the job was how people viewed the job content of their jobs; essentially, what we do on the job. The satisfiers were reflected by the higher-order needs of Maslow's Hierarchy and ERG theory—achievement, recognition, responsibility for a task, professional advancement, and growth. The central theme of dissatisfiers was that they represented feelings about the work environment. Thus, dissatisfiers were related to salary and working conditions; the lower-order needs of Maslow's Hierarchy.

The researchers additionally determined that factors preventing dissatisfaction do not necessarily lead to satisfaction, but simply to removing or preventing dissatisfaction resulting in a neutral state. They called dissatisfiers **hygiene factors** and satisfiers **motivators** (Figure 3.4). Hygiene, as a general term refers to conditions that maintain health. You can think of Herzberg's Hygiene factors as those elements of work that are necessary for maintaining health, such as money to buy food, and good working conditions (e.g., clean, safe). Motivator factors are those that give you a reason to perform, such as wanting to be recognized or feeling challenged to excel.

The research showed that motivator factors were necessary for satisfaction at work. In contrast, hygiene factors were only necessary for holding off dissatisfaction—having them did not lead to job satisfaction, but not having them led to dissatisfaction. Similarly, a lack of motivator factors did not lead to dissatisfaction, but instead to a neutral state of no job satisfaction.

As a consequence of their findings that the presence of hygiene factors without motivator factors did not lead to job satisfaction, Herzberg et al. determined that dissatisfaction and satisfaction are not opposites on a continuum. By distinguishing between hygiene factors, which are conditions of the job or external factors that influence people's perceptions of their jobs, and motivators, which are how people relate to their work or internal factors, Herzberg and colleagues were the first to identify extrinsic versus intrinsic motivation (Salancik & Pfeffer, 1978).

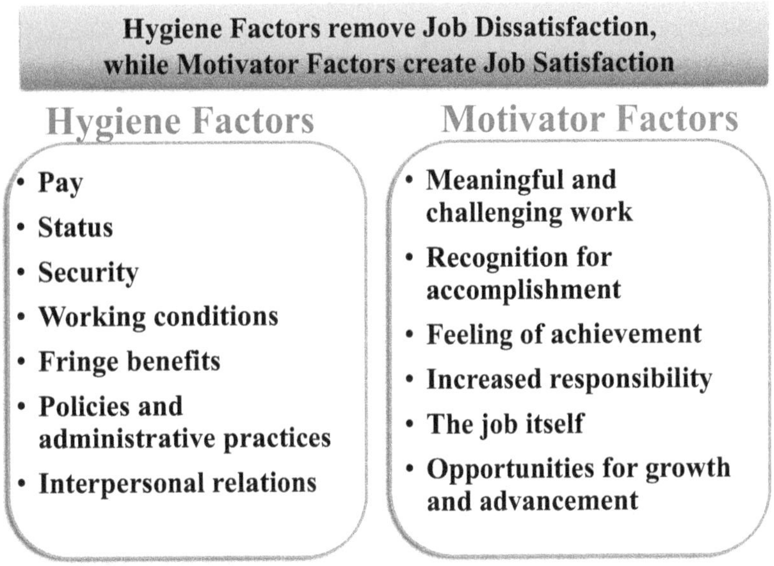

Hygiene Factors remove Job Dissatisfaction, while Motivator Factors create Job Satisfaction

Hygiene Factors

- **Pay**
- **Status**
- **Security**
- **Working conditions**
- **Fringe benefits**
- **Policies and administrative practices**
- **Interpersonal relations**

Motivator Factors

- **Meaningful and challenging work**
- **Recognition for accomplishment**
- **Feeling of achievement**
- **Increased responsibility**
- **The job itself**
- **Opportunities for growth and advancement**

FIGURE 3.4   Hygiene and Motivator Factors.

Courtesy Zinta Byrne. Source: Herzberg, Mausner, and Snyderman (1959)

The distinguishing characteristic of the Hygiene-Motivator or Two-Factor Theory is its focus on dissatisfiers, aspects of the work environment, and satisfiers, mechanisms for achievement and growth.

Applying Motivation-Hygiene Theory

Katt and Condly (2009) applied motivation-hygiene to the classroom to determine what motivates students or what prevents their motivation. Their participants were 125 students (26% male, 69% female) from a large university in the southeastern part of the United States. After receiving descriptions and explanations of their feelings about class, motivation levels, and specific incidents that evoked different feelings about class work, the researchers coded and analyzed the responses. Most cited motivators included achievement, recognition for achievement, professor demonstrating concern, and relevant course work. Most frequently noted hygiene factors were class management (e.g., professor preparation and control of the class, unclear expectations, disrespectful class environment), problems attributed to oneself (e.g., lack of preparation, procrastination), and class policy (e.g., attendance and late work policies, fairness of assessments, clarity of course assignments). Students reported hygiene factors as the incidents that most negatively affected them, whereas motivators were noted as incidents that made them feel particularly good. Students did not mention motivators (e.g., achievement, lack of recognition) as sources of negative feelings. The authors concluded their findings provided support for the dual action of motivators and hygiene factors, and the applicability of the two-factor theory to situations other than the workplace.

How do Managers Use Motivation-Hygiene Theory in the workplace?

To use the motivation-hygiene theory, managers must address both satisfiers (motivator factors) and dissatisfiers (hygiene factors) at the same time.
Step One: Evaluate and understand employees' perceptions

1. Job tasks—Is the work meaningful and challenging; can employees gain a feeling of accomplishment from the job tasks?

2. Recognition—Are employees recognized for what they do?

3. Opportunities within the organization—Is there upward or lateral mobility? Are there opportunities for development?

4. Pay—When comparing to others in and outside the organization, do they understand why they are paid what they are? Is the pay fair? Is the pay appropriate given the work?

5. Working conditions—Are they safe, clean, and comfortable?

6. Benefits—Do employees receive adequate health benefits? Is there financial security such as a retirement plan?

7. Policies and decision-making procedures—Are decision-making policies transparent and understandable?

8. Interpersonal relations—Do employees get along with their boss and colleagues? Is there a lot of conflict in the office?

The key differences between Herzberg's two-factor model and ERG theory include: (a) ERG is about what factors in general spark motivation, whereas the two-factor model is about what motivates us to feel satisfied (or not) at work, and (b) the way factors are organized—ERG uses levels from concrete (e.g., physical needs) to emotional (e.g., esteem needs), and in contrast the two-factor model divides factors in half between concrete (e.g., policies, pay) and emotional (e.g., meaningful).

Evaluations of perceptions can be accomplished with internal surveys (quick polls) or through external firms that frequently run opinion/attitude surveys for the organization. Once mangers have an idea of how employees perceive their motivation and hygiene factors, they can take actions to eliminate the dissatisfiers (or reduce them) and increase missing satisfiers.

Step Two: Reduce or remove dissatisfiers
Managers can use internal or external resources to reduce dissatisfiers in the workplace. For example, they can determine if employees' pay can be appropriately adjusted if necessary (e.g., is it competitive), or provide comparison information to employees so they can see that they actually make a very good salary comparatively. Pay can be a sensitive topic for many employees—some believe they should make more no matter what the comparative data says and others understand why their pay is appropriate, but they are embarrassed or frustrated that they cannot find ways to make more.

Similarly, managers can make adjustments in other areas to reduce dissatisfiers. For example, working conditions may need an upgrade for safety concerns or for improving the general feel and comfort level of the workplace. Some changes do not require major investments of money; they can be as simple as rearranging the office configuration to improve communication, minimize noise, improve lighting, or reduce feelings of cramping and overcrowding. Efforts such as these can reduce or remove dissatisfiers.

Step Three: Boost satisfiers
Effective management involves more than just reducing dissatisfaction. Effective management also demands the simultaneous

attention to increasing satisfiers. Managers can use job redesign strategies to improve satisfiers. Theories such as job characteristic theory, can be used to improve satisfiers like meaningfulness at work and increased responsibility.

Expectancy Theory or VIE Theory

Moving away from the satisfaction of specific needs, Vroom (1964) proposed a theory of motivation focused on how people determine whether and when they will take action in a particular direction. Expectancy theory, also called VIE theory, proposes that people make a calculative or rational decision to be motivated depending on three beliefs (Figure 3.5).

Valence refers to the value given to a particular outcome; in Figure 3.5, the outcome is reward for performance. Thus, in Figure 3.5 valence is the perceived value of the rewards we expect in return for our performance. According to Vroom (1964), the strength of the valence is not the value of the object itself, but rather the *anticipated satisfaction in the outcome* that creates the value. In this case, the value is the satisfaction of getting the reward in return for performance, not the actual reward itself.

Instrumentality refers to the belief that actions and efforts taken to achieve or obtain the outcome will be rewarded. Instrumentality is an internal assumption or assessment that performance will and does result in a reward.

Expectancy refers to the belief that actions and efforts will actually influence levels of performance. Vroom noted that this does not mean outcomes remain within people's direct control; it means they have an expectation that their efforts will have an effect on obtaining the desired outcome. Stated another way, if you don't believe your efforts will lead to a higher level of performance (e.g., work more, accomplish more), you're less likely to continue those efforts.

Putting these three beliefs into an example in the classroom (Figure 3.6) may make the theory more clear:

1. Getting an A in the course will be incredibly satisfying (Valence)—good grades matter to me and I value what good grades do for me

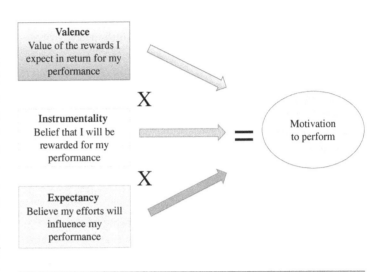

FIGURE 3.5   Expectancy Theory or VIE Theory.

Courtesy Zinta Byrne. Source: Vroom (1964)

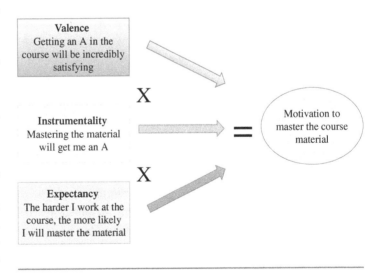

FIGURE 3.6   Example of VIE Theory for Mastering Course Material.

Courtesy Zinta Byrne

2. I believe that mastering the course material will get me an A (Instrumentality)—I will be rewarded with an A for mastering the course material

3. The harder I work at the course, the more likely I will master the material (Expectancy)—I believe my efforts (working hard to learn the material) will influence my level of mastery.

Note, the difference between instrumentality and expectancy. Instrumentality is about being rewarded and expectancy is about your efforts making a difference. Thus, instrumentality comes from outside oneself—someone has to reward you, whereas expectancy comes from inside of oneself—it's solely about you.

Given these three conditions, I am motivated to master the course material. Essentially, the theory might be stated this way If I work hard, I'll master the material; if I master the material, I'll get an A; getting an A will be incredibly satisfying. If I work hard, I'll master the material = expectancy. If I master the material, I'll get an A = instrumentality. Getting an A will be satisfying = valence. Note that you're not rewarded for working hard (i.e., performance)—you're rewarded for mastering the material (i.e., the outcome of your performance).

The theory applies to whatever grade is considered valuable, not just an "A" as used in this example. For some students and some classes, a "C" or passing grade is extremely valuable!

The Mathematical Formula: An In-depth Look at VIE Theory

Vroom (1964) stipulated that the relationship between the three beliefs (valence, instrumentality, expectancy) can be expressed as a mathematical formula (depicted in a variety of ways). In the formula, Valence differs by the value people attach to rewards, as well as a preference among outcomes at any point in time (thus Valence is not static). This value can be denoted in a variety of ways depending on how it is measured. For example, a researcher may ask participants to rate the value of various rewards on a scale of 1 to 10, with 10 denoting the highest value.

In the formula, Expectancy is the probability (ranging from 0 = the outcome will not follow, to 1 = the outcome will definitely follow) that one's efforts will lead to the outcome. Expectancy, therefore, refers to a guess or prediction about the future; an estimate of confidence that given a certain amount of effort a particular level of performance may be achieved. This guess or estimate is not unlike you guessing how much work might be involved in studying for an exam—estimates such as "I'll study for the next three days before the exam and I can probably get an A" function as a probability estimate of achieving an A on the exam.

Within the formula, Instrumentality represents the probability that performance will lead to the outcome. For example, if an organization instituted a pay freeze, we can estimate the probability of being rewarded for performance during the pay freeze at either 0 or very close to 0. Likewise, if your previous attempts to pass the exams in the course have failed, assuming you're honest with yourself, you're more likely to estimate a low probability of passing the next exam than a high probability of passing.

At any time, an outcome can have a Valence, Instrumentality, or Expectancy of zero, which indicates (1) indifference to attaining the outcome, (2) attainment of the outcome may be out of your control and therefore may not happen (resulting in a zero probability), or (3) that efforts may not lead to the outcome (resulting in a zero probability). Since the formula is multiplicative, if at any time one of the three factors is zero, the result is no motivation to perform or strive toward the outcome. Vroom labeled the result of the formula *Force*—the behavior on the part of the person. Thus, the Force on the person to perform (i.e., the motivation to take action and/or persist) is a function of the Valence, Instrumentality, and Expectancy of attaining the outcome associated with such performance.

The formula and explanation of the formula are far more complicated than need be for appreciating the basic assumptions of VIE theory and its application. Indeed, meta-analytic results of studies testing Expectancy Theory have shown the three factors contributing to Force (i.e., Valence, Instrumentality, Expectancy) relate more strongly to outcomes such as performance than to each other as the theory assumed. Meta-analytic results refer to the outcome of **meta-analysis**, a statistical procedure for combining the results of many studies on a particular topic. The goal of meta-analysis is to summarize the results by describing the patterns that emerge. Furthermore, the results suggested that the three factors were best used as individual **predictors**, as opposed to combined in a multiplicative formula as originally proposed (see Van Eerde & Thierry, 1996). However, regardless of the research findings, the basic understanding from the theory remains simply that the strength of our actions depends on the expectation that the act will result in some desirable outcome, and that we can act to achieve the outcome.

© Neirfy/Shutterstock.com

Stated in simple workplace terms, expectancy theory says that you will be motivated to work if you believe your efforts will lead to some desired level of performance, and that your efforts will result in some kind of reward that you value or care about. Performance, however, is rarely rewarded in such simplistic ways—reward for performance is usually also dependent on seniority, skill level, demand, economic conditions, pay cycles, and other external criteria unrelated to one's pure level of performance or effort. Research suggests that expectancy theory is best used to predict motivation levels *within* people as opposed to *between* people (or across groups; Van Eerde & Thierry, 1996), thus suggesting the broad application to organizations is somewhat limited.

The distinguishing characteristic of VIE Theory is the focus on what the individual values and his or her estimates about whether what is valued can actually be obtained.

Exercise 3.3

Draw the VIE model with three new examples of motivational situations specific to you. For example, if you want to become a good swimmer or a good runner, draw a VIE model to explain your motivation to become good at swimming or running.

How Do Managers Use Expectancy Theory in the Workplace?

Understanding what employees' value is a first step toward using VIE at work—the rewards offered at work must be of value to employees. Some organizations, for example, have turned to **cafeteria-style benefits**, which means that employees can choose between several options, tailoring their benefits to match their needs. For example, a young family of four can choose a health insurance plan that provides coverage for children, whereas a couple with no children can choose a health plan that only covers the two of them.

Providing adequate information about how performance can lead to desired outcomes that are rewarded is equally important. Making sure rewards are indeed directly tied to performance makes it easier to communicate the instrumentality of performing. This information can be provided in communications, appraisal meetings, or casual conversations reinforcing the various paths to linking performance to outcomes. Making it clear what level of accomplishment or performance leads to what kind of reward is essential in giving employees instrumentality. Lastly, training and development opportunities may be important for improving employees' expectancy—believing we can do the work that is necessary to influence performance requires the skill to do the work and the confidence, or self-efficacy (belief in our ability to do the tasks) that we can actually accomplish the task. Employees typically confuse expectancy and instrumentality. Just because you work hard doesn't mean the company will reward you for that hard work.

Job Characteristics Theory

Intent on understanding how characteristics of the job motivate employees, Hackman and Oldham (1976) proposed the job characteristics theory, a broad-based theory for explaining how efforts at changing the job result in positive outcomes, such as satisfaction and **intrinsic motivation**. Hackman and Oldham suggested that five core job dimensions trigger three critical psychological states that result in personal and work outcomes (see Figure 3.7). Let's walk through the components of the model, one section at a time.

Core Job Dimensions

Skill Variety refers to the extent to which the job requires a number of different skills for completion. For example, jobs such as university professor, fireman, police-woman, nurse, doctor, landscaper, or air traffic controller all require a number of different skills such as typing, reading, fast decision-making, situational diagnostic skills, client interactions, skills in diffusing volatile situations, creativity in mixing materials, or attending to a number of sources of information and sorting through them to determine which is most critical in that moment. There are thousands of different jobs (see **O*NET**) that require different combinations and variety of skills.

Task Identity refers to the extent to which finishing all the job tasks results in a complete and identifiable whole product. For example, individuals working on "black boxes" in government defense industries, such as communication, only know what goes into the box. The black box is not necessarily an actual box; it's a phrase that signifies an independent unit designed to receive certain inputs and generate specific outputs, but who or what provides the inputs and what or who uses the output remain unknown to the designers. Thus, in

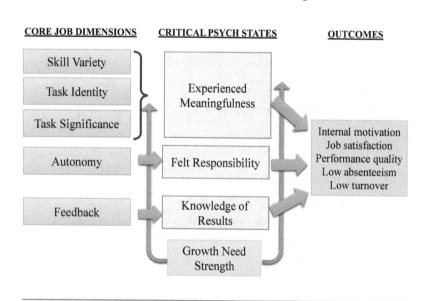

FIGURE 3.7 Job Characteristics Theory.

Courtesy Zinta Byrne. Source: Hackman and Oldham (1976)

the example of communications, the employees creating the communication unit have very low task identity because they only know which communication mechanisms they installed within the independent box, but they do not know where it goes, how it is used, who uses it, or why.

Task Significance refers to how much impact the job has on others in the organization or on the organization itself. For example, employees who understand how the completion of their job affects others' ability to do their jobs, and ultimately how what they do ties into the organization's success, have high task significance.

Autonomy refers to how much freedom, independence, control, or discretion the employee has to perform his or her work and when to schedule the work. For example, many individuals working as checkers at grocery stores have very little autonomy in their jobs—they are told when to be there, how long they need to work, how to do the job, and what to say to customers. In contrast, politicians are considered to have a great deal of autonomy scheduling meetings when convenient, meeting with **constituencies**, and deciding how long they need to be in attendance at various decision-making sessions. Professors at universities, doctors, and lawyers are known for having significant levels of autonomy.

Example of a job with skill variety, task identity, task significance, autonomy, and feedback.

© Gorodenkoff/Shutterstock.com

Feedback refers to the amount of information the employee gets from the job, and "the degree to which carrying out the work activities required by the job results in the individual obtaining direct and clear information about the effectiveness of his or her performance" (Hackman & Oldham, 1976, p. 258). So what exactly does this mean? Some tasks provide immediate feedback on whether they were completed successfully or effectively. For example, computer programmers developing simple code enjoy knowing right away whether their program worked or not because the program either runs or fails; what the program was supposed to do either happens or does not happen. In contrast, landscapers do not know how well they have done their job because they can't tell right away if what they planted will take hold and grow or if the drip irrigation system they installed will work consistently a few weeks from now.

Critical Psychological States

Three dimensions, skill variety, task identity, and task significance, combine to foster the psychological state of experienced meaningfulness of the work. *Experienced meaningfulness* refers to the extent to which the employee experiences the job as worthwhile, valuable, and meaningful. The degree to which the employee has skill variety, task identity, and task significance determines how much the employee feels or experiences meaningfulness at work.

The degree to which the job has autonomy determines how much *felt responsibility* the employee has for the work outcomes. The extent to which the job outcomes or results rely on the person's own efforts, initiative, and decisions, indicates how much felt responsibility the person will have—the more that the results rely on the person, the more felt responsibility. If the job outcomes depend on being told what to do, how to do it, and when, the person doing the job will have a lessened sense of felt responsibility.

Have you ever felt your course instructor was just giving you busy work? What part(s) of the job characteristics theory is/are missing in that situation? If you could give your instructor feedback on how to increase your motivation on the task, what would you say?

Feedback from the work or job tasks provides *knowledge of results*. Using the computer example from above, the feedback the computer programmer receives not only says if the program works (effectiveness) but also gives the employee the outcome (the results of the program), leading to high knowledge of results. In the case of the landscaper, knowledge of results is low because the product of the effort cannot be seen for months or years, and only if the landscaper can return to the site to see the original installation. Thus, feedback from the job itself results in either high or low knowledge of results. If the job provides a lot of immediate feedback (e.g., knowing whether the job was complete and done well), knowledge of results is high.

Outcomes

The potential for the job to create internal motivation within an employee is highest when employees perceive all core job dimensions as high. The effect of the dimensions on motivation is multiplicative, like VIE theory. A near-zero score on any one of these core job dimensions results in low levels of motivation. Thus, the combination of the core job dimensions describes the motivating potential of the job—when they are high, the job has a high potential to trigger the psychological states that motivate the worker; when the dimensions are low, the job has a low motivating potential. Hackman and Oldham referred to the motivating potential of a job as how much or to what degree the core dimensions are met on the job. The authors further specified that the motivating potential of a job was equal to (skill variety + task identity + task significance)/3 × autonomy × feedback.

An example of how job characteristics theory might work with motivation at school includes working on a class project—like a senior design project. In 2015, Colorado State University engineering students from mechanical and electrical engineering built an all-electric vehicle called the Formula SAE race car, to compete against other student designed and built cars at the SAE International competition. Each of the nine team members had to apply a variety of skills, such as decision-making, reading, writing, electric writing, mechanical problem solving, and so on, to collaboratively work on the project. The team was responsible for all aspects of the project including budget, fund-raising, design, construction, and so on. Because the team was relatively small and a lot had to be done in a small amount of time, each member had to identify tasks and complete them from start to finish in collaboration with others (task identity). It was clear how each member's work on the project impacted each other—if one person did not get the wheels on properly, the other could not test the steering system (task significance). Team members worked independently as well, figuring out how to complete their part of the project and getting it done on schedule (autonomy). Part of demonstrating their learning is showing they can work autonomously. With a project like this, you knew right away if what you did worked or did not—as you tested, did the wheels move, the lights flash the way they are supposed to, and did the car battery propel the car fast enough (feedback). Thus, the core job dimensions of JCT were all clearly present in this example. Needless to say, the team members reported high levels of meaningfulness in what they were doing, felt very responsible for their part of the project, knew whether what they were doing was working; hence, they were highly motivated as demonstrated by the more than 30,000 hours of work it took to complete the project—including a custom-designed battery power system!

Hackman and Oldham (1976) also proposed that the relationship between the core job dimensions and the psychological states, as well as the relationship between the psychological states and the resulting outcomes were moderated by an individual difference variable called *growth need strength* (hence the arrows from growth need strength up to the arrows between the dimensions and state, and states and outcome in Figure 3.7). Growth need strength refers to the need for personal growth and development, and for challenging and stimulating work. The Job Characteristics theory proposed that people with high growth need strength have a high need for personal growth and development in their jobs, and the more the job can provide that, the more motivated the employee will become. Moderation means that the effect of core job dimensions on psychological states is *dependent* on the level of growth need strength. Likewise, the effect of psychological states on resulting outcomes is dependent on the level of growth need strength. Hackman and Oldham (1975) explained the moderation as "people who strongly value and desire personal feelings of accomplishment and growth should respond very positively to a job which is high on the core dimensions; individuals who do not value personal growth and accomplishment may find such a job anxiety arousing and may be uncomfortably 'stretched' by it" (p.160). An early critique of the job characteristics theory reports it of little value to those with low growth need strength, since the motivational potential of core job dimensions is dramatically reduced for such individuals (Roberts & Glick, 1981).

Hackman and Oldham's (1976) original analyses of their proposed model (shown in Figure 3.7), revealed a few differences in the model than what they hypothesized. In particular, felt responsibility was not only predicted by autonomy, but also predicted by the other core dimensions at near equal levels. They also found that of the core dimensions, skill variety, task identity, and task significance were the strongest and most reliable predictors of psychological states and resulting outcomes. They found support for psychological states mediating between core dimensions and outcomes. Lastly, the authors found support for growth need strength moderating relationships between core dimensions and psychological states, and psychological states relating to outcomes. Substantial additional research has been conducted testing and applying the theory, with findings generally supporting the overall model but mixed findings for both the **mediating** psychological states and the **moderating** power of growth need strength—some support it and some do not (e.g., Champoux, 1991; DeVaro, Li, & Brookshire, 2007; Evans & Ondrack, 1991; Fried & Ferris, 1987; Johns, Xie, & Fang, 1992; Tiegs, Tetrick, & Fried, 1992). Recent studies have shown the moderating effect of growth need strength only works in combination with other constructs like personality factors, such as openness to experience (de Jong, van der Velde, & Jansen, 2001). Other critiques included lack of consistent findings for the mediating role of the psychological states, effects of situational variables reducing the generalizability of the theory, and whether the motivational potential is truly the result of a multiplicative calculation or additive calculation (Fried & Ferris, 1987; Johns et al., 1992; Kelly, 1992). Hence, the theory may have more conceptual value than practical or empirical utility.

Quick research methods/stats refresher: A mediator is a variable that enables one variable to relate to another—it explains why one variable affects another. For example, in the JCT, the reason why skill variety leads to higher motivation is because skill variety creates a sense of meaningfulness at work and the more we feel we're doing something meaningful, the more motivated we are to work harder. Thus, our sense of meaningfulness explains why using a variety of skills in our job leads us to feel motivated to work hard.

A moderator is a variable that increases or decreases the effect of one variable on another. In simple terms, whenever you say in psychology "it depends", you're talking about a moderator variable. For example, using what you learned in Chapter 2, do organizations recruit from colleges? The answer is that it depends on whether the organization is hiring for a job in which college students might be appropriate. In this case, the moderating variable is the type of job the organization is recruiting for. The more the job is oriented towards college students, the more likely the organization recruits from colleges.

How do Managers use Job Characteristics Theory in the Workplace?

Critiques aside, job characteristics theory offers managers insight into how to change aspects of their employees' jobs to boost their motivation and satisfaction at work. In a study of 283 employees, Piccolo and Colquitt (2006) demonstrated that components of the theory explained how leaders excite employees to engage in beneficial job behaviors such as task performance and **organizational citizenship behaviors** (helping behaviors that support performance in the organization). Thus, leaders can foster higher levels of performance and commitment at work by focusing on modifying their employees' core job dimensions (i.e., increasing skill variety or increasing autonomy).

To support the use of job characteristics theory in practice, Hackman and Oldham (1975) developed the job diagnostic survey (JDS). The JDS was designed to evaluate existing jobs on how their design would lead to the core job dimensions and psychological states of the job characteristics theory. Employees take the JDS, responding to items on a 1 = low to 7 = high response scale (see Table 3.2). The JDS comprises a seven-part instrument that uses different formats specifically created to reduce confounding across content areas within the instrument.

TABLE 3.2 Components of the Job Diagnostic Survey

To what extent does your job require you to work closely with other people (e.g., clients, or others in the organization?)						
1	2	3	4	5	6	7
Very little; dealing with other people is not at all necessary.			Moderately; some dealing with others is necessary.			Very much; dealing with other people is absolutely essential and critical.

⋮

⋮

To what extent does your job permit you to decide on your own how to go about doing the work?						
1	2	3	4	5	6	7
Very little; the job gives me almost no personal say about how and when the work is done.			Moderate autonomy; many things are not under my control but I can make some decisions about the work.			Very much; the job allows me almost complete control and responsibility to decide how and when to do it.

⋮

⋮

(Continued)

TABLE 3.2   Components of the Job Diagnostic Survey   (*Continued*)

To what extent does your job require you to work closely with other people (e.g., clients, or others in the organization?)

To what extent is your job a complete piece of work that has whole and identifiable pieces, with an obvious beginning and end? (e.g., you do more than just a small part of the overall work, which is completed by others)

1	2	3	4	5	6	7
My job is only a tiny part of the overall piece of the work. I cannot see the results of what I do in the final product.			My job is a moderate-sized chunk of the overall piece of work. I can see some of the results of what I do in the final product.			My job involves doing the entire job, from start to finish; the results of my work can easily be seen in the final product.

⋮

⋮

How accurate is the statement in describing your job?

1	2	3	4	5	6	7
Very Inaccurate	Moderately Inaccurate	Slightly Inaccurate	Uncertain	Slightly Accurate	Mostly Accurate	Very Accurate

1.   The job requires a lot of cooperative work with other people.

2.   The job is arranged so that I do not have the chance to do an entire piece of work from beginning to end.

3.   The job gives me considerable opportunity for independence and freedom in how I do the work.

⋮

⋮

How much do you agree with the statement?

1	**2**	**3**	**4**	**5**	**6**	**7**

1.   I often have trouble figuring out whether I'm going well or poorly on this job.

2.   Whether or not this job gets done right is clearly my responsibility.

⋮

⋮

(*Continued*)

TABLE 3.2   Components of the Job Diagnostic Survey   *(Continued)*

To what extent does your job require you to work closely with other people (e.g., clients, or others in the organization?)						
How satisfied are you with this aspect of your job?						
1	2	3	4	5	6	7
Extremely Dissatisfied	Dissatisfied	Slightly Dissatisfied	Neutral	Slightly Satisfied	Satisfied	Extremely Satisfied
1.	The amount of job security I have.					
2.	The amount of personal growth and development I get in doing my job.					
3.	The amount of independent thought and action I can exercise in my job					

Courtesy Zinta Byrne. Source: Hackman and Oldham (1975)

The distinguishing feature of Job Characteristics Theory is the focus on factors or dimensions of the job leading to psychological states that trigger satisfaction and motivation.

The JDS asks about job components and attitudes about work experiences to get at people's ratings of the psychological states.

Results from the JDS may be graphed to show comparatively how employees perceive each job component. In Figure 3.8, the results of the JDS suggest the job role should be modified to increase task identity and autonomy.

To increase skill and task variety, managers can combine job tasks such that a single employee's responsibility increases covering more of the job, eliminating the need for two different employees each doing only one aspect of the job. For example, a senior nurse can do both the tasks required of a nurse and at other times teach workshops to more junior nurses on essential aspects of the job that are hard to understand without years of experience. Thus, the advanced nurse occasionally using teaching skills increases skill use while removing the need for another person to teach the workshops. To increase autonomy, managers can give employees freedom over when to complete a set of job tasks, as long as the criteria for completion are clear. For example, software development engineers often have substantial autonomy. Some jobs simply cannot be done at the employees' choosing or in the manner the employee wishes (e.g., some jobs have strict procedures that must be followed in order and at a specific time).

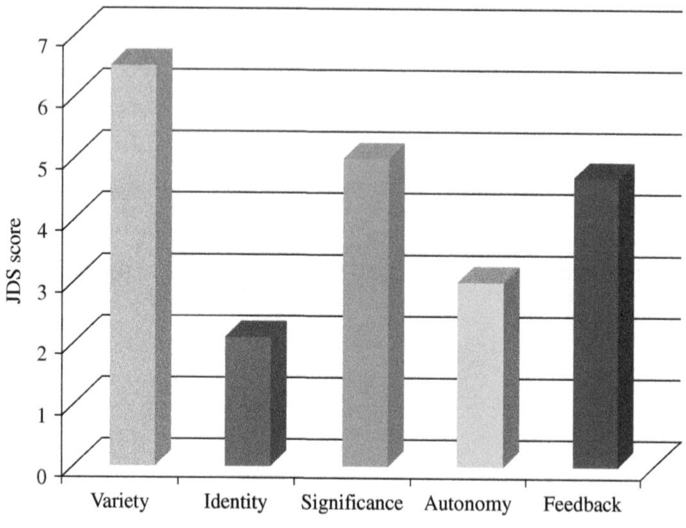

FIGURE 3.8   Sample of Results from the JDS.

Courtesy Zinta Byrne

Exercise 3.4

Draw the Job Characteristics Theory, labeling and explaining what each dimension of JCT means. Using your own words, summarize what the theory basically says about motivation.

Job Redesign Options

Job redesign options can be used with any of the broad-based theories to increase motivation at work. Options include job rotation, job enrichment, job enlargement, flextime, job sharing, and telecommuting. Job redesign approaches are particularly effective for improving satisfiers identified in Herzberg's two-factor theory.

Job rotation refers to an approach to job redesign where employees move to other departments or units within the organization that have the same job title or configuration of job tasks. In job rotation (also called **cross-training**; Figure 3.9), employees do not necessarily learn an entirely new job (although in some cases they can); at a minimum they may learn a few new skills or processes. Job rotation can be as simple as switching to another comparable position within the same unit or division, just to experience a new group and learn a few new techniques or approaches to the job.

During medical training, Doctors are expected to rotate through a variety of areas (orthopedics, cardiac, pulmonary) to practice their training and develop a choice of specialty for their residency application.

Barista and cash register worker trade positions to increase skill variety and ensure staffing needs can be met when one is absent.

FIGURE 3.9   Examples of Job Rotation.

© Photographee.eu/Shutterstock, Inc.; © Monkey Business Images/Shutterstock, Inc.; © CandyBox Images/Shutterstock, Inc.

Job rotation can be as complicated as rotating to entirely different jobs within one's educational scope (Figure 3.9). For example, job rotation is sometimes implemented for top level executives or senior administrators in organizations, to teach them how every division or large unit is run before promoting them to the next level in the organization, a level that requires knowledge of the underlying units. For instance, to prepare a Chief Executive Officer (CEO) for the position, the organization may place the CEO on a job rotation cycle for a few years, running (or job shadowing) the marketing department, manufacturing, sales, and other key divisions. Job rotation is positively associated with increases in promotions and salary (Campion, Cheraskin, & Stevens, 1994), possibly because of the breadth and depth of skills and knowledge that come from rotating through a variety of positions. Job rotation is not feasible when the underlying knowledge or potential skill for the job does not exist. For example, accountants in hospitals are not rotated into a cardiac surgeon's position. Likewise, surgeons are not rotated into the chief financial officer position.

Another approach to job redesign is *job enrichment*, which means enriching or expanding the job to make it more fulfilling by satisfying higher order needs on Maslow's hierarchy (e.g., esteem, self-actualization). One approach to job enrichment, called vertical loading, includes adding more tasks to an employee's job and giving the employee more responsibility and freedom to decide how and when to perform the tasks (thus adding autonomy). Connected tasks typically completed by separate employees can be combined such that one person does all the connected tasks, providing a clearer picture of how the job fits into the overall project. For example, if José in accounting handles client billing and receivables, job enrichment would include not only billing the clients but also talking with them when they have questions about their bills, rather than turning them over to someone in customer service who has no knowledge of the details of the client's financial arrangement with the organization.

Unions do not like job enrichment because employees are given more responsibility, but not necessarily given more pay and a higher-level job title.

Job enlargement, considered another form of job enrichment, refers to growing the current job without increasing responsibility. This would involve adding more tasks or greater task variety, but not adding more responsibility such as supervising others or adding control over the schedule or process for job completion. For example, an implementer at a landscaping company may, in addition to planting the required plants in the location noted by the designer, lay the bark and place the drip lines. As you might imagine, some people are not excited about job enlargement because the general outcome of job enlargement is that more is expected without an increase in pay or better job title.

Other redesign options for increasing motivators may include restructuring the job to allow for *flextime*, which refers to a flexible work schedule. For example, employees within certain units who work 8-hour shifts could start work any time between 7:00 a.m. and 9:00 a.m., and leave any time between 4:00 p.m. and 6:00 p.m. Thus, the employee can decide when to show up for work as long as the start time falls between 7 and 9 in the morning. Employees remain responsible for working the required number of hours per day and/or per week, but they can determine with some freedom when to start. Flextime varies by organization and group, thereby accommodating the needs of the organization.

Job sharing creates another redesign option that offers employees a different type of work flexibility. Job sharing involves taking a single job and assigning two half-time people such that two people work together to complete the job requirements. For example, Sharon may work on Monday and Tuesday, and half a day Wednesday, whereas Amy may work half a day on Wednesday, and all day Thursday and Friday. This particular arrangement works well for employees with family obligations and also benefits the organization by keeping valued employees on the payroll.

Telecommuting or the virtual office allows employees to do their job from any location, thus not requiring that it be done only at the office. Telecommuting requires that employees have the equipment they need to do the job, such as the ability to connect with others at work when needed or to the Internet. Most telecommuters have a computer linked to the office via an Internet connection, phones to allow for conference calls, and printers, faxes, or other forms of equipment that may be needed depending on the type of work performed. Jobs involving information processing or knowledge-related tasks may be easily executed virtually, away from the office. Clearly some jobs cannot be accomplished using a telecommuting or virtual office arrangement. Jobs such as manufacturing, outdoor manual labor, or jobs that require the work be completed at a specific job site (e.g., construction, laboratory, hospital) to name a few, cannot be configured as telecommute or virtual office jobs.

Job Redesign includes:
(a) job rotation
(b) job enrichment
(c) job enlargement
(d) flextime
(e) job sharing
(f) telecommuting

Which form of job redesign would you prefer? Why?

Exercise 3.5

List the broad-based theories of motivation and provide a brief statement of what each theory explains/says.

Narrow-based Theories of Motivation

Intrinsic/Extrinsic Motivation

Porter and Lawler (1968) defined intrinsic motivation as people doing things because those things are interesting and satisfying, whereas **extrinsic motivation** is about people doing things because those things are externally rewarded (e.g., pay, incentive, recognition from others). Satisfaction in this case comes from being rewarded rather than from doing the activity itself.

Cognitive Evaluation Theory and Self-Determination Theory

In an odd twist of findings, research shows the more you are rewarded for doing an activity you inherently enjoy, the less motivated you become to do the activity for its own sake (Deci, 1975). The reward interferes with your love of the task and now to continue feeling motivated, you require more of the external reward rather than your internal satisfaction to keep doing the task. Cognitive evaluation theory was proposed to explain how and why these extrinsic rewards seem to undermine intrinsic motivation. According to the theory (Deci, 1975; Deci & Ryan, 1980), feelings of competence and autonomy underlie intrinsic motivation, which is motivation propelled by internal interest and spontaneous satisfaction from an activity, rather than motivation driven by an external reward or payment from an external source, called extrinsic motivation (Porter & Lawler, 1968).

Indeed, research shows challenging tasks are intrinsically motivating (e.g., Danner & Lonky, 1981), and that positive internal feedback of achieving challenge tasks promotes a sense of competence (Fisher, 1978; Ryan, 1982) that fosters intrinsic motivation (Deci, Koestner, & Ryan, 1999). Cognitive evaluation theory suggests that external rewards diminish feelings of autonomy, which changes the nature of the activity from being within one's control to being controlled by others, leading to the undermining of intrinsic motivation. Results of meta-analyses support the general conclusion that external tangible rewards reduce intrinsic motivation for interesting tasks (Deci et al., 1999). In contrast, external rewards in the form of positive and noncontrolling feedback (i.e., does not feel manipulative or with a hidden agenda) tend to increase intrinsic motivation. When positive feedback is received with the perception that its intent is to manipulate or control behavior, the feedback backfires and reduces intrinsic motivation just like tangible external rewards. How do you increase intrinsic motivation? Provide autonomy over the task; intrinsic motivation seems to increase with increases in task autonomy (Zuckerman et al., 1978). In addition to having a sense of autonomy, feelings of competence also play a role in intrinsic motivation (Danner & Lonky, 1981). Feedback increases feelings of competence and consequentially increases intrinsic motivation (Deci, 1975; Ryan, 1982).

The distinguishing characteristic of cognitive evaluation and self-determination theory is the focus on the difference between intrinsic and extrinsic motivation, and that people have an innate tendency toward and need for being intrinsically motivated.

Self-determination theory extends cognitive evaluation theory by describing internal and external motivation in greater detail (Deci & Ryan, 1985; Gagne & Deci, 2005; Ryan & Deci, 2000). Self-determination theory is actually made up of five mini-theories (see Deci & Ryan, 2012), but one in particular, basic needs theory, is particularly useful in the workplace. Basic needs theory (Ryan, Sheldon, Kasser, & Deci, 1996) proposes that people seek to fulfill three universal needs: autonomy, competence, and relatedness. The

Self-determination theory has been used to explain motivation in gaming environments. It turns out players who perceive high levels of in-game autonomy (e.g., choice over actions, tasks undertaken), high competence (e.g., opportunity to acquire new skills, challenges, intuitive controls), report higher motivation to play and greater satisfaction in playing (Ryan, Rigby, & Przybylski, 2006). Furthermore, those in multiplayer online games reported higher need for relatedness, another component of self-determination theory.

theory suggests people are often motivated even when the task is not intrinsically interesting because they understand and strongly value the benefit their behavior ultimately provides, or because their behavior is fully integrated into their identity such that it is self-determined. Self-determination theory builds on the fundamental belief that humans have innate tendencies toward intrinsic motivation, by satisfying three needs (i.e., competence, autonomy, and relatedness) that are important for triggering and enhancing intrinsic motivation (Gagne & Deci, 2005; Ryan & Deci, 2000). As long as people interpret their work environment as (a) supportive of their feelings of competence, (b) giving them self-control (i.e., autonomy), and (c) characterized by a sense of relatedness, they will believe that their actions or behaviors are self-determined and intrinsically motivated (Ryan & Deci, 2000).

So how does self-determination theory apply to an educational setting? Researchers have shown that students assigned to master material in order to teach it later, were more intrinsically motivated and learned more than students assigned material with the expectation of taking a test to assess mastery (Niemiec & Ryan, 2009). Students in autonomy-supported class environments report higher intrinsic motivation, competence, and self-esteem than those in courses where instructors are more control-oriented and limit students' autonomy (Deci, Schwartz, Sheinman, & Ryan, 1981).

Self-determination has also been shown to apply to non-Western cultures. In a four study paper, Jang, Reeve, Ryan, and Kim, 2009 examined the applicability of self-determination theory to Korean students, who tend more towards collectivism (i.e., focused on fitting into a group) than western students (i.e., focused on individualism). The authors found that Korean students were likely to benefit from autonomy-supportive learning climates, just like their western culture peers.

How Do Managers Use Intrinsic/Extrinsic Motivation in the Workplace?

Managers should explore what employees find interesting about a task or activity and then provide the tools, resources, and feedback to encourage higher levels of mastery and enjoyment from task accomplishment. If employees are not in the right job, a job they find interesting, or in a job that fails to provide interesting work most of the time, finding another job that is a better match may be the right next step. In some organizations, switching jobs is not difficult; however, in others, switching is not an option due to the size of the organization, types of skills needed across jobs, and other constraints. In such cases, job redesign strategies may be appropriate for changing tasks to create more interest for employees. Also, applying strategies for thinking about the work differently may be appropriate. For example, helping employees see how the current tasks they have may lead to future opportunities that otherwise are unavailable may create an intrinsic interest in the current tasks because they can be now seen as stepping stones for a desired future job.

According to self-determination theory, people want to be self-directed—they want to have some control over how they do their work and accomplish the job objectives. Not all jobs allow for complete discretion, but when possible, managers can give employees a chance to provide input on how to do their work best. For example, at Toyota Auto Company, employees are encouraged to brainstorm how to improve their work and tasks, and they are encouraged to provide those suggestions to their managers. Because these employees are the ones actually doing the work (as opposed to the manager), they are in the best position to offer suggestions for how to do it better—to increase efficiency and quality. The organization rewards the employees with verbal recognition and helps give them a sense of ownership in the job and the quality of the final product. Thus, Toyota's approach applies both self-determination theory and the job characteristics theory.

Self-determination theory also includes the need for competence or mastery; employees want to be good at what they do and they inherently want to improve. Managers can provide development opportunities for employees to improve their skills, develop new skills related to their jobs, and provide resources to do so (either free classes and workshops, or funds for taking classes or buying books). Job rotation is a good example of a job design strategy managers can use to give their employees an opportunity to develop and learn new skills, while still continuing to strengthen and use the ones they have.

Accordingly, managers can promote intrinsic motivation by applying self-determination theory (and goal setting theory, as well), and by heeding the consistent finding that extrinsically rewarding something that is already intrinsically rewarding to someone will reduce motivation to perform, and to perform at higher levels.

Take a look at RSA Animate's YouTube video on "Drive: The surprising truth about what motivates us". https://www.youtube.com/watch?v=u6XAPnuFjJc This animated sketch was drawn to illustrate Daniel Pink's talk on the essentials of self-determination theory.

Regulatory Theories

Regulatory theories are based on **homeostatic physiological mechanisms** (e.g., Cannon, 1929), which state that people seek or are driven to balance or resolve **dissonance** (discomfort), preferring a state of **homeostasis** or equilibrium. Control theory is a general theory of regulation (derived from a number of disciplines and applied in various forms in engineering, mathematics, medicine, and economics) that can be applied to understanding what motivates people toward accomplishing a particular state or goal (Carver & Scheier, 1982). Very simply, in psychology, regulatory theories say we are constantly monitoring our environment and are motivated to make adjustments to feel most comfortable.

Control theory says that using a specific standard or referent comparison point, we compare perceptions or measures of the current state to the standard, adjust efforts based on the difference between the current and the standard, and thereby create a new state which is then measured or perceived and re-compared to the standard to determine how far off or discrepant the current state is from the standard. The room thermostat serves as a common example for understanding control theory, shown in the Figure 3.10. The terminology in the figure: standard, comparator, sensor, effector, and output, are commonly used in control theory models.

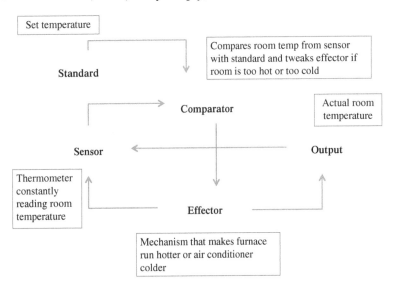

FIGURE 3.10   Control Theory.

Courtesy Zinta Byrne. Source: Carver and Scheier (1982)

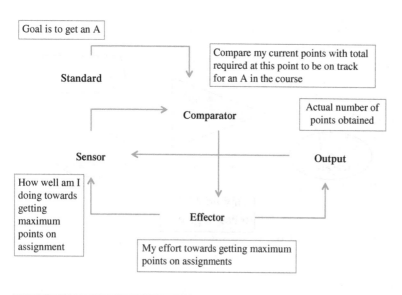

FIGURE 3.11   Applying Control Theory to an Educational Example.

Courtesy Zinta Byrne

The standard is set by you, your boss, the organization, or some outside group. For example, if your goal is to lose 20.5 kilos (about 45 lbs), that becomes your standard. If your job requires you deliver 40 packages by 8PM, that is the standard in this regulatory model. The comparator is the difference between where you are now and the standard. Thus, if you stand on a scale (a sensor), you can compare the number on the scale with your standard.

The theory can also easily be applied to education (see Figure 3.11).

How Do Managers Use Control Theory in the Workplace?

An example of how managers can use control theory comes from a medium sized organization located in the Midwestern region of the United States. The organization established a goal (i.e., the goal is the "standard" in the regulatory model) of wanting to be in the top quarter of the normative database of their industry on their **employee engagement** scores (Byrne, 2015). Employee engagement refers to a psychological state of motivation at work, where we are physically, cognitively, and emotionally absorbed and focused on the work (Kahn, 1990). The value for engagement (comparator) reported in the normative database to which the organization compared itself was provided by a large consulting firm. Based on all the organizations with which the consulting firm worked, this organization's scores on engagement were below the 50th percentile. Because of the low scores, the organization set out to determine what was causing their low scores and how to raise them. They worked internally on a number of projects, training supervisors to offer more support, developed stronger teams using team-building exercises, reevaluated their pay system, restructured jobs to improve their meaningfulness and challenge levels, and implemented a number of other solutions that were recommended to them for increasing their scores (combined, these actions make up the effector). After several months, the vendor surveyed (the survey is the sensor) them again on engagement and found some improvements (the result of the efforts, which is the "output" or the new engagement score), but the organization was still below the top quarter cutoff. The organization conducted more internal investigations to find out what else they could do to influence and encourage higher engagement scores. After implementing additional solutions (effector), the vendor resurveyed (sensor) them and the organization was thrilled to find their scores (output) were nearly at the required cutoff mark (standard) to be considered in the top quarter. This ongoing surveying (sensor), testing against the norm (comparator), doubling efforts to track down gaps in the system and apply solutions to boost engagement (effector) can all be placed within the control theory model.

The comparative cycle, or feedback loop, is control theory's distinguishing characteristic—it's what separates it from all other motivation theories.

Goal-setting Theory

Goals are a source of motivation (Locke, 1968)—they propel people in a particular direction. Goals tell us in what direction to go, for how long, and with how much intensity (Earley, Wojnaroski, & Prest, 1987). However, research has shown that for goals to have their maximum motivational potential, they must be specific and challenging, and the person with the goal must accept the goal.

First, a goal must be specific for it to move us in a particular direction. Being told "do your best" is a nonspecific goal. Specific goals, such as "score a 90% on the next exam", lead to better performance because they provide a standard to which we must achieve—an end point or a measure for knowing when we have reached the goal. Thus, deciding to get an A in the course tells us what to aim for and also when we get there. A specific goal helps you determine what is important and requires attention, versus what can wait—thus, specific goals clarify priorities.

Second, a goal must be challenging. The more difficult the goal, the higher the performance level to achieve the goal (Locke, 1997; Mento, Steel, & Karren, 1987; Wright, 1990). It turns out a major predictor of an employee's goal-level is his or her past performance and ability (Wofford, Goodwin, & Premack, 1992), as well as level of task-specific self-esteem (high esteem results in choosing more difficult goals). A difficult goal requires greater effort and persistence than does an easy goal.

Third, we have to accept the goal. Assigned goals can easily be ignored because you do not internalize them or feel responsible for achieving them. By taking part in setting the goal, you can choose the difficulty level, the specifics of the goal, and take ownership of the goal—it becomes personal.

Employees with goals tend to focus their attention toward goal achievement, exert more effort, persist, and develop strategies to achieve the goal more than employees who do not have goals (Locke, Shaw, Saari, & Latham, 1981). The same is true for groups of employees—that is, a group having a group goal (Durham, Knight, & Locke, 1997; O'Leary-Kelly, Martocchio, & Frink, 1994; Weingart, 1992). However, with tasks that are complex or novel, goal-setting seems to interfere with performance (Wood, Mento, & Locke, 1987).

People tend to have different orientations to goal-setting: mastery or performance (Dweck, 1986). Those with a **mastery-goal orientation** are more interested in setting goals related to learning (e.g., I'd like to learn how this works) as opposed to performance goals, which are more about doing well (e.g., getting an A). Those with a mastery-goal orientation are more likely to set harder goals, and seek feedback and training than those with a **performance-goal orientation**. Those with a performance-goal orientation tend to get more done (Figure 3.12).

FIGURE 3.12   Performance-goal Orientation.

© Keepsmiling4u/Shutterstock, Inc.

> **Exercise 3.6**
>
> Draw a model of control theory using an example relevant to a goal you have.

How Do Managers Use Goal-Setting in the Workplace?

For goal setting to work, employees must be committed or attached to achieving their goal (Tubbs, 1994), receive feedback on their progress toward the goal (Erez, 1977), and possess the skills and ability to achieve the goal (Mitchell & Daniels, 2003). Managers can involve their employees in the goal setting process, ensure the goals are aligned with the organizational goals, make sure goals set by employees are of an appropriate challenge level, and, lastly, confirm that the goals are specific. Additionally, by working together to set the goals, managers and their employees can determine what kind of feedback is needed and when it would be most helpful, and how to determine when the goal has been accomplished. Mini-goals, interim milestones, or subgoals are valuable with long-term projects. Mini- or interim goals help people focus on a specific goal that is within their sights, giving them interim feedback on progress toward the larger goal. Furthermore is that managers need to support and monitor their employees to ensure they have the resources and encouragement needed to make progress toward goal achievement. If employees lack the necessary skills or knowledge to achieve a particular goal, managers can work with them to obtain the skills and knowledge (e.g., make training available, modify goal to incorporate a development/learning cycle).

If a goal must be assigned and cannot be established in a participatory way, managers need to make sure employees receiving these assigned goals understand the rationale behind the goal and how they can best be successful toward achieving the goal. Goals that initially appear unrealistic or unachievable will not be met if employees cannot at least understand why such goals were set and find ways of feeling successful at making progress toward the goal, even if it cannot ultimately be met. Regardless of the country's culture, employees with a high need for achievement, an individual tendency to want to accomplish challenging goals, will do better if given an opportunity to structure the goal (Byrne et al., 2004).

Managers may want to match employees' goal orientation to task objectives. For example, some tasks are complex and require that the employee become an expert. In these cases, employees with a mastery-goal orientation may perform at a higher level than those with a performance-goal orientation, whose focus is on getting the job done quickly. Projects that must be completed well and quickly but not necessarily to an expert level may be best handed over to performance-goal oriented employees (Winters & Latham, 1996).

As opposed to matching the employee with the task objective, another way to use the mastery versus performance perspective is to frame the goal to match the employee's orientation (Seijts & Latham, 2012). For example, a school district in Northern Colorado sought to implement environmental sustainability principles by designing and building all new schools to meet sustainability requirements. The problem was that no one in the district and none of the builders in the community knew anything about sustainability principles. Learning about sustainability is a mastery goal. However, many of the employees who would be involved in building and maintaining the schools favored performance goals. Therefore, for the

What type of goal-orientation do you prefer—mastery or performance? If you like to do better than other students in the class or be the first one done, you lean towards performance orientation. If you prefer to get it right, even if you're the last one done, you lean toward mastery orientation.

performance-oriented employees, the district supervisor established goals such as, track down three new types of low-flush toilets by the end of the month, pick four new types of electrical wiring systems for lighting that saves 50% in energy, and obtain bids from at least three different architectural firms with proven credentials for building sustainable buildings. To achieve these goals, employees had to learn about sustainability, but they did so while achieving their performance goals. Had these employees been told "go learn about sustainability," the project would probably still be in the idea phase. For those with a mastery-orientation, the supervisor asked them to develop two new processes for how to integrate feedback from the utilities, community, and other stakeholders. Their goal, in contrast to their performance-oriented peers, was focused on learning and discovery.

Equity Theory

Equity theory was initially proposed as *inequity* theory by Adams (1963). Because people seek equity rather than inequity, the theory became known as equity theory.

Equity theory is partially based on Festinger's (1957) cognitive dissonance theory, which says that people generally prefer consistency between their emotions, behavior, or cognitions (i.e., thoughts). When our emotions are inconsistent with our behaviors, the result is dissonance or an uncomfortable state of anxiety, which propels us to either change the emotions or change the behavior to resolve the dissonance. Psychological dissonance is an unpleasant tension, which drives or motivates the person to reduce the unpleasant state. Thus, for you to experience dissonance, the cognitions have to be contradictory, causing enough tension to drive you to reduce the tension. A common example of cognitive dissonance is people who believe smoking is detrimental to their health, yet smoke five packs of cigarettes per day. To reduce the resulting tension of the inconsistency between beliefs and behaviors, they will either stop believing that smoking is bad or will stop smoking.

Equity theory is also partially based on social comparison theory (Festinger, 1954). Social comparison theory says that we compare ourselves to other people to evaluate and understand our opinions and abilities given a certain situation. Adams framed equity theory in terms of people developing a perceived ratio of outcomes (what they get out of their investment at work, such as intrinsic rewards or pay) to inputs[1] (their investments at work—their perceived contribution to the job). People compare their outcome/input ratios to the corresponding ratios of someone else, or to themselves at an earlier time (e.g., what happened in a previous job). Adams suggested that equity exists when a person's outcome/input ratio is the same as someone else's outcome/input ratio (see Figure 3.13).

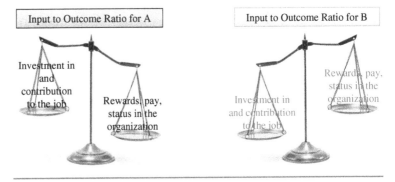

FIGURE 3.13   Theory of Inequity.

© zendograph/Shutterstock.com

---

[1] Adams' incorporates far more into what may be considered or perceived as an input and an outcome, but that has been omitted here to keep the theory simple and understandable.

For example, suppose Pat and Deepti work together. If Deepti (Person B using Figure 3.13) put more time and effort into completing a specific task than did Pat (Person A using Figure 3.13), but got much less in return than did Pat (so Pat was paid twice as much at Deepti for doing less), the result is inequity. Deepti would consider the situation an underpayment—having received less than what was put into the job compared to Pat. According to the theory, Pat would consider the situation an overpayment—having received more than what was put into the job in comparison to Deepti (in reality, though, Pat would unlikely consider being overpaid since we generally feel we deserve more than we get).

Here is a slightly different example where the inputs and outcomes are more subtle than task completion and pay. Suppose Pauline is a manager and assigns Sofia, her new employee, to a key client project. Sofia has only been working for Pauline for two months. Mona has been working for Pauline for three years and still has yet to be assigned to a key client project. From Mona's perspective, Sofia does not deserve to be assigned to a client project before her because Sofia has not been there as long, has not demonstrated the same commitment to Pauline as Mona has, and probably has not yet demonstrated whether she can perform the job. Mona would see this situation as inequitable (unfair) based on a comparison of her expertise, commitment to Pauline, and length of time performing on the job, in comparison to Sofia.

The comparison of one's input/output ratio to another's is equity theory's distinguishing characteristic.

Equity theory requires a comparison between inputs and outcomes, and between you and a referent or comparison other, either oneself or another person. Thus, you can feel an outcome is unfair because based on what you've been given in the past for your efforts, you *deserved* more this time. The comparison is between your input/output ratio today and your input/output ratio from the past.

Based on cognitive dissonance theory, equity theory attempts to explain what happens after inequity is perceived. The theory suggests inequity causes psychological tension, and the person doing the comparing wants to restore balance between inputs and outcomes (or the input/outcome ratio) to relieve the tension. To do so, the person will follow one of several options: (a) alter the outcome/input ratio by working harder, working less, or asking for more from the organization to compensate the inequity; (b) change the comparison person's outcomes/inputs ratio if possible; (c) withdraw from the relationship or situation (i.e., change jobs, quit the group); (d) cognitively reevaluate the outcome/input ratio (e.g., rationalize the workload relative to the outcomes, reassess the value of the outcomes; or (e) change the referent or comparison other—pick someone else as the point of comparison.

Can you remember a time when you felt you studied really hard for an exam, but didn't do as well as your friend who didn't study as hard as you did? Use equity theory to explain why you felt the situation was unfair.

A substantial amount of research has accumulated on equity theory over the years. Results from this research show employees do react to perceptions of inequity in work situations, typically responding with dissatisfaction, less commitment to the organization, lower trust levels, a reduction in job performance behaviors (such as doing the job itself or helping others at work to get a project done), increased withdrawal behaviors like contemplating quitting or just mentally checking-out on the job, and overall higher negative emotional reactions (see a meta-analysis by Colquitt, Conlon, Wesson, Porter, & Ng, 2001).

How Do Managers Use Equity Theory in the Workplace?

Knowing that people constantly compare themselves to others at work in terms of how much and what kind of work they do and what they get from the organization in return is valuable to keep in mind because their resultant evaluation of this comparison drives their thoughts and behaviors. They are either motivated to work harder, work less, change other's workload, or potentially leave the job or organization. Since employees are going to make these comparisons whether desirable or not, managers can use their understanding of equity theory to help employees make the best comparisons they can make, rather than comparisons based on erroneous information. For example, managers can make as much information as possible about salary comparisons across industries, locations, jobs, and pay scales within the company available to employees and explain how their salary or pay was derived and how it measures up to the appropriate comparison person or group.

Managers can make expectations for performance clear by providing examples of the type of performance behaviors and contributions desired by the organization that can result in a variety of rewards or outcomes. They can also provide hypothetical examples of how and when some compensation arrangements may be more appropriate depending on the type of work, responsibility, or performance level demonstrated. The point is not to have employees mastering detailed information about their peers, but rather to help employees use the right information to understand how their own contribution is perceived.

Setting appropriate expectations about the job, what is valuable and what is not, and how reward decisions are made puts employees in the right position make appropriate comparisons. They may still make comparisons that end up with them feeling underpaid (e.g., compare self to performer at next level in the organizational hierarchy), but managers can help guide employees toward the right referent, even if that referent is themselves at a prior time.

Additionally, reminding employees that they may not be in the best position to see and know everything that their peers do on the job may help them to recognize that even if it appears they are doing more than their referent others and getting less in return, that may not be the reality. Employees perceiving inequity are not always motivated to work productively for the organization; they seek to repair the unfairness and that means their motivation can be targeted at rectifying the inequity by either working more, working less, or worse case, sabotaging someone else's productivity. Managers can ask employees about the comparisons they are making, how they see their contributions to the organization, and what outcomes they feel they are receiving in exchange. Asking these questions can help the manager understand the comparisons the employee is making. Such information allows managers to clarify for the employee whether the comparisons are accurate. Sometimes, we compare ourselves to people beyond our scope or job level, creating an inappropriate comparison that results in feelings of inequity every time. By creating appropriate comparisons, employees can remain motivated at work.

Why does the bossy-pushy tactic used by the SecureWorks Sales VP work with the sales force? What theory or theories of motivation do you think are triggered for the sales people?

Company Example 3.2   An Unusual Way of Motivating Sales People at SecureWorks

In 2002, salespeople at SecureWorks, an Atlanta based company selling security-related software, were told if they did not meet their sales quota in 3 months, they would be fired. In addition, each salesperson's performance data (i.e., number of sales) was shared publically and shamed for not making their numbers. Ironically, the salespeople themselves actually thrived under this bullying motivation strategy and showed a surprising level of loyalty to the new Vice President who implemented these motivational tactics. Research shared by Cummings, Gengler, Preciphs, and Stewart (2004) who wrote the story on SecureWorks in *Fortune Small Business*, suggests that people in jobs like sales where performance is easily measured may be inspired by this aggressive mentality; others not so much. Furthermore, sales teams were required to meet at 7 a.m. for 2 hours of role play and training, given feedback on the spot, and required to work until after 7 p.m.—the more client-facing time, the more likely they would sell enough to make quota. The fear of being humiliated in front of others can be highly demotivating for some, but inspire performance in others. The reward for responding to such tactics can also be reinforcing; since the new tactics were in place salespeople at SecureWorks started making three to four times their previous annual salaries.

Chapter Summary

When you consider the motivational theories reviewed in this chapter, a number of options exist for researchers and managers in understanding what motivates employees at work and how to increase and maintain high levels of motivation. For example, money does work as a motivator for some employees and particularly when considering the levels of Maslow's Hierarchy or Herzberg's Hygiene-Motivators theory. However, money applied to intrinsically rewarding work may squash or reduce intrinsic motivation. Likewise, if money is not what someone values or if someone perceives that whatever he or she does is unlikely to result in the performance necessary to obtain the increase in salary (expectancy theory), money will not be a motivator. Motivation is more complex than a single solution (like giving more money) that can be automatically applied to every situation under the assumption that it will work every time. Researchers exploring new psychological mechanisms for how motivation works and managers deciding how to sustain high levels of motivation at work need to consider all the different theories and current research findings at their disposal.

Figure 3.14 provides a visual summary of the key concepts from Chapter 3.

The visual summary shows that motivation theories have different foci—either explaining how our needs are met or why and how aspects of our jobs move us to behave in one way or another. The source of our motivation might be internal, external, or perhaps a little removed from us (an indirect influence). These theories of motivation can be categorized as broad or narrowly focused, but regardless they all tell us about the direction, intensity, and amount of time we spend at a task or behaving in a certain way. Our motivation is aimed at achieving some target, which has some consequence associated with it. In the workplace, that consequence is generally performance.

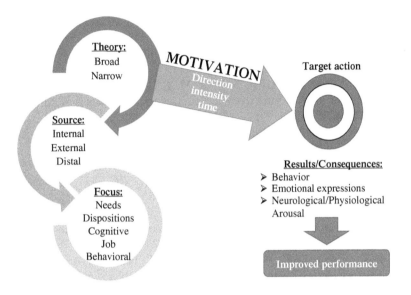

FIGURE 3.14   Visual Summary of Chapter 3.

Courtesy Zinta Byrne

Discussion Questions

1. If managers cannot motivate employees, they need to motivate them-selves, what is the value of all these motivation theories and explaining how managers apply them?

2. A lot of motivation theories look like they are basically saying that the more people have to do, the more motivated they are. First, do you agree with that summarizing statement—if so, why, if not, why not? Second, if that is the case, why do we need different theories to tell us this same simple message? What more are the models and theories saying than "get more busy" to be more motivated?

3. Should we be pushing for more motivation at work? How does that clash with or connect with the trend toward more life outside of work, more time off, and more fun?

References

Adams, J. (1963). Towards an understanding of inequity. *The Journal of Abnormal And Social Psychology, 67*(5), 422–436. doi:10.1037/h0040968

Alderfer, C. P. (1969). An empirical test of a new theory of human needs. *Organizational Behavior & Human Performance, 4*(2), 142–175.

Arnolds, C. A., & Boshoff, C. (2002). Compensation, esteem valence and job perfor-mance: An empirical assessment of Alderfer's ERG theory. *The International Journal of Human Resource Management, 13*(4), 697–719. doi:10.1080/09585190210125868

Byrne, Z. S. (2015). *Understanding employee engagement: Theory, research, and prac-tice*. New York, NY: Routledge/Taylor & Francis Group.

Byrne, Z. S., Mueller-Hanson, R., Cardador, J., Thornton, G. III, Schuler, H., Frintrup, A., & Fox, S. (2004). Measuring achievement motivation: Tests of equivalency for English, German, and Israeli versions of the achievement motivation inventory. *Personality and Individual Differences, 37,* 203–217.

Campion, M. A., Cheraskin, L., & Stevens, M. J. (1994). Career-related antecedents and outcomes of job rotation. *Academy of Management Journal, 37*(6), 1518–1542. doi:10.2307/256797

Cannon, W. B. (1929). Organization for physiological homeostasis. *Physiological Reviews, IX*(3), 399–431.

Champoux, J. E. (1991). A multivariate test of the Job Characteristics Theory of Work Motivation. *Journal of Organizational Behavior, 12*(5), 431–446. doi:10.1002/job.4030120507

Carver, C. S., & Scheier, M. F. (1982). Control theory: A useful conceptual framework for personality–social, clinical, and health psychology. *Psychological Bulletin, 92*(1), 111–135. doi:10.1037/0033-2909.92.1.111

Colquitt, J. A., Conlon, D. E., Wesson, M. J., Porter, C. H., & Ng, K. (2001). Justice at the millennium: A meta-analytic review of 25 years of organizational justice research. *Journal of Applied Psychology, 86*(3), 425–445. doi:10.1037/0021-9010.86.3.425

Danner, F. W., & Lonky, E. (1981). A cognitive-developmental approach to the effects of rewards on intrinsic motivation. *Child Development, 52*(3), 1043–1052. doi:10.2307/1129110

Deci, E. L. (1975). *Intrinsic motivation.* New York, NY: Plenum Press.

Deci, E. L., & Ryan, R. M. (1980). Self-determination theory: When mind mediates behavior. *Journal of Mind And Behavior, 1*(1), 33–43.

Deci, E. L., Koestner, R., & Ryan, R. M. (1999). A meta-analytic review of experiments examining the effects of extrinsic rewards on intrinsic motivation. *Psychological Bulletin, 125*(6), 627–668. doi:10.1037/0033-2909.125.6.627

Deci, E. L., & Ryan, R. M. (1985). *Intrinsic motivation and self-determination in human behavior.* New York, NY: Plenum Press.

Deci, E. L., & Ryan, R. M. (2012). Self-determination theory. In P. A. M. Van Lange, A. W. Kruglanski, & E. T. Higgins (Eds.), *Handbook of theories in social psychology* (Vol. 1, pp. 416–437). Thousand Oaks, CA: SAGE.

Deci, E. L., Schwartz, A. J., Sheinman, L., & Ryan, R. M. (1981). An instrument to assess adults' orientations toward control versus autonomy with children: Reflections on intrinsic motivation and perceived competence. *Journal of Educational Psychology 73,* 642–650.

de Jong, R. D., van der Velde, M. G., & Jansen, P. W. (2001). Openness to experience and growth need strength as moderators between job characteristics and satisfaction. *International Journal of Selection and Assessment, 9*(4), 350–356. doi:10.1111/1468-2389.00186

DeVaro, J., Li, R., & Brookshire, D. (2007). Analysing the job characteristics model: New support from a cross-section of establishments. *International Journal of Human Resource Management, 18*(6), 986–1003. doi:10.1080/09585190701321211

Durham, C. C., Knight, D., & Locke, E. A. (1997). Effects of leader role, team-set goal difficulty, efficacy, and tactics on team effectiveness. *Organizational Behavior and Human Decision Processes, 72*(2), 203–231. doi:10.1006/obhd.1997.2739

Dweck, C. S. (1986). Motivational processes affecting learning. *American Psychologist, 41*(10), 1040–1048. doi:10.1037/0003-066X.41.10.1040

Earley, P., Wojnaroski, P., & Prest, W. (1987). Task planning and energy expended: Exploration of how goals influence performance. *Journal of Applied Psychology, 72*(1), 107–114. doi:10.1037/0021-9010.72.1.107

Erez, M. (1977). Feedback: A necessary condition for the goal setting-performance relationship. *Journal of Applied Psychology, 62*(5), 624–627. doi:10.1037/0021-9010.62.5.624

Evans, M. G., & Ondrack, D. A. (1991). The motivational potential of jobs: Is a multiplicative model necessary? *Psychological Reports*, *69*(2), 659–672. doi:10.2466/PR0.69.6.659-672

Festinger, L. (1954). A theory of social comparison processes. *Human Relations*, *7*, 117–140. doi:10.1177/001872675400700202

Festinger, L. (1957). *A theory of cognitive dissonance*. Stanford, CA: Stanford University Press.

Fisher, C. D. (1978). The effects of personal control, competence, and extrinsic reward systems on intrinsic motivation. *Organizational Behavior & Human Performance*, *21*(3), 273–288. doi:10.1016/0030-5073(78)90054-5

Ford, M. E. (1992). *Motivating humans: Goals, emotions, and personal agency beliefs*. Thousand Oaks, CA: Sage.

Frese, M., & Zapf, D. (1994). Action as the core of work psychology: A German approach. In H. C. Triandis, M. D. Dunnette, & L. M. Hough (Eds.), *Handbook of industrial and organizational psychology*, (2nd ed., Vol. 4, pp. 271–340). Palo Alto, CA: Consulting Psychologists Press.

Fried, Y., & Ferris, G. R. (1987). The validity of the Job Characteristics Model: A review and meta-analysis. *Personnel Psychology*, *40*(2), 287–322. doi:10.1111/j.1744-6570.1987.tb00605.x

Gagné, M., & Deci, E. L. (2005). Self-determination theory and work motivation. *Journal of Organizational Behavior*, *26*(4), 331–362. doi:10.1002/job.322

Hackman, J., & Oldham, G. R. (1975). Development of the Job Diagnostic Survey. *Journal of Applied Psychology*, *60*(2), 159–170. doi:10.1037/h0076546

Hackman, J., & Oldham, G. R. (1976). Motivation through the design of work: Test of a theory. *Organizational Behavior & Human Performance*, *16*(2), 250–279. doi:10.1016/0030-5073(76)90016–7

Hall, D. T., & Nougaim, K. E. (1968). An examination of Maslow's Need Hierarchy in an organizational setting. *Organizational Behavior & Human Performance*, *3*(1), 12–35.

Herzberg, F., Mausner, B., & Snyderman, B. B. (1959). *Motivation to work*. Oxford, England: John Wiley.

Jang, H., Reeve, J., Ryan, R. M., & Kim, A. (2009). Can self-determination theory explain what underlies the productive, satisfying learning experiences of collectivistically oriented Korean students? *Journal of Educational Psychology*, *101*(3), 644–661. doi: 10.1037/a0014241

Johns, G., Xie, J., & Fang, Y. (1992). Mediating and moderating effects in job design. *Journal of Management*, *18*(4), 657–676. doi:10.1177/014920639201800404

Kahn, W. A. (1990). Psychological conditions of personal engagement and disengagement at work. *Academy of Management Journal, 33*, 692–724.

Kanfer, R. (1990). Motivation theory and industrial and organizational psychology. In M. D. Dunnette & L. M. Hough (Eds.), *Handbook of industrial and organizational psychology*, (2nd ed., Vol. 1, pp. 75–170). Palo Alto, CA: Consulting Psychologists Press.

Katt, J. A., & Condly, S. J. (2009). A preliminary study of classroom motivators and de-motivators from a motivation-hygiene perspective. *Communication Education*, *58*(2), 213–234. doi:10.1080/03634520802511472

Kelly, J. E. (1992). Does job re-design theory explain job re-design outcomes? *Human Relations*, *45*(8), 753–774. doi:10.1177/001872679204500801

Locke, E. A. (1968). Toward a theory of task motivation and incentives. *Organizational Behavior & Human Performance*, *3*(2), 157–189. doi:10.1016/0030-5073(68)90004-4

Locke. E. A. (1997). The motivation to work: What we know. *Advances in Motivation and Achievement, 10,* 375–412.

Locke, E. A., Shaw, K. N., Saari, L. M., & Latham, G. P. (1981). Goal setting and task performance: 1969–1980. *Psychological Bulletin*, *90*(1), 125–152. doi:10.1037/0033-2909.90.1.125

Luthans, F. (1998). *Organizational Behavior.* Singapore: McGraw–Hill.

Maslow, A. H. (1948). "Higher" and "lower" needs. *Journal of Psychology: Interdisciplinary and Applied, 25,* 433–436. doi:10.1080/00223980.1948.9917386

Mento, A. J., Steel, R. P., & Karren, R. J. (1987). A meta-analytic study of the effects of goal setting on task performance: 1966–1984. *Organizational Behavior and Human Decision Processes, 39*(1), 52–83. doi:10.1016/0749-5978(87)90045-8

Mitchell, T. R., & Daniels, D. (2003). Motivation. In W. C. Borman, D. R. Ilgen, & R. J. Klimoski (Eds.), *Handbook of psychology: Industrial and organizational psychology,* (Vol. 12, pp. 225–254). Hoboken, NJ: John Wiley & Sons.

Niemiec, C. P., & Ryan, R. M. (2009). Autonomy, competence, and relatedness in the classroom: Applying self-determination theory to educational practice. *Theory and Research in Education, 7*(2), 133–144.

O'Leary-Kelly, A. M., Martocchio, J. J., & Frink, D. D. (1994). A review of the influence of group goals on group performance. *Academy of Management Journal, 37*(5), 1285–1301. doi:10.2307/256673

Piccolo, R. F., & Colquitt, J. A. (2006). Transformational leadership and job behaviors: The mediating role of core job characteristics. *Academy of Management Journal, 49,* 327–340. doi: 10.5465/AMJ.2006.20786079

Pinder, C. G. (1998). *Work motivation in organizational behavior.* Upper Saddle River, NJ: Prentice-HalL.

Porter, L. W., & Lawler, E. E. III. (1968). *Managerial attitudes and performance.* Homewood, IL: Irwin-Dorsey.

Robbins, S. P. (1998). *Organizational behavior: Concepts, controversies, applications.* Upper Saddle River, NJ: Prentice-Hall.

Roberts, K. H., & Glick, W. (1981). The job characteristics approach to task design: A critical review. *Journal of Applied Psychology, 66*(2), 193–217. doi:10.1037/0021-9010.66.2.193

Ryan, R. M. (1982). Control and information in the intrapersonal sphere: An extension of cognitive evaluation theory. *Journal of Personality and Social Psychology, 43*(3), 450–461. doi:10.1037/0022-3514.43.3.450

Ryan, R. M., & Deci, E. L. (2000). Self-determination theory and the facilitation of intrinsic motivation, social development, and well-being. *American Psychologist, 55,* 68–78. doi: 10.1037//0003-066X.55.1.68

Ryan, R. M., Rigby, C. S., & Przybylski, A. (2006). The motivational pull of video games: A self-determination theory approach. *Motivation and Emotion, 30*(4), 347–363. doi: 10.1007/s11031-006-9051-8

Ryan, R. M., Sheldon, K. M., Kasser, T., & Deci, E. L. (1996). All goals are not created equal: An organismic perspective on the nature of goals and their regulation. In P. M. Gollwitzer & J. A. Bargh (Eds.), *The psychology of action: Linking cognition and motivation to behavior* (pp. 7–26). New York, NY: Guilford Press.

Salancik, G. R., & Pfeffer, J. (1978). A social information processing approach to job attitudes and task design. *Administrative Science Quarterly, 23*(2), 224–253. doi:10.2307/2392563

Seijts, G. H., & Latham, G. P. (2012). Knowing when to set learning versus performance goals. *Organizational Dynamics, 41*(1), 1–6. doi:10.1016/j.orgdyn.2011.12.001

Taormina, R. J., & Gao, J. H. (2013). Maslow and the motivation hierarchy: Measuring satisfaction of the needs. *The American Journal of Psychology, 126*(2), 155–177. doi: 10.5406/amerjpsyc.126.2.0155

Tiegs, R. B., Tetrick, L. E., & Fried, Y. (1992). Growth need strength and context satisfactions as moderators of the relations of the job characteristics model. *Journal of Management, 18*(3), 575–593. doi:10.1177/014920639201800308

Tubbs, M. (1994). Commitment and the role of ability in motivation: Comment on Wright, O'Leary-Kelly, Cortina, Klein, and Hollenbeck (1994). *Journal of Applied Psychology, 79*(6), 804–811. doi:10.1037/0021-9010.79.6.804

Van Eerde, W., & Thierry, H. (1996). Vroom's expectancy models and work-related criteria: A meta-analysis. *Journal of Applied Psychology, 81*(5), 575–586. doi:10.1037/0021-9010.81.5.575

Vroom, V. H. (1964). *Work and motivation.* Oxford, England: Wiley.

Wanous, J. P., & Zwany, A. (1977). A cross-sectional test of need hierarchy theory. *Organizational Behavior & Human Performance, 18*(1), 78–97. doi:10.1016/0030-5073(77)90019-8

Weingart, L. R. (1992). Impact of group goals, task component complexity, effort, and planning on group performance. *Journal of Applied Psychology, 77*(5), 682–693. doi:10.1037/0021-9010.77.5.682

Winters, D., & Latham, G. P. (1996). The effect of learning versus outcome goals on a simple versus a complex task. *Group & Organization Management, 21*(2), 236–250. doi:10.1177/1059601196212007

Wofford, J. C., Goodwin, V. L., & Premack, S. (1992). Meta-analysis of the antecedents of personal goal level and of the antecedents and consequences of goal commitment. *Journal of Management, 18*(3), 595–615. doi:10.1177/014920639201800309

Wood, R. E., Mento, A. J., & Locke, E. A. (1987). Task complexity as a moderator of goal effects: A meta-analysis. *Journal of Applied Psychology, 72*(3), 416–425. doi:10.1037/0021-9010.72.3.416

Wright, P. M. (1990). Operationalization of goal difficulty as a moderator of the goal difficulty-performance relationship. *Journal of Applied Psychology, 75*(3), 227–234. doi:10.1037/0021-9010.75.3.227

Zuckerman, M., Porac, J. J., Lathin, D. D., & Deci, E. L. (1978). On the importance of self-determination for intrinsically-motivated behavior. *Personality and Social Psychology Bulletin, 4*(3), 443–446. doi:10.1177/014616727800400317

CHAPTER 4

Predicting Feelings and Behaviors at Work: Attitudes

Learning Outcomes

After studying this chapter you should be able to explain:

Watch https://www.youtube.com/watch?v=cBp9j5B1gc0 to get an overall view/sense of how attitudes dominate our lives.

1. Major job attitudes organizational psychologists and managers care about, and why they are considered important.

2. The role attitudes have at work.

3. How job attitudes predict other job attitudes and behaviors at work.

4. How organizations use different approaches to assess attitudes in the workplace.

Mini-Quiz: Attitudes

As an introduction to this chapter, please take the following mini-quiz (answers are in the back of the book). As you read the questions and consider the answers *before* diving into the chapter, you'll challenge yourself before you master the content, a process that helps facilitate learning for long-term retention. Some questions may have more than one correct answer. Don't worry if you cannot answer all questions correctly on your first try. By the time you read through the chapter and spend some of your own time thinking about these concepts, you should be able to determine the best answers. Try the quiz again after you finish reading the chapter.

1. Which of the following diagrams best represents attitudes?
   a. A
   b. B
   c. C

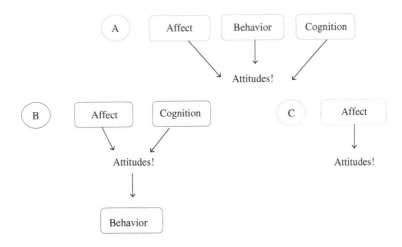

Courtesy Zinta Byrne.

2. Attitudes can be formed by:
   a. Looking around and seeing what's acceptable to other people
   b. Thinking about what our friends would do and think
   c. Looking back on our own behavior and thinking about why we might have done what we did
   d. Our own past experiences

3. Attitudes lead to
   a. Other work attitudes.
   b. Employees' behavior.
   c. Nothing; they are an end in themselves.
   d. Important outcomes of socialization.

4. (Choose one of the following): Job satisfaction, Commitment, Turn-over _____ is the most widely and commonly studied job attitude and the one most often assessed in organizations.

5. If you are a manager and you want to change your employees' attitudes about their jobs, you are going to be more successful if you:
   a. Focus on something the employees care about, and use strong arguments and logical reasoning to explain why their jobs are so important
   b. Highlight how the employees' attitudes are inconsistent with how they want to act on the job (e.g., employees feel fatigued and dissatisfied, yet want to be highly energetic and productive sales people)

c. Conduct an employee satisfaction survey

d. Unfortunately, the attitudes are unlikely to change no matter what you do

Overview

Organizations frequently want to know employees' attitudes at work—such as, how satisfied are you? Are you committed to the organization—will you stay or are you thinking of quitting soon? An organization's leaders care about employees' job attitudes because they believe that job attitudes predict behavior at work, and for the most part, they are correct. Because of this belief, you'll see surveys like the mini-example below (Table 4.1):

Take the following short survey and use the response scale below to indicate your response.

TABLE 4.1 Mini Attitudes Survey

Strongly Disagree	Disagree	Somewhat Disagree	Neutral	Somewhat Agree	Agree	Strongly Agree
1	2	3	4	5	6	7

Item	Your Response
1. I am willing to put in a great deal of effort to help my organization succeed.	
2. I feel like I belong here at my organization.	
3. In my present job, I believe there are opportunities to get ahead.	
4. I feel I am paid fairly for the amount of work I do.	
5. I feel happy at my job.	

What job attitude(s) do you think the questions in Table 4.1 are getting at?

These items above are examples of typical questions you may be asked to indicate your attitude toward your organization and your job. One or more of the questions asks you how you feel about the job or the organization. Another asks you to judge the level of effort you want to exert on behalf of the organization. Job attitudes are about the organization, supervisor, and work itself. So a logical question you might have is whether job attitudes are just simply opinions about work?

What Exactly Are Attitudes?

Attitudes are summary evaluations of a psychological object, such as a person, people, place, or event. These evaluations are based on beliefs, feelings, and/or on past behavior, either ours' or others'. Attitudes derive from internal states that are not directly observable, but can be inferred or determined from observable behavior, such as facial expressions or body language (e.g., smiling; see Figure 4.1). The attitude represents an internal state, inferred from the favorable or unfavorable response

FIGURE 4.1 Inferring Attitudes through Observation

© StockLite/Shutterstock, Inc.; © Jason Stitt/Shutterstock, Inc.; © Monkey Business Images/Shutterstock, Inc.

displayed toward another person or group. In this example, the psychological object being evaluated is the other person or group. Attitudes can be good or bad, harmful or beneficial, pleasant or unpleasant, and likeable or dislikeable about an object, event, or place (Fishbein, 1963). Accordingly, attitudes may be considered opinions.

Some researchers have argued that job attitudes are not *only* situationally determined (caused within and by a specific situation, such as experiencing a rude person), but are also dispositionally determined (caused within the person), which means that we may have a tendency toward specific attitudes or direction of attitude (Salancik & Pfeffer, 1978; Staw & Ross, 1985). For example, some people, no matter what the job, seem to get very absorbed in their work and their **job involvement** level is relatively stable over time regardless of the job (Lodahl & Kejnar, 1965). Their consistent level of involvement at work, regardless of the job, suggests they are predisposed or inclined to be involved at work because of their personality.

Given the seeming complexity of attitudes, researchers have attempted to delineate what goes into attitudes; that is, they seem to have emotional components, thinking or cognitive components, but then also behaviors have been associated with attitudes. In an effort to clearly state what makes up an attitude, researchers proposed the tripartite view.

Why do organizations care about your job attitudes?

Tripartite View of Attitudes

A long-held, but no longer dominant view of attitudes is that they are a combination of affective, cognitive, and behavioral (Figure 4.2) responses to a psychological object. After much debate over the years, consensus turned toward considering behavior an outcome of attitudes rather than a component (Figure 4.3). That said, lingering debate in some circles continues as to whether behavior remains some part of the core of an attitude; hence, both perspectives are provided here.

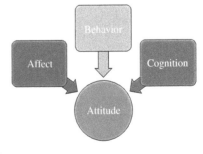

FIGURE 4.2 Tripartite View of Attitudes: Affect, Behavior, and Cognition

Courtesy Zinta Byrne.

Affect refers to emotion—we feel positively or negatively toward an object. For example, how you feel about a particular coworker determines your attitude about your coworker and potentially influences your attitude about all coworkers. Maybe you have had a particularly hard time working with that coworker. Maybe that coworker's consistent rude and disrespectful treatment toward you causes you to feel hurt or angry after every interaction. Your negative feelings about working with this coworker most likely manifest as a negative attitude about the coworker.

A *behavioral* response is an action—an observable behavior. Suppose you are enjoying a lively discussion with a group of coworkers when another person, someone who is not your friend but a friend of one your coworkers, walks up to the group and starts joining in the conversation. If you immediately turn and walk away from the group, even though you were in the midst of saying something, your action provides a behavioral demonstration of your attitude. In this example, is the demonstrated attitude about the newcomer or about being interrupted? If you first looked at the newcomer in disgust and then walked away, we might conclude that your attitude was specifically about the newcomer, though it still could be about being interrupted. Your attitudes can be inferred from your behavior, but unless the behavior is very clearly targeted at a particular object (in this case the newcomer) we're hard pressed to figure out what specifically your attitude is toward or what it is.

Cognition means thinking or judgment. You may classify an object as positive or negative based on its properties. For example, suppose your employer has a policy that says for every extra hour you work, you can earn extra pay, but only as long as your boss asks you to work overtime. You would probably judge the policy as favorable. In contrast, another example may be that there is an agreement at work, almost like a policy, that says if people have to leave work early to pick up their children at day care, they are excused—it's okay for them to leave and those who remain either complete the leftover work or reschedule to accommodate the coworker who left. If you are the parent leaving to pick up your children, you might think this policy represents family-friendly support from the organization. But what if you don't have children? The policy only applies to some people and not others, and is therefore based only on whether you have children, not based on anything work related. In addition, though likely unintended, it punishes those who do not have children because they end up doing more work and their non-work needs are not respected. Most likely, if you're in this position you'd judge this policy as unfavorable. You might even develop a negative attitude towards your coworkers who have small children, even though they are simply taking advantage of an existing resource or policy provided by the organization.

Although this tripartite view of attitudes is appealing because of its simplicity and apparent comprehensiveness, as mentioned previously it is no longer the dominant perspective on attitudes (Figure 4.3). A reason why the tripartite perspective fell out of favor is that the three dimensions were not as highly correlated as would be expected given all three dimensions were supposedly equally essential to making up an attitude. It seems the behavioral actions once considered a part of an attitude are truly best thought of as following from the emotional and cognitive dimensions of the attitude. Behaviors are, therefore, considered outcomes of attitudes (Tesser & Shaffer, 1990).

Breaking attitudes down into an affect and cognitive component might make sense, but for many the concept can still be confusing because the way we talk about attitudes in everyday language implies they are behaviors or objects.

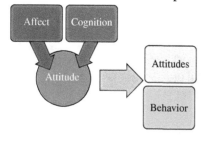

FIGURE 4.3   The More Accurate View of Attitudes

Courtesy Zinta Byrne.

Attitudes are evaluations of psychological objects (such as people or places), based on beliefs, feelings, and past experiences that lead to a behavioral manifestation of those emotions and cognitions.

How We Talk About Attitudes

Accordingly, learning about attitudes as they are discussed and studied in organizational sciences can be a bit challenging. It sometimes seems as we refer to attitudes as behaviors, actions, or objects, our lay understanding of attitude interferes with our ability to understand them scientifically. For example, in everyday speech we might say things like "don't give me an attitude, here, I'm just sharing what happened," "he had a generally good attitude," or "they have a negative attitude about proposals." Attitude in everyday speech is often used as if it is a temperament; like a characteristic of our personality, style, or approach. However, that is not how attitude is used or referred to in the scientific study of attitudes. You won't see a scientific paper discuss job involvement, fairness, or support as "the attitude of job involvement" or "the attitude of support." Instead, you'll see "Employees reporting high job involvement…" or "People care a lot about fairness in the workplace…perceptions of fairness were rated high." Similarly, "supervisors who provided organizational support reported having employees who were high performers." Yet, as you'll read in the next sections, job involvement, fairness, and organizational support are considered job attitudes—they are evaluations of people, places, events, or objects at work.

Learning about attitudes is not just an academic exercise—when we understand what goes into forming an attitude, we gain insight into how to potentially influence them or change them, a key goal of business leaders in organizations.

Exercise 4.1

Now that you have read this section on what attitudes are, in your own words describe what an attitude is and give some examples of attitudes you have.

How Are Attitudes Formed?

Attitudes do not exist until an individual experiences the person, people, place, or event, and then responds (Allport, 1935; Katz & Stotland, 1959; Krech & Crutchfield, 1948). For example, what is your attitude toward working in a factory? If you haven't yet worked in a factory, you may not have an attitude about that type of work. Or suppose you conjure up an image that looks something like Figure 4.4, where you envision yourself standing at a loud machine inside a windowless warehouse. Maybe you've seen an image like that in a movie.

But what if factory work looks more like Figure 4.5, where everything is automated, your role is to monitor a computer that crunches data for manufacturing, and the room is clean and quiet?

FIGURE 4.4   Factory Equipment

©Pavel L Photo and Video/Shutterstock, Inc.

FIGURE 4.5 Computer Servers

©Shchipkova Elena/Shutterstock, Inc.

FIGURE 4.6 Self-Perception Using Past and Present

©Tatiana Frank/Shutterstock, Inc.

Your attitude may initially form based on information from others, or photos like Figures 4.4 or 4.5, but might not truly solidify or take full shape (either strongly positive or negative) until you actually experience the object—in this case, a factory.

To explain how we form attitudes, let's turn to several theories including self-perception theory and social information processing theory. These theories also provide initial starting points for predicting and changing attitudes, which extends their value beyond understanding to application.

Self-Perception Theory

Self-perception theory (Bem, 1967) suggests that our attitudes are formed by considering our own behavior (almost as if you are a third-party or outside observer). We decide what attitudes we must have been experiencing to have caused our specific behavior or action. In other words, what attitude must have existed to produce our current behavior? People can consider their behavior after-the-fact and determine what their attitudes must have been to create the behavior they displayed, almost as if looking at themselves in a mirror of the past (Figure 4.6).

An implication of self-perception theory, supported with research evidence (Bem & McConnell, 1970), is that people may espouse one attitude before a particular behavior has occurred, but then espouse another attitude after the behavior occurred. They use their behavior to determine their true attitude. For example, I might say I like detailed work involving numbers. But if I put off every project that requires me to spend hours in the details, or I try delegating it to someone else, I might infer from my own behavior that I really do not like detailed work involving numbers. After all, if I did, I wouldn't keep trying to get out of doing the work or putting it off.

In addition to people using their own behavior as an indicator of their attitude, they also turn to the contextual environment and their peers to determine what attitudes to form. That is, people also form their attitudes from their interactions with those around them.

Social Information Processing Theory

Social information processing theory (Salancik & Pfeffer, 1978) says that people use the environmental cues around them and their social interactions with others (e.g., what others say or do) to determine their own attitudes. Cues from the environment may include: a supervisor disciplining a coworker, what coworkers say, and other information available within the work environment. For example, the supervisor's actions provide information about acceptable and unacceptable behavior, as well as provide information about the supervisor herself (e.g., she holds people accountable). Direct statements from coworkers, such as "things are so unfair around here" are also cues that influence attitudes. Maybe you haven't thought much about the fairness of the workplace until your closest friend and coworker starts complaining about how unfair it is. Calling attention to concerns in the workplace, such as policies or changes, makes the concerns more salient thereby influencing job attitudes. For instance, managers attempting to be open about the company's performance may point out that the organization's stock price keeps dropping. These statements make the loss in value more obvious to employees, who may otherwise have not been paying attention to the value of the company stock. As a consequence, employees may develop a negative attitude about the value of the company.

How Do Managers Use These Explanations of Attitudes in the Workplace?

Managers can use explanations of attitudes in the workplace to determine when employee attitudes are formed about various aspects of work, and use those explanations to understand what might be driving employees' responses. For example, knowing that employees form their attitudes by using the information in their contextual environment (social information processing theory), managers should tap into the shared perceptions of subordinates (via anonymous survey, casual conversation) or shared perceptions of multiple workgroups regarding the work environment. Thus, instead of assuming that some employees purposefully take on a negative attitude, managers can apply social information processing theory to recognize that employees take cues from the environment. This information can result in better decisions and actions on the part of the manager. For instance, recognizing that one employee's negative attitude about an upcoming organizational change can affect others in the group might lead a manager to spend more time communicating the benefits of the change.

Self-perception theory can be used during efforts to change workplace practices and norms. Knowing that people may form an attitude consistent with ongoing behavior, managers can assign their employees tasks that require specific actions hopefully leading them to the desired attitude. Take note, however, that changing attitudes or trying to implant them can backfire.

Changing attitudes tends to be only one of the key concerns of organizational leaders. Another is predicting employees' attitudes because they are assumed to ultimately predict employee behavior.

Why do our attitudes change?

Why Do We Care about Attitudes at Work?

Organizations want to know employees' attitudes because they believe those attitudes predict behavior. For example, most organizational leaders believe that satisfied employees are high-performing employees. Thus, organizations most often measure attitudes, specifically job satisfaction, as part of annual opinion surveys. Those in charge of the surveys, such as human resource managers, use the resulting scores to tell them whether they need to take actions to improve the attitudes they measured. The organization's ultimate goal is to increase employee performance. Leaders believe they can accomplish the goal by keeping employees' job attitudes, like satisfaction, high. Their beliefs are not far from reality, though not all attitudes influence performance to the direct degree that most organizational leaders think. We review attitudes and their influence in organizations in the next sections.

Organizations care about your job attitudes because they believe these attitudes relate to your behavior, specifically your job performance.

Exercise 4.2

What are the theories we use to explain how attitudes form? Given an example of each.

Which Job Attitudes Do Organizations Care about?

Employees have many attitudes toward their jobs, but a few, in particular, tend to be the focus of attention in organizations. Job attitudes most studied within organizations include job involvement, fairness, organizational support, trust, job satisfaction, commitment, and turnover intentions (i.e., plans to quit).

There is no particular way to categorize or structure attitudes (like that provided in Chapter 3 for theories of motivation). To make sense of the attitudes, you can structure them by which tend to be considered predictors versus which tend to be considered outcomes. Note, however, that although we can categorize these attitudes as predictors versus outcomes for the sake of learning them, they are all attitudes, which means they are not exclusively predictors or outcomes.

Organizations consider the following attitudes predictors: job involvement, support, trust, and fairness. Organizations seek ways to increase outcome attitudes or behaviors by manipulating these predictors. These predictors are wonderful in and of themselves, thus regardless of what else they might lead to or affect, having job involvement, support, trust, and attitudes of fairness are all great for both employee and organization. Organizations typically consider the following attitudes outcomes: job satisfaction, commitment, and turnover intentions, although job satisfaction and commitment can also be predictors themselves. For example, commitment to the organization predicts job performance.

To help cement your understanding of each job attitude, a short paragraph expressing how the attitude is seen at work, what can be done to foster it, and

To refresh your memory of experiments: a predictor is considered an independent variable. Independent variables in experiments are manipulated and measured, and they are assumed to occur first in the causal chain of events. After manipulating the independent variable, you then measure the dependent variable to see what effect the independent variable had on the dependent variable, sometimes called the outcome. For example, suppose your boss gives you a very exciting project to work on, and you, being excited,

(Continued)

what attitudes or behaviors it promotes is provided after the **consequences (outcomes)** and **antecedents (predictors)** of each attitude. Because some attitudes are talked about in the sections that follow before they are actually defined or described in detail, you're encouraged to jump to their definition and jump back, and/or look them up in the glossary at the end of the book.

Job Attitudes as Predictors

Remember from courses you might have had in research methods, predictors are constructs we use to determine when another variable will occur—they happen before the variable of interest. Accordingly, they forecast or foretell what will happen next. The following variables are frequently used as predictors in research on workplace behavior and attitudes.

Job Involvement

Job involvement refers to the centrality of work in one's life and to how important work is to one's self-identity and self-image (Lawler & Hall, 1970; Lodahl & Kejner, 1965). Sample items assessing job involvement are shown in Table 4.2. Thus, the more job involvement we feel, the more central work is to our lives and the more our identity is associated with that job. Consider a pastor (i.e., person of religious faith leading a congregation)—the pastor's work is very central to what the pastor believes, feels, and does every day. There is essentially no, or very little, separation between a pastor and the pastor's job. In this situation, the pastor's job involvement is probably pretty high. In contrast, consider a person who identifies with raising a family and sees that as their primary responsibility and life-calling. That individual's self-identity and self-image is tied to raising a family—not to work associated with a corporation. In this case, job involvement would be assumed to be quite low.

Consequences or Outcomes of Job Involvement

Consequences or outcomes of job involvement include other job attitudes such as satisfaction and commitment (also see Mathieu & Zajac, 1990), work–life conflict, and job stress. Job involvement is not highly correlated with job performance or effort at work, but does contribute to job performance to a degree (Dalal, Baysinger, Brummel, & LeBreton, 2012).

work diligently and with high quality, producing a great report that your boss really likes. Suppose this is in contrast to the not-so-exciting projects you've received in the past, where your work was not as good and you took a lot longer to complete the work. Your boss can predict the quality and speed with which you complete a project (your quality and speed are the outcome) by how excited you are about the project (your excitement is the predictor).

TABLE 4.2 Sample Items Used for Assessing Job Involvement

The most important things that happen to me involve my present job.
I am very much involved personally in my job.
Most of my interests are centered around my job.

Source: Kanungo, 1982.

Antecedents or Predictors of Job Involvement

Results from meta-analyses (e.g., Brown, 1996) show that predictors of job involvement include job characteristics (e.g., skill variety, feedback, task significance, job challenge, task complexity), and supervisory variables such as support (e.g., flexible schedule when needed, resources to help on a big project). Ways organizations can increase job involvement include boosting both individual and organizational efforts with career planning (e.g., Orpen & Pool, 1995). Demographic variables (e.g., education, age, sex) are largely unrelated to job involvement, which means job involvement levels between younger and older employees, for example, does not vary just because of their age. Their level of job involvement may be systematically different, but it's not because of their age—there is some other factor that explains their differing job involvement levels, such as length of time working or stage of life (e.g., not yet having family responsibilities vs. having a lot of family responsibilities).

Meta-analyses are studies of studies. Instead of using new data, a meta-analysis uses the statistical results reported in multiple studies conducted on that same concept (e.g., job involvement) to determine what can be concluded across these studies.

Job Involvement in the Workplace   An employee who reports high levels of the attitude job involvement is more likely to report high levels of the attitudes commitment and job satisfaction, and low levels of work conflict or job stress (although we know that job stress may be due to many other factors beyond our control). Thus, managers will want to foster high job involvement in their employees as it relates to them being satisfied at work and potentially less stressed. Ways to foster job involvement include redesigning employees' jobs so they use a variety of job skills and by providing support in the form of necessary job resources and flexibility in the job schedule. Using the example of lots of family responsibilities, having a flexible job schedule can allow an employee to have high job involvement while also being involved with the family. The best way to determine how to increase an employee's job involvement is to ask! What works for one employee, may not work for another.

Fairness

Fairness at work, also called organizational justice, refers to at least three to four different types of perceptions.

Distributive justice refers to employees' perceptions of the fairness of decisions (Deutsch, 1975). To determine if a decision outcome (like whether you get a raise or promotion) is fair, employees compare what they received for their work versus what others like them received for similar work. Thus, the evaluation of whether the result of a decision is fair is based on a comparison to others—what do you perceive they did to get what they got, and how does that compare to what you did to get what you got. Remember, their evaluation/comparison is based on their perception, which may not be accurate. For instance, you might think they did not work as hard as you did, but maybe in reality they worked harder than you, but you just can't see their work. People also judge the distributive fairness of a decision by determining whether they got what they think they deserved. Thus, we do not always compare ourselves to others to judge fairness—we sometimes base our judgment on what we feel we deserve.

Procedural fairness is the perception of how fair the process (assuming there is one) is that was used to make the job-related decision (Thibaut & Walker, 1975). Employees consider a number of aspects of the process to determine its fairness. These include whether the process (a) preserves unbiased decision making, (b) is applied consistently across people and time, (c) ensures accurate information is used, (d) allows for corrections for inaccurate decisions, (e) conforms to ethical standards, and (f) provides a mechanism to incorporate and account for the views of all parties affected by the decision (Leventhal, 1980). Let's walk through this: if the process used to decide who gets a promotion ensures there are no favorites, you don't jump through a harder hurdle than others, does not consider hearsay or gossip as valid information, has a way to correct an honest mistake if it occurs, does not allow back-door deals, and the people who will report to the newly promoted person have some input—the process will likely be considered fair.

Interactional justice is about the fairness of treatment received during the implementation of the decision (Bies & Moag, 1986). It refers to whether employees feel treated with dignity and respect when being told about the decision, why the decision was made the way it was, and what the decision means for them. Interactional *justice* has also been divided into a two-part construct, which is where the "at least three to four" types of justice statement comes from: *interpersonal justice*, which refers to how much people feel they are treated with politeness, respect, and dignity; and *informational justice*, which refers to the adequacy of explanations given for decisions and why the outcomes were distributed as they were (Greenberg, 1993).

Organizational justice has also been viewed as a multifoci model (Byrne, 1999; Byrne & Cropanzano, 2000), where instead of focusing on the type of justice, the emphasis is on the entity or person considered responsible for justice. Accordingly, one might consider that justice is either from the organization or from the supervisor, resulting in multiple foci of justice. A variation of this delineation of justice appears as an agent-system view (Colquitt, Conlon, Wesson, Porter, & Ng, 2001). Regardless, the three types of fairness delineated above (distributive, procedural, interactional) remain prominent in the literature. What this research points out is that people care a lot about fairness in the workplace.

People are concerned with whether they are paid fairly, treated respectfully, and given the same opportunities as others. Employees reflect on whether the organization cares about their welfare, whether they can meet their needs for control and belonging, and whether the organization is ethical in how it handles business (Colquitt, Greenberg, Zapata-Phelan, 2005). It turns out that fairness is a pretty important attitude/judgment in the workplace and plays a big role in predicting many different outcomes.

Sample items for assessing the different types of justice are shown in Table 4.3.

TABLE 4.3   Sample Items Used to Assess Fairness

Distributive justice	To what extent are you fairly rewarded considering the responsibilities you have?
	To what extent are you fairly rewarded for the amount of effort you put forth?
	To what extent does your outcome reflect what you contributed to the organization?

(Continued)

TABLE 4.3   Sample Items Used to Assess Fairness (*Continued*)

Procedural justice	To what extent have you been able to express your views and feelings during decision-making procedures?
	To what extent has the company developed procedures been designed to generate standards so that decisions can be made with consistency?
	To what extent has the company developed procedures that collect accurate information needed for making decisions?
Interpersonal justice	To what extent has your boss treated you politely?
	To what extent have you been treated with dignity?
Informational justice	To what extent has your boss been candid in his/her communications with you?
	To what extent has your boss explained the procedures thoroughly?

Courtesy Zinta Byrne. Source: Moorman, 1991 and Colquitt, 2001.

Consequences or Outcomes of Fairness

The results of two meta-analyses (Cohen-Charash & Spector, 2001; Colquitt et al., 2001) show that all three forms of fairness are positively correlated with satisfaction, job performance, organizational support, citizenship behaviors (i.e., going above and beyond the job expectations), organizational commitment, and trust in the organization, supervisor, and coworkers. All three types of fairness are negatively correlated with withdrawal behaviors (behaviors associated with minimizing one's involvement and interactions at work), turnover intentions, counterproductive work behavior, and negative emotions (e.g., disgust) at work.

Fairness is also positively related to organizational practices such as, giving employees voice (i.e., input, feedback), communication, and **affirmative action** (i.e., rectify imbalances related to race, gender, or ethnicity). Procedural and interactional fairness, in particular, have been shown to reduce negative perceptions of organizational politics (intentional acts to promote self-interest at the expense of others) by creating trust in leaders and enforcing nonbias decision-making (Byrne, 2005).

Antecedents or Predictors of Fairness

Leaders who have mutually respectful relationships with their subordinates tend to provide them with an opportunity for **voice** or expression (Bhal & Gulati, 2004; Daly & Geyer, 1994), which creates trust, a prerequisite for the development of an attitude of fairness (Lewicki, Wiethoff, & Tomlinson, 2005). Employees who have close relationships with their supervisors and groups at work develop an identity with them, as well as feelings of self-worth that lead to fairness attitudes

(Lind & Tyler, 1988). Thus, strong, positive relations at work support the development of positive attitudes of fairness at work.

Fairness in the Workplace   Employees who hold attitudes of fairness about their work assignments, the procedures used to make those assignments, and how they are treated by their supervisors report high commitment to their organizations, trust others, and work to positively support the organization. In contrast, employees who evaluate their work as unfair have been known to sabotage the work, act out with negative emotions, and generally disrupt working relations. They do not trust the organization. Ways that managers can increase fairness attitudes are by being transparent in their decision-making, sharing how decisions are made and explaining why they made the decision they made, and by asking their employees for their opinions and taking action on suggestions. Over-structuring policies is not necessarily the best approach; instead applying fairness given the specific circumstances and treating employees as individuals will be perceived as more fair than just applying a single rigid policy to everyone (Cropanzano & Byrne, 2001). Making sure employees are rewarded commensurate with their efforts and accomplishments will also foster a positive attitude of fairness. Managers need to keep in mind that employees will see things as unfair if they feel they haven't been given what they believe they deserve—therefore, it is worth the time to find out what employees think they have done and deserve. If their perceptions are out of line, helping them understand what is more realistic is a valuable effort. Because fairness is about perceptions, managers need to remain cognizant of what employees can see, can't see, and won't know about the workplace (e.g., other's contributions, qualifications)—thus recognizing why some perceptions of unfairness may arise.

Theories Specific to Fairness

A variety of theories have been used to explain why employees' attitudes about fairness relate to their performance or intentions to stay (i.e., negative relationship with turnover intentions), most of which come from other fields such as social psychology and some of which are explained in the next section. However, there are at least three well-known theories of fairness that help us predict how we think employees will respond: equity theory, group value model, and fairness heuristic theory.

Equity Theory   Recall from Chapter 3 that equity theory says people compute in their heads a ratio of what they receive for their efforts to how much effort they contributed. If their contribution outweighs what they receive in exchange, an evaluation of inequity occurs and they react with anger. If the outcome/input ratio is in their favor, i.e., they get more out than they put in, they will

feel guilty. However, the theory includes one more important evaluation. At its heart, social comparison theory (Festinger, 1954) forms the foundation of equity theory (Adams, 1965). Social comparison theory says that we compare ourselves to others to evaluate and understand our opinions and abilities given a certain situation. Like needing a mirror to see whether we look okay, we use our comparisons with others to adjust and judge the validity of our opinions and the quality of our abilities. Equity theory uses this natural drive for comparison to suggest that people compare their outputs/inputs ratio to that of another person. If someone else is getting more than you but you contributed more, you will judge the situation as inequitable, feel angry about it, and try to alleviate the negative feelings by restoring equity—or restoring a balance. Similarly, if you get more than others did but you contributed less, you will feel guilty and try to work harder to make up the difference, or in some cases buy them benefits such as their lunch, coffee, or cover them for an extra day off. In practice, however, researchers found that people rarely feel guilty when overcompensated. Equity theory has been used to explain distributive justice.

Group Value Model—Relational Model—Fairness Heuristic Theory

The group value model, renamed the relational model, and later again reformulated as the group engagement model (Lind & Tyler, 1988; Tyler & Blader, 2002; Tyler & Lind, 1992) proposed that people care about their status in groups and their collaboration with others. As a result, they care about fairness because it conveys information about their position or relationship within the group. Fairness heuristic theory (Lind, Kulik, Ambrose, & de Vera Park, 1993) builds on these relational models and says that fairness perceptions form a heuristic or rule of thumb for whether to accept decisions made by authority figures. People rely on their perception of the fairness of the decision to determine if the authority is legitimate and the decision should be accepted.

Why can you feel that a decision is fair even if it's not in your favor?

Organizational Support

Organizational support refers to employees' perceptions and beliefs their organization cares about their personal well-being and values their contribution (Eisenberger, Huntington, Hutchinson, & Sowa, 1986). An example of items assessing organizational support are shown in Table 4.4.

TABLE 4.4   Sample Items Used to Assess Organizational Support

My organization cares about my opinions.
My organization really cares about my well-being.
Help is available from my organization when I have a problem.
My organization would forgive an honest mistake on my part.

Courtesy Zinta Byrne. Source: Eisenberger, Cummings, Armeli, & Lynch, 1997.

Consequences or Outcomes of Organizational Support

Consequences or outcomes of organizational support include commitment, job satisfaction, job involvement, job performance, and retention (low turnover intentions; Rhoades & Eisenberger, 2002; Riggle, Edmondson, & Hansen, 2009).

Antecedents or Predictors of Organizational Support

Meta-analytic studies show that organizational support is positively predicted by fairness and favorable job conditions, such as job security and low job stress (e.g., Rhoades & Eisenberger, 2002). Correlations between fairness and perceptions of organizational support tend to be moderately high (e.g., $r = .59$ to $r = .68$, Rhoades & Eisenberger, 2002), especially when compared to the relationship between other constructs and support. These findings indicate that employees who perceive fairness may also tend to perceive support and vice versa, and increasing fairness may be a good approach to also increasing perceptions of organizational support (e.g., Byrne, Pitts, Wilson, & Steiner, 2012). That said, keep in mind that correlation does not mean causation; thus, it is possible that engaging in practices shown to positively relate to fairness will not necessarily be accompanied by increased perceived support.

Organizational Support in the Workplace Employees with positive evaluations of organizational support report feeling cared for by the organization. Consequently, they commit themselves to the organization, feel satisfied at work, get involved in their jobs, and perform at high levels. Ways to foster an attitude of organizational support include asking employees if they need help, structuring the work environment and schedule to support the employees' needs, and making sure that decisions are made fairly and are communicated.

Theories Specific to Organizational Support

Organizational support theory (Eisenberger et al., 1986) suggests that people attribute human-like characteristics to the organization and in doing so develop a relationship with the organization much like people develop friendships. That is, underlying organizational support theory is the concept that people naturally reciprocate favorable treatment (e.g., someone gives you a gift and you automatically want to give one in return) and desire favorable treatment in return. Thus, when the organization appears to show concern for them and value them through actions that convey consideration, employees reciprocate with commitment and performance. Hence, an application of organizational support theory is to teach supervisors, managers, and leaders within the organization to convey concern and appreciation for employees. Additionally, managers need to understand and know what they can provide in support of employees, such as what policies and programs are open to employees, how much flexibility managers can give them, and what is and is not at the manager's discretion. In showing support, managers and leaders can foster employees' beliefs that the organization itself values them and that in turn promotes a desire in the employees to perform and demonstrate high job involvement. Clearly, the concern and appreciation should be genuine, otherwise employees learn to distrust their managers and leaders, and ultimately the organization.

Exercise 4.3

What is the difference between fairness and organizational support? Under what circumstances would you have an attitude of fairness instead of support, and/or vice-versa? Can you have both attitudes at the same time, but in opposite directions?

Trust

Trust has been conceptualized in a number of ways: as an individual difference construct (i.e., a propensity to trust; Mayer, Davis, & Schoorman, 1995; Rotter, 1980), an attitude (Giffin, 1967), a feature of institutions (i.e., an organization engenders trust; Bradach & Eccles, 1989), or a feature of interactions (i.e., trust lies in the relationship between individuals; Lewicki & Bunker, 1996; Schoorman, Mayer, & Davis, 2007). Trust is also generally defined as a psychological state in which an individual is willing to be vulnerable to the organization or a person with the expectation that the vulnerability will lead to positive intentions on the part of the organization or other person (Mayer et al., 1995; Rousseau, Sitkin, Burt, & Camerer, 1998). Stated another way, trust is the willingness to be vulnerable to another person because the other person has shown to be predictable and ethical, and to have good intentions. Trust has been correlated with organizational performance and employee job attitudes (Dirks & Ferrin, 2001; Davis, Schoorman, Mayer, & Hwee Hoon, 2000), such as job satisfaction and commitment (Campbell, Simpson, Boldry, & Rubin, 2010).

Trusting someone is different from being confident in that person, or in being able to predict what that person will say or do (Mayer et al., 1995). Trust forms a critical foundation for long-term mutually beneficial relationships (Deutsch, 1958). Quite a few researchers agree with conceptualizing trust as a psychological state (Kramer, 1999); however, others continue assessing trust as something other than a state (i.e., feature of institution or person).

Furthermore, trust is studied in a variety of forms, such as a cognitive-based trust (expecting reliability and dependability of another's actions) and an affect-based trust (the emotional tie or bond between a person and entity or other person; McAllister, 1995). An example of a survey item that might be used to assess cognitive-based trust is "I can rely on this person not to make my job more difficult by careless work" (McAllister, 1995, p.37). Compare that to an item used for assessing affect-based trust: "We have a sharing relationship. We can both freely share our ideas, feelings, and hopes" (McAllister, 1995, p.37). According to McAllister (1995) cognitive-based trust leads to affect-based trust. Trust can also be toward specific foci such as the organization, supervisor, and coworkers (Mayer et al., 1995; Nyhan & Marlowe, 1997).

Trust in one's supervisor provides a key indicator of the quality of the supervisor-subordinate relationship (Graen & Uhl-Bien, 1995) and a core component of a leader's ability to be effective (Zand, 1972). Trust is also essential among coworkers or teammates, as it provides the necessary bridge between employees needing to collaborate and rely on each other for completing a task or developing a new idea (McAllister, 1995; Zand, 1972). As a result of trust, team performance is much higher than when trust is lacking (Larson & LaFasto, 1989). An example of the types of questionnaire items assessing trust are included in Table 4.5.

TABLE 4.5   Sample Items Used for Assessing Trust

If I had my way, I wouldn't let [organization, person] have any influence over issues that are important to me (Reverse scored).
I would be willing to let [organization, person] have complete control over my future in this company.
I would be comfortable giving [organization, person] a task or problem which was critical to me, even if I could not monitor their actions.

Courtesy Zinta Byrne; Source: Mayer & Davis, 1999.

Much of the trust literature fails to specify the exact kind of trust assessed, making the interpretation and summation of results challenging. In the next two sections, when the type of trust is identified in the literature, is is explicitly mentioned in that section.

Consequences or Outcomes of Trust

Trust in management, one's supervisor, and coworkers are all positively related to job satisfaction and organizational commitment (Cook & Wall, 1980), though trust in supervisor and in coworkers are not as strongly related to organizational commitment as is trust in management (Yoon & Hanjun, 2011). Trust in the organization is positively correlated with organizational commitment, and job satisfaction, whereas trust in supervisor is related to task performance and organizational citizenship behaviors (Aryee, Budhwar, & Chen, 2002). Trust is also positively associated with organizational effectiveness (Kegan, 1971). Trust in organizations is negatively correlated with turnover intentions; thus, employees with low trust in the organization are likely to quit. Trusting the leaders of the organization is associated with employees (a) demonstrating citizenship behaviors, (b) wanting to stay and be committed to the organization, (c) feeling satisfied at work, and (d) feeling they can commit to the decisions leaders make (Byrne, Pitts, Chiaburu, & Steiner, 2011; Dirks & Ferrin, 2002).

Antecedents or Predictors of Trust

Predictors of trust in management and trust in supervisors include goal clarity and work autonomy (Yoon & Hanjun, 2011). Fairness in organizations has also been shown to predict trust in the organization and in the supervisor (Aryee et al., 2002; Byrne, Pitts, Wilson, & Steiner, 2012; Connell, Ferres, & Travaglione, 2003). However, when fairness was compared to leadership and perceptions of organizational support in predicting trust in managers, support was the strongest predictor of the three (Connell et al., 2003). Thus, leaders can foster trust from their employees by implementing fair procedures, providing support, and involving employees in the decision making process (Dirks & Ferrin, 2002). Word of caution - if you ask for input to help you make a decision, make it clear that you are just asking for input and may or may not use all the input you get. Otherwise, if you do not clearly take their input and directly use it to make the decision they think you should make, they will be angry you asked for their input. So to preserve fairness and trust, be clear on what kind of input you're seeking and how you might use it (or not use all of it).

Why would trust in management have different consequences than trust in supervisors?

Distrust and Destroying Trust

Distrust is a recurring problem in organizations (Sitkin & Roth, 1993), and unfortunately because of the nature of distrust, people aren't necessarily willing to report that they don't trust their organization or boss (they distrust their anonymity on the survey!). Researchers do have some idea of distrust at work, however. A 2014 survey called the *Work and Well-being Survey* conducted by the American Psychological Association (APA) reported that 24% of those sampled ($N = 1562$; United States only) do not trust their employer and 32% felt their employer was not always honest and truthful (APA, 2014).

So what exactly is distrust? Distrust refers to feeling that another person does not have the best intentions and may actually have negative or harmful intentions towards you (Govier, 1994). Electronic monitoring, such as when people act like customers but are actually secretly monitoring performance, being forced to keep log books to prove stated actions (e.g., laws in the United States require truck drivers to log their hours on the road), and other surveillance actions tend to foster and promote a climate of distrust among employees (Kramer, 1999). Many of these systems were initially intended to create or improve overall trust; however, the unintended message sent to employees is that they cannot be trusted.

Trust is easier to destroy than it is to develop and promote (Barber, 1983); hence, efforts to promote trust, such as electronic keystroke monitoring designed to balance workload, must be carefully evaluated for their unintended consequences; in this case, conveying a lack of trust. Events or actions that destroy or damage trust tend to be salient and memorable, which means they are more likely to have a stronger effect on the recipient than trust building actions that are often more subtle (Slovic, 1993). Individuals in subordinate roles also tend to be more sensitive to whether their supervisors' actions are trustworthy or not because of their dependence and vulnerability due to their lower status in the organization's hierarchy (Kramer, 1996). Thus, actions that the supervisor may not think would hurt trust actually end up damaging established trust levels.

The findings from Kramer's (1996) study suggest that supervisors must be cognizant of the potential effect of their own behavior on others and reassure subordinates through openness and direct conversation that their decisions are made with positive intentions. Of course, this communication won't work if the supervisor's actions do not match his or her words. In a follow-up of their 2014 *Work and Well-being Survey* results, the APA noted their study revealed three key predictors of trust: employees' level of involvement with the organization, recognition from the organization, and how well the organization communicates (Gavett, 2014). It stands to reason that improvements in these three areas may be associated with improvements in trust, though the APA survey was not an experiment assessing causation, but rather a survey assessing correlation.

Trust in the Workplace   Employees with a positive attitude of trust (high trust) are more likely to commit to the organization and report high job satisfaction, whereas employees with a negative attitude of trust (low trust) are likely to quit. Ways to increase positive trust include providing autonomy and goal clarity, and support employees' needs for flexible work schedules or help from coworkers. To avoid developing the attitude of distrust in employees, managers can reiterate their intentions when making decisions, communicate frequently, and ask employees to share their concerns to create opportunities for rectifying misunderstandings.

Watch https://www.ted.com/talks/frances_frei_how_to_build_and_rebuild_trust to see a great Ted Talk on trust - building and rebuilding trust.

Exercise 4.4

In a brief few statements, explain whether trust and fairness are the same attitude. Give examples to make your explanation clear.

Job Attitudes as Outcomes

Outcomes follow after other variables in time—they are the consequences or results of the attitudes and behaviors that happen before them. Thus, the following attitudes are typically studied as outcomes or consequences in the study of the workplace, though many can also serve as antecedents of other job attitudes.

Job Satisfaction

Job satisfaction refers to a positive evaluation of one's job tasks, pay, coworkers, and overall appraisal of one's job (Locke, 1976). Job satisfaction is probably the most widely researched topic in organizational psychology (Judge, Parker, Colbert, Heller, & Ilies, 2002) because of the many attitudes and behaviors tied to job satisfaction, and organizations' interest in and assumptions about how central satisfaction is to employees' performance. Research has shown that job satisfaction is similarly perceived across countries, making it a universal work attitude (Judge et al., 2002).

Why is it so easy to destroy trust?

Initially, job satisfaction was studied as a general overall satisfaction with work, comfort with the work environment, and a lack of boredom on the job (Locke, 1976). The Hawthorne studies discussed in Chapter 1 began as studies of the work environment but showed that workers have attitudes about their work, and satisfaction with the work was one of the first attitudes identified along with several others related to management (Locke, 1976).

Job satisfaction has additionally been divided into multiple dimensions including pay, work, promotions, recognition and rewards, benefits, work environment or conditions, company or organization, management or supervision, and coworkers. Even though specific types of satisfaction matter, overall job satisfaction still plays an important role in understanding employees' attitudes at work, and therefore, general job satisfaction scales are still used to assess employees' overall job satisfaction (Spector, 1985).

Look up the MSQ at http://vpr.psych.umn.edu/instruments/msq-minnesota-satisfaction-questionnaire and click on the various forms and manual at the bottom of the web page.

An example of the types of items used to measure job satisfaction are included in Table 4.6. The Minnesota Satisfaction Questionnaire (MSQ) is a popular measure of different forms of job satisfaction. The MSQ comes in different formats and includes questions similar to those in Table 4.6. Individuals respond to the items on a 5-point scale from "very dissatisfied" to "very satisfied".

TABLE 4.6 Sample Items Used to Assess Job Satisfaction

Being able to keep busy all the time.
The chance to tell people what to do.
The working conditions.

Consequences or Outcomes of Job Satisfaction

Job satisfaction is negatively related to people's intentions to quit. It is also negatively related to job stress, such as lack of clarity about what is expected or inconsistent demands from the boss. Job satisfaction is positively related to organizational commitment, job performance, and citizenship behaviors (Brown & Peterson, 1993; Judge et al., 2002).

Antecedents or Predictors of Job Satisfaction

Job characteristics theory (Hackman & Oldham, 1976) discussed in Chapter 3 suggests jobs that have intrinsically motivating characteristics such as autonomy, task identity, and skill variety lead to high levels of job satisfaction. Research has shown that these job characteristics do positively and moderately relate to job satisfaction (correlations range between .24 and .34; Loher, Noe, Moeller, & Fitzgerald, 1985). Therefore, organizational leaders believe they have the ability to affect job satisfaction by changing characteristics of the job through efforts like job redesign.

Job Satisfaction in the Workplace   Employees who display an attitude of satisfaction with their jobs are likely to become committed to the organization and demonstrate high job performance, and less likely to quit the organization. Managers wanting to increase employee job satisfaction may focus their energy on redesigning jobs to provide opportunities for employees to use a variety of skills, and to help them see how their work fits into the bigger organizational picture.

Theories Specific to Job Satisfaction

Quite a few different theories have been used to explain what leads to job satisfaction and relationships between job satisfaction and other constructs. For example, the job characteristics theory (Hackman & Oldham, 1976) suggests that aspects of the work environment trigger key psychological states, which develop the attitude of job satisfaction.

Researchers have determined that people do not necessarily have the same level of satisfaction with each dimension of work (e.g., pay, supervisor, coworkers, environment). For example, you can be satisfied with your coworkers, but not with your pay or company benefits (Judge, Piccolo, Podsakoff, Shaw, & Rich, 2010). Additionally, some aspects of the job or work environment are more valuable to you than others and the value differs by person (Locke, 1976). For example, who you work with might be very valuable to you because you care about your connection with others at work, whereas recognition is not as important or valuable because you don't like being the center of attention. Locke (1976) referred to this varying value across job dimensions as *range of affect theory*. Level of satisfaction is a function of how valuable that aspect of work is to the employee and the degree to which the job has that aspect.

Some theorists base their propositions about job satisfaction and its relationship with other constructs on a discrepancy model of job satisfaction, proposing that job satisfaction is the result of evaluating the discrepancy between what one wants or expects versus what one has. For example, you'd compare your current job to what you had before or what you think the ideal job should be (e.g., Ilgen, 1971; Porter, 1961). Another discrepancy model is the met-expectations hypothesis (Porter & Steers, 1973). Met-expectations hypothesis is a variation of Vroom's Expectancy Theory (discussed in Chapter 3) and suggests that as long as your expectations are met, you're satisfied. However, if your expectations are not met, you'll be dissatisfied.

Still others argue that satisfaction develops from having your needs met (e.g., Maslow, 1948, Hierarchy of Needs; see Chapter 3). Similarly, Herzberg's Two-Factor or Motivator-Hygiene Theory (Herzberg, 1968; Herzberg, Mausner, & Snyderman, 1959) suggested that employees could be equally satisfied and dissatisfied with work depending on whether they felt they had adequate resources and benefits at work. Remember that the motivator factors included aspects of work considered sources of satisfaction such as achievement, recognition, or status. Hygiene factors included contextual work factors such as working conditions, relations with others, and pay, and were considered a source of dissatisfaction when not present or adequate. Thus, the theory posited that satisfaction was the positive evaluation of having your needs met. Even though Maslow's Hierarchy and Herzberg's Motivator-Hygiene theory have been used as theories of motivation, they are about what motivates you to get what you need to become satisfied.

Commitment

Commitment to the organization, also called organizational commitment, refers to an emotional attachment or identification with the organization and its values. Employees who are committed to their organizations report feeling like they belong at the organization. They feel attached and obligated to stay, and are involved in the organization (Allen & Meyer, 1990). Commitment has further been described as a strong belief in the organization's goals and values, a willingness to exert extra effort on behalf of the organization, and a strong desire to maintain membership within the organization (Mowday, Steers, & Porter, 1979).

Cross-cultural research evidence based on meta-analysis suggests that commitment is a similar construct across different countries (Meyer, Stanley, Jackson, McInnis, Maltin, & Sheppard, 2012). Though the average commitment ratings may be similar, there is variability, which suggests organizations operating in multiple countries may find slightly different employee commitment levels across their country surveys. Because meta-analysis shows commitment is considered and understood the same way from country to country (i.e., it means the same thing no matter what country you're from or live in), when differences in ratings occur (higher in one country versus another), they are *actual* differences and cannot be explained away as simply different interpretations of the construct based on language or cultural norms.

Employees can be committed in one of three ways: affective, normative, and continuance commitment (Allen & Meyer, 1990 see Table 4.7 for sample items). The three types of commitment are related to each other, though not so strongly that they could be considered the same construct (Meyer, Stanley, Herscovitch, & Topolnytsky, 2002).

Affective commitment refers to an employee's emotional attachment, identification with, and involvement with the organization (Allen & Meyer, 1990). This form of commitment represents how employees feel about their organization and whether those feelings give rise to a sense of belonging.

Why do some motivation theories explain how and why we develop a positive attitude of job satisfaction?

TABLE 4.7   Sample Items Used for Assessing Commitment

Organizational commitment	I would be happy to spend the rest of my career with this organization.
	This organization has a great deal of personal meaning to me.
Affective commitment	I really feel as if this organization's problems are my own.
Continuance commitment	If I had not already put so much of myself into this organization, I might consider working elsewhere.
Normative commitment	I would feel guilty if I left my organization now.

Courtesy Zinta Byrne. Source: Meyer, Allen, & Smith 1993, and Mowday, Steers, & Porter, 1979.

Normative commitment refers to how much an employee feels obligated to stay with the organization (Allen & Meyer, 1990). Employees may feel obligated for a number of reasons, including values that suggest once you are employed with an organization you should stay for a certain amount of time, or you have friends and family at work and don't want to leave them.

Continuance commitment refers to employees staying with the organization because they feel the cost of leaving is too high relative to the cost of staying. This form of commitment has also been called calculative commitment (Mathieu & Zajac, 1990) because of the assessment of the relative costs of staying versus leaving. In times of high unemployment, alternative work opportunities may not exist; consequently, employees may believe the cost of leaving is too high because they are unlikely to find another job or may not beat out the competition for whatever jobs do exist. It may also be the case that employees do not want to leave their current employer because of the many bonuses and benefit packages the organization currently offers, benefits the employees would have to give up if they went elsewhere.

Though researchers study these three forms of commitment (i.e., affective, normative, and continuance; Jaros, 1997), organizations and practitioners most often simply refer to commitment without specifying which type. In general, it is understood or assumed that they are referring to affective commitment. In addition to the three types of commitment, researchers have found employees form their attitude of affective commitment about and directed toward a specific target: the organization, supervisor, coworker, occupation, or other targets within the organization (Becker, 1992). These targets matter most when trying to determine what types of organizational change or improvement projects to implement. For example, if employees in a single unit or division report reasonably high organizational commitment, but low supervisory commitment, the organization would do well to address specific issues at the supervisor's level as opposed to organizational policies or structure.

Consequences or Outcomes of Commitment

Organizational leaders believe that employees' organizational commitment determines who stays and who leaves the organization (Mathieu & Zajac, 1990).

They are not wrong—committed employees do report low turnover intentions and they tend to perform citizenship behaviors (Meyer et al., 2002). Outcomes of affective and normative commitment include turnover, job performance, citizenship behavior, and stress. These constructs are more highly correlated with affective and normative commitment than with continuous commitment (Meyer et al., 2002). Occupational and union commitments also positively relate to affective commitment (Mathieu & Zajac, 1990). Occupational commitment refers to commitment to one's occupation, like nurse, teacher, or engineer. Union commitment refers to commitment to one's union (i.e., an organized group of workers lobbying for better pay and work conditions), like the American Civil Liberties Union, the United Food and Commercial Workers International Union, United Service Workers Union, European Trade Union, Cyprus Workers' Confederation, or the Korean Railway Workers Union, just to name a few.

Antecedents or Predictors of Commitment

Work experience constructs considered predictors of commitment, like organizational support, leadership, **role ambiguity**, **role conflict**, and fairness are all correlated with the different forms of commitment, in particular affective and normative (Meyer et al., 2002). Of these predictors, fairness and organizational support show the highest correlations with affective and normative commitment. Rhoades, Eisenberger, and Armeli (2001) demonstrated that perceived organizational support predicts affective commitment. Unlike these other two forms of commitment, continuance commitment does not show high correlations with any constructs assessed in various meta-analytic studies (e.g., Allen & Meyer, 1996). Thus, researchers find it easier to predict levels of the attitudes affective and normative commitment than continuance commitment.

> Why do you think commitment is considered a different attitude than satisfaction?

Neither Outcome nor Predictor of Commitment

There are some variables that are considered neither an outcome nor a predictor of commitment. For example, demographics such as gender and education are not highly related to any of the forms of commitment; thus, they are not considered outcomes or predictors of commitment (Mathieu & Zajac, 1990; Meyer et al., 2002). Satisfaction and commitment are considered reciprocally related, which means evidence does not exist to support one causing the other (Currivan, 1999).

Commitment in the Workplace   Employees who display a positive attitude of commitment at work demonstrate high job performance, and are less likely to want to quit their jobs. Managers wishing to increase commitment in their employees can offer support through showing concern, providing extra job resources, and making sure employees understand job expectations to reduce role ambiguity.

> ### Exercise 4.5
>
> Create two tables that have commitment, trust, fairness, and support on the rows and columns. In the first table cells, write what the attitudes have in common. In the second table cells, write how the attitudes differ from each other.

Turnover Intentions

Why are employees committed to their organizations? How do we explain their commitment?

Turnover intentions refer to plans or motivations to quit the job or organization. They are considered a form of withdrawal behavior (Porter & Steers, 1973). Withdrawal behaviors, or actions to pull oneself out of one's job or the organization psychologically, physically, or both, include absenteeism, **psychological withdrawal**, turnover intentions, early departure from work or lateness, and actual turnover (Podsakoff, LePine, & LePine, 2007).

Turnover can be very costly for businesses, averaging billions of U.S. dollars per year (Mathis & Jackson, 2003). Some of those financial costs are irreplaceable—when people with valuable knowledge, skills, and ability leave the organization, replacing the knowledge gap can take years. Hiring new people incurs a cost, as does training them. Additionally, costs add up as productivity losses accumulate between the time the turnover occurs and the time the new hire becomes productive (O'Connell & Mei-Chuan, 2007).

Furthermore, when employees quit, those who remain pick up the workload until a replacement is hired and trained, and the burden on the "survivors" is a form of cost as well. Specifically, as the workload increases, so do the stress and errors on the job (Jex, 1998; O'Connell & Mei-Chuan, 2007). As the stress increases for the remaining employees, their job satisfaction drops, their productivity drops, and their intentions to quit increase (Podsakoff et al., 2007). The loss of employees may not be a fast road to losing the entire employee group as these falling dominoes may suggest, but for an organization already squeezed for staff or who already has overloaded and stressed employees, the cascading effect of one employee leaving does occur and should not be ignored.

Dysfunctional turnover occurs when an employee wants to quit, but the organization would rather keep them (Dalton, Krackhardt, & Porter, 1981). There are cases, however, where everyone is relieved when some employee in particular leaves—possibly the employee who never did their share of the work or the one who could not get along with anyone. *Functional* or *optimal turnover* occurs when an employee wants to leave and the organization is all too happy to let them go (Abelson & Baysinger, 1984; Dalton, Todor, & Krackhardt, 1982). Functional turnover is not without costs (e.g., costs of having to replace people, extra workload on those who are still there); however, the gains typically outweigh the costs. Retirements can be considered functional turnover for the organization; however, for the employees who

remain, the loss of experience and knowledge retirees' take with them can have a negative impact.

Voluntary turnover refers to choosing to quit as opposed to being asked or forced to quit such as during a layoff, which is called involuntary turnover. Assessing involuntary turnover is easy—the organization has made the decision for you that you are leaving. In contrast, determining if employees have the attitude of voluntary turnover intentions is not as simple as just asking people if they want to quit, though that is usually at least one of the questions asked to assess turnover intentions. Why isn't it easy to just ask? Because people are often afraid to answer honestly out of fear that if they do, they may suffer some negative consequence, such as losing good or challenging assignments, no opportunities for raises, have their hours cut, or become ignored. An example of the types of items used to assess turnover intentions are shown in Table 4.8.

Consequences or Outcomes of Turnover Intentions

Turnover intentions are strongly related to actual turnover behavior (Tett & Meyer, 1993), and shown to be immediate precursors to actual turnover (Mobley, Horner, & Hollingsworth, 1978). Thus people who have intentions to leave, tend to act on those intentions; however, intentions to quit do not always result in actual turnover (Podsakoff et al., 2007; Tett & Meyer, 1993). There are many reasons for wanting to quit but not actually going through with it, including concerns such as lack of job alternatives, leaving family and friends, reduction in benefits or health-care options, or fear of moving and starting over.

Antecedents or Predictors of Turnover Intentions

Both job satisfaction and organizational commitment are negatively related to and lead to turnover intentions, with commitment being more strongly related to turnover than job satisfaction (e.g., comparing $r = -.51$ between commitment and turnover intentions with $r = -.04$ between satisfaction and turnover intentions; Podsakoff et al., 2007). Thus, as job satisfaction and commitment drop, intentions to quit go up. Similarly, both job satisfaction and organizational commitment are negatively related to withdrawal behaviors (excluding turnover and turnover intentions), though the strengths of the relationships are much weaker than those between satisfaction and commitment with turnover intentions. As compared to pay, supervisory, and coworker satisfaction, work satisfaction has the highest relationship with turnover amongst these forms of satisfaction (Griffeth, Hom, & Gaertner, 2000).

Organizational justice predicts turnover intentions; the more fair the workplace, the less employees consider leaving (e.g., Byrne, 2005; Colquitt et al., 2001).

TABLE 4.8 Sample Items Used for Assessing Turnover Intentions

How often do you think about quitting this organization?
How likely are you to search for a position with another employer?
How likely are you to leave the organization in the next year?

Job redesign efforts such as job enrichment and job rotation (Chapter 3) can reduce dysfunctional turnover (McEvoy & Cascio, 1985), as can reducing turnover through better selection practices, realistic job previews (i.e., getting a realistic as opposed to glorified idea of the job entails before taking it), and improving person–organization fit (O'Connell & Mei-Chuan, 2007; Premack & Wanous, 1985). Efforts to increase job satisfaction and commitment can also reduce dysfunctional turnover (Podsakoff et al., 2007). However, the same findings are not applicable for increasing functional turnover (Williams, 1999).

Functional turnover can be encouraged by rewarding good performers and ensuring that bad performers are not rewarded (called rewards contingency: rewards dependent on some criteria—in this case, performance; see Williams, 1999), because poor performers who are not rewarded tend to leave if they can (Williams & Livingstone, 1994). Williams (1999) found that the more pay was tied to performance, such as being on 100% commission, the higher the probability that poor performers would leave and the organization would rejoice in their voluntary departure (functional turnover). Those who were good performers paid on 100% commission did well because they were rewarded for their performance, and thus had no desire to quit. On the flip side, high performers who are not sufficiently rewarded tend to leave.

Demographic variables such as education, marital status, race, and age are weakly negatively correlated with turnover. Women and men tend to quit at comparable rates (Griffeth et al., 2000).

Turnover in the Workplace   Without considering alternative job offers and/or other outstanding reasons for quitting, employees who have an attitude of intending to quit tend to experience low job satisfaction and commitment, and are less inclined to stay once a good opportunity to leave presents itself. Ways to reduce intentions to quit include increasing employees' job satisfaction. Because there are a variety of reasons why people develop turnover intentions, a good first step is to find out what is going on with each employee—for example, assess their job satisfaction and ask about concerns or challenges at home and at work to determine if there are outside factors driving employees to consider quitting.

Theories Specific to Turnover

Several researchers have taken different approaches to answering the question of what causes people to want to quit, resulting in a few theoretical models of turnover reviewed in this next section.

Why do you think commitment is more strongly related to turnover intentions than satisfaction is to turnover intentions?

Mobley's (1977) Turnover Model   One approach to understanding turnover decisions incorporates job dissatisfaction, thinking of quitting, evaluating options, and then deciding whether to leave (see Figure 4.7; Mobley, 1977).

In Mobley's (1977) model of turnover, each step represents a decision point where an employee determines whether to take the next step. People do not necessarily go through each step or deliberate for much time on each step. The starting point serves as an important contribution of this model—if the job is dissatisfying, you begin to think about quitting. With new technology and social

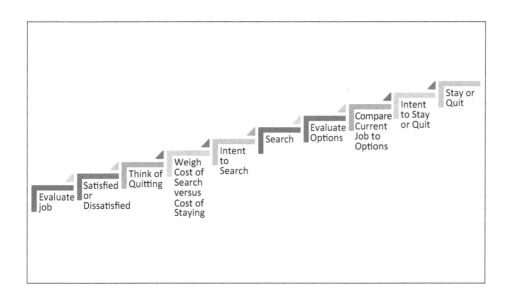

FIGURE 4.7   Mobley's Turnover Model

Courtesy Zinta Byrne. Source: Mobley, 1977.

media such as Google, LinkedIn, and Monster.com making it easier to find a job, the steps of Mobley's model may require some reordering. Specifically, it may be that as part of evaluating their current job, employees search the Internet for alternatives and based on what they find, develop attitudes of dissatisfaction and intentions to quit.

Other models of turnover do not follow a linear step-wise progression like Mobley's, such as Jackofsky's (1984) model reviewed next.

Jackofsky's (1984) Turnover Model   Jackofsky's (1984) model of turnover is really oriented towards job turnover, which focuses on either taking a different job in the same organization or taking a *job* in another organization. Jacofsky proposed that people take the first step toward considering leaving after experiencing dissatisfaction, a desirability to move, or because it is easy to change jobs (Figure 4.8).

A key component of Jackofsky's (1984) model is the inclusion of job performance as an indirect trigger to feelings of job (dis) satisfaction. Specifically, researchers have shown that when performance is the basis for rewards, satisfaction and dissatisfaction are closely tied to performance. For example, high performers who are paid accordingly tend to be satisfied, whereas high performers who do not feel adequately paid for their level of performance tend to be dissatisfied and seek alternative job opportunities. Importantly, high performers may find it easier to leave than low performers because high performers are desirable to other organizations, making alternative jobs easier to find. Thus, higher levels of job

FIGURE 4.8   Jackofsky's Turnover Model

© nitsawan katerattanakul/Shutterstock.com; © Rawpixel.com/Shutterstock.com performance are associated with a higher number of unsolicited job offers or efforts at recruitment. In general, Jackofsky proposed that both low and high performers are likely to leave, but what causes them to leave differs. Job satisfaction moderates the relationship between performance and turnover such that as highly and acceptable performing employees' satisfaction increases, they are less likely to quit than are the lowest performers.

Employees might find it easy to leave after unexpectedly being recruited by another organization, or finding job hunting on the Internet is easier than expected. People may consider their satisfaction level with the current job only after they have been recruited or made aware of other alternatives (such as when a friend shares a job advertisement). Possibly only then do they decide to take the next step toward actively considering leaving their job or the organization. Ease of leaving also requires consideration of one's age, job complexity or level, and characteristics of the current labor market.

Another nonlinear, nonstep oriented model of turnover is Lee and Mitchell's (1994) unfolding model, which suggests that people may be encouraged to considering leaving the organization as an outcome of one of four decision-triggers.

Lee and Mitchell's (1994) Unfolding Model of Turnover Lee and Mitchell's (1994) unfolding model of turnover (Figure 4.9) has been used for understanding why people unexpectedly leave the organization.

A decision rule might be "I won't take a job where I have to go in to the office before 10AM"

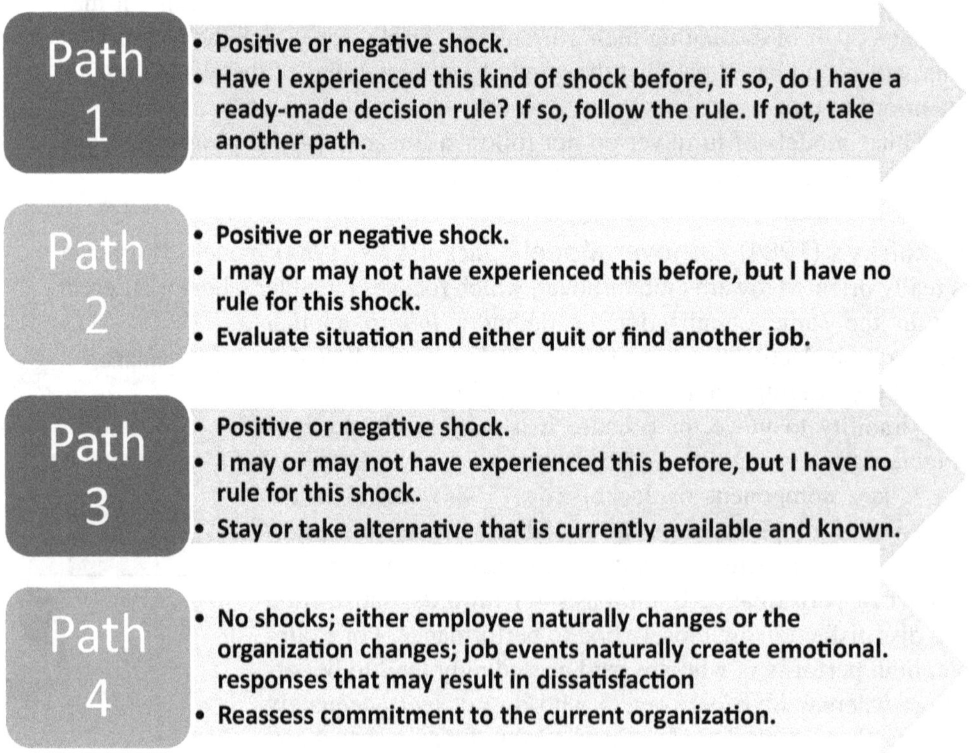

Path 1
- Positive or negative shock.
- Have I experienced this kind of shock before, if so, do I have a ready-made decision rule? If so, follow the rule. If not, take another path.

Path 2
- Positive or negative shock.
- I may or may not have experienced this before, but I have no rule for this shock.
- Evaluate situation and either quit or find another job.

Path 3
- Positive or negative shock.
- I may or may not have experienced this before, but I have no rule for this shock.
- Stay or take alternative that is currently available and known.

Path 4
- No shocks; either employee naturally changes or the organization changes; job events naturally create emotional. responses that may result in dissatisfaction
- Reassess commitment to the current organization.

FIGURE 4.9 Unfolding Model of Turnover

Courtesy Zinta Byrne. Source: Lee and Mitchell, 1994.

The Unfolding Model of Turnover suggests that people take one of four paths toward deciding whether to quit or stay with the organization. A "shock" is introduced and causes an employee to reflect on his or her job. A shock is a "distinguishable event that jars employees toward deliberate judgments about their jobs . . . and must be interpreted and integrated into the person's system of beliefs" (Lee & Mitchell, 1994, p. 60). Shocks are not necessarily negative. They can include pregnancy, aging parents, missed promotion, obtained promotion, buying a new house, company asks you to lie about their product, or any life-changing event that causes an individual to rethink their current job position. Once a shock is introduced, an employee may (or may not) consider leaving the job as one potential option. If leaving is considered an option, the employee may begin to look for alternative jobs. Figure 4.9 depicts a simplified version of the four decision paths an employee may go through. The different decision paths require different amounts of deliberation (may be easy to decide or more difficult). The model is more complicated than shown here, but this shows the basic idea that employees' experience shocks and consider what to do based on the shocks.

Why might turnover intentions be hard to predict?

Summary of Attitudes

With so many attitudes, you might be struggling to make sense out of how they all fit together or possibly even whether they fit together. The next section provides a summary of the attitudes discussed in the above sections, as well as a graphic for how they all fit together.

The previous sections provide a review of quite a few different job attitudes. Table 4.9 provides a handy summary of the attitudes reviewed and their definitions.

All the attitudes shown in Table 4.9 tend to show up as crucial for the productive functioning of an organization. Employees' levels of these attitudes can determine the success of leaders' efforts to make organizational changes. They play a role in whether employees decide to invest their full selves at work or if employees, instead, just work for pay and put their passionate efforts elsewhere. Attitudes, such as job satisfaction and turnover intentions, are essential in a consistent and productive workforce—high levels of turnover can be destructive to the intellectual wealth of an organization; those with the knowledge leaving the organization take critical information and capability with them, leaving the organization unable to sustain its levels of innovation and/or performance. Balanced levels of turnover can be productive and move the intellectual wealth of the organization forward. Lastly, employees' perceptions of the level of support they receive are related to several of the other attitudes. Thus, employees' attitudes play a big role in the success of the organization because they serve an important function in the work lives of employees.

How Attitudes Fit Together

Figure 4.10 illustrates the general relationships between the various attitudes described in the previous section, with the addition of a few variables often considered as predictors or outcomes but are not themselves considered attitudes. For example, job characteristics are not considered attitudes, but appear in the Figure because employees develop attitudes about work (e.g., job satisfaction) as a consequence of job characteristics.

TABLE 4.9   Quick Definitions of Job Attitudes

Attitude	Brief Definition
Job involvement	The centrality of work in one's life and to how important work is to one's self identity and self-image.
Fairness or justice	*Distributive justice:* Fairness of decisions; compared to others, was the decision appropriate.
	Procedural justice: Fairness of processes used to make decisions; does the process ensure unbiased decisions, apply consistently to everyone, allow for appeals to correct mistakes, rely on accurate information, conform to ethical standards, and ensure all people affected are considered.
	Interactional justice: Fairness of treatment during procedure implementation; treated with dignity and respect (interpersonal justice), given adequate explanations (informational justice).
Organizational support	Employees' perceptions and beliefs that their organization cares about their personal well-being and values their contribution.
Trust	Willingness to be vulnerable to another because the other person has shown him or herself to be predictable, ethical, and with good intentions. (Conceptualized in a number of forms, such as affect- and cognitive-based, feature of institution)
Job satisfaction	Positive evaluation of one's job tasks, pay, coworkers, and overall appraisal of one's job.
Commitment	Emotional attachment or identification with the organization and its values, such that you feel you belong, and feel attached to the organization and its people. (Conceptualized in a number of forms, such as affective or normative commitment).
Turnover intentions	Considered a form of withdrawal, they are intentions or motivations to quit the job or organization. (Can have dysfunctional and functional turnover).

The illustration in Figure 4.10 depicts the basic direction in which the relationships have been studied or proposed, but should not to be interpreted as a causal model of the relationships between all the variables. Rather than memorize the Figure, possibly the most helpful way to make sense of all the attitudes is to recognize that things that support our work and us, tend to lead to how we feel about work. For example, getting organizational support, such as being able to start your job at 9AM instead of 8AM so you can drop off the kids at daycare, allows you to be more involved at work (job involvement), which leads to less work-life conflict and less job stress. And, the more support the organization gives you to help you do your job, the less likely you are to plan to quit (turnover intentions), and the fewer intentions/plans you have for quitting, the less likely you are to actually quit. It is also the case that the more support you have, the higher your job satisfaction and commitment, and

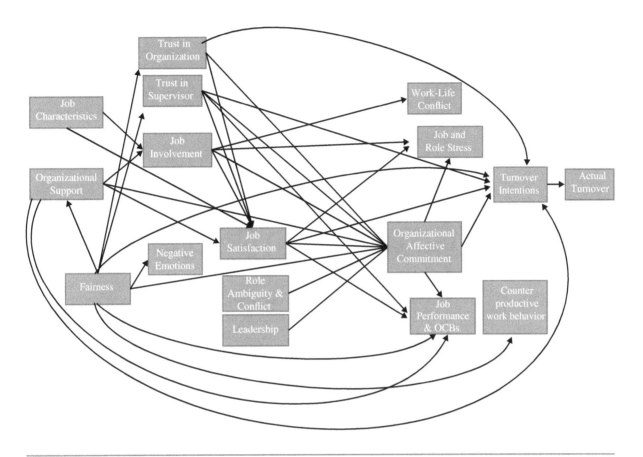

FIGURE 4.10   Making Sense of the Job Attitudes

Courtesy Zinta Byrne.

the higher your job performance. These are all relationships shown by arrows leading away from organizational support.

You can conclude from Figure 4.10 that the study of attitudes can be complicated because of the many relationships between the attitudes themselves. You may ask, "if they are all related, why bother studying them separately?" Though attitudes have many relationships with other attitudes and behaviors, they are unique and contribute to a rich understanding of how people feel and think about their work and workplace, and what behaviors consequently follow thereafter. Thus, although the overall Figure looks like a bowl of spaghetti noodles with square meatballs, like spaghetti, each thread is an individual piece that contributes to the understanding of attitudes at work.

Exercise 4.6

Figure 4.10 is a big mess—draw a picture of how you see the attitudes relating to each other; a picture that makes the MOST sense to you and one you can more easily remember than Figure 4.10 here.

What Theories Explain Job or Work Attitudes?

Aside from the specific theories mentioned for specific attitudes (e.g., range of affect theory for job satisfaction), some theories can be used with any work attitude to explain how it is formed, changed, or relates to other attitudes or behaviors. Let's review those next.

Social Information Processing Theory and Self-Perception Theory

Social information processing theory (Salancik & Pfeffer, 1978) suggests that people adapt their evaluations of the workplace to their social context, using information from their own past and from the current situation. Thus, employees develop or shift their attitude based on the available information at that time. For example, one source of information is your own action—are you enjoying work or not, are you staying at work or thinking about leaving? Self-perception theory (Bem, 1967) suggests that information about your own actions from the past informs your attitudes in the present. Another source of information is other people in the work environment. What are others saying about their satisfaction or commitment or trust? Each employee considers what they hear about the work environment and incorporates that information into their own feelings and thoughts. Thus, what you hear your friends and coworkers saying about their satisfaction affects your own thoughts and feelings about your level of satisfaction.

Social Exchange Theory

Social exchange theory (Blau, 1964) is another theoretical framework used with several different work attitudes. The theory says that people form relationships with an entity (organization) or person, through a series of obligations and reciprocal fulfillments of the obligations that over time build trust between the partners. For example, the organization provides a salary, benefits, and support, and expects that in exchange employees will attend work regularly, perform, and commit to helping the organization achieve its goals. The employees may work extra if a project must be rushed, commit to only working for that organization, and strive for innovation and productivity to accelerate the organization's goals toward an even greater mission. The employee expects the organization to reciprocate with promotional opportunities, bonus pay and raises, and to offer job security. This cycle of exchanges forms a bond—a social exchange relationship where what is exchanged is not always financial or tangible, but has lasting implications for both the employee and organization. For example, a social commodity might be status, recognition, or feelings of belongingness on the part of the organization, and commitment and citizenship behavior on the part of the employee. Thus, organizations can create obligations by offering fairness and organizational support, which can work as effectively as pay. Applied to job attitudes, social exchange theory suggests that employees exchange positive job attitudes (like commitment or trust) for support, resources, fairness, and benefits.

Affective Events Theory

Affective events theory (Weiss & Cropanzano, 1996) suggests that our emotional reactions to work events influence our attitudes. Our first reaction to work events is immediate and emotional. As time passes between the initial event and our first reaction, we think about what happened and develop a cognitive interpretation or appraisal of the event. Affective events theory emphasizes the role of emotions in conjunction with cognition and social cues in forming job attitudes. The important contribution of this theory in understanding attitudes is its emphasis on emotions. Outward display of emotions are typically discouraged in many work environments (though varies by job); big displays of anger, frustration, or fear are discouraged and only controlled levels of humor are tolerated. However, people do experience emotions whether they display them or not, which means according to affective events theory, employees are forming and changing their attitudes as they experience the workplace. By recognizing events trigger emotional responses that influence attitudes, organizational leaders can create situations that promote specific feelings in an effort to foster or guide specific attitudes. For example, organizations that promote and encourage appropriate fun at work may be inadvertently raising levels of job satisfaction.

How Do Managers Use These Theories in the Workplace?

Managers may use theories to understand the current situation and then take action to change the state of affairs. Social information processing theory, self-perception theory, social exchange theory, and affective events theory might all be used to explain why employees adopt certain job attitudes. Job attitudes, such as commitment or perceptions of fairness, ultimately determine behavior. For instance, employees who perceive the workplace as unfair will respond by either rectifying the unfairness or leaving. Accordingly, managers can use the principles of social exchange theory to recognize that when employees are given something, like support, they feel obligated to give back. Therefore, providing fairness, support, and good leadership should be related to positive attitudes and behaviors from employees.

Knowing via social information processing theory that employees turn to others around them to determine what attitude is appropriate, managers can attempt to understand employees' attitudes by gauging the attitudes of the group or organizational unit as a whole.

Lastly, managers can use affective events theory to recognize that big change events at work will create emotional turmoil for employees—work events create emotional responses that influence attitudes. Change frequently creates ambiguity, frustration, and sometimes fear. Be ready for these emotional responses and take proactive actions, such as meeting with employees and putting support mechanisms in place before acting on preplanned change events.

Ultimately, however, the goal of many leaders and managers is to change attitudes—not just understand them. Although understanding is helpful and provides perspective, leaders and managers want to move attitudes in a positive direction with the hopes that positive work outcomes result.

How Can Attitudes Be Changed?

Attitudes can be relatively stable, but they can be changed. For example, job satisfaction has been considered a relatively stable attitude when measured over several jobs (Locke, 1976). However, there are some theories that suggest attitudes can be changed, including the elaboration likelihood model (ELM) and cognitive dissonance.

Elaboration Likelihood Model

ELM is a dual-process (two-path) model that explains how we change attitudes (Petty & Cacioppo, 1996). The model assumes that we want to hold an attitude we believe is right or desirable. We take one path, the central route, when we have the time and ability to think carefully on the situation and information given to decide whether to change our attitude so that we can hold the "desirable" attitude (see Figure 4.11). We take this path when we are motivated to process the information given to us.

We take the other path, the peripheral route, when we do not have the time or ability to think carefully and must quickly decide whether to change our attitude or not (Figure 4.11). Thus, we take the peripheral route when we lack the motivation to elaborate on the information. The disadvantage of the peripheral route is that if attitude change occurs, it is temporary and susceptible to counterattacks or efforts to change the attitude in another direction. The central route tends to produce more stable and long-lasting attitude change that is resistant to efforts to change it back or in another direction.

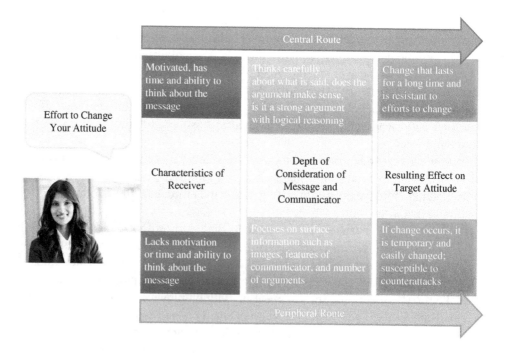

FIGURE 4.11   Elaboration Likelihood Model (ELM)

©michaeljung/Shutterstock, Inc. Courtesy Zinta Byrne.

Hence, the central and peripheral routes of processing can be used to change attitudes, depending on the characteristics of the audience and the goal. Knowing the characteristics of the receiver of the message is essential for deciding which path to take. By the way, your decision as to which path you'll take is not necessarily conscious.

A good example of ELM in practice is television advertisements for medical products. People watch television to relax; not to think carefully about what they are hearing or seeing. Advertisements pushing medical products use actors dressed as doctors (white lab coat), with a fake name badge of Dr. Whomever, and share high-level benefits for the product, typically emphasizing the emotional benefits of taking the product: "why suffer from blinding headaches; take 'headache-away' three times a day…" Similarly, medical products are advertised and, in the United States, the manufacturers are required to share their many side effects during the commercial. Counting on your lack of motivation to focus on the content of the advertisement, they list off 20 or more side effects, sandwiching possible death in the middle of lesser side effects, all the while showing you loving couples laughing, families playing, pets, and babies, to distract you from listening to the long list of painful and debilitating side effects. At the end of the commercial, all you remember is how pleasant the people were and how this product seems to make them feel better. The problem with these advertisements is that they take the peripheral route to persuasion, which results in only a temporary attitude change susceptible to counterattacks. That means companies wanting to convince of the side-effects of these drugs and get you to not use them could do so during the day when you have time and energy to evaluate carefully provided evidence, a real doctor, and careful messaging. These "counterattacks" on your attitude about the drugs is likely to be effective.

Although this example is one from everyday life and hopefully helps to clarify how ELM works, our goal in this book is to understand how to use these theories in the workplace. Therefore, the next example shows how we can use ELM in the workplace.

Using ELM in the Workplace

An example of ELM in the workplace is when the organizational leaders want to implement a large change that will affect everyone's jobs. Often these changes are not up for discussion; employees do not get to vote whether the change will occur. Many people do not like change. In such situations, the well-informed charismatic Chief Executive Officer holds group meetings with employees towards the end of the day (when everyone is tired) to explain the change and attempt to get employees to change their negative feelings about change into a positive attitude of acceptance. The CEO is usually dressed in a sophisticated suit and surrounded by a well-dressed Vice President and several other executives, all dressed in their sophisticated suits. Slide shows of pictures of a glorious future are shown on large screens behind the line-up of executives, catchy music is playing, lights are flashing and shining like a disco dance floor, and the messages are simple and punctuated: "The New Us *is* the New You!" Between the slides and slogans, the CEO and team share several details such as you being reassigned to a new team, a few will be let go due to the restructuring, and people will need to work a little extra to make the new change work. However, at the end of the meeting, as you walk back to your desk singing that catchy little tune they played, all you remember were the lights, the flashy slogans, feeling good about what you heard. The future really does look bright!

But your positive attitude about the pending organizational change will only be temporary and/or susceptible to attack. Thus, if early the next day your coworkers who did not attend the presentation attack the reassignments, layoffs, and extra hours without additional pay, all for a new future that benefits the "suits" and not you, you might quickly change your attitude about the pending organizational change.

Previously in the chapter, we reviewed how we form our attitudes using self-perception theory. On a similar track as self-perception theory using our own thoughts about our actions, cognitive dissonance is a theory concerning thoughts and actions that can be used for changing attitudes.

Cognitive Dissonance

Cognitive dissonance refers to an inconsistency between our thoughts and statements with our actions, which creates feelings of tension and anxiety (Festinger, 1962). People are motivated to present a consistent image. They want their behavior to match what they say and they want to behave or speak consistently with how they have done so in the past. When people behave in a way that is inconsistent with what they say (e.g., enacting corrupt policies while espousing how fair they are), it creates an internal anxiety—a dissonance. Festinger (1962) proposed that cognitive dissonance is powerful enough to cause people to either change their behavior or change their thinking (attitude) to get to a state of consistency or homeostasis.

An example of how dissonance can be used to create attitude change is shown in an **intervention** designed to increase the use of safety seatbelts in automobiles. Geller, Hickman, and Pettinger (2004) attempted to link seatbelt use on airplanes with the use of seatbelts in cars. Over a 17-year study, 1258 flight attendants were given a card that politely asked them to read an important safety message at the end of the flight (see Figure 4.12). The card was presented on 528 flights, and read on 223 of those flights. Only three of the attendants refused to accept the card.

Although the authors of the study did not measure the number of passengers who subsequently buckled up in their cars once on the ground, they did receive a personal letter from at least one passenger who put on the seat belt in the subsequent taxi ride and was saved by the belt after the taxi hydroplaned and crashed. Geller et al. concluded that by linking the message of seatbelt behavior in an auto with a related behavior the recipient had already performed (i.e., the passenger on a plan), an inconsistent

** Airlines have been exemplary promoters of seatbelt use.

** Please, at the end of the trip, would someone in your flight crew announce the buckle-up reminder below. This announcement will show that your airline cares about transportation safety.

FIGURE 4.12 Example of Safety Prompt

©zhu difeng/Shutterstock, Inc. Courtesy Zinta Byrne

or hypocritical condition would be created if the same passenger then got in a car and failed to use the auto safety belt.

Again, this example provides a nice understanding of dissonance in a societal context, but what about the workplace? The next example provides an opportunity to see how cognitive dissonance might be applied in the workplace.

Using Dissonance in the Workplace

A frequently occurring example of cognitive dissonance in the workplace is with newly promoted managers. Before promotion, they commiserated with their coworkers about the policies for workload and breaks that seemed harsh to employees. They ranted about how if they were in management, they would *never* implement policies like these and as soon as they had a chance, they would eliminate these "brutal" policies. Yet, shortly after promotion, these new managers realize that even though they personally still disagree with those policies, as managers they have to keep them in place to meet budget and get their teams to achieve the expected performance levels. Their actions are now inconsistent with their previous statements and true feelings, creating cognitive dissonance. To relieve the dissonance, these new managers typically change their thoughts about the policies because they cannot change the policies. Typically, they'll begin rationalizing to their employees why the policies aren't so bad after all, which relieves their dissonance. Their words (policy is really okay) are now consistent with their actions (enforcing the policies).

One way managers can use dissonance is to recruit key employees, those who are often considered the most influential in a group, and involve them in creating a new policy. By being an active player in setting what might be a controversial policy, the employees develop actions—creating and supporting a new policy—that result in a cognitive dissonance. They can't complain about policy; after all, they were part of creating it. Instead, they will rationalize with their peers why the policy is actually good for them in an effort to relieve their own dissonance. This strategy is not necessarily manipulative—the employees' involvement ultimately creates a better policy.

As noted previously, we care about attitudes at work because we assume they predict our behavior. This assumption is not without support: a classic theory in social psychology, the theory of planned behavior (Ajzen & Fishbein, 1977) explains that our attitudes do predict our behavior, though the prediction is more effective for specific behaviors tied to the attitudes about those behaviors than it is for general behaviors.

Theory of Planned Behavior

A widely accepted and well-studied model of attitudes and behavior prediction is the theory of planned behavior (Ajzen, 1991; Ajzen & Fishbein, 1980; see Figure 4.13). The theory of planned behavior offers another explanation for why someone might be willing to behave in a certain way or change his or her behaviors (like smoking) as a result of his or her attitudes. The theory reinforces our reasons for caring about attitudes at work: because we think they lead to important behaviors, and we think we can change those behaviors.

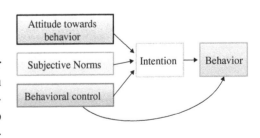

FIGURE 4.13   Theory of Planned Behavior

Courtesy Zinta Byrne. Source: Ajzen and Fishbein, 1980.

The theory says that a person's behavior is determined by his or her intentions (motivation) to perform the behavior. The stronger the intention/motivation to perform the behavior, the more likely it will occur. Intention is the willingness to try or to put effort toward something.

The best predictors of individuals' intentions are their:

1. Attitudes toward the specific behavior

2. Subjective norms

3. Perceived behavioral control

For the theory to work, you must first have a specific attitude toward a particular behavior. For example, an attitude about being on time for work every day. The attitude can be either favorable or unfavorable. Second, you must have a belief about how the people you care about will view the given behavior—"what will those I care about think if I am on time for work every day?" This second component, subjective norms, refers to the social pressure you perceive exists for you to perform the behavior. Third, you have to believe that you can decide whether to perform the behavior or not perform the behavior. For example, if you do not believe you have the opportunity or the resources (e.g., time, money, skills, ability) to perform the behavior, then taking the actions—doing the behavior—is not within your behavioral control. Accordingly, the theory works well for specific behaviors, like completing a term paper.

Sometimes seeing how a theory applies to an everyday class situation makes it easier to understand. Let's apply the theory of planned behavior to students' working on a term paper (Figure 4.14).

In this example (a) students who like the term paper assignment, (b) believe that their friends will think them smart if they work on the paper, and (c) believe they are capable of writing the paper and have all the information they need to do so, will (d) develop intentions to work on the term paper, which ultimately (e) lead to them actually working on the paper. In contrast, students who believe their friends will think they're not cool if they work on the paper are ultimately unlikely to have strong intentions to complete the paper. Those intentions are lessened even more if they also do not feel they understand the assignment (i.e., lacking behavioral control).

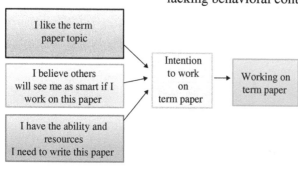

FIGURE 4.14   Applying the Theory of Planned Behavior to Students' Term Papers

Courtesy Zinta Byrne.

Substantial research evidence supports the theory of planned behavior. Furthermore, social attitudes, such as favorability toward or against a particular religion, conservation, or stereotypes display only weak relationships with specific behaviors. In contrast, job attitudes display reliably strong relationships with relevant job behaviors. Researchers suggest that job attitudes are more accessible or salient than social attitudes because we constantly experience our jobs. How we feel about the experience of work is brought to our attention regularly. Furthermore, for many people, their job is personal; it's an identity (Hulin & Judge, 2003). Thus, we have a greater ability to connect our general attitude about our job to our specific job behaviors.

So the theory of planned behavior provides an opportunity to connect employees' job attitudes with their specific behaviors, but organizations want to predict and change a lot of employees' attitudes at one time, and not just specific ones associated with targeted behaviors. The organization wants to change broad behaviors, like overall performance, including task performance and citizenship behaviors (i.e., helping). Designing change efforts based on ELM, cognitive dissonance, or the theory of planned behavior for an entire organization at one time is simply not possible, nor would such efforts necessarily result in the desired outcome. So how does an organization get at a large percentage, if not all, of its employees?

Exercise 4.7

Explain the three general theories that explain how attitudes are formed and the theories we use to explain how we change attitudes. How are the form-attitude theories similar to and different from the change-attitude theories?

How Do Organizations Assess Employee Attitudes?

Human resource managers, **organizational development** managers, or external consultants hired by organizations use surveys and sometimes focus groups to assess job attitudes, and potentially begin to change them.

Surveys: The Most Popular Method

Surveys are the most popular method for assessing job attitudes because they have several advantages including: fast to execute and complete, can be given to thousands of people worldwide at the same time, provide quantitative data for fast analysis, and can be given repeatedly for comparison (compare scores across units or organizations) or trending (seeing trends or patterns of relationships over time).

Disadvantages of surveys include that you get what you ask for—that is, people can only answer the question that is asked of them. Therefore, if the questions on the survey are unclear or not applicable and there is no ability to choose a response like "not applicable" or "don't understand," or to explain oneself on the survey, the response may not actually reflect what a person thinks. Thus, you as the survey giver have no idea that's the case because there is no place for the person to say that the question was unclear. Additionally, some people do not trust surveys and so they respond with mostly neutral answers or they skip most of the questions. There is no way to know by looking at the raw data whether the answers provided are legitimate or represent someone not answering honestly. Why would people respond dishonestly rather than just not complete the survey? Because some organizations reward employees for responding to the survey—there may be an organizational goal for the percentage of employees responding to a survey, and hitting that goal results in bonus pay. Thus, there is not necessarily incentive to respond meaningfully, only to respond. A lie scale, which is a scale specifically added to surveys to try to catch random responses, are usually not included (unless a researcher or academician is conducting the survey) and are not in and of themselves a fool proof way to catch responses that look legitimate but actually are not. Other reasons to provide answers that may not accurately represent your true response include feeling the survey is not confidential, not anonymous, will reflect negatively on you and/or your organization, instigate retaliation, or might cause your boss or organization to make a change that you don't want. For example, if you're asked whether your workload is adequate, and you say "yes", you might be afraid your boss will increase your workload because it's adequate - you should be working harder than that. Instead of answering yes, you answer "overwhelmed."

Other methodological issues remain with collecting data from employees on a single survey at a single collection point such as **common method bias**. Common method bias refers to variability in the data resulting solely due to the method of measurement and not due to true differences in responses, and then using those scores to interpret correlations between them (Campbell & Fiske, 1959). Thus, instead of interpreting true differences or similarities in people's responses, you are instead being fooled by numbers that covary only because the questions were all asked at the same time. Common method variance or bias potentially occurs on organizational surveys because these surveys are nearly always collected at a single point in time and in one sitting. If this method problem exists, why do organizations not address the problem? Because the people giving the survey may not have been trained in psychological measurement and thus do not know about common method bias, or there may be too many logistical challenges with trying to implement strategies to avoid common method variance (Podsakoff, MacKenzie, Lee, & Podsakoff, 2003, provide a number of strategies). Strategies include procedural approaches (e.g., getting responses on predictor and outcome variables from different sources like subordinates and supervisors, breaking up the survey in half and waiting a few weeks between halves) and statistical approaches (see Podsakoff et al., 2003 for details).

© Andrey_Popov/Shutterstock.com

Another potential disadvantage with organizational surveys is not asking enough items to adequately assess the construct (e.g., a single item asking about supervisory relations probably will not capture the full scope of the relationship). There are several other methodological problems with a single survey implementation that are too expansive to cover here (see a good textbook on psychological measurement, such as Cohen, Swerdlik, and Sturman's, 2013, *Psychological Testing and Assessment: An Introduction to Tests and Measurements*).

Do the advantages of a single survey outweigh the disadvantages? For many organizations, the answer is "yes." The human resource leaders or organizational development leaders want a snapshot of employees' attitudes and they want it fast, and many may not be aware of the methodological biases that contaminate their results. The alternatives to single point surveys are, for the most part, impractical for large organizations. For example, interviewing employees, focus groups, experiments, or observations are logistically impractical for large organizations, unless only a subset or sampling of employees are included and there is no rush for the data.

What should an organization do then if the alternatives are impractical, but using single surveys is problematic? The answer is complex, but there are strategies organizations can take to contribute to resolving the problem. For example, the individuals giving the surveys should be trained in psychological measurement and experts in survey methodology. They can use a number of strategies and apply creative solutions in collaboration with the organization to accurately assess employees' attitudes. If the results are important and will guide key decisions that translate into costly solutions, spending the time and money on a well-developed survey created and executed by an expert is worth the investment.

Surveys provide another important advantage, however, despite some of their potential disadvantages. Organizations like to see how they compare with other similar firms, and survey companies can provide this benchmarking data by conducting large surveys across many organizations.

Benchmarks or Normative Data

Many large consulting firms offer **benchmarks** for comparison, which means they have used the same survey with hundreds of other organizations and can provide comparisons between your organization's results and all these other organizations combined (Figure 4.15). Benchmarking specifically refers to the process of comparing results from business to business.

Organizations generally see tremendous value in benchmarking because they believe they can compare how they are doing relative to their peers. This is very similar to wanting to know what the average score on the latest exam was and how many people got an "A." Knowing this, you can determine where your score is relative to others to get an idea of how you're doing in comparison.

There are, however, several disadvantages to benchmarking when conducted by outside firms using a method of combining organizations' data, and providing a general mean score as the comparison point. Most of the disadvantages fall into measurement concerns and the statistical significance of the comparisons. For example, what does it mean to compare a score of 4.5 to 4.6? Is there actually any real difference between these two numbers on a 1–5 scale? Most likely not, but with a sample of thousands, the statistics might say there is a significant statistical difference. But is there any practical difference? Probably not. Additionally, as an organization compares its scores to the benchmark, is there any information on what other potential factors might have existed to influence the scores of the other organizations included in the benchmark? Nope, since many benchmarking firms do not collect contextual information when gathering survey scores. It's possible there might be one very large organization included in the benchmark that is

Series of Items	Your Score	Diff	Financial Industry	Healthcare Industry	All
Satisfaction	4.1	⬇	4.5	4.3	4.3
Benefits	4.0	⬇	4.7	4.2	4.3
Supervisors	3.4	⬇	5.0	4.7	4.4
Coworkers	5.0	⬆	4.1	4.8	4.6

FIGURE 4.15   Snapshot of Benchmarking

Courtesy Zinta Byrne.

skewing the scores and you won't know it. You also wouldn't know if one or more organizations in the benchmark recently underwent big changes that artificially boosted their scores at the time of the benchmark survey, nor if the business cycle for when the other samples were collected was substantially different from yours.

Benchmarking is seductive—most organizations want to know how they compare to others like them and they consider a difference in scores between 4.5 and 4.6 to be meaningful. They want to be able to say whether they are competitive in the market, just as you want to say whether you're top in your class. According to Festinger (1954), we all engage in social comparison, comparing ourselves to others, and benchmarking is a form of social comparison but on the organization level. Thus, although there are several methodological concerns with benchmarking, organizations will use them to judge where they stand in the marketplace relative to their peers and the competition. Rather than ignore benchmarks, organizations can use them as rough guides to get an idea of where they stand relative to others, and then use more rigorous methods to explore why and where differences should or should not exist.

Chapter Summary

Organizations care about your attitudes at work because they seem to be related to and predict many valuable job behaviors such as performance and engagement. Attitudes such as job satisfaction, commitment, job involvement, turnover intentions, trust, and fairness have been the focus of much research attention and for good reasons. Together these attitudes essentially make up your feelings and cognitions at work. A number of theories have been proposed to explain how your attitudes form about your work and how those attitudes are related to each other and to behaviors you demonstrate relevant to the organization's goals. Lastly, it turns out that attitudes can be assessed and changed, though some are more difficult to change than others (e.g., commitment vs. satisfaction), and some are influenced by a number of different factors that are unrelated to what happens at work and not necessarily predictable (e.g., turnover intentions).

Why is collecting responses on a single survey and then analyzing the correlations between those responses a problem?

The implications for job or work attitudes for organizations and the leaders within are that employees form attitudes at work, enter into work with attitudes already formed, and change their attitudes about work as a result of their interactions with others and with the organization itself. Because of the power of attitudes to influence how people behave at work, organizations and their leaders pay attention to them, as should you.

Figure 4.16 provides a visual summary of the key concepts from chapter 4.

The summary shows that various antecedents promote different job attitudes, which have various outcomes including more attitudes, work behaviors, and/or stress (to name a few). The location of arrows suggests a causal path, from antecedents to a first set of outcomes that become mediators for the final outcomes (e.g., work behaviors). Attitudes can lead to other attitudes, as well as to behavioral outcomes such as performance or quitting. Although the summary diagram shows this linear causal chain, in reality the summary could have been a big circle where everything leads to everything else. However, such a summary becomes hard to read.

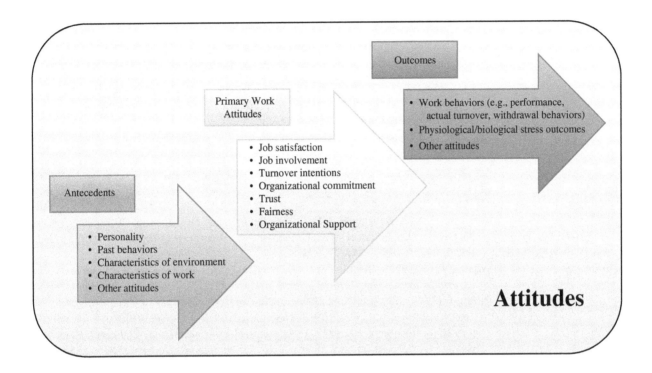

FIGURE 4.16   Visual Summary of Chapter 4

Courtesy Zinta Byrne.

Discussion Questions

1. If attitudes are interrelated and there is no true starting point, why is it helpful to talk about one attitude predicting another? In what ways is describing attitudes in a causal linear chain helpful, and not helpful, to organizational leaders and/or practitioners?

2. Which of the attitudes referred to in this chapter do you think is the MOST important to understand, predict, or change for an organization to be successful? Why this/these attitudes and not the others?

3. Under which conditions do you see elaboration likelihood working more effectively than the theory of planned behavior in changing attitudes? Now provide conditions for the reverse—when is the theory of planned behavior more effective in explaining attitude change over the elaboration likelihood model?

4. Even though the chapter offers some disadvantages to benchmarking, why do you think organizations continue to insist on using them? What does the benchmark provide them? Use theories of motivation from the previous chapter to explain how and why benchmarking has the power it has in organizations.

5. Given the gig economy, where people do not necessarily work beyond an independent contractor status, do you think understanding attitudes at work

will remain important to follow and understand? Does our focus on attitudes at work matter anymore in the gig economy? If not, why not? If so, why? Do you think how we focus on the attitudes will change? In what way(s)?

6. What are some reasons why measuring job attitudes can be difficult? What alternative methods are there for measuring or getting at employees' job attitudes? Which is best?

References

Abelson, M. A., & Baysinger, B. D. (1984). Optimal and Dysfunctional Turnover: Toward an Organizational Level Model. *Academy of Management Review, 9*(2), 331–341. doi:10.5465/AMR.1984.4277675

Adams, J. S. (1965). Inequity in social exchange. In L. Berkowitz (Ed.), *Advances in experimental social psychology* (Vol. 2, pp. 267–299). New York, NY: Academic Press.

Ajzen, I. (1991). The theory of planned behavior. *Organizational Behavior and Human Decision Processes, 50*(2), 179–211. doi:10.1016/0749-5978(91)90020-T

Ajzen, I., & Fishbein, M. (1977). Attitude-behavior relations: A theoretical analysis and review of empirical research. *Psychological Bulletin, 84*(5), 888–918. doi:10.1037/0033-2909.84.5.888

Ajzen I., & Fishbein, M. (1980). *Understanding attitudes and predicting social behavior.* Englewood-Cliffs, NJ: Prentice-Hall.

Allen, N. J., & Meyer, J. P. (1990). The measurement and antecedents of affective, continuance and normative commitment to the organization. *Journal of Occupational Psychology, 63*(1), 1–18. doi:10.1111/j.2044-8325.1990.tb00506.x

Allen, N. J., & Meyer, J. P. (1996). Affective, continuance, and normative commitment to the organization: An examination of construct validity. *Journal of Vocational Behavior, 49*(3), 252–276.

Allport, G. W. (1935). Attitudes. In C. Murchison (Ed.), *Handbook of social psychology* (pp. 798–844). Worcester, MA: Clark University Press.

APA (2014). *2014 Work and well-being survey.* Washington, DC: American Psychological Association.

Aryee, S., Budhwar, P. S., & Chen, Z. (2002). Trust as a mediator of the relationship between organizational justice and work outcomes: Test of a social exchange model. *Journal of Organizational Behavior, 23*(3), 267–286. doi:10.1002/job.138

Barber, B. (1983). *The logic and limits of trust* (Vol. 96). New Brunswick, NJ: Rutgers University Press.

Becker, T. E. (1992). Foci and bases of commitment: Are they distinctions worth making? *Academy of Management Journal, 35*(1), 232–244. doi:10.2307/256481

Bem, D. J. (1967). Self-perception: An alternative interpretation of cognitive dissonance phenomena. *Psychological Review, 74*(3), 183–200. doi:10.1037/h0024835

Bem, D. J., & McConnell, H. (1970). Testing the self-perception explanation of dissonance phenomena: On the salience of premanipulation attitudes. *Journal of Personality and Social Psychology, 14*(1), 23–31. doi:10.1037/h0020916

Bhal, K. T., & Gulati, N. (2004). Leader member exchange and perceived justice: The mediating impact of voice. *Indian Journal of Industrial Relations, 40*(1), 1–16.

Bies, R. J., & Moag, J. S. (1986). Interactional justice: Communication criteria of fairness. In R. J. Lewicki, B. H. Sheppard, & M. H. Bazerman (Eds.), *Research on negotiation in organizations* (Vol. 1, pp. 43–55). Greenwich, CT: JAI Press.

Blau, P. M. (1964). *Exchange and power in social life.* New York, NY: Wiley.

Bradach, J. L. & Eccles, R. G. (1989). Price, authority, and trust: From ideal types to plural forms. *Annual Review of Sociology, 15*, 97–118. doi:10.1146/annurev.so.15.080189.000525

Brown, S. P. (1996). A meta-analysis and review of organizational research on job involvement. *Psychological Bulletin, 120*(2), 235–255. doi:10.1037/0033-2909.120.2.235

Brown, S. P., & Peterson, R. A. (1993). Antecedents and consequences of salesperson job satisfaction: Meta-analysis and assessment of causal effects. *Journal of Marketing Research, 30*(1), 63–77. doi:10.2307/3172514

Byrne, Z. S. (1999, April). *How do procedural and interactional justice influence multiple levels of organizational outcomes?* Symposium presentation at the 14th annual conference of the Society of Industrial and Organizational Psychology, Atlanta, GA.

Byrne, Z. S. (2005). Fairness reduces the negative effects of organizational politics on turnover intentions, citizenship behavior and job performance. *Journal of Business and Psychology, 20,* 175–200.

Byrne, Z. S., & Cropanzano, R. (2000, April). *To which source do I attribute this fairness? Differential effects of multi-foci justice on organizational work behaviors.* Presented at the 15th annual conference of the Society of Industrial and Organizational Psychology, New Orleans, LA.

Byrne, Z., Pitts, V., Chiaburu, D., & Steiner, Z. (2011). Managerial trustworthiness and social exchange with the organization. *Journal of Managerial Psychology, 26,* 108–122.

Byrne, Z. S., Pitts, V. E., Wilson, C. M., & Steiner, Z. J. (2012). Trusting the fair supervisor: The role of supervisory support in performance appraisals. *Human Resource Management Journal, 22,*129–147.

Campbell, D. T., & Fiske, D. W. (1959). Convergent and discriminant validation by the multitrait-multimethod matrix. *Psychological Bulletin, 56*(2), 81–105. doi:10.1037/h0046016

Campbell, L., Simpson, J. A., Boldry, J. G., & Rubin, H. (2010). Trust, variability in relationship evaluations, and relationships processes. *Journal of Personality and Social Psychology, 99,*14–31. doi:10.1037/a0019714

Cohen-Charash, Y., & Spector, P. E. (2001). The role of justice in organizations: A meta-analysis. *Organizational Behavior and Human Decision Processes, 86*(2), 278–321. doi:10.1006/obhd.2001.2958

Cohen, R. J., Swerdlik, M. E., & Sturman, E. (2013). *Psychological testing and assessment: An introduction to tests and measurement.* New York, NY: McGraw-Hill.

Colquitt, J. A. (2001). On the dimensionality of organizational justice: A construct validation of a measure. *Journal of Applied Psychology, 86*(3), 386–400. doi:10.1037/0021-9010.86.3.386

Colquitt, J. A., Conlon, D. E., Wesson, M. J., Porter, C. H., & Ng, K. (2001). Justice at the millennium: A meta-analytic review of 25 years of organizational justice research. *Journal of Applied Psychology, 86*(3), 425–445. doi:10.1037/0021-9010.86.3.425

Colquitt, J. A., Greenberg, J., & Zapata-Phelan, C. P. (2005). What is organizational justice? A historical overview. In J. Greenberg & J. A. Colquitt (Eds.), *Handbook of organizational justice* (pp. 3–56). Mahwah, NJ: Lawrence Erlbaum Associates Publishers.

Connell, J., Ferres, N., & Travaglione, T. (2003). Engendering trust in manager-subordinate relationships: Predictors and outcomes. *Personnel Review, 32,* 569–587. doi:10.1108/00483480310488342

Cook, J., & Wall, T. (1980). New work attitude measures of trust, organizational commitment and personal need non-fulfillment. *Journal of Occupational Psychology, 53*(1), 39–52.

Cropanzano, R., & Byrne, Z. S. (2001). When it's time to stop writing procedures. An inquiry into procedural injustice. *Human Resource Management Review, 11,* 31–54.

Currivan, D. B. (1999). The causal order of job satisfaction and organizational commitment in models of employee turnover. *Human Resource Management Review, 9*(4), 495–524. doi:10.1016/S1053-4822(99)00031-5

Dalton, D. R., Krackhardt, D. M., & Porter, L. W. (1981). Functional turnover: An empirical assessment. *Journal of Applied Psychology, 66*(6), 716–721. doi:10.1037/0021-9010.66.6.716

Dalton, D. R., Todor, W. D., & Krackhardt, D. M. (1982). Turnover overstated: The functional taxonomy. *Academy of Management Review, 7*(1), 117–123. doi:10.5465/AMR.1982.4285499

Daly, J. P., & Geyer, P. D. (1994). The role of fairness in implementing large-scale change: Employee evaluations of process and outcome in seven facility relocations. *Journal of Organizational Behavior, 15*(7), 623–638. doi:10.1002/job.4030150706

Davis, J. H., Schoorman, F., Mayer, R. C., & Hwee Hoon, T. (2000). The trusted general manager and business unit performance: Empirical evidence of a competitive advantage. *Strategic Management Journal, 21*(5), 563–577.

Deutsch, M. (1958). Trust and suspicion. *Journal of Conflict Resolution, 2,* 265–279. doi:10.1177/002200275800200401

Deutsch, M. (1975). Equity, equality, and need: What determines which value will be used as the basis of distributive justice? *Journal of Social Issues, 31,* 137–149. http://onlinelibrary.wiley.com/journal/10.1111/%28ISSN%291540-4560

Dirks, K. T., & Ferrin, D. L. (2001). The role of trust in organizational settings. *Organization Science, 12*(4), 450–467. doi:10.1287/orsc.12.4.450.10640

Dirks, K. T., & Ferrin, D. L. (2002). Trust in leadership: Meta-analytic findings and implications for research and practice. *Journal of Applied Psychology, 87*(4), 611–628.

Eisenberger, R., Cummings, J., Armeli, S., & Lynch, P. (1997). Perceived organizational support, discretionary treatment, and job satisfaction. *Journal of Applied Psychology, 82*(5), 812–820. doi:10.1037/0021-9010.82.5.812

Eisenberger, R., Huntington, R., Hutchison, S., & Sowa, D. (1986). Perceived organizational support. *Journal of Applied Psychology, 71,* 500–507.

Festinger, L. (1954). A theory of social comparison processes. *Human Relations, 7*117–7140. doi:10.1177/001872675400700202

Festinger, L. (1962). Cognitive dissonance. *Scientific American, 207*(4), 93–107.

Fishbein, M. (1963). An investigation of the relationship between beliefs about an object and an attitude toward that object. *Human Relations, 16,* 233–239.

Gavett, G. (April 28, 2014). Why a quarter of Americans don't trust their employers. Retrieved from http://blogs.hbr.org/2014/04/why-a-quarter-of-americans-dont-trust-their-employers/?utm_source=feedburner&utm_medium=feed&utm_campaign=Feed%3A+harvardbusiness+%28HBR.org%29

Geller, E., Hickman, J. S., & Pettinger, C. B. (2004). The Airline Lifesaver: A 17-year analysis of a technique to prompt the delivery of a safety message. *Journal of Safety Research, 35*(4), 357–366. doi:10.1016/j.jsr.2004.04.002

Giffin, K. (1967). The contribution of studies of source credibility to a theory of interpersonal trust in the communication process. *Psychological Bulletin, 68*(2), 104–120. doi:10.1037/h0024833

Govier, T. (1994). Is it a jungle out there? Trust, distrust and the construction of social reality. *Dialogue, 33,* 237–252. doi:10.1017/S0012217300010519

Graen, G. B., & Uhl-Bien, M. (1995). Relationship-based approach to leadership: Development of leader-member exchange (LMX) theory of leadership over 25 years: Applying a multi-level multi-domain perspective. *The Leadership Quarterly, 6*(2), 219–247. doi:10.1016/1048-9843(95)90036-5

Greenberg, J. (1993). The social side of fairness: Interpersonal and informational classes of organizational justice. In R. Cropanzano (Ed.), *Justice in the workplace:*

Approaching fairness in human resource management (pp. 79–103). Hillsdale, NJ: Lawrence Erlbaum Associates.

Griffeth, R. W., Hom, P. W., & Gaertner, S. (2000). A meta-analysis of antecedents and correlates of employee turnover: Update, moderator tests, and research implications for the next millennium. *Journal of Management, 26*(3), 463–488.

Hackman, J., & Oldham, G. R. (1976). Motivation through the design of work: Test of a theory. *Organizational Behavior & Human Performance, 16*(2), 250–279. doi:10.1016/0030-5073(76)90016-7

Herzberg, F. (1968). One more time: How do you motivate employees? *Harvard Business Review, 46*(1), 53–62.

Herzberg, F., Mausner, B., & Snyderman, B. B. (1959). *Motivation to work.* Oxford, England: John Wiley.

Hulin, C. L., & Judge, T. A. (2003). Job attitudes. In W. C. Borman, D. R. Ilgen, R. J. Klimoski (Eds.), *Handbook of psychology: Industrial and organizational psychology, Vol. 12* (pp. 255–276). Hoboken, NJ: Wiley.

Ilgen, D. R. (1971). Satisfaction with performance as a function of the initial level of expected performance and the deviation from expectations. *Organizational Behavior & Human Performance, 6*(3), 345–361.

Jackofsky, E. F. (1984). Turnover and job performance: An integrated process model. *Academy of Management Review, 9*(1), 74–83. doi:10.5465/AMR.1984.4277940

Jaros, S. J. (1997). An assessment of Meyer and Allen's (1991) three-component model of organizational commitment and turnover intentions. *Journal of Vocational Behavior, 51,* 319–337.

Jex, S. M. (1998). *Stress and job performance: Theory, research, and implications for managerial practice.* Thousand Oaks, CA: Sage.

Judge, T. A., Parker, S. K., Colbert, A. E., Heller, D., & Ilies, R. (2002). Job satisfaction: A cross-cultural review. In N. Anderson, D. S. Ones, H. Sinangil, C. Viswesvaran (Eds.), *Handbook of industrial, work and organizational psychology, Volume 2: Organizational psychology* (pp. 25–52). Thousand Oaks, CA: Sage.

Judge, T. A., Piccolo, R. F., Podsakoff, N. P., Shaw, J. C., & Rich, B. L. (2010). The relationship between pay and job satisfaction: A meta-analysis of the literature. *Journal of Vocational Behavior, 77*(2), 157–167. doi:10.1016/j.jvb.2010.04.002

Kanungo, R. N. (1982). Measurement of job and work involvement. *Journal of Applied Psychology, 67,* 341–349. doi:0021-9010/82/6703-0341

Katz, D, & Stotland, E. (1959). A preliminary statement to a theory of attitude structure and change. In S. Koch (Ed.), *Psychology: A study of a science* (Vol.3, pp. 423–475). New York: McGraw-Hill.

Kegan, D. L. (1971). Organizational development: Description, issues, and some research results. *Academy of Management Journal, 14*(4), 453–464. doi:10.2307/255060

Kramer, R. M. (1999). Trust and distrust in organizations: Emerging perspectives, enduring questions. *Annual Review of Psychology, 50,* 569–598. doi:10.1146/annurev. psych.50.1.569

Krech, D., & Crutchfield, R. S. (1948). *Theory and problems of social psychology.* New York: McGraw-Hill.

Larson, C. E., & LaFasto, F. J. (1989). *Teamwork: What must go right/what can go wrong.* Thousand Oaks, CA: Sage.

Lawler, E. E., & Hall, D. T. (1970). Relationship of job characteristics to job involvement, satisfaction, and intrinsic motivation. *Journal of Applied Psychology, 54*(4), 305–312. doi:10.1037/h0029692

Lee, T. W., & Mitchell, T. R. (1994). An alternative approach: The unfolding model of voluntary employee turnover. *The Academy of Management Review, 19*(1), 51–89. doi:10.2307/258835

Leventhal, G. S. (1980). What should be done with equity theory? In K. J. Gergen, M. S. Greenberg, & R. H. Willis (Eds.), *Social exchange: Advances in theory and research* (pp. 27–55). New York: Plenum Press.

Lewicki, R. J., & Bunker, B. B. (1996). Developing and maintaining trust in work relationships. In R. M. Kramer & T. R. Tyler (Eds.), *Trust in organizations: Frontiers of theory and research,* (pp. 114–139). Thousand Oaks, CA: Sage.

Lewicki, R. J., Wiethoff, C., & Tomlinson, E. C. (2005). What is the role of trust in organizational justice? In J. Greenberg & J. A. Colquitt (Eds.), *Handbook of organizational justice* (pp. 247–272). Mahwah, NJ: Lawrence Erlbaum Associates Publishers.

Lind, E., Kulik, C. T., Ambrose, M., & de Vera Park, M. V. (1993). Individual and corporate dispute resolution: Using procedural fairness as a decision heuristic. *Administrative Science Quarterly, 38*(2), 224–251. doi:10.2307/2393412

Lind, E. A., & Tyler, T. (1988). *The social psychology of procedural justice.* New York: NY: Plenum Press.

Locke, E. A. (1976). The nature and causes of job satisfaction. In M. D. Dunnette (Ed.), *Handbook of industrial and organizational psychology* (pp. 1297–1349). Chicago, IL: Rand McNally.

Lodahl, T. M., & Kejnar, M. (1965). The definition and measurement of job involvement. *Journal of Applied Psychology, 49*(1), 24–33. doi:10.1037/h0021692

Loher, B. T., Noe, R. A., Moeller, N. L., & Fitzgerald, M. P. (1985). A meta-analysis of the relation of job characteristics to job satisfaction. *Journal of Applied Psychology, 70*(2), 280–289. doi:10.1037/0021-9010.70.2.280

Maslow, A. H. (1948). 'Higher' and 'lower' needs. *Journal of Psychology: Interdisciplinary and Applied, 25,* 433–436. doi:10.1080/00223980.1948.9917386

Mathieu, J. E., & Zajac, D. M. (1990). A review and meta-analysis of the antecedents, correlates, and consequences of organizational commitment. *Psychological Bulletin, 108*(2), 171–194. doi:10.1037/0033-2909.108.2.171

Mathis, R. L., & Jackson, J. H. (2003). *Human resource management* (10th ed.). Mason, OH: Thompson/South-Western.

Mayer, R. C., & Davis, J. H. (1999). The effect of the performance appraisal system on trust for management: A field quasi-experiment. *Journal of Applied Psychology, 84*(1), 123–136. doi:10.1037/0021-9010.84.1.123

Mayer, R. C., Davis, J. H., & Schoorman, F. D. 1995. An integrative model of organizational trust. *Academy of Management Review, 20,* 709–734.

McAllister, D. J. (1995). Affect-and cognition-based trust as foundations for interpersonal cooperation in organizations. *Academy of Management Journal, 38,* 24–59. doi:10.2307/256727

McEvoy, G. M., & Cascio, W. F. (1985). Strategies for reducing employee turnover: A meta-analysis. *Journal of Applied Psychology, 70*(2), 342–353. doi:10.1037/0021-9010.70.2.342

Meyer, J. P., Allen, M. W., & Smith, C. (1993). Commitment to organizations and occupations: Extension and test of a three-component conceptualization. *Journal of Applied Psychology, 78,* 538–551.

Meyer, J. P., Stanley, D. J., Herscovitch, L., & Topolnytsky, L. (2002). Affective, continuance, and normative commitment to the organization: A meta-analysis of antecedents, correlates, and consequences. *Journal of Vocational Behavior, 61*(1), 20–52. doi:10.1006/jvbe.2001.1842

Meyer, J. P., Stanley, D. J., Jackson, T. A., McInnis, K. J., Maltin, E. R., & Sheppard, L. (2012). Affective, normative, and continuance commitment levels across cultures: A meta-analysis. *Journal of Vocational Behavior, 80*(2), 225–245. doi:10.1016/j.jvb.2011.09.005

Minnesota Satisfaction Questionnaire. (n.d.) Retrieved from https://www.psych.umn.edu/psylabs/vpr/msqinf.htm

Mobley, W. H. (1977). Intermediate linkages in the relationship between job satisfaction and employee turnover. *Journal of Applied Psychology, 62*(2), 237–240. doi:10.1037/0021-9010.62.2.237

Mobley, W. H., Horner, S. O., & Hollingsworth, A. T. (1978). An evaluation of precursors of hospital employee turnover. *Journal of Applied Psychology, 63,* 408–414.

Moorman, R. H. (1991). Relationship between organizational justice and organizational citizenship behaviors: Do fairness perceptions influence employee citizenship? *Journal of Applied Psychology, 76*(6), 845–855. doi:10.1037/0021-9010.76.6.845

Mowday, R. T., Steers, R. M., & Porter, L. W. (1979). The measurement of organizational commitment. *Journal of Vocational Behavior, 14*(2), 224–247. doi:10.1016/0001-8791(79)90072-1

Nyhan, R. C., & Marlowe., H. A. Jr. (1997). Development and psychometric properties of the organizational. *Evaluation Review, 21*(5), 614–636.

O'Connell, M., & Mei-Chuan, K. (2007). The cost of employee turnover. *Industrial Management, 49*(1), 14–19.

Orpen, C., & Pool, J. (1995). The joint effects of individual career planning and organizational career management on employee job performance and job involvement. *Studia Psychologica, 37*(1), 27–29.

Petty, R. E., & Cacioppo, J. T. (1996). *Attitudes and persuasion: Classic and contemporary approaches.* Boulder, CO: Westview Press.

Podsakoff, N. P., LePine, J. A., & LePine, M. A. (2007). Differential challenge stressor-hindrance stressor relationships with job attitudes, turnover intentions, and withdrawal behavior: A meta-analysis. *Journal of Applied Psychology, 92,* 438–454. doi:10.1037/0021-9010.92.2.438

Podsakoff, P. M., MacKenzie, S. B., Lee, J., & Podsakoff, N. P. (2003). Common method biases in behavioral research: A critical review of the literature and recommended remedies. *Journal of Applied Psychology, 88*(5), 879–903. doi:10.1037/0021-9010.88.5.879

Porter, L. W. (1961). A study of perceived need satisfactions in bottom and middle management jobs. *Journal of Applied Psychology, 45*(1), 1–10. doi:10.1037/h0043121

Porter, L.W., & Steers, R. M. (1973). Organizational, work, and personal factors in employee turnover and absenteeism. *Psychological Bulletin, 80*(2), 151–176. doi:10.1037/h0034829

Premack, S. L., & Wanous, J. P. (1985). A meta-analysis of realistic job preview experiments. *Journal of Applied Psychology, 70*(4), 706–719. doi:10.1037/0021-9010.70.4.706

Rhoades, L., & Eisenberger, R. (2002). Perceived organizational support: A review of the literature. *Journal of Applied Psychology, 87*(4), 698–714. doi:10.1037/0021-9010.87.4.698

Rhoades, L., Eisenberger, R., & Armeli, S. (2001). Affective commitment to the organization: The contribution of perceived organizational support. *Journal of Applied Psychology, 86,* 825–836.

Riggle, R. J., Edmondson, D. R., & Hansen, J. D. (2009). A meta-analysis of the relationship between perceived organizational support and job outcomes: 20 years of research. *Journal of Business Research, 62*(10), 1027–1030. doi:10.1016/j.jbusres.2008.05.003

Rotter, J. B. (1980). Interpersonal trust, trustworthiness, and gullibility. *American Psychologist, 35,* 1–7. doi:10.1037/0003-066X.35.1.1

Rousseau, D. M., Sitkin, S. B., Burt, R. S., & Camerer, C. (1998). Not so different after all: A cross-discipline view of trust. *Academy of Management Review, 23,* 393–404. doi:10.5465/AMR.1998.926617

Salancik, G. R., & Pfeffer, J. (1978). A social information processing approach to job attitudes and task design. *Administrative Science Quarterly, 23*(2), 224–253. doi:10.2307/2392563

Schoorman, F. D., Mayer, R. C., & Davis, J. H. (2007). An integrative model of organizational trust: Past, present, and future. *Academy of Management Review, 32,* 344–354. doi:10.5465/AMR.2007.24348410

Sitkin, S. B., & Roth, N. L. (1993). Explaining the limited effectiveness of legalistic 'remedies' for trust/distrust. *Organization Science, 4*(3), 367–392. doi:10.1287/orsc.4.3.367

Slovic, P. (1993). Perceived risk, trust, and democracy. *Risk Analysis, 13*(6), 675–682. doi:10.1111/j.1539-6924.1993.tb01329.x

Spector, P. E. (1985). Measurement of human service staff satisfaction: Development of the Job Satisfaction Survey. *American Journal of Community Psychology, 13*(6), 693–713. doi:10.1007/BF00929796

Staw, B. M., & Ross, J. (1985). Stability in the midst of change: A dispositional approach to job attitudes. *Journal of Applied Psychology, 70*(3), 469–480. doi:10.1037/0021-9010.70.3.469

Tesser, A., & Shaffer, D. R. (1990). Attitudes and attitude change. *Annual Review of Psychology, 41,* 479–523.

Tett, R. P. & Meyer, J. P. (1993). Job satisfaction, organizational commitment, turnover intention, and turnover: Path analyses based on meta-analytic findings. *Personnel Psychology, 46,* 259–293.

Thibaut, J., & Walker, L. (1975). *Procedural justice: A psychological analysis.* Hillsdale, NJ: Lawrence Erlbaum Associates.

Tyler, T. R., & Blader, S. L. (2002). Terms of engagement: Why do people invest themselves in work? In H. Sondak (Ed.), *Toward phenomenology of groups and group membership* (pp. 115–140). New York, NY: Elsevier Science. doi:10.1016/S1534-0856(02)04006-9

Tyler, T. R., & Lind, E. (1992). A relational model of authority in groups. In M. P. Zanna (Ed.), *Advances in experimental social psychology, Vol. 25* (pp. 115–191). San Diego, CA: Academic Press. doi:10.1016/S0065-2601(08)60283-X

Weiss, H. M., & Cropanzano, R. (1996). Affective events theory: A theoretical discussion of the structure, causes and consequences of affective experiences at work. In B. M. Staw, L. L. Cummings (Eds.), *Research in organizational behavior: An annual series of analytical essays and critical reviews, Vol. 19* (pp. 1–74). Greenwich, CT: JAI Press.

Williams, C. R. (1999). Reward contingency, unemployment, and functional turnover. *Human Resource Management Review, 9*(4), 549–576. doi:10.1016/S1053-4822(99)00033-9

Williams, C. R., & Livingstone, L. (1994). Another look at the relationship between performance and voluntary turnover. *Academy Of Management Journal, 37*(2), 269–298. doi:10.2307/256830

Yoon Jik, C., & Hanjun, P. (2011). Exploring the relationships among trust, employee satisfaction, and organizational commitment. *Public Management Review, 13*(4), 551–573. doi:10.1080/14719037.2010.525033

Zand, D. E. (1972). Trust and managerial problem solving. *Administrative Science Quarterly, 17*(2), 229–239.

CHAPTER 5

Doing the Job and Then Some: Performance

Learning Outcomes

After studying this chapter you should be able to explain:

1. What comprises performance on the job and in organizations, versus what it is not considered performance in organizations.

2. The different types of job performance behaviors and their effects in organizations.

3. How performance is managed.

4. How performance is encouraged.

Mini-Quiz: Performance

As an introduction to this chapter, please take the following mini-quiz (answers are in the back of the book). As you read the questions and consider the answers *before* diving into the chapter, you'll challenge yourself before you master the content, a process that helps facilitate learning for long-term retention. Some questions may have more than one correct answer. Don't worry if you cannot answer all questions correctly on your first try. By the time you read the chapter and spend some of your own time thinking about these concepts, you should be able to determine the best answers. Try the quiz again after you finish reading the chapter.

1. Which of the following are correct about this statement: When we think about employee "performance", it includes only what a person is expected to do and that they do it well.
    a. True! We can only monitor and consider what employees are expected to do based on the descriptions of their jobs.
    b. Not always—"performance" can also include voluntary and extra tasks that are outside of a person's normal job.
    c. False. There are many different ways to view performance, such as adaptability, completing specific tasks, and broad skills like communication.
    d. Performance is not only tasks. We can understand performance better when we split it into *utility, efficiency, and productivity.*

2. You manage an employee who is known for taking particularly long breaks. This person can get rather chatty with other workers and often distracts them from what they are supposed to be doing. You have spoken with your employee about this, but the situation doesn't seem to be improving. This troublesome employee is best described as:
    a. Having low motivation
    b. Being unethical
    c. Engaging in counterproductive behavior
    d. Using "extra-role" behaviors

3. As a leader in your organization, how can you help manage employee performance?
    a. Performance appraisals
    b. Consistent punishment
    c. Giving feedback
    d. Setting goals

4. You are a manager at a local grocery store and it is that time of year to have meetings with employees to talk about their performance—annual performance appraisal time! What can you do to make these meetings more successful?
    a. Clearly identify which behaviors were considered and rated when making the feedback report
    b. Have employees reflect on their own performance and evaluate their own performance
    c. Give the employee one, overall score. This is easier to understand and talk about
    d. Go through training yourself to better understand biases and common errors that people make when evaluating others

5. How can you help employees improve their performance?
    a. Focus on changing employees' personalities
    b. Provide opportunities to get more experience
    c. Pay people more money
    d. Do whatever it takes to make employees happy (i.e., have high satisfaction)

Overview

Although understanding and measuring job performance is usually a topic relegated to the industrial psychology domain, we study it here in organizational psychology because of its centrality to organizational topics. Given the tremendous value organizations place on employee performance, your ability to manage your own performance at work can determine your overall job success. It also determines the success of the organization. Organizational leaders care about employee performance because the business thrives on employees achieving the organization's goals. Performance in organizations represents a key component of organizational functioning. Employees go to work to do their jobs—to perform. Although there are many other things employees do while at work, their number one responsibility is to perform to achieve organizational goals. Therefore, understanding job performance and **performance management** becomes essential for developing effective teams, managing projects to successful completion, and for employees themselves in navigating work expectations.

Organizations spend time and money managing performance at work and developing strategies for how to get the highest performance out of all their employees. Annual and quarterly performance reviews determine raises and promotion opportunities, and ultimately connect with organizational performance that drives **market share** or company market value.

What is Performance in Organizations?

Performance refers to an employee's aggregated or accumulative behaviors aimed toward meeting organizational goals. As such, performance encompasses employees fulfilling job tasks and expectations in a way that positively contributes to the organization's objectives. Thus, job performance represents a collection of behaviors or actions as opposed to a single behavior. However, employees spend little time just performing *tasks*. They also perform many other behaviors that contribute to the organization, thus "task performance" is an insufficient term to capture all of what job performance entails (Murphy, 1989).

Because there is not only ONE job within and across organizations, job performance as a broad construct is not one thing. It differs from organization to organization and differs across job families. A job family refers to a group of jobs that are similar in some global way, but different in specific skill requirement and expectations. For example, *skilled craft jobs* is a job family and the jobs that fit into that family include, carpenter, painter, plumber, electrician, and locksmith. As a consequence, defining job performance in general requires broad terms that can encompass all jobs within a family and within multiple families of jobs.

Employees view performance as the expectations organizations have of them, for which they receive in exchange rewards on the job, such as pay. In contrast, organizations view performance as the difference between survival and demise. Survival can mean beating the competition and winning market share at the lowest cost. Thus performance takes on a broader definition for organizations, incorporating not only what the employee accomplishes, but how efficiently and effectively the employee accomplishes the work.

Campbell (1990) suggested that to understand all the components of performance (i.e., the action or behavior that produces results for the organization) from both the employee and organization's view, we need to divide performance into effectiveness, productivity, and utility. In addition, however, efficiency also plays a part in understanding performance. We've already reviewed how performance is defined; so let's review effectiveness, efficiency (which plays a role in determining productivity), productivity, and utility.

Effectiveness refers to an evaluation of how well the job is done. In the example in Table 5.1, Judy, who works at a local coffee shop where her job is to make coffee, is considered effective because she makes coffee that people request. Effectiveness is an evaluation of results that is made by others and is not typically within the control of the employee. In Judy's case, her coffee (the result of her

TABLE 5.1 Chart of Performance, Effectiveness, Efficiency, and Utility

Term	Definition	Examples
Performance	Goal relevant actions that are under employee's control • What you do on the job. • What you are hired to do	Judy makes coffee. Dr. Tym teaches 3 classes. Paramedic gives emergency first aid.
Effectiveness	An evaluation of what is produced or accomplished. • How *well* you get the job done • Do your results work, do they have an impact?	Judy makes good coffee that people request. His 2nd time running the company, Steve Jobs developed a new vision for Apple, Inc. and that moved the company from near bankruptcy to a leading role in high technology innovation. Thus, as CEO, he was very effective.
Efficiency	• How *much* you get done relative to what you were given • Output relative to inputs	Judy can make 3 cups in the time it takes Bob to make 1. Juanita is given 20 pages to write 3 documents, but writes 4 four using only 15 pages. Alexander is given 20 pages to write 3 documents, but only writes 2 using all 20 pages. Alexander is less efficient.
Productivity	Ratio of effectiveness to the cost of effectiveness • What is the cost of achieving that effectiveness?	Judy makes coffee people like, with no waste, and the coffee grounds do not cost much compared to what the company can charge per cup of coffee Judy makes. Amazon.com spends money on perfecting its ordering and shipping systems, but their ability to process orders and ship them fast makes them the largest and most shopped-at book store, resulting in the largest market share of the book retailer market.
Utility	The value of work and level of performance, effectiveness, or productivity • Does your performance give the organization something it wants?	Judy makes coffee people want, with no waste, and fast, and the organization she works for is a coffee shop.

Courtesy Zinta Byrne.

performance) is evaluated by the customers and by her bosses. She might make coffee that she likes, but if the customers do not like it, she will not be considered effective at her job of making coffee. How effective Judy is, however, says nothing about whether she is wasteful—can she make a lot of coffee using the available resources? The answer to this question lies in her efficiency.

Efficiency refers to how much is accomplished relative to the resources provided. Accordingly, high efficiency results when more can be accomplished with what is given. For example, if Juanita is asked to write three reports and is given only 20 pages to do so, if she can write four reports in less than 20 pages, she might be considered efficient. In comparison, if Jianguo is also given only 20 pages to three documents but he can barely complete two using all 20 pages, he is considered much less efficient than Juanita. In this example, the quality of the work produced is not assessed. To account for both effectiveness and efficiency, we turn to productivity.

Productivity refers to the relationship between effectiveness and the cost of achieving that level of effectiveness (Mahoney, 1988). Thus, productivity considers what it costs to achieve the observed level of effectiveness. For example, if Judy can make coffee that people want fast and with little waste, and the coffee grounds she uses do not cost much relative to what her employer can charge per cup of coffee, we can say that Judy is quite productive. The cost of making the coffee is outweighed by how many cups she can make and what the company can charge in exchange per cup. Productivity, therefore, takes into account efficiency of performance. If Judy gets the job done faster than Derek, but she tends to make mistakes that require remaking the coffee and extra time cleaning up, Judy is not considered efficient. Derek may be slower, but if his work is of high quality such that no one has to remake the coffee or clean up after him, he might end up being more efficient than Judy, and therefore, in the end, more productive. Now, although we have assessed their productivity, whether what Judy and Derek are doing is considered valuable to the organization or not refers to the utility of their work.

Last, *utility* refers to the value of the work at a certain level—does the organization want and expect this work? Suppose Judy (from the examples in Table 5.1) is not a barista but actually a dental hygienist in a dentist's office. The utility of Judy's coffee making is very low because her job is not to make a lot of good coffee, and make it fast. Utility may vary by situation. For example, if the dentist is hosting a workshop about the benefits of brushing, Judy's excellent coffee making may have high utility at that time because the goal of the workshop is to get people drinking coffee so that the dentist can demonstrate how teeth color can change just after drinking a single cup of coffee.

Understanding how organizations view performance is useful when considering their success and its implications on individual employees (e.g., whether they have jobs or not). However, the evaluation of an individual's work behavior requires detailing the components of performance.

Why is defining performance in organizations difficult?

Exercise 5.1

Create a table like Table 5.1 using your own words to define performance, effectiveness, efficiency, productivity, and utility, and provide examples for each using your own experiences (can be from a job, school, sports, church, or other situation that works for you).

How is Performance Described in Organizations?

Two examples of job performance taxonomies (groupings of components) include Campbell's (1990) model comprising eight different dimensions, and Murphy's (1989) **taxonomy** of four different dimensions. These taxonomy were put forth to clarify what job performance is and what it is not. Although both models were originally oriented toward the military, they are general enough to be used outside of the military context and can serve as excellent starting points for understanding performance. Table 5.2 shows the two taxonomies side-by-side.

Campbell's Taxonomy

Campbell's (1990) taxonomy was designed to help improve the selection and placement system in the U.S. Army, with an ultimate goal towards improving productivity.

Job-specific task proficiency refers to core job tasks associated with a specific job and typically identified in a job description (if one exists). For example, tasks may include writing an employee handbook, driving a city bus, or developing a new accounting process.

Non-job-specific tasks are those that all jobs require within a job family. For example, all university professors must teach, but what they teach and how, falls under job-specific tasks. All managers are expected to motivate their employees, but how they do so is not specified.

Facilitating peer and team performance includes behaviors such as helping coworkers, helping the boss, and boosting morale (cheery, supportive). Individuals who work alone will have little importance given to this factor on their performance evaluation.

Effort is just what you would think: the amount of energy, force, exertion, or attempts a job requires.

TABLE 5.2   Side-by-side Comparison of Campbell's & Murphy's Job Performance Taxonomies

Campbell (1990)	Murphy (1989)
• Job-specific task proficiency • Non-job-specific task proficiency • Facilitating Peer and Team Performance • Effort • Written and oral communication • Supervision/leadership • Management/administration	• Individual and team task performance: made up of job proficiency, which in turn, includes both general skills and task-related knowledge
• Personal or self-discipline (e.g., controlling outbursts, following rules, safety violations)	• Interpersonal relations behaviors
	• Down-time (e.g., leads to missing work) • Destructive/hazardous (e.g., safety violations, accidents, sabotage)

Courtesy Zinta Byrne. Source: Campbell (1990) and Murphy (1989).

Campbell separated *written and oral communication* from job-specific and non-job-specific task proficiency; however, these separations may not be necessary for many job environments. Campbell separated them to call attention to some jobs in which these skills are critical and form the central focus of the jobs. Jobs such as book author, copy editor, or speech writer are mostly comprised of writing. For other jobs, like food server, landscaper, or accountant, these skills help but are not central to success on the job.

Campbell specifically separated supervision and administration roles from all others to focus attention on behaviors that are not typically considered performance behaviors of direct employees. These behaviors are unique to supervisory roles, but still make up performance; hence, they belong in the taxonomy. For example, behaviors such as role modeling, goal setting, face-to-face interactions to boost motivation, training, and recognizing and rewarding behavior are considered supervision-like behaviors and fit into the *Supervision/Leadership* dimension. The *management/administrative* category includes coordination and controlling behaviors such as making job assignments, representing the unit at higher level meetings, overcoming crises that stand in the way of goal accomplishment for the team, controlling the budget, and organizing resources across groups.

Personal discipline refers to your ability to control emotional outbursts, follow rules, avoid safety violations, and avoid engaging in work behaviors that hurt the organization (see counterproductive work behaviors in the next section).

The eight levels of Campbell's model were intended to be sufficient to describe the top of the hierarchy in all jobs of the Dictionary of Occupational Titles.

Murphy's Taxonomy

Murphy's (1989) taxonomy was developed using U.S. Navy personnel jobs (i.e., enlisted ranks) as an illustration of an approach to defining dimensions of job performance (see Murphy, 1989 for details). His intent was not to develop a taxonomy for military use, but instead his purpose was to illustrate a methodology for showing how each dimensions is measured. The result of his project was a taxonomy of job performance for the Navy. The model shows how overall effectiveness in the job is determined by four broad dimensions of performance.

Individual and Team Task Performance is made up of job proficiency, which is further composed of general skills and task-related knowledge. When compared to Campbell's taxonomy, this broad dimension incorporates all behaviors reflected in Campbell's job-specific task proficiency, non-job-specific task proficiency, facilitating peer and team performance, effort, written and oral communication, supervision/leadership, and management/administration.

Interpersonal Relations behaviors include all interpersonal interactions and mirrors Campbell's personal or self-discipline. The face-to-face interpersonal interactions between supervisor and subordinate noted as part of Campbell's dimension of Supervision/leadership would also be incorporated in this dimension of Murphy's model.

Murphy classified behaviors that inhibit or limit effectiveness on the job into two categories: down-time behaviors and destructive behaviors.

Down-time behaviors refer to what happens off the job (e.g., party on Sunday night) that leads to work absence or withdrawal.

Destructive behaviors include safety violations, accidents, and sabotage.

Although Campbell's and Murphy's taxonomies of performance are well-known, there are other models of job performance that have been proposed, that were not designed using military samples.

Other Models of Performance

There are many other models of job performance (see Campbell, 1994). For example, there exists a taxonomy of adaptive performance, which focuses on training and selecting for ability to adjust to physical work environments, handling emergencies, or handling ambiguity (see Pulakos, Arad, Donovan, & Plamondon, 2000, see Table 5.3). Another is the taxonomy of managerial performance consisting of 18 dimensions (Table 5.4) such as planning and organization (see Borman & Brush, 1993).

Why would organizations use productivity (as defined in Table 5.1) instead of either Campbell's or Murphy's taxonomy of performance?

TABLE 5.3   Adaptive Performance

The Eight Dimensions of Adaptive Performance (Pulakos, Arad, Donovan, & Plamondon, 2000)
Handling emergencies or crisis situations
Handling work stress
Solving problems creatively
Dealing with uncertain and unpredictable situations
Learning work tasks, technologies, and procedures
Demonstrating interpersonal adaptability
Demonstrating cultural adaptability
Demonstrating physically oriented adaptability

Courtesy Zinta Byrne. Source: Pulakos et al. (2000).

TABLE 5.4   Borman & Brush's Taxonomy of Managerial Performance

Borman & Brush (1993)	
Planning & Organizing	Decision making & problem solving
Guiding, directing, motivating, & giving feedback	Staffing
Training, coaching, & developing	Persisting towards goals
Communicating effectively	Crisis & stress management
Representing the organization	Commitment
Technical proficiency	Monitoring & controlling resources (includes people)
Administration & Paperwork	Delegating
Maintaining good relations	Selling/influencing
Coordinating resources	Collecting & interpreting data

Courtesy Zinta Byrne. Source: Borman and Brush (1993).

Do Employees Only Perform Expected Job Behaviors?

Some employees only demonstrate those behaviors that directly contribute to the completion of their specific job and nothing more. However, researchers determined that many employees voluntarily do much more than required, and these extra behaviors make a significant contribution to the overall functioning of the organization. *Extra-role performance behaviors* refer to actions employees take that contribute to the overall functioning of the organization and potentially the organization's goals, but that generally fall outside of the specific stated job requirements or defined job role (Katz, 1964). These behaviors may add to what is expected or formally defined; hence, the term "extra-role"—they are extra or in addition to the defined role. Research supports a direct connection between these extra job performance behaviors and effectiveness at work (Podsakoff, Ahearne, & MacKenzie, 1997; Podsakoff, MacKenzie, Paine, & Bachrach, 2000). Therefore, these extra behaviors are important even though they may or may not be explicitly specified in documented job descriptions and thus may not be explicitly rewarded.

Why would you voluntarily perform extra-role performance behaviors? What would be the motivation in doing so?

Organizational Citizenship Behaviors

Extra job performance has also been called organizational citizenship behaviors (OCBs; Smith, Organ, & Near, 1983). OCBs are considered another form of performance that contributes to the functioning of the organization. When originally defined, OCBs were considered a type of performance, rarely if ever formally recognized during the performance appraisal. Thus, even though employees were demonstrating OCBs, they did so without formal recognition or reward, thus OCBs were meant to capture this category of voluntary extra-role performance. Since its original introduction, scholars of OCBs acknowledge that these performance behaviors may actually be recognized and rewarded in the appraisal system (Organ, 1997), depending on the supervisor and/or organization. Organ's typology represents one way of describing OCBs and is shown in Table 5.5.

Another view suggests that OCBs represent general helping behaviors that improve organizational efficiency and effectiveness, but are targeted to benefit a particular individual or the organization (Williams & Anderson, 1991). OCBOs (O for organization) are OCBs beneficial to the organization, in general. These include conscientious behaviors, such as giving advance notice if late or absent from work, and adhering to established rules. OCBIs (I for individuals) are OCBs beneficial to specific or targeted individuals. For example, helping individuals when they are absent or taking personal interest in others are both forms of OCBI. You may see OCBS (S for supervisor) or OCBCW (CW for coworkers) in various studies assessing OCBs targeted to benefit the supervisor specifically or one's coworkers (see Cheung, 2013; Suazo & Stone-Romero, 2011).

Considering a different categorization for citizenship, Borman (2004) offered a conceptual taxonomy that incorporated the previous approaches to citizenship behavior. He believed all views of citizenship could be summarized into three essential conceptual categories: personal support to others, support to the organization, and conscientious behaviors (shown in Table 5.6).

TABLE 5.5   Organ's Taxonomy of Organizational Citizenship Behaviors

Dimension	Definition	Example
Altruism	Helping behaviors, prosocial behaviors.	Volunteering to help a coworker get his/her job done, even if it means you have to stay late and miss an evening out.
Civic Virtue	Doing things that support the organization and being a good representative of the organization. Could include defending the organization	Attending the community meeting and defending your organization when others in the room begin criticizing the organization. Participating in recruitment efforts.
Conscientiousness	Thinking ahead of what might be needed and acting accordingly.	Arriving to meetings on time or early; phoning ahead when you're running late for a meeting; paying attention to document requirements so all formatting is correct before the review process.
Courtesy	Consideration of others	Checking in with coworkers to see how they are doing on a long assignment. Letting others know where and how to reach you when a big project is in the works and you have to step out.
Sportsmanship	Being a "good sport"; not complaining even if justified	Helping a coworker implement their project after your proposed project was rejected, even though your project was liked more by the team overall.

Courtesy Zinta Byrne. Source: Organ (1997).

TABLE 5.6   Borman's Conceptual Model of Citizenship Behavior

Borman's Summary Model of Citizenship Behavior

Personal Support
- Helping others through suggestions, teaching, role modeling, or offering emotional support for personal problems.
- Accepting feedback, keeping others informed of upcoming events that may affect them, and prioritizing team interests ahead of one's own.
- Demonstrating consideration, courtesy, tactfulness, and satisfaction and confidence in others.

Organizational Support
- Defending and promoting the organization, showing loyalty and satisfaction with the organization despite temporary hardships or setbacks.
- Supporting the organization's mission and objectives, complying with organizational rules and procedures that are reasonable, and offering ideas for improving the organization.

Conscientious Initiative
- Persisting with extra effort despite difficult conditions.
- Taking the initiative to do what is needed even when the duties required are outside what is normally expected or part of one's standard duties, and also doing more than asked.
- Developing knowledge and skills by taking advantage of opportunities within and outside of the organization, as well as using one's own time and resources to do so.

Courtesy Zinta Byrne; Source Borman (2004).

Contextual Performance

Another term for extra-role and OCB performance behaviors is contextual performance, which refers to other activities that do not fall under task performance, but are still important for organizational effectiveness (Borman & Motowidlo, 1993). Contextual performance includes volunteering, extra enthusiasm or effort to complete tasks successfully, helping, following organizational rules, and endorsing, supporting, or defending organizational objectives. The focus is not so much on whether the behaviors contribute to the core of the job, but on the initiative taken to do them. Variability in contextual performance is due to employees' volition or predisposition to take on extra tasks, whereas variability in task performance is generally due to employees' knowledge, skills, and abilities on the job. Contextual performance is considered a broader concept than OCB, though many researchers and practitioners now seem to use the terms interchangeably.

Borman and Motowidlo (1993) developed 16 items designed to assess contextual performance, reproduced here with some slight modifications (Table 5.7). Their study was designed to assess military personnel (in the United States) and therefore, items that specifically referred to military concepts can be modified to fit the general work context.

© cpaulfell/Shutterstock.com

Extra-role, contextual performance, or OCBs do contribute to the functioning of the organization and ultimately to the organization's overall productivity and effectiveness both in the U.S. and internationally (e.g., Hui, Lee, & Rousseau, 2004; Lievens & Anseel, 2004; Tierney, Bauer, & Potter, 2002). However, experienced managers are more likely to value these extra performance behaviors to a greater degree than are less experienced managers (Befort & Hattrup, 2003). Managerial experience refers to how long

---

TABLE 5.7 Scale for Contextual Performance

1. Comply with instructions even when supervisors are not present
2. Cooperate with others in the team
3. Persist in overcoming obstacles to complete a task
4. Display proper military appearance and bearing
5. Volunteer for additional tasks
6. Follow proper procedures and avoid unauthorized shortcuts
7. Look for a challenging assignment
8. Offer to help others accomplish their work
9. Pay close attention to important details
10. Defend the supervisor's decisions
11. Render proper courtesy
12. Support and encourage a coworker with a problem
13. Take the initiative to solve a work problem
14. Exercise personal discipline and self-control
15. Tackle a difficult work assignment with enthusiasm
16. Volunteer to do more than the job requires to help others or to contribute to the group's effectiveness

Courtesy Zinta Byrne; Source Borman and Motowidlo (1993).

someone has been a manager and in how many roles the person has served as a manager across the organization or across industries. It seems this greater level of experience allows managers to develop an appreciation for the contribution that extra-role behaviors provide to their teams and the organization overall (McCall, Lombardo, & Morrison, 1988).

Supervisors tend to consider contextual performance in their ratings of employee general job performance (Johnson, 2001), even though many researchers have suggested these performance behaviors are mostly overlooked. Unfortunately, the supervisors may be more inclined to view OCBs demonstrated by male employees as extra behaviors, whereas when demonstrated by women, the same OCBs are thought of as part of doing the job (Heilman & Chen, 2005; Kidder & Parks, 2001). Additionally, not all managers consider OCBs or contextual performance as "extra" or beyond the job description even for their male employees. Managers may view many of these contributions as essential for top performance, blurring the lines between "expected" and "doing more than expected". These differences in expectations create challenges for performance appraisal, making communication between employees and management critical—discussions of job expectations and what makes for excellent versus only good performance are essential.

In summary, extra-role, contextual performance, and citizenship performance behaviors all include nonrequired behaviors that contribute to the organization's effectiveness (Motowidlo, 2000).

Several performance models or taxonomies, as provided in this chapter, were based on work with the U.S. military—that's because the military sponsored a number of research centers, since at least World War I, to provide effective selection, classification, training, and leadership solutions.

What is Not Performance in Organizations?

Performance, as a broad term, is not simply employees' accumulated behavior at work (Motowidlo, 2003). People do many things at work over the course of a work day, some of which do not help or promote achieving organizational goals. These behaviors are not considered job performance because they do not contribute to the organization or toward fulfilling the job requirements, and they are not just the opposite of job performance or OCBs (Dalal, 2005). Instead, they are called *counterproductive work behaviors*.

Counterproductive Work Behaviors

Counterproductive work behaviors, such as taking excessively long breaks or negative gossiping, are intentionally negative actions that cause harm to the organization or its members in some way (Robinson & Bennett, 1995). Examples of counterproductive work behaviors include: avoiding work, purposefully incorrectly performing tasks, aggression, verbal abuse such as being rude and insulting, theft, sexual harassment, rumor spreading, sabotage, and disruptive behavior (e.g., Spector & Fox, 2002). The category of destructive/hazardous behaviors from Murphy's (1989) taxonomy of job performance may be considered comprising counterproductive work behaviors. Like OCBs, counterproductive work behavior can be directed at a person, multiple people, or the organization (e.g., Dalal, Lam, Weiss, Welch, & Hulin, 2009).

Several scholars have made efforts to categorize counterproductive work behaviors, but no one model of categories has become the standard. Robinson

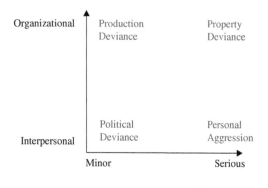

FIGURE 5.1 Deviant Workplace Behaviors (adapted from Robinson & Bennett, 1995)

and Bennett's (1995) typology of deviant workplace behaviors is one example of the many classification systems, as is Abué, Rousseau, Mama, and Morin's (2009) typology of counterproductive behavior in teams.

Deviant Workplace Behaviors

Robinson and Bennett (1995) referred to counterproductive work behaviors as employee deviance. Based on their study of a number of different samples, they developed a four quadrant model (Figure 5.1 and Table 5.8).

Team Counterproductive Behaviors

Work teams (discussed in Chapter 7) may possess their own specific type of counterproductive work behavior, targeted at disrupting the internal functioning of the team as opposed to the organization. Specifically, counterproductive behavior in teams can fall into one of four categories: parasitism, interpersonal aggression, boastfulness, and misuse of team resources (Aubé et al., 2009).

Parasitism involves team members trying to get others to do their work. They may reduce their own efforts, pretend to be occupied with something to force others to take on the task or responsibility, be absent for longer than needed, or claim an illness or family event that requires leaving work early or being away from work for periods of time. *Interpersonal aggression*

TABLE 5.8 Typology of Counterproductive Work Behaviors

Quadrant Label	Example Behaviors	Level	Severity
Production Deviance	Leaving early, before your shift is over Taking long and excessive breaks Slowing work pace intentionally Wasteful behaviour	Organizational	Minor
Political Deviance	Show bias and favoritism Gossip and spread rumors Blame others for work failures Intentionally try to get ahead at the expense of others	Interpersonal	Minor
Property Deviance	Destroy equipment Accept bribes Lie about when you worked Steal office supplies and other products from the company	Organizational	Serious
Personal Aggression	Sexual harassment Office harassment Verbal abuse and rudeness Stealing from coworkers or supervisor Placing coworkers or supervisor in direct physical harm	Interpersonal	Serious

Courtesy Zinta Byrne. Source: Robinson and Bennett (1995).

refers to negative behaviors toward other team members such as denigrating a team member, spreading rumors, gossiping behind team members' backs, and making discriminatory or prejudicial statements about a team member. *Boastfulness* is just what it seems—boasting, bragging, or over-exaggerating one's own contributions in comparison to those of other team members. These behaviors become harmful because: they involve taking credit for others' work, claiming the team's success as solely due to one's own efforts, minimizing team members' contributions, publically bragging about one's own achievements and thus minimizing and putting down the achievements of other members of the group, and blaming others for mistakes, thereby removing oneself from any responsibility for things gone wrong. Lastly, *misuse of resources* represents a category comprising behaviors directed toward inappropriate use of material and equipment designed for team use. This may include wasting office supplies or raw material needed for producing the team product, carelessly damaging materials without a sense of responsibility, not following safety regulations when using equipment, and demonstrating a general lack of responsibility about the efficient use of limited resources that must be shared by the entire team. Results of studies on the team typology of counterproductive behaviors have shown they negatively affect team performance (Aubé & Rousseau, 2011).

Why are counterproductive work behaviors not considered just the opposite of job performance or contextual performance?

All counterproductive work behaviors negatively affect the organization's ability to meet its goals. Ultimately, managers are responsible for supervising performance to keep employees working effectively, efficiently, and hopefully, also demonstrating those valuable extra-role behaviors.

Exercise 5.2

Compare and contrast citizenship behavior with contextual performance, and compare/contrast those with counterproductive work behavior. Give an example of each.

How Do We Manage Performance?

Performance management is about how organizations use appraisals and feedback to make performance-based decisions and improve employee performance. Performance management refers to a "systematic, data-oriented approach to managing people at work that relies on positive reinforcement as the major way to maximizing performance" (Daniels, 1989, p.4). Appraisals are the evaluations themselves and they typically fall within the responsibility of the employee's immediate supervisor. In **self-managed teams**, employees may contribute to the appraisal of each team member by providing feedback, but there is usually one lead person or a single manager who is responsible for assigning the final performance rating that dictates raises or promotion opportunities.

Appraisals can have many different purposes including contributing to the quality of staffing and administrative decisions such as promotions or pay raises, helping employees make better job fit decisions (e.g., a bad performance appraisal may be indicative of poor skill to job match), contributing to continued socialization and developing employees' attachment to the organization, or serving a legal function for organizations by providing documentation of poor or questionable performance (Murphy & Cleveland, 1995). When "done effectively, performance management communicates what's important to the organization, drives employees to achieve results, and implements the organization's strategy" (Pulakos & O'Leary, 2011, p.147)

In organizations where appraisals are used, managers conduct performance appraisals once per year or twice per year at best, and they evaluate their employees based on the past accumulative performance. The assumption with this model is that performance is stable over time. However, within-person variability exists—people do not perform at the same level day in and day out (see Borman, 1991; Fisher & Noble, 2004; Stewart & Nandkeolyar, 2006). Furthermore, assessments made over a long period of time show that as people learn their jobs, their performance increases and stabilizes (Ployhart & Hakel, 1998). Researchers have also found that the complexity of the job factors into the stability, where employees can perform at a more stable level in simple jobs than more highly complex jobs where performance levels fluctuate more (Sturman, Cheramie, & Cashen, 2005). Unfortunately, although substantial research evidence has now confirmed that performance is variable, appraisal systems still assume that performance is stable.

The appraisal meeting where the appraisal is discussed between employee and manager (Figure 5.2) presents another aspect of the entire performance management system, in addition to the actual measurement of performance. Substantial research has shown that employees' perceptions of the fairness of the appraisal process, and how fairly they are treated during the appraisal meeting, affects whether they accept the feedback (e.g., Leung, Su, & Morris, 2001).

The more the manager knows and understands the rating system and the use of the ratings within the organization, knows the employee's job expectations and processes, understands how to convey fairness during the appraisal process, and is trained to observe and evaluate performance, the better the overall evaluation and the more likely the manager can help the employee understand how to improve their performance. The appraisal meeting provides an opportunity for the manager to clarify confusions with the feedback, and for the employee to ask questions about the feedback and opportunities for improvement.

The purpose of measuring and communicating performance components is to change

Ask questions during your performance appraisal meeting to get a better understanding of how you were assessed, what the criteria are for good performance, and how can you improve to exceed organizational expectations. The more involved you are in managing your own performance, the more satisfied you'll be with the outcome.

FIGURE 5.2 The Appraisal Meeting

© Jeanette Dietl/Shutterstock, Inc.

performance, or more specifically, increase and improve it. There are a number of different ways that organizations and managers can manage performance, but one interesting approach uses the principles of operant conditioning—or reinforcement.

Using Operant Conditioning to Change Performance

Based on the works of Skinner's (1972) behavioral modification and operant conditioning, Daniels (1989) suggested that to positively affect change in employees' job performance, one must focus on changing behavior by paying attention to both the antecedents of performance (i.e., triggers, things that cause performance) and the consequences of performance (i.e., what happens after a person performs; Figure 5.3). Operant conditioning is a learning process that involves changing the likelihood of a response by influencing the consequences of that response through the manipulation of antecedents and rewards. Consequences are either positive or negative.

Antecedents to performance generally include job design, goals and priorities, policies, resources (e.g., tools, work environment), training and education, norms or actions of the group, and communications such as feedback or delegations. Daniels proposed three classes of antecedents that have the most powerful effect on employees' job performance: (a) those that describe expectations, such as job descriptions or well specified delegation, and standards for job performance; (b) those historically associated with specific consequences such as making a quota and receiving a bonus directly tied to achieving that quota; and (c) behaviors that happened just before the desired performance, such as a client asking for advice or a solution.

Antecedents get their power from the consequences themselves; thus, an antecedent triggers behavior but unless the consequence reinforces the behavior, the antecedent loses its power to trigger the behavior again (Daniels, 1989; Skinner, 1972). For example, if there are unintended positive consequences associated with undesirable behavior (such as more attention), don't be surprised if the undesired behavior continues. The opposite is also true. If desirable consequences are associated with performance, you can expect that performance to continue. Not all consequences are created equal—some consequences increase behavior whereas others decrease behavior.

Consequences that remove something negative or provide something positive will increase behavior. Consequences that cause something negative or withhold something positive decrease behavior.

According to operant conditioning, employees' performance can be modified by paying attention to the consequences within the work environment associated with their performance. For example, good performers

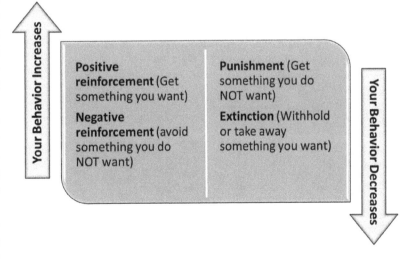

FIGURE 5.3   Performance Management

Courtesy Zinta Byrne. Source: Daniels (1989).

are often given more assignments and responsibility because they get the job done quickly and efficiently. However, more assignments and more responsibility without accompanying pay or time off can, for some, be a form of punishment—these employees feel punished for working hard; the harder they work, the more they are given, while others who aren't getting the job done are given less to do. What might seem like a positive reward by management to show the top performer that their work is appreciated turns out to be a form of punishment and the result is the top performer withdraws behavior at work to offset the added workload and perceived inequity. Rather than encourage even more work (which is what the manager might have had in mind by giving more responsibility to the employee), this punishment decreases the amount of work the employee does. A better approach in this case might be to acknowledge the high performer's good work and ask them what motivates them to keep working at that level—do they want more responsibility, recognition, or something else within your means? Table 5.9 provides examples of positive and negative reinforcement. The consequence serves as a reinforcement for the antecedent behavior.

TABLE 5.9   Examples of Using Antecedent/Consequence Management

Antecedent	Behavior #1	Consequence	Reinforcement	Result	Subsequent Behavior
Want to do well in class	Read the chapter	Do well on chapter homework	Positive	Behavior #1 increases	Read more chapters
Want boss's positive attention	Make suggestions for improving the job	Boss rewards you	Positive	Behavior #1 increases	Make more suggestions
Lazy	Complain about the hard work	Boss reassigns hard job to others	Negative	Behavior #1 increases	Complain more about the hard work
Want to avoid failing the next exam	Study for the exam	Avoid failing the next exam	Negative	Behavior #1 increases	Study for the next exam
Want to avoid losing points to poor attendance	Show up to class	Avoid losing points	Negative	Behavior #1 increases	Show up to class every time
Want to do well in class	Study for the exam	Fail the exam	Punishment	Behavior #1 decreases	Will not study for the next exam
Want boss's positive attention	Make suggestions for improving the job	Boss ignores suggestion even though previously acknowledged them	Extinction	Behavior #1 decreases	Stop making suggestions

The complaining employee serves as a great example of how consequences reinforce undesired behavior (see Daniels, p. 27–28). Often managers pay most attention to those employees who complain the most. These employees create a lot of managerial headaches because of their complaints. The problem, however, is that these complainers make their issues the most salient and urgent for resolution, leaving the good worker without managerial attention. What results is that the manager ends up paying attention to the complainers and not to those who actually work hard and deserve attention. Without knowing it, the manager has reinforced the complainers' behaviors and the complainers will continue to complain, if not complain even more. Table 5.9 provides examples of negative reinforcement, which increase performance by taking away a negative consequence. For example, being embarrassed in class is a negative consequence, something you don't want. To take away that negative consequence, you don't ask questions in class—thus you avoid showing that you are not prepared and avoid being embarrassed. By avoiding being embarrassed, you increase the behavior of staying quiet in class (not asking questions).

Consequences are most effective when they occur while employees are performing the desired (or undesired) action or shortly thereafter. Thus, bonuses given months after the excellent performance, raises given at the end of the year, and annual performance evaluations that refer to performance behaviors from a year ago do little to change employees' behavior. Thus, how performance is evaluated and when it is acknowledged makes a big difference in whether it is stifled or encouraged.

Exercise 5.3

Create your own version of Table 5.9 using the same headings as Table 5.9, but insert your own antecedents and behaviors.

How Do We Evaluate Performance?

Evaluating performance is a bit complex. There are a number of different approaches and rating systems, many customized within the organization. Much of the power in performance management is embedded within the assessment process, the measurement and evaluation of performance. There are a few recommended practices for assessment and for encouraging performance in organizations.

The main outcome of performance appraisal is feedback for employees on how well they are meeting expectations and what they might do differently to improve or grow. As Murphy and Cleveland (1995) noted, appraisal can have many purposes (e.g., improve performance, position for promotion, political fights, position for dismissal); however, for simplicity, let's just focus on the use of appraisal for improving performance.

For employees to receive feedback, the feedback giver (the evaluator) must be appropriately trained on giving feedback using the appraisal form chosen or developed by the organization. Most appraisal forms are general and incorporate rating scales from 1–3 or 1–5 corresponding with "needs improvement" to "exceeds job expectations" or similar such anchors. Some organizations, however, have check boxes instead of rating scales simply to indicate whether the employee meets or does not meet the expectation.

The categories rated depend on the organization, the position, and what is valued in the organization in terms of competencies or behaviors. For example, in the 1990s Hewlett–Packard (HP) included a "Teamwork" category on many of the appraisals, emphasizing that not only is individual performance important but so is contribution to the team, conducting oneself as a respectable team player, and balancing the need to get one's own work done with the need to help team members and meet the team goals. The categories selected on appraisal forms usually map onto the knowledge, skills, and abilities that employees must have and demonstrate for effective performance in their job class or job family (e.g., first level engineer, second level engineer, master engineer, distinguished engineer).

Many problems with appraisal systems, whether online or paper, lie within the scale anchors and how employees are rated within each category. The anchors and expectations for ratings are unclear, leaving managers to figure out on their own whether an employee is excellent or just very good (Longenecker, 1989). Many of the problems with ratings include errors such as halo, recency, and first impression effects (Ivancevich, 1979). Halo errors represent a cognitive bias that refers to creating an overall impression of an individual based on a single characteristic, rather than on that individual's actual performance. For example, if you think Bob is a funny, energetic person and you generally like him, you'll probably rate his performance on a specific task higher than you should because of your overall positive impression of him. Likewise, the recency effect is also a bias that can be seen when a manager rates an employee based only on their most recent performance, such as the last few months, thereby failing to consider performance across the entire year. For example, if Ming-Li failed to complete several job tasks within the last month, you're likely to rate performance lower on the evaluation regardless of the fact that Ming-Li delivered work on time every month of the last year up until this past month. Lastly, just as everyone forms a first impression when meeting others, managers form a first impression of an employee. Importantly here is that this first impression may subsequently influence the manager's rating of the employee's overall performance, causing the manager to discount or overlook performance over time. As an example, suppose Boris, new to the team, demonstrates high respect for all team members, takes on extra work tasks, keeps a clean desk, and for the first week of work shows up an hour before everyone else. These behaviors are sure to create a positive impression of Boris for the boss. That positive impression may carry over for quite some time, even though as the months progress Boris avoids taking on extra work, shows up on time instead of early, and ignores some team members. If the early performance is more salient than the recent decline in performance, the first impression may outweigh recency effects. Though halo, recency, and first impression biases form naturally and are not the result of "bad management," they can be controlled with knowledge and skill development for managers.

Some managers may be more harsh or lenient than others, unable to withhold personal biases, or fail to observe enough behavior to make an accurate rating. These errors and inconsistencies amongst managers make comparisons across employees tough for the management team since none of the ratings are based on the same criteria, and leave employees feeling unfairly evaluated. Organizations can reduce such rating errors by offering training for their managers on accurate performance rating (e.g., Cardy & Dobbins, 1994; Davis & Mount, 1984; Ivancevich, 1979; Latham, Wexley, & Pursell, 1975). Frame-of-reference training also reduces halo and leniency errors (Day & Sulsky, 1995; Sulsky & Day, 1992; Woehr, 1994). In frame-of-reference training, managers read vignettes of poor, average, and good performers, and practice providing performance feedback for each employee. The managers receive evaluations on the accuracy of their ratings, with the intent to help them calibrate or align their ratings with each other. A study of 149 managers from 22 different U.S. manufacturing and service organizations provided the following list of rating competencies (groups of knowledge, skills, and abilities) necessary for effective appraisals (see Table 5.10; Fink & Longenecker, 1998).

Despite the evidence that training makes a difference, few organizations put the time and effort into this important skill-building training for managers (Grote, 1996). Reasons why organizations may not train their managers include assuming managers already know how to conduct appraisals, lack of resources for training (e.g., money, trainers to do the training, time), or ineffective leaders who are unaware of the complexity of conducting effective appraisals (Fink & Longenecker, 1998).

Similar challenges with appraisals exist internationally, and training is noted as a critical and essential tool for ensuring accurate appraisals in the global work environment (Appelbaum, Roy, & Gilliland, 2011). Considering the multinational nature of many companies, the cultural components of the workplace such as value for hierarchy or teams versus individual success matter in the appraisal context as do different legal requirements—countries differ in the amount of

TABLE 5.10   Managerial Competencies Required for Effective Performance Appraisal

Knowledge	Must know the purpose of the rating form, the procedure for using the rating form, and shortcomings associated with the organizational appraisal system. Also includes knowledge of legal and compliance requirements; must understand what makes a defensible appraisal and inappropriate reference to race, sex, age, national origin, religion, or disability.
Communication	Includes written and verbal skills. Must be able to communicate job duties and clarify performance expectations, which means they must understand what their employees do and the scope of each position. Be able to write about specific behaviors and consequences, write for creating atmosphere that encourages two-way discussion, and removing ambiguity.
Decision-making	Must have effective decision-making skills and demonstrate sound judgment. Training and practice in how to make rating decisions can help improve decision-making.
Coaching	Must demonstrate the ability to coach (ongoing, not just once a year) any type of performance situation. Includes development and career guidance or counseling. Includes knowing how to give feedback, tracking and recording employees' performance, and how to effectively praise. Helping with short- and long-term goal setting, career progression, and development strategies
Delegation	Must be able to effectively delegate and empower employees. Creating accountability, clarifying goals, and ensuring employee has resources and power to complete the delegation.
Observational	Managers must be able to objectively observe behavior, document observations regularly, and recognize critical performance dimensions.
Conflict resolution	Must be able to resolve conflicts, problem-solve for collaborative solutions. Must be able to handle employees who react negatively to their appraisal by creating atmosphere of trust—this depends heavily on a fair appraisal and a fair process.

legal oversight and accountability for human or personnel management. For example, Europe has a requirement that organizations operating in Europe must establish European Work Councils, which consist of employees who represent the European employees of the company and who are consulted before human resource practices are approved. These bodies or groups are similar to unions, who protect employees' rights and enforce consistent policies. Similarly, laws established in South Africa in 1996 require that organizations put performance management systems in place to ensure organizations are run effectively and efficiently.

There are many mechanisms for specifying how managers should evaluate and rate their employees' performance. Most are covered in detail in books on Industrial Psychology. However, as an organizational psychologist and organizational behavior specialist, it helps to have some understanding of what goes into some assessment tools because how employees are rated affects their motivation (Chapter 3) and their attitudes (Chapter 4), as well as their performance (this chapter).

Behavioral Anchor Rating Scale

Another problem inherent in performance appraisals is the lack of clearly identified behaviors associated with a particular rating on the scale. One type of performance appraisal scale recommended as good practice and that provides clearly identified behaviors for consistent ratings is the behaviorally anchored rating scale (BARS) or behavior observation scales (BOS). The scale provides specific behaviors representative of gradations of performance. Although BARS are time consuming to develop, these forms of rating scales provide clear anchors for both employees and managers using the scales. The performance dimensions of the BARS are developed by those using the system, resulting in more accurate descriptions than appraisals developed at the corporate office far removed from the actual job and person being rated. However, BARS focus on rating behaviors as opposed to measuring or quantifying output, which means they are best for jobs where there is a direct connection between behaviors and output (Lee, 1985).

A five-step process describes how BARS are developed (Cocanougher & Ivancevich, 1978).

1. People who know about the job describe specific examples of effective and ineffective performance behaviors.

2. A review team (usually group of managers supervising employees in these jobs) is put in place to evaluate all the behaviors accumulated in step 1, reducing them by removing redundancies or refining the list to key examples. The goal is to reduce the list to 5–12 dimensions.

3. This list of 5–12 dimensions is then given to a different group of managers and/or employees who have extensive knowledge of the job. Their task is to assign the behaviors to the appropriate dimensions, which determines which behaviors to retain or discard. Specifically, behaviors that are assigned to the same dimensions as what the group in step 2 did are retained for that dimension. Those not assigned to the same

dimension are either discarded or reevaluated. By having this second group review the behaviors and pick which dimension they believe the behavior represents, the BARS developers can be more confident that the behavior is a good representation of the dimension because it was independently identified by a second group. This step determines which behaviors best represent which dimensions for the final BARS.

4. The second group then assigns points to the behaviors to reflect how well the behaviors represent performance on their particular dimension. Level of agreement between raters is then assessed—higher agreement means the behavior is retained as the representative behavior for the dimension. This is done for each dimension.

5. The remaining behaviors are then used as the behavioral anchors for performance on each dimension. Each dimension receives its own BARS such as that shown in Figure 5.4, which shows a BARS for Team Work.

Appraisals may not, however, incorporate BARS because they are customized for the specific job family or job and organization—they require time and money to develop and to ensure accuracy and differentiation between the different anchors. Additionally, each set of BARS are only applicable to the job for which they are created—thus, the system may not easily be used across jobs or divisions in the organization depending on the specificity of the various behaviors identified or uniqueness of the job.

Just as there are varying opinions as to how employees are rated and using what tools, as well as what behaviors should be rated, there are also differing opinions as to who should do the actual rating.

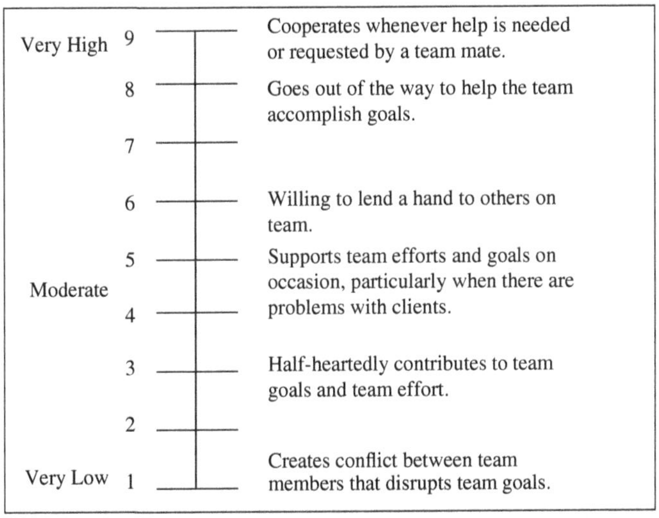

> If the organization doesn't have BARS, ask your boss for examples of behaviors that top performers demonstrate, just so you can get your own examples of what behaviors are considered excellent.

Very High	9	Cooperates whenever help is needed or requested by a team mate.
	8	Goes out of the way to help the team accomplish goals.
	7	
	6	Willing to lend a hand to others on team.
	5	Supports team efforts and goals on occasion, particularly when there are
Moderate	4	problems with clients.
	3	Half-heartedly contributes to team goals and team effort.
	2	
Very Low	1	Creates conflict between team members that disrupts team goals.

FIGURE 5.4 Example of a BARS Performance Rating for the Team Work Dimension

Courtesy Zinta Byrne. Source: Cocanougher and Ivancevich (1978).

Who Should Do the Rating?

Typically, one's boss or supervisor is responsible for conducting the performance evaluation and review session. However, research supports that a variety of sources rating an employee can contribute to a better overall performance evaluation (Conway & Huffcutt, 1997), including other-assessment, self-assessment, and peer-assessment.

Other-Assessment

Why is evaluating performance hard and potentially complicated?

Multisource rating systems (e.g., 360 degree ratings, where the employee, peers, subordinates, bosses, and clients provide performance ratings) have become more popular in organizations (Bracken & Church, 2013). Some argue that the strength of the **360-degree feedback** lies in discussing the discrepancies between how individuals rate themselves and how others rate them. Since job performance is a function of aptitude, task understanding, decision-making, persistence, and facilitating the performance of others, how others perceive one's performance is a valuable source of information for self-improvement (Nilsen & Campbell, 1993). Additionally, the 360-degree ratings by peers and managers have been positively correlated with job performance (Beehr, Ivanitskaya, Hansen, Erofeev, & Gudanowski, 2001), suggesting these ratings may be particularly relevant. In other countries, however, 360-degree feedback may not be as valued because the idea of getting subordinates' feedback on a superior's performance may violate cultural values and norms (e.g., Fletcher & Perry, 2002). For example, Hofstede (1980) determined that Serbians rate their national culture very high on **power distance**. Power distance is one of Hofstede's dimensions of culture that describes the degree to which the society accepts power differences in organizations or institutions. A high power distance culture accepts that power is distributed unevenly. In organizations, lower levels within the organization accept and respect that higher levels in the organization have more power and authority (Hofstede, Hofstede, & Minkov, 2010). The implications for 360-degree feedback is that Serbians respect the inaccessibility and authority of superiors, such that it would be considered a violation of their cultural norms to ask lower levels in the power structure for feedback on the performance of employees at higher levels in the organization.

Self-Assessment

Employees can participate in self-assessment, which refers to them evaluating their own performance. We tend to believe we perform at a higher rate than others do, probably for ego preservation and consequences of the **fundamental attribution error**. The fundamental attribution error occurs when we attribute our successes to internal factors and failures to external factors, but attribute others' successes to external factors and failures to internal factors (Ross, 1977). Despite generally higher ratings of our own performance, it turns out these ratings tend not to display halo errors (Thornton, 1980). Self-ratings appear different from supervisor ratings because employees see themselves differently than do supervisors (Thornton, 1980). Such self-assessments can play a valuable role in developmental discussions as opposed to the evaluative or administrative component of the meeting (Greguras, Robie, Schleichea, & Goff, 2003). Self-assessment has been used by Chief Executive Officers (CEOs) who use the tool to facilitate communications between themselves and their board members with the goal of helping the CEOs improve (Athitakis, 2013).

Peer-Assessment

Coworkers often provide feedback on their peers, thus providing peer-assessment used for the evaluation process. Sometimes the process is formal, and calculations of **inter-rater agreement** (i.e., agreement of ratings between multiple peers) are made to determine the extent to which peers agree on specific ratings of specific behaviors. Sometimes the process is informal where the supervisor solicits feedback from peers and uses whatever information is volunteered by coworkers. Similar to the difference in perception between self- and supervisory-ratings of job performance, peers have a different perspective on what is and is not good job performance, which can also differ from the supervisor's view (Borman, 1974; Holzbach, 1978; Shore, Shore, & Thornton, 1992). Even though they may have different ideas of what is good and bad job performance, it turns out peers often provide similar ratings as supervisors (Conway & Huffcutt, 1997).

Although many organizations debate how to manage performance, there is not much debate over how to get the best performance out of employees. Several approaches have been proposed and tested, including those that involve manipulating the work environment to boost motivation and job attitudes, such as job satisfaction.

How Do We Encourage High Performance?

Encouraging performance requires understanding its specific components so that efforts to increase it can be appropriately targeted. People differ in performance as a function of three determinants: procedural knowledge and skill, declarative knowledge, and motivation (Campbell, 1990). *Procedural knowledge and skill* refers to knowing how to do a task, and understanding what needs to be done and how. Procedural knowledge and skill requires *declarative knowledge*, which refers to the facts—understanding the requirements of the task. For example, students learning to be physicians spend years first gaining the declarative knowledge for their profession. They must first learn physiology and anatomy, chemistry, biology, and neuroscience before they learn how these systems combine. They must develop a substantial knowledge base before they begin to learn how to perform surgery. They may then spend years in residency practicing and developing their procedural knowledge before they become independent physicians capable of performing surgery.

Researchers have argued that differences in performance are most likely a function of differences in declarative and procedural knowledge, and motivation (Campbell, McCloy, Oppler, & Sager, 1993), which again suggests that if you can pinpoint which area is causing the performance gap, you can focus energies on resolving those gaps. Employees who know what to do, but not how, need training. Employees who know what to do but do not want to may be helped by some of the principles discussed in Chapter 3 on Motivation.

Watch https://www.ted.com/talks/adam_grant_the_surprising_habits_of_original_thinkers? to get some perspective on creative performers.

Motivation to perform is created both internally and externally. Though both were discussed in Chapter 3, other aspects of the work environment are specific to affecting motivation to perform.

Company Example 5.1	Deloitte Reinvents Their Performance Management System

Deloitte employs about 287,000 people in their multinational professional services company. In 2015, Deloitte determined through internal surveys that their performance management system was cumbersome and not driving desired outcomes like performance. Their performance management system was previously designed to set cascading goals at the start of the year and then determine if people met their objectives at the end of the year. This process involved about two million hours or more of employees time per year! Rather than continue with 360° ratings, or getting multiple people's ratings of employees (which turned out to be inconsistent depending on what they thought was being rated), Deloitte changed their system to only ask the project lead to provide four statements about each employee—statements focused on their own actions with respect to the employee—thus, asking them what they would do with the employee, as opposed to what they "think" about the employee. Rather than wait until the end of the year to conduct performance reviews, because Deloitte's business is project-based, they conduct reviews at the end of every project. In addition, employees themselves are encouraged to ask about their performance and not wait for the project lead to initiate the discussion. Lastly, the system was changed to encourage and focus on the conversation about performance rather than conducting a single review and producing a number and a report to quantify/objectify each employee.

Work Environment

When considering performance and the work environment, a fair and supportive workplace can encourage employees to demonstrate OCBs and contextual performance (Moorman, 1991). Additionally, work environments where employees feel their employers have met their obligations tend to perform at high levels, as do employees in low-constraint (i.e., see section below on minimizing constraints) work environments. Work environments fraught with organizational politics tend to inhibit performance, and therefore positive work climates are essential. The next section reviews various aspects of the work environment that play a role in promoting high employee job performance.

Support and Fairness

Social exchange theory (Blau, 1964) and **psychological contracts** (Rousseau, 1990) have been used to explain why employees demonstrate performance and extra-role behaviors when provided with fair and supportive work environments. Using social exchange theory, Byrne, Pitts, Chiaburu, and Steiner (2011) demonstrated that 119 full-time employees (working for a U.S.-based firm) who perceived their managers as trustworthy and as providing support reported having high job performance and commitment to their organization. Social exchange theory suggests that these employees reciprocated the support they received with high job performance.

Similarly using social exchange theory, Hon and Lu (2013) studied 232 service employees in multinational hotels in China and found a positive relationship between fair leaders and their employees' job performance. They argued that employees exchanged job performance for the fairness received from their leaders. Organizational support consistently and positively predicts job performance, and just happens to be grounded in social exchange theory (e.g., Darolia, Kumari, & Darolia, 2010). Thus, fairness and support appear to encourage high performance, as explained by social exchange theory.

Fulfilled Obligations

A psychological contract is defined as individual beliefs employees have about reciprocal obligations between them and their organization (Rousseau, 1990). Employees have certain expectations about what organizations should provide (e.g., fairness, promotions, pay) and organizations have expectations of its employees (e.g., hard work, conscientiousness, commitment). Importantly, these joint expectations are unspoken and unwritten—they are assumed to exist. Using psychological contract theory, which describes this two-way relationship of assumed obligations, Tsui, Lin, and Yu (2013) showed that 361 Taiwanese employees perceiving a fulfilled contract (employer meets its end of the bargain) demonstrated high job performance and commitment. When psychological contracts are violated (employer fails to deliver on employees' expectations) employees respond by withdrawing their performance behaviors (Suazo, 2009).

How Do Managers Apply Fairness, Support, and Obligations?

Managers can apply social exchange theory and psychological contract theory to the work environment in efforts to encourage higher levels of job performance. Recognizing that employees perform in exchange for fairness, support, autonomy, pay, and other benefits, enables managers to focus their efforts on getting these benefits or redesigning jobs to allow for these benefits. Additionally, restating the benefits that the organization provides clarifies the psychological contract and calls attention to how the organization has fulfilled employees' expectations. Managers might also take the extra step by having a discussion with employees to find out what they feel the organization expects of them and what they expect of the organization. Clarifying these underlying, unspoken expectations can help avoid future misunderstandings.

Organizational Politics

Another aspect of work environments is the political nature of decisions and agreements. Work environments fraught with perceptions of organizational politics, where individuals or groups of individuals take actions to advance their own positions at the expense of others, discourage OCBs. The more employees perceive the environment to be political (therefore less fair; Byrne, 2005), the less likely they are to demonstrate OCBs (Witt, Kacmar, Carlson, & Zivnuska, 2002). Thus, empirical evidence supports relationships between positive aspects of the work environment and high job performance.

Elements that Increase Job Satisfaction

Job performance is positively related (about $r = .30$) to job satisfaction (Judge, Thoresen, Bono, & Patton, 2001). Thus, any improvements made to the job that enhance job satisfaction may also coincide with improvements in job performance. As noted in Chapter 3 on Motivation, enriching core job dimensions as noted in the Job Characteristics Theory results in job satisfaction. Many of the redesign approaches noted in Chapter 3 have the positive consequence of adding to the social exchange relationship and demonstrating fulfillment of psychological contract.

Case Study on Climate and Job Performance

Though empirical evidence is hard to come by, at least one case study shows that performance improves when the **organizational climate** improves (Houldsworth & Machin, 2008). Organizational climate refers to how individuals in organizations experience and make sense of their work environment (Schneider, 2000), and what components go into creating a shared organizational experience. It refers to the day-to-day procedures, policies, routines, and rewards that people experience regularly while working every day (Jones & James, 1979; Rentsch, 1990; Schneider, 1990).

BELRON, a large organization that installs and repairs glass for automobiles, has companies under a variety of names (e.g., Carglass, Autoglass, O'Brien) in 30 different countries. They attribute their growth in performance to positive improvements in their organizational climate directly driven by leadership development. The leadership development was focused on making a positive and high-performing climate. They assessed climate along six dimensions:

- Flexibility: minimal bureaucracy, foster innovation
- Responsibility: autonomy and risk (reasonable amount) are encouraged
- Standards: high standards, with continual improvement
- Rewards: rewards/recognition are performance-based
- Clarity: mission and roles are clear
- Team commitment: pride, dedication, and cooperation are felt by team members

BERLON gives annual climate surveys to determine the gaps in climate, and to focus development workshops on the low scoring areas. The results of the climate surveys are then reviewed and managers' areas are grouped into one of the following four levels by number of weaknesses in climate dimensions (i.e., gaps in climate): (1) high-performing (at most 1 gap only), (2) energizing (at most two gaps only), (3) neutral (at most three gaps only), and (4) demotivating (have many gaps in climate). BELRON reported that when their climate was improved through leadership development programs, demotivating climates were transformed into high-performing climates in about four years. Profits resulting from increased employee performance were reportedly 125% higher than before the leadership program. Although the study at BELRON was not rigorous enough to determine causation or rule out possible alternative explanations, they did note that as their climate improved and was rated more positively by employees and clients, the performance of the organization also improved.

Exercise 5.4

In a brief few statements, describe the various methods of evaluating performance by comparing and contrasting their strengths and weaknesses. You might consider creating a table to organize your comparisons.

Minimizing Constraints

Issues with job performance may not be a simple gap in declarative or procedural knowledge, or even motivation. Problems with performance may arise from situational environmental constraints at work, constraints beyond an employee's control. Researchers have identified at least 11 general situations at work or things done at work that when constrained cause negative work performance (Peters & O'Connor, 1980, 1988; Spector & Jex, 1998). Constraints related to these identified areas need not all be present at the same time, nor apply to every work situation.

1. Job-related information
   - ❏ Information from a variety of sources, which is needed for the job assignment.

2. Tools and equipment
   - ❏ Specific equipment, tools, or machines that are needed to do the job.

3. Materials and supplies

4. Budgetary support
   - ❏ Financial support and resources to do the job; this may include travel, long-distance or international travel, job-related entertainment, hiring new personnel or retaining existing personnel, hiring temp workers. Does not include one's own salary.

5. Required services or help from others

6. Task preparation
   - ❏ Includes previous training or education that is relevant to the job.

7. Time availability
   - ❏ Time needed to do the job when taking into consideration interruptions, time constraints imposed on the task, unnecessary meetings, and non-job-related distractions.

8. Work environment
   - ❏ Physical components of the job such as lighting, safety, noise, temperature, comfort in general.

9. Scheduling of activities

10. Transportation

11. Job-related authority

Research has shown that employee performance ratings in low-constrained work environments are higher than for those in high-constrained work situations (Steel & Mento, 1986). Thus, performance can be encouraged by attempting to remove constraints proactively or once they are encountered.

Work or Job Experience

Another way to encourage high job performance is to increase job experience. Level of job experience positively affects job knowledge, which positively influences job performance (Schmidt, Hunter, & Outerbridge, 1986). Increases in job experience not only lead to higher gains in overall job knowledge, but also to improvements in job skills. Thus, more relevant high quality work experience seems to translate into higher job performance (Quiñones, Ford, & Teachout, 1995), but only up to a certain point (McDaniel, Schmidt, & Hunter, 1988). On average, after about three years on the job no major gains in performance are made due to increased experience on the job. Job experience, though, is not just about time in the role. One can gain valuable job experience through a variety of assignments (like job rotation) that create learning opportunities and chances to practice implementing declarative knowledge.

Non-manipulatable Factors Associated with High Performance

There are other factors associated with high performance that organizations should know about but cannot easily change. **Conscientiousness** (a personality trait characterized by efficiency, dependability, and self-discipline) predicts job performance (Barrick & Mount, 1991), but changing someone's level of conscientiousness is essentially not possible or incredibly hard to do. Likewise, people with extroverted personalities tend to demonstrate higher performance levels in jobs that require extraversion (e.g., managers, sales professionals), but one's level of extraversion is hard, if not impossible, to change. There are a number of studies examining the personality correlates of OCBs and/or performance including international studies such as Bourdage, Lee, Lee, and Shin's (2012) study using a sample of 262 Korean employees (they found conscientiousness predicted OCBs), that suggest personality traits can be strong predictors of high job performance. Though personality cannot be easily manipulated by the organization, knowing that certain personalities are related to high performance may allow organizations to create work teams that are composed of at least one person with personality traits that predict performance, in an effort to have that person encourage others to perform at the same level. This form of purposefully staging encouragement is like deliberately using peer pressure to drive behavior. By pairing employees with complementary personalities and skills, the organization can generate higher overall team performance, rather than just high individual performance.

Why should we focus on performance appraisals in organizational psychology and organizational behavior?

How Do Managers Use the Information in this Chapter in the Workplace?

Of all the chapters thus far, this one might be the most applicable for managers and easily/readily applied. Managers can use the theories and taxonomies in this chapter in several ways. Managers can use effectiveness, efficiency, productivity, and utility to clarify expectations for performance for employees. By clearly identifying what each means, providing examples relevant to employees' jobs, and explaining how their relative importance to the job (i.e., is it more important for employees to be efficient or effective?), managers can help employees understand what is expected and how they will be evaluated. The taxonomies of performance might be used to develop a performance management and appraisal model. Namely managers can set up a rubric for evaluating performance based on the different performance categories within either Campbell's or Murphy's model—depending on the relevancy of the model to the specific job. Similarly, specifying what is considered task performance versus extra-role helps employees understand what they will get credit for doing and what might be considered going above and beyond—AFTER the required job tasks are completed. Employees who focus most of their energy on OCBs at the expense of doing the required tasks are often confused why their performance rating was low. Managers can use these performance taxonomies to explain why and bring employees back on track as to what is expected.

Though it might be obvious, some employees may not understand what counterproductive performance behaviors are—for example, some might think that taking long breaks, taking extra office supplies home for personal use, and telling a white lie about when they were actually working is just par for the course. After all, they worked hard and deserve a little extra time off—and if they were paid more, they would not have to take supplies home. Regardless, these "rationalized" behaviors are counterproductive and managers can use Robinson and Bennett's typology to show employees what kinds of behaviors are not acceptable.

Additionally, explaining the taxonomies to employees is one thing, but managers can reinforce what is truly desired behavior versus not desired behavior by applying operant conditioning every day. Thus, if the explanation of expectations and performance behaviors in terms of taxonomies is just too complex and over-academic for employees to grasp, managers can role model or identify a role model to demonstrate behaviors, and use positive and negative reinforcement consistently to help employees learn what is and is not rewarded performance at work.

To ensure managers are effective at coaching and evaluating their employees' performance, they need training and guidance on how to conduct effective appraisals. Thus, like employees needing taxonomies or clear understanding of expected competencies and behaviors for performing at work, so do managers in their task of managing employee performance. The Managerial Competencies provided by Fink and Longenecker (Table 5.8) can be used by organizations as a taxonomy of managerial performance behaviors for managing performance. If your organization does not provide this kind of training and you are a manager wanting to manage performance well, why not seek outside training courses to develop these skills.

In addition to your own skill development, being conscious that your ratings of your employees' behavior may differ from theirs and/or their peers, you can seek peer-assessments and self-assessments from your employees before providing their appraisals. Getting employees' self-assessments of performance can also help you discuss psychological contracts to ensure perceived fairness and provide support for your employee, in addition to finding out what constraints your employees feel they have in accomplishing their tasks.

Chapter Summary

Performance in organizations is important for employees and the organization alike. There are many aspects of performance that must be understood and considered, all the way from how performance is defined in the organization, to how it is measured and evaluated, how the results of the evaluation are shared with the employee, and how the performance ratings are used within the organizational system. Consequently, the management of performance is complex and sometimes overwhelming.

Regardless of its complexity, managers cannot afford simply to leave performance management up to the human resources manager or department. Taking an active role in understanding performance and engaging in self-development for accurate performance appraisal are worthy exercises with long-term payoffs. Pulakos and O'Leary (2011) recently argued that the best performance management systems provide standards for ratings, frame-of-reference training or calibration training, and communication skills training. The best results are achieved through well-developed manager–employee communication using a straightforward performance-rating tool. They further proposed that the focus of attention of performance management should be on how managers and employees relate and communicate regarding expectations and ongoing continuous feedback, and that it is this communication, built on performance standards and solid managerial skills, that make for a good performance management system. Others additionally suggest that appropriate accountability must be inherent in the appraisal system to ensure proper communication and use of objective standards for performance; standards designed to meet the organization's goals (Lewis, 2011). You as the participant in the performance appraisal can take an active role in fostering good communication, asking to understand the performance rating system, and holding yourself accountable for meeting and exceeding standards for performance.

Figure 5.5 provides a visual summary of the key concepts from Chapter 5.

The visual shows how various factors including knowledge and skill, motivation, aspects of the work environment, work experience, constraints (or lack thereof), and one's personality feed into one's performance-related behaviors. Thus, there are many different elements of the person and work environment that affect performance. Additionally, performance management in the form of feedback on one's performance and reinforcement to either encourage or discourage performance behaviors can increase or decrease work behaviors. Counterproductive work behaviors are a form of performance behaviors, but

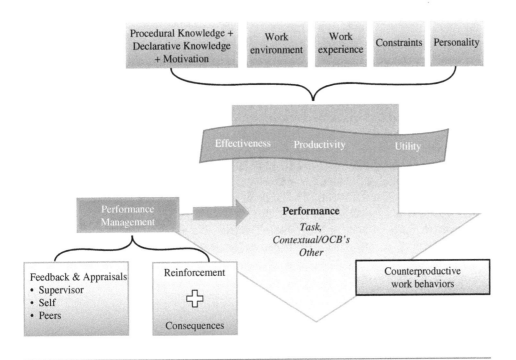

FIGURE 5.5   Visual Summary of Chapter 5

Courtesy Zinta Byrne.

not ones that are encouraged. Thus, the visual includes the critical components of the chapter in the form of a flowchart.

Discussion Questions

1. What makes performance so hard to manage?

2. A lot of the focus on performance management lies with the supervisor. But what responsibility does the employee have in managing their own performance? If you could redesign performance management, how would you do it to make the responsibility for performance management a joint effort between employee and supervisor?

3. Counterproductive work behaviors are very costly for organizations and sometimes hurtful to many people. What do you think is the best way to stop people from directing their motivation towards counterproductive behaviors, and instead get them motivated towards performing positive productive work behaviors?

4. Knowing about psychology—that we are susceptible to halo effects and other biases in our judgment, can we truly separate extra-role and contextual performance from job performance that meets/fulfills the specified job description (assuming one exists)? If there is no job description, how do you decide what performance crosses the line from on-the-job expected performance to extra-role? Does it make sense to categorize these performance behavior types?

References

Appelbaum, S. H., Roy, M., & Gilliland, T. (2011). Globalization of performance appraisals: Theory and applications. *Management Decision, 49*(4), 570–585. doi: 10.1108/00251741111126495

Athitakis, M. (2013). Self-study. *Associations Now, 9*(8), 56–61.

Aubé, C., & Rousseau, V. (2011). Interpersonal aggression and team effectiveness: The mediating role of team goal commitment. *Journal of Occupational and Organizational Psychology, 84*(3), 565–580. doi:10.1348/096317910X492568

Aubé, C., Rousseau, V., Mama, C., & Morin, E. M. (2009). Counterproductive behaviors and psychological well-being: The moderating effect of task interdependence. *Journal of Business and Psychology, 24,* 351–361. doi: 10.1007/s10869-009- 9113-5

Barrick, M. R., & Mount, M. K. (1991). The Big Five personality dimensions and job performance: A meta-analysis. *Personnel Psychology, 44*(1), 1–26. doi:10.1111/j.1744-6570.1991.tb00688.x

Beehr, T. A., Ivanitskaya, L., Hansen, C. P., Erofeev, D., & Gudanowski, D. M. (2001). Evaluation of 360 degree feedback ratings: Relationships with each other and with performance and selection predictors. *Journal of Organizational Behavior, 22*(7), 775–788. doi:10.1002/job.113

Befort, N., & Hattrup, K. (2003). Valuing task and contextual performance: Experience, job roles, and ratings of the importance of job behaviors. *Applied H.R.M. Research, 8*(1–2), 17–32.

Blau, P. (1964). *Exchange and power in social life.* New York, NY: Wiley.

Borman, W. C. (1974). The rating of individuals in organizations: An alternate approach. *Organizational Behavior & Human Performance, 12*(1), 105–124.

Borman, W. C., (1991). Job behavior, performance, and effectiveness. In M. D. Dunnette & L. M. Hough (Eds.), *Handbook of industrial and organizational psychology* (2nd ed., Vol. 2, pp. 271–326). Palo Alto, CA: Consulting Psychologists Press.

Borman, W. C. (2004). The concept of organizational citizenship. *Current Directions in Psychological Science, 13,* 238–241.

Borman, W. C., & Brush, D. H. (1993). More progress toward a taxonomy of managerial performance requirements. *Human Performance, 6*(1), 1–21. doi:10.1207/s15327043hup0601_1

Borman, W. C., & Motowidlo, S. J. (1993). Expanding the criterion domain to include elements of contextual performance. In N. Schmitt, et al. (Eds.), *Personnel selection in organizations,* (pp. 71–98). San Francisco, CA: Jossey-Bass.

Bourdage, J. S., Lee, K., Lee, J., & Shin, K. (2012). Motives for organizational citizenship behavior: Personality correlates and coworker ratings of OCB. *Human Performance, 25*(3), 179–200. doi:10.1080/08959285.2012.683904

Bracken, D. W., & Church, A. H. (2013). The "New" performance management paradigm: Capitalizing on the unrealized potential of 360 degree feedback. *People & Strategy, 36*(2), 34–40.

Byrne, Z. S. (2005). Fairness reduces the negative effects of organizational politics on turnover intentions, citizenship behavior and job performance. *Journal of Business and Psychology, 20,* 175–200.

Byrne, Z., Pitts, V., Chiaburu, D., & Steiner, Z. (2011). Managerial trustworthiness and social exchange with the organization. *Journal Of Managerial Psychology, 26*(2), 108–122. doi:10.1108/02683941111102155

Campbell, J. P. (1990). Modeling the performance prediction problem in industrial and organizational psychology. In M. D. Dunnette & L. M. Hough (Eds.), *Handbook of industrial and organizational psychology,* (2nd ed., Vol. 1, pp. 687–732). Palo Alto, CA: Consulting Psychologists Press.

Campbell, J. P. (1994). Alternative models of job performance and their implications for selection and classification. In M. G. Rumsey, C. B. Walker, & J. Harris (Eds.), *Personnel selection and classification* (pp. 33–51). Hillsdale, NJ: Lawrence Erlbaum Associates.

Campbell, J. P., McCloy, R. A., Oppler, S. H., & Sager, C. E. (1993), A theory of performance. In N. Schmitt & W. C. Borman (Eds.), *Personnel selection in organizations* (pp.35–70). San Francisco, CA: Jossey-Bass.

Cardy, R. L., & Dobbins, G. H. (1994). *Performance appraisal: Alternative perspectives.* Cincinnati, OH: South-Western Publishing Company.

Cheung, M. Y. (2013). The mediating role of perceived organizational support in the effects of interpersonal and informational justice on organizational citizenship behaviors. *Leadership & Organization Development Journal*, *34*(6), 551–572. doi:10.1108/LODJ-11-2011-0114

Cocanougher, A., & Ivancevich, J. M. (1978). "BARS" performance rating for sales force personnel. *Journal of Marketing*, *42*(3), 87–95.

Conway, J. M., & Huffcutt, A. I. (1997). Psychometric properties of multisource performance ratings: A meta-analysis of subordinate, supervisor, peer, and self-ratings. *Human Performance*, *10*(4), 331–360. doi:10.1207/s15327043hup1004_2

Dalal, R. S. (2005). A meta-analysis of the relationship between organizational citizenship behavior and counterproductive work behavior. *Journal of Applied Psychology*, *90*(6), 1241–1255. doi:10.1037/0021-9010.90.6.1241

Dalal, R. S., Lam, H., Weiss, H. M., Welch, E. R., & Hulin, C. L. (2009). A within-person approach to work behavior and performance: Concurrent and lagged citizenship-counterproductivity associations, and dynamic relationships with affect and overall job performance. *Academy of Management Journal*, *52*(5), 1051–1066. doi:10.5465/AMJ.2009.44636148

Daniels, A. C. (1989). *Performance management: Improving quality productivity through positive reinforcement* (3rd ed.). Tucker, GA: Performance Management Publications.

Darolia, C. R., Kumari, P., & Darolia, S. (2010). Perceived organizational support, work motivation, and organizational commitment as determinants of job performance. *Journal of the Indian Academy of Applied Psychology*, *36*(1), 69–78.

Davis, B. L., & Mount, M. K. (1984). Effectiveness of performance appraisal training using computer assisted instruction and behavior modeling. *Personnel Psychology*, *37*(3), 439–452. doi:10.1111/j.1744-6570.1984.tb00521.x

Day, D. V., & Sulsky, L. M. (1995). Effects of frame-of-reference training and information configuration on memory organization and rating accuracy. *Journal of Applied Psychology*, *80*(1), 158–167. doi:10.1037/0021-9010.80.1.158

Fink, L. S., & Longenecker, C. (1998). Training as a performance appraisal improvement strategy. *The Career Development International*, *3*(6), 243–251. doi:10.1108/13620439810234509

Fisher, C. D., & Noble, C. S. (2004). A within-person examination of correlates of performance and emotions while working. *Human Performance*, *17*(2), 145–168. doi:10.1207/s15327043hup1702_2

Fletcher, C., & Perry, E. L. (2002). Performance appraisal and feedback: A consideration of national culture and a review of contemporary research and future trends. In N. Anderson, D. S. Ones, H. Sinangil, C. Viswesvaran (Eds.), *Handbook of industrial, work and organizational psychology: Personnel psychology* (Vol. 1, pp. 127–144). Thousand Oaks, CA: Sage Publications Ltd.

Greguras, G. J., Robie, C., Schleicher, D. J., & Goff, M. (2003). A field study of the effects of rating purpose on the quality of multisource ratings. *Personnel Psychology*, *56*(1), 1–21. doi:10.1111/j.1744-6570.2003.tb00141.x

Grote, R. C. (1996). *The complete guide to performance appraisal.* New York, NY: AMACOM.

Heilman, M. E., & Chen, J. J. (2005). Same behavior, different consequences: Reactions to men's and women's altruistic citizenship behavior. *Journal of Applied Psychology, 90*(3), 431–441. doi:10.1037/0021-9010.90.3.431

Hofstede, G. (1980). Motivation, leadership, and organization: Do American theories apply abroad? *Organizational Dynamics*, 42–63. doi: 0090-2616/80/0014-0042

Hofstede, G., Hofstede, G. J., & Minkov, M. (2010). *Cultures and organizations: Software of the mind* (3rd ed.). New York, NY: McGraw-Hill

Holzbach, R. L. (1978). Rater bias in performance ratings: Superior, self-, and peer ratings. *Journal of Applied Psychology, 63*(5), 579–588. doi:10.1037/0021-9010.63.5.579

Hon, A. Y., & Lu, L. (2013). Be good for love or for money? The roles of justice in the Chinese hotel industry. *International Journal of Contemporary Hospitality Management, 25*(6), 883–902. doi:10.1108/IJCHM-09-2012-0174

Houldsworth, E., & Machin, S. (2008). Leadership team performance management: The case of BELRON. *Team Performance Management, 14*(3/4), 118–133.

Hui, C., Lee, C., & Rousseau, D. M. (2004). Psychological contract and organizational citizenship behavior in China: Investigating generalizability and instrumentality. *Journal of Applied Psychology, 89*(2), 311–321. doi:10.1037/0021-9010.89.2.311

Ivancevich, J. M. (1979). Longitudinal study of the effects of rater training on psychometric error in ratings. *Journal of Applied Psychology, 64*(5), 502–508. doi:10.1037/0021-9010.64.5.502

Johnson, J. W. (2001). The relative importance of task and contextual performance dimensions to supervisor judgments of overall performance. *Journal of Applied Psychology, 86*(5), 984–996. doi:10.1037/0021-9010.86.5.984

Jones, A. P., & James, L. R. (1979). Psychological climate: Dimensions and relationships of individual and aggregated work environment perceptions. *Organizational Behavior and Human Performance, 23,* 201–250.

Judge, T. A., Thoresen, C. J., Bono, J. E., & Patton, G. K. (2001). The job satisfaction–job performance relationship: A qualitative and quantitative review. *Psychological Bulletin, 127*(3), 376–407. doi:10.1037/0033-2909.127.3.376

Katz, D. (1964). The motivational basis of organizational behavior. *Behavioral Science, 9*(2), 131–146. doi:10.1002/bs.3830090206

Kidder, D. L., & Parks, J. (2001). The good soldier: Who is s(he)? *Journal of Organizational Behavior, 22*(8), 939–959. doi:10.1002/job.119

Latham, G. P., Wexley, K. N., & Pursell, E. D. (1975). Training managers to minimize rating errors in the observation of behavior. *Journal of Applied Psychology, 60*(5), 550–555. doi:10.1037/0021-9010.60.5.550

Lee, C. (1985). Increasing performance appraisal effectiveness: Matching task types, appraisal process, and rater training. *Academy of Management Review, 10*(2), 322–331. doi:10.5465/AMR.1985.4278235

Leung, K., Su, S., & Morris, M. W. (2001). When is criticism not constructive? The roles of fairness perceptions and dispositional attributions in employee acceptance of critical supervisory feedback. *Human Relations, 54*(9), 1155–1187. doi:10.1177/0018726701549002

Lewis, R. E. (2011). Accountability is key to effective performance appraisal systems. *Industrial & Organizational Psychology, 4*(2), 173–175. doi:10.1111/j.1754-9434.2011.01318.x

Lievens, F., & Anseel, F. (2004). Confirmatory factor analysis and invariance of an organizational citizenship behaviour measure across samples in a Dutch-speaking context. *Journal of Occupational And Organizational Psychology, 77*(3), 299–306. doi:10.1348/0963179041752727

Longenecker, C. O. (1989). Truth or consequences: Politics and performance appraisal. *Business Horizons, 32,* 76–83.

Mahoney, T. A. (1988). Productivity defined: The relativity of efficiency, effectiveness, and change. In J. P. Campbell, et al., & Associates (Eds.), *Productivity in organizations: New perspectives from industrial and organizational psychology* (pp. 13–39). San Francisco, CA: Jossey-Bass Publishers.

McCall, M. W., Lombardo, M. M., & Morrison, A. M. (1988). *The lessons of experience: How successful executives develop on the job.* Lexington, MA: Lexington Books.

McDaniel, M. A., Schmidt, F. L., & Hunter, J. E. (1988). Job experience correlates of job performance. *Journal of Applied Psychology, 73*(2), 327–330. doi:10.1037/0021-9010.73.2.327

Moorman, R. H. (1991). Relationship between organizational justice and organizational citizenship behaviors: Do fairness perceptions influence employee citizenship? *Journal of Applied Psychology, 76*(6), 845–855. doi:10.1037/0021-9010.76.6.845

Motowidlo, S. J. (2000). Some basic issues related to contextual performance and organizational citizenship behavior in human resource management. *Human Resource Management Review, 10*(1), 115–126. doi:10.1016/S1053-4822(99)00042-X

Motowidlo, S. J. (2003). Job performance. In W. C. Borman, D. R. Ilgen, & R. J. Klimoski (Eds.), *Handbook of psychology: Industrial and organizational psychology* (Vol. 12, pp. 39–53). Hoboken, NJ: Wiley.

Murphy, K. R. (1989). Dimensions of job performance. In R. F. Dillon, & J. W. Pellegrino (Eds.), *Testing: Theoretical and applied perspectives* (pp. 218–247). New York, NY: Praeger Publishers.

Murphy, K. R., & Cleveland, J. N. (1995). *Understanding performance appraisal: Social, organizational, and goal-based perspectives.* Thousand Oaks, CA: Sage.

Nilsen, D., & Campbell, D. P. (1993). Self-observer rating discrepancies: Once an overrater, always an overrater? *Human Resource Management, 32*(2/3), 265–281.

Organ, D. W. (1997). Organizational citizenship behavior: It's construct clean-up time. *Human Performance, 10*(2), 85–97. doi:10.1207/s15327043hup1002_2

Peters, L. H., & O'Connor, E. J. (1980). Situational constraints and work outcomes: The influences of a frequently overlooked construct. *Academy of Management Review, 5*(3), 391–398. doi:10.5465/AMR.1980.4288856

Peters, L. H., & O'Connor, E. J. (1988). Measuring work obstacles: Procedures, issues, and implications. In F. Schoorman, & B. Schneider (Eds.), *Facilitating work effectiveness* (pp. 105–123). Lexington, MA: Lexington Books/D.C. Heath and Com.

Ployhart, R. E., & Hakel, M. D. (1998). The substantive nature of performance variability: Predicting interindividual differences in intraindividual performance. *Personnel Psychology, 51*(4), 859–901. doi:10.1111/j.1744-6570.1998.tb00744.x

Podsakoff, P. M., Ahearne, M., & MacKenzie, S. B. (1997). Organizational citizenship behavior and the quantity and quality of work group performance. *Journal of Applied Psychology, 82*(2), 262–270. doi:10.1037/0021-9010.82.2.262

Podsakoff, P. M., MacKenzie, S. B., Paine, J., & Bachrach, D. G. (2000). Organizational citizenship behaviors: A critical review of the theoretical and empirical literature and suggestions for future research. *Journal of Management, 26*(3), 513–563. doi:10.1177/014920630002600307

Pulakos, E. D., Arad, S., Donovan, M. A., & Plamondon, K. E. (2000). Adaptability in the workplace: Development of a taxonomy of adaptive performance. *Journal of Applied Psychology, 85*(4), 612–624. doi:10.1037/0021-9010.85.4.612

Pulakos, E. D., & O'leary, R. S. (2011). Why is performance management broken? *Industrial & Organizational Psychology, 4*(2), 146–164. doi:10.1111/j.1754-9434.2011.01315.x

Quiñones, M. A., Ford, J., & Teachout, M. S. (1995). The relationship between work experience and job performance: A conceptual and meta-analytic review. *Personnel Psychology, 48*(4), 887–910. doi:10.1111/j.1744-6570.1995.tb01785.x

Rentsch, J. R. (1990). Climate and culture: Interaction and qualitative differences in organizational meanings. *Journal of Applied Psychology, 75,* 668–681.

Robinson, S. L., & Bennett, R. J. (1995). A typology of deviant workplace behaviors: A multidimensional scaling study. *Academy of Management Journal, 38*(2), 555–572. doi:10.2307/256693

Rousseau, D. M. (1990). New hire perceptions of their own and their employer's obligations: A study of psychological contracts. *Journal of Organizational Behavior, 11*(5), 389–400. doi:10.1002/job.4030110506

Ross, L. (1977). The intuitive psychologist and his shortcomings: Distortions in the attribution process. In L. Berkowitz (Ed.), *Advances in experimental social psychology,* (Vol. 10, pp. 173–220). New York, NY: Academic Press.

Schmidt, F. L., Hunter, J. E., & Outerbridge, A. N. (1986). Impact of job experience and ability on job knowledge, work sample performance, and supervisory ratings of job performance. *Journal of Applied Psychology, 71*(3), 432–439. doi:10.1037/0021-9010.71.3.432

Shore, T. H., Shore, L. M., & Thornton, G. C. (1992). Construct validity of self- and peer evaluations of performance dimensions in an assessment center. *Journal of Applied Psychology, 77*(1), 42–54. doi:10.1037/0021-9010.77.1.42

Skinner, B. F. (1972). *Cumulative record: A selection of papers* (3rd ed.). East Norwalk, CT: Appleton-Century-Crofts.

Smith, C., Organ, D. W., & Near, J. P. (1983). Organizational citizenship behavior: Its nature and antecedents. *Journal of Applied Psychology, 68*(4), 653–663. doi:10.1037/0021-9010.68.4.653

Schneider, B. (1990). The climate for service: An application of the climate construct. In B. Schneider (Ed.), *Organizational climate and culture* (pp. 383–412). San Francisco, CA: Jossey-Bass.

Schneider, B. (2000). The psychological life of organizations. In N.M. Ashkanasy, C. P. M. Wilderom, & M. F. Peterson (Eds.), *Handbook of organizational culture & climate* (pp. xvii–xxi). Thousand Oaks, CA: Sage.

Spector, P. E., & Fox, S. (2002). An emotion-centered model of voluntary work behavior: Some parallels between counterproductive work behavior and organizational citizenship behavior. *Human Resource Management Review, 12*(2), 269–292. doi:10.1016/S1053-4822(02)00049-9

Spector, P. E., & Jex, S. M. (1998). Development of four self-report measures of job stressors and strain: Interpersonal Conflict at Work Scale, Organizational Constraints Scale, Quantitative Workload Inventory, and Physical Symptoms Inventory. *Journal of Occupational Health Psychology, 3*(4), 356–367. doi:10.1037/1076-8998.3.4.356

Steel, R. P., & Mento, A. J. (1986). Impact of situational constraints on subjective and objective criteria of managerial job performance. *Organizational Behavior and Human Decision Processes, 37*(2), 254–265. doi:10.1016/0749-5978(86)90054-3

Stewart, G. L., & Nandkeolyar, A. K. (2006). Adaptation and intraindividual variation in sales outcomes: Exploring the interactive effects of personality and environmental opportunity. *Personnel Psychology, 59*(2), 307–332.

Sturman, M. C., Cheramie, R. A., & Cashen, L. H. (2005). The impact of job complexity and performance measurement on the temporal consistency, stability, and test-retest reliability of employee job performance ratings. *Journal of Applied Psychology, 90*(2), 269–283. doi:10.1037/0021-9010.90.2.269

Suazo, M. M. (2009). The mediating role of psychological contract violation on the relations between psychological contract breach and work-related attitudes and behaviors. *Journal of Managerial Psychology, 24*(2), 136–160. doi:10.1108/02683940910928856

Suazo, M. M., & Stone-Romero, E. F. (2011). Implications of psychological contract breach: A perceived organizational support perspective. *Journal of Managerial Psychology, 26*(5), 366–382. doi:10.1108/02683941111138994

Sulsky, L. M., & Day, D. V. (1992). Frame-of-reference training and cognitive categorization: An empirical investigation of rater memory issues. *Journal of Applied Psychology, 77*(4), 501–510. doi:10.1037/0021-9010.77.4.501

Thornton, G. C. (1980). Psychometric properties of self-appraisals of job performance. *Personnel Psychology, 33*(2), 363–271. doi:10.1111/j.1744–6570.1980.tb02348.x

Tierney, P., Bauer, T. N., & Potter, R. E. (2002). Extra-role behavior among Mexican employees: The impact of LMX, group acceptance, and job attitudes. *International Journal of Selection And Assessment, 10*(4), 292–303. doi:10.1111/1468-2389.00219

Tsui, P., Lin, Y., & Yu, T. (2013). The influence of psychological contract and organizational commitment on hospitality employee performance. *Social Behavior and Personality, 41*(3), 443–452. doi:10.2224/sbp.2013.41.3.443

Williams, L. J., & Anderson, S. E. (1991). Job satisfaction and organizational commitment as predictors of organizational citizenship and in-role behaviors. *Journal of Management, 17*(3), 601–617. doi:10.1177/014920639101700305

Witt, L. A., Kacmar, M., Carlson, D. S., & Zivnuska, S. (2002). Interactive effects of personality and organizational politics on contextual performance. *Journal of Organizational Behavior, 23*(8), 911–926. doi:10.1002/job.172

Woehr, D. J. (1994). Understanding frame-of-reference training: The impact of training on the recall of performance information. *Journal of Applied Psychology, 79*(4), 525–534. doi:10.1037/0021-9010.79.4.525

CHAPTER 6

The Toll Work Takes:
Occupational Stress

Learning Outcomes

After studying this chapter, you should be able to:

1. Define occupational stress.

2. Explain why the occupational stress process is important to understand within the context of organizations.

3. Identify common job stressors, their consequences (strains), and explain, using at least one or two theories of stress, how stressors create strains.

4. Develop a customized stress-management program for yourself by synthesizing the explanations of existing models of job stress and recommended actions.

Mini-Quiz: Occupational Stress

As an introduction to this chapter, please take the following mini-quiz (answers are in the back of the book). As you read the questions and consider the answers *before* diving into the chapter, you'll challenge yourself before you master the content, a process that helps facilitate learning for long-term retention. Some questions may have more than one correct answer. Don't worry if you cannot answer all questions correctly on your first try. By the time you read the chapter and spend some of your own time thinking about these concepts, you should be able to determine the best answers. Try the quiz again after you finish reading the chapter.

1. Which of the following *best* characterizes how people generally talk about "stress" at work?
   a. Having a headache from balancing too many projects at work
   b. Struggling with an ongoing conflict with a coworker
   c. Feeling like you just cannot live up to your boss' expectations while working on a project
   d. Lifting heavy boxes all day as the main part of your job

2. What sorts of factors affect how we experience stress?
   a. Personality
   b. Individual coping mechanisms
   c. Continued exposure to stressful events
   d. Having support from others

3. True or false: Stress can actually be good for employee performance.
   a. True! Eustress can create a positive energy for accomplishing work goals.
   b. It depends—some level of eustress is good for people, but distress most often leads to negative consequences.
   c. True, although eustress is rare and hardly ever discussed.
   d. False, stress feels negative in the moment, and inhibits performance.

4. Why should organizations care about stress?
   a. Stress is related to many job attitudes, such as job satisfaction and turnover intentions.
   b. While stress has negative individual outcomes, it doesn't typically affect employee performance, so organizations really shouldn't be too concerned.
   c. When employees are stressed, they are more likely to cause accidents so for safety reasons, organizations should care about stress.
   d. Organizations incur higher health-care costs due to stress-related injuries and illnesses.

5. Stress is not only about physiological responses but about a/an _____ the situation.
   a. Appraisal of
   b. Biological response to
   c. Instantaneous reaction to
   d. The cause of responses to

Overview

Research indicates that being exposed to negative **stressors** (e.g., daily hassles, constant change events, chronic conflict with coworkers) eventually causes harm in employees (e.g., negative health consequences), ultimately negatively impacting the organization. This impact to the organization typically occurs in the form of high costs for healthcare, high absenteeism and withdrawal from work, high turnover rates, accidents on the job (which of course negatively affects employees themselves), and reduced productivity and effectiveness. There is no doubt that negative affects of stress have consequences regardless of the context, but in this chapter, we focus exclusively on the effects of stress in the workplace.

Though the primary focus of this chapter is on organizations and employees therein, you can probably identify with what is said in this chapter because as a student you likely feel stress much, if not most, of the time. The National College Health Assessment of 2005 found that across 33 campuses, 32% of students rated stress the number one factor affecting their individual performance. Because the educational experience involves exposure to varying stressors, such as exams, varying workloads, friends, or work-school-life balancing pressures over prolonged periods, stress is sometimes hard to manage. The upside, however, is that you *can* manage stress.

What Is Stress?

Definitions of stress have varied over time and across disciplines. Defined as a stimulus, stress refers to the aspects of the environment that trigger either positive or negative responses. In this case, you can think of stress as an independent variable in an experiment. For example, time pressure or work conflicts are the stimuli that bring about headaches and anxiety. However, conceptualizing stress as a stimulus ignores the evidence that not everyone reacts in the same way to the same stimuli. Some react to time pressure with anxiety. When they do, we think of negative stress, called **distress** (Selye, 1982), which occurs when stimuli are perceived as threats (Figure 6.1). However, other people meet time pressure with excitement, seeing the pressure as a challenge to work harder and faster. This stress is considered positive or good stress, called **eustress** (Selye, 1982), that may result when stimuli are perceived as positively challenging and effective coping mechanisms can be applied to take on the challenge.

FIGURE 6.1 Stress at Work

© Rob Marmion/Shutterstock, Inc.

Although eustress exists, most stress research tends to focus on distress because the consequences can be so debilitating. Since the emphasis is on the negative response, sometimes those negative reactions are called stress. In this case, stress is defined as a response to stimuli. For instance, anxiety, headaches, or neck pain can indicate that stress exists for an individual. If you use stress defined as the response, you can think of stress as a dependent variable in an experiment. When we study stress in the workplace, we call it occupational stress.

What Is Occupational Stress?

Occupational stress specifically refers to the process whereby work or job-related stress responses are triggered by factors at work that may be situational, contextual/environmental, or psychological/social, and that force employees to deviate from their normal feelings or behaviors (Beehr & Newman, 1978; Caplan, 1975).

The National Institute for Occupational Health and Safety (NIOSH) is a U.S. federal agency within the Center for Disease Control and Prevention. NIOSH focuses on research and recommendations for preventing worker injury and illness, and uses a response-based definition of stress when it defines occupational stress as the "harmful physical and emotional responses that occur when the requirements of the job do not match the capabilities, resources, or needs of the worker" (NIOSH 99-101). NIOSH reports that about one third or more of workers they surveyed in the United States report high stress. Similarly, the European Agency for Safety and Health at Work reports that of surveyed workers in 2005, work-related stress is the second most reported health issue, affecting at least 22% of respondents.

Because there are so many different ways that the word "stress" has been used, the stimulus-response terminology is used in the occupational health discipline and the organizational psychology and behavior fields to avoid confusion. Occupational health psychology is a discipline dedicated to the study of health, well-being, and safety in the workplace (e.g., offices, agricultural settings, manufacturing), and stress is just one of the major topics of focus within this branch of knowledge. The word *stressor* is used to describe the various stimuli that evoke a response indicative of stress (Kahn & Byosiere, 1992), such as adverse physiological changes, task-related demands, physical symptoms, or psychological tension. The response or reaction to the stressor is called the **strain**.

Strains fit into three categories: psychological, physical, and behavioral. A psychological strain may be feelings of anxiety. Physical strains include pulled muscles in the back or neck, a headache, or heart palpitations. A behavioral strain may take the form of yelling or being aggressive toward one's work colleagues perhaps pushing them or crowding their space. Any stimulus can produce a response in any one particular individual, but stress researchers study what affects most individuals so they can generalize their recommendations to large groups and organizations.

Additionally, scholars in organizational psychology and behavior focusing on occupational stress tend look at the stress process as an interaction between people and their social environment, known as the *psychosocial perspective* of stress. The psychosocial perspective is grounded in the transactional definition of stress (Lazarus, 1966), which suggests that how people appraise their social environment triggers a psychological response and this interaction generates a reaction. For example, if you judge your coworkers performing better than you as a threat, you might withdraw either physically (i.e., ask to relocate your desk, call in sick) or psychologically (i.e., give up caring about your performance), or both. If, however, you judge your coworkers' efforts to outperform you as a challenge, you will advance toward the challenge by working harder and more efficiently, perhaps learning new skills to boost your results beyond theirs.

The psychosocial perspective takes the transactional model one step further by saying that not only do people appraise their environment and then respond based on the appraisal, their appraisal depends on their psychological state and their social environment, primarily made up of demands, job characteristics, or relationships at work. The transactional model emphasizes the appraisal component of the process. Thus, perceptions of control and the availability of social support make a difference as to the appraisal of job demands, as either

Think about what creates the stress process for you. What are the stressors, what are the strains? Do you have control over any of the stressors?

challenging or harmful, and to the appraisal of coping mechanisms (Fleming, Baum, & Singer, 1984), whether effective or not. Regardless of the appraisal, however, everyone experiences stress outcomes.

Although everyone experiences stress outcomes (i.e., strains), they do not experience them all to the same degree, and they are not all triggered by the same cause. That leads us to consider the various types of stress, next.

Exercise 6.1

Using your own words, define stress, occupational stress, stressors, and strains.

General Types of Stress

There are a number of different types of stress characterized by how long they endure: acute, episodic acute, and chronic. *Acute stress* arises from immediate job tasks, brief conflicts or disagreements with coworkers or the boss, the rush of getting a project done on time, or time pressures like missing your train by 3 minutes. Acute stress is short lived, can be a threat or challenge, and creates similar reactions such as anxiety, anger, headaches, back pain, upset stomach, fast heart rate, and shortness of breath to name a few. Everyone experiences acute stress, both in positive forms (e.g., excitement of winning a race) and negative forms (e.g., near car accident or an angry customer yelling at you). Acute stress occurs infrequently.

Episodic acute stress occurs somewhat frequently, but remains acute. This stress can develop from having an overly scheduled life where a time-gap between appointments does not exist, juggling too many demands across many areas of work and life, taking on more than resources or time allows, and worrying excessively about uncontrollable events or people. Each episode of stress is short-lived, hence "acute," but these events occur frequently. Episodic acute stress is not always negative; those who thrive on the thrill of busy excitement or being the center of activity experience episodic acute stress as a positive state. Unlike acute stress, not everyone experiences episodic acute stress. Jobs in which one might experience episodic acute stress include surgeon, nurse, restaurant server, fire fighter, manager, pilot, or police officer. Episodic acute stress occurs more frequently than acute stress, but is not constant like chronic stress.

Chronic stress tends to be negative, experienced as a day-to-day, long-term drain caused by ongoing work, health, family, personal, or financial problems that cannot easily be resolved. For example, a workplace overwhelmed with corruption or negative work politics, an abusive manager or coworker, or a work environment that is consistently hot, dirty, or physically unsafe (e.g., large manufacturing equipment in constant motion) can create chronic stress. Chronic stress is considered dangerous because people are unable to remove or resolve the issues that cause the stress, leaving them with few options for relieving strains. Some resolve the negative consequences of stress through destructive solutions such as substance abuse, violence, or suicide. Chronic stress most typically results in detrimental health consequences. Jobs wherein one might experience chronic stress include air traffic controller, oil rig worker, emergency room doctor, or meat processing plant worker.

Workplace stressors can be acute, episodic acute, and chronic, thus workplace stressors tend to be characterized based on their source rather than how long they

Watch how stress can actually change your brain - https://www.ted.com/talks/madhumita_murgia_how_stress_affects_your_brain

last or how frequently they occur. Workplace stressors also come in many forms, including those related to the work role and those that span between work and home.

Types of Workplace Stressors

Workplace stressors come in various forms such as job role-related, workload, family/work integration (time-based/strain-based conflict), and job security (Table 6.1).

TABLE 6.1   Work-Specific Stressors

Term	Definition	Example
Role conflict	Disagreement or inconsistent demands from sources; different expectations for your role or roles	Supervisor says customers are never wrong and to give them whatever they ask for, but then also tells you that it's your job to manage customer costs by not giving in to customer requests
Role overload	Too many different roles that you're expected to fill at the same time	You are a customer service representative while also acting as the team lead and the team accountant; being the office manager at the same time as administrative assistant while also managing the technology requests
Role ambiguity	Lack of clarity about the role and consequences of performance in the role; uncertainty about what performance behaviors will fulfill the role expectations	New job; an existing job that you are new to; job scope is changing; the organization is going through changes so it's unclear what your job is in the new structure
Role workload	Can be role underload or role overload—both can result from irregular workflow; can be actual load or perception of the load	Seasonal work (holidays in retail usually produce excessive overload) or outdoor efforts are paced by the weather (road construction in snow climates can only be done during the nonsnow months). Role underload may be experienced by being overqualified for a job and then not being given enough responsibility in the job
Time-based/ strain-based conflict	Conflict that results between or across work and nonwork domains. One of the most common domain cross-overs is work and family.	Time-based: number of hours at work take away from ability to see your family Strain-based: anger, headaches, back pain from job prevent dancing with partner
Job insecurity	Ongoing prospect or perceived threat of losing your job; threats can be economical or advancements in technology	Organization constantly downsizes or rightsizes to appease stakeholders or shareholders; some industries more susceptible than others (e.g., manufacturing); automation or other innovations reduce number of workers needed
Shift work	Work that occurs during hours that cross from day into night or vice versa, or that changes from day to day or week to week	Many, if not most, service jobs (particularly in retail and entertainment); seasonal work; transportation industry, healthcare, and work that can be continued 24 hours per day, 7 days per week (e.g., mining, fishing).

Role Stressors

Workplace stressors often present themselves as role stressors (Kahn, Wolfe, Quinn, Snoek, & Rosenthal, 1964). A job role is the position a person holds at work, such as supervisor, cashier, coworker, team leader, or technician. In its academic definition, a role is a set of socially accepted behaviors for a specific context (Glazer & Beehr, 2005). Importantly, the pattern or set of behaviors in the role is socially determined and accepted, which means that roles are not defined solely by the individual. As such, the expectations are created and molded by the people who have a stake in what you accomplish within that role. Additionally, people generally occupy more than one role at work—that of employee, subordinate (you have a boss), supervisor (you are a boss to others), coworker, temporary team or project lead, or customer (can be internal or external). Each role has expectations for what work tasks should be achieved as part of the role or within the boundaries of that role.

Role Conflict

Why is chronic stress more dangerous than episodic acute stress?

Role conflict occurs when incompatible or competing sets of expectations have been communicated for the job or tasks associated with the job. These incompatible expectations may be from multiple bosses, such as when an employee has one supervisor in one location but also has a reporting relationship with another supervisor in another location. For example, some engineers report to both a marketing manager and a manager responsible for the engineering development. Multiple expectations generated from the multiple roles that each person holds creates the stress. For instance, an employee can be a subordinate, supervisor, and coworker, all at the same time. Expectations across these different roles may be incompatible making the prioritization or resolution of some problems particularly difficult. The employee may not be able to perform all expected sets of behaviors at the same time. A good illustration of this is José, the team lead for a new car design project. José has been told by the design boss to take as much time as needed because the design must be of the highest quality to pass the quality design inspection. In conflict with the design boss, the manufacturing team is telling José that the design has to be ready in the next month and that the quality is not critical because the manufacturing process is constrained anyway. Therefore, José should design what manufacturing can build, rather than a high-quality design that will be discarded once it gets to manufacturing. In this situation, José has competing expectations—on one hand, the expectation is to produce the highest quality during the design stage and ignore time constraints; on the other hand, the expectation is to produce a design constrained by what manufacturing can build and do so quickly.

Juggling work roles with the expectations from roles at home (e.g., wife, husband, partner, parent, child, cook, tutor) is considered role conflict and tends to be subgrouped under the label of work-life or work-family conflict. Contrary to what some people may think, many of these juggling challenges are not self-inflicted. According to a recent article in *Bloomberg Businessweek*, a weekly business magazine, employers now expect employees to log into the computer to check e-mail between the hours of 11 p.m. and

2 a.m. (see "Work-Life Balance and the New Night Shift" by Brad Stone at businessweek.com). Though it is not the organization's responsibility to make people's home life functional, the strains that result from conflicts between the work and home roles ultimately affect the organization. Outcomes of role conflict, such as reduced employee productivity, employee absences, and lack of attention at work, can have detrimental effects especially where worker safety is concerned. Therefore, most organizations recognize and attempt to support employees' efforts to manage these role conflicts. A role stressor that employees expect organizations to take responsibility for includes role overload.

Role Overload

Role overload occurs when the expectations or responsibilities of the role exceed the available resources or are unreasonable for one person to achieve (Sales, 1970). Resources include materials, individual abilities, or qualifications. An example of a role overload situation might be a graduate teaching assistant who thought the role involved helping the professor, but is instead left to teach the course without the professor present. Another example might be working in a seasonal job stocking inventory, but this time the boss asks you to also be responsible for managing other stockers, as well as selling the merchandise. Having expectations exceeding what we can currently achieve creates a different stressor for us than not understanding what those expectations actually are.

Role Ambiguity

Role ambiguity occurs with unclear expectations for the role. Specifically, you experience role ambiguity when you cannot determine whether or how you perform within the role will result in an expected outcome, because the objectives for the role are unclear. For instance, there may be insufficient, misleading, or too little information available to determine the actual role (Rizzo, House, & Lirtzman, 1970). A simple example of experiencing role ambiguity might be your first job at the local coffee shop. You know you have to work the register and serve coffee, but you might be unclear about what else is involved, such as whether you just pour the coffee or also deliver it to the table, and whether you are also responsible for clearing the tables after people have finished with their coffee - or do they clear their own tables. Hence, role ambiguity is about the lack of clarity regarding the assignments, objectives, duties, scope of the job, and responsibilities needed to fulfill the role (Beehr & Glazer, 2005). You do not know whether the way you do the job will result in accomplishing the goals, because the objective or purpose of the work is unclear. Understanding how those tasks combine into a role that supports the organization may be unclear because of the newness of the job role, changes in the job structure, or changes to the organization itself. It may be that in your efforts to perform in a way that achieves the goal, you take on more than expected of the job—namely because the expectations are so unclear. However, taking on more than can be achieved given the role or not having enough to do within the role falls under role workload stressors.

Role overload is not the same as work overload. Role overload is having too many roles to fill and each role fails to provide enough resources to achieve the role expectations. Work overload is simply having too much to do.

Role Workload

Workload is just that—the amount of work an employee has and is expected to complete. Employees' negative experience of workload associated with their role falls under two different categories: role underload and role overload. Role underload refers to the perceptions of not having enough to do, not being given enough responsibility, or being overqualified for the job such that the job is boring (Shultz, Wang, & Olson, 2010). In a study of 1,383 individuals reporting underload at work, 34% experienced backaches, 18% headaches, 22% muscular pain in their arms or legs, 23% fatigue, and 15% felt irritable (Shultz et al., 2010). Thus, even though these study participants reported severe boredom at their jobs, they still suffered a significant number of strains due to underload stress.

Role overload refers to having too much to do, too much responsibility for the role, or being underqualified and as a consequence feeling overwhelmed in the role (Shultz et al., 2010). In comparison to the figures for underload, of the 1,132 who reported overload, 46% experience backaches, 25% headaches, 28% muscular pain in their arms or legs, 33% fatigue, and 21% felt irritable (Shultz et al., 2010). Importantly, the difference between the two groups across these strains is not large; both groups experience strains.

Outcomes of Role Stressors

The role stressors discussed above relate to a number of challenging and detrimental consequences or strains. For example, results of meta-analysis show that role ambiguity is associated with low organizational commitment ($r = -.48$), low job satisfaction ($r = -.41$), high job tension ($r = .30$), and intentions to quit ($r = .31$; Örtqvist & Wincent, 2006). Likewise, from the same meta-analysis role conflict is negatively associated with organizational commitment ($r = -.36$) and job satisfaction ($r = -.40$), and positively associated with tension at work ($r = .43$) and intentions to quit ($r = .37$). Though role overload has shown the same pattern of relationships as role conflict and ambiguity, the strengths of these relationships with role overload are weaker than with role ambiguity and role conflict (Jackson & Schuler, 1985; Örtqvist & Wincent, 2006). In contrast, role overload is more highly correlated with emotional exhaustion ($r = .46$) than is role conflict ($r = .12$) and role ambiguity ($r = .22$). All three role stressors are positively related to emotional exhaustion, with role overload demonstrating the strongest relationship (Örtqvist & Wincent, 2006). No surprise, high levels of role ambiguity are associated with low job performance ($r = -.39$; Örtqvist & Wincent, 2006).

Having very little autonomy and little perceived control on the job are both strongly related to role conflict and role ambiguity, as is having little or no ability to participate in management decisions or direction (Spector, 1986). In sum, role stressors lead to a number of negative consequences for employees and their organization, and yet most can be avoided, at least to some degree. Some stressors that cannot be easily avoided or managed by the organization include workplace stressors, such as perceived job insecurity and shift work.

Other Workplace Stressors

In addition to role stressors, employees experience several other workplace stressors (see Table 6.1) that negatively affect their ability to perform at work, including perceived job insecurity, family/work integration, time-based/strain-based conflict, and shift work.

Job Insecurity

Either the real or perceived threat of losing your job, **job insecurity**, creates anxiety over the prospect of having to look for another job, finding new sources of financial support, losing insurance or other benefits, and a host of other consequences that losing your job might create. Just anticipating the loss of your job creates feelings of insecurity, regardless of whether that anticipation is justified or not. Job insecurity refers to the concern over the continuity or long-term potential (i.e., permanence) of your job (Davy, Kinicki, & Scheck, 1997; Heaney, Israel, & House, 1994).

Perceptions of job insecurity negatively affect your physical and mental health, in addition to your job attitudes such as commitment, job satisfaction, and turnover intentions (Sverke, Hellgren, & Näswall, 2002). Many different factors contribute to you perceiving job insecurity, including the current state of the job market, changes in the organization that create ambiguity, and family responsibilities (Keim, Landis, Pierce, & Earnest, 2014).

Time-based/Strain-based Conflict

When the responsibilities and demands from work and nonwork domains conflict, employees experience either time-based or strain-based conflict (Greenhaus & Beutell, 1985). The most commonly studied nonwork domain is home or family.

Time-based conflict occurs when the number of hours demanded by work interferes with the ability to meet the demands from home or the family, and vice versa; it can occur when the family demands time that interferes with the job demands. Since time is a limited resource, whatever one domain consumes cannot be used by the other domain.

Strain-based conflict occurs when your energy is depleted or you are physically incapacitated in a way that negatively affects your ability to engage in activity across domains. The strains can be physical or mental. For example, suffering anxiety from major conflicts with coworkers at work might make it particularly challenging to enjoy a relaxing evening at home (not until you can relieve that anxiety). Similarly, back pain caused from a weekend of yard chores may make sitting for 2 hours in an important meeting at work difficult. The strains need not be caused by stressors associated with work—they are simply strains experienced in one domain that negatively affect performance in the other domain.

Perceptions of job insecurity, and time-based and strain-based conflict can all occur as a result of shift work, another type of workplace stressor.

Shift Work

With the globalization of work and technology incorporated into nearly every job, employers expect their employees to work in shifts that differ from old

Working with coworkers to whom you are sexually attracted can create a stressor of its own at work, and not just for you. Research shows that workplace gossip about the relationship can cause stress for coworkers, the lower status relationship partners get short changed on promotions or advancement opportunities after the relationship ends, and cross-hierarchical relationships create concerns about unfair advantages for the lower status partner in the romantic relationship (Chan-Serafin, Teo, Minbashian, Cheng, & Wang, 2017; Cowan & Horan, 2014; Malachowski, Chory, & Claus, 2012). In general, many organizations now have policies about romantic relationships, such as not being allowed to work for a romantic partner, to manage stress and perceptions of injustice See https://www.ted.com/talks/amy_nicole_baker_7_common_questions_about_workplace_romance for a good Ted Talk about workplace romance.

style traditional farming hours (i.e., daylight only) or otherwise known as the 8 a.m.–5 p.m. workday (although if you have ever worked on a farm, you know the day starts long before 8AM and ends long after 5PM). Instead, employees' work hours cross from day into night and vice versa. Shift work explicitly refers to any configuration of working hours such as 4 a.m.–1 p.m., 8 a.m.–5 p.m., 6 p.m.–3 a.m., or 9 p.m.–6 a.m., which is not necessarily consistent from day to day or week to week. Many of these different shifts occur in occupations such as agriculture, medicine, transportation, travel, entertainment, law enforcement or services such as fire and power/utilities, and retail. When viewing Figure 6.2, think of your favorite coffee shop or breakfast restaurant that opens at 5 a.m. Those who open the restaurant have to be there by 3 a.m. to set up.

These days, nearly every industry has shift workers. Shift work varies by number of extended hours. For example, some nursing shifts are 12–14 hours per day for 3 consecutive days. Pilots and flight attendants may work for 2 days consecutively, followed by 2 days off. Shift work also varies by the number of days, placement of days, and beginning and ending times of the shift.

Shift work, in and of itself, is not necessarily a psychological stressor—some nurses, for example, prefer 12- to 14-hour days because they can get their work week completed within a few days, leaving a couple of days during the week for

FIGURE 6.2 Shift Work

accomplishing tasks that can only be completed during a Monday–Friday week or old style "banking hours" between 7 a.m. and 4 p.m. These nurses may also enjoy the full days away from work rather than only a few hours per day. Thus, with these 12- to 14-hour shifts, they can more easily balance their work-life domains and avoid time-based conflicts.

However, shift work does present its own risks; the physical and psychological toll that shift work can take, disrupting natural sleep patterns, social life, and eating patterns can have detrimental effects for employees and their organization. For instance, medical interns who work more than 24 hours consecutively in a single shift with every other shift an extended cycle make 21% more serious medical errors and 5.6 times as many diagnostic errors than those on a reduced schedule of no more than 16 consecutive hours (Landrigan et al., 2004). Research conducted in the 1960s demonstrated people have internal body clocks that run on a 24- 25-hour cycle, independent of external cues (Smith, Folkard, & Fuller, 2003). Thus, any schedule forced to disrupt this natural cycle (called circadian rhythms) will have consequences. For example, international travel to areas differing by 5–9 hours from one's local time causes a forced shift in sleep cycles, with a required shift again on return. Jet lag is the common term used for summing up the exhaustion associated with these time shifts, from which it can take days to adjust and recover. Similarly, working late shifts one week and then early morning shifts the next, creates significant adjustment challenges. According to Smith et al. (2003), shift work affects sleep cycles the most, both in terms of the quantity and quality, which can have long-term consequences to cognitive and physical functioning.

Because of the negative long-term consequences resulting from shift work, some occupations have begun instituting guidelines capping the length of shifts. For example, the Accreditation Council for Graduate Medical Education (ACGME) in the United States implemented a cap on the number of hours medical residents and interns (i.e., medical doctors in their first year of training) can work as part of their training shifts. The cap was originally set at a maximum 30 consecutive hours and no more than 80 hours per week (Cromie, 2006). That number has since dropped to 16 consecutive hours as an outcome of a 2011 rule passed by the ACGME. Where did the 16-hour cutoff come from? Research showed that doctors' performance began to deteriorate at about the 16-hour cutoff (Landrigan et al., 2004), hence the use of 16 hours as the maximum shift length.

Similarly, in 2013 the United States Department of Transportation's Federal Motor Carrier Safety Administration announced federal regulations to limit the average workweek for truck drivers to 70 hours, down from 82 hours per week. Truckers reaching their 70-hour limit are required to rest for 34 consecutive hours (including two nights) before they can start the next shift. Lastly, truck drivers are limited to 11 hours of daily driving in a 14-hour workday. Both drivers and their organizations are subject to severe fines for each offense (see the Federal Motor Carrier Safety Administration website for the most up to date regulations; §395.3 in particular for maximum driving times).

Tolerance for Shift Work?

Though shift work has many negative consequences, some people seem to handle the changes in sleep cycles necessary to accommodate shift work more easily than others do. Research has shown that people under the age of 45, men, those with sleep vigor and flexibility (ability to overcome drowsiness; can be morning or evening person), and extroverts, seem somewhat more tolerant or able to cope with shift work and changes in shifts. This is in comparison to employees over 45 years of age, women (whose reproductive cycles can be affected by shift work), and those with strong preferences for morning hours (includes introverts in general; see Smith et al., 2003, for a complete review as well as suggestions for interventions when shift work is required).

Technology

Another workplace stressor is technology. Technology has dramatically changed the face of organizations and the global workforce in the last several decades (Larson, 2007). Changes in how the organization operates include expectations for workers to be available at any time, all the time, and have unrestricted access to technology. When workers go home, they do not necessarily leave work at the office. They may continue by logging into e-mail or finishing a report on their computer. Similarly, employees on vacation are often "checking in" with the office through their e-mail or voice mail systems. Role expectations have incorporated technology access such that many jobs now require and expect employees to be available 24 hours per day, 7 days per week (i.e., 24 × 7).

In addition to expectations for availability or access to employees 24 × 7, the adoption of technology is itself a psychological stressor. Employees may not feel comfortable with the constant use of various types of technology (that often change regularly), and may experience overload as they are expected to accomplish more under the assumption that technology creates higher efficiency. Higher efficiency may be achievable if employees have adequate job control, however, technology itself can both increase and decrease job control for workers, depending on the type of work and whether the technology functions properly (Coovert & Thompson, 2003). In other words, technology can limit your ability to get your job done. Every computer malfunction in a job that relies on using the computer equals lost productivity. Additionally, technology has changed social interactions among employees, decreasing the need for face-to-face communication and replacing it with virtual interfaces (Taha & Calwell, 1993). As a consequence of reducing face-to-face interactions, employees' social networks and support systems are often reduced, leaving them feeling isolated (Hampton, Sessions, & Her, 2011). People need social support (Dickerson & Zoccola, 2009), and isolation can have detrimental effects (Fiorillo & Sabatini, 2011; Karelina & DeVries, 2011).

The excessive use of technology can also create physical problems for employees (Coovert & Thompson, 2003). Repetitive motion disorders such as **carpal tunnel syndrome** can occur. Carpal tunnel syndrome refers to a compression of the median nerve in the carpal tunnel where the nerve passes through the wrist into the hand. Other physical problems, such as back and shoulder muscle aches, eyestrain, neck strain, and hearing loss may all develop just from sitting at the computer and typing day in and day out. Carrying a laptop in a shoulder bag for extended periods of time produces strain on the back, arms, and neck—even when the laptop is as light as 3 lbs (1.36 kg). Various disciplines, such as ergonomics and human factors, are dedicated to understanding the impact of work configurations and technology on employees.

Why does knowing the different types of work stressors matter to organizations?

Discrimination

Employees who experience discrimination or harassment in any form suffer negative strains, which impact their ability to function at their best at work. Employees may be subject to bullying and discrimination for language, religion, gender, sexual orientation, age, or race. For example, in a recent study, Daly et al. (2018) found of the 585 participants in their study, Arabic-speaking employees experienced more discrimination than the Vietnamese or Chinese participants. Chinese participants reported being bullied more than Vietnamese or Arabic-speaking respondents. All participants over 45 years of age reported more bullying than respondents under the age of 45. For all respondents, frequency of experienced discrimination was directly associated with levels of strains. Similarly, a recent study examining discrimination against women of color showed that workplace discrimination was directly connected with their reports of high psychological distress, which results in poor work and health outcomes (Velez, Cox, Polihronakis, & Moradi, 2018). Employees are also discriminated against for their weight. Researchers have shown that weight discrimination is directly related to stress at a biological level—cortisol levels for weight-based discrimination were 33% higher than those not discriminated against for their weight (Jackson, Kirschbaum, & Steptoe, 2016).

Consequently, workplace stressors resulting in various physical and psychological strains can negatively impact organizations and their members. Thus, understanding and knowing about occupational stress is essential for maximizing organizational effectiveness and health.

Exercise 6.2

Compare and contrast the different types of role stress, and role stress in general from the other types of work stress, such as shift work. Give an example of each.

Why Do We Need to Know about Occupational Stress in Organizations?

Occupational stress is pervasive and affects nearly every organization in a negative way. We study occupational stress in organizations because we believe, based on evidence accumulated thus far, that being constantly exposed to stress eventually causes harm in employees (Figure 6.3). In turn, this impact on employees has a negative effect on the organization in the form of high cost of healthcare, high absenteeism and turnover, on the job accidents, reduced productivity, and reduced team effectiveness.

Occupational stress can take many forms and not always those that cause employees to be absent from work or respond to surveys with "yes, I'm feeling very stressed due to work." How often have you continued working even when you felt overwhelmed and probably started developing symptoms of

FIGURE 6.3 Effects of Stress

Clockwise: © Creativa Images/Shutterstock, Inc.; © Piotr Marcinski/Shutterstock, Inc.; © d13/Shutterstock, Inc.; © Zurijeta/Shutterstock, Inc.

You can't eliminate work stress, but you might be able to manage the effects of stressors. Find stress management classes and techniques to manage and cope with your stress levels. Stress theories or frameworks presented in this text may provide ideas on where to direct your stress management energy.

a cold? Many people do not have paid days off for illness or the financial security to take a few days off without pay to recover from the consequences of stress.

An examination of over 92,000 workers revealed those indicating high stress levels reported health-care costs of up to 8.6% higher than workers reporting low stress levels (Goetzel et al., 2012). These health-care costs were attributed solely to the differences in stress and not all the negative health consequences associated with stress. Specifically, Goetzel and colleagues (2012) removed from the calculations those with high blood pressure, depression, high body weight, alcohol consumption, or tobacco use that could be associated with stress and mismanaged stress but have their own significant and unique health costs. When problems related to stress and its mismanagement were all combined, health costs increased up to 214%! Stress costs both employees and organizations.

It is evident that stress has a negative impact on people and work. Ways to prevent stressors and deal with the aftermath of stressors result from an understanding of the stress process. A number of theories of stress have been developed that provide insight into how to prevent and manage stress.

What Are the Theories of Job Stress

Theories of job stress help us think about what factors play a role in creating stress for employees and how they may react to the stress in ways that affect the organization or that bring about harm to themselves. Thus, the value of the theories is their comprehensive statement of when people react, in what ways they react, what they react to, and why. Theories tested in practice provide additional confidence that they work to guide employees, managers, and organizations in developing new strategies for dealing with and proactively stopping new stressors from developing.

Selye's Model

Many students learn that reactions to stressors are represented by the general adaptation syndrome (GAS; Selye, 1946), typically presented with a graph depicting how the body responds to demands. Selye (1946) proposed the body responds to positive or negative stressors following the same process. GAS is made up of three stages that progress over time, as shown in Figure 6.4. The first stage, called alarm, occurs when it becomes apparent there is something to which you need to react. The body responds with increased heart rate, blood pressure, and tightening of muscles. The second stage, resistance, involves the body resisting the stressor by adapting and trying to return the body to a relaxed and balanced state. The body resists the stressor, but may do so at the expense of the body's ability to handle other additional stressors. Selye argued that if this stage takes too long, the body drains all its reserves and becomes depleted, entering the third stage called exhaustion. In this stage, the body collapses.

Selye (1946) proposed that the alarm stage was further divided into two phases: shock and counter-shock. Shock refers to a sudden and intense internal response. Selye described it as actual damage to the internal system at a physical and biological level. Counter-shock refers to a secondary shock that occurs when the system realizes the stressor is not going away.

There are, however, a number of problems with using Selye's GAS to understand workplace stress. First, how people respond to stress differs due to a variety of factors including personality, learned coping skills, and initial health status. For example, anxious people tend to perceive stressors in their environment more so than relaxed people do (Lazarus, 1966). Accordingly, anxious people or those with high-strung personalities may follow a different pattern than the GAS model suggests. Additionally, researches have since determined that the body adopts new setpoints for homeostasis in response to constant stressors (Sterling & Eyer, 1988). The second significant problem with Selye's model is that researchers have found it is rare, if ever possible, for the body to deplete all resources due to sustained stress. Rather, instead of

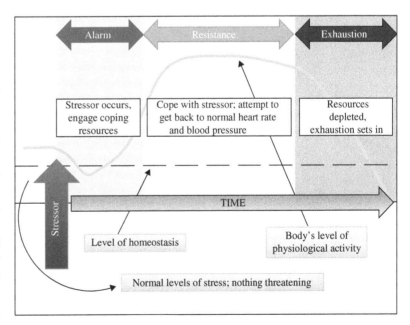

FIGURE 6.4   Selye's General Adaptation Syndrome

Courtesy Zinta Byrne. Source: Selye, 1946.

running out of resources, the body constantly draws from itself to respond, creating a stress-response that is more damaging than the original stressor itself (Sapolsky, 1998). That is, constantly using energy to handle chronic stress means continuously elevating the blood pressure, increasing muscle tension, and flooding the system with excess hormones and an activation of the immune system. The consequence is that the body starts to attack or damage itself (Sapolsky, 1998) rather than run out of steam.

Aside from the specific criticisms of Selye's model, treating stress as a response only (or as a dependent variable only) becomes problematic for predicting what will cause a reaction because different stimuli can create the same reaction. For example, headaches result from numerous causes such as eyestrain caused when forgetting one's reading glasses or from caffeine withdrawal, but we would not consider these specific situations as inducing work-related stress the way we might time pressures or personnel conflicts. Additionally, people respond differently to stimuli depending on their own characteristics and, how they interpret the work environment.

To acknowledge that neither a stimulus alone or response only definition is sufficient, the transactional definition of stress suggests that stress is a process in which people appraise situations and events as harmful, threatening, or challenging, and then cope with those perceptions (Folkman, Lazarus, Dunkel-Schetter, DeLongis, & Gruen, 1986; Lazarus, DeLongis, Folkman, & Gruen, 1985). Given this definition, stress is not necessarily negative, but instead relies on a person's interpretation of events. Thus, an individual's perception, cognitive appraisal, determines if external stimuli are viewed as challenges or threats.

Transactional Model of Stress

When people encounter a situation at work, Lazarus and colleagues (1966; Folkman et al., 1986; Lazarus et al., 1985) suggested they first engage in a primary appraisal. This involves asking the question "am I okay," or "is this a troubling situation?" People evaluate whether the situation feels threatening or challenging to them. If the situation appears threatening, people enter a secondary appraisal in which they determine what they need to or can do about the situation, thereby choosing their coping mechanism. If challenging, people enter a secondary appraisal, determining how to confront the challenge, again choosing their coping mechanism. Once they have acted to change the situation, they reappraise its effectiveness and engage in primary appraisal of the "new" situation (see Figure 6.5).

The implications of Lazarus' model are that stress is not an absolute

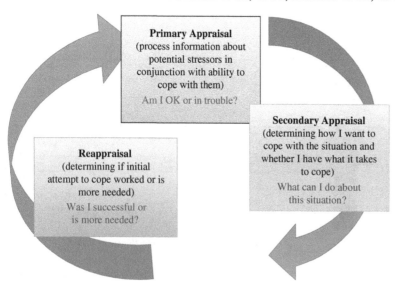

FIGURE 6.5   Lazarus' Transaction Model of Stress

Courtesy Zinta Byrne. Source: Lazarus, 1966.

state or event that affects everyone identically—how one interprets the event determines whether one experiences it as a positive or negative stressor. The interaction between the person and environment, and individualized cognitive appraisal may partly explain why some college students fall apart during exam week, whereas others thrive on the challenge. Some students see deadlines and test taking as highly stressful, whereas others see deadlines as effective end-goals or as an opportunity to demonstrate their mastery of the course material.

Main Contribution of the Model

The main contribution of the Transactional Model of Stress is that it describes the response to stressors as an individualized appraisal of a situation. Cognitive appraisal is a key feature of this model, as opposed to a physiological only response, which forms Selye's (1946) original model of stress. Thus, people *think* about their situation and stressors, and do not just react with an increased heart rate.

McGrath's (1976) Model of Job Stress

Although we can apply Lazarus' model to the workplace, the model narrowly focuses on the appraisal of the situation. McGrath's (1976) model of job stress incorporates and extends Lazarus' model to describe stress in organizations that follows a closed-loop cycle whereby four processes connect four stages of assessment (Figure 6.6).

The four stages include that you:

1. encounter a *situation* at work

2. assess the *perceived situation* for its potential to lead to an undesirable state

3. engage in *response selection*, which involves making a decision about how to respond to the situation

4. implement your response demonstrating a particular *behavior* in the hopes that the situation will improve

The four processes that connect these stages include the following:

A. *appraisal process*, the same as Lazarus' *primary appraisal* step in which you figure out whether the situation poses a possible threat

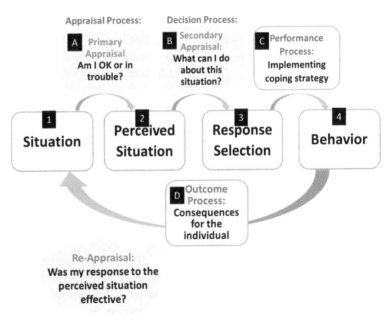

FIGURE 6.6   McGrath's (1976) Model of Job Stress (Adapted)

Courtesy Zinta Byrne. Source: McGrath, 1976.

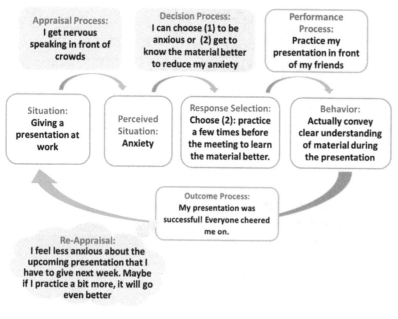

FIGURE 6.7 Example of McGrath's Model Applied to Presentation Situation

Courtesy Zinta Byrne.

B. *decision process*, which is where you choose alternative responses for coping with the situation, the same as Lazarus' secondary appraisal

C. *performance process* (also called the response process) represents your actual response, where you implement one of your response alternatives

D. *outcome process*, which shows that your behavior when responding to the stressor connects back to the original situation; changing the conditions you experienced thereby causing a new appraisal

This overall cycle represents how you change as you cope with the situation and then reassess. Figure 6.7 shows an example of McGrath's model applied to giving a presentation in class.

Main Contribution of the Model

Perhaps the main contribution of McGrath's model of job stress is its emphasis on stress processes in the workplace: that stress is an iterative cycle between people and their work environment, and that as one responds to the stress, the original stressful situation changes.

The ISR Model of Job Stress

McGrath's model, though influential, seemed focused on just the stress appraisal and coping cycle. What McGrath's model fails to incorporate are the many factors within organizations that play a role in creating the stressful situations that trigger coping responses.

Kahn and his colleagues (French & Kahn, 1962; Katz & Kahn, 1978) at the Institute for Social Research (ISR) of the University of Michigan developed a model of stress, which they called the ISR Model, to guide their ongoing research (see Figure 6.8). The model was introduced as a broad guideline for how categories of concepts were hypothesized to relate to one another.

The model suggests that variables within the objective work environment affect the psychological work environment (how the employee experiences work), which then gives rise to physiological, behavioral, or affective responses in the employee. For example, people who must work across teams within the organization (part of the job structure or objective work environment) may report feeling incompatible work demands on their time from the various teams (which is how they experience that part of their job), which results in them feeling anxious (response or reaction) about the incompatible demands. The consequence of them feeling anxious is that they develop headaches and pulled neck muscles, which represents the health consequences in the model.

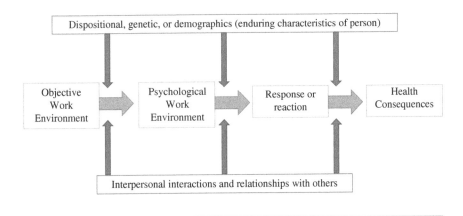

FIGURE 6.8   ISR Model of Job Stress

Courtesy Zinta Byrne. Source: Katz & Kahn, 1978.

People vary, however, in their personality and how they interact or relate to others at work, and these factors (individual personality, relationships) affect how each step in the model is perceived and experienced (shown as moderators in the model; Chapter 3 page 70 has a side-bar on what a moderator variable is, in case you forgot). For instance, employees who have a difficult relationship with their coworkers experience working across groups very differently from those who have excellent relationships and welcome the cross-group collaboration. Figure 6.9 provides an illustration of how the model might look when applied to Jody, a 25-year old manager at a local health club.

Main Contribution of the Model

The ISR model generated a lot of research into stress at work because it comprehensively incorporated work characteristics, both objective and subjective (how

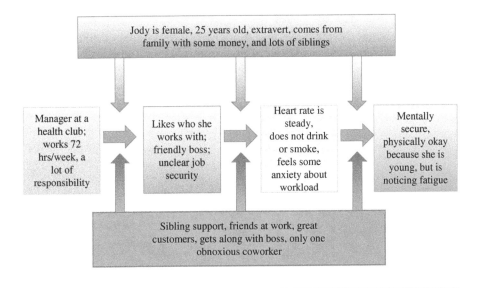

FIGURE 6.9   ISR Model Using Individual as Example

Courtesy Zinta Byrne.

the person experiences work), and modeled the stress-response cycle. The model included antecedents, the stress reaction, and the response, with appropriate person-by-environment interactions or moderators. It seems that all subsequent job stress models built on the ISR model as a foundation, becoming more comprehensive but also more complicated.

Beehr & Newman's (1978) Model of Job Stress

Beehr and Newman (1978) conducted a review of the job stress literature and proposed a model to capture the important passage of time within which stress mechanisms play out. The flow of events varies over time and situation, and mechanisms (e.g., responding and the consequences of the response) occur at various points in the chain. Their model shown in Figure 6.10, illustrates how the stress facets, conceptual dimensions encompassing a number of variables, may be related.

The *personal characteristics* facet includes personality traits, physical condition of the person (e.g., current health issues), developmental life-stage (e.g., young with no kids, middle-age with children), and general demographics such as age, sex, and occupation.

The *environmental characteristics* facet includes features of the job, such as general workload, level of responsibility or authority, design of the tasks, and pace of work; role demands, such as role ambiguity, clarity, or overload; organizational characteristics, such as company size, job security, climate, reward systems, management norms; and the organization's external demands and conditions, such as type of customers, regulatory agencies that oversee the organization, wealth of the company, technological scope and use, and geographic location of the organization.

The *stress processes* facet includes the psychological and physical ways in which people respond to stress such as perceptions, evaluation or appraisal of the situation, and cognitions about past or present situations, and chemical, neurological, and physiological responses.

People consequences include psychological and physical health such as depression, anger, headaches, gastrointestinal problems, or fatigue, and behavioral

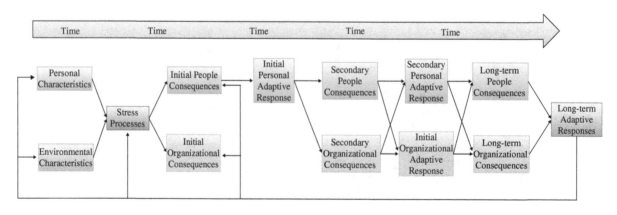

FIGURE 6.10   Beehr and Newman's Model of Job Stress

Courtesy Zinta Byrne. Source: Beehr & Newman, 1978.

consequences such as drug or substance abuse, excessive risk-taking behavior, and stealing or vandalism.

Organizational consequences are changes in profits, materials, productivity, and increased or conflicts with unions or regulatory boards.

Lastly, the *adaptive responses* facet is divided into the personal and organizational adaptive responses. Personal adaptive responses include meditation, stress-management, social support, biofeedback, drug or alcohol abuse treatment, and physical activity. Organizational adaptive responses include job redesign, reorganization of structure, changes in reward systems, increases in health-care services, or increasing communication. Third-party adaptive responses may also factor into the cycle and these include legislation that forces organizations to change their health-care plans or work schedule.

Here is how the model works: characteristics of the work environment, such as an ineffective boss, combined with one's inability to tolerate poor leadership (personal characteristic) lead to the experience of stress. That stress leads to an immediate consequence (people consequence), such as high blood pressure and complaining about the supervisor. That experience of stress also leads to a consequence at the organization in the form of low morale that may affect sales. Because of the complaining and high blood pressure, the employee may psychologically withdraw from work (initial adaptive response). That withdrawal leads to low motivation and increased sick days, which triggers a reduction in productivity in the group (secondary organizational consequence). The organization may respond with incentives for performance or policies to regulate absenteeism that lead to additional reactions from the employee. This cycle of responses and consequences can continue such that over time, if the stress is unresolved, there may be permanent negative health consequences for employees and loss of revenue and reputation for the organization (long-term people and organizational consequences). At the end of the cycle is a long-term adaptive response. Long-term responses can include the implementation of stress-management processes or programs, leadership development programs, task-forces to determine the initial causes of stress at work, and efforts to legislate work-life quality, such as instituting an official end of day time (e.g., Norwegians end their work day at 6 p.m.). Adaptive responses may also be unhealthy (e.g., substance abuse), but do remove or change the effects of the stressor.

Beehr and Newman's (1978) model can be challenging to read because of its many cross-over paths. Therefore, an alternative view of the model is shown in Figure 6.11 simplifying the paths and clarifying the characteristics of each facet. Note that the model illustrates a cycle, in which adaptive responses create changes in the environment that trigger personal and environmental adaptive responses. Hence, the model inherently assumes the passage of time.

Main Contribution of the Model

An important contribution of Beehr and Newman's model, which is often depicted by a simpler model without the sequence of primary and secondary responses and consequences, is its emphasis on the process over time—that the job stress process is one that occurs over time and involves various interactions between the person and the work environment. Additionally, this model appears to be one of the most comprehensive models of stress, capturing the complexity and

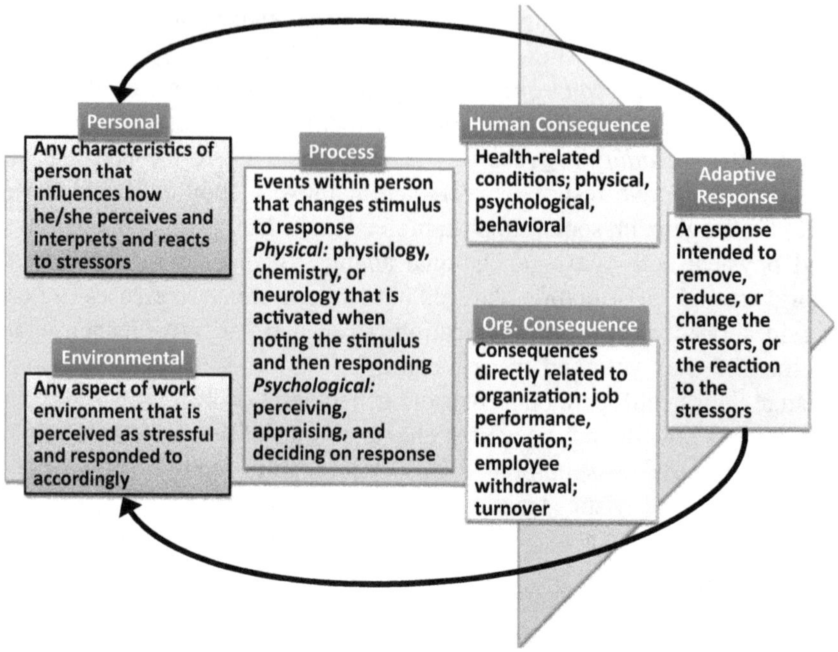

FIGURE 6.11   Another Variation on Beehr and Newman's Model of Stress

Courtesy Zinta Byrne. Source: Beehr & Newman, 1978.

interrelatedness of the many factors and facets of life and work that join together to create stress responses.

Exercise 6.3

What makes Beehr and Newman's Model of Job Stress an improvement over the basic ISR model?

Karasek's (1979) Model of Job Stress

Inconsistent findings about the impact of job stress led Karasek (1979) to propose a stress model in which two constructs, job control and job demands, interact to predict when employees experience their highest levels of stress. The model predicts that with increasing job demands and decreasing job control or decision latitude (i.e., decision authority, skill level, opportunity to control aspects of the job), job strains increase, as depicted in Figure 6.12. Decision latitude includes learning new things, freedom to make decisions, ability to participate in decisions, having a say in the job, and opportunity to be creative in problem-solving. Job demands include fast-paced work, a high workload, excessive time pressure, lack of time to complete the job, and having to work hard to do the job itself (Karasek, 1979).

   In addition Karasek also hypothesized that when both job demands and decision latitude are high, the job situation instigates problem-solving action and employees develop new behaviors on and off the job to handle the job situation. He called this situation one in which the job is active (Figure 6.13). When both job demands and decision latitude are low, the job is passive—problem-solving decreases (makes sense if there are few problems to solve) and employees may develop a sense of learned helplessness or general apathy toward the job (see Figure 6.13). Researchers have since shown that work underload, not having enough challenging work (likely a passive job), can be a high job stressor because of boredom, causing a lack of overall stimulation, which in turn negatively affects sleep patterns (Kelly & Cooper, 1981; Poulton, 1978).

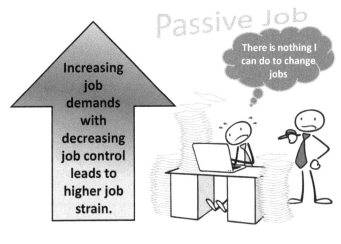

FIGURE 6.12   Job Strain As a Function of Job Demands and Decision Latitude

© Robert Kneschke/Shutterstock.com

Main Contribution of the Model

A contribution of Karasek's (1979) model was that previous researchers had failed to consider *both* demands and job control or ability to meet the demands when examining job strain. Karasek examined the results of previous studies showing top executives in higher status jobs with tremendous pressure reporting higher job satisfaction than employees in lower status jobs with considerably less pressure. The results seemed paradoxical. You would expect those with high job pressure and a lot of responsibility to report lower job satisfaction as an outcome of all the job tension, than people with few responsibilities. The assumption in previous research was a simple linear relationship: as job demands go up, so should job strain. But the relationship was not that simple. Hence, an important contribution of this model in predicting job strain is the ratio of job demands to job control or decision latitude.

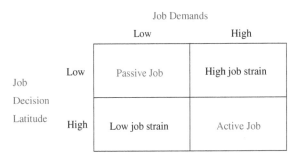

FIGURE 6.13   Active and Passive Jobs within Karasek's Model

Variants of High Demands Models

A number of models have been proposed that are variations on the basic theme: excessive demands and lack of resources results in strains. These theories include a **person–environment fit** theory and the effort-reward imbalance model of stress.

Person–Environment Fit Theory (Harrison, 1978)

Another model of stress to consider the interaction between people and their environment is the person–environment (P–E) fit theory (Harrison, 1978). The P–E fit theory suggests strains are experienced when a lack of congruency between the person and his or her environment exists in the form of demands in excess of and incongruent with what a person can handle, or in the form of an incongruence between a person's needs and what the environment supplies. Incongruence can occur either objectively (an actual lack of resources, excess demands, or lack of abilities) or subjectively (perceived lack or excess) across both person and environment components. For instance, a person may have an excess of demands, have an actual ability to deal with the demands, but perceive not having the ability; thus, creating a mismatch between the objective environment and subjective person. Consistent with Karasek's (1979) model, strains increase as demands exceed resources and the fit between the person and the work decreases (Edwards, 1996; Edwards & Harrison, 1993).

Siegrist (1996) Effort-Reward Imbalance Model of Job Stress

The effort–reward imbalance model is similar to equity theory (Deutsch, 1975) in that it proposes an imbalance within a reciprocal relationship between employee contributions or effort and rewards. However, rather than propose the ensuing experience is a perception of lack of fairness, the effort–reward imbalance model suggests the outcome of the perceived imbalance is strain. The model suggests that work interactions are based on exchanges of efforts (e.g., fulfilling job demands) and rewards (e.g., esteem, control, or money). When these two factors are not in balance, especially when there are high efforts and low rewards, employees experience work strains such as anxiety or anger. An important contribution of the model, therefore, is the emphasis that people want to be rewarded for their efforts, and when they feel they are not rewarded properly, they experience threats to their well-being and health.

For example, employees feeling they have demonstrated high levels of effort but received little in return report a variety of health complaints (Bosma, Peter, Siegrist, & Marmot, 1998). Furthermore, in the same study, the employees who felt they were putting in more than they received (Figure 6.14) were more likely to develop heart disease up to 6 years later than were those who did not report putting in high effort and receiving low rewards (Siegrist, Peter, Junge, Cremer, & Seidel, 1990). Thus, the strain resulting from the perceived imbalance created long-term health consequences lasting several years.

How much you get out of the job

How much effort you put into the job

FIGURE 6.14 Effort–Reward Imbalance

© zendograph / Shutterstock.com

Exercise 6.4

How is the Effort-Reward Imbalance Model of Job Stress different from inequity theory from the previous chapters?

Recent Theories

Most of the theories of stress reviewed thus far were introduced in the 1960s and 1970s. Recent models of stress include the Conservation of Resources theory (Hobfoll, 1989), the Job Demands-Resources Model (Demerouti, Bakker, Nachreiner, & Schaufeli, 2001), and the allostatic load model of stress (McEwen & Stellar, 1993).

Conservation of Resources

The Conservation of Resources model (Hobfoll, 1989) suggests that people prefer health and pleasure, and in their pursuit of maintaining these positive states, they load up on and conserve positive physical, social, and psychological resources. Resources include the capability to get more resources such as the mastery of knowledge or skills, positive energy such as self-esteem, and financial resources obtained through work. Stress is a threat to those resources, either to maintaining them or to accumulating more. When confronted with stressors that threaten the resources, the model proposes people attempt to minimize the loss.

Hence, overall the model says when not confronted by stressors, people attempt to stockpile resources to offset anticipated future loss of resources during stressful events. When confronted by stressors, they try to minimize the loss of resources by protecting themselves, withdrawing, or through other conservation behaviors. The model is a forward thinking approach with a long-term outlook as opposed to a short-term reactionary only model, like Selye's GAS model.

Why is it valuable to review and understand older theories of stress, when newer ones are available?

Job Demands-Resources

The job demands-resources model (JD-R: Demerouti et al., 2001) is similar to the Conservation of Resources model, and builds on Karasek's (1979) model of stress combined with the Effort–Reward Imbalance Model by Siegrist (1996). The JD-R proposes that resources buffer the energy depletion of job demands. If sufficient resources are lacking to offset the demands, employees experience burnout. In this model, job demands are considered physical, social, or organizational factors that require sustained attention. Demands, however, come at a cost to the employee. Resources are considered anything on the job that reduces those demands. Resources, like demands, can be physical, social, or organizational factors. Job control, an important aspect of Karasek's model, is included in job resources.

Both the Conservation of Resources and JD-R models of stress suggest that organizations may play a role in enabling employees to accumulate needed resources and manage job demands. Several approaches have been suggested including those with multiple phased or tiered plans.

Allostatic Load

When people experience stressors for a longtime, such as with chronic stress, their bodies adjust and seek homeostasis to the ongoing strains by maintaining body functions at these elevated and/or tense levels. For example, people may experience high blood pressure (i.e., hypertension), and elevated levels of anxiety as a result of chronic stress. Rather than relaxing these responses periodically, the body adjusts to this new norm creating a new resting state of high anxiety and hypertension. The allostatic load model of stress (McEwen & Stellar, 1993) was proposed to explain this new normal in the body in response to ongoing stressors. The model is a little more complex than the simple explanation provided here (see Ganster & Rosen, 2013 for more detail); however, what is most important to understand is that the allostatic load model represents an interdisciplinary (e.g., applied psychology, biology, physiology) theory for understanding the interaction between our physiological and cognitive response to stressors, and is one of the newer perspectives on the stress process.

How Do Managers Use These Theories in the Workplace?

People respond to stressors differently, thus having an understanding of the various theories presented here might help managers determine how best to support and work with their employees. For instance, recognizing as a manager whether you are setting up your employees for one or more of the various role stressors can help you clarify job expectations, better determine what is and is not with the scope of the job, and also what kind of support you need to give to help employees negotiate the challenges of the job.

As a manager, your job might be to help employees think through (out loud) how to handle the challenges of a stressful job. For example, an employee who tends to think through situations before reacting might find it helpful to discuss how to handle additional work stressors by walking through the transactional model of stress—what information are they considering that makes them feel threatened by the situation? Can you help reframe the appraisal as a nonthreat? Applying McGrath's model might mean considering more steps in the appraisal process. That is, what are the ways your employee chose to handle the additional work stressors? Are there potentially other ways of handling the situation that with managerial help, such as additional resources or alternative approaches, could result in a less anxiety provoking outcome?

Sometimes employees are just not aware of what they can and cannot ask for; thus, as a manager, you can help brainstorm new ideas knowing what kind of resources you can make available to help your employees. For some employees, a more in-depth conversation about personal and environmental characteristics might be in order, and in that case, you might turn to the ISR model to guide your conversation and efforts to help. For instance, if it turns out that your employee is from a large and close-knit family but is new to the area and thus has no access to family for support, you might consider assigning the employee to a team of coworkers who can help the new employee learn the job and also find friendly support while getting acquainted with the area. Once settled in, this new employee can be put on more independent or individual assignments without quite as much team involvement. During conversations with your employees, you might figure out that a more complex model like Beehr and Newman's should be used as a reference because the organization is providing adaptive responses that may not be helpful. As a manager, you are part of the organization, which means you might be engaging in job redesign, for example, that is actually going to make things worse for your employee—having conversations with your employees can help you determine their responses and yours, and find a better solution. In other cases, the solution might be as simple as giving your employee a little more job control, consistent with Karasek's model.

Hence, the different theoretical models can act as guides for managers to think about how stressors in the workplace occur, their source, and how their employees might respond. There are ways, however, that organizations as a whole can respond to occupational stress.

What Can Organizations Do about Occupational Stress?

Organizational researchers (e.g., Cooper, Dewe, & O'Driscoll, 2001; Quillan-Wolever & Wolever, 2003) have suggested a three-tiered prevention or intervention approach: primary, secondary, tertiary to managing stress at work.

Primary Interventions

Primary interventions (or solutions) focus on reductions in the sources of stress, such as the work environment itself, the structure of the organization, technology, and the structure of the job. Their focus is on prevention by changing the job environment rather than the person (Semmer, 2011). Efforts in job redesign and role restructuring, like incorporating flextime (i.e., allowing employees to start and stop their work day during a range rather than a single set time; for instance, start any time between 5 a.m. and 7 a.m.) or compressed work weeks (work four 10-hour days instead of five 8-hour days), can alleviate some role stressors.

In organizations where flextime is possible, the organization itself saves time and expenses by not having to enforce strict schedules, especially if those work hours are not essential to work function. For instance, lawyers, engineers, or professors may not have jobs that necessitate strict start and stop times; whereas nurses, restaurant servers, assembly line workers, drivers for shipping/distribution firms, or other shift work and customer service jobs may be limited to a strict start and stop time because of changing of shifts, laws, or coverage issues.

Aside from scheduling redesign, changes to the physical work space to reduce noise or distractions, restructuring lines of authority to provide more job control, and increasing employee participation in decisions that directly affect their ability to do their jobs (Cooper et al., 2001) may be other options that relieve stress. With an adequate assessment of the source of stressors, organizations can proactively establish work plans that either reduce or eliminate stressors.

Secondary Interventions

Secondary interventions focus on changing the effect stressors have on employees, as opposed to changing the work environment that creates the stressors. For example, solutions include helping employees learn muscle-relaxation techniques, meditation, or other relaxation and stress-management strategies that involve physical movement. Secondary approaches are the most common interventions to stress management in organizations (Dewe, 1994), perhaps because they are the cheapest for organizations. These solutions put the ownership of stress coping and management on the employee, thus eliminating the need for the organization to address structural sources of stress (such as redesigning everyone's jobs, changing lines of responsibility, or investing in fixes to the work environment like new furniture, air units, or lighting).

Stress-management approaches are about using stress relief techniques on a regular basis, proactively, rather than just using relief techniques when already feeling stressed. With a stress-management approach, employees plan and schedule time to take care of future anticipated stress; stress that has not yet occurred. Practicing stress management is hard because people generally do not think about stress when they are not experiencing job stress. However, if they give some thought to it, employees can usually predict what times of year, workloads, or situations are likely to create feelings of stress, simply based on experiences.

In managing stress proactively, one has to identify stress relievers and stress triggers. Stress relievers are those actions or thoughts that can be healthy or unhealthy. They include what we automatically do when feeling stressed. For example, some people turn to exercise to relieve stress, whereas others may turn to food or substance use (e.g., alcohol, cigarettes, drugs).

A key question to ask yourself is whether what you do when you're feeling stressed helps or ultimately makes things worse. For example, many who turn to a few drinks to relieve their stress find it only helps temporarily. Having a few drinks may ultimately make the situation worse for them, because they end up doing something else while under the influence that then adds to additional stress (e.g., getting into a fight, overspending via online shopping). A great stress reliever is some form of relaxation that directly addresses the physical tension in the body that is automatically triggered by the stress response cycle, but that doesn't itself lead to negative consequences elsewhere (Figure 6.15). For instance, exercise, massage, or meditation can relax the physical tension in muscles that is triggered during the stress response. Laughter has been shown to lead to general muscle relaxation for up to 45 minutes after the initial laughter event, and to an increase in production of stress fighting hormones (Berk et al., 1989; Fry, 1992; Paskind, 1932). Hence, laughter is a terrific stress reliever.

Relaxation techniques can be simple and many can be used most anytime and anywhere. Practicing stress management relief techniques can prevent a buildup of anxiety and overall tension, and thus, make it easier to emotionally and physi-

Which techniques do you find work for you? Why?

cally handle stress as it comes. Two things stress management trainers suggest employees keep in mind: (1) don't be overwhelmed by managing the stress—just make the techniques realistic and regular; and (2) choose stress relievers that generate the biggest gain in relief. Hence, choosing those with the fastest and strongest relief effect (e.g., exercise, meditation) may be the best to practice regularly.

Organizations can sponsor relaxation training, biofeedback training (using instruments that measure physiology to make people more aware of how their bodies respond to stress and to relaxation strategies), and stress inoculation training (a form of cognitive-behavioral therapy that builds resistance to stress effects through managed exposure to stressful events).

As an illustration, a stress inoculation training program (e.g., Keyes, 1995) may be to, first, help employees become more aware of their emotional and behavioral reactions to stressors. Second, once employees are aware their reactions are based on their appraisal of the stressors, the next step is to develop their relaxation, problem-solving, cognitive restructuring, and decision-making skills and practice so these techniques can be used easily and without a lot of thought during a stressful event. Lastly, employees are put through simulations of stressful situations so they can practice and tryout their healthy coping skills.

Organizations sometimes introduce wellness programs to encourage health promotion (Ganster, Mayes, Sime, & Tharp, 1995), but again, these programs are designed to put the responsibility for stress management in the hands of the employees.

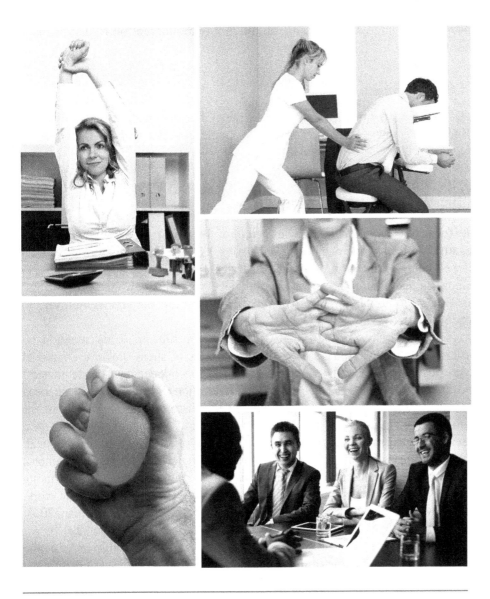

Watch https://www.ted.com/talks/kelly_mcgonigal_how_to_make_stress_your_friend to see how stress might actually be good for your health.

FIGURE 6.15   Stress Management and Relievers

Clockwise: © Robert Kneschke/Shutterstock, Inc.; © wavebreakmedia/Shutterstock, Inc.; © David Mckee/Shutterstock, Inc.; © Robert Kneschke/Shutterstock, Inc.; © Pressmaster/Shuttertock, Inc.

Tertiary Interventions

Tertiary approaches to managing stress at work are focused on how to deal with the stressful event after it has created the strains; thus, what to do about treating the consequences of stress. Tertiary approaches may include recommending employees to **employee assistance programs** (EAPs, programs established by human resources to provide short-term counseling or related assistance), providing referrals to counseling professionals, or encouraging time off from work. EAPs are sometimes external services provided to the organization, internal services provided by the organization, or a combination of both with connections to local hospitals and community health centers to make referrals easy and affordable (Dewe, 1994). Of the three intervention levels, this one is the most costly to organization; therefore, they have a vested interest in focusing on the first two intervention levels: primary and secondary.

Ask for help—your organization may have options that you have never considered and aren't aware of.

Exercise 6.5

Describe what organizations can do about occupational stress—develop unique examples for all three levels—examples not mentioned in the book.

Chapter Summary

The focus of occupational stress has been, for the most part, on how work stress negatively affects workers' general well-being, as well as the organization's overall well-being in the form of lost productivity. There is no doubt that people do respond in many different ways to varying levels of what they appraise as stressors. Organizations support efforts to relieve stressors and help train employees to cope with distress.

Nelson and Simmons (2003) argue it may be time to focus attention on eustress—the positive effects of positive appraisals of stress. Positive emotional states, positive energy, and a pleasurable response to work demands create physical and emotional well-being, engagement, and innovation (Byrne, 2015). As opposed to stress management focusing on coping with distress, Nelson and Simmons (2003), as well as others (e.g., Quick & Quick, 1984; Quick et al., 1997), suggest that stress management should be rooted in the ideas of effective time management, learned optimism, social support, and eustress generation (see Nelson & Simmons, 2003, for a full discussion). Organizations can take an active role in facilitating eustress and many have already begun by instigating play, social events at work, and allowing employees to design their work environments (e.g., Berkeman, 2013; Brotherton, 1996; Nel & Spies, 2007; Vijay & Vazirani, 2011; Witham, 2013).

Why would an organization implement secondary or tertiary interventions over primary interventions?

Perhaps what matters most here is that stress *is* a manageable process and *you* can play an active role in managing your own stress responses. Though you cannot eliminate stress in your life, nor would you want to, you can develop skills for how you perceive the work environment (whether a threat or challenge) and practice coping in ways that promotes your health rather than tear it down.

Figure 6.16 shows a visual summary of the key concepts reviewed in Chapter 6.

The visual summary reminds us that the objective (e.g., heat, noise, time pressure) and psychological (i.e., our experience) environment factors influence our appraisal of the situation. Do we perceive the environment as a threat or a positive challenge? Our appraisal gives rise to a response. The large hour glass reminds us that stress is a process that occurs overtime, and triggers primary and secondary outcomes. Primary outcomes are individual strains that we experience ourselves, whereas the secondary outcomes are those that affect the organization overall. Thus, we are not alone in the effects of stress—the organization for whom we work is affected by how we respond and cope with stressors. Lastly, support is essential for managing and handling the strains we experience. Substantial research shows support is a key factor in healthy stress management and coping.

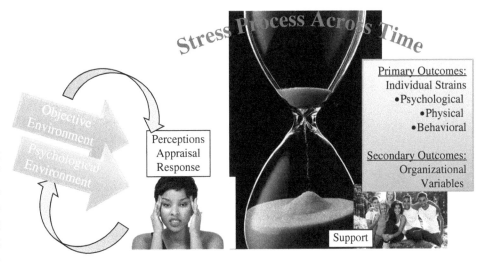

FIGURE 6.16   Visual Summary of Chapter 6

© Sanjay Deva/Shutterstock, Inc.; ©sergign/Shutterstock, Inc.; ©oliveromg/Shutterstock, Inc. Courtesy Zinta Byrne.

Discussion Questions

1. Stress is an overall health topic, so why do we focus so much effort on specific stress related to what happens in our jobs/occupations? Is there something unique or special about occupational stress that suggests we must deal with it separately from overall general life stress?

2. There are so many theories of stress at work. What might be a simplified overall model that combines the essential components of all the models, something that you can find more useable yet specific enough to occupational health? That is, what are the essential parts of models that you think absolutely must be considered when explaining stress at work? How do they all combine?

3. Given that we keep studying more stress at work—it seems that the current plans and strategies for handling stress are not working. First, do you agree with that? Are we experiencing more and more stress at work regardless of available interventions? Second, if you agree, why is it that the strategies outlined in the textbook are not working? In your opinion, what is missing? What would make primary, secondary, and tertiary interventions successful?

References

Beehr, T. A., & Glazer, S. (2005). Organizational role stress. In J. Barling, E. K. Kelloway, & M. R. Frone (Eds.), *Handbook of work stress* (pp.7–34). Thousand Oaks, CA: Sage.

Beehr, T. A., & Newman, J. E. (1978). Job stress, employee health, and organizational effectiveness: A facet analysis, model, and literature review. *Personnel Psychology, 31*(4), 665–699. doi:10.1111/j.1744-6570.1978.tb02118.x

Berk, L., Tan, S., Fry, W., Napier, B., Lee, J., Hubbard, R., & ... Eby, W. (1989). Neuroendocrine and stress hormone changes during mirthful laughter. *The American Journal of the Medical Sciences, 298*(6), 390–396.

Berkeman, O. (2013, December 12). Who Goes to Work to Have Fun? *New York Times.* p. A35.

Bosma, H., Peter, R., Siegrist, J., & Mannot, M. (1998). Two alternative job stress models and the risk of coronary heart disease. *American Journal of Public Health, 88,* 68–74.

Brotherton, P. (1996). The company that plays together... (cover story). *HR Magazine, 41*(12), 76.

Byrne, Z. S. (2015). *Understanding employee engagement: Theory, research, and practice.* New York, NY: Routledge/Taylor & Francis Group.

Caplan, R. D. (1975*). Job demands and worker health: Main effects and occupational differences.* Rockville, MD: U.S. Dept. of Health, Education, and Welfare, Public Health Service, Center for Disease Control, National Institute for Occupational Safety and Health.

Chan-Serafin, S., Teo, L., Minbashian, A., Cheng, D., & Wang, L. (2017). The perils of dating your boss: The role of hierarchical workplace romance and sex on evaluators' career advancement decisions for lower status romance participants. *Journal of Social and Personal Relationships, 34*(3), 309–333.

Cooper, C. L., Dewe, P. J., & O'Driscoll, M. P. (2001). *Organizational stress: A review and critique of theory, research, and applications.* Thousand Oaks, CA: Sage.

Coovert, M. D., & Thompson, L. F. (2003). Technology and workplace health. In J. C. Quick & L. E. Tetrick (Eds.), *Handbook of occupational health psychology* (pp. 221–242). Washington, DC: American Psychological Association.

Cowan, R. L., & Horan, S. M. (2014). Love at the office? Understanding workplace romance disclosures and reactions from the coworker perspective. *Western Journal of Communication, 78*(2), 238–253.

Cromie, W. J. (2006). Interns continue to work overly long shifts, study finds. Retrieved from the Harvard Gazette Archives at http://www.news.harvard.edu/gazette/2006/09.14/99-sleepyinterns.html

Daly, A., Carey, R. N., Darcey, E., Chih, H., LaMontagne, A. D., Milner, A., & Reid, A. (2018). Workplace psychosocial stressors experienced by migrant workers in Australia: A cross-sectional study. *PLoS ONE, 13(9),* 1–19. doi: 10.1371/journal.pone.0203998

Davy, J. A., Kinicki, A. J., & Scheck, C. L. (1997). A test of job security's direct and mediated effects on withdrawal cognitions. *Journal of Organizational Behavior, 18,* 323–349.

Demerouti, E., Bakker, A. B., Nachreiner, F., & Schaufeli, W. B. (2001). The job demands-resources model of burnout. *Journal of Applied Psychology, 86*(3), 499–512. doi:10.1037/0021-9010.86.3.499

Deutsch, M. (1975). Equity, equality, and need: What determines which value will be used as the basis of distributive justice? *Journal of Social Issues, 31*(3), 137–149.

Dewe, P. (1994). EAPs and stress management. *Personnel Review, 23*(7), 21–32.

Dickerson, S. S., & Zoccola, P. M. (2009). Toward a biology of social support. In S. J. Lopez, C. R. Snyder (Eds.), *Oxford handbook of positive psychology (2nd ed.)* (pp. 519–526). New York, NY: Oxford University Press.

Edwards, J. R. (1996). An examination of competing versions of the person–environment fit approach to stress. *Academy Of Management Journal, 39*(2), 292–339. doi:10.2307/256782

Edwards, J. R., & Van Harrison, R. R. (1993). Job demands and worker health: Three-dimensional reexamination of the relationship between person-environment fit and strain. *Journal of Applied Psychology, 78*(4), 628–648. doi:10.1037/0021-9010. 78.4.628

Fiorillo, D., & Sabatini, F. (2011). Quality and quantity: The role of social interactions in self-reported individual health. *Social Science & Medicine, 73*(11), 1644–1652. doi:10.1016/j.socscimed.2011.09.007

Fleming, R., Baum, A., & Singer, J. E. (1984). Toward an integrative approach to the study of stress. *Journal of Personality and Social Psychology, 46*(4), 939–949. doi:10.1037/0022-3514.46.4.939

Folkman, S., Lazarus, R. S., Dunkel-Schetter, C., DeLongis, A., & Gruen, R. J. (1986). Dynamics of a stressful encounter: Cognitive appraisal, coping, and encounter outcomes. *Journal of Personality And Social Psychology, 50*(5), 992–1003. doi:10.1037/0022-3514.50.5.992

French, J. R. P., Jr., & Kahn, R. L. (1962). A programmatic approach to studying the industrial environment and mental health. *The Journal of Social Issues, 18,* 1–47.

Fry, W. (1992). The physiologic effects of humor, mirth, and laughter. *JAMA: The Journal of the American Medical Association, 267*(13), 1857–1858.

Ganster, D. C., Mayes, B. T., Sime, W. E., & Tharp, G. D. (1982). Managing organizational stress: A field experiment. *Journal of Applied Psychology, 67*(5), 533–542. doi:10.1037/0021-9010.67.5.533

Ganster, D. C., & Rosen, C. C. (2013). Work stress and employee health: A multidisciplinary review. *Journal of Management, 39(5)*, 1085-1122. doi: 10.1177/0149206313475815

Goetzel, R. Z., Xiaofei, P., Tabrizi, M. J., Henke, R. M., Kowlessar, N., Nelson, C. F., & Metz, R. (2012). Ten modifiable health risk factors are linked to more than one-fifth of employer-employee health care spending. *Health Affairs, 31*(11), 2474–2483. doi:10.1377/hlthaff.2011.0819

Greenhaus, J. H., & Beutell, N. J. (1985). Sources of conflict between work and family roles. *Academy of Management Review, 10,* 76–88.

Hampton, K. N., Sessions, L. F., & Her, E. (2011). Core networks, social isolation, and new media: How internet and mobile phone use is related to network size and diversity. *Information, Communication & Society, 14*(1), 130–155. doi:10.1080/13691 18X.2010.513417

Harrison, R. V. (1978). Person-environment fit and job stress. In C. L. Cooper & R. Paye (Eds.), *Stress at work* (pp. 175–205). New York, NY: Wiley.

Heaney, C. A., Israel, B. A., & House, J. S. (1994). Chronic job insecurity among automobile workers: Effects on job satisfaction and health. *Social Science & Medicine, 38,* 1431–1437.

HobfollS, S.E. (1989). Conservation of resources: A new attempt at conceptualizing stress. *American Psychologist, 44*(3), 513–524. doi:10.1037/0003/066X.44.3.513

Jackson, S. E., Kirschbaum, C., & Steptoe, A. (2016). Perceived weight discrimination and chronic biochemical stress: A population-based study using cortisol in scalp hair. *Obesity, 24*(12), 2515-2521. doi:10.1002/oby.21657

Jackson, S. E., & Schuler, R. S. (1985). A meta-analysis and conceptual critique of research on role ambiguity and role conflict in work settings. *Organizational Behavior and Human Decision Processes, 36*(1), 16–78. doi:10.1016/0749-5978(85)90020-2

Kahn, R. L., & Byosiere, P. (1992). Stress in organizations. In M. D. Dunnette, L. M. Hough (Eds.), *Handbook of industrial and organizational psychology, Vol. 3 (2nd ed.)* (pp. 571–650). Palo Alto, CA: Consulting Psychologists Press.

Kahn, R. L., Wolfe, D. M., Quinn, K. P., Snoek, J. D., & Rosenthal, R. A. (1964). *Organizational stress: Studies in role conflict and ambiguity.* New York: Wiley.

Karelina, K., & DeVries, A. (2011). Modeling social influences on human health. *Psychosomatic Medicine, 73*(1), 67–74. doi:10.1097/PSY.0b013e3182002116

Karasek, R. A. (1979). Job demands, job decision latitude, and mental strain: Implications for job redesign. *Administrative Science Quarterly, 24*(2), 285–308.

Katz, D., & Kahn, R. L. (1978). *The social psychology of organizations.* New York, NY: Wiley.

Keim, A. C., Landis, R. S., Pierce, C. A., & Earnest, D. R. (2014). Why do employees worry about their jobs? A meta-analytic review of predictors of job insecurity. *Journal of Occupational Health Psychology, 19*(3), 269–290. doi:10.1037/a0036743

Kelly, M., & Cooper, C. L. (1981). Stress among Blue Collar Workers. *Employee Relations, 3*(2), 6–9.

Keyes, J. B. (1995). Stress inoculation training for staff working with persons with mental retardation: A model program. In L. R. Murphy, J. J. Hurrell, Jr., S. L. Sauter, & G. P. Keita (Eds.), *Job stress interventions* (pp. 45–56). Washington, DC: American Psychological Association.

Landrigan, C. P., Rothschild, J. M., Cronin, J. W., Kaushal, R., Burdick, E., Katz, J. T., Lilly, C. M.,…Czeisler, C. A. (2004). Effects of reducing interns' work hours on serious medical errors in intensive care units. *New England Journal of Medicine, 351,* 1838–1848.

Larson, C. F. (2007). 50 Years of change in industrial research and technology management. *Research Technology Management, 50*(1), 26–31.

Lazarus, R. S. (1966). *Psychological stress and the coping process.* New York, NY: McGraw-Hill.

Lazarus, R. S., DeLongis, A., Folkman, S., & Gruen, R. (1985). Stress and adaptational outcomes: The problem of confounded measures. *American Psychologist, 40*(7), 770–779. doi:10.1037/0003-066X.40.7.770

Malachowski, C. C., Chory, R. M., & Claus, C. J. (2012). Mixing pleasure with work: Employee perceptions of and responses to workplace romance. *Western Journal of Communication, 76*(4), 358–379.

McEwen, B. S., & Stellar, E. (1993). Stress and the individual: Mechanisms leading to disease. *Archives of Internal Medicine, 153*(18), 2093-2101.

McGrath, J. E. (1976). Stress and behavior in organizations. In M. Dunnette (Ed.), *Handbook of industrial and organizational psychology* (Vol.1, pp. 1351–1396). Chicago, IL: Rand McNally.

Nel, D., & Spies, G. M. (2007). The use of play therapy mediums in a stress management program with corporate employees. *Journal of Workplace Behavioral Health, 22*(1), 33–51. doi:10.1300/J490v22n01_03

Nelson, D. L., & Simmons, B. L. (2003). Health psychology and work stress: A more positive approach. In J. Quick, L. E. Tetrick (Eds.), *Handbook of occupational health psychology* (pp. 97–119). Washington, DC: American Psychological Association. doi:10.1037/10474-005

NIOSH 99-101 *Stress at work.* Retrieved from http://www.cdc.gov/niosh/docs/99-101/

Örtqvist, D., & Wincent, J. (2006). Prominent consequences of role stress: A meta-analytic review. *International Journal of Stress Management, 13*(4), 399–422. doi:10.1037/1072-5245.13.4.399

Paskind, H. A. (1932). Effect of laughter on muscle tone. *Archives of Neurology & Psychiatry, 28,* 623–628.

Poulton, E. (1978). Blue collar stressors. In C. Cooper & R. Payne (Eds.), *Stress at work.* New York, NY: Wiley.

Quick, J. C., & Quick, J. D. (1984). *Organizational stress and preventive management.* New York: McGraw-hill.

Quick, J. C., Quick, J. D., Nelson, D. L., & Hurrell, J. J. Jr. (1997). *Preventive stress management in organizations.* American Psychological Association: Washington, DC.

Quillan-Wolever, R. E., & Wolever, M. E. (2003). Stress management at work. In J. C. Quick & L. E. Tetrick (Eds.), *Handbook of occupational health psychology* (pp. 355–375). Washington, DC: American Psychological Association.

Rizzo, J. R., House, R. J., & Lirtzman, S. I. (1970). Role conflict and ambiguity in complex organizations. *Administrative Science Quarterly, 15*(2), 150–163. doi:10.2307/2391486

Sales, S. M. (1970). Some effects of role overload and role underload. *Organizational Behavior & Human Performance, 5*(6), 592–608. doi:10.1016/0030-5073(70)90042-5

Sapolsky, R. M. (1998). *Why zebras don't get ulcers.* New York, NY: Henry Holt and Company.

Selye, H. (1946). The general adaptation syndrome and the diseases of adaptation. *Journal of Clinical Endrocrinology & Metabolism, 6*(2), 117–190.

Selye, H. (1982). History and present status of the stress concept. *Handbook of stress: Theoretical and clinical aspects, 2,* 7–20.

Semmer, N.K. (2011). Job stress interventions and organization of work. In J. Quick, L.E. Tetrick (Eds.), *Handbook of occupational health psychology (2nd ed.)* (pp. 299–318). Washington, DC: American Psychological Association.

Shultz, K. S., Wang, M., & Olson, D. A. (2010). Role overload and underload in relation to occupational stress and health. *Stress and Health: Journal of the International Society for the Investigation of Stress, 26*(2), 99–111. doi:10.1002/smi.1268

Siegrist, J. (1996). Adverse health effects of high-effort/low-reward conditions. *Journal of Occupational Health Psychology, 1*(1), 27–41. doi:10.1037/1076-8998.1.1.27

Siegrist, J., Peter, R., Junge, A., Cremer, P., & Seidel, D. (1990). Low status control, high effort at work and ischemic heart disease: Prospective evidence from blue-collar men. *Social Science and Medicine, 31,* 1127–1134.

Smith, C. S., Folkard, S., & Fuller, J. A. (2003). Shiftwork and working hours. In J. C. Quick & L. E. Tetrick (Eds.), *Handbook of occupational health psychology* (pp. 163–184). Washington, DC: American Psychological Association.

Spector, P. E. (1986). Perceived control by employees: A meta-analysis of studies concerning autonomy and participation at work. *Human Relations, 39*(11), 1005–1016. doi:10.1177/001872678603901104

Sverke, M., Hellgren, J., & Näswall, K. (2002). No security: A meta-analysis and review of job insecurity and its consequences. *Journal of Occupational Health Psychology, 7*(3), 242–264. doi:10.1037/1076-8998.7.3.242

Taha, L. H., & Calwell, B. S. (1993). Social isolation and integration in electronic environments. *Behaviour & Information Technology, 12*(5), 276–283. doi:10.1080/01449299308924391

Velez, B. L., Cox, R., Jr., Polihronakis, C. J., & Moradi, B. (2018). Discrimination, work outcomes, and mental health among women of color: The protective role of womanist attitudes. *Journal of Counseling Psychology, 65*(2), 178–193. doi: 10.1037/cou0000274

Vijay, M., & Vazirani, N. (2011). Emerging paradigm - Fun in workplace to alleviate stress. *SIES Journal of Management, 7*(2), 24–30.

Witham, T. (2013). Having fun. *Credit Union Management, 36*(11), 42–43.

PART II

Running the Organization Using Teams and Leaders

CHAPTER 7

Being Part of a Group: Teams

Learning Outcomes

After studying this chapter you should be able to:

1. Discuss the different types of teams that exist in organizations and identify their strengths and weaknesses.

2. Evaluate when organizations should and should not use teams.

3. Judge when teams are designed to be effective versus ineffective.

Mini-Quiz: Teams

As an introduction to this chapter, please take the following mini-quiz (answers are in the back of the book). As you read the questions and consider the answers *before* diving into the chapter, you'll challenge yourself before you master the content, a process that helps facilitate learning for long-term retention. Some questions may have more than one correct answer. Don't worry if you cannot answer all questions correctly on your first try. By the time you read through the chapter and spend some of your own time thinking about these concepts, you should be able to determine the best answers. Try the quiz again after you finish reading the chapter.

1. Which of the following can be classified as a "team"?
    a. Two people who are working on a project together.
    b. Three coworkers who have been e-mailing each other to resolve a problem with one of the company policies.

      c. The finance department.

      d. A manager and the employees the manager supervises.

2. True or false: Diversity in teams is highly desirable.

      a. False. Diverse teams often experience higher levels of conflict than non-diverse teams, which is not desirable for organizations.

      b. True. Having a variety of personalities, backgrounds, and skills can lead to greater team effectiveness.

3. What makes for an effective self-managed team?

      a. Teams need some sort of leader; if they are "self-managed" they will fail.

      b. Clarifying the processes in the team, such as how to make decisions.

      c. Selecting team members who are experts and can work independently.

      d. Selecting team members who all have similar skills so they can work closely together to complete a given task.

4. What special challenges do virtual teams face?

      a. Because communication can be so much easier and quicker virtually, teams can be very large, making it more difficult to keep up with everyone.

      b. Having a strong leader.

      c. Training employees to deal with conflict.

      d. Not having the ability to put "a face" to the people with whom you interact and work.

5. _____ are social guidelines for how to act in a particular group and when violated, may result in the group rejecting that particular team member.

Overview

Chances are if you work for an organization with more than 10 people, you yourself or some of your employees work in a team. **Teams** comprise two or more people working together to accomplish a common set of goals. Organizations use teams because they believe people performing on a task together are often more effective than people working as individuals. Indeed, teams can play a critical role in accomplishing a lot of work in a short amount of time. When the job requires a variety of skills, judgments, and experience, it appears teams outperform individuals working alone (e.g., Glassop, 2002). They accomplish more in teams than alone because of the team climate (positive or performance oriented), the help that team members provide, the excitement of working with others, and the inability to get everything done alone.

However, not all projects that require the completion of several tasks are well suited for the team approach. There are also situations where people accomplish more when working alone, such as when that person's expertise, and that expertise alone, is required. For example, a jewelry maker, glass blower, or pharmacist generally do not work in teams to design a necklace, produce a unique carafe, or mix a prescription. Other situations where teams can be inappropriate include joint editing of documents. Multiple team members editing a document together usually experience high inefficiency and frustration. When too many people edit the document at the same time, the document becomes unreadable and takes an exponentially longer amount of time to complete as compared to a single person editing the document (regardless of the technology used).

It turns out, the secret to effective teams includes knowing when to use them and for what purpose.

What Are Teams?

Numerous definitions for teams exist perhaps because so many variations of groups exist (Figure 7.1). Teams vary by size, structure (the stable patterns of relationships among members: McGrath, 1964), and purpose. One of the early definitions of teams offered by Katzenbach and Smith (1992) states that a team is "a small number of people with complementary skills who are committed to a common purpose, performance goals, and approach for which they hold themselves mutually accountable" (p. 5). However, as the focus on teams in organizations has grown, the definition has expanded to include **interdependence** *among team members*. Guzzo (1995) notes that teams must engage in task-based

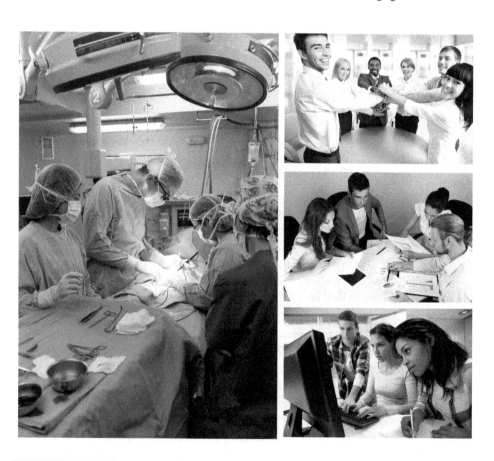

FIGURE 7.1 Teams

Clockwise: © Franck Boston/Shutterstock, Inc.; © Africa Studio/Shutterstock, Inc.; © Goodluz/Shutterstock, Inc.; © Konstantin Chagin/Shutterstock, Inc.

interdependence, which means that to successfully complete the group task, members must interact with each other by exchanging information, sharing resources, and coordination. Sundstrom and colleagues (Sundstrom, de Meuse, & Futrell, 1990; Sundstrom, McIntyre, Halfhill, & Richards, 2000) incorporate this idea by defining teams as an interdependent collection of individuals, who see themselves as a team and who share responsibility for outcomes.

Kozlowski and Bell (2013) proposed that groups comprise two or more individuals who:

- perform organizationally relevant work tasks
- share one or more common work-related goals
- interact on a social basis
- have tasks that are interdependent
- maintain and manage boundaries between themselves and other groups
- are embedded in an organizational context that sets boundaries, constrains the team, and influences exchanges between the team and other groups or units.

They also note that teams share a number of features about their members including:

- Interdependence
- Belonging to existing work units
- Specialized yet complementary roles
- Complementary expertise
- Reporting to the same manager
- Working the same shift or work period
- A history of working together
- Potentially sharing physical work space or work location.

The common elements in definitions of teams in the workplace can be combined to create a single definition: a team is a collection of interdependent members, who see themselves as a group, who work together to accomplish a common goal, and who manage their relationships within the constraints of the organization.

Given this definition, teams can have many different features associated with them, such as their size, structure, member characteristics, and where they are located.

Given this definition, are the teams you are often asked to form in classes actually considered "teams"? Explain why or why not.

Features of Teams

Teams have features that affect how well they function and how communication occurs. Features include team size, structure, composition (i.e., membership), and location (i.e., colocated or geographically dispersed).

Size

Because team size affects communication patterns, effectiveness of the leader, budgets, production speeds, and more, size is an important variable for researchers to include in their studies and for managers to focus on when determining team structure.

A team is usually not considered a team until there are two or more members. Although no magic number exists for team size (Guzzo & Shea, 1992; Hackman, 1987), some suggest that effective teams range between 2 and 25 people, with most possessing less than 10 members. The most effective teams have no more members than necessary required for the task, but a general rule of thumb is to have between 7 and 9 members (Curral, Forrester, Dawson, & West, 2001; Katzenbach, 2000; Katzenbach & Smith, 1993). Smaller teams may lack the necessary diversity of skills and expertise, or perspective that contributes to innovation and effectiveness (Curral et al., 2001). The larger the group, the harder for members to interact and hold group discussions, share information, and make decisions. Large teams sometimes have more resources, skills, energy, and variety of knowledge or expertise than small teams, but these additions are only useful if the team needs these features and if coordination among members can be effectively managed.

Team size affects team members themselves, making management more challenging. Specifically, large teams are associated with lower team-member job satisfaction, higher negative emotions experienced on the job, and lower levels of overall mental well-being than smaller teams (Campion, Medsker, & Higgs, 1993; Hausknecht, Trevor, & Howard, 2009; Markham, Dansereau, & Alutto, 1982; Wegge, Roth, Neubach, Schmidt, & Kanfer, 2008). What's a *large* team? No set number determines what makes a team large; instead, researchers suggest that when teams are larger than previously sized or large relative to the task and organization, they are considered "large" (Markham, et al., 1982). As team size increases, the quality of the group experience tends to deteriorate and members begin demonstrating counterproductive behaviors within the team (Aubé, Rousseau, & Tremblay, 2011).

Not all large teams deteriorate. Teams can be very large and consequently develop subteams within them that reduce their large feel. For example, groups that organize large events, such as the World Triathalon Corporation who puts together the IronMan Triathlon or Amaury Sport Organisation who puts together Le Tour de France cycling race, may include hundreds of people overall. However, they are divided into smaller groups, subteams, with specialized functions. Incidentally, large organizations usually arrange themselves with large units divided into smaller units, which eventually are subdivided into teams of 5–7 people.

Within those groups or subgroups, members might arrange themselves by their roles, which alters the structure of the group.

Think of teams on which you've served, participated, or been a member. How big were they? Can you remember a time when the team was too large for comfort? If so, how many were on the team and why did the team size seem too big? If the team wasn't too big, what made it just right or potentially too small?

Structure

The structure of the team refers to team member roles and how those roles relate to one another and to the organization as a whole (McGrath, 1964). Roles can be specific and differentiated patterns of behavior that may require particular knowledge and skill (such as team leader or team treasurer). For example, specific and differentiated patterns include leader, social reinforcement (cheerleader), workflow coordinator (taskmaster), and joker or comic relief (Hackman, 1992). Roles also include unspecified behaviors that everyone shares (Kozlowski & Bell, 2013), such as "team member."

The division of work, horizontal or vertical, affects the structure and composition of the team. Horizontal division of labor refers to each person in the team handling different parts of a group task, with no one person responsible for the entire task completion. With vertical division of labor, each person in the team handles one part of the task, but in contrast to horizontal division, team members take responsibility for how the entire team accomplishes that group task. For instance, in many restaurants waiters or waitresses (now most often called servers) and the hosts are assigned as a team based on their shift (what time they are scheduled). All servers share the responsibility of serving all customers. They may have assigned sections of seating in the restaurant, handling different parts of the restaurant clientele, but they share the responsibility. Therefore, they clear tables when needed or help serve food to the customers seated in that section if needed. The host, in contrast, is responsible for the efficiency of the entire shift because it is their duty to manage the seating assignments and not over-seat or under-seat any one section over another. The servers handle their tasks and the hosts handle theirs, but the host's responsibility includes the success of the entire shift. In this example, the servers represent horizontal division of labor and the host, relative to the servers, represents a vertical division of labor. Sometimes division of labor is determined by where the team is located or the specific composition of the group members, rather than by task.

Composition

Composition refers to the properties of the team based on its membership. Properties include the diversity and location of members.

Diversity of membership in teams includes the variety of skills, knowledge, experience level, and ability of team members, as well as demographic features. Thus, diversity incorporates more than just members' sex, age, cultural background, or language base (e.g., Hispanic, German, isiZulu).

The best teams take into consideration the skill mix of the members. A team comprising complementary skills among its members does better than a team where too many members share the same skill sets or expertise (Katzenbach & Smith, 1993). Diversity of members' skills is better for creative and intellectual tasks than is homogeneity of skills and may help performance overall. In addition, teams work most effectively when they collectively have problem-solving capability, the right technical or functional expertise relevant to the task they are given, decision-making capability, and interpersonal skills. Cross-functional teams are a good example of a type of team that takes advantage of diversity of skills among members. Such teams are made up of employees from various functional areas across the organization, such as marketing, technical writing, customer service, production, design, and manufacturing. Most often the employees work at the same organizational hierarchical level; hence, they are peers, but not within the same team. The assumption behind **cross-functional** teams is that the diversity of cognitive biases and approaches to problem solving, as well as variety of knowledge and skill sets, should make the team more effective than one without cross-functional representation (Jackson, May, & Whitney, 1995).

Diversity of personality has also been shown to support high levels of team effectiveness. For example, without considering the nature of the task, it may be best to include both introverts and extraverts on a team, as opposed to only one or the other (Stewart & Barrick, 2004).

What have you experienced with diversity of team members? Was there a group composition that you remember working well? Think of lab teams or other groups to which you've been assigned—what was the composition of the team members? Did your experiences differ between situations where you might have been randomly assigned (like in class) versus deliberately assigned (based on your gender, class level, or experience) to a team?

Although much can be gained with team diversity, differences can lead to conflicts, misunderstandings, and general frustrations in working together that result in decreased job satisfaction and high team member turnover (Roberge & van Dick, 2010). For example, societal contexts overlapping with skill variety and organizational contexts complicate diversity (Jackson, et al., 1995). Societal contexts include how individuals are socialized within their cultural communities, for example within their religion, language, gender, and ethnicity. Organizational contexts include socialization within occupational units; for example, nurses and engineers have different occupational values and norms. Differences in cultural upbringing and norms can introduce misunderstandings that take time to resolve. Thus, the values you developed growing up, the different skills you have to do your job, and where within the organization you work, may all factor into the ease with which you function on a team. The more different the values, skills, and expectations of the organizational units, the more challenge diversity creates in communication and effective teamwork.

Whether the diversity of team members positively or negatively affects the team or its performance can depend on the team task (Kozlowski & Bell, 2013). Some types of tasks may be best handled by a homogenous team composition (McGrath, 1964; Neuman & Wright, 1999). For example, tasks that involve complex communications with highly interdependent tasks, issues laden with racial or political tensions that only serve to further ignite sensitivities, or must be completed fast may not be well suited to a highly heterogeneous team.

Colocated or Geographically Dispersed

Composition of teams includes whether members are located together or apart from each other (Figure 7.2). Colocated teams are those whose members work in the same office and interact with one another face-to-face (Ahuja & Gavin, 2003).

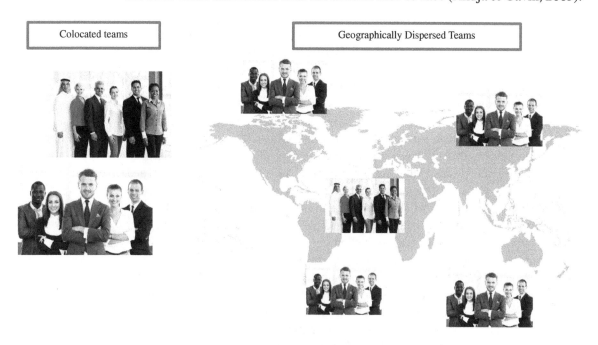

FIGURE 7.2 Colocated and Geographically Dispersed Teams

Top image (repeated): © michaeljung/Shutterstock, Inc.; bottom image (repeated) © OPOLJA/Shutterstock, Inc.; Background map: © RAEVSKY/Shutterstock, Inc.

They may also on occasion interact through the computer or phone, but most of their interactions are categorized as face-to-face. Most research results, unless explicitly stated as applying to **virtual teams**, are for colocated workgroups or teams. Geographically dispersed teams, typically called virtual teams, are those whose members are separated by time and distance, such that they are forced to interact with one another through technology such as the computer or phone (Martins, Gilson, & Maynard, 2004; Townsend, DeMarie, & Hendrickson, 1998).

Virtual teams need not be permanent configurations. With both temporary and permanent virtual teams, organizations can take advantage of making most effective use of their talented employees without having to relocate them to different parts of the country just for a particular project. Thus, travel expenses, relocation expense, and greater access to global markets are all benefits of geographically dispersed teams (Bell & Kozlowski, 2002; Cascio, 2000; Kristof, Brown, Sims, & Smith, 1995). Similar to the organization benefiting, employees themselves benefit from reduced living expenses (i.e., being able to live in cheaper parts of the country) and commute time, and increased work flexibility (Martins et al., 2004).

When virtual teams have been compared to colocated teams, however, virtual teams sometimes produce less, in particular when a lot of coordination is required such as with a very complex task (Straus & McGrath, 1994). Additionally, the nature of the virtual environment can make managerial issues more challenging to handle. For instance, team members may perceive higher levels of isolation or lack of trust in their coworkers, which negatively affects progress on interdependent tasks. Interpersonal communication may be reduced or inhibited because of the computer or electronic interface (Cascio, 2000; Kirkman, Rosen, Gibson, Tesluk, & McPherson, 2002; Lebie, Rhoades, & McGrath, 1996; Martins et al., 2004; Powell, Piccoli, & Ives, 2004). Thus, managing virtual teams requires additional efforts in relationship development and establishing team trust, as well as ensuring access to effective communication technology that boosts the feeling of social presence. Webcam enabled communication, for instance, contributes to relationship maintenance beyond simple texting.

The different features of teams combine to create many different categories or typologies of teams. Thus, a number of team types have been established to help make sense of how teams are composed and what teams do.

What Kinds of Teams Exist?

Some teams are formed to make recommendations or to advise others. Such teams include **task forces**, **quality circles**, or safety groups. Task forces are temporary groups established to solve a particular problem, like how to assign shared space and equipment or develop a plan for distributing grant funds. Quality circles are temporary groups of diverse members across the organization established to focus on a quality issue, such as obtaining and maintaining zero defects. Safety groups are another type of quality circle whose specific focus is on reducing safety violations, improving the use of safety equipment, and designing work such that it can be accomplished in the most safe manner possible (e.g., redesigning arrangement of equipment). Task forces and quality circles quickly determine how to solve a problem, or to review criteria that need to be met. They then make a recommendation for how to meet the criteria. Teams with the goal of making one or more recommendations usually operate on a specific timeline, whereas quality circles and safety groups generally have no deadline.

Why is it important to consider the structure of a team?

Other teams complete projects or manage projects, as opposed to just making recommendations. For example, manufacturing, design and development, operations, marketing, sales, customer service, and accounting teams complete a particular task or set of tasks. In contrast, management or administrative teams run operations—they themselves do not necessarily produce a product or outcome, but instead supervise other teams to complete the work, through delegation and overseeing the schedule or resources of the teams.

Teams do not fall into just one type category; thus, categories are not exclusive. As you read the sections below, you'll see that some teams are representative of a number of different types.

Traditional

Traditional teams have a leader and members who work face-to-face in the same office. The team leader focuses on establishing processes, team relations, maintaining schedules, collecting and giving performance feedback, and finding resources for the team (Kozlowski & Bell, 2013). Traditional teams may be considered production teams or project teams, where team members produce the materials or finished products of the organization. For example, production or project teams include engineering teams, building construction or landscaping crews, or assembly workers in a manufacturing or assembly plant. When people refer to teams at work, traditional teams usually come to mind first.

Self-Managed

In contrast to traditional teams, **self-managed teams** do not have a designated leader or manager. Consequently, they are sometimes called leaderless teams. They can be either semi- or fully-autonomous. If semiautonomous, a leader may provide the overall goal for what the team should achieve, but the members decide among themselves how to accomplish the higher level directive. Fully autonomous teams establish their own goals within the overall objective of the organization as a whole, in addition to determining for themselves how to accomplish those goals.

In self-managed teams, members are generally responsible for management functions such as scheduling workload across team members, solving personnel problems and conflicts, and scheduling and conducting team meetings (Hackman, 1986). Self-managed teams have been used in a number of settings at work such as task forces, quality circles, or new venture groups (group formed to pursue a new line of business that disbands after the new venture has formed). Sometimes, because team members struggle with performance management issues and organizations often require that a single person be charged with managing budgets for salaries, a manager may be appointed to oversee these administrative duties for one or more self-managed teams.

Think back on a team to which you were assigned for a class project. Would you classify the team as self-managed? If so, why? If not, who managed your team?

When established, self-managed teams can be very effective, but are not infallible (Neck, Stewart, & Manz, 1996). Challenges with strong team member personalities, lack of clear authority or mechanisms for accountability within the group, unclear decision-making procedures, member conflict, and loss of mentoring or coaching from someone not directly affected by the work itself all present areas for failure for newly established self-managed groups (Laiken, 1994). Establishing a **leaderless team** depends on first training members on how to handle peer conflicts and make decisions, and how to hold each other accountable in productive ways (Laiken, 1994).

Successful self-managed teams are usually composed of highly educated, self-motivated, self-directed experts or specialists able to work independently, as well as with others, but who have an established reputation for their expertise and self-directed capabilities (Barry, 1991). Given a flexible work environment, clear goals, and room to achieve the goals, self-managed teams comprising these types of individuals enjoy high productivity and success for the organization (Barry, 1991).

For self-managed teams to succeed, the team members should be trained on communication, establishing project schedules and workload balance, developing group processes, and managing personal conflict. Without a leader, the members of the self-managed team must be able to handle group dynamics and possess process skills of their own. Barry (1991) suggests that successful self-managed teams adopt a form of distributed leadership, where members take on parts of the leadership role depending on their specific strengths and capabilities. For example, if one team member is particularly good at organizing and scheduling, that team member may take on this role for the team. Another may be good at resolving conflict between individuals, and thus when conflict develops team members seek consultation from that particular member. A different team member's strengths may lie in interacting with external partners, negotiating for resources, and communicating progress. Hence, that person takes on those responsibilities for the group. Lastly, one of the other team members may be particularly good at developing group processes, and thus this member takes on the role of developing and managing group processes that keep the team functioning smoothly. Other management functions may require assignment, such as responsibility for the budget. Each self-managed team must determine for itself what tasks within the management role are applicable to their group, and then decide how to divide those tasks among the team members.

Virtual

The location of a team is a feature of teams that also dictates to some extent how team members communicate. Some teams are composed of members across a variety of geographic locations or even different organizations, such as with collaborative teams (e.g., World Cup, Olympics, Samsung Affiliates). As a consequence, most of their communications transpire via electronic mechanisms such as phone, Internet, and e-mail (often referred to as **computer-mediated communication**). With advancements in technology, team members can communicate relatively effortlessly, increasing the freedom to

© Rawpixel.com/Shutterstock.com

grow teams to sizes that can reduce feelings of interpersonal connection. For example, teams of 100 or more are not uncommon, though effectively collaborating with this many people at a time results in significant challenge (Gratton & Erickson, 2007), as noted previously in this chapter.

Virtual communication does not require geographic separation of team members, but geographically dispersed teams require virtual communication. Employees can communicate virtually while occasionally traveling, to accommodate work schedule flexibility, or to increase productivity as workers telecommute and work at home. Sometimes, team members can be one office apart and still prefer to use computer-mediated communication (Hollingshead & McGrath, 1995). Virtual teams, however, do not just use computer communication for convenience—they depend on it.

For team members to be effective in a virtual team arrangement, they must develop rich mechanisms for communication despite the limits of the communication medium (Carlson & Zmud, 1999). Theorists have argued for some time that electronic media inhibit the ability to convey the subtle cues that nonverbal behavior such as facial expressions or hand gestures can offer (Culnan & Markus, 1987; Daft & Lengel, 1984). Although emoticons such as a smiley face ☺ are used in an attempt to convey nonverbal emotional cues, they are limited and often misunderstood (Kahai & Cooper, 2003). Chapter 10 on Communication provides more information about nonverbal cues.

Although being a part of a virtual team can add challenges such as how to communicate effectively, scholars and practitioners have developed several best practices for virtual teams.

Best Practices for Virtual Teams

Gratton and Erickson (2007) identified several best practices for keeping virtual teams of large sizes, geographically dispersed, and diverse, highly collaborative. Their best practices fall within four categories: executive support, human resource practices, strength of the team leader, and the structure of the team.

First, *executive support* refers to having executives of the organization demonstrate supportive and collaborative behaviors among themselves and with others. These executives invest in building social relationships across members of the organization. For example, Gratton and Erickson note that Royal Bank of Scotland designed their offices in an open floor plan with lots of open spaces and meeting areas. They set up their collective buildings like a university campus or open-space mall with shops, restaurants or food courts, exercise areas, and open fields for a quick game of soccer. The physical arrangement and overall feel of the work environment encourages open conversation, and frequent interaction both on a professional and social level. Executives model collaborative behavior by frequently interacting within these open spaces, and they provide coaching on teamwork for those who report to them.

Second, *human resource practices* that have the biggest effect on collaboration include training in collaborative behavior skills and support for informal community building. Skills necessary for collaboration incorporate appreciating others, engaging in purposeful conversation, resolving conflicts, and program management. Training for the following collaborative skills is essential: teamwork (holding each other accountable, resolving conflicts), emotional intelligence (awareness of one's own emotions and those of others, as well as how to regulate one's emotions), networking or establishing mutually beneficial relationships and communication. Furthermore, by sponsoring events that support the surrounding community, highly collaborative organizations can demonstrate support and responsibility for the employees' families and friends.

Third, groups sustaining high collaboration despite their large sizes and geographic separation do so with a *strong leader*. Strong leaders flex with the situation, demonstrating both task- and relationship-oriented skills (discussed in more detail in Chapter 8 and 9). According to Gratton and Erickson (2007), a strong leader is one who makes the goals of the group clear, clarifies the tasks required for accomplishing the goal, clarifies responsibilities among team members, and manages the project plan (e.g., schedule and resources). Strong leaders demonstrate well-developed relationship skills, follow through on conversations that resolve issues and build support, and use good communication skills (e.g., listening, asking questions).

Lastly, how the team is *structured* plays a part in effective collaborative teams. Gratton and Erickson (2007) suggest teams that capitalize on existing relationships increase their chances for success. Specifically, when team members already have a relationship with each other and then add new members to the group, they are able to build these new connections faster than if all members are new to one another. Having at least 20%–40% of the team members already knowing each other before the team forms can produce strong team collaboration from the start of the project. There is a downside to teams composed of several friends—when the subgroups are too tight, they become reluctant to allow new members to join or they allow new membership but maintain exclusive clicks.

> If employees work in virtual teams, why would an open campus workplace facilitate collaboration amongst employees?

Virtuoso

Unlike most other teams, virtuoso teams do not seek consensus and team harmony, nor do they last long. Virtuoso teams consist of elite experts specially convened to accomplish an ambitious and highly risky goal (Fischer & Boynton, 2005). They follow an aggressive schedule, seem uncharacteristically intense, and they deliver results. Such teams do not last long because of the frenetic pace; most members burnout or lose their energy. The members are hand-picked for the specific purpose of accomplishing a certain project goal. The virtuoso team is not accountable in the same way as traditional teams. For example, they have permission to break rules. In addition, team members are not chosen for their stellar personalities. Instead, their selection into the group depends on their expertise, desire to take on the toughest challenges, dive into risk at any cost, and willingness to stand their ground. These people do not give in or agree to get along; thus, conflict regularly ensures. Members of virtuoso teams are forced to work together under very strict and tight time constraints.

Fischer and Boynton (2005) offer the following comparison between traditional and virtuoso teams (Table 7.1). A couple of examples Fischer and Boynton offer as virtuoso teams include the team who developed the first Cray computer (aptly named after the team leader Seymour Cray), and Microsoft's Xbox team.

Of all the team types reviewed thus far, none are as vague in their expected outcomes as the advisory or time-limited team.

TABLE 7.1 Traditional Versus Virtuoso Teams

Traditional Team	Virtuoso Team
Members chosen for their availability or ability to fill a gap	Members are chosen for their expertise and skill—generally considered specialists
Emphasizes the group at the expense of individualism; solutions chosen based on consensus	Emphasizes individuals; encourages competition between members; solutions chosen based on merit—the best idea wins
Task-oriented	Idea-oriented
Members work individually and can communicate via e-mail, phone, or other virtual mechanisms; politeness is expected	Members work interdependently, frequently, in close proximity; politeness is discarded for honesty and directness
Focuses on meeting the needs and expectations of the average customer	Focuses on meeting the needs and expectations of the sophisticated customer
Decisions based on market knowledge; affirm common stereotypes	Decisions defy market knowledge; reject common stereotypes

Courtesy Zinta Byrne. Source: Fischer and Boynton, 2005.

Advisory or Time-Limited

Advisory teams have no authority or responsibility for implementing solutions; instead, they simply make recommendations. Examples of advisory groups are problem-solving teams, quality circles, or selection committees.

Problem-solving teams are designed for that purpose only—to solve a specific problem. They are usually made up of team members from across the organization, in particular the units or divisions of the organization affected by the problem, or who may need to play a role in solving the problem. Problem-solving teams may meet for an hour or two per week, sometimes more depending on the severity of the problem, until the problem is solved. The group then either disbands or works on a new problem, sometimes swapping out team members for others depending on expertise needed for solving the new problem.

Quality circles were popular in the 1980s when manufacturing plants were driven to reduce errors and waste and to boost production and profit. As mentioned above, quality circles comprise advisory teams of diverse members across the organization established to focus on resolving quality concerns and making recommendations for maintaining quality.

Investigative groups are also advisory teams. For example, allegations of abuse or misconduct are usually investigated by a special team pulled together to find the cause of the event or nature of allegations, and then advise on the best course of action to resolve the situation.

Action or performance teams make up another type of time-limited team that forms to complete complex performances. Thus, instead of advising or producing a specific product, these teams perform today and then disband. For instance, military crews, surgery teams, rescue units, musical bands, or circuses make up action teams. Though some of these teams perform together for many years, they do eventually disband.

Management teams can be considered a special type of advisory team because the members typically do not produce a tangible product for the organization. Instead, they achieve their productivity by advising and guiding others to accomplish tasks. However, most advisory team members do not have authority, which makes the management team unique. Thus, like nonmanagement advisory teams, management teams such as the board of directors or the chief executives of an organization (often referred to as the **C-suite**) advise, coach, and plan, but unlike a nonmanagement advisory team, the management group has the authority to turn their advice into a directive and delegate tasks to achieve the "advice."

Although teams are configured differently depending on their type and features, how these characteristics come together can be a bit confusing. There may be many ways of combining features and types of teams, yet only a few theoretical models of teams have been proposed and studied in the research literature. Some of these models were derived from theory only, whereas others were derived from industry—from actual teams in the field. Both are valuable in understanding what makes teams and then later, how we create the most effective teams in the workplace.

Exercise 7.1

The book refers to five different types of teams. Create a table that has each type of team listed in the columns and rows. In the diagonal cell, write the definition of the type of team. In the lower triangle of the table, jot down what makes each team type different from the another. In the upper triangle of the matrix, write down what the team types have in common.

How Are Teams Formed?

Teams form through a variety of processes, with no single approach appearing best. Additionally, teams change over time making it difficult to identify how they initially formed. Furthermore, studying teams in natural settings to determine how they form is complicated because of lack of access, timing, confounding the study by being a participant, and other methodological and practical challenges. Thus, understanding exactly how teams form remains an open research question. A few scholars have developed models of team formation from research or based on group theory, several of which are explained in this section.

Tuckman

Tuckman's (1965) model of how teams form (Figure 7.3) is one of the first and most often mentioned, even though it is now considered dated and research has since indicated that not all groups follow this progression (Kozlowski & Bell, 2013). Because it is so well known and was for many years the only model of group formation taught, many people still refer to it and therefore, there is value in knowing and understanding the model.

Tuckman suggested that teams go through five distinct and sequential steps of development.

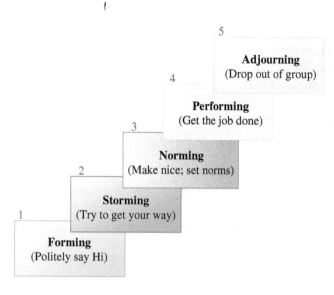

FIGURE 7.3 Tuckman's Model of Team Formation

Courtesy Zinta Byrne. Source: Tuckman, 1965.

Stage 1: Forming

In the Forming stage, politeness dominates and members try to orient themselves into the group. Issues such as uncertainty around the purpose of the group, how the group will be structured, and who will lead, dominate the initial stage of formation. Even in preassigned groups, such as units in the military, uncertainty still remains over how each member fits in with the team and over the leader's characteristics, and this climate of uncertainty promotes an environment of "getting to know each other." Generally, first names are exchanged and potentially some nervous discussion about the uncertainty in the team takes place.

Stage 2: Storming

In the Storming stage, members become comfortable with each other and try to influence the group to best fit their own needs. They may become assertive about the group's direction and what role they want to fulfill in the group. This stage is usually marked by some internal conflict and power struggle, as members try to vie for control over the direction and structure of the group. The personalities of team members become important as teams with all dominant personalities can be stuck in this stage for a while fighting over who will be in control, whereas teams with a mix and several agreeable personality types will resolve their conflicts faster (e.g., Graziano, Jenson-Campbell, & Hair, 1996; Stewart & Barrick, 2004).

Stage 3: Norming

The Norming stage is characterized by members reconciling conflicts from the storming stage, and developing a common purpose. Members begin to establish norms and identify their roles, determining the different functions the group members can fulfill. Communication patterns emerge, and norms for behavior, dress, and process may also begin to emerge. Relationships between members form and the team begins to demonstrate a sense of identity and cohesiveness.

Stage 4: Performing

Members begin fulfilling their roles and working toward completion of the task in the performing stage. At this point, the team is fully functional and working toward task completion, as opposed to focusing entirely on how members get along. Not all groups get to this stage because of their inability to resolve issues at the earlier stages of formation. Depending on the purpose of the team, it will either continue performing or complete the task and move toward adjourning, a stage that Tuckman added later (Tuckman & Jensen, 1977) after he proposed these first four stages.

Stage 5: Adjourning

In this stage, members begin to disengage, distancing themselves from the team and reducing their activities within the group. For groups with a short-lived purpose who complete their tasks, the adjourning stage occurs quite naturally and expectedly. For teams designed to function for a longtime, this stage includes the challenges of some members leaving, others staying, and sometimes new members joining to replace those who have left. Teams that have been together for a longtime may struggle with the distancing of a member or two, and hurt feelings may cause an increase in conflict and a renegotiation of roles. Leaving members may either positively or negatively influence new members, or they may leave without much effect. Sometimes the adjourning stage throws the team back into the forming and storming stages, depending on how many members adjourn, which roles are now vacant in the group, and the qualities of the new member joining the team.

The distinguishing characteristic of Tuckman's model is the rhyming stages that follow a strict linear progression.

Although Tuckman's model is easy to remember, it is not without criticisms.

Criticisms of Tuckman's Model

Tuckman developed his model based on therapy groups, where members who have never met come together, but not for a group task; they join because of a common goal of improving their mental health. Such teams, however, struggle with their own interpersonal interactions more so than task achievement, which dominates most typical work teams. Tuckman's theory of team development remains appealing because few models of team development exist. That said, the model fails in relevancy or applicability to most organizational teams because of the nature of the groups that served as the model's foundation (Kozlowski & Bell, 2013).

Furthermore, although Tuckman's model is most memorable because of its cute rhyming stage names, the model is not very helpful when considering teams that must often develop quickly, such as flight crews or medical teams. Fast forming teams have no time to traverse through the pre-stages of development before performing; they must perform immediately. In some cases, like a medical team or flight crew, job roles (e.g., chief surgeon, pilot) dictate team roles and norms allowing the team to skip the forming, storming, and norming stages. In other cases, such as emergency rescue or natural disaster fighting teams, the teams may not have prescribed leader roles or norms that facilitate skipping formation steps.

The model assumes a linear progression through the stages, however, some teams engage in all stages at all times, continuously storming and norming, while performing and also losing or introducing new members along the way.

Lastly, the model does not take into consideration what norms or rules may exists for teams within the organization, norms that predetermine who does what in a team and how teams operate.

In response to many of the criticism to Tuckman's model, subsequent attempts to develop models resulted in researchers either building on components of Tuckman's but changing some minor aspect, or developing completely different types of frameworks.

Subsequent Models to Tuckman's

For a while, subsequent models to Tuckman have kept a similar pattern of linear progression. For instance, Hare (1976) suggested that teams define their situation, develop new skills, develop roles, and then complete the work accordingly,

Why is there value in learning Tuckman's model if there are so many criticisms of the model?

in that order. Similarly, LaCoursiere (1980) suggested teams go through orientation, dissatisfaction, resolution, production, and termination stages.

McGrath (1984) proposed that teams develop in stages comprising both task and interpersonal activities:

Stage I. *generate*: generate plans (task) as well as values and goals (interpersonal)

Stage II. *choose*: choose alternatives and policies (task) and agree on values and goals (interpersonal)

Stage III. *negotiate*: resolve conflicts of viewpoints (task) by developing norms and allocating roles (interpersonal)

Stage IV. *execute:* perform the tasks (task) and establish and maintain cohesiveness (interpersonal)

To illustrate how his developmental sequence incorporating both task and interpersonal activity maps conceptually onto Tuckman's stages of team development, McGrath presented a model similar to that shown in Figure 7.4.

Teams can change over time and operate within the contextual environment of the organization that influences their processes. However, previous models failed to consider the contextual environment, or factors that affect team processes. Thus, Gersick (1988) took a different approach to studying teams.

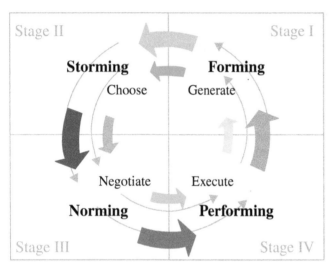

FIGURE 7.4   Integrated Stages of Group Development

Courtesy Zinta Byrne. Source: McGrath, 1984

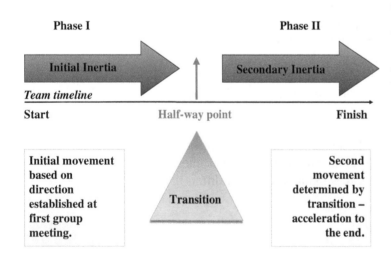

FIGURE 7.5   Punctuated Equilibrium Model

Courtesy Zinta Byrne. Source: Gersick, 1988.

Gersick

Given that Tuckman's model did not fit for many organizational teams, Gersick (1988) examined eight naturally occurring different teams, following them around for a variety of timeframes associated with the life of the team. Specifically, she studied three graduate management teams (lifespan of 7–11 days), a community fundraising committee (lifespan of 3 months), a task force at a bank (lifespan of 34 days), hospital administrators (lifespan of 12 weeks), psychiatrists and social workers (lifespan of 9 weeks), and a team of university faculty and administrators (lifespan of 6 months). She found that all teams, regardless of lifespan, size, or type, progressed through a similar path of activity all based on their timeline.

Gersick labeled her model the Punctuated Equilibrium Model (see Figure 7.5 for an illustration). It helps to visualize the model when reading the description of each phase of the model.

During the first phase, teams meet, establish a direction, and then experience an initial period of inertia (or activity) along that direction. This may look something like the first stages of Tuckman's model, with members deciding on the project outcomes, when they'll meet next, and members' roles.

At about the half-way point in the project schedule, the team undergoes a transition (almost a panic), in which they set a revised direction for the second phase, a secondary inertia marked by fast and furious work to complete the project. This transition point is characterized by a concentrated burst of activity wherein members drop their old patterns of behavior, adopt new perspectives on their work, and make much more progress than they did in the early phase. The team may at this point reconceptualize the problem they are supposed to solve, draw on new ideas, and reframe their accrued experiences.

Once the team enters into the second phase, the members continue the momentum from the transition point and work to complete the task.

Regardless of type of group, Gersick found that they each developed a pattern of behavior and worked consistently with those patterns for a longtime—those periods of inertia. Consistent across groups, the timing of the transition always occurred at their halfway mark on their calendar for the project. You might ask "what about groups without a schedule?" Gersick argued that the half-way point is a natural phenomenon and thus, does not require an actual schedule. She proposed that we hit half-way points in many areas of our lives, such as hitting mid-life changes in perspective as part of adult development (Jacques, 1955).

However, like Tuckman's model, Gersick's also does not apply to all teams. For example, the model does not fit well for teams expected to be in place for years with no clear end date, or teams that must begin performing immediately, such as cockpit or flight crews, rescue teams, or emergency medical teams. Teams like these may have to perform with consistent force from start to finish, rather than an initial effort with a burst to the end.

The previous models talk about the formation of teams, but not all teams end and there is a period where teams must maintain themselves. Additionally, before we can understand what makes for an effective team, we must recognize that some practices or aspects of teams develop while they are forming, that then later influence their effectiveness. This next section reviews that in-between stage, when teams are forming and developing the norms that will determine their effectiveness.

> Think back on a team to which you were assigned for a class project. Did your group fit into Gersick's model?

How Do Teams Maintzain Themselves?

Once teams are formed, they stay together to perform, to achieve their goal. In all models of team formation, part of the model includes some period of time when the group is no longer forming but not disbanding. Thus, teams maintain themselves during cycles of performance and they do so using norms.

Norms: Rules for Behavior

When teams form, they establish group norms that direct and regulate individual behavior within the group (Hackman, 1992). Norms are the rules or guidelines for how people should behave and respond to stimuli in the environment. For example, norms determine whether it's okay to speak out against a decision made by the group leader or how much communication is expected among team members before decisions are made. Our behaviors are shaped by the collective group, and therefore the norms or standards for behavior that the group establishes (typically during socialization and when the team forms) should not be ignored. Norms do not apply to people's internal thoughts and feelings, but may apply to externally voiced thoughts and feelings. Thus, group norms may prevent a member from expressing anger as a behavior, but these norms do not necessarily stop that member from feeling intense internal anger (private beliefs and attitudes; Hackman, 1992).

Norms matter in teams because team members tend to regulate each other's use of group resources and behavior, to either foster or promote desired behavior, or to stop undesirable behavior, all of which contribute to team maintenance. When group members deviate from the norms too much, other members pull them back in line, reject them, or accommodate the change to the norm (Levine, 1989). "Pulling back in line" means trying to correct the member's behavior by telling the member about the inappropriate behavior or firmly expressing disapproval. Nearly every student can describe the situation of sitting in a classroom where the professor is trying to explain a complex idea and two people start talking to each other in hushed tones. As the two students continue and begin distracting others around them, a few students here and there will turn to stare at the couple for a few moments, frowning at them, and then turning back toward the instructor. This stare-down will occur a number of times until the talking students either see these stares and stop or someone asks them to stop talking. Staring at the talking couple or actually telling them to stop talking are efforts to keep to the norm that no one talks while the professor talks. You are mistaken if you think the stare-down technique only happens in the classroom; you will find the same correcting behavior in boardrooms and meeting rooms across organizations.

Norms generally take time to develop, though some may be introduced quickly, as needed, if specific behaviors must be regulated for immediate team success. For example, some groups may determine that a new norm *now* exists because of a reoccurring problem in the group, such as lack of acknowledgment when a decision has been made. Thus, a group may say "we keep running into the problem where we make a decision, but no one restates it so we end up revisiting the decision again. From here on out, let's document when a decision is made and what our decision is, so we can stop revisiting the same decision over and over again."

Violating Norms

Although in general, members adhere to group norms, they are sometimes ignored. Members may violate norms when the norm goes against their personal beliefs. Additionally, how and whether norms are upheld depends on the status of the member. High-status members include those highly regarded for their expertise, experience, or personality, or those with extensive seniority. These members tend to enjoy positive personal power as a result of their likability or ability, or because of accumulated experience in the organization and/or the team. High-status members resist pressures to conform to the group norms more than

Why is Gersick's model not actually a model of team development? What does the model actually describe/explain?

do the low-status members, and as a result, have more freedom to deviate from the norms, up to a point (Hackman, 1992). Low-status members, in contrast, are not regarded well for one reason or another. For instance, new team members are often initially considered low-status group members because they have not yet proven their abilities and skills, and have not yet demonstrated how they can do more for the group than other members can.

Deviants are members who consistently violate group norms. Usually, the group does not accept the constant violation of norms and eventually, if the violation continues, rejects the group member. Rejecting group members may take the form of ostracizing them (Williams & Sommer, 1997), usually after the more subtle attempts to change behavior fail. With ostracism, all communication with the deviating member is stopped, and everyone ignores the person. Nevertheless, group members are rarely physically removed from the group (Hackman, 1992).

Changing the Majority View

Deviants or members who consistently and aggressively violate the groups norms can play a valuable function in the group, which may result in them being accommodated by the rest of the team. Those who routinely violate the norms help establish the boundary conditions for group behavior. By acting out, they help the group determine acceptable behavior. The group may make adjustments or accommodate the pushes against the norms, thereby altering the group norms. Thus, under certain conditions, when group members who initially follow the norms begin to push back against them, they can influence the direction of the group (Levine, 1989; Maass, West, & Cialdini, 1987; Moscovici, 1980; Moscovici, Lage, & Naffrechoux, 1969). Research suggests that minority members, a small group within the larger group, who push back against the norms, can be influential when they present a clear, consistent, and credible alternative to the normative thinking; an alternative that is easy to understand yet hard to dismiss because of its clear value. Minority members (can be as few as two people in a group of five) can sway the majority when they present:

1. A clear and unambiguous alternative position that cannot be reconciled with the status quo and thus not easily ignored.

2. Their position or viewpoint in a consistent manner over time, without wavering.

3. A cohesive, unified group that sticks together, presenting a single viewpoint.

4. An ability to avoid becoming deviants as a permanent role in the group.

5. A position that is consistent with dominant cultural values.

A single minority member will generally be unsuccessful swaying the group majority; however, add one person to the minority team and now you have two people pushing back on the majority norms. By presenting a clear alternative view to the majority, a view not easily swept aside by "how we do things here," and an alternative that offers a logical or rational viewpoint that is hard to ignore, the minority can force the majority to consider the position.

However, if the minority viewpoint changes, becomes erratic, or creates confusion, the firmness of the alternative viewpoint becomes weakened. Continuing to put forth a consistent unified view highlights the strength of the minority group's resolve—they believe in this position. When people believe so firmly in a position that they will not sway from it and they consistently and continuously put that position forward to the majority, the strength of their conviction cannot be ignored. The majority members will start to wonder "what do they know that keeps them so firm to that position?" If the minority members are labeled as group deviants, they lose their ability to influence the majority because once labeled *deviants*, they can be ignored and not taken seriously. After all, there are norms for how to deal with deviants, norms that are accepted by the group. Thus, minority members must avoid being labeled as deviants. Lastly, espousing a position consistent with current societal norms lends strength to the minority view as it is difficult to change the majority if your position is not well accepted.

Why are deviant team members sometimes valuable in creating positive group norms?

So, you now know how teams are formed, what features make up teams, the various types of teams that may exist, and how norms play a role in maintaining teams. The practical application of teams, however, is dependent on these factors coming together to create an effective team.

What Makes for an Effective Team?

Teams are everywhere, which makes it important to focus on their effectiveness. Just getting the job done is not the same as being effective, as discussed under job performance in Chapter 5. To get the most out of using a team, they must be designed to be effective, in addition to having the right combination of team members. For example, Hackman (see Coutu & Beschloss, 2009) proposed five conditions that leaders need for building an effective team:

1. Real teams.
   - ❏ You need to know who is on the team and who is not.
2. Compelling vision or direction.
   - ❏ Team members need to know the team's goal and agree on what they are supposed to be doing; there needs to be a clear agenda.
3. Enabling structures.
   - ❏ The structure of the team matters, which includes the mix of team members in terms of personalities and skills. Enforceable and clear norms are necessary.
4. Supportive organization.
   - ❏ The team needs to be embedded within an organization that provides an infrastructure such as information technology, human resources, reward systems, and mechanisms for obtaining resources.
5. Expert coaching.
   - ❏ Teams need coaching as a team, not just the individuals within the team. Functional processes are needed for the team, and coaching to create appropriate processes throughout the life of the project is essential.

Company Example 7.1 T-Mobile's Customer Service Teams

To ensure teams are effective, T-Mobile, the brand name for mobile communication and a subsidiary of Germany's Deutsche Telekom AG, a team-based performance appraisal system is used for evaluating customer service teams. Individual performance is still evaluated and recognized, but teams are recognized for their performance and in a big way (Dixon, 2018). Because team members are evaluated on the success of the team as well as their own individual success, they are motivated to help weaker/newer employees learn the job. The performance tools weigh team performance higher than individual performance to encourage teamwork. Additionally, teams hold weekly meetings to share best practices, and help each other learn how to handle customer service challenges, further encouraging collaboration. According to the company, the model works as evidenced by their increased customer service ratings and higher employee retention (see Dixon, 2018).

In addition to teams being designed for effectiveness, team members themselves play a role in creating their own group's effectiveness (Katzenbach & Smith, 1993). Specifically, in their research on teams Katzenbach and Smith found that the best teams are those where members share information and insights, make decisions that support the effectiveness of each member, and reinforce their own performance standards. The best teams require mutual accountability between members, such as calling out members who perform below standards or seem to be slacking off at times. Best teams also include members who rely on one another for discussion and debate, count on joint contributions to accomplishing team goals, and who expect a level of commitment to the purpose or goal of the team from one another. In summary, Katzenbach and Smith offered eight processes that several successful teams shared (Figure 7.6).

In a more recent effort to clarify what makes teams effective, Pentland (2012) determined that communication appears central to team success, and identified five defining communication patterns effective teams share:

1. All team members talk and listen equally and in short contributions.

2. Members interact with each other and not just with or via a team leader.

3. Members interact with each other face-to-face, using energetic expressions and gestures.

4. Side conversations are common within the team.

5. Members occasionally break from the group to obtain outside information and then bring it back into the group.

© 4 PM production/Shutterstock.com

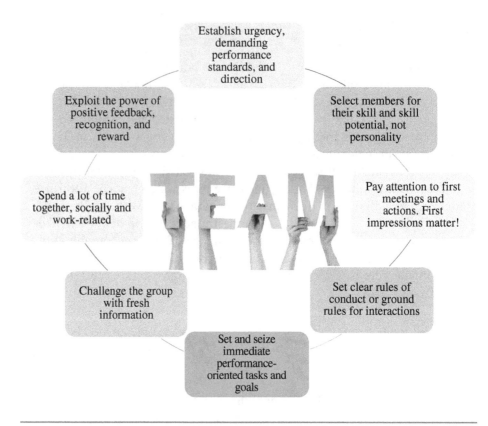

FIGURE 7.6 What Makes A Successful Team?

Courtesy Zinta Byrne. Background image: © Nelosa/Shutterstock, Inc.

Watch https://www.ted.com/ talks/drew_humphreys_ how_machine_learning_ can_teach_us_to_ build_more_effective_ teams#t-29353 for a great Ted Talk about effective teams and how to build and manage effective teams.

When combining Hackman's, Katzenbach and Smith, and Pentland's recommendations for effective teams, we can conclude that leaders must establish at least five critical conditions, team members need to embrace at least eight essential processes for working together, and team members' communication patterns should match at least five criteria. But is that enough to make effective teams?

Additional research indicates there is more to effective teams than just what the leader establishes, the team processes, and how team members talk to each other. For example, team members' collective cognitive ability contributes to team effectiveness (e.g., LePine, Hollenbeck, Ilgen, & Hedlund, 1997), especially when the team task is new versus well-rehearsed (such as a task the team always works on). Team cognition, the collective knowledge of the group, also depends, to a degree, on the quality of interpersonal relationships within the group (Curşeu, Schalk, & Wessel, 2008).

Social relationships among team members also make a difference in the effectiveness of the team. The widespread use of short-lived task forces (e.g., ad hoc committees, auditing teams) and cross-functional teams (Guzzo, 1995; Mohrman & Cohen, 1995) often brings together individuals who have never met (Ancona & Caldwell, 1990). Therefore, developing ways to encourage relationship building is essential. For instance, applying the speed-dating approach to studying the importance of relationships within groups, Curşeu, Kenis, Raab, and Brandes (2010) found that teams who formed and socialized via the team-dating mechanism reported higher teamwork quality, more effective team processes, and more collective cognitive knowledge sharing than groups formed by maximizing diversity of membership and no team-speed-dating. Speed team-dating refers to a paradigm where one team member interacts with another member for 2 minutes and then switches to interact with another member, eventually interacting with each member of the team for 2 minutes apiece. The implications of Curşeu et al.'s (2010) study are that teams may be most effective when they have purposefully arranged for building social relationships that allow for the development of trust and connection outside of the team task.

Researchers have also determined that team member personality, in addition to cognitive ability and social relationships, can make a positive contribution to team effectiveness. For instance, team-level conscientiousness plays a role in team effectiveness, specifically in performance, creativity, and decision-making (Barrick, Stewart, Neubert, & Mount, 1998; Barry & Stewart, 1997). The same researchers also noted that teams made up of members with high levels of extraversion, agreeableness, openness to experience, and emotional stability demonstrate high team performance. Unfortunately, if one member in the group is particularly low on any of these personality traits

© dotshock/Shutterstock.com

relative to the other members, the entire team performance suffers. Most likely, the team performance suffers because the other members high on these traits struggle to accommodate the less agreeable or less extraverted team member.

Although social relationships can be developed, as demonstrated by Curşeu et al. (2010), cognitive ability and personality are usually considered mostly determined; therefore, what's one to do if the team does not have a high collective cognitive ability or the "right" combination of personalities? In a recent interview (Coutu & Beschloss, 2009), Hackman, an expert in teams, noted that the most effective teams are those that train together and stay together for a while. By training together and working together, they come to know each other well, emphasizing the importance of relationships among team members. To keep the team challenging itself, Hackman suggested that one member take on the role of deviant, to keep forcing the group out of complacency. Thus, although changes to cognitive ability and personality are not likely, a team that trains together learns how to adapt and flex to each member's persona, recognizes which members may be better suited for which team tasks, develops effective communication patterns, and builds trusting relationships that can benefit from the devil's advocate or deviant perspective without creating destructive conflict.

A few other factors, in addition to characteristics of the team members themselves, have been shown to affect team effectiveness, including: adequate team resources (Bishop, Scott, & Burroughs, 2000); trusting environment between team members (DeOrtentiis, Summers, Ammeter, Douglas, & Ferris, 2013);

positive and supportive team climate (González-Romá, Fortes-Ferreira, & Peiró, 2009); core job dimensions such as autonomy, skill variety, task identity, and task significance (Campion, Papper, & Medsker, 1996); and team efficacy, which refers to team members having confidence that they can, as a team, succeed (Gibson, Randel, & Earley, 2000).

So how do you combine and make sense of all these research findings together to make an effective team? Various theoretical models have been offered to depict team processes, factors, and functions that play a role in team effectiveness. The next section reviews a number of models of team effectiveness.

Exercise 7.2

Explain what makes teams effective and the role norms play in team effectiveness.

Theories of Group/Team Effectiveness

Theories or models of group effectiveness may be either based on primary research studies conducted by the model author(s) or offered as prescriptions for what *should* be the best way to create effective teams tend to include more components (i.e., both internal and external factors), making them a bit more comprehensive. You can use both sets of theories or models of team effectiveness to figure out how to make your own team effective or how to improve the overall effectiveness of the teams in your organization. Theoretical models also provide a fast visual clarification to how all the components that affect teams fit together, making communication about teams easier.

Theories and research studies tend to build on one another. Thus, later models incorporate the assumptions and components of earlier models, which make exposure to the models in chronological order an effective approach for learning them and understanding how they may be used in organizations. Hence, we start with one of the first models of teams introduced in the organizational literature.

McGrath

In one of the first series of models of teams, McGrath (1964) proposed a cycle for teams in which inputs (member characteristics, group structure, and task or environmental characteristics) affect group interaction processes, which in turn change group performance, development of group norms, and the group members themselves (shown in Figure 7.7). He called this model "one cycle of a continuous process" (p. 71) and labeled it "Frame of Reference for Analysis of Groups" (p. 69).

Group composition included the characteristics of team members such as age, sex, skills, abilities, and cultural backgrounds.

Group structure referred to the relationships between team members, such as friendships, roles, power, and communication patterns.

Environment and task characteristics referred to the work environment in which a group functioned, including the nature of the group tasks.

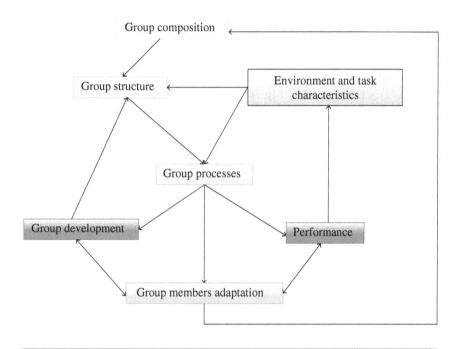

FIGURE 7.7 McGrath's Frame of Reference for Analysis of Groups

Courtesy Zinta Byrne. Source: McGrath, 1964.

Group processes referred to the activities group members engaged in and their interactions with each other.

McGrath additionally suggested that group processes resulted in three outcomes:

- *performance*, which included the quality and quantity of output of the group.

- *group development*, which referred to changes in the groups shared beliefs, attitudes, and goals.

- *group members adaptation* (he called this outcome "effects on group members"), which refers to how the group processes change members themselves including their attitudes, personality, and abilities.

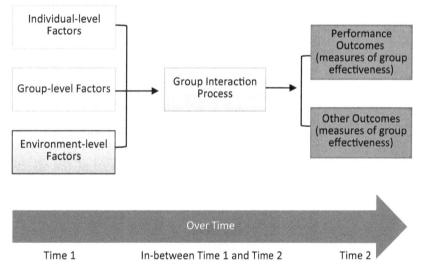

FIGURE 7.8 McGrath's Model for Team Effectiveness

Courtesy Zinta Byrne. Source: McGrath, 1984.

McGrath's model is more often depicted as shown in Figure 7.8, perhaps because the original model was visually more complicated, and this follow-up shows a progression in his thinking about the processes of teams.

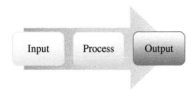

FIGURE 7.9 The Basic Input-Process-Output Model

Courtesy Zinta Byrne.

Figure 7.8 shows McGrath's essential model of team effectiveness, which suggests that over time, individual factors (attitudes, personality), group factors (team composition, size), and work-context called environmental factors (group task, reward system) flow into or affect group processes, which in turn affect the team's results such as effectiveness, performance, or satisfaction. If you compare the elements of the model shown in Figure 7.7 and 7.8, you can see that Figure 7.8 is a simplified presentation, but contains all the same components. McGrath (1964) referred to his general model of team functioning as a cycle of "input, process and output" (p. 71), which is depicted in Figure 7.9, and forms the foundation of many subsequent group models.

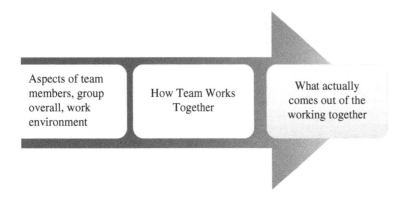

FIGURE 7.10 Input-Process-Output Model in Basic Terms

Courtesy Zinta Byrne.

The distinguishing characteristic of McGrath's model is that teams follow an input-process-output cycle.

Figure 7.10 depicts the same general input-process-output model phrased in terms of what each box conveys.

Nearly all team effectiveness models developed after McGrath's (1964) depict the basic input-process-output model, with variations in the form of moderators and mediators; for example, process in Figure 7.9 and Figure 7.10 is a mediator. Mediators explain how or why input variables affect output variables. For example, the relationship between leadership and employee satisfaction is explained by employees' commitment to their organization, which develops as a result of good leadership (Yousef, 2000). In the case of McGrath's model, team processes explain how aspects of team members and the work environment affect the team's output. Moderators are variables upon which the strength of relationships between variables depends. For example, the relationship between proactive personality (i.e., tendency to seek out and act on opportunities to create change) and training outcomes is dependent on age; the effects are stronger with younger adults than older (Bertolino, Truxillo, & Fraccaroli, 2011).

Gladstein

Because she felt research on high-performing teams had become stagnated, Gladstein (1984) studied 326 individuals representing 100 intact teams in a marketing division of a large organization in an effort to develop a new and better model of team effectiveness, based on "real" teams. The result of her study was that she proposed a model based on McGrath's (1964) input-process-output model (shown in Figure 7.11), thus building on his work, yet extending it based on her own new findings.

As part of her study, she asked participants questions about group norms, team size, leadership, role clarity, and group skills. She also asked how long people worked for the organization and in their jobs to assess group-level factors that affect how the team members interact with one another. For organizational-level factors, she asked about the reward systems, supervisory behaviors, organizational training, and market growth of the organization. These variables together were also hypothesized to affect how the team interacted with one another.

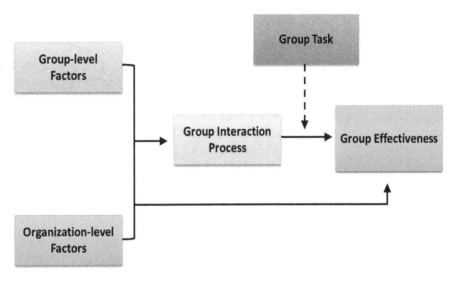

Gladstein proposed that *group-level factors* (e.g., group composition, structure of the group such as their roles and size) and *organization-level factors* (e.g., resources available such as training or consulting, and organizational structure such as supervisory control) influence how the group interacts in addition to

FIGURE 7.11   Gladstein's Model of Team Effectiveness

Courtesy Zinta Byrne. Source: Gladstein, 1984.

affecting the *effectiveness of the group* (hence the direct arrows to group interaction process and group effectiveness from group-level and organization-level factors).

Group interaction process specifically referred to how the team members communicated with each other, their supportiveness, the level of their interpersonal conflict, how they worked on tasks, their decision-making processes, and how they managed interactions with other groups.

Gladstein additionally proposed that the nature of the *group task* (the overall group project) would affect how much the group interaction processes affected group effectiveness. Accordingly, the relationship between group interaction process and group effectiveness was dependent on the group task. She measured group task as a combination of the complexity, interdependence, and certainty of the task. The dashed line in Figure 7.11 indicates this relationship was hypothesized but failed to receive empirical support in her actual data. Lastly, she measured group performance, group-member satisfaction, and sales revenue, which combined made up her measure of group effectiveness.

Gladstein originally set out to determine which variables in the model had the most influence on effectiveness because the firm that hired her wanted to know how to increase team performance to be more competitive in their market space. Some of the teams in the organization performed well, whereas others did not. Thus, the goal of her project was to determine how to predict and improve team effectiveness, to provide upper management with a set of recommendations. Her results supported her hypothesized model, although specific details about what fell into each box were not exactly as she proposed. The dashed line in Figure 7.11 indicates what Gladstein originally proposed, but did not find significant results for - thus, group task did not ultimately moderate the relationship between group interaction process and group effectiveness.

The distinguishing characteristic of Gladstein's model is its development based on actual intact teams.

Uniqueness of the model

Unique to Gladstein's model is that hers is based on a theoretical framework (McGrath, 1964) tested using a field sample. Her study examined a variety of teams as they currently operate, as opposed to a single team and as opposed to how they *should* theoretically operate. Several later models suggest what "should" be the best way to improve team effectiveness (Hackman's model), or what all models combined theoretically suggest is related to effectiveness. The models are not based on what actually occurs in organizations.

Hackman

In an effort to prescribe how groups should be designed and function for maximum effectiveness, Hackman introduced a model that identifies factors designed to enhance (or reduce) the effectiveness of the group, with the intent of understanding what produces constructive change (Figure 7.12).

A prescribed model is not based on field experience—how teams actually work—but describes how they *should* be designed to work effectively, based on theory and accumulated empirical evidence.

Walking through the Figure, one box at a time:

Group-level factors, or group design, included core job dimensions that foster motivation and feedback on whether the group performs. No surprise, this part of the model draws from the job characteristics theory core job dimensions proposed by Hackman and Oldham (1976), since this Hackman is the very same (J. Richard Hackman). Group-level factors also include the composition of the group in terms of experience, knowledge, size, diversity (should not be a homogenous group), group norms (specifically those that support self-regulation and planning), and interpersonal skills (ability to work with others). Additionally, group-level factors incorporate attention to a learning environment and system for obtaining and transferring important and necessary information among group members and between groups.

Organization-level factors, or organizational context, refer foremost to a supportive organizational reward system. A supportive reward system incorporates challenge, consequences for performance, and rewards that focus on the group as opposed to the individual.

Group synergy refers to the group members using their energy and talents well, such that their interactions expand their capabilities and contribute to group functioning. Synergy is gained when the group results exceed the individual contributions of each member alone. "Synergy among members results

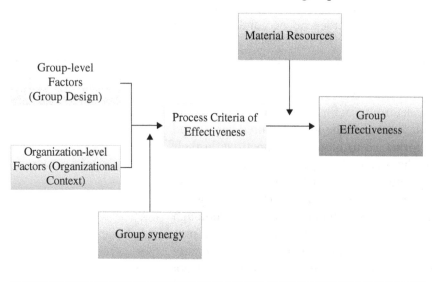

FIGURE 7.12   Hackman's Normative Model of Team Effectiveness.

Courtesy Zinta Byrne. Source: Hackman, 1987

in group outcomes that may be quite different from those that would be obtained by simply adding up the contributions of individual members" (Hackman, 1987, p. 322). Group synergy, how the group members work together and interact with one another, may result in more efficient processes and increases in motivation because the group determines how to coordinate their efforts well and avoid the lost time and energy that coordination takes. Part of group synergy comes about from shared commitment to the team, which generates a kind of excitement and value for group membership.

Process criteria of effectiveness refers to the effort the team applies to the group task, the collective group knowledge and skill applied to the task, and the appropriateness of the strategies used by the group to accomplish the task. Strategies include dividing the work into subgroups, brainstorming first about how to complete the project, or creating a quality check cycle for projects where objectives change frequently before the final deadline. Hackman referred to this part of the model as "the hurdles the group must overcome to be effective."

Resources, or material resources as Hackman called it, are the materials necessary for completing the group task. These include equipment, space, tools, raw materials, money, or people to sufficiently achieve the task.

Group effectiveness in the model results from meeting three criteria: (1) the groups' output must exceed performance standards of those receiving the output; (2) the social processes invoked during task completion must maintain or enhance the capability of the group to work together again; and (3) the experience of working in the group must satisfy the group members as opposed to frustrate them and leave them disgusted or disillusioned.

> The distinguishing characteristics of Hackman's Normative model are its prescription for how teams should function to be effective and its emphasis on team member relational experiences.

Uniqueness of the model

Hackman's model describes what it will take to improve teams; how to increase the probability that they will perform at higher levels. Thus, the model does not describe how teams actually work or what has been seen in teams, but rather how they should be to achieve high effectiveness. Another unique feature of Hackman's model is an emphasis on group synergy and resources. Hackman's definition of group effectiveness was quite different from other models. Specifically, as opposed to just measuring the amount produced or the quality of performance, Hackman believed that the effectiveness could only be understood by evaluating how well the output met the expectations of the client, how well the group worked together, and whether the journey to produce the output was a good one. Thus, even if a group produced a product the client loved, but the members hated each other thereafter, he felt the group effectiveness was very low—to Hackman, group models are social and personal; they are not just about objective criteria. This tri-part evaluation that makes up the assessment of team or group effectiveness is a unique feature of Hackman's model relative to the other models of group effectiveness.

Another key differentiator is the mediator—process criteria of effectiveness. In other models, this process variable is about how the team interacts, which in Hackman's model is incorporated more within the group synergy variable. Additionally, Hackman emphasized the resources necessary for the team to complete the work, whereas other models do not mention resources.

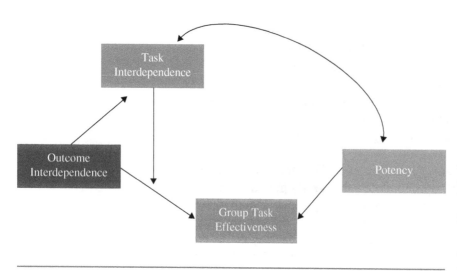

FIGURE 7.13 Shea and Guzzo's Model of Team Effectiveness

Courtesy Zinta Byrne. Source: Shea and Guzzo, 1987.

Shea and Guzzo

Coming more from a perspective of how teams are managed versus just what makes them effective, Shea and Guzzo (1987) presented their model (Figure 7.13) based on an examination of a large national corporation with what could be considered 800 teams (800 retail outlet stores).

In their model, *task interdependence* refers to how much interaction group members have on their actual job tasks. For example, a recent class was assigned a Group Wiki project, where teams of students were to develop a Wiki for a specific topic within organizational psychology (e.g., leadership). A Wiki is a web application that allows people from anywhere (as long as they can get to it on the Internet) to contribute content of any kind (written, pictures, audio). Low-task interdependence was demonstrated by groups of students who structured their work so that they divided the topic content into pieces such that each member worked on his or her piece independently, without needing the others to complete their work. At the end of the class, they combined the parts to create a final document. There was no interaction or reliance on one another to get the task done. In contrast, groups that worked on all parts together, needing one another's contribution to complete each paragraph or section, demonstrated high-task interdependence. Thus, task interdependence is about someone else's output forming your input, and vice-versa, in order to complete the task. The task cannot be done without both contributions - you are dependent on each other.

Outcome interdependence refers to when the completed task accomplished by the entire group results in an outcome important to and shared by the group members. For example, outcomes may be things like rewards or punishments. The more that group members rely on each other for their outcome (e.g., group lounge, group microwave, group bonus), the more one deviant member negatively affects the group. If one person does not perform, the entire group fails to get the group reward. Olympic relay teams are a good example of this. If one member of the relay fails to perform for whatever reason, the entire team suffers the loss; not just that team member.

Potency refers to group members' collective belief that they can be effective. They believe they have, as a group, what it takes to succeed (e.g., skills, resources, feedback). Potency is correlated with task interdependence (hence the double-sided arrow), such that increases in task interdependence allow members to see each other's work and as a result, see that they have skills in the group to get the job done. This interdependence and visibility of each other's skills increases their belief that they can succeed on the task. Likewise, increases in potency affect how the team organizes their interdependent tasks—they believe they have what it takes to succeed, and this affects how they rely on each other's contributions to the task (increasing interdependence).

Shea and Guzzo also noted that the effectiveness of the group provides feedback to team members on how successful they are, thus indirectly reinforcing their belief that they can succeed (success increases one's belief that success is achievable).

The distinguishing characteristic of Shea and Guzzo's model is the emphasis on interdependence between team members.

Uniqueness of the model

Shea and Guzzo's model differs from the other models by its simplicity and emphasis placed on interdependence. Shea and Guzzo focused on explaining why groups succeed or fail, developing their theoretical model from a review of the literature and from their own experiences. They then applied their theory to understanding a national retail organization, which makes this model similar to Gladstein's in that it tests a theory of teams in the field. The results of Shea and Guzzo's surveys asking about task interdependence, potency, and outcome interdependence (to a lesser extent) provided general support for their model, with the importance of outcome interdependence emphasized. Their model is also unique because it focuses on a specific part of team effectiveness—the relationships within the group more so than the effects of the contextual environment or organization on employees. Thus, their model is not as broad or big-picture as some of the other team models presented earlier.

Campion, Medsker, and Higgs

Pulling many previous models of teams together, Campion et al. (1993) conducted a review of the literature and proposed a comprehensive model of team effectiveness (Figure 7.14).

Campion and colleagues tested the model on five employees per group, randomly selected out of 80 groups across five geographical units of a financial services company in the United States. Group sizes varied from 6 to 30 members, but only five per team were necessary for the study. Each group performed the same tasks, which included clerical and processing work such as sorting, coding, handling customer inquiries, and quality checks. All jobs were considered interdependent. All groups followed similar organizational policies and practices, making them comparable. The sample was disproportionately women (96%) and only 1.6% had a college degree or more, whereas the managers included in the sample nearly all had a college degree (92.6%; 77 of the 80 groups had managers included in the sample).

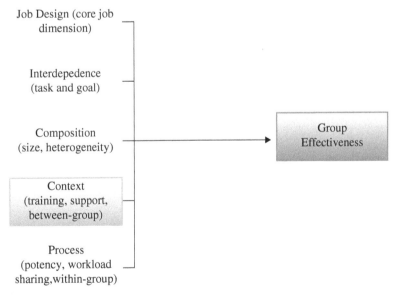

FIGURE 7.14   Campion, Medsker, and Higgs' Model of Team Effectiveness

Courtesy Zinta Byrne. Source: Campion, Medsker, and Higgs, 1993.

The distinguishing characteristic of Campbell et al.'s model is it serves as a simple summary model of several well-known models of group effectiveness.

Campion et al.'s results showed all variables except interdependence related to employee and manager ratings of group effectiveness, which was measured as productivity (how much of the assigned work did not get finished), employee satisfaction, and managers' judgments of effectiveness (quality of work, productivity, managers' perceptions of satisfaction of team members). Within *context*, between-group communications did not relate to group effectiveness. Task identity within *job design* also did not relate to any of the group effectiveness measures, but all other job design variables did (e.g., task identity). Similarly, within *composition*, heterogeneity did not relate to any of the group effectiveness measures, but probably because the sample was 96% female, same level of education, and same skillset or job tasks (thus a very homogenous composition).

In conclusion, the model shown in Figure 7.14 was, for the most part, supported by the data suggesting that these categories of work or characteristics of work (job design, composition, context) predict group effectiveness.

Uniqueness of the model

Campion and colleagues' model was developed from a work redesign perspective, which makes their focus on understanding the job characteristics (i.e., core job dimensions of the job characteristics theory) of effective work groups. They specifically pulled from the theoretical literature the characteristics of work hypothesized to relate to group effectiveness. Campion et al.'s model is based on Gladstein's (1984), Hackman's (1987), Guzzo and Shea's (1992), and Tannenbaum, Beard, and Salas' (1992) models of group effectiveness.

Missing from Campion et al.'s model, but shown in the models upon which it is based, are moderators and mediator variables—that is, there are no variables upon which predictors of group effectiveness are dependent or variables that explain why predictors are related to group effectiveness. An example of a moderator might be group size, whether job design is more important when the group is large versus small. An example of a mediator might be that communication skills explain why context influences effectiveness.

Thus, one value of Campion and colleagues' model is its apparent simplicity—you can easily talk about what makes for group effectiveness using this model. The simplicity, unfortunately, can also hide the true complexity of teams; hence, more value is gained out of Campion et al.'s model when you understand the models upon which theirs is based.

Exercise 7.3

Compare and contrast the following team models: McGrath, Gladstein, Hackman, Shea, and Guzzo.

Effective Virtual Teams

None of the previously reviewed models discuss factors necessary for effective virtual teams.

Furst, Reeves, Rosen, and Blackburn (2004) argued that virtual teams are presented with certain challenges that in-person teams are not; namely, logistical problems (e.g., communication), interpersonal relationship building, and technology difficulties. Resulting from their longitudinal study of six virtual teams in a large food distribution company, the authors developed the following guidelines, embedded within Tuckman's stages of team development, for facilitating effective virtual teams.

1. During the forming stage, provide realistic team previews of what it might look like to work in a virtual team, have experienced team members coach new team members, develop team identity, develop a clear mission, and secure upper/senior management support.

2. During the storming stage, conduct in-person face-to-face team building, train members on conflict resolution practices and skills, and obtain mediation for conflicts that team members are not able to resolve themselves with their newly developing skills.

3. During the norming stage, specify task requirements, hold team members accountable, create schedules and completion dates, facilitate information sharing by establishing procedures for sharing information, and assign a team coach who has skills in being a virtual member and in managing a virtual team.

4. During the performing stage, provide resources and support for the team to perform as needed, and foster a culture that supports and values virtual team work.

Virtual teams rely on computers to communicate; however, teams using computer-mediated communication are not necessarily effective when it comes to decision-making. For instance, Carey and Kacmar (1997) conducted a study examining groups using **teleconferencing** compared to in-person decision-making groups, to determine the effects of the electronic system on overall group functioning. They found, despite the complexity (simple or not) of the task, the teleconferencing groups took longer to complete a task than did face-to-face groups. Teleconferencing for complex tasks was related to more errors in solutions than in-person problem solving. Both types of groups (teleconferencing vs. face-to-face) had correct solutions for simple tasks. Furthermore, group members in the face-to-face groups were more satisfied with group interactions than were those in the teleconferencing groups. Additionally, information overload was rated higher with teleconferencing than with face-to-face communication. Lastly, members of face-to-face groups reported more contributions to transactions (a contribution or communication directly related to the task) and social contributions (a communication not task related) between group members than in teleconferenced groups.

Carey and Kacmar's findings are consistent with a 2002 meta-analysis, wherein researchers determined that computer-mediated communication was related to decreased effectiveness, increased time for task completion, and decreased satisfaction with the group, as compared to face-to-face communication (Baltes, Dickson, Sherman, Bauer, & LaGanke, 2002). Relationships were moderated by variables such as group size, time limitations, task type, and anonymity, indicating that effectiveness of virtual teams was dependent on group size, time limits, type of task, and anonymity. The authors recommended seriously considering these findings before putting computer-mediated communications in place for group processes Marlow, Lacerenza, and Salas (2017) recently

Reflecting back on the various models of group effectiveness, why (when) would you choose one model over another? For what type of situation, research question, or challenge is one model better or more helpful than the others? Which ones? Which situations? Create a table to identify each model and identify the situation the model is best suited for.

leveraged an extended input-process-output model called the input-mediator-output-input framework (Ilgen, Hollenbeck, Johnson, & Jundt, 2005), to theorize that understanding how to make virtual teams effective requires greater attention on their communication patterns and constraints. Specifically, they suggested that virtual communication is not a yes-no construct; rather virtuality lies on a continuum from complete black-box communication to a hybrid of face-to-face/electronic communication.

Like all the recommendations before this one, the recommendations here do not apply to all teams. Because there are so many different kinds of teams and combinations of contextual environments, no one model works for all.

How Do Managers Use These Theories in the Workplace?

Managing teams is a challenge because you are not just focused on one person, but a group of several people who all bring their own needs, personalities, competencies, strengths, and weaknesses to the table. How they combine to be effective is very much like putting puzzle pieces together. Managers can use the theories in this section to guide them as to what they should be considering when working with their teams. For example, the various models basically suggest that factors/aspects about the individuals themselves, the group, and the work environment come together to influence how the team members interact with each other and with the organization, and those interactions determine the group's performance and ultimate satisfaction with the team. Nearly all the models indicate that you have to consider how the team adapts/interacts and works over time—a single snapshot will not give you an accurate picture of the team. The models vary by how detailed or comprehensive they are. For example, Shea and Guzzo offer a narrowly focused perspective on teams, whereas Campion et al. give a very high level and broad perspective on teams. Managers wanting to step back and think more globally about how all their various teams are working and what general areas of resources or processes they need to focus on over the next fiscal year might find Campion et al.'s model helpful. Managers wanting to work with one team in particular that seems to be struggling might consider the more narrow focus of Shea and Guzzo's model, or consider the group synergy component of Hackman's normative model.

When Are Teams NOT Effective?

There are times when implementing teams, regardless of type, is not the way to go. Some tasks are better completed by a single individual than by a group of people who struggle to coordinate efforts, or when there is not enough reason for multiple people working together. If the work to be done does not require interdependency or one person needing to work with another, there is no reason to form a team.

When first forming, teams are generally not effective (Coutu & Beschloss, 2009) unless they are trained to form instant high-function teams, like cockpit crews and medical emergency teams. The ineffectiveness of most teams when first forming is mostly due to their inexperience with each other. Projects or tasks that require high levels of creativity are best completed by individuals, because teams in this case hinder and interrupt the creative thought process.

Based on a review of the readings, ineffective teams share a few characteristics shown in Figure 7.15, most of which many of us have experienced at one time or another.

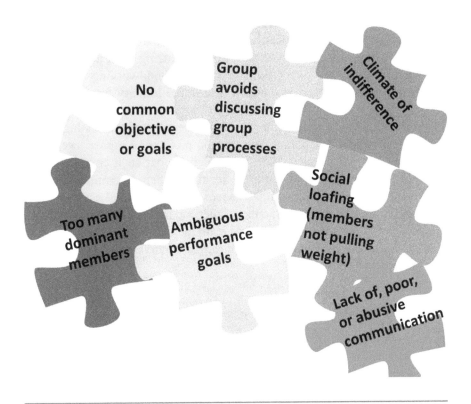

FIGURE 7.15   Ineffective Teams

Courtesy Zinta Byrne.

When Should You NOT Form Teams?

As mentioned, there are times when it may not make sense to form a team (Hackman, 1987). Thus, before forming a team, managers should consider the following questions:

1. What specifically is the task that must be completed?
2. What are the expectations for accomplishing the task and for doing it well?
3. Is there a manager or leader for this team, or should it be self-managed?
4. What are the benefits of having a team work on this task, what are the disadvantages?

If the answer to these questions suggests a team is the right approach, these follow-up questions should be asked:

5. How should the team be composed?
6. What resources are necessary and available?
7. How can the team be supported?

Why is it particularly challenging to have an effective virtual team?

There are times when teams are implemented regardless of whether the task requires a team or whether the team will succeed given the resources, management, and goals. No doubt as a student, you've likely been forced to engage in team projects even then the project could have been better completed alone.

The purpose for teams in education, however, tends to be different from in organizations (e.g., learn communication skills, exposure to challenges of teamwork). Teams are often formed for the sake of experiencing what it means to be in a work team. Because teamwork skills must be learned, working in teams as part of class projects can help you develop at least preliminary familiarity with the skills.

Within an organization, teams may be created because of preexisting norms for using the team approach to complete specific projects or higher level managers may have demanded that a team be formed. Under such conditions, the best course of action might be to form the team and then determine how best to accomplish the work given the circumstances. Members could establish processes and strategies that allow for the most independent work, while still maintaining a facade of being a team. By training team members and paying attention to what makes for an effective and ineffective team, members could work to make the team as effective as possible.

Chapter Summary

Teams are made up of two or more employees working together to accomplish a common goal or set of goals. Team members are often dependent on one another for some aspect of their jobs, though they can work independently to a degree and still consider themselves as part of a team. Teams vary in size, structure, membership, and location (some are 100% virtual, some are 100% colocated, and some are a hybrid). Teams can be managed by a supervisor or manager, self-managed, temporary, permanent, or time-limited and for advisory purposes only. Each type of team and type of configuration has its strengths and weaknesses; therefore, the design of teams is dependent on the goals for the team.

Organizations typically use teams when they believe that more people on a task are better than one and when a task is too big for one person to achieve alone. Some tasks or projects are not well suited for a team approach; they are better off completed by a single individual with specific skills and knowledge needed for that task. A number of theories have been proposed for how teams form and what makes for an effective team. However, the actual study of teams in organizations is challenging and interventions are hard to test because of the complexity of teams and the inability to control or hold constant the environment and factors that affect team dynamics.

Figure 7.16 provides a visual summary of the key concepts from Chapter 7.

The visual summary shows teams can vary in terms of their types and how they are formed, and that a number of factors contribute to and affect the effectiveness of teams. These factors are shown as leading into or pointing to the center circle of teams. At the top of the visual summary is the basic group model of various inputs leading to group processes which then lead to outputs. Most group models are built on this basic foundational IPO model. Essentially, everything you need to know about teams in organizations appears

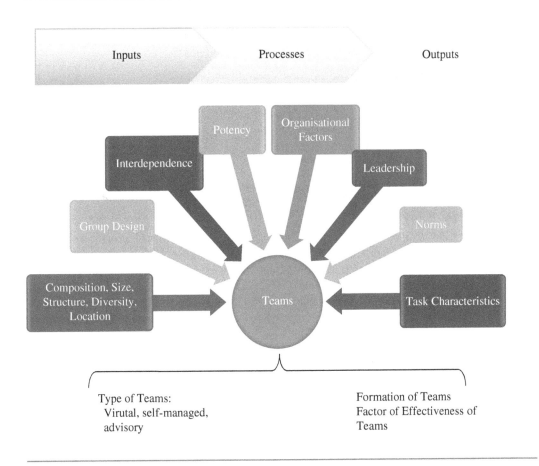

FIGURE 7.16   Visual Summary of Chapter 7.

Courtesy Zinta Byrne.

in this visual summary for Chapter 7. Of course, the details are not in the visual summary—such as what is comprised in organizational factors or group design, for example.

Discussion Questions

1. Teams appear relevant to the workplace and much research reviewed in the chapter suggests they work effectively. If so, why do most college students hate teamwork? If you could tell your instructors what to do differently in their team assignments, what would you share to make the team project a better experience and more useful for you as a student?

2. Effective teams require a lot of outside structure and support, such as a supportive organization and a compelling vision or direction. Pentland (p. 223 of this chapter) offered specific communication patterns of effective teams. What do you as a team member need to contribute or do on a team to ensure it is successful—beyond these communication patterns? What responsibility do you have as a member of a team to that team to ensure its success? Do you have this responsibility on every team you join or are assigned to?

3. What makes a team ineffective, and why? How do you work around those factors that contribute to team ineffectiveness?

4. How can you avoid Gersick's punctuated equilibrium hitting your project at the mid-point of the timeline, leaving you to scramble in the end to get it done? What strategies, perhaps some from Chapter 3 on motivation, would you put in place to make the overall project more efficient and balance the workload more?

References

Ahuja, M. K., & Galvin, J. E. (2003). Socialization in virtual groups. *Journal of Management, 29* (2), 161–185.

Ancona, D. G., & Caldwell, D. (1990). Improving the performance of new product teams. *Research Technology Management, 35*(2), 25–29.

Aubé, C., Rousseau, V., & Tremblay, S. (2011). Team size and quality of group experience: The more the merrier? *Group Dynamics: Theory, Research, and Practice, 15*(4), 357–375. doi:10.1037/a0025400

Baltes, B. B., Dickson, M. W., Sherman, M. P., Bauer, C. C., & LaGanke, J. (2002). Computer-mediated communication and group decision making: A meta-analysis. *Organizational Behavior and Human Decision Processes, 87*(1), 156–179. doi:10.1006/obhd.2001.2961

Barrick, M. R., Stewart, G. L., Neubert, M. J., & Mount, M. K. (1998). Relating member ability and personality to work-team processes and team effectiveness. *Journal of Applied Psychology, 83*(3), 377–391. doi:10.1037/0021-9010.83.3.377

Barry, D. (1991). Managing the bossless team: Lessons in distributed leadership. *Organizational Dynamics, 20*(1), 31–47. doi:10.1016/0090-2616(91)90081-J

Barry, B., & Stewart, G. L. (1997). Composition, process, and performance in self-managed groups: The role of personality. *Journal of Applied Psychology, 82*(1), 62–78. doi:10.1037/0021-9010.82.1.62

Bell, B. S., & Kozlowski, S. J. (2002). A typology of virtual teams: Implications for effective leadership. *Group & Organization Management, 27*(1), 14–49. doi:10.1177/1059601102027001003

Bertolino, M., Truxillo, D. M., & Fraccaroli, F. (2011). Age as moderator of the relationship of proactive personality with training motivation, perceived career development from training, and training behavioral intentions. *Journal of Organizational Behavior, 32*(2), 248–263. doi:10.1002/job.670

Bishop, J. W., Scott, K., & Burroughts, S. M. (2000). Support, commitment, and employee outcomes in a team environement. *Journal of Management, 26*(6), 1113–1132. doi:10.1177/014920630002600603.

Campion, M. A., Medsker, G. J., & Higgs, A. (1993). Relations between work group characteristics and effectiveness: Implications for designing effective work groups. *Personnel Psychology, 46*(4), 823–850. doi:10.1111/j.1744-6570.1993.tb01571.x

Campion, M. A., Papper, E. M., & Medsker, G. J. (1996). Relations between work team characteristics and effectiveness: A replication and extension. *Personnel Psychology, 49*(2), 429–452. doi:10.1111/j.1744-6570.1996.tb01806.x

Carey, J. M., & Kacmar, C. J. (1997). The impact of communication mode and task complexity on small group performance and member satisfaction. *Computers in Human Behavior, 13*(1), 23–49. doi:10.1016/S0747-5632(96)00027-1

Carlson, J. R., & Zmud, R. W. (1999). Channel expansion theory and the experiential nature of media richness perceptions. *Academy of Management Journal, 42,* 153–170.

Cascio, W. F. (2000). Managing a virtual workplace. *Academy of Management Executive, 14,* 81–90.

Coutu, D., & Beschloss, M. (2009). Why teams DON'T work. *Harvard Business Review, 87*(5), 98–105.

Culnan, M. J., & Markus, M. L. (1987). Information technologies. In F. M. Jablin, L. L. Putnam, K. H. Roberts, & L. W. Porter (Eds.), *Handbook of organizational communication: An interdisciplinary perspective.* (pp. 420–443). Newbury Park, CA: Sage.

Curral, L. A., Forrester, R. H., Dawson, J. F., & West, M. A. (2001). It's what you do and the way that you do it: Team task, team size, and innovation-related group processes. *European Journal of Work and Organizational Psychology, 10*(2), 187–204. doi:10.1080/13594320143000627

Curşeu, P. L., Kenis, P., Raab, J., & Brandes, U. (2010). Composing effective teams through team dating. *Organization Studies, 31*(7), 873–894. doi:10.1177/0170840610373195

Curşeu, P. L., Schalk, R., & Wessel, I. (2008). How do virtual teams process information? A literature review and implications for management. *Journal of Managerial Psychology, 23*(6), 628–652. doi:10.1108/02683940810894729

Daft, R. L., & Lengel, R. H. (1984). Information richness: A new approach to managerial behavior and organization design. *Research in Organizational Behavior, 6,* 191–233.

DeOrtentiis, P. S., Summers, J. K., Ammeter, A. P., Douglas, C., & Ferris, G. R. (2013). Cohesion and satisfaction as mediators of the team trust—Team effectiveness relationship: An interdependence theory perspective. *The Career Development International, 18*(5), 521–543. doi:10.1108/CDI-03-2013-0035

Dixon, M. (2018). Reinventing Customer Service. *Harvard Business Review, 96*(6), 82–90.

Fischer, B., & Boynton, A. (2005). Virtuoso teams. (cover story). *Harvard Business Review, 83*(7/8), 116–123.

Furst, S. A., Reeves, M., Rosen, B., & Blackburn, R. S. (2004). Managing the life cycle of virtual teams. *Academy Of Management Executive, 18*(2), 6–20. doi:10.5465/AME.2004.13837468

Gersick, C. J. (1988). Time and transition in work teams: Toward a new model of group development. *Academy of Management Journal, 31*(1), 9–41. doi:10.2307/256496

Gibson, C. B., Randel, A. E., & Earley, P. (2000). Understanding group efficacy: An empirical test of multiple assessment methods. *Group & Organization Management, 25*(1), 67–97. doi:10.1177/1059601100251005

Gladstein, D. L. (1984). Groups in context: A model of task group effectiveness. *Administrative Science Quarterly,* (3), 3–27.

Glassop, L. I. (2002). The organizational benefits of teams. *Human Relations, 55*(2), 225–249. doi:10.1177/0018726702055002184

González-Romá, V., Fortes-Ferreira, L., & Peiró, J. M. (2009). Team climate, climate strength and team performance. A longitudinal study. *Journal of Occupational and Organizational Psychology, 82*(3), 511–536. doi:10.1348/096317908X370025

Gratton, L., & Erickson, T. J. (2007). 8 ways to build collaborative teams. *Harvard Business Review, 85*(11), 100–109.

Graziano, W. G., Jensen-Campbell, L. A., & Hair, E. C. (1996). Perceiving interpersonal conflict and reacting to it: The case for agreeableness. *Journal of Personality and Social Psychology, 70*(4), 820–835. doi:10.1037/0022-3514.70.4.820.

Guzzo, R. A. (1995). Introduction: At the intersection of team effectiveness and decision making. In R. A. Guzzo & E. Salas (Eds.), *Team effectiveness and decision making in organizations* (pp. 1–8). San Francisco, CA: Jossey-Bass.

Guzzo, R. A., & Shea, G. P. (1992). Group performance and intergroup relations in organizations. In M. D. Dunnette, L. M. Hough (Eds.), *Handbook of industrial and organizational psychology* (2nd ed., Vol. 3, pp. 269–313). Palo Alto, CA: Consulting Psychologists Press.

Hackman, J. R (1986). The psychology of self-management in organizations. In M. S. Pallack & R O. Perloff (Eds.), *Psychology and work: Productivity, change, and employment.* Washington, DC: American Psychological Association.

Hackman, J. R (1987). The design of work teams. In J. W. Lorsch (Ed.), *Handbook of organizational behavior* (pp. 315–342). Englewood Cliffs, NJ: Prentice-Hall.

Hackman, J. (1992). Group influences on individuals in organizations. In M. D. Dunnette, & L. M. Hough (Eds.), *Handbook of industrial and organizational psychology* (2nd ed., Vol. 3, pp. 199–267). Palo Alto, CA: Consulting Psychologists Press.

Hackman, J., & Oldham, G. R. (1976). Motivation through the design of work: Test of a theory. *Organizational Behavior & Human Performance, 16*(2), 250–279. doi:10.1016/0030-5073(76)90016-7

Hare, A. P. (1976). *Handbook of small group research* (2nd ed.). New York, NY: Free Press.

Hausknecht, J. P., Trevor, C. O., & Howard, M. J. (2009). Unit-level voluntary turnover rates and customer service quality: Implications of group cohesiveness, newcomer concentration, and size. *Journal of Applied Psychology, 94*(4), 1068–1075. doi:10.1037/a0015898

Hollingshead, A. B., & McGrath, J. E. (1995). Computer-assisted groups: A critical review of the empirical research. In R. A. Guzzo & E. Salas (Eds.), *Team effectiveness and decision making in organizations* (pp. 46–78). San Francisco, CA: Jossey-Bass.

Ilgen, D. R., Hollenbeck, J. R., Johnson, M., & Jundt, D. (2005). Teams in organizations: From input-process-output models to IMOI models. *Annual Review of Psychology, 56*, 517–543.

Jackson, S. E., May, K. E., & Whitney, K. (1995). Understanding the dynamics of diversity in decision-making teams. In R. A. Guzzo, E. Salas, & Associates (Eds.), *Team effectiveness and decision making in organizations,* (pp. 2014–2261). San Francisco, CA: Jossey-Bass.

Jaques, E. (1955). Death and the mid-life crisis. *International Journal of Psychoanalysis, 46,* 502–514.

Kahai, S. S., & Cooper, R. B. (2003). Exploring the core concepts of media richness theory: The impact of cue multiplicity and feedback immediacy on decision quality. *Journal of Management Information Systems, 20,* 263–299.

Katzenbach, J. R., & Smith, D. K. (1992). Why teams matter. *Mckinsey Quarterly,* (3), 3–27.

Katzenbach, J. R., & Smith, D. K. (1993). The discipline of teams. *Harvard Business Review, 71*(2), 111–120.

Katzenbach, J. R. (2000). Peak performance: Aligning the hearts and minds of your employees. Boston, MA: Harvard Business School Press Books.

Kirkman, B. L., Rosen, B., Gibson, C. B., Tesluk, P. E., & McPherson, S. O. (2002). Five challenges to virtual team success: Lessons from Sabre, Inc. *Academy of Management Executive, 16*(3), 67–79.

Kozlowski, S. J., & Bell, B. S. (2013). Work groups and teams in organizations. In N. W. Schmitt, S. Highhouse, & I. B. Weiner (Eds.), *Handbook of psychology, Vol. 12: Industrial and organizational psychology* (2nd ed., pp. 412–469). Hoboken, NJ: John Wiley & Sons Inc.

Kristof, A. L., Brown, K. G., Sims, H. P. Jr., & Smith, K. A. (1995). The virtual team: A case study and inductive model. *Advances in Interdisciplinary Studies of Work Teams, 2,* 229–253.

LaCoursiere, R. B. (1980). *The life cycle of groups: Group developmental stage theory.* New York, NY: Human Sciences Press.

Laiken, M. E. (1994). The myth of the self-managing team. *Organization Development Journal, 12*(2), 29–34.

Lebie, L., Rhoades, J. A., McGrath, J. E. (1996). Interaction process in computer-mediated and face-to-face groups. *Computer Supported Cooperative Work, 4,* 127–152.

LePine, J. A., Hollenbeck, J. R., Ilgen, D. R., & Hedlund, J. (1997). Effects of individual differences on the performance of hierarchical decision-making teams: Much more than g. *Journal of Applied Psychology, 82*(5), 803–811. doi:10.1037/0021-9010.82.5.803.

Levine, J. M. (1989). Reaction to opinion deviance in small groups. In P. B. Paulus (Ed.), *Psychology of group influence* (2nd ed., pp. 187–232). Hillsdale, NJ: Erlbaum.

Maass, A., West, S. G., & Cialdini, R. B. (1987). Minority influence and conversion. In C. Hendrick (Ed.), *Group processes: The review of personality and social psychology* (Vol. 8, pp. 55–79). Sage Publications.

Markham, S. E., Dansereau, F., & Alutto, J. A. (1982). Group size and absenteeism rates: A longitudinal analysis. *Academy of Management Journal, 25*(4), 921–927. doi:10.2307/256108.

Marlow, S. L., Lacerenza, C. N., & Salas, E. (2017). Communication in virtual teams: a conceptual framework and research agenda. *Human Resource Management Review, 27,* 575-589.

Martins, L. L., Gilson, L. L., & Maynard, M. T. (2004). Virtual teams: What do we know and where do we go from here? *Journal of Management, 30* (6), 805–835.

McGrath, J. E. (1964). *Social psychology: A brief introduction.* New York, NY: Holt, Rinehart, and Winston.

McGrath, J. E. (1984). *Groups: Interaction and performance.* Englewood Cliffs, NJ: Prentice Hall.

Mohrman, S. A., & Cohen, S. G. (1995). When people get out of the box: New relationships, new systems. In A. Howard (Ed.), *The changing nature of work* (pp. 365–410). San Francisco, CA: Jossey-Bass.

Moscovici, S. (1980). Toward a theory of conversion behavior. In L. Berkowitz (Ed.), *Advances in experimental social psychology, 13,* 209–239. New York, NY: Academic Press.

Moscovici, S. S., Lage, E. E., & Naffrechoux, M. M. (1969). Influence of a consistent minority on the responses of a majority in a color perception task. *Sociometry, 32*(4), 365–380. doi:10.2307/2786541

Neck, C. P., Stewart, G. L., & Manz, C. C. (1996). Self-leaders within self-leading teams: Toward an optimal equilibrium. In M. M. Beyerlein, D. A. Johnson, & S. T. Beyerlein (Eds.), *Advances in interdisciplinary studies of work teams: Team leadership* (Vol. 3, pp. 43–65). Elsevier Science/JAI Press.

Neuman, G. A., & Wright, J. (1999). Team effectiveness: Beyond skills and cognitive ability. *Journal of Applied Psychology, 84*(3), 376–389. doi:10.1037/0021-9010.84.3.376.

Pentland, A. (2012). The new science of building great teams: The chemistry of high-performing groups is no longer a mystery. *Harvard Business Review, 90*(4), 60–70.

Powell, A., Piccoli, G., & Ives, B. (2004). Virtual teams: A review of the current literature and directions for future research. *The DATA BASE for Advances in Information Systems, 35*(1), 6–36.

Roberge, M., & van Dick, R. (2010). Recognizing the benefits of diversity: When and how does diversity increase group performance? *Human Resource Management Review, 20*(4), 295–308. doi:10.1016/j.hrmr.2009.09.002

Shea, G. P., & Guzzo, R. A. (1987). Group effectiveness: What really matters?. *Sloan Management Review, 28*(3), 25–31.

Stewart, G. L., & Barrick, M. R. (2004). Four lessons learned from the person-situation debate: A review and research agenda. In B. Schneider, & D. Smith (Eds.), *Personality and organizations* (pp. 61–85). Mahwah, NJ: Lawrence Erlbaum Associates Publishers.

Straus, S. G., & McGrath, J. E. (1994). Does the medium matter? The interaction of task type and technology on group performance and member reactions. *Journal of Applied Psychology, 79*(1), 87–97. doi:10.1037/0021-9010.79.1.87

Sundstrom, E., de Meuse, K. P., & Futrell, D. (1990). Work teams: Applications and effectiveness. *American Psychologist, 45*(2), 120–133. doi:10.1037/0003-066X.45.2.120

Sundstrom, E., McIntyre, M., Halfhill, T., & Richards, H. (2000). Work groups: From the Hawthorne studies to work teams of the 1990s and beyond. *Group Dynamics: Theory, Research, And Practice, 4*(1), 44–67. doi:10.1037/1089-2699.4.1.44

Tannenbaum, S. I., Beard, R. L., & Salas, E. (1992). Team building and its influence on team effectiveness: An examination of conceptual and empirical developments. In K. Kelley (Ed.), *Issues, theory, and research in industrial/organizational psychology* (pp. 117–153). Oxford, England: North-Holland. doi:10.1016/S0166-4115(08)62601-1

Townsend, A. M., DeMarie, S. M., & Hendrickson, A. R. (1998). Virtual teams: Technology and the workplace of the future. *Academy of Management Executive, 12*(3), 17–29. doi:10.5465/AME.1998.1109047

Tuckman, B. W. (1965). Developmental sequence in small groups. *Psychological Bulletin, 63*(6), 384–399. doi:10.1037/h0022100

Tuckman, B. W., & Jensen, M. A. (1977). Stages of small-group development revisited. *Group & Organization Studies, 2*(4), 419–427. doi:10.1177/105960117700200404

Wegge, J., Roth, C., Neubach, B., Schmidt, K., & Kanfer, R. (2008). Age and gender diversity as determinants of performance and health in a public organization: The role of task complexity and group size. *Journal of Applied Psychology, 93*(6), 1301–1313. doi:10.1037/a0012680

Williams, K. D., & Sommer, K. L. (1997). Social ostracism by coworkers: Does rejection lead to loafing or compensation? *Personality and Social Psychology Bulletin, 23*(7), 693–706. doi:10.1177/0146167297237003

Yousef, D. A. (2000). Organizational commitment: A mediator of the relationships of leadership behavior with job satisfaction and performance in a non-western country. *Journal of Managerial Psychology, 15*(1–2), 6–28. doi:10.1108/02683940010305270

CHAPTER 8

Running the Organization: Management

Learning Outcomes

After studying this chapter you should be able to:

1. Explain the differences between management and leadership.
2. Describe the role of managers in organizations.
3. Describe the type of management functions typically executed in organizations.
4. Explain what it takes to become a manager.
5. Explain how teams may be able to manage themselves.

Mini-Quiz: Management

As an introduction to this chapter, please take the following mini-quiz (answers are in the back of the book). As you read the questions and consider the answers *before* diving into the chapter, you'll challenge yourself before you master the content, a process that helps facilitate learning for long-term retention. Some questions may have more than one correct answer. Don't worry if you cannot answer all questions correctly on your first try. By the time you read through the chapter and spend some of your own time thinking about these concepts, you should be able to determine the best answers. Try the quiz again after you finish reading the chapter.

1. You are the manager of a regional hospital. Which of the following would be among your primary responsibilities?
    a. Helping teams of nurses set and achieve organizational level goals
    b. Working with others on the administrative team to create a mission and value statement for the organization
    c. Hiring and training new staff
    d. Developing new processes that contribute to a positive work environment at the hospital

2. Leaders and managers can differ in:
    a. Personality
    b. Work tasks
    c. They aren't really different
    d. Focusing on people versus tasks

3. As a manager, you want to help your team members perform their jobs well. Giving feedback is an essential part of accomplishing this goal. What do we know about feedback that can help you advise your employees?
    a. Written feedback and defining negative consequences for poor performance are most effective
    b. Incorporating simple goals for improvement is important
    c. You should meet frequently with employees, rather than just once a year to do an annual review
    d. When working with a team, individual goals (rather than team goals) are most important for performance

4. When giving feedback and helping develop employees, focusing on _____ will be more effective than focusing only on trying to overcome weaknesses.

5. How have management practices changed since the early 1900s when we started studying how to manage people?
   a. Management currently operates much like the military, using a "command and control" mentality
   b. Management today focuses on stability and highly structured systems
   c. Management today tries to embrace flexibility
   d. Management today is most concerned with the end result, or "management by objective"

Overview

Organizations always have managers. Besides the time when you might have worked for yourself, when have you not had a manager? Even small businesses, perhaps family owned, have someone in charge, someone responsible for the success of the organization. A quick Internet search shows there are any misconceptions about what managers do. Managers are employees with supervisory responsibilities over a project team that works to achieve its goal, on time, and with the expected quality. In many cases, managers and leaders are one in the same. But as you'll read in this chapter and the next, leadership includes a number of additional skills beyond management. Similarly, management emphasizes several operational and **project management** skills that leaders usually de-emphasize when focusing on leadership activities. Can managers be leaders? Yes. Can leaders be managers? Yes. To clarify essential skills for managing organizations, this chapter focuses on management.

What is a manager? Watch this TEDx talk at https://www.youtube.com/watch?v=jFG7jqJXbno&feature=youtu.be

What is Management?

Management is the generic term used to describe the group of managers in an organization who oversee work schedules, staffing, project coordination, and other similar tasks associated with ensuring that the work that needs to be done to achieve the mission and vision, actually gets done. A vision or mission (a statement of why the organization was formed) guides in what direction work efforts should go.[1] For example, a mission may be to produce the number one car in the country (car manufacturer) or provide progressive, high-quality health care delivered by expert clinical teams who are compassionate (hospital). Missions and visions are sometimes intertwined. For instance, Ford Motor Company's Mission and Vision is "One team, One Plan, and One Goal". BMW's mission statement is "The BMW Group is the world's leading provider of premium products and premium services for individual mobility." BMW's strategy for achieving this mission is "to be profitable and to enhance long-term value in times of change." Accordingly, management refers to the people in the organization responsible for achieving the vision or mission.

However, you may sometimes hear people talk about management as a function or a job, as opposed to using the term to refer to the actual group of managers.

---

[1] see Chapter 9 and 13 to learn more about Vision and Mission.

Management as the function of bringing projects to completion by coordinating time-lines and people has been practiced long before the industrial era (Drucker, 1954). For instance, Egyptians managed the building of pyramids over 4700 years ago. However, in organizational science we tend to refer to the history of management as only dating back to the industrial period in the United States, Asia, and Europe (as a rule, usually between 1830 and 1950; Cummings & Bridgman, 2011). During the industrial period, workers were hired in factories or manufacturing settings, agricultural environments, and in construction. The combination of many workers focusing on single projects required the study of management practices to ensure maximum productivity and minimal waste. Thus, although "management" has been around for a very longtime, the discipline of management, the formal study of management, did not blossom until the early 1900s with the creation of large organizations as part of the focus on production during the industrial era (Kotter, 1990).

Although management practices of the early 1900s are not exactly the same as they are today, a number of the underlying concepts remain the same. Shown in Table 8.1, Rodrigues (2001) provided a thorough comparison between management principles espoused by Fayol in the 1940s and those of today.

A simple summary of Rodrigues' comparison suggests that management practices of the early 1900s focused mainly on:

- Stability
- Control
- Centralization
- Independence or loner problem solving
- Authority
- Structure
- Keeping everyone in place and on track

As times have changed and markets have become more volatile with change, the management has shifted to:

- Embrace flexibility
- Empowerment
- Participation
- Decentralization
- Group or team problem solving
- Transforming to meet the needs of today and tomorrow

Thus, management is still about getting the work done and ensuring it is done within budget, on time, to the quality and specifications required; it's just that how it is done has changed.

Management no longer models the "command and control" military style approach. Command and control refers to a style of management where someone in a position of authority (a commander) maintains control over the people underneath him or her (e.g., employees) by issuing commands that are obeyed

TABLE 8.1   Principles of Management in the 1940s and 20th Century

Principles of Management in the 1940s	Principles of Management in the Twentieth century
Work is most efficient if divided into small parts and assigned to workers with specialized skills	Work is treated as a project, where one person may complete multiple parts requiring a variety of skills
The boss has the authority and responsibility and it's not shared with employees; managers control the work rather than coordinate	Participative management, self-managed teams, and employees with autonomy perform better; managers coordinate and empower
Organizations are run following explicit rules and policies that maintain order and control	Organizations still need policies to keep coordination efforts in sync, but employees are guided toward creativity and held in check with informal, group norms
Employees report to one boss only and take direction only from that boss	Employees may report to a number of different managers at one time, or none if they are part of a self-managed team
Each team has one goal such that everyone works toward the same plan at the same time and the boss decides the course of action with no input from the team	Teams provide input into their direction, where multiple functions may reside with one group working toward a few complimentary goals
Employees must be fully committed to the objectives of the organization (which tend to be very stable) to the point that they sacrifice their own goals	An effort is made to align employees' goals with those of the organization (which tend to change regularly), demonstrating commitment to the employees
Do not underpay or overpay employees, but keep pay motivational	Performance-based pay ensures that employees are paid for their hard, high-quality work
Balance between centralization and decentralization, where upper management makes the broad plans and lower-level management translates those into tactical plans	Decisions are made with whomever has the expertise to make them, and as such, problem-solving groups are formed
Communication and decisions follow the chain of command up and down—lateral (peer to peer) communication does not occur unless approved and required	Flatter organizational structures and faster speed of business call for greater flexibility in communication and decision patterns, resulting in a less-formalized organization
There shall be order—everything must be in the right place at the right time, with the right employee on it; control is for the sake of control, even if it's very inefficient	Efficiency of control ensures everything is in the right place when it needs to be allowing for greater flexibility internally and efficient coordination; greater internal communication
Employees must be committed and comply; fairness is important from managers because it results in commitment	Fairness is important and managers earn their employees commitment by sharing in the ownership of the organization
The goal is to keep employees for as long as possible to reduce turnover and inefficiencies of training new people; hiring and keeping to retirement is the goal	Some turnover is expected and even desired in some industries (e.g., fast-food); employees do not stay until retirement; downsizing or rightsizing is ongoing
Managers should manage and come up with all the ideas	Problem-solving groups come up with ideas
Morale must be maintained at high levels at all times	Morale is expected to fluctuate and that's okay

Courtesy Zinta Byrne.

without question. Though the military maintains hierarchical chains of command (i.e., Second Lieutenant, First Lieutenant, Captain, Major), leaders in many military institutions today are taught to empower their troops and engage in a leadership style that makes their people *want* to follow, as opposed to just following because they are told to do so (Larsson, 2012). Respect for military command remains crucial; there are times when commands need immediate implementation without questions. However, the military of today (regardless of country) tends to emphasize earning the troop's followership in addition to commanding with authority.

A well-known practice of management that is not as popular as when it was introduced is the concept of "management by objectives" or MBO (introduced by Drucker, 1954). MBO refers to a process or style of management that focuses on the end results rather than how the results are achieved. MBO focuses on the goals and purpose of the tasks rather than on the tasks themselves. If you simplify MBO to its bare bones, you could say that it is simply the process of goal setting. MBO assumes that workers are capable and skilled enough to determine for themselves how to accomplish their work and that all they need are clear goals. A number of articles published since the method was introduced have found mixed and less than supportive results (e.g., Aplin, Schoderbeck, & Schoderbeck, 1979; Carroll & Tosi, 1970; Ivancevich, 1972; Jamieson, 1973; Kondrasuk, Flagler, Morrow, & Thompson, 1984; Tosi & Carroll, 1968). Regardless of the lack of consistent support for the MBO approach, hundreds of articles and books have been written that include the idea of MBO, as well as recent studies incorporating the concept into team management (Antoni, 2005; Fulk, Bell, & Bodie, 2011). Because the concept is so ingrained in the literature and in popular management materials, you will most likely run into the idea either at work or in your scholarly efforts.

What Differentiates Management from Leadership?

Management is not necessarily the same concept as leadership, though the two overlap. A basic difference between management and leadership is that you *manage* projects and tasks, but you *lead* people. Though a bit simplistic, stating the difference in this way captures the differentiator between management and leadership. Although management involves people, the primary objective of management is to accomplish the task or project. The primary emphasis in leadership is on influencing people to focus on achieving organizational goals while achieving their own goals, as well as on creating a supportive work climate where people want to accomplish the work at hand. Managers can lead and leaders can manage. Therefore, you shouldn't assume that a "manager" cannot also be a "leader."

© Keepsmiling4u/Shutterstock.com

TABLE 8.2   What Managers and Leaders Do

What Management is Focused On	What Leadership is Focused On
Project goals	Company vision
Standardization, order, consistency	Innovation, initiating change, introducing controlled chaos
Day-to-day schedules; relatively short-term outlook	5–10 year projections; relatively long-term outlook
Planning a project including scheduling and budgeting	Integration of several product project plans and how they fit into the overall corporate strategy
Assigning tasks to people based on their competencies and to meet the schedule	Exciting people about the overall mission of the organization; providing the dreams
Doing what needs to be done and motivating employees to get the job done	Inspiring others to want to do what needs to be done and to go beyond the job description
Reacting to daily or weekly delays, problems, or people issues; working on the details of completing tasks and projects	Proactively determining in what direction to take the organization and how to do so in the time needed and to meet stakeholder objectives
Taking secured risks with clear payoffs	Taking calculated but aggressive risks with unclear payoffs

Courtesy Zinta Byrne. Source: Kotter, 1990.

These two concepts, management and leadership, are often used interchangeably. Furthermore, within organizations employees rarely think explicitly about the difference between management and leadership. The concepts are separated here for the purposes of clearly understanding what it takes to manage versus lead the organization. The savvy manager or leader might also benefit from thinking about the delineation.

Several scholars have offered their views on the distinction between the focus of management and of leadership. Table 8.2, based on Kotter (1990), refers to the opposing behaviors of managers and leaders.

In contrast, Table 8.3, based on Zaleznik (1977), refers to the personality characteristics or traits that distinguish managers from leaders. Though included here, most current theories of leadership have discarded viewing leadership as attributed to an inborn temperament or trait (see last row of Table 8.3).

Turning away from the personality or traits of managers or leaders, recent work has focused on comparing the two constructs by the themes that emerged during interviews with actual managers and leaders who described their jobs and how they do their jobs. For instance, Toor (2011) interviewed 49 leaders (42 men, 7 female) of various stature (e.g., manager, director, chief executive officer, managing partner), across a variety of firms in the construction industry in Singapore, including architectural and engineering consulting. He conducted thematic network analysis (i.e., analysis of the themes or patterns that emerge from the interviews[2]) explicitly for developing a model of the differences between management and leadership. Figure 8.1 illustrates his basic model. Toor's actual model included arrows between the management and leadership sides of the

---

[2] see Braun and Clarke, 2006, for a good "how to" paper on thematic analysis in psychological research.

TABLE 8.3   Personality Characteristics Often Attributed to Managers Versus Leaders

A Manager . . .	A Leader . . .
Is a problem solver	Directs affairs; gives direction
Uses accumulated experience to get things done and create order	Serves as instruments of learning for trial and error, creating disorder
Adopts impersonal attitudes toward goals, which arise out of necessity	Adopts a personal and active attitude toward goals, which arise out of a desire to fulfill a need or dream
Accepts how people think or do not think about things; does not attempt change	Changes the way people think about what is desirable, possible, and necessary
Views work as a process that involves a combination of people and ideas, that when combined and controlled achieves a goal	Views work as an opportunity to develop new ideas, to excite others about the many possible options, and create a new goal together
Prefers to work with people, but maintains a low level of emotional investment	Prefers to work with ideas, but focuses on what the ideas mean to people and how the ideas affect them
Strives to convert win–lose into win–win	Strives for identification between employees and the organizational goals, to move everyone to develop new unexplored ideas
Regulates existing order—strives for maintenance and homeostasis	Creates chaos
Is balanced and well-developed since childhood; forms and maintains widely distributed attachments or relationships	Struggled with a difficult upbringing; usually struggles with neuroses; establishes and yet also breaks intense one-to-one relationships

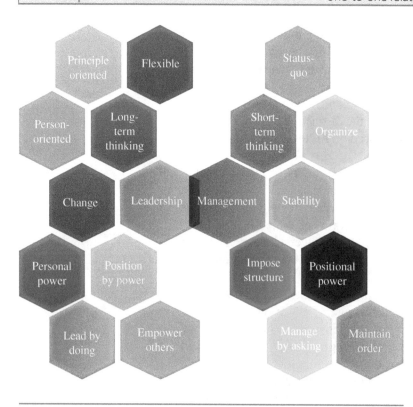

model suggesting levels of differences in functional (e.g., stability vs. change), conceptual (e.g., long-term vs. short-term), definitional (e.g., flexible vs. status-quo), and behavioral (e.g., lead by doing vs. manage by asking) themes.

For simplicity, the themes are included in the illustration in Figure 8.1, but the arrows are not. Emergent themes in the model included that leaders are more flexible and open to change than managers, and managers are more rigid and order-seeking than leaders. There was also some overlap between management and leadership, as shown by the slight overlap between the leadership and management hexagons in Figure 8.1.

Though Kotter, Zaleznik, and Toor sought broad and comprehensive distinctions between leaders and managers, Jacques, Garger, and Thomas

FIGURE 8.1   Toor's Thematic Network of Leadership and Management

Courtesy Zinta Byrne.

(2008) suggested that managers are very simply differentiated from leaders by their desire to demonstrate a higher concern for the task and task accomplishment than concern for people. In contrast, leaders demonstrate a higher concern for people. Similarly, a few writings on management judged against leadership suggest that management is more about skills and the use of tools to accomplish tasks, whereas leadership is about competencies such as self-awareness, embracing diversity, ability to influence, encouraging challenge, and demonstrating adaptability and consistency (e.g., Knight, 2005).

Other researchers, however, argue that real differences between management and leadership simply do not exist. For example, Fagiano (1997), in a short memo to members of the *American Management Association*, described the difference between the two functions in the form of a fable about an octopus and a goose. The octopus symbolizes management where the octopus' brain serves as the director for its arms, with each arm accomplishing a lot on its own. The arms do not know what to do without the octopus brain sending directive signals. There is no shared knowledge of vision between arms; each acts independently. When the octopus tires, production stops. This presents the *classical* view of management. The goose symbolizes leadership, one day developing a vision that if the flock flies somewhere else, it can find better weather conditions than currently exist. The goose shares this vision of flying to better weather conditions with the flock. Geese in the flock catch on, becoming excited by the vision, and adopt the same vision. The lead goose shares the vision so completely that all the geese in the flock have the knowledge of where to fly to get to good weather conditions. Thus, each goose in the flock knows the way and can do it alone, but they all decide to go together as a team. When the lead goose tires, another takes up the lead and keeps the flock moving forward toward the good weather. Fagiano noted, however, that although this story suggests that managers and leaders are very different, just as an octopus is different from a goose, if these differences truly exist between managers and leaders, then one must question how there can be so many highly successful managers achieving organization-wide results since this achievement assumes having good vision? He concluded that the only way this could be achieved is if octopuses can fly and geese can have at least eight arms. His point was that managers can lead and leaders can manage.

Though overlap exists, the distinguishing differences between a manager and a leader include that managers tend to focus on day-to-day operations, resolving immediate problems, and coordinating resources within projects; in comparison, leaders tend to focus more on strategizing long-term goals, resolving crises at the organizational level, and coordinating resources for the entire organization.

What *Exactly* Do Managers Do?

- Meetings
- Coaching underperformers
- Helping engage workers
- Emails

Where Manager's Spend Time/Week

With the next chapter focused on what exactly leaders do, let's turn to focusing on what exactly managers do. Managers translate the higher level vision of the company's leaders into actionable plans that can be executed and completed. A high-level vision, such as "number one in the industry" is not an actionable goal. Someone has to translate this into steps that can be taken to become number one in the industry. For instance, the manager must ask: "What does it mean to be number one? In which industry? How far away are we from being number one? What specifically do we need to do to close the gap?" The answers to these questions inform the **project plans** that employees at the lowest levels of the organization can follow.

To manage in an organization means to oversee employees in the accomplishment of a set of tasks, by a certain time, meeting specific expectations or criteria. Toward this effort, managers may also manage other managers. In large organizations, there may be several layers of managers managing other managers, who manage individual employees on project teams. Sometimes a visual illustration of how everyone is connected within an organization makes the layers of management easier to understand (Figure 8.2). Below is a figure depicting a portion of an organization's hierarchical chart showing a couple levels of management. A hierarchical chart shows who reports to who.

The actual tasks that managers complete vary by level within the organization, by organization, and by industry. In general, managers allocate or assign resources to one or more teams or project units within the organization, assign staff to each aspect of the project, and keep track of progress so they can readjust schedules, move resources around, or make other changes as needed to keep the project on schedule and within budget or resource quota. Sometimes trade-off decisions must be made, such as deciding to move the resources from one project to another. Resources (e.g., material needed for manufacturing, staff) may at times fail to meet the quality expected, which creates additional costs, delays, or other problems that require solving. Often the manager is responsible for deciding how to solve the problem, whether to use the existing resources or whether to escalate the problem to a higher level of management.

In some organizations, however, managers are not given the responsibility to make decisions when problems in the schedule, task completion, or resources develop. In such organizations, managers control and monitor the schedule by ensuring that the right number of people are assigned to complete each task in the plan. But, when it comes to the task of deciding what to do when a problem occurs, the boss above them develops the schedule, resolves timing and resource issues, and makes the key decisions as to whether one project is impacted to save another. Though this sounds like a system made for people with "authority issues," knowing who is responsible for what decisions and who is accountable if the decision was a bad one can be positive for the organization.

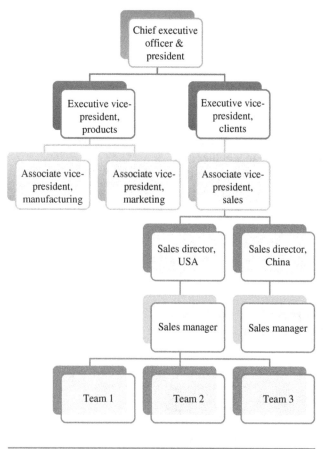

FIGURE 8.2 Hierarchical Chart

Courtesy Zinta Byrne.

Managers are responsible for their team's completion of tasks and for the team members themselves.

Exercise 8.1

In your own words, write a few sentences about what a manager is, what a leader is, and how the two differ but can also overlap.

Project Management

When given the authority to make trade-off decisions, managers manage projects. Project management involves the optimization of resources, including people, information, and materials, necessary for the completion of a project corresponding to a specific schedule. Project management is a transactional or task-oriented activity, typically focused on one project. A single project may be to design and produce the next lite beer (e.g., Heineken, based in the Netherlands), produce a dye for leather that won't rub off on your hand and fits in with the rest of the dye's produced by the company (e.g., BASF, based in Germany), or create a new sales incentive program to excite sales representatives to sell more by the end of the quarter (any organization with a sales force; e.g., Agilent Technologies in the United States, Toyota in Japan, or Lenovo in China).

Why is it valuable to know that many scholars consider managers different from leaders?

Managers practice project management, which Larson and Drexler (2010) suggested is comprised of four phases or stages:

1. Defining
    ❑ Goals, resources, and the scope of the project are defined.

2. Planning
    ❑ Steps are created for achieving the project goals and the relevant people for working on each step are identified. This stage also includes developing risk management plans (i.e., plans that identify potential risks to project completion and how to handle those risks if they are realized), contingency plans (i.e., other actions that can be taken should unexpected events delay the project), and scheduling, as well as constructing communication plans and budget.

3. Executing
    ❑ The project takes place, timelines are evaluated, and budgets carefully maintained. **Status reports** are regularly generated to keep upper level management and clients informed on progress. Revisions to the project plan are made, as needed, while the project progresses.

4. Termination
    ❑ The project is completed and the product or outcome is transferred to its new owner (i.e., client or next team).

To keep track of these four stages, managers may develop a project plan using different computer software tools (e.g., MicroSoft Project, Tenrox, Clarizen, FastTrack, OmniPlan) or charts, such as a **Gantt chart** (Figure 8.3) or **PERT chart** (Figure 8.4). Regardless of which type of chart is developed, the chart's value lies in the visual depiction of the schedule, allowing managers and employees to see, in a single view, the entire scope of the project, interdependencies, and critical points (e.g., events or dates that affect the entire project

Fancy fan production March 2012-December 2012

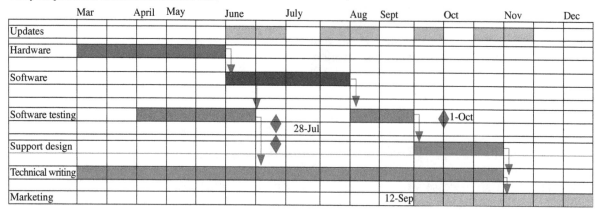

FIGURE 8.3 Segment of a Gantt Chart

Courtesy Zinta Byrne

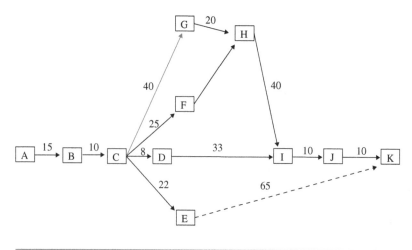

FIGURE 8.4 PERT Chart

Courtesy Zinta Byrne.

timeline). Though you may initially struggle finding a visual chart like the ones illustrated here informative, with training and practice reading Gantt and PERT charts, you might come to find these visual aids tremendously helpful. By gaining an instant assessment of whether the project is on schedule or identifying who is dependent on who, you can quickly determine if more attention should be directed toward one group of employees, resource, or critical point over another.

Gantt charts, like the segment of a chart shown in Figure 8.3, are named after Henry Gantt, the industrial engineer who in the early 1900s developed the scheduling method. Gantt worked for Frederick Winslow Taylor (of Taylorism in Chapter 1) and created the first project management chart to support the production of the first Ford automobile (Lock, 2013). The Gantt chart provides a clear view of the amount of time each group works on their portion of the project. A linked Gantt chart, such as the one in Figure 8.3, also shows which groups are dependent on each other (the arrows), and where critical points are in the schedule (the diamonds) that if they are delayed, the entire project is delayed.

A PERT (Program Evaluation and Review Technique) chart, shown in Figure 8.4, includes at least three parts: a starting event, the activity required, and the signifying end event. PERT charts often include low and high estimate completion dates or time estimates. The PERT chart makes the amount of time for activities visually clear and can show how much flexibility any one project component has before it hits a critical due date. The benefit of exact time costs shown in the chart along the lines allows for calculations of critical paths and cost of delays. The unit of time is dependent on the project. For example, in Figure 8.4, the units might be hours, days, weeks, or months. Dotted lines are used to depict inactivity and red lines show critical paths (a path, which if delayed, puts the entire project on hold).

Using charts or other project management tools (there are hundreds available), managers ensure the project achieves its goals. Managers anticipate the many possible ways the project could fail, and prepare alternative actions should those problems occur. Anticipating issues and readying a plan to address them (called **contingency planning**) allows the manager to smoothly adjust and handle the many potential hiccups that occur along the way, achieving success in the end. A good resource for learning about project management and reading more about these charts is Lock's (2013) book on Project Management.

Interview with a Former Program Manager

Some organizations hire people into a very specific role called **program manager**. As opposed to project management, which involves being responsible for managing a specific group of people working on a single project, a program manager is responsible for managing the production of a solution or product that has many associated projects. A program manager engages in project management on a large scale, coordinating several different projects that are all interconnected. For example, to produce a new lightweight sport jacket, Xtep, based in China, has a project team that develops the fabric, a different project team designs the various styles, another project team makes and tests the finished jacket, and another project team markets the jacket internationally. A program manager coordinates across these different project teams; in this case, to ensure a final jacket is completed on the time schedule dictated by upper management or sometimes the sales/marketing teams.

An example of what a program manager does may provide clarity regarding the differences between a project manager and a program manager, but also on what project management can entail. The following excerpt is from an interview with a former program manager. The interview provides valuable insight into the complex coordination efforts of project management, and what some challenges and concerns are with coordinating resources and schedules across multiple projects. Note that although the interview refers to creating the overall schedule, later the interview (not captured here) the program manager discussed how that schedule is constantly updated and modified to accommodate changes in the individual project teams as the overall program progresses.

> "I managed the overall production of a new mini-computer server. As the Program Manager, I coordinated all the schedules for all the components that came together for that single program (i.e., multiple projects that come together to make up an entire product or solution offered by the organization). This means that I combined all the individual component schedules into one big one, allowing me to see what fit together and what didn't. I communicated between groups delivering different parts of the project, and shared progress of all the parts of the project with upper levels of management. I developed an overall project schedule by asking all managers involved to provide me a projection of when they

Managers use planning tools to help keep track of deliverables, resources, critical paths, and contingencies. However, you don't have to be a manager to appreciate the benefit of tracking goals and schedules—remember goal-setting in Chapter 3?

© ESB Professional/Shutterstock.com

could deliver their pieces, such as finished software, the final hardware product (the machine itself), completed technical manuals, a support plan that included training support engineers to handle customer problems, and marketing plans for how and when the product would be priced and advertised. Each of those managers was responsible for managing their own teams of employees and their own project schedules, and to develop a plan that could potentially meet the projected end-date established by the company leaders. If the target end-date could not be achieved, I worked with these managers to determine the best possible plan and negotiated with leaders on what was achievable given the most aggressive timing. I asked each manager to map out their best case scenario – the absolute best project plan possible assuming no mistakes or delays. I also asked for them to indicate anticipated or potential delays, effect of the delays, and to provide several contingency plans for handling those potential delays. I then combined all projections together to create a dependency tree (who was dependent on whom), and timelines identifying when critical points in the schedule would occur where we didn't have enough resources or too many sitting idle waiting for one team to finish something that another team needed. I also created budget plans based on what the managers gave me. I added key checkpoints into the schedule where I needed to confirm that each team was on track and able to deliver according to the plan. I added meetings for regular communication between groups, and meetings for updating upper level management on the overall project progress. In addition, by having all schedules combined onto one big project plan, I could identify potential gaps, delays, and other issues resulting from the coordination of multiple independent groups. I shared this overall plan with the individual team managers and asked them to point out where they thought they might run into a problem if some resource or dependency wasn't delivered on time or to the expected quality. Finally, something always goes wrong, so I built a contingency plan that mapped out what we would do if at different points in the schedule something did go wrong; like a delay that was out of our control. The schedule, with some wiggle room and buffers added in to accommodate the anticipated (but undesirable) delays, was given to upper management. Within each project team, the managers managed their individual team members; tracking deliverables, scheduled time off, crunch times, and dependencies. These managers were responsible for ensuring that their people met their project deliverables on time. They were responsible for communicating timelines, problems, or accomplishments to others, like me – the Program Manager. But I never managed or interacted with their employees. I only worked with the managers of all these teams. In total, I think I managed at least 10 different managers at the same time, while also 'managing' the upper management."

Why would the program manager develop a contingency plan if everyone provided their best plan for achieving the goal?

As you might conclude from the interview excerpt, program management makes sense for large organizations where multiple projects come together to create an overall product, or potentially many products. Program management, therefore, is rarely used in small or family run businesses where the number of projects is naturally limited. In these cases, managers engage in project management and there is no need to hire a program manager. Additionally worth noting is that program managers are often used to facilitate the execution of multi-year research grants in academic institutions - though they are more often called "project managers" in those settings. The National Science Foundation, a U.S. government agency that funds research, has program managers who are responsible for getting proposals reviewed by external experts and for recommending multi-million dollar funding initiatives (see www.nsf.gov/about/how.jsp)

Ilgen & Knowlton, 1980; LePine & Van Dyne, 2001; Martinko & Gardner, 1987). If the manager believes the employee's poor performance resulted from a lack of effort, desire, or some other factor within the employee's control, the response is not as favorable as when the poor performance was believed to come about from something outside of the employee's control (e.g., sick). Unfortunately, we are all susceptible to the fundamental attribution error (Ross, 1977). The fundamental attribution error occurs when we attribute our successes to internal factors and our failures to external factors, but attribute others' successes to external factors and their failures to internal factors (Ross, 1977). This error, sometimes referred to as dispositional vs. situational inference, can easily occur because we often lack insight into what others are doing or why, whereas we always have an "insider's" perspective on our own situation and intentions.

Consequently, managers handling employees' poor performance may be more likely to attribute the poor performance to internal factors (controllable) than external (uncontrollable) factors. Other errors of managing performance (several were reviewed in Chapter 5 under Evaluating Performance), such as halo effects are attributed to overall positive feelings about the person (Cooper, 1981). The manager's relationship with the employee, therefore, can also factor into how their performance is managed or perceived (Dobbins & Russell, 1986; Fedor & Rowland, 1989). A well-developed relationship could create an emotional attachment that over time gets in the way of giving honest, unbiased feedback (Axelrod, Handfield-Jones, & Michaels., 2002; Murphy & Anhalt, 1992), including negative feedback. A good relationship can help a manager determine the actual cause of poor performance. In Mueller-Hanson and Pulakos's (2018) book on driving performance, they identify two main types of performance failures: behavioral or task, which may occur because of employees' lack of will (i.e., motivation), skill, or the environment (e.g., lack of accountability, heavy workload). Thus, the first step in managing performance is understanding what drives performance.

Giving Negative Performance Feedback

Giving positive feedback to good performers is easy because the employee is expected to receive the feedback favorably. In contrast, managers often prefer not to give negative feedback to poor performers out of fear of a negative reaction, or worse yet, bullying allegations. Cunningham (2007) reported a rise in false bullying allegations in Europe, where organizations put programs in place that encouraged employees to file complaints against their managers when the manager did something wrong. However, it appeared that some, in particular poor performers receiving negative performance feedback, abused the system by filing false bullying claims. Consequently, managers in such work climates became reluctant to provide negative feedback and manage poor performance. Instead, they sought to move the poor performer to another position in a different unit, all to

"Is this about your negative performance review?"

© Cartoon Resource/Shutterstock.com

avoid the potential of complaints or a grievance filed against them. In effect, good managers were discouraged from appropriately helping their employees find ways to improve their performance. Even if accusations of bullying do not follow, managers are reluctant to give negative feedback out of a fear for how the employee will react.

Though it may not feel this way to the manager, *not* providing candid and accurate feedback to employees is a form of showing disrespect for the employee, while also being unfair to higher performing employees (Axelrod et al., 2002). The underperforming employee fails to learn how to receive the necessary information for self-development and improvement, and is unable to make informed decisions about their career. The higher performing employees have to put up with a poor performer who is "getting away with it," resulting in more work for everyone but the poor performer, and potentially a drop in employee morale.

Because of how emotionally exhausting and difficult giving negative feedback can feel, performance management tends to take center-stage for managers. This is especially true for managers who lack appropriate skills in handling these potentially sensitive or threatening situations. A recent effort to develop a positive approach to performance appraisal is promising and worth sharing here. Bouskila-Yam and Kluger (2011) collaborated with a multinational corporation based in Israel, called SodaStream, to develop a performance appraisal system called Strength-Based Performance Appraisal (SBPA). Rather than focus on people's weaknesses during the appraisal, the approach focuses on employees' strengths, and how to use them to fortify areas of weakness. Out of the 700 employees in the organization, 90 participated in the project (26 managers and 64 employees). The SBPA incorporated the following seven different principles or tools: Feedforward, reflected best self, happiness research, the 3:1 principle, developing strengths, win–win approach, and positive organizational core and collective efficacy (shown in Table 8.4).

After implementation, reactions within SodaStream to the SBPA included: quality time to review the evaluation, positive focus on strengths, satisfaction with the appropriateness of focus, and clarification of expectations. Disadvantages of the SBPA included that it was time intensive and hard to use (Bouskila-Yam & Kluger, 2011). To facilitate its use, Aguinis, Gottfredson, and Joo (2012) developed recommendations for delivering feedback using the strengths-based approach. Although, the effectiveness of both the SBPA and recommendations for its use are unknown at this time because of lack of research evidence, the general idea and reactions from SodaStream suggest the SBPA offers a promising approach for helping managers through the performance appraisal process, which might help in handling poor performers.

A valuable skill is delivering both positive and negative feedback. Even as a student, this skill can be very helpful on team-based class projects.

Coaching Poor Performers

Though managers are expected to handle poor performers and programs like SBPA may help with identifying the cause and solutions for poor performance, research has noted that many first-line or front-line managers (those directly responsible for managing workers as opposed to managers who supervise other managers) are reluctant to deal with poor performers (Axelrod, et al., 2002). Both the employee receiving the feedback and the manager giving it may feel

TABLE 8.4   Seven Principles or Tools of Strength-Based Performance Appraisal (SBPA)

Principle or Tool	Definition
Feedforward Interview (FFI)	Multipurpose interview designed to build relationships with the manager and organization by leveraging Appreciative Interviewing, a technique of Appreciative Inquiry (an approach to organizational improvement that focuses on what's working well rather than what's not working).
	Employees (1) reflect on positive work experiences, (2) describe what made them feel full of energy, (3) identify the peak moment of excitement in that work, (4) determine what conditions existed that made that positive experience happen, and (5) identify what current behaviors and plans the employee has, if taken into the immediate future, could create those positive conditions again.
Reflected Best Self Feedback (RBSF)	A strengths-based approach that says people excel when they know their unique strengths and learn to expand them and apply them to various situations. Assumes progress is a function of building on one's strengths.
Happiness Research	Being happy creates a positive attitude in employees that allows them to be more open to others and to creativity. Happy employees perform, so this approach leverages the 3:1 principle (below).
The 3:1 principle	Happy people have a 3:1 ratio of positive to negative emotions. With a higher number of positive emotional experiences to negative, people are more able to hear, accept, and learn from negative but useful feedback. Positive feedback should be directed toward promotion behaviors (creativity), whereas negative feedback should be directed toward prevention behaviors (adhering to safety, orderliness) to take advantage of the self-regulatory focus of positive moods.
Develop strengths	Every day for 2 weeks, employees write down three good things that happened to them, along with why those things happened. Then find a new way each day to use strengths. The result? A happier and higher performing employee.
Win–win	Demonstration of concern for others' needs and goals, in addition to one's own, when developing solutions or negotiating a solution. Win–win is part of FFI when describing both process and outcome that are beneficial for the storyteller. Also embedded in goal setting with manager—design goals that support the interest of the company and of the employee.
Positive Organizational Core and Collective Efficacy	The SBPA should align with organizational goals and support organizational intent, as well as be consistent for the organization. Thus, the use of Appreciative Inquiry is not just at the individual level, but also considering the organization itself.

Courtesy Zinta Byrne.

threatened to receive and deliver (respectively) negative information, with both sides wishing to protect their personal and professional self-esteem. Rosen and Tesser (1970) called this the mum-effect; keeping mum (or silent) when having to transmit or receive bad news, an outcome of ambiguous social norms concerning how to behave when giving or receiving unpleasant news (Fisher, 1979; Tesser, Rosen, & Tesser, 1971). Situations wherein negative feedback is shared can be emotionally stressful for both parties (Smith, Harrington, & Houghton, 2000).

To understand how managers can effectively manage poor performance, Goodhew, Cammock, and Hamilton (2008) interviewed 32 managers about their strategies for handling poor performers. The authors found that not all managers could explain how they handled their poor performers. However, for those who could, they noted that poor performance served as a trigger that led to three primary actions:

1. *Talk to the individual about the performance issue.* This involved reiterating overall expectations and explaining why the performance was considered poor.

2. *Address the actual problem.* This involved determining first what problem is creating the poor performance, and then removing obstacles or road blocks that might be creating poor performance, providing training to address a lack of skill or knowledge, and offering encouragement and seeking motivational strategies to address potential lack of motivation.

3. *Let the employee perform.* After taking the first two actions, the next step is to allow the employee to try again, while monitoring for performance improvements.

Not all interviewed managers considered or viewed performance the same way—some considered it an outcome of motivation and others considered it a process. Some managers were inconsistent in how they handled poor performance, which can be problematic. Consistency is important for maintaining perceptions of fairness (Chapter 4; Kim & Rubianty, 2011) and for potentially avoiding lawsuits over prejudicial treatment (Gillespie & Parry, 2006; Liden & Mitchell, 1985).

By treating every performance situation consistently, as a developmental opportunity, poor performance may be managed into better performance. Taking a coaching approach, Hersey and Goldsmith (1980) proposed the ACHIEVE model for assessing and managing performance problems (shown in Figure 8.6).

The ACHIEVE model may help managers manage their employees' performance more effectively by helping employees identify what problems are hindering their performance and how to solve them. The manager walks through each step asking a question to identify the problem:

1. Is it an ability problem, where the employee lacks the appropriate skills or knowledge required for the task? (Ability)

2. It is a problem with a lack of understanding about what is expected in this role? (Clarity)

3. What organizational support may be needed here? (Help)

4. Is there a lack of incentives for the employee? (Incentive)

5. Has the employee received coaching and feedback to help guide performance levels? (Evaluation)

6. Has the employee been evaluated fairly—have decisions been made that adhere to legal policies such that the manager is not maliciously

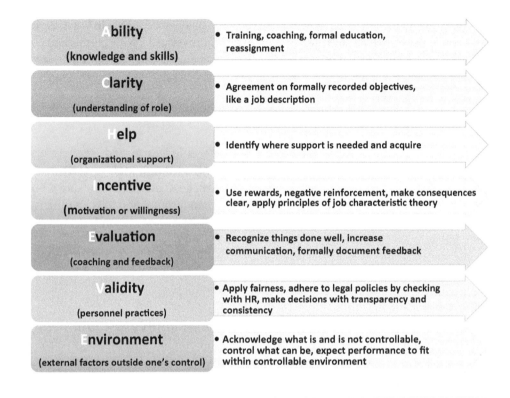

Ability
(knowledge and skills)
- Training, coaching, formal education, reassignment

Clarity
(understanding of role)
- Agreement on formally recorded objectives, like a job description

Help
(organizational support)
- Identify where support is needed and acquire

Incentive
(motivation or willingness)
- Use rewards, negative reinforcement, make consequences clear, apply principles of job characteristic theory

Evaluation
(coaching and feedback)
- Recognize things done well, increase communication, formally document feedback

Validity
(personnel practices)
- Apply fairness, adhere to legal policies by checking with HR, make decisions with transparency and consistency

Environment
(external factors outside one's control)
- Acknowledge what is and is not controllable, control what can be, expect performance to fit within controllable environment

FIGURE 8.6   ACHIEVE Model

Courtesy Zinta Byrne. Source: Hersey & Goldmsith, 1980.

(but rather accidentally due to ignorance or inappropriate applications) making biased decisions that are not in the employee's favor? (Validity)

7. Is the employee's performance suffering because of uncontrollable consequences? (Environment)

The most important aspects of this model include first identifying the performance problem, and second, developing an appropriate solution. The model ensures that employees learn to identify the performance issue along with why it exists, and then learn how to solve the problem.

Although it may feel as though the model is hard to remember or implement, keep in mind that the goal is to figure out first "why" an employee might be having a performance problem and then second "what can we do about it."

Coaching poor performers, though, is not just about employees who have either an ability problem or lack of clarity surrounding what is expected of them. In some cases, poor performance is due to illness, problems occurring outside of work, or maybe even due to a personality conflict (or more challenging, a personality disorder). Understanding why an employee is struggling is a first step to identifying what to do next. For employees with health concerns, issues outside of work, and even those with personality conflicts, the best bet might be to encourage them to seek support and help from employee assistance programs or human resource management in the company. As a manager, you would do well to ask the employee if it is okay to include someone from human resource management to help brainstorm best and most effective ideas for performance improvement. With permission to include these other folks in the performance discussion meeting, you as a manager not only have immediate support, but help in brainstorming effective next steps.

Encouraging Meaning at Work

Managers are in a unique position to encourage employees to find meaningfulness at work, which ultimately leads to positive job attitudes, high performance, and overall employee well-being. Specifically, managers' direct relationship with their employees and their direct control over their employees jobs facilitates their ability to, first, understand what meaningfulness at work might look like for their employees and then, second, to actually mold the work environment to support meaning at work. Through conversation, managers can explore with their employees what excites them about work, what helps them understanding their contribution to work, and whether their employees are clear on the importance for their contributions. Using the job redesign approaches (reviewed in Chapter 3), managers can work with employees to ensure they have skill variety at work, design the job so that the employee can complete the whole job (from start to finish; i.e., task identity), can see directly how their work contributes to a bigger impact (task significance), and ensure they have some autonomy on the job that is appropriate to the task and their level of responsibility. Research shows that meaningfulness can be derived from the job characteristics (Hackman & Oldham, 1976). To further promote opportunities for experiencing meaning at work, managers can develop mentorship programs and career development tracks such as job rotations that advance cross-training of employees.

Byrne (2015) noted several actions that can be taken to cultivate a work environment that supports meaningfulness. Ones that managers might have direct control over and can provide include

- Resources—such as encouraging employees to attend training sessions, providing information to help employees be more innovative and autonomous at work.

- Managing work stressors—this might include incorporating scheduling flexibility to allow workers to more readily balance their work and family demands.

- Reiterating company mission—this involves ensuring employees know what the mission is and how their work fits into and supports the mission (task significance).

- Promoting fit—ensuring employees feel they fit with the current work environment and job; this could include promoting a climate of inclusion, valuing diverse opinions and orientations, and finding a good match between personality, ability, and skills with the job.

Although managers cannot create meaningfulness at work for employees, they can foster and promote a work environment that empowers and enables employees to find and create meaningfulness at work.

Exercise 8.2

Imagine yourself working with someone who is not performing well and it is negatively impacting you and the team you are on. Create a situation from your past experiences, either a real one from a job, sports team, or class project. Now, using the ACHIEVE model, describe how you will give that person feedback to improve performance. Write out the steps you will take and what you will say. Do you think this model would work to improve this person's performance? What are its strengths and weaknesses?

How Do You Become A Manager?

How do managers become managers in your workplace?

In many organizations, you may become a manager by being promoted or hired into the position. Exceptions include the military, where students who attend the military academies typically enter as cadets to become officers, the military equivalent of a manager and a leader. In the craft trades, such as plumbing or carpentry, you can manage other members of your trade only after you achieve the level of Master, which requires years of apprenticeship under the tutelage of a Master and then several years as a Journeyman or completion of trade school. Hence, a few paths exist for moving into management depending on the industry and organization.

Succession Planning

Becoming a manager may depend on existing staffing plans. Most staffing plans, especially for large organizations, require **succession planning**, which refers to determining how each management position will be filled when the individual currently occupying the role leaves for whatever reason (e.g., promotion, turnover, lateral move, demotion or firing). Succession planning becomes more important the higher up in the organizational management structure you go because of the challenges in identifying a replacement. The higher you go in the organization hierarchy, where managers supervise and direct other managers, the position typically requires a greater breadth of knowledge and experience, years of training as managers of smaller projects or units, and potentially experience in management overseas (especially with multinational companies). Hence, very few people tend to qualify for these positions; they must either be groomed or prepared in advance for the opportunity to apply for such a position, or be hired from outside the organization. In contrast, at lower levels of the organization, there may be a reasonably large number of people who wish to apply and who have the background, experience, and aptitude for the job. Management jobs with direct supervision of employees who are not managers themselves (i.e., they have no management responsibility) frequently do not require previous management experience.

In organizations where succession plans are required, top executives are asked to identify a few individuals who, with training and targeted experiences, can be groomed for the job such that they can apply once the position is vacated. In such cases, these identified individuals are given targeted assignments that build their breadth of experience, challenge them, build their management capability, and help them gain other key insights or knowledge to make them a good manager/leader. Furthermore, by having a number of identified individuals groomed for potential succession, the current executive can see who handles challenges best, whether there may be others with untapped potential, and who might serve as alternative successors should circumstances change in the interim (e.g., an identified high potential gets hired by a competitor). In addition to identifying **high potentials**, the organization may ask for a few individuals to apply for these opportunities to ensure a fair process overall and allow previously unknown, but highly qualified candidates to come forward.

External Candidates

When internal candidates are not available or a position is considered difficult to fill, organizations may open the position to external applicants, indicating that they are willing to hire from outside the organization directly into a management position. Several organizations, such as the government in some countries, are required to consider external applicants even if they are confident they want to hire from within. In comparison, organizations such as family run businesses may only hire from within and are not required by law to open their positions to external candidates.

Whether forced or not, some organizations open their positions to outside candidates because they want to bring new ideas into the organization and a way to do so is to hire someone from the outside. You typically see this in universities. By hiring graduates from other universities, the department and university can bring in new ideas, new approaches, and potentially additional stature.

Another reason to hire an external candidate is to facilitate a change effort—you hire the type of manager you seek to create a new or different organizational culture. In some cases, an organization has created a new position for which no one internally fits because the position or role is so new. Thus, opening the position to external candidates may attract a qualified individual who can fulfill the specific needs of the new role.

Skills Required

Why should organizations actively plan to promote employees to management roles?

Once hired, being a manager involves developing and using a variety of skills, such as effective time management, self-awareness or self-understanding (i.e., knowing your strengths and weaknesses, as well as your limitations; see Bourner, 1996), self-regulation or emotional-regulation (i.e., managing and regulating one's emotions), communication (both written and oral), negotiation, conflict management, influence skills (see Cialdini, 2009), and project management, to name just a few. An increasing valuable skill for managers to develop is in creating an inclusive work environment. Although debate continues in the United States as to the legal rights of lesbian, gay, bisexual, transgender, and queer (LGBTQ) individuals, many businesses favor inclusive work environments and that means as a manager, you're likely to manage an individual who identifies LGBTQ (Zugelder

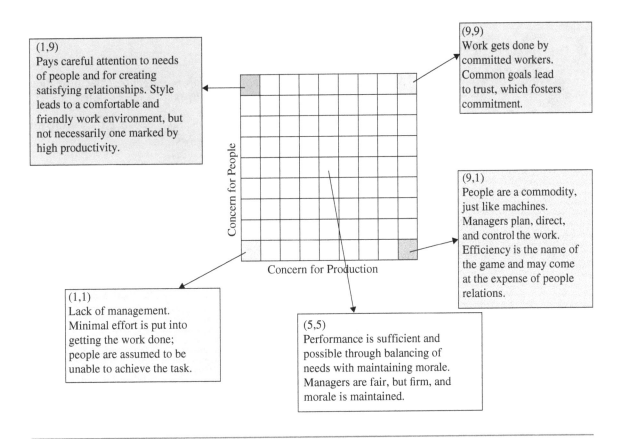

(1,9)
Pays careful attention to needs of people and for creating satisfying relationships. Style leads to a comfortable and friendly work environment, but not necessarily one marked by high productivity.

(9,9)
Work gets done by committed workers. Common goals lead to trust, which fosters commitment.

Concern for People

Concern for Production

(9,1)
People are a commodity, just like machines. Managers plan, direct, and control the work. Efficiency is the name of the game and may come at the expense of people relations.

(1,1)
Lack of management. Minimal effort is put into getting the work done; people are assumed to be unable to achieve the task.

(5,5)
Performance is sufficient and possible through balancing of needs with maintaining morale. Managers are fair, but firm, and morale is maintained.

FIGURE 8.7   Managerial Grid

Courtesy Zinta Byrne.

& Champagne, 2018). An important skill to learn is recognizing discrimination based on sexual orientation and identity. There may be behaviors/words used in work contexts that require you as a manager to address them quickly, and/or complaints made that may or may not be justified (i.e., misunderstanding rather than true intent). As a manager, you cannot "make" people like each other, but you can require professionalism. An abundance of books and materials exist for identifying critical management skills and how to develop them.

Among the many skills required of managers, balancing between people management and task management has received substantial attention in the academic literature. Developed to explain how leaders should behave, Blake, Mouton's, and Bidwell's (1962) managerial grid (the version illustrated in Figure 8.7 is adapted from Blake, Mouton, Barnes, & Greiner, 1964, and Blake & Mouton, 1982a, 1982b) is among the most well-known models depicting the balance between a focus on employees versus a focus on task completion. The model is based on the idea that managers vary from 1 to 9 in their concern for people and from 1 to 9 in their concern for production. Consequently, the grid has two axes: (1) organizational needs for production and profit, called *concern for production* and (2) human needs for mature and healthy relationships, called *concern for people*. Using varying levels on each axes, the authors categorized management styles into five different categories.

Blake, Mouton, and Bidwell (1962) labeled the five categories of management styles in the following way:

- The 1,9 managers were called *country club management* because they sought to maximize relations and focused little on actual productivity.

- The 9,9 managers were called *team management* because they were all about the team accomplishing as much as possible.

- The 9,1 manager is considered authoritarian or *task management*, because this type of manager focuses on getting the job done at all costs, even if that means stomping on employees to do so. There is little concern for the needs of employees, as those only get in the way of production.

- The 5,5 manager was considered *dampened pendulum* because the focus was on the middle of the road, on balancing the organizational needs with the people needs, and meeting long-term production and retention goals. This type of manager is described as working hard enough to get results but not pushing too hard as to come across as hard-nosed, but also not letting people off too easily (Blake & Mouton, 1975).

- The 1,1 managers were the *impoverished management*, also known as laissez-faire, because they did only the minimum required to lead their teams to production and paid little if any attention to the needs of the team members. These are the managers who have "checked out" or are simply in a bad job fit—they don't want to be managers, so they don't try.

Blake and Mouton (1982a) advocated for the 9,9 manager, suggesting that behavior consistent with the team management style would be most effective.

Being a manager is still easier for men than for women, even though more women are now in management than ever before (U.S. Department of Labor Statistics for 2018). Although women make up about 57% of the workforce, they only represent 34% of the managerial jobs and only 24% are chief executives (Women's Bureau in the U.S. Department of Labor, see https://www.dol.gov/wb/stats/stats_data.htm). So why are so few women in management roles? Baumgartner and Schneider (2010) reviewed the literature and found six essential issues (though there are undoubtedly more) preventing women from breaking through the glass ceiling. The glass ceiling refers to a perceived barrier that seems to prevent qualified people from getting a job in the high ranks of an organization, but is not explicitly identified in the policies or decision-making practices. Thus, although people are told they can be promoted and they can see that others are being promoted, they themselves seem to hit this clear barrier—they can see where they want to go, but they just cannot get there. The six essential issues include:

1. Men still prevent women from getting access to the network.

2. Women are still considered the primary caretaker by society, which means the burden of balancing family and professional demands falls on their shoulders resulting in overwhelming sacrifices not experienced by their male counterparts.

3. The role of mentoring remains unclear in the literature; although mentoring has been connected with success, that is not the case for all women and it depends on who is doing the mentoring (male vs. female).

4. There is no support offered from those who manage to get through the glass ceiling.

5. The literature is contradictory as to effective leadership styles; women acting like women are penalized, as are women acting like men—it is a no win situation.

6. Women are opting out.

In their interviews of a handful of women who have broken through the glass ceiling, Baumgartner and Schneider obtained suggestions for how to tackle the six issues above. Some of the suggestions included: promote yourself, detach from the stereotypes, create a strong support system for yourself, use effective listening skills, determination, prioritize, and trust your mentors to name a few. Note that none of the suggestions included acting like a man!

Exercise 8.3

Using Blake and Mouton's managerial grid, using your own words describe the five categories of management styles and give an example of each from your own experience or from a friend's experience.

What Are Self-Managed Teams?

The entire chapter has thus far focused on the specific role of manager, occupied by a single individual, but not all teams have such a role or person. As noted in Chapter 7, self-managed teams are groups of employees who manage themselves rather than having a formally appointed manager who manages them. Self-managed teams have the power and authority to determine how to perform their work, according to what schedule, and who exactly on the team does what (Erez, LePine, & Elms, 2002). Though the design or makeup of the team can vary (Mohrman, Cohen, & Mohrman, 1995), self-managed teams divide and rotate the various management responsibilities among team members. Thus, one team member may take responsibility for the team schedule, one may handle the budget and sign purchase orders or take care of other budgetary expenses, one may provide status updates to upper management, one may direct all communications with other teams such as marketing or sales, and another may control the team's resources. These responsibilities might rotate among members every quarter (i.e., every 3 months), only some responsibilities may rotate such as team scheduling or status updating, or some responsibilities could remain with one member throughout the life of the team. Researchers have shown that rotating responsibilities for leading the team promotes a climate of shared leadership (Mohrman et al., 1995), in addition to fostering perceptions of fairness and social responsibility norms (Kerr, 1983); hence, self-managed teams should consider adopting the rotation model.

Though called "self-managed," such teams are rarely 100% self-managed (Laiken, 1994). A manager who oversees the self-managed team and potentially

Why might it be helpful to hire a manager from outside the organization?

other teams within the same functional unit (e.g., marketing, production) typically handles performance reviews and pay determination for self-managed teams. In some cases, the team members may provide developmental support to each other through a type of peer review. However, each team member is generally given an individual annual review that is not shared with the other team members and that addresses specific performance issues or challenges unique to that individual. In this case, the manager who oversees the appraisal for that self-managed team might have to rely on input or feedback from team members to complete the individual performance review, since their involvement in the day-to-day operations and management of the team is limited.

The distinguishing characteristics of self-managed teams are the lack of a formal manager scheduling assignments and the resolution of personnel issues.

In addition to the potential differences in how performance appraisals are handled in self-managed teams versus traditional teams, compensation may also differ between the two types of teams. For instance, some self-managed teams are compensated based on what the entire team as a unit achieves, even though employees may prefer and seek compensation and reward based on their individual performance. Such preferences are usually culturally determined—some cultures value group performance over individual performance and expect compensation to match their value system. Although individuals may have their preferences, how group members are paid is up to the organization.

So far, much of the focus in this section on self-managed teams has been on how they are different from traditionally managed teams. However, performance management, problem employee management, project management, and other issues noted previously in this chapter are all relevant for self-managed teams. The biggest difference between self-managed teams and nonself-managed teams is that employees self-manage their tasks, schedules, and deliverables, and take ownership for resolving their internal team problems, as opposed to a dedicated manager handling these tasks. Additionally, just like membership on a traditionally managed team, membership on a self-managed team may require flexibility, negotiation skills, willingness to make compromises for the benefit of the group, greater skill breadth, and tolerance for ambiguity.

How Do We Transition from Management to Leadership?

Now that we've fully explored the topic of management, understanding how to transition from management to leadership serves as an important lead into the next chapter, which focuses on leadership.

Manikutty (2003) offered five transitions the manager must make to become a leader. This plan of transitions requires attention to self-development and self-awareness (not unlike what Schmidt & Tannenbaum proposed in 1960), and on adopting a new perspective.

The manager must transition from:

1. Managing facts and data to managing emotions.
   - ❏ Managers typically collect and analyze data, assuming that decisions based solely on data are best. However, transitioning into leadership means valuing and leveraging emotions, and taking them into

consideration when making decisions. Decisions are not always best when they rely only on data, just as they are not always best when relying entirely on emotions.

2. Managing emotions to generating emotions.
   ❏ Managing emotions is not enough—the leader must generate emotions, moving people to action through passion, excitement, anger, fear, or insecurity. Different situations call for different emotions and leaders must recognize which emotion is called for and how to generate it.

© Nako Photography/Shutterstock.com

Watch https://www.ted.com/talks/susan_colantuono_the_career_advice_you_probably_didn_t_get? to hear about women and transitioning from management to leadership.

3. Following standards to setting standards.
   ❏ Sometimes leaders must set new standards to achieve an exciting and innovative future, breaking existing standards or rules. Managers are typically rewarded for playing by the rules, but leaders sometimes excel when breaking them or going around them; however, being unethical is still considered unprofessional and leads to poor decisions and choices..

4. A position of realism to fantasy—dreamer.
   ❏ Managers are required by the nature of their responsibilities to be practical and realistic, to even err on the side of conservatism to ensure they meet their budget and time goals. However, leaders are supposed to be dreamers; envisioning a future that no one has yet considered and that may be just out of reach. Additionally, the dream must be achievable at some level or it remains a dream.

5. Narrowly focused decisions that maximize one parameter, to compromising when needed.
   ❏ Managers are expected to seek ways to maximize the potential of their approach because they aren't asked to take the full picture into consideration. However, leaders must keep all aspects of the business in mind, which means having to make short-term compromises for long-term gains, or other kinds of trade-offs that serve the bigger picture.

Exercise 8.4

Now that you have read the chapter, explain how you become a manager, what a manager is, and how manager's transition to become leaders.

Chapter Summary

Although combining management and leadership together makes sense given the overlap of concepts, separating them facilitates learning the two topic areas. In this chapter, we focused on management, the next chapter focuses on Leadership. Management and the role of being a manager are about the actual

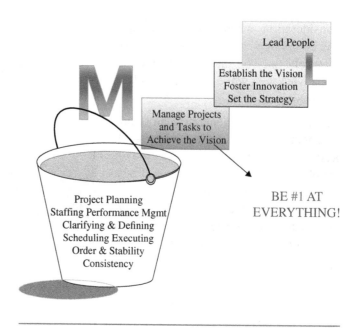

FIGURE 8.8   Visual Summary of Chapter 8

Courtesy Zinta Byrne.

work of the organization; getting the job done. As you advance from the bucket of management responsibilities, both leaders and managers can set organizational strategy, in general, leaders establish strategy and vision, and management executes on the strategy and vision. There are different types of managers and different tasks that managers take on, such as project management that achieves organizational performance. Managing employees' performance and maximizing their potential falls within the responsibility of managers. Without such efforts, employees may not be properly aligned toward achieving the organizational goals and may not be organized in a way to perform their tasks most effectively or efficiently. Becoming a good manager requires a number of different skills, knowledge of a variety of content areas, and ability, but ultimately you can learn how to become a good manager.

Figure 8.8 provides a visual summary of the key concepts from Chapter 8.

The idea with this visual is that managerial tasks are essentially contained within one big bucket—the job of the manager is to project plan, ensure appropriate staffing and assign those folks to tasks, while monitoring the schedule. Additionally, the manager clarifies and defines for employees what it means to achieve the organization's vision. Managers provide the stability and structure that employees need to stay focused and know, at all times, on what they need to work and what has to be done. In the visual, once you step outside the bucket, you begin to get into that which differentiates management from leadership. Leaders focus on the bigger picture; the vision, the long-term plan of where the organization needs to go 5 to 10 years from now. Thus, the leader's role is not as constrained as the manager's role. Keep in mind, this differentiation between the manager and leader is, in some organizations, superficial—managers lead and leaders manage, but in some organizations, leaders might do more leading/ visioning than managing.

Discussion Questions

1. What is the utility, if any, of separating management from leadership? Argue for keeping them distinct as they are in the chapter, or for combining them as others do. What are the implications of your view of management/leadership (either as separate or combined concepts) on the organization overall, the employees in the organization, and on the manager/leader directly?

2. What is the difference between project management and program management? In which situations do you envision them being the same thing?

3. Assume you are one of the HR directors at Uber or Lyft, where most of the workers are the independent contractors doing the driving. If you have to manage their performance and/or give them negative feedback, how would you frame it and do it? Would you be able to apply the ACHIEVE model? If not, why not? If so, how would you modify the model to fit with this gig work?

4. Given that many millennials and workers of the most recent generations reportedly feel they should be promoted to management within a year of starting work, should we move to self-managed teams? If so, how do you envision that would work in the bigger picture of the organization? If not, why not? Can you think of any company or industry where entirely self-managed teams could work?

5. Think of a class project or assignment that you have been given recently—something that you knew at the start of the semester or quarter that was due at the end of the term. Using a project plan of some kind, like a Gantt chart, PERT chart, excel, or even just a hand-drawn diagram, map out the project including tasks, due dates, contingency planning (e.g., unexpected quiz or additional project, lost backup disk), team members (if it is a group project), and overall goals/resources. What can you gain from planning your projects to this level of detail in advance of the project, even when the project may not involve outside dependencies? What do you think the impact would be on overall project timing if you did this with a team (i.e., think of Gersick's punctuated equilibrium model from Chapter 7).

References

Aguinis, H., Gottfredson, R. K., & Joo, H. (2012). Delivering effective performance feedback: The strengths-based approach. *Human Performance, 55,* 105–111. doi:10.1016/j.bushor.2011.10.004

Alvero, A. M., Bucklin, B. R., & Austin, J. (2001). An objective review of the effectiveness and essential characteristics of performance feedback in organizational settings. *Journal of Organizational Behavior Management, 21*(1), 3–29. doi:10.1300/J075v21n01_02

Antoni, C. (2005). Management by objectives–an effective tool for teamwork?. *International Journal of Human Resource Management, 16*(2), 174–184. doi:10.1080/0958519042000311381

Aplin, J. C. Jr., Schoderbeck, C. G., & Schoderbeck, P. P. (1979). Tough-minded management by objectives. *Human Resource Management, 18*(2), 9–13.

Axelrod, B., Handfield-Jones, H., & Michaels, E. (2002). A new game plan for C players. *Harvard Business Review, 80*(1), 80–88.

Baumgartner, M. S., & Schneider, D. E. (2010). Perceptions of women in management: A thematic analysis of razing the glass ceiling. *Journal of Career Development, 37*(2), 559–576. doi:10.1177/0894845309352242

Blake, R. R., & Mouton, J. S. (1975). An overview of the Grid®. *Training and Development Journal, 29,* 29–37.

Blake, R. R., & Mouton, J. S. (1982a). A comparative analysis of situationalism and 9,9 management by principle. *Organizational Dynamics, 10*(4), 20–43. doi:10.1016/0090-2616(82)90027-4

Blake, R. R., & Mouton, J. S. (1982b). How to choose a leadership style. *Training & Development Journal, 36*(2), 38–47.

Blake, R. R., Mouton, J. S., Barnes, L. B., & Greiner, L. E. (1964). Breakthrough in organization development. *Harvard Business Review, 42*(6), 133–155.

Blake, R. R., Mouton, J. S., & Bidwell, A. C. (1962). Managerial grid. *Advanced Management - Office Executive, 1*(9), 12–15.

Bourner, T. (1996). Effective management and the development of self-awareness: A plain manager's guide. *The Career Development International, 1*(4), 14–18. doi:10.1108/13620439610114270

Bouskila-Yam, O., & Kluger, A. N. (2011). Strength-based performance appraisal and goal setting. *Human Resource Management Review, 21*(2), 137–147. doi:10.1016/j.hrmr.2010.09.001

Byrne, Z. S. (2015). Understanding employee engagement: Theory, research, and practice. New York, NY: Routledge/Taylor & Francis Group.

Carroll, S. R., & Tosi, H. L. (1970). Goal characteristics and personality factors in a management-by-objectives program. *Administrative Science Quarterly, 15*(3), 295–305.

Cialdini, R. B. (2009). *Influence: Science and Practice* (5th ed.). Boston, MA: Pearson Education.

Cooper, W. H. (1981). Ubiquitous halo. *Psychological Bulletin, 90*(2), 218–244. doi:10.1037/0033-2909.90.2.218

Cummings, S., & Bridgman, T. (2011). The relevant past: Why the history of management should be critical for our future. *Academy of Management Learning & Education, 10*(1), 77–93. doi:10.5465/AMLE.2011.59513274

Cunningham, I. (2007). Is honest feedback always a good idea? And why is there concern about bullying? *Development and Learning in Organizations, 22*(1), 5–7.

Dobbins, G. H., & Russell, J. M. (1986). The biasing effects of subordinate likeableness on leaders' responses to poor performers: A laboratory and a field study. *Personnel Psychology, 39*(4), 759–777.

Drucker, P. F. (1954). *The practice of management.* New York, NY: Harper & Brothers.

Erez, A., LePine, J. A., & Elms, H. (2002). Effects of rotated leadership and peer evaluation on the functioning and effectiveness of self-managed teams: A quasi-experiment. *Personnel Psychology, 55*(4), 929–948. doi:10.1111/j.1744-6570.2002.tb00135.x

Fagiano, D. (1997). Managers vs leaders: A corporate fable. *Management Review, 86*(10), 5.

Fayol, H. (1949). *General and industrial management.* New York, NY: Pitman.

Fedor, D. B., & Rowland, K. M. (1989). Investigating supervisor attributions of subordinate performance. *Journal of Management, 15*(3), 405.

Fisher, C. D. (1979). Transmission of positive and negative feedback to subordinates: A laboratory investigation. *Journal of Applied Psychology, 64*(5), 533–540. doi:10.1037/0021-9010.64.5.533

Fulk, H., Bell, R. L., & Bodie, N. (2011). Team management by objectives: Enhancing developing teams' performance. *Journal of Management Policy & Practice, 12*(3), 17–26.

Gillespie, T. L., & Parry, R. O. (2006). Fuel for litigation? Links between procedural justice and multisource feedback. *Journal of Managerial Issues, 18*(4), 530–546.

Goodhew, G. W., Cammock, P. A., & Hamilton, R. T. (2008). The management of poor performance by front-line managers. *Journal of Management Development, 27*(9), 951–962.

Green, S. G., & Liden, R. C. (1980). Contextual and attributional influences on control decisions. *Journal of Applied Psychology, 65*(4), 453–458.

Green, S. G., & Mitchell, T. R. (1979). Attributional processes of leaders in leader–member interactions. *Organizational Behavior & Human Performance, 23*(3), 429–458. doi:10.1016/0030-5073(79)90008-4

Hackman, J., & Oldham, G. R. (1976). Motivation through the design of work: Test of a theory. *Organizational Behavior & Human Performance, 16*(2), 250–279.

Hackman, J., & Oldham, G. R. (1980). *Work redesign.* Reading, MA: Addison-Wesley.

Hersey, P., & Goldsmith, M. (1980). A situational approach to performance planning. *Training & Development Journal, 34*(11), 38.

Ilgen, D. R., Fisher, C. D., & Taylor, M. (1979). Consequences of individual feedback on behavior in organizations. *Journal of Applied Psychology, 64*(4), 349–371. doi:10.1037/0021-9010.64.4.349

Ilgen, D. R., & Knowlton, W. A. Jr. (1980). Performance attributional effects on feedback from superiors. *Organizational Behavior & Human Performance, 25*(3), 441–456.

Ivancevich, J. M. (1972). A longitudinal assessment of management by objectives. *Administrative Science Quarterly, 17*(1), 126–138.

Jacques, P. H., Garger, J., & Thomas, M. (2008). Assessing leader behaviors in project managers. *Management Research News, 31*(1), 4–11.

Jamieson, B. D. (1973). Behavioral problems with management by objectives. *Academy of Management Journal, 16*(3), 496–505. doi:10.2307/255009

Johnson, S., & Blanchard, K. (1982). The one minute manager. New York, NY: Blanchard Family Partnership.

Kerr, N. L. (1983). Motivation losses in small groups: A social dilemma analysis. *Journal of Personality and Social Psychology, 45*(4), 819–828. doi:10.1037/0022-3514.45.4.819

Kim, S., & Rubianty, D. (2011). Perceived fairness of performance appraisals in the federal government: Does it Matter? *Review of Public Personnel Administration, 31*(4), 329–348. doi:10.1177/0734371X11428903

Kleingeld, A., van Mierlo, H., & Arends, L. (2011). The effect of goal setting on group performance: A meta-analysis. *Journal of Applied Psychology, 96*(6), 1289–1304. doi:10.1037/a0024315

Knight, J. (2005). All leaders manage, but not all managers lead. *Engineering Management, 15*(1), 36,37.

Kondrasuk, J. N., Flagler, K., Morrow, D., & Thompson, P. (1984). The effects of management by objectives on organization results. *Group & Organization Studies, 9*(4), 531–539.

Kotter, J. P. (1990). What leaders really do. *Harvard Business Review, 68*(3), 103–111.

Laiken, M. E. (1994). The myth of the self-managing team. *Organization Development Journal, 12*(2), 29–34.

Larson, J. R. (1986). Supervisors' performance feedback to subordinates: The impact of subordinate performance valence and outcome dependence. *Organizational Behavior and Human Decision Processes, 37*(3), 391–408. doi:10.1016/0749-5978(86)90037-3

Larson, E., & Drexler, J. A. Jr. (2010). Project management in real time: A service-learning project. *Journal of Management Education, 34*(4), 551–573. doi:10.1177/1052562909335860

Larsson, G. (2012). Leader development in a natural context. In J. H. Laurence & M. D. Matthews (Eds.), *The Oxford handbook of military psychology* (pp. 187–196). New York, NY: Oxford University Press. doi:10.1093/oxfordhb/9780195399325.013.0069

Lepine, J. A., & Van Dyne, L. (2001). Peer responses to low performers: An attributional model of helping in the context of groups. *Academy of Management Review, 26*(1), 67–84. doi:10.5465/AMR.2001.4011953

Liden, R. C., & Mitchell, T. R. (1985). Reactions to feedback: The role of attributions. *Academy of Management Journal, 28*(2), 291–308. doi:10.2307/256202

Lock, D. (2013). *Project Management* (10th ed.). Surrey, England: Ashgate Publishing Ltd.

Manikutty, S. S. (2003). From a manager to a leader: Bridging a Gulf or jumping a chasm? *Vikalpa: The Journal For Decision Makers, 28*(4), 53–61.

Martinko, M. J., & Gardner, W. L. (1987). The leader/member attribution process. *Academy of Management Review, 12*(2), 235–249. doi:10.5465/AMR.1987.4307811

Mohrman, S., Cohen, S. G., & Mohrman, A. R. (1995). *Designing team-based organizations: New forms for knowledge work.* San Francisco, CA: Jossey-Bass.

Mueller-Hanson, R. A., & Pulakos, E. D. (2018). Transforming performance management to drive performance: An evidence-based roadmap. NY: Routledge

Murphy, K. R., & Anhalt, R. L. (1992). Is halo error a property of the rater, ratees, or the specific behaviors observed? *Journal of Applied Psychology, 77*(4), 494–500. doi:10.1037/0021-9010.77.4.494

Nadler, D. A. (1979). The effects of feedback on task group behavior: A review of the experimental research. *Organizational Behavior & Human Performance, 23*(3), 309–338. doi:10.1016/0030-5073(79)90001-1

Rodrigues, C. A. (2001). Fayol's 14 principles of management then and now: A framework for managing today's organizations effectively. *Management Decision, 39*(10), 880–890.

Rosen, S., & Tesser, A. (1970). On reluctance to communicate undesirable information: The MUM effect. *Sociometry, 33*(3), 253–263. doi:10.2307/2786156

Ross, L. (1977). The intuitive psychologist and his shortcomings: Distortions in the attribution process. In L. Berkowitz (Ed.), *Advances in experimental social psychology* (Vol. 10, pp. 173–220). New York, NY: Academic Press.

Schmidt, W. H., & Tannenbaum, R. R. (1960). Management of differences. *Harvard Business Review, 38*(6), 107–115.

Smith, W. J., Harrington, K., & Houghton, J. D. (2000). Predictors of performance appraisal discomfort: A preliminary examination. *Public Personnel Management, 29*(1), 21–32.

Smither, J. W., London, M., & Reilly, R. R. (2005). Does performance improve following multisource feedback? A theoretical model, meta-analysis, and review of empirical findings. *Personnel Psychology, 58*(1), 33–66.

Tesser, A., Rosen, S., & Tesser, M. (1971). On the reluctance to communicate undesirable messages (the MUM effect): A field study. *Psychological Reports, 29*(2), 651–654. doi:10.2466/pr0.1971.29.2.651

Toor, S. (2011). Differentiating leadership from management: An empirical investigation of leaders and managers. *Leadership & Management in Engineering, 11*(4), 310–320. doi:10.1061/(ASCE)LM.1943-5630.0000138

Tosi, H. L., & Carroll, S. J. (1968). Managerial reaction to management by objectives. *Academy of Management Journal, 11*(4), 415–426. doi:10.2307/254890

Wilk, L. A., & Redmon, W. K. (1998). The effects of feedback and goal setting on the productivity and satisfaction of university admissions staff. *Journal of Organizational Behavior Management, 18*(1), 45–68. doi:10.1300/J075v18n01_04

Zaleznik, A. (1977). Managers and leaders: Are they different? *Harvard Business Review, 55*(3), 67–78.

Zugelder, M. T., & Champagne, P. J. (2018). A management approach to LGBT employment: Diversity, inclusion and respect. *Journal of Business Diversity, 18*(1), 40–50.

Taking the Organization into the Future: Leadership

CHAPTER 9

Learning Outcomes

After studying this chapter, you should be able to explain:

1. What leadership is and what it means to be a leader.
2. The difference between leadership and management.
3. The differences and similarities between trait, behavioral, and situational theories of leadership.
4. How leaders are developed.
5. What happens when an organization has an ineffective leader.

Mini-Quiz: Leadership

As an introduction to this chapter, please take the following mini-quiz (answers are in the back of the book). As you read the questions and consider the answers *before* diving into the chapter, you'll challenge yourself before you master the content, a process that helps facilitate learning for long-term retention. Some questions may have more than one correct answer. Don't worry if you cannot answer all questions correctly on your first try. By the time you read through the chapter and spend some of your own time thinking about these concepts, you should be able to determine the best answers. Try the quiz again after you finish reading the chapter.

1. As a leader of an organization, it is your job to influence people, attaining their buy-in for the organization's goals and direction. What technique is going to be most effective when gaining employee buy-in to your vision and mission?
   a. Coerce them—if people know there are negative consequences, they will fall in line and do what they are supposed to do for the organization.
   b. Reward them—if you give bonuses and other rewards, employees will like you and help drive organizational goals.
   c. Make it known you are the leader—if you use the "because I am the leader and I say so" mentality, employees will know who's boss and will complete tasks that you ask them to do.
   d. Consistently share information—when you share information that employees want and need, they will accept you as a leader and will more readily follow you.

2. True or false: Leaders are born, not made.
   a. False. The "trait" approach to leadership is not supported as a solo explanation for leadership; we can definitely train people to be better leaders.
   b. True. Personality is the most important factor for being a good leader.

3. What will help you be a better leader?
   a. Being intelligent
   b. Focusing on tasks rather than people/relationships
   c. Asking for input and involving your employees when making decisions
   d. Act in ways that are consistent with your own values

4. If you were going to train a group of management-level employees to be better leaders, which approach is most effective?:
   a. Select the employees of the managers and have them help explain what leadership they need
   b. Use traditional learning, such as reading books on leadership and having classes that employees can sign up for
   c. Pair employees with a mentor
   d. Provide opportunities after the training to follow-up with leaders and have them reflect on how they have changed

5. What might your organization face if it has a somewhat abusive or dictatorial leader?
   a. High turnover and people leaving the organization
   b. High prevalence of employee health problems
   c. Employees experiencing unusually high levels of stress at home as well as at work
   d. Employees performing better on the job

Overview

Leaders of organizations have fascinated the general population and academicians for years.

What makes a good leader? Why do bad leaders often have many followers? We are intrigued with the ability or power of persuasion and loyalty that leaders seem to have and attract. Some leaders have substantial visibility, such as leaders of countries or leaders of large firms such as those generally reported in the global and local media. Others, though perhaps just as influential, garner less visibility but still move their organizations toward contributing to the economy of their country, nation, state, or town. Anthropological studies show that even when societies do not have institutionalized leaders (like a chief, ruler, or elected official), there are always people who rise to the occasion and initiate action, playing a central role in decision making and acting as a leader. Thus, leadership, the term given to encompass the role of leaders, seems to be a natural concept. You could ask, however, if it's so natural, why are there so many of us who can't do it well? This chapter explores what it takes to lead (Figure 9.1).

FIGURE 9.1 Leadership

© Jaromir Chalabala/Shutterstock, Inc.

What does it Mean to Lead an Organization?

Leading an organization is different from managing one. As a leader, you develop the vision and mission of an organization, and then inspire your employees to follow and to join in achieving that mission. As noted in Chapter 8, managing an organization refers to the operations, to allocating the right resources to the right task to achieve the vision and mission of the organization. Kotter (1988), considered an authority on leadership, noted in his book "*The Leadership Factor*" that effective leadership involves:

1. Creating an agenda for change that includes developing:
   - ❑ A vision for what can and should be
   - ❑ A vision that takes into account the long-term interests of everyone involved
   - ❑ A strategy for achieving the vision
   - ❑ A strategy that takes into account all the relevant organizational and environmental forces

2. Building a strong implementation network that includes
   - ❑ Supportive relationships with key sources of power that are needed for implementing the strategy

❏ Relationships strong enough to elicit cooperation, compliance, and teamwork
❏ A highly motivated core group of people
❏ A core group committed to making the vision a reality

In contrast, Kotter suggested that effective management involves:

1. Planning
   ❏ Logically deducing the means to achieve a given end or goal

2. Budgeting
   ❏ The planning process associated with the organization's finances

3. Organizing
   ❏ Creating a formal structure to accomplish the plans
   ❏ Staffing the plan with qualified managers who, in turn, staff their teams
   ❏ Clearly defining each employee's role
   ❏ Providing everyone with financial and career incentives
   ❏ Delegating appropriate authority to employees

4. Controlling
   ❏ Looking out for deviations from the plan and using formal authority to get back on track

Notice the contrast between what Kotter says effective leadership is versus what effective management entails. As explained in Chapter 8, however, management and leadership are not necessarily mutually exclusive; yet as clearly illustrated by Kotter, they are not necessarily interchangeable. The degree to which they overlap depends on the nature of the organization, industry, and specific leader/manager. Management and leadership could be thought of on a continuum, where the extreme ends represent the manager without leader responsibility (left endpoint) and the leader without management responsibility (right endpoint) (Figure 9.2).

The developmental focus of military academies in the United States illustrates the continuum well. For example, at WestPoint Military Academy and the Air Force Academy cadets are trained on the philosophy that leadership is developed in each individual (thus not an inborn trait), and strengthens as they mature through the training program and management ranks. Cadets begin by first learning what it takes to be a good follower. The next step requires they manage and mentor junior cadets and peers. As they advance from year to year through their academic training, they develop the skills for leading and directing larger groups of junior cadets and peers in various aspects of military exercises or in classroom activities. Military academies exist to develop leaders; the philosophy being that all military personnel are, in some form, leaders. At graduation, the newly

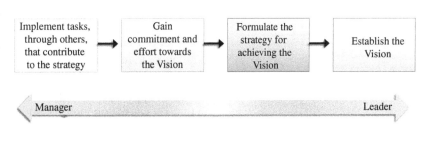

FIGURE 9.2   Continuum of Management to Leadership

Courtesy Zinta Byrne.

minted military officers see themselves as leaders, as do their peers. Although the example here describes military academies in the United States, it appears that the same leader philosophy and general developmental training model apply to military academies in other countries (e.g., China, Russia, South Africa).

Some organizations, like military academies and universities, are designed to produce leaders, while organizations hire them. Regardless of which institution you work for, having the knowledge of what makes up leadership provides insight into evaluating the appropriateness of who is hired. So the next logical questions include, what *is* leadership and what does it look like?

What is Leadership and What Does It Look Like?

Leaders are expected to provide strategic direction and vision for their organization, regardless of whether they work in a business or military unit. They should have a plan for what the organization wants to achieve in 5–10 years (less for a startup company), and what is needed to get there. Employees expect leaders to secure and obtain necessary resources, have a clear idea of what success means, and generate excitement to achieve that success. Unfortunately for leaders, employees' expectations of what they can do and what they are capable of tend to be high regardless of industry or size of organization. Not only are leaders expected to bring resources into the organization to achieve its goals, they also need to know how to keep unwanted problems out of the organization (i.e., boundary management).

Gilmore (1982) suggested that leadership is really about boundary management. As a leader, your job is to protect the organization from the influence of external entities pressuring the organization to change or adopt outside values and standards, while ensuring the adoption of new ideas and positive influences associated with the vision occur within the organization. Leaders focus on exciting employees to innovate and to transform work into something meaningful (Zaleznik, 1977). A leader influences, motivates, and enables others to make their unique contributions toward the organization's effectiveness and ultimately its success.

How Do Leaders Influence Others?

Leaders' jobs require influencing others; to convince others the organization's direction is the right one, the best one, and the path they have chosen will lead to success for the organization as a whole. The extent to which the leader can influence followers depends on their power. Power refers to the source or nature of influence. Subordinates or followers can respond to power in three different ways: compliance, identification, and acceptance or internalization. *Compliance* refers to doing what you're told but not doing it willingly—you do it just to fulfill the request and get past the moment. *Identification* refers to doing what the leader wants you to do because you identify with them; you feel as though you are similar in some way to the leader and, therefore, you feel that what you're asked to do makes sense. *Acceptance* or *internationalization*, the strongest and most long lasting influence, refers to doing what the leader wants because you believe it's the right thing to do. French and Raven (1959) introduced six sources of power upon which leaders can draw to influence their followers (Table 9.1).

TABLE 9.1 Sources of Power

Source of Power	Definition	Example	Type of Influence	Effectiveness
Coercive	Influence through punishing people. This power base is dependent on creating fear. The follower reacts to the fear that some negative consequence will occur if they fail to comply.	Dismiss or suspend, demote, assign unpleasant tasks, withhold key information	Formal; based on authority or position	Not very; only obtain compliance and only if the consequence is severe enough.
Reward	Opposite of coercive power. Leader gives rewards to get followers to do what's desired.	Pay raise, bonus, recognition, promotion, interesting work, preferred shift	Formal; based on authority or position	Not very; only obtain compliance and only if the reward is valued.
Legitimate (also called Positional)	Influence through the position the leader holds. Includes the ability to use both coercive and reward power.	Supervisor, police officer, military leader, school teacher	Formal; based on authority or position	Not very; only obtain compliance and mostly when the authority is direct vs. indirect.
Expert	Influence is through knowledge or the perception of knowledge. Followers listen to the leader because of their expertise.	Professors, world-renowned experts, top engineer or designer	Personal; based on what the leader possesses	Moderate, depending on whether the knowledge applies to that situation. Might get acceptance.
Referent	Influence comes through followers liking or admiring the leader.	Charismatic leaders; celebrities marketing products	Personal; based on what the leader possesses	Moderate; May get identification.
Informational	Influence by having information that others need or want. The leader is influential only when they have the needed information.	Assistants	Personal; based on what the leader possesses	Moderate, depending on the consistency of having needed information. May get acceptance.

Courtesy Zinta Byrne. Source: French and Raven, 1959.

Our understanding of how leaders develop and use power to influence others came from years of studying how employees follow. We have had a long fascination with leadership, which traces back hundreds of years.

Exercise 9.1

In your own words, write a few sentences about what it means for leaders to lead and how they do it—how do they get others to do what they want?

What Do We Know About Leadership?

Leadership is probably among the oldest preoccupations of human beings, with traces of the captivation with leadership in Egyptian hieroglyphics, Greek myths, and various religious documents such as the Bible and Koran.

Although interest in leadership dates far back in history, the scientific study of leadership did not start until the 1930s and 1940s. Since then, it has undergone many changes, from focusing on specific traits leaders possess, to their individual behaviors, to an emphasis on leaders' complex relationships with the employees of the organization. Leadership scholars have been trying to understand why some people become leaders and others do not, why some are effective when others are not, and whether leadership actually makes a difference. As an outcome of their studies, several theories of leadership have emerged; theories that facilitate leadership development and improving organizational effectiveness.

Why should leaders vary their source of power?

Theories of Leadership

A number of theories of leadership have been developed over the years, as research scholars have studied how leaders develop, influence employees, and make decisions. The following section organizes theories by their emphasis and their development in time, such that each subsection illustrates the progression of the field and our thinking about leaders. Recognizing how our understanding of leadership has developed and evolved helps us to formulate for ourselves what behaviors, types of relations with followers, and personal characteristics might lead to positive responses from our followers/subordinates.

You'll often find that business leaders tend to latch onto a popular theory and then fail to revise their view even as scholars refute the theories and propose new, better theories. For instance, believing that leaders are born and not made is a common misperception, yet there are many who still feel that you can't learn to be a good leader. Their perspective is that if you do not start out with "natural" leadership abilities, you can't develop them later.

Leadership theories help clarify why and how leadership develops in organizations, providing insight into formulating models for ourselves about what behaviors, types of relationships with followers, and personal characteristics make for good leadership that excites followers.

Additionally, learning the leadership theories enables you to build your own models of leadership that fit your own situation. By gaining insight into how leading scholars explain why leaders affect their followers, given a new situation, you can chart your own path for influencing your followers.

To get a handle on the development of leadership theories, the scholarly work can be divided into at least three approaches:

1. Trait approach, which focuses on the enduring traits leaders must possess.

2. Behavioral approach, which focuses on how leaders should act and what specific behaviors they should display to be considered leaders.

3. Contingency approach, which focuses on how leaders should change their style to match the needs of the situation.

Most recent approaches to leadership incorporate theories from disciplines outside of psychology and organizational behavior to describe a complex relationship between the leader and follower, and the environment. These theories extend beyond the three approaches, trait, behavioral, and situational, and have been collectively grouped into what is simply called "new leadership theories," for lack of a better term (Bryman, 1992, p.21).

Traits Make the Leader: The Trait Approach

The earliest view of leadership, introduced as the "great man" theory (Carlyle, 1907), proposed that great leaders possess specific enduring and inherent traits, setting them apart from everyone else. Only a handful of men possess these traits. Specifically, the theory stated that leadership resides inside the person (specifically men, sorry ladies)—you are either born a leader or you are not. This fundamental belief, that to be a great leader you must possess certain traits (traits that you cannot acquire or develop later), could be traced back to Galton's (1869) work that suggested leaders were extraordinary people. However, great leaders were identified even before Galton; leaders such as Egyptian Pharaohs and the heroes of Greek mythology. Many recognized leaders such as Moses, Frederick Nietzsche, Sitting Bull, Winston Churchill, Abraham Lincoln, Catherine the Great, King Henry IV, Queen Elizabeth, Martin Luther King, Albert Einstein, and Gandhi—the list goes on—are described as having specific traits that set them apart from all other people (a few examples shown in Figure 9.3).

Though the great man perspective had popular appeal for a while, early empirical research was unsupportive of any single trait, cluster of traits, or even demographic characteristics (e.g., height, education) that could predict leadership across situations (Mann, 1959; Stogdill, 1948). Researchers found that although traits such as intelligence, initiative, and self-confidence were indeed related to leadership, their importance depended upon the specifics of the situation, meaning that no single trait or set of traits could predict leadership across situations. The overall outcome of this early critical work on the trait approach (e.g., Jennings, 1943; Newstetter, Feldstein, & Newcomb, 1938) was to squelch it and favor, instead, other approaches to understanding leadership (e.g., behavioral, contingency, both explained in the next sections). Researchers concluded that leadership must result from an interaction between the person and the situation. Traits are not harmful to good leadership; they simply aren't the only explanation for a leader's success or failure, which is what the great man theory espoused.

Pharaoh Tutankhamun's funeral mask, ruled around 1324 B.C.

Roman Emperor, Julius Caesar, ruled in 46–44 B.C.

Sitting Bull holding a peace pipe, circa 1885

Dalai Lama, Italy, Rome 10/2006

FIGURE 9.3   A Few Great Man Leaders

Even though researchers clarified that traits alone do not make the leader, the fascination with whether leaders have unique traits remains. Resurgence in examining traits and leadership can be attributed to the advent of meta-analytic studies (e.g., Judge Ilies, Bono, & Gerhardt, 2002; Judge, Colbert, & Ilies, 2004; Lord, De Vader, & Alliger , 1986), because looking at the results of many studies across a variety of situations combined revealed new insight into traits of effective leaders. Results of meta-analyses (i.e., Judge et al., 2002; Lord et al., 1986) have shown correlations between leadership and several traits such as extroversion, openness to experience, intelligence, dominance, and conscientiousness.

Similarly, a recent meta-analysis showed that interpersonal skills, oral and written communication, decision-making, and management skills (such as project management) are consistent predictors of effective leadership (Hoffman, Woehr, Maldagen-Youngjohn, & Lyons, 2011). A common theme emerging across a number of reviews is that good leaders display self-confidence, integrity, and emotional balance or maturity, regardless of situation (Bass, 1990; Daft, 1999; House & Aditya, 1997; Kirkpatrick & Locke, 1991; Northouse, 1997; Stogdill, 1948; Yukl, 1998; Yukl & Van Fleet, 1992). Thus, using meta-analyses, researchers refuted the argument that no single trait or cluster of traits can predict leadership across situations because results showed consistent correlations between leadership and specific traits among a number of studies conducted in a variety of settings. These cumulative findings suggest that traits may serve a role in identifying effective leaders, but do not necessarily *make* the leader. Despite these research findings, people are still fascinated with and convinced that leaders are special and born with unique traits.

Intelligence

Research by Carol Dweck suggests that having a growth mindset removes the idea of having a fixed level of intelligence; see her work at https://mindsetonline.com/index.html

In one of the earliest scholarly reviews of the research on leadership, Mann (1959) determined that intelligence and good leadership were highly related. It turns out that Mann was onto something as recent meta-analyses (Judge, et al., 2002; Lord, et al., 1986) have confirmed that leadership is indeed correlated with intelligence across a number of studies. In yet another meta-analysis, Ilies, Gerhardt, and Le (2004) demonstrated that the combination of intelligence and personality factors strongly relates to leadership emergence (i.e., being perceived as a leader), and that genetic differences partially explain differences in leader emergence. Thus, personality and intelligence are, to a degree, inherited and this inheritance influences whether you are perceived as being leader-like. A recent study shows, however, that intelligence has nothing to do with success and that personality trumps intelligence (see Heckman & Kautz, 2012).

The Big-Five

Judge and his colleagues (2002) used meta-analysis techniques to empirically examine the research on the relationships between leadership in general, leadership emergence, and leadership effectiveness, and the five-factor model of personality (also called the Big-Five), which includes Openness to experience, Conscientiousness, Extraversion, Agreeableness, and Neuroticism (Tupes & Christal, 1992). First, the term "leadership" in general is a nonspecific reference to leadership. In contrast, "leadership emergence" is a specific term that refers to when individuals rise up, take charge, or assume leadership roles, as opposed to being officially appointed into the role. Leader or leadership emergence relies on whether the leaders are perceived as a leader, without necessarily knowing much about their actual performance. Leader effectiveness refers to how well the leader leads, taking into consideration their actual achievements and performance (Lord et al., 1986).

Second, the big-five personality traits are defined as follows. Openness to experience reflects an artistic, imaginative, introspective, and curious personality. Conscientiousness personality is described as efficient, planful, dependable, dutiful, and self-disciplined. Extraversion reflects the energetic, cheerful, and engaging person who loves socializing and is energized by being with others. Agreeableness reflects the appreciative, giving, trusting, noncritical, and sympathetic personality. Lastly, neuroticism reflects the anxious, unstable, touchy, moody, and self-defeating personality (McCrae & Costa, 1997; McCrae & John, 1992).

Judge and colleagues reviewed the qualitative and quantitative results of studies published from 1887 to 1999, searching for those that met the inclusion criteria for their meta-analysis (e.g., studied the five-factor model of personality, had the necessary statistical data). Their search and screening process resulted in a final set of 78 studies. The results of their analyses showed that Extraversion was most strongly correlated with leadership in general (ρ, the average correlation across all studies, was .31), followed by Conscientiousness, Neuroticism, and Openness to Experience. These results confirm Mann's (1959) original findings that showed extroversion and interpersonal sensitivity related to leadership (Mann, 1959). Agreeableness was very weakly correlated ($\rho = .08$) with leadership. Only Agreeableness was not correlated with leader emergence; all other big-five personality factors were correlated with leader emergence and leader effectiveness (with Neuroticism negatively correlated). The authors further showed, however, that these relationships were not the same across all settings, which included organizations, government, and students. Only Extraversion correlated with leadership across all settings.

Although intelligence and the big-five personality traits tend to be the most often studied characteristics of leaders, other traits appear unique between leaders and nonleaders.

Traits Besides Big-Five and Intelligence

Characteristics besides the big-five personality traits and intelligence found to differentiate between leaders and nonleaders include internal locus of control (whether you believe that you can influence life events; Rotter, 1966), trait anxiety (tendency toward general nervousness and high anxiety under stress; Spielberger, 1972), general self-efficacy (belief in your overall ability to perform toward goals; Shelton, 1990), and optimism (Popper, Amit, Gal, Mishkal-Sinai, & Lisak, 2004).

Personality traits other than the big-five that have garnered substantial research attention included the authoritarian personality, power orientation, and Machiavellianism (Bass, 1990).

Authoritarian personalities are described as politically and religiously conservative, power seeking, emotionally regulated or perceived as cold, discriminatory or appearing hostile toward other groups in particular minority groups, and rigid or resistant to change. These authoritarian leaders come across as in charge, in control, and stern; they won't tolerate weakness. Power orientation refers to people's attitudes toward power, where some seek it and others do not. Those seeking power use it to motivate others to get what they want, always finding the best way to have power over or control over the situation and others. These are the individuals who seem to maneuver the political system, and get regular promotions. When power is used solely for the benefit of the leader, it comes across as abuse and quickly backfires. In contrast, using the power to help followers or the organization, overall, is considered entrepreneurial and positive (Bass, 1990; Fodor & Riordan, 1995). Research shows that leaders who both seek and use power can be effective (O'Brien & Harary, 1977; Shaw & Harkey, 1976), in particular when the situation calls for social power (power through positive relationships) versus technical expertise (e.g., expert power; House & Singh, 1987).

Still more personality traits factored into explanations of leadership including **narcissism** (Rosenthal & Pittinsky, 2006), **sociopathic personality** (Cangemi & Pfohl, 2009), combinations resulting from the Myers-Briggs Type Indicator (e.g., Hautala, 2008), and several factors rated on the California Psychological Inventory such as dominance (Hogan, 1978). Those with high levels of **social–emotional intelligence**, the ability to understand and identify emotions in oneself and others and use that information to interpret the most effective response (Gardner, 1978; Salovey & Mayer, 1989), appear to be most adaptable and most popular in peer and subordinate ratings of good leaders (Ilies et al. 2004). Furthermore, leaders with high emotional intelligence are most effective in encouraging follower performance in collectivistic, feminine, and high uncertainty avoidance cultures (Miao, Humphrey, & Qian, 2018).

In sum, even though the big man theory was discarded many years ago, researchers' fascination with unique personality characteristics that may help identify good leaders has generated a tremendous body of literature and some very interesting findings.

Physical Traits

The fascination with leaders does not stop with personality, however. An interesting twist to the study of leaders' unique characteristics was recently demonstrated by Wong, Ormiston, and Haselhuhn (2011). The authors examined whether facial characteristics of Chief Executive Officers (CEOs) were related to their organization's financial performance. Before you read what they found, let's try a quick experiment. Figure 9.4 shows two faces—one wider relative to its length (left image in Figure 9.4) and the other longer than it is wide (right image in Figure 9.4). After looking at the pictures, which of the two CEOs do you think achieved the greatest financial performance for their organization?

Wong and colleagues did not show faces to study participants. Instead, to get the width by length ratio they measured the faces of CEOs using published photos (98% of their sample was Caucasian). They then examined the archival data of company performance records associated with each CEO. The results of their data analyses revealed that CEOs whose faces were wider than they were long achieved greater financial performance for their firms than did CEOs whose faces were longer than they were wide. Well, did you guess right?

Wong et al.'s results were moderated by (dependent on) the decision-making dynamics of the firm; the more simple the decision-making processes (i.e., the

FIGURE 9.4   Wider Than Long and Longer Than Wide Male Faces

Left: © CURAphotography/Shutterstock, Inc.; Right: © CURAphotographer/Shutterstock.com

less flexible, see issues as black and white), the more the CEO's face structure predicted firm performance. The authors argued that men with a higher width-to-height facial ratio (i.e., wide face) appear more aggressive and physically imposing, and as such present a more domineering (hence, perceived power-ful) impression than their counterparts with a lower width-to-height facial ratio (i.e., long narrow face). Take a look at the photos here. Which of these CEOs do you think achieved the greatest financial performance for their organization? (Figure 9.5).

Wong et al. (2011) reported that race did not alter the results of their faces width to length ratio study, suggesting that you should have considered those on the left more successful in achieving higher company financial performance than those on the right in Figure 9.5.

Although it may be fascinating to know that a CEO with a wide face appears domineering, you cannot change your face shape (without major surgery) and it's unclear if women with wider than long faces share the same CEO success. Similarly, though some personality traits may be suppressed or held in check, it is unlikely you can completely change your personality to become what is consid-ered leader-material. For example, if you're an introvert who prefers to be alone, for how long can you "play" being an extravert who enjoys being around people all day before you tire out? Likewise, if you're an extravert, how hard is it to fake being an introvert? Most people will tell you that even for personality traits they really want to change, they simply can't.

Since we are unable to easily change who we are, the trait approach may seem useless in understanding and developing leaders. Not so—its value is in helping to understand what people might expect of a leader based on what characteristics the leader appears to possess. Research shows that people are fairly accurate in judg-ing someone's personality, just by looking at the person or based on other short encounters (e.g., Albright, Kenny, & Malloy, 1998; Gosling, 2008; Naumann, Vazire, Rentfrow, & Gosling, 2009). For example, study participants have

FIGURE 9.5   Does Skin Color Affect Your Judgement?

Top left: © George Rudy/Shutterstock.com; Top right: © kurhan/Shutterstock.com; Bottom left: © KK Tan/Shutterstock.com; Bottom right: © Asier Romero/Shutterstock.com

accurately judged cooperativeness (Stirrat & Perrett, 2010), **criminality** (Valla, Ceci, & Williams, 2011), and aggressiveness (Carre, McCormick, & Mondloch, 2009) using facial photos only. This work carries over into the leadership domain where after brief exposure to photos, research participants accurately judged **leader emergence** (e.g., Antonakis & Dalgas, 2009; Mueller & Mazur, 1996; Zebrowitz & Montare, 2005). The implications of these findings are that individuals may form expectations about effective leadership based on what personality traits they believe matter for leadership, regardless of whether those beliefs are accurate. Additionally, if used in leader development, leaders can be trained to recognize where and how their personality is perceived by others.

Where judging people by their looks fails us horribly is in our implicit (and sometimes explicit) biases triggered by appearances. In a study of Black women senior-level corporate professionals, researchers found continued reports of subtle racism and themes of racial microaggression (Holder, Jackson, & Ponterotto, 2015). Modern racism occurs frequently in the form of microaggressions, "brief and commonplace daily verbal, behavioral, and environmental indignities, whether intentional or unintentional, that communicate hostile, derogatory, or negative

The trait approach to leadership proposes that leaders possess unique traits or characteristics that set them apart from all others, enabling them to be great leaders.

racial slights and insults" (Sue et al., 2007, p. 273). The accumulation of racial microaggressions not only results in psychological harm to the targeted individual, but affects their careers and feeds stereotypes. For example, Black women are stereotyped as hostile, aggressive, and intellectually inferior, preventing their ascent to upper levels in organizations (Holder et al., 2015). Therefore, judging leader traits and success by looking at them is not an advisable or desired approach.

Exercise 9.2

What is the trait approach of leadership and what are the traits associated with leaders?

Behavior Makes the Leader: The Behavioral Approach

The trait approach to explaining leadership offered interesting results, but little real clarification as to what makes a good leader. Thus, researchers turned to examining what behaviors leaders displayed and focused on whether patterns existed that would explain what separates a leader from a nonleader. Likert (1961) proposed that high performing leaders differed from those who seemed to struggle, in that the successful leaders developed supportive relationships with their followers. These relationships enabled upward and downward communication, and created influence among followers that was otherwise nonexistent. The supportive leader helped the employees feel personally important and understand how they contributed to the organization's mission. Consequently, these leaders excited their employees to pursue the organization's mission, engage in their work group, and achieve high performance goals. Likert additionally suggested that the leader's workgroup was critical to success because group loyalty produces trust, better communication, and support. Though few researchers seem to refer back to Likert's initial theorizing on how successful leaders behave, many of his concepts appear to have been incorporated in recent theories of leadership.

The idea of leaders providing support appears in many theories such as consideration versus initiating structure, the vertical dyad linkage, and servant leadership, all discussed in the next sections.

Consideration versus Initiating Structure

Some of the earliest works considered part of the behavioral approach include the Ohio State University studies of leadership. In 1945, the Personnel Research Board at Ohio State University sponsored a number of studies that examined leadership (Shartle, 1950). This project involved developing a measure of leadership called the Leader Behavior Description Questionnaire (LBDQ; Hemphill, 1950), and then used the measure to assess which behaviors were most often displayed by effective leaders (Fleishman, 1953a; Halpin & Winer, 1957).

Researchers found the behaviors displayed most clustered into two categories: *consideration* and *initiating structure* (Figure 9.6). Consideration behaviors comprise those where the leader shows careful attention to employees' feelings and displays general concern for followers' well-being. Leaders who demonstrate consideration behaviors express appreciation for good work, care about

Why is it important NOT to assume leaders look a certain way?

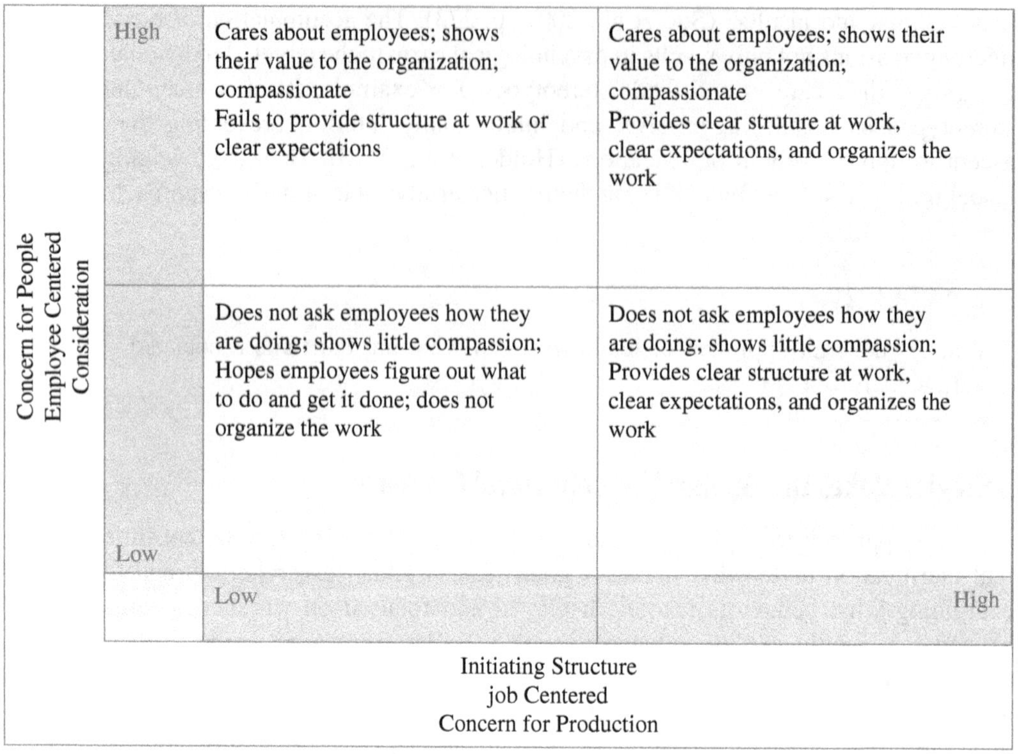

	High	Cares about employees; shows their value to the organization; compassionate Fails to provide structure at work or clear expectations	Cares about employees; shows their value to the organization; compassionate Provides clear struture at work, clear expectations, and organizes the work
Concern for People Employee Centered Consideration		Does not ask employees how they are doing; shows little compassion; Hopes employees figure out what to do and get it done; does not organize the work	Does not ask employees how they are doing; shows little compassion; Provides clear structure at work, clear expectations, and organizes the work
	Low		
		Low	High

Initiating Structure
job Centered
Concern for Production

FIGURE 9.6   Consideration vs. Initiating Structure

Courtesy Zinta Byrne.

job satisfaction, maintain employees' self-esteem by treating them as peers, and involve employees in decision-making processes (Bass, 1990). Initiating structure refers to how much the leader organizes work, maintains standards, and develops the details for how work should be done and by when. Such a leader has clear communication, but tends not to involve followers in decision-making. The goal of the leader exhibiting initiating structure behaviors is to get the work organized and done (Bass, 1990).

This two-component model of leadership was popular for quite some time, with many studies launched to examine under what conditions leaders demonstrated either consideration or initiating structure, or both high consideration and high initiating structure behaviors (Fleishman, 1953b, 1995). Though the Ohio State Studies are most often cited for this model, comparable work was ongoing concurrently at the University of Michigan (Blake, Mouton, & Bidwell, 1962; Likert, 1961) and at Harvard (Bales, 1954). The outcome of those studies was two other variations of this two-factor model: employee-centered and production-centered (generally synonymous with consideration and initiating structure, respectively; see Figure 9.6) and person- and task-oriented behaviors (again, quite similar to consideration and initiating structure, respectively). Because these models were also quite well-liked at the time, you may see them in published articles and books, even though their use has fallen out of favor, likely because of their simplicity.

Recently, however, Judge, Piccolo, and Ilies (2004) conducted a meta-analysis of the research on the consideration/initiating structure model of leadership, demonstrating the validity of the two-component model, and essentially resurrecting it for use. Culling through hundreds of studies to select those that met the inclusion criteria (i.e., studied the constructs and included statistical results necessary for a meta-analysis), Judge et al. examined a final set of 130 studies. Their results showed that consideration more strongly predicts effective leadership than does initiating structure (which we could argue is a characteristic of management). They also found that consideration was more strongly associated with follower satisfaction than was initiating structure, whereas initiating structure was more strongly related to performance than was consideration. Additionally important about this study is Judge and colleagues' demonstration that these two leader behaviors are robust and indicate effective leadership across measures, time, and sources of assessment, despite that most leadership researchers have long since dismissed this two-factor model of leadership as an artifact or mere historical relic. Several other two-factor models were also popular for a while, and those too have also been long dismissed.

Why is it beneficial to learn about the trait approach to leadership, if it's not really used much anymore?

Other Two-factor Models

The consideration versus initiating structure model was not the only two-factor or two-component model developed to explain how leaders should or do behave. Another two-factor classification includes authoritarian or autocratic versus democratic (Lewin & Lippitt, 1938). A number of models fit within this classification including the managerial grid (concern for production vs. concern for people) discussed in Chapter 8 (and therefore not be repeated here), Theory X and Theory Y (McGregor, 1960), and directive versus participative leadership (Berlew & Heller, 1983).

Theory X/Theory Y (sometimes written as Theory X/Y; Figure 9.7) refers to two types of leaders (McGregor, 1960):

1. an authoritarian or autocratic leader whose approach maintains tight controls and who believes that employees needed to be told what to do (Theory X manager).

2. a leader who approaches leading using a liberal or democratic style, believing employees' developmental needs should be met and that the manager should empower employees to achieve their best (Theory Y manager).

Theory X Manager

Theory Y Manager

FIGURE 9.7 Theory X/Theory Y managers

Left © alphaspirit/Shutterstock.com; Right © fizkes/Shutterstock.com

Recent research on Theory X/Y shows that managers who were considered Theory X type managers failed to develop the interpersonal relationships that managers who were considered Theory Y developed, and that such interpersonal relationships were positively indicative of high organizational commitment among employees (Şahin, 2012). Thus, Theory Y managers' seem to foster organizational commitment in their employees. Theory X managers display more apprehension in interpersonal communications than do Theory Y managers (Russ, 2013), which may explain these research findings.

Somewhat similar to the Theory X manager style, directive leadership refers to the leader making the decisions and expecting the group to follow the decisions. In contrast, participative leadership refers to the leader equalizing decision-making, seeking input from followers and involving them in the decision process though not releasing responsibility for the decision to the group. The leader remains a leader, but involves the group and encourages members to participate in problem solving, discussions, and formulating the decision, similar to the Theory Y manager.

The behavioral approach to leadership proposes that the effectiveness of leaders is dependent on how they behave and what specific actions they take that demonstrate their strength as leaders.

Instead of forcing leadership behavior into separate categories, Tannenbaum and Schmidt (1958) proposed that leadership behaviors belong on a continuum from subordinate-centered to boss-centered (shown in Figure 9.8). Similar to the autocratic-democratic, or directive-participative two-factor models, the continuum of leadership behaviors suggests leaders have a range of behaviors that vary from controlling to hands-off. The difference between this leadership model and those previously proposed lies in that Tannenbaum and Schmidt were explicit about the variable behaviors in-between the two extreme endpoints, whereas other

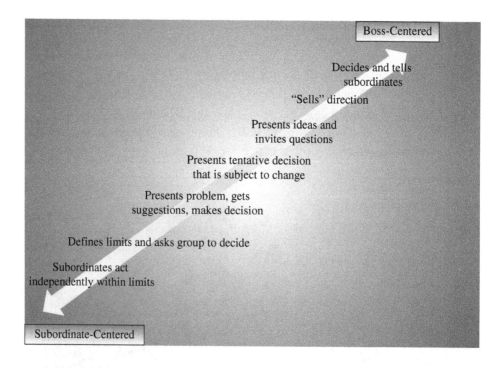

FIGURE 9.8 Continuum from Subordinate-Centered to Boss-Centered Leadership

Courtesy Zinta Byrne.

authors may have also felt the same but did not make the continuum of behavior as explicit. Instead, their models reflected more of a bipolar model of leadership.

Furthermore, Tannenbaum and Schmidt suggested that the most effective leader was one who "maintains a high batting average in accurately assessing the forces that determine what his most appropriate behavior at any given time should be and in actually being able to behave accordingly" (p. 101). This perspective provides a nice transition into the situational leadership approach, otherwise called the contingency approach, which refers to a leader who takes the situation into account.

Exercise 9.3

What is the behavioral approach of leadership? Different models have been proposed to explain the behaviors of leaders—draw them and briefly state what they essentially say about leadership.

Situation Makes the Leader: The Situational Approach

Though the behavioral approach to understanding leadership was instrumental in moving away from the "great man" concept and recognizing that how leaders treat their employees makes a difference, the idea that one set of behaviors is appropriate for every situation also falls short of explaining leadership. Not every situation calls for an authoritarian leadership style or a leader with innovative product ideas.

Fiedler's Contingency Model

Fiedler's (1964) contingency model of leadership represents one of the earliest theories of leadership that took into consideration both the leader's style and the demands of the situation. The model assumes leaders possess a fixed style, either task-oriented or relationship-oriented. Thus, to be effective, the leader must be placed in a situation that calls for their specific style. The model additionally suggests that the leader's effectiveness is dependent on situational control, which is defined as the degree to which the situation *allows* the leader to influence the group's behavior using the leader's unique style. In other words, some situations are conducive to task-oriented style leadership, such as those requiring structure (like a manufacturing plant), whereas in other situations the employees do not need as much task structure but instead need to feel valued (for example, high school teachers).

To use Fiedler's model, one must first identify whether the leader has a more relationship-oriented style or task-oriented style, and then second, consider the situation. Three situational factors impact the leader's ability to influence followers: (1) relationships with followers, (2) the power of influence that the leader's position allows, and (3) the structure of the task that the group needs to accomplish. Figure 9.9 shows which type of leadership style influences the group to perform well, given various combinations of the three situational factors (high vs. low, or strong vs. weak).

Fiedler suggested the most important of the three situational factors to consider was the relationship the leader has with group members. High and low levels of this situational factor (the relations row in Figure 9.9) are combined with structure of the task and positional power of the leader, resulting in eight octants. The best scenario is one in which the leader is liked by the group, the tasks are structured, and the leader has quite a bit of power (Octant I). It is most difficult for a leader to influence the group to high performance levels when the leader is not well liked (very poor relations), the tasks are structured or only vaguely structured, and the leader's power is weak (octants VI and VIII).

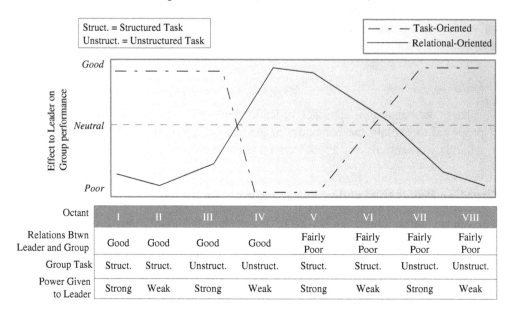

FIGURE 9.9 Fiedler's Contingency Model

Courtesy Zinta Byrne. Source: Fiedler, 1962, 1967, and Chemers et al., 1973.

To determine the leader's orientation (task vs. relational), Fiedler developed a measure called the Esteem for Least Preferred Coworker (LPC). The name can be confusing—the way it works is that the leader is asked to think of all people with whom the leader has ever worked, and using the 16–20 item LPC measure (see Figure 9.10 for sample items) describe the one with whom the leader would prefer to work with the least. Items are on a bipolar continuum, such as pleasant to unpleasant or gloomy to cheerful. The favorable pole items are scored with 8's and the unfavorable pole items with 1's. The sum of the item ratings gives a LPC score. A high LPC score (e.g., 120) means the leader considers even his or her least preferred coworker as someone who is actually pleasant, friendly, self-assured, cheerful, and enthusiastic. A high LPC score indicates a relational-oriented leader, whereas a low LPC score (e.g., 44) designates a task-oriented leader (Chemers, 1973). High LPC leaders are characterized as considerate and passive, and their influence results in good group performance when the conditions are moderately favorable—Octants IV through VI. Low LPC leaders are considered controlling, managing and directive, and work best in the worst and best favorable situations for the leader—Octants VII through VIII, and I through III.

A favorable situation exists when the leader is generally accepted and trusted by subordinates (good leader-member relations), the tasks for which individuals are responsible are clear and fully understood through formalization

Pleasant	1	2	3	4	5	6	7	8	Unpleasant
Friendly	1	2	3	4	5	6	7	8	Unfriendly
Tense	8	7	6	5	4	3	2	1	Relaxed
Open	1	2	3	4	5	6	7	8	Guarded
Gloomy	8	7	6	5	4	3	2	1	Cheerful

FIGURE 9.10 Sample of Items From Least Preferred Coworker (LPC)

and direction (high task structure), and the leader's power is recognized by senior management (strong position of power). Juxtapose that with the unfavorable situation characterized by the leader lacking acceptance or trust by subordinates (poor leader–member relations), the tasks for which individuals are responsible are unclear and not fully understood because of a lack of formalization and an absence of direction (low task structure), and the leader's power is not recognized by senior management (weak position power). In either a favorable or unfavorable situation, the leader with the task-oriented style should be the most effective. When the situation variables are mixed (i.e., moderately unfavorable and moderately favorable), the relations-oriented leader approach should be most effective. This leader will provide clear direction. When the situation is unfavorable, it's clear why the task-oriented leader is best. Relations are not good and people need structure. They need a leader to guide them to get the job done and win over senior management. So why is the task-oriented leader best for favorable situations? Because in a favorable situation, the leader-member relations are good, the task structure is high, and the position power is strong. This combination makes for an environment in which individuals are prepared to be guided by given a goal or direction, and they expect to be told what to do.

Research has questioned the validity of the LPC and Fiedler's suppositions that it assesses leadership style (Hare, Hare, & Blumberg, 1998; Kennedy, Houston, Korsgaard, & Gallo, 1987). Additionally, a meta-analysis conducted in the early 1990s showed that although contingency theory originally predicted that Octant I through III favored the low-LPC leader, studies reviewed in the meta-analysis showed that they were nearly equally effective, with the low-LPC leader only slightly more effective than the high-LPC leader. The analyses also showed that it wasn't until Octant VII before the low-LPC leader again overtook the high-LPC leader in effectiveness. Thus, the scope of effectiveness for the high-LPC leader was from Octants I through VII, and for low-LPC leaders, Octants I through III, and VIII (Schriesheim, Tepper, & Tetrault, 1994).

Fiedler's Contingency Model was important at its time because it suggested that leaders must consider the contextual environment. Theories that came after incorporated attention to the situation, though not in the same way that Fiedler did.

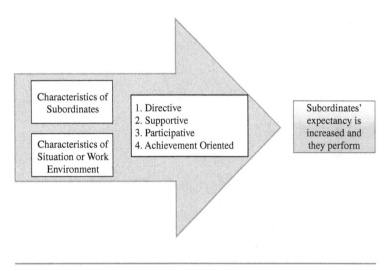

FIGURE 9.11 House's Path Goal Theory

Courtesy Zinta Byrne.

Why is the Contingency model of leadership valuable to understand/ learn if it's so complex and other theories have been proposed afterwards?

Path Goal Theory

Instead of relying on an ideal environment to encourage employees to perform, Path Goal Theory (House, 1971) suggested the leader creates the right environment. The theory suggests that leaders get employees motivated to perform by clarifying and endorsing the path that employees need to take toward successful goal achievement, and by increasing the value of attaining that goal for employees. When you understand how you can be successful in achieving a particular goal, and you value the goal that you're trying to achieve, the elements of expectancy theory (covered in Chapter 3 on Motivation) are maximized, and the outcome is that you are more likely to act toward achieving that goal. Path Goal Theory says that the leader provides that understanding and value. As stated by House (p. 324), "the motivational functions of the leader consist of increasing personal pay-offs to subordinates for work-goal attainment, and making the path to these pay-offs easier to travel by clarifying it, reducing road blocks and pit falls, and increasing the opportunities for personal satisfaction en route." When leaders clarify the path-goal relationship, they reduce role ambiguity (making it clear what employees are supposed to do), which in turn increases their motivation (Figure 9.11).

Meta-analyses results (Wofford & Liska, 1993), however, demonstrate that Path Goal Theory is not well supported. In general, leader behaviors (e.g., empowering, clarifying path to goal) were hypothesized to influence subordinate effectiveness depending on situational factors, but these findings were not consistently supported. Thus, we turn to other theories of how the leader and situation interact to influence follower behavior.

Vroom-Yetton-Jago

As mentioned previously, researchers have identified that leaders should be directive or participative, but just making this statement lacks clarification on when and with which situations the different styles of leadership are most effective. To help in this matter, Vroom and Yetton (1974) developed a model to guide a leader's decision as to when to use which form of leadership style. Recognizing that different situations call for different leadership approaches, Vroom and Yetton proposed that based on yes–no answers to a series of questions about a problem, the choice as to which style, directive or participative, becomes clear. For example, the first question to ask is whether it matters if one solution is qualitatively better than another—thus, this question focuses on the quality of the solution. If the answer is no, the next question asks, is the acceptance of the decision by subordinates important for effective implementation of the solution? If, however, the answer to the first question was yes, then the next step is to ask yourself whether you have sufficient information to make a high-quality decision. To determine if you can make that high-quality decision, you ask yourself a series of seven questions:

A. Is quality required?
B. Do I have enough information to make a quality decision?
C. Is the problem structured?
D. Do employees need to accept the decision to implement the solution effectively?
E. Will employees accept it if I make the decision alone?
F. Are employees' goals for solving this problem aligned with the organization's?
G. Will there be conflict among employees if we go with a preferred solution?

The overall flowchart of the series of yes–no questions that Vroom and Yetton developed looks something like Figure 9.12, where each decision in the diagram represents a choice of either one or more "rules" from which to select. An example rule is, you solve the problem or make the decision yourself. There are seven rules. The problem is stated and then the questions (A through G) are asked, depending on the answer to the previous question.

The decision flowchart becomes difficult to read very quickly, with each yes–no decision breaking into two paths (the no path is represented with a dashed red arrow, the yes path with a solid black arrow). Consequently, the practical utility of the model is questionable.

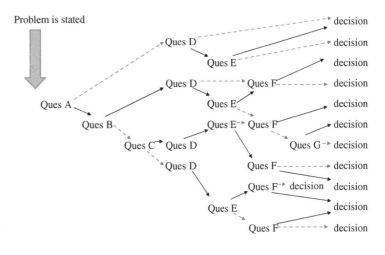

FIGURE 9.12   Vroom, Yetton, Yago Decision Tree

Courtesy Zinta Byrne. Source: Vroom and Yetton, 1974.

Put very simply, the most effective leadership style of directive, participative, or somewhere in between for solving a particular problem depends on whether a high-quality decision is required and whether the leader is trying to get employees' acceptance for the decision (as opposed to just getting compliance). Vroom and Jago (1988) identified five different decision styles that could be exhibited to handle the problem (Table 9.2), and these decision styles range from directive to participative.

Although initial studies by Vroom and colleagues supported the decision-tree model, later studies criticized methodological flaws, such as testing decisions on simplified situations and using retrospective decisions (Ayman, Chemers, & Fiedler, 1995). Additionally, managers made different choices depending on whether the problem concerned a single individual or a group. Vroom and Yetton (1973) and Vroom and Jago (1974) added to the original model (hence the name Vroom-Yetton-Jago) by considering additional contingency factors, such as whether employees had the knowledge and time to engage in problem solving, and whether geographic dispersion was a

TABLE 9.2   Five Decision Styles

Decision Style	Action
Autocratic I	Problem is solved by the person who has the necessary information at the time.
Autocratic II	Leader makes the decision, but first asks for helpful information from subordinates.
Consultative I	Leader shares problem with subordinates to get their input, one at a time, but then makes decision on his or her own, and may or may not use the input received.
Consultative II	Leader shares problem with subordinates as a group to get their input, but then makes decision on his or her own, and may or may not use the input received.
Group I	Leader shares problem with subordinates as a group to get their input, and a decision is then made together. Leader facilitates the group, but does not push an agenda.

Courtesy Zinta Byrne. Source: Vroom & Jago, 1988.

The situational approach to leadership suggests that leaders must change their style depending on the demands of the situation. Thus, the effectiveness of the leader is an outcome of the interaction between the leader and situation.

factor in the decision-making process since location affects the quality of directive versus participative decision making. Though Vroom and Jago improved the validity of the original model (Jago, Ettling, & Vroom, 1985), they also complicated it by changing the yes-no answers to a 5-point rating system. Recent research using rigorous scientific approaches has shown limited support for the model (see Field & Andrews, 1998; Field & House, 1990; Parker, 1999). Perhaps, the model's greatest value is when it is used for training managers and leaders to be more deliberate in their decision-making.

> **Exercise 9.4**
>
> Compare and contrast the situational leadership theories. What distinguishes them from each other, what do they have in common, and in what situations specifically would the theories be most useful? For example, when would you use Fiedler's model over Path Goal Theory?

Newer Leadership Theories

Newer leadership theories have been developed based on what we've learned in the past using the theories reviewed thus far. By advancing the idea that leadership results from a combination of the leader, the leader's behavior, and the situation, new theories use the initial propositions that (a) leaders possessed unique characteristics or traits (not necessarily inborn), (b) leader behaviors affect followers, and (c) the situation sets the context for when the unique combination of traits with behaviors will have the most powerful effect. In addition, new theories acknowledge that leaders have unique relationships with their followers. The vertical dyad linkage is a great example of a theory that acknowledges the unique relationship leaders have with their followers.

Vertical Dyad Linkage

Unlike previous approaches to understanding leadership, where the focus was on how the leader influenced a group of followers, the Vertical Dyad Linkage approach (Dansereau, Cashman, & Graen, 1973) proposed that the leader forms special relationships with each follower (employee), and that these relationships influence the leader's behaviors. Thus, the leader will act differently with different members of the overall team and the best way to understand leadership is to focus on these relationships. The distinguishing feature of this model is the focus on the dyadic relationship between the leader and a member of the follower group (in organizations, this is typically the leader's direct subordinates). Past leadership theories reviewed thus far suggested the leader is consistent with group members, but the Vertical Dyad Linkage model suggests this is not the case. Additionally, group members in turn behave differently as a result of how the leader treats them, resulting in a reciprocal or dyadic connection (i.e., linkage) between the leader's behavior and each group member's behavior. The model is based on social exchange theory (Blau, 1964; also see Graen & Uhl-Bien, 1995), which states that individuals form a relationship wherein "one" obligates the "other" to reciprocate by the one first supplying services or some kind of benefit (not financial) that the "other" finds valuable. Through the norms of reciprocity (Gouldner, 1960), the "other" then responds to the obligation by reciprocating with something of comparable value. This back and forth giving and receiving sets up a pattern of trust whereby each party expects and assumes the other person will at some point reciprocate.

Social exchange does not rely on financial or contractual agreements, which are considered principles of an economic exchange. For instance, you sign an employment contract with your employer wherein you agree to perform in exchange for a salary. Instead, social exchange is based on the trade of services or products of social value, such as supervisory support in return for performance at work. Additionally, there is no time element to social exchanges—the reciprocation need not occur immediately, but should happen at some point after the initial receipt of services that obligate the return. In the case of the vertical dyad linkage, the leader gives the subordinate attention and support (Dansereau, Graen, & Haga, 1975) and the subordinate may reciprocate with high performance and insights on morale and worker motivations to which the leader is otherwise not privy. Those without a vertical link to the leader do not enjoy this give and take relationship with the leader.

Advances to Vertical Dyad Linkage theory were based on a longitudinal study (Dansereau et al., 1975) that made a distinction between leaders and supervisors, separated group members into the "in-group" (people close to and preferred by the leader) and the "out-group" (people not close to or preferred by the leader) and identified the leader-subordinate relationship as a "superior-member exchange" (p. 72). Specifically, supervisors were considered equivalent to managers, and the distinction between leader and manager is similar to that described in Chapter 8 and in the beginning of this chapter. The longitudinal study revealed that membership in the in-group meant receiving more and complete information from the supervisor, and being included in decision making. Being a member of the out-group meant not getting as much attention as the in-group and not having as much support from the supervisor as those in the in-group. Lastly, out-group members reported having problems with the supervisor and supervisors reported having problems with out-group subordinates' understanding of expectations, which did not occur with the in-group (Figure 9.13). This vertical dyad linkage between the supervisor and subordinate, characterized by a social exchange relationship, was later called leader–member exchange (LMX: Graen & Schiemann, 1978).

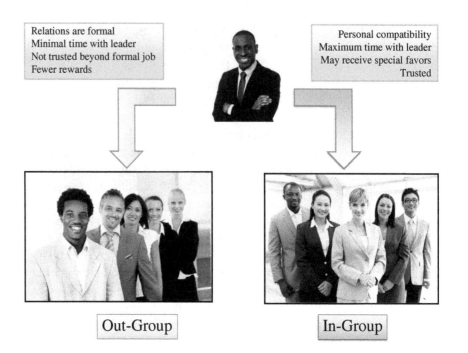

FIGURE 9.13 Vertical Dyad Linkage

Clockwise: © stockyimages/Shutterstock, Inc.; © Andrey_Popov/Shutterstock, Inc.; © Rawpixel/Shutterstock, Inc.

Why is Vroom-Yetton-Jago's model still valuable today?

LMX has long since replaced Vertical Dyad Linkage, and remains an influential theory of leadership at a micro-level—leader/follower relationship, as opposed to leader/many followers. Many studies support the propositions of LMX. For example, recent work on cross-culture studies have shown the social exchange nature of the LMX relationship across cultures appears universal, demonstrating that at least this theory developed in the United States is applicable in other cultural contexts—that is, there were no cultural differences in recognizing LMX exists. However, the effects of LMX on employee citizenship behavior, job satisfaction, and turnover intentions are stronger in Western cultures than Eastern, but that LMX effects on task performance (i.e., doing the job you're hired to do) appear no different across cultures (Rockstuhl, Dulebohn, Ang, & Shore, 2012). Additionally, recent meta-analyses results show that leader behaviors, rather than the subordinate perceptions or actions, essentially determine the quality of LMX (Dulebohn, Bommer, Liden, Brouer, & Ferris, 2012). Thus, the LMX leader who rewards, coaches, provides direction, and encourages participation is more likely to have strong LMX relationships because such behaviors suggest the leader cares about the employee. The behaviors most noted in forming strong LMX relations include transactional and transformational—reviewed next.

Charismatic, Transactional, and Transformational Leadership

Even though the "great man" theory has long been put to rest, recent approaches to leadership brought back the idea that effective leaders tend to have extraordinary qualities *in addition to* behaving in effective ways, and this combination has a powerful effect on followers and the relationships that ensue. Charismatic and transformational leadership (Bass, 1985; Burns, 1978) incorporate attention to the influence of the situation, but they also suggest effective leaders in specific situations rely on traits or characteristics not everyone possesses, though can develop.

Charismatic leadership theory (Burns, 1978; Fromm, 1941) proposes charismatic leaders are confident, convey a sense of strong purpose, are articulate about their goals, and able to emotionally excite followers about their goal (Bass, 1990). Good examples of charismatic leaders include Nelson Mandela, Eva Peron, and Bill Clinton. They are characterized by their visionary and ideological goals, savvy style that exudes confidence (Figure 9.14), and an undeniable ability to use their gift for communication to inspire employees to create and achieve (Conger & Kanungo, 1987). The key attribute of the charismatic leader is that followers are overwhelmingly drawn to and attracted to this person in a near cult-like manner, hanging onto the

FIGURE 9.14   Charismatic Leaders

leader's every word (Trice & Beyer, 1986), and as a consequence of the leader's charisma, followers do as the leader wants. Examples of charismatic leaders in history include people like Martin Luther King Jr., Mahatma Gandhi, and Nelson Mandela. Whether you or your politics favor these folks (or not), Bill Clinton, Ronald Reagan, Bernadette Devlin, and Manny Pacquiao have been considered charismatic by various groups. What they all have in common is the ability to inspire their followers through words. Different from trait theories of leadership, consideration as a charismatic leader requires the leader behave in a way that causes people to perceive and attribute charisma to the leader—thus, the leader is considered charismatic because of their behavior, not because of the position they serve or simply because they are a leader (Conger & Kanungo, 1987; House, Woycke, & Fodor, 1988). The concept of a charismatic leader is not new—it has existed for quite some time in Greek and Biblical writings, as well as political and sociological studies (see Conger & Kanungo, 1987, for a review); however, within the workplace, the introduction of the concept is given credit to the works of Burns and Bass in the 70s and 80s.

Transformational leadership theory incorporates charismatic leadership and puts forth that leadership requires the ability to align subordinates' goals with those of the organization, providing an inspiring vision that motivates employees to take ownership of the success of the organization and perform beyond their own original expectations (Bass, 1985). Furthermore, transformational leadership style is delineated into four competencies: *inspirational motivation*, which refers to the ability to communicate clearly and effectively in such a way that followers are inspired to achieve; *idealized influence*, which refers to being a role model for followers by displaying strong ethical principles and emphasizing group gains over individual benefits; *individualized consideration*, the way in which leaders treat employees as individuals, demonstrating an appreciation for their unique contributions and needs; and, *intellectual stimulation*, the ability to encourage employees to believe in their own creativity and push them to challenge their own thinking. The transformational leader exhibits these four competencies to encourage employees to higher levels of performance than they have previously displayed, and do so without the use of coercive power or promises of some reward, such as higher pay that may temporarily motivate, but loses its effect over time (see Chapter 3 on Motivation). Their focus on positive relations with employees leads to a high quality leader-follower interaction that positively relates to employee mental health (Montano, Reeske, Franke, & Hüffmeier, 2017). Examples of transformational leaders include Michael Bloomberg, Richard Branson, Julius Caesar, Adolf Hitler, and Elon Musk.

Transformational leadership is often contrasted with transactional leadership (Burns, 1978), though the two styles may complement one another. Transactional leadership is exemplified by attention to the tasks that need accomplishing and are accomplished through a transaction exchange relationship with followers (i.e., task completion traded for rewards; Burns, 1978). The leader who uses a purely transactional leadership style explains what is needed to get the task done, and then exchanges rewards, benefits, and other tangible offerings to motivate followers to complete the tasks. Examples of transactional leaders include Charles de Gaulle, Bill Gates, and Norman Schwarzkopf.

The effect of transformational leadership, the focus on the joint ownership of organizational success, on followers is somewhat dependent on one's country culture. Research by Leong and Fischer (2011) shows that how transformational leadership is perceived varies by culture because of cultural expectations. For example, egalitarian cultures expect leaders to take care of employees, whereas mastery cultures expect leaders to be domineering and directive, telling employees what to do. In cultures that expect leaders to empower their followers, transformational leadership is viewed more positively than in cultures where the leader is expected to act more transactional or even dictatorial. Contrary to Leong et al.'s findings, however, other research suggests that transformational leaders are equally valued regardless of culture (Javidan, Dorfman, de Luque, & House, 2006). Perhaps a good way to reconcile the differing conclusions is to acknowledge that in some cases, transformation leadership might be viewed positively and in others, it might not be considered as powerful as transactional leadership. Your best bet is to pay attention to the country culture and general work environment, and ask questions about how things work.

Transformational leadership has sparked tremendous research interest. Recent work has extended the theory into other forms of transformational leadership most appropriate for efforts in environmental sustainability and social responsibility—corporations recognizing their impact on community and attempting to control negative effects while maximizing positive.

Servant Leadership   As an extension to transformational leadership, servant leadership is typified by leaders attending to their followers and building trust rather than just transforming followers' beliefs and behaviors to align them with organizational goals (Ehrhart, 2004; Greenleaf, 1970; van Dierendonck, 2011). This form of leadership adds a component of social responsibility to transformational leadership (Graham, 1991), while incorporating elements of transformational leadership such as vision, pioneering, and encouragement (Russell & Stone, 2002). Examples of servant leaders include Mother Teresa, Mahatma Gandhi, Martin Luther King, Jr., and Abraham Lincoln. The biggest difference between transformational and servant leadership is the focus of the leader's and subordinates' attention; transformational leaders and followers focus on the leader and on the goals of the organization, whereas servant leaders and their followers focus on the development of the followers (Graham, 1991; Parolini, Patterson, & Winston, 2009; Stone & Russell, 2004). Servant leaders are perceived as putting their followers' needs above their own. Servant leadership contributes to the perspective that leaders influence their subordinates by emphasizing the relationship and empowering subordinates through trust.

Although servant leadership has garnished some recent interest in the literature, transformational leadership has remained one of the most prominent leader theories for some time. The most recent addition to the leader theory portfolio is full range leadership theory and authentic leadership theory, which are both extensions of transformational leadership theory.

Full Range Leadership Theory

Transformational leadership theory fostered a lot of excitement among practitioners and researchers, alike, because it reenergized the interest in leader traits or characteristics that make for exceptional leadership and aimed the spotlight on the leader's relationship with followers. The next few theories continue to expand on transformational leadership theory and illustrate how leadership theories have become nearly exclusively focused on the leader and followers, as opposed to the situation, as was so heavily featured in the contingency models of leadership, such as Fiedler's Contingency Theory.

Bass and colleagues (Avolio, 1999; Avolio & Bass, 1991; Avolio, Waldman, & Yammarino, 1991; Bass, 1998; Bass & Avolio, 1994) expanded transformational leadership theory to include nine core factors: five transformational, three transactional, and one nontransactional laissez-faire leadership component. The five transformational elements include *idealized influence attributed*, which refers to the leader's charisma and being viewed as ethical; *idealized influence behavior*, which refers to the leader's charismatic actions centered on core values and beliefs aligned with the mission; *inspirational motivation, intellectual stimulation*, and *individualized consideration* as described previously under transformational leadership. Transactional leadership included: *contingent reward leadership*, which refers to the leader's attention to role clarity and providing material or psychological rewards in exchange for performance; *management-by-exception active*, which refers to how actively vigil the leader is in ensuring standards are met; and *management-by-exception passive*, which refers to leaders who intervene only when employees do not comply with the standards. The *nontransactional laissez-faire leadership* component refers to the deliberate absence of actions such as a leader avoiding decision making, giving up responsibility when it should be retained, or not using authority when they should.

The full range theory of leadership proposes every leader has varying degrees of these nine factors, and depending on the balance of factors, the leaders is either a role model or a nonleader. Avolio (1999) also proposed four principles at the core of leadership. Principle 1 states good leaders balance the management of their vulnerabilities, embracing and confronting them rather than avoiding them. Principle 2 reinforces the idea of the relationship between leaders and followers as based on commitment rather than compliance. Principle 3 focuses on how the leaders we trust most are those with whom we identify and those we see as vulnerable. Lastly, Principle 4 states good leaders understand the situation from all perspectives and manage the situation successfully.

The full range leadership theory received its name because it attempted to pull together theories that described the full scope of behaviors leaders could exhibit for effective leadership. Thus, combining transformational, transactional, charismatic, and laissez-faire leadership styles created a single theoretical framework of leadership components. As a precursor to authentic leadership theory, described next, Avolio (1999) offered the additional four principles (described in the previous paragraph) to move leadership theories in the direction of ethical leadership. The four principles are captured in the authentic leadership theory, one of the last and most recent theories of leadership proposed in the literature.

Authentic Leadership Theory

Authentic leadership theory offers an improvement to ethical and transformational leadership (Avolio, Gardner, Walumbwa, Luthans, & May, 2004), and is one of the most recently introduced theories of leadership; hence, the least well studied. Authentic leadership is defined as a process wherein the leader acts consistently with their personal beliefs and values, which in turn foster trust and attributions of credibility. The core of authentic leadership avoids describing leaders' behavior in prescribed ways, but rather suggests that as they become more genuine, they become more self-aware and remain true to themselves.

Highly authentic leaders are those who know themselves. They know their weaknesses and strengths, how they react given different situations, their beliefs and values and when those are critical to their core self, and how to interact with others in an open and original way. Additionally, Avolio et al. describe authentic leaders as those who are not only aware of themselves and others', but also aware of the context or situation (Figure 9.15). Consistent in the presentation of their persona to followers and leaders at organizational levels above them, they demonstrate a lack of political maneuvering often seen when leaders act one way with employees but another way with leaders or other colleagues higher up in the organizational hierarchy. Authentic leadership draws from transformational leadership through connecting with follower's values and beliefs, and showing them how their values and beliefs can be incorporated into a joint vision. Authentic leaders lead by example, role modeling how to be a leader, and by focusing on what is right and ethical or moral, not necessarily focusing on profitability at the expense of all other routes to effectiveness. Examples of authentic leaders might include Howard Schultz, Anne Mulcahy, Eleanor Roosevelt, and Ed Whitacre. Some suggest Barack Obama fits into this type of leadership style, as well.

With regards to how they motivate their followers, the authentic leader does so by engaging employees in identifying with them on a personal level and through encouraging a social identification with the organization. As described in these ways, authentic leaders may at times be vulnerable to criticism because they have exposed and

FIGURE 9.15 Authentic Leadership

made transparent their values and beliefs. However, because authentic leaders understand themselves and appreciate others' values, strengths, and weaknesses, they may use the criticism to develop stronger relationships with others or even improve their own approach or themselves. Such leaders create hope, trust, optimism, and positive energy, resulting in a positive interchange between the leader and followers (Avolio et al., 2004).

> Authentic leaders sound almost too amazing to be true, yet they do exist. Can you think of a leader or supervisor you have had who fits at least some of the descriptions of the authentic leader?

Preliminary results of research studies show that authentic leadership is positively related to job satisfaction, job performance, commitment, and team outcomes (e.g., Hannah, Walumbwa, & Fry, 2011; Peterson, Walumbwa, Avolio, & Hannah, 2012; Peus, Wesche, Streicher, Braun, & Frey, 2012; Wang, Sui, Luthans, Wang, & Wu, 2014). Yet, so are other forms of leadership, such as transformational and charismatic (Chiaburu, Smith, Wang, & Zimmerman, 2014; Conger, 2013). The unique facet of authentic leadership that sets it apart from all previous theories is its core emphasis on moral and ethical leadership (Avolio & Wernsing, 2008). A relatively new dilemma for authentic leadership theory is the very notion of authenticity (Fine, 2017). Leaders who identify as LGBTQ may struggle with being fully authentic in work environments where norms reinforce heterosexuality and male/female stereotypes, such that being authentic carries career and potential personal risk.

> Fine (2017) provides a comprehensive challenge of authentic leadership theory for the LGBTQ community.

Other theories of leadership may incorporate some of the components of authentic leadership, such as establishing a joint vision or being open (e.g., transformational, full range), but none include an emphasis on ethical leadership, transparency of values and beliefs, or on consistency between actions, communications, values, and beliefs, which all make for moral and ethical leadership. Because of the newness of the theory, not many studies have examined authentic leadership theory as of yet.

Exercise 9.5

How is the full range model of leadership different from its predecessors? What makes the vertical-dyad model different from transformational leadership theory? Before moving on to the next pages, develop a matrix that lists the different theories comprising full range and vertical-dyad, and fill the cells with the characteristics of those theories that make them unique from one another.

> A recent meta-analyses shows that transformational leadership and authentic leadership are highly correlated, as are transformational and ethical leadership. Additionally, if you want to predict/explain citizenship behavior, engagement, job satisfaction, commitment, trust, or LMX, including a measure of servant leadership with one of these other forms of leadership would be advised. See Hoch, Bommer, Dulebohn, and Wu's 2018 meta-analysis for all the details.

Complexity Theory of Leadership

Though not really a theory of leadership per se, complexity theory of leadership recognizes the dynamic forces that push on organizations and their leaders, creating an unpredictability to what is needed from leaders and when. Complexity theory refers to a science of dynamic and natural interactions, characterized by uncertainty, unpredictability, and complexity (Marion & Uhl-Bien, 2001). It is not actually a single theory, but rather describes *an approach* used in many fields, not just organizational psychology or organizational behavior. Complexity science proposes that we view "organizations as complex adaptive systems composed of a diversity of agents who interact with one another, mutually affect one another, and in doing so generate novel behavior for the system as a whole" (p. 390). Thus, leadership under this approach is (a) exemplified by understanding and drawing on the dynamic and interactive relationship between employees with each other and their work environment; (b) recognizing that planning, controlling, and predicting every aspect of the organization and its direction is simply not possible; and (c) creating the right conditions for employees to innovate.

Like authentic leadership, complexity theory of leadership suggests that transformational, transactional, and servant leadership theories are not enough to reflect the dynamic interchange between leaders, followers, and the environment necessary for leaders to create and maintain effective organizations. Leaders must be flexible and cocreators of the work environment, handling changes as they occur and adapting their approach in a behavior by situation by trait interaction. Complexity theory concedes that continuous change, adaption, and innovation are necessary for flourishing, and when applied to leadership, complexity theory provides the framework for moving leadership beyond a static set of behaviors and traits. By attempting to control the environment through exhibiting prescribed behaviors or determined traits, the leader prevents employees from expressing the creativity necessary for innovation and discovery. At the core of complexity theory is adaptation—the leader must be flexible and adaptive to the needs of the every changing, unpredictable organizational environment. Clearly, given the nonprescriptive nature of the theory, complexity leadership requires unique leader training (e.g., Keene, 2000). Like authentic leadership theory, few studies have yet examined complexity theory of leadership; therefore, little can be concluded thus far about the effectiveness of complexity theory of leadership over other forms of leadership, such as authentic leadership.

Strategic Leadership

The last theory to include under "New Leadership Theories" is strategic leadership, defined as "a person's ability to anticipate, envision, maintain flexibility, think strategically, and work with others to initiate changes that will create a viable future for the organization" (Ireland & Hitt, 2005, p. 63). Strategic leadership comprises six components, which when completed successfully culminate in a vision and strategic direction (see Chapter 13 for Strategy) for the organization that secures its competitive advantage. At the core of this approach is the acceptance that environments and economic conditions are unpredictable and always will be, not unlike that described in complexity theory of leadership. Additionally, the strategic leader represents a concept beyond a position or rank; instead, the concept signifies a leader who empowers employees and stakeholders to partner with them to develop answers to the challenges that lie ahead. Thus, effective strategic leadership entails innovative leadership practices that capitalize on learning from the past, while maximizing future potential through flexibility and a clear vision or direction for the future. The theory does not draw from the previous trait, behavioral, or situational leadership theories, but instead focuses on how a leader must keep the organization focusing on its strategy.

Ireland and Hitt proposed the following six components of strategic leadership:

1. *creating the organization's purpose and vision* (the reason the organization exists; described more in Chapter 13)

2. *developing, using, and maintaining core competencies,* which refers to resources, skills, and capability (what the organization is known for producing or offering)

3. *growing* **human capital**, which refers to developing the knowledge and skills of employees in the organization so they fulfill their potential and become organizational citizens, rather than just laborers

4. *shaping and sustaining an effective organizational culture*, which refers to the set of norms, values, and shared beliefs that exist in an organization. In an effective culture, employees recognize the changing nature of economic markets and outside forces on the organization, and as citizens of the organization they keep it innovative, progressive, and competitive.

5. *embracing and emphasizing ethical practices*

6. *establishing balanced organizational controls*, which are the formal and informal procedures leaders use to maintain employee performance.

The new theories of leadership take into account previous models proposing the importance of leader traits and behaviors, and the situation, but also emphasize the leader-follower relationship and the authenticity of the leader.

Thus, strategic leadership embraces the responsibilities of the leader, as opposed to focusing on how the leader should act or be.

Making Sense of All the Models

With so many leadership models, a summarizing chart of their distinguishing characteristics and practical use comes in handy. Table 9.3 provides an alphabetized summary of the theories reviewed in the above sections, what you can use to recognize the theory, and the theory's practical value.

TABLE 9.3   Summary of Theories of Leadership

Theory	Distinguishing Characteristics	Use in Practice
Authentic	"Real" and "genuine"; core emphasis is on moral and ethical	Being authentic requires a strong personality and capacity for being moral, ethical, consistent, and transparent. This framework is good for training. Being an authentic leader is great for situations where trust was previously an issue or the past leaders were unethical.
Charismatic, Transactional, Transformational	Directive vs. Visionary and Savvy	There's a place and time for being directive and focusing on task accomplishment, vs. being dreamy and suave. The practical utility of this theory is to learn how to be whichever style is needed at that time, because they each work. Transformational tends to be effective across situations.
Complexity theory	Direction in the midst of unpredictability	This theory can be applied to leadership in start-ups and situations where change is the norm (e.g., environmental sustainability).
Consideration vs. Initiating Structure	Caring, people-oriented vs. directive, assigning standards for efficiency.	Figure out what kind of leader you are, and use that strength. However, also take time to develop skills in the opposing style, so that you can draw on them when the situation requires. Consideration is more strongly related to motivated followers, but structure is more strongly related to follower performance.

(continued)

TABLE 9.3 Summary of Theories of Leadership (*continued*)

Theory	Distinguishing Characteristics	Use in Practice
Fiedler's Contingency	Least Preferred Coworker; leader style is fixed	Learn your style as a manager and only accept leadership in a situation that fits your style, or where you can modify the situation to fit your style. The LPC and its accompanying theory have limited practical use.
Full Range	Combination of traits and transformational	This model is great for training. Its direct practical utility beyond that is unclear as of yet.
Path Goal Theory	Leaders show you the way	Not many practical uses exist for this theory since the research hasn't supported its suppositions.
Strategic leadership	Strategy	The practical use of this model is in situations where the future is the focus—such as when the organization is in an entrepreneurial state. The framework is good for organizations charting a new course.
Theory X/Y	Authoritarian vs. democratic	Theory Y managers convey more fairness and greater employee commitment than Theory X managers. The theory might have limited practical utility beyond identifying a more autocratic vs. democratic style.
Trait	Known as the "great man theory" of leadership. Leaders tend to have distinctive traits.	Recognize that some people still believe traits make the leader; so, if you don't have "the trait" you'll have to work harder to convince supporters to pick you for leadership roles and to see you as a leader while you're in that role. Some traits are useful in predicting leader emergence, such as extraversion and conscientiousness.
Vertical Dyad Linkage	Leader-follower relationship	Replaced by LMX. The practical utility of the theory is that the best approach for a follower is to get into the in-group of the leader because this will lead to better assignments and insider information about the organization. For the leader, the best use of the theory is to form leader member relations since these will lead to more information and helpful subordinates.
Vroom-Yetton-Jago	Decision-tree	This theory is hard to use because you cannot turn to the decision-tree to determine every choice before the decision must be made. The potential value of this theory lies in training purposes — leaders can be coached on how to be more deliberate in their decision-making.

Courtesy Zinta Byrne.

Aside from the knowledge we've gained from the progression of theories of leadership, we also know that leadership must be considered within the culture it sits, and that the gender of the leader does matter. Research on both areas is reviewed next.

Country or National Culture

Though changing over the last decade, most of what we understand about leadership has been derived from studies in Western cultures. For example, Takahashi, Ishikawa, and Kanai (2012) argue that leadership differs in Japan because of the cultural differences. Japanese culture is characterized as **collectivistic** (Hofstede, 1991), which means that people care more about fitting in, the tendency is think "we" rather than "I", there is an emphasis on belonging and getting along with others rather than on being independent, and there is an emphasis on loyalty, obligation, duty, and social stability (Hofstede, 1983). Hence, Takahashi et al. suggested that leadership in Japan is influenced by the powerful social relationships between leaders and their employees, more so than in **individualistic** cultures where making one's own decision and striving for uniqueness is of greatest value. The results of their study showed that some leadership theories carry over to the Japanese work context (e.g., leader–member exchange, contingency theories), whereas others such as transformational leadership do not work as well, indicating that leadership theories are context/culture dependent.

Like Japan, China is considered a collectivistic culture as well (Hofstede, 1991), yet studies within China led to different conclusions than those by Takahashi et al., in Japan, indicating that something other than just culture makes a difference. Leung and Bozionelos (2004) studied 101 Chinese men and women working in the Hong Kong area, examining perceptions of leadership and personality. They were interested in which of the Big-Five personality traits and characteristics of transformational leadership were considered most prototypical of an effective leader in China. They found that effective leaders were considered by followers as those who were extraverted, conscientious, agreeable, emotionally stable (so low scores on Neuroticism), and open to new experiences, in this order of importance. Effective leaders were also perceived as being transformational in style. Importantly, however, although they expected gender differences, the authors found none in employees' prototypes—both men and women reported the same personality and style characteristics of effective leaders.

Differences were found, however, in the importance of personality traits by gender. Specifically, men rated extraversion and then conscientiousness as the top two personality traits for leaders, whereas the women rated extraversion and then agreeableness as the top two personality traits. These findings suggest that leadership studies in Western cultures may be relevant, at least to some degree, in Eastern cultures—that is, the Western studies should not be completely discounted; many of the results do seem to apply to leaders across the globe. Still, others have found evidence that caution in applying Western beliefs to Eastern cultures is necessary, as implicit prototypes of effective leaders may not carry over. For instance, Harms, Han, and Chen (2012) showed that Western culture participants implicitly associated leadership effectiveness with emotional positivity, intelligence, and dominance. These perceived characteristics of effective leaders were, however, not predictive of actual leader effectiveness of Chinese CEOs—actual leader effectiveness was associated with risk taking, replicating previous study findings, and was not one of the characteristics that Western raters applied to effective leadership. Regardless, their research adds to previous work demonstrating similar cultural findings (e.g., Albright et al., 1997).

The conclusion here is that national/country culture plays a role in the interpretation of and expectations of leadership, and that assuming theories developing in the United States should port over to other countries leads to errors. A blatant example of this might be assuming leadership theories developed in the U.S. apply to countries like Saudi Arabia, where up until very recently, the "born into leadership" philosophy was alive and well (Kattan et al., 2016). Thus, unless you are male and born into a royal family or very wealthy family, you can never be a leader. Research is needed to test the theories and determine if relationships found in U.S. research hold up in studies across cultures. Leung and Bozionelos' (2004) findings suggest that most theories should be applicable, but Takahashi et al.'s suggested they need to be tested. Therefore, caution should be used when attempting to apply leadership theories in countries other than where they were studied in the research literature.

Sex

"Gender" is often interchanged with "sex" however, the two terms are indeed different. Gender refers to social roles and sex refers to biological and physiological characteristics. For many years, gender stereotypes have been strongly reinforced such that being female required also conveying feminine characteristics and mannerisms, and being male required conveying masculine characteristics and behaviors. While these strong stereotypes are being actively challenged in todays society (e.g., bisexual, transgender), much of the research in leadership has not caught up - hence gender differences studied to date are primarily sex differences - between males and females. There are a few exceptions. Specifically, Morton (2017) found that followers with strong negative attitudes towards gay men rated gay male leaders as less effective than heterosexual male leaders. Followers without negative attitudes towards gay men rated both gay male leaders and heterosexual male leaders equally effective. A popular and long held assumption is that men make better leaders than do women. But is it true that men are better leaders than women? Recent research shows that men seem to think so, but are reluctant to explicitly rate men leaders more highly than they do women leaders. In an interesting study, Latu and colleagues (2011) examined 301 college students (70% female, 44% Caucasian, 31% African–American, 13% Asian) asking them to group lists of positive and negative workplace traits into four categories: female, male, good, or bad. Using an implicit association test (a test that assesses implicit or felt but not expressed attitudes rather than explicit, expressed attitudes), the authors found that male participants demonstrated greater levels of implicit associations between men and leader success than women and leader success. The opposite was true for female participants; they implicitly associated females with greater success than men. The difference in the association was greater for men—that is, they were more likely to report a greater level of association between men and success than women were with women and success (hence, women were harder on women than men were on women!). Neither group explicitly rated any one gender as more successful than the other.

The implications of their findings for leadership are that if men implicitly associate men with being stronger leaders than women, they are more likely to unconsciously choose and reward men for their leader behavior than are women. Additionally, though their explicit ratings were nonbiased, the results of the study show that people still think differently about the abilities of men and women to lead, which may affect other decisions and actions that indirectly and over the long run affect women's ability to take on top leadership roles.

Studies of women leaders (Figure 9.16) have shown that those who appear stereotypically masculine (e.g., no make-up, conservative dark suit) tend to be perceived as more competent than those who appear stereotypically feminine

Can you think of a time when you had a good male boss and a time when you had a good female boss? What made them good bosses? What about a boss who did not identify as male or female (e.g., both, neither)?

(Sczesny & Kühnen, 2004; Sczesny, Spreemann, & Stahlberg, 2006). Consistent with these findings, women who were rated as attractive were considered less capable as leaders than those considered less attractive or unattractive (Eagly & Karau, 2002; Langlois et al., 2000). Little, if any, research thus far has been conducted on transgender leaders' and whether they are more, less, or equally effective.

Rule and Ambady (2009) conducted a study where participants judged pictures of 20 female CEOs and 46 male CEOs, rating them on perceived leadership, competence, dominance, facial maturity (i.e., baby-face, which is considered round faced, large eyes, small nose, high forehead, and small chin indicates less maturity; Zebrowitz & Montepare, 2005), likeability, and trustworthiness. They found there were no differences between the genders' ratings except that men rated male CEOs higher in dominance and facial maturity than female CEOs. Dominance and facial maturity are corre-

FIGURE 9.16   Female Leaders

Right: © wernerimages/Shutterstock, Inc.; Left: © Jeanette Dietl/Shutterstock, Inc.

lated (Zebrowitz, 1997), which may also explain Wong et al.'s (2011) findings regarding facial height to length ratio (discussed previously in this chapter).

Rule and Ambady also demonstrated that CEOs who were rated as competent and likely to succeed based on facial appearance (i.e., masculine, mature), led companies that were more profitable—this was the same for both men and women CEOs.

Do you think that these cumulative results suggest that to be a successful woman CEO you must forgo all makeup? Look at Figure 9.17, and pick the face you think looks most trustworthy, competent, and likeable.

A recent study by Etcoff et al. (2011) showed that women executives wearing a moderate amount of makeup were considered more trustworthy, competent, and likeable than those wearing no makeup, a little makeup (natural look), and a lot of makeup (glamorous look). These conclusions were achieved after participants were shown three women's faces with and without makeup for 250 milliseconds. Even after longer inspection, the results were the same. In Figure 9.17, the amount of makeup worn increases from left to right, with the first image on the left wearing virtually no makeup, the second sports a natural look, the third is more dramatic, and the fourth would be considered a lot of makeup. Although the faces shown in Figure 9.17 are not those from Etcoff et al.'s study, they are similar in the amount of makeup shown.

Why should a leader consider the national or country culture of employees?

With so many theories about leaders and research findings about differences in perceptions of success based on culture and gender, determining how to develop good leaders may seem a daunting task. Thankfully, there are a number

FIGURE 9.17   Differences in Makeup (Faces are approximately the same size)

Left: © Subbotina Anna/Shutterstock, Inc.; Middle left: © via khorzhevska/Shutterstock, Inc.; Middle right: © Yuri Shevtsov/Shutterstock, Inc.; Right: © Valua Vitaly/Shutterstock, Inc.

of books available on how to become a leader, although most are based on either a single organization and their anecdotal findings of leadership training, or on the philosophies of the book author who may provide little empirical foundation.

How do we Develop Good Leaders?

Some researchers have noted that the practice of leadership development supersedes the research on leadership development (Day, 2001), which suggests that some practice is not evidence-based.

However, a recent meta-analysis showed that leadership training is indeed effective. Data from 335 independent studies showed that leadership training can improve on the job leadership behaviors and performance, and lead to increases in subordinate outcomes (Lacerenza et al., 2017). Researchers have found cultural differences in leadership - namely, in China, ethical leaders must be both a moral person and a moral manager. Showing you are a moral person means exhibiting a fully moral person including kind-hearted, compassionate, and altruistic (Zhu, Zheng, He, Wang, & Zhang, 2017). Demonstrating moral management includes treating followers with respect and dignity. Both must be present and aligned to have credibility as an ethical leader, according to this cross-cultural research.

The review in Table 9.4 provides a summary of what we know to date about leadership development and training from available published empirical studies.

In summary:

- Manager training is effective, especially for lower levels of management (as opposed to top organizational leaders) and when tailored to the skill level and personality of the manager.

- There's a bigger payoff for the organization when training lower levels of management than higher levels.

- Managers can be trained to be transformational and these changes bring about higher organizational performance.

- Mentoring of leaders makes a difference in training and should accompany traditional training methods.

- Nonclassroom training methods, such as role playing and challenging assignments are effective and perhaps more so than classroom training.

- How you measure training effectiveness makes a difference in the conclusions.

- After event reviews (i.e., structured reflections) of behavior can add to the effects of leader development programs on the leader.

So what can you, as a manager, do with this information? First, recognize that getting training early as a new manager is perhaps one of the best strategies for helping you and helping your organization. Second, if the only training your organization offers is traditional classroom style training, find nontraditional leader development programs that may be available through local community colleges, chamber of commerce, or management clubs. Programs that offer role-playing, ropes courses, and other challenging exercises will complement what your organization can offer you. Third, find a mentor. Your organization may not offer a formal mentor program, but there may be more senior managers/leaders willing to informally mentor you, or you might find a local mentoring program, again, through local community services such as the chamber of commerce. Lastly, ask your organization for training. It's in their best interest for you to succeed, so ask to find out what is available and then take advantage and sign up for whatever training you can.

Getting the training you need or the opportunities you need is especially true for women leaders and leaders identifying with gender minority groups (e.g., LGBTQ).

Don't wait for training to come to you—take initiative and find the training you need to become an excellent manager and leader. Just taking the initiative demonstrates you are leader material, willing to take on whatever challenge awaits you.

> **Exercise 9.6**
>
> Table 9.4 provides a review of a fair number of studies. In your own words, what is the main take-away conclusion about leadership from those studies combined?

TABLE 9.4 Review of Leadership Development Studies in Chronological Order

Authors	What did they find?	Implications of Findings?
Burke & Day (1986)	Meta-analytical results show that general management training is effective in improving motivation and overall performance. Self-awareness training was fairly effective in changing manager's behavior.	Overall, management training has a positive effect and therefore, should be implemented.
Kelloway & Barling (2000)	The authors reviewed a number of studies that they and others conducted, and found that training leaders to be transformational is effective. Leaders who received training, with follow-up sessions, led their organizations to higher performance levels.	You can train leaders to be transformational, using either workshops or counseling sessions. Don't overwhelm learners—make small changes at a time, ones that fit into the daily routine. Follow-up training with feedback and expectations for change.

(continued)

TABLE 9.4 Review of Leadership Development Studies in Chronological Order *(continued)*

Authors	What did they find?	Implications of Findings?
Arthur, Bennett, Edens, & Bell (2003)	Meta-analytic results show that training for leaders is effective, and that the method of training, skill or tasks that leaders are trained on, and the criteria used to evaluate success of training were all related to reported levels of training effectiveness. For example, lecture method of training was effective for several types of skills and tasks, and behavioral training (like a simulator) was particularly effective for learning psychomotor skills such as operating machinery. Lecture style training is effective, in particular for cognitive-based and interpersonal skill training.	It matters how you measure the effectiveness of training because different things, such as ability and opportunity to perform the new skill, will have an impact on whether you see improvement or not. When it comes to learning tasks, it helps to match the style of training to the style of task—e.g., for cognitive skills, use a lecture style; for skills that require psychomotor action (like operating machinery), use behavioral training such as simulators or other hands-on training.
Collins & Holton (2004)	Meta-analytic findings show management training is effective depending on the objective and specific outcomes. They found wide variations in the success of programs.	Some programs are effective and some are not. Knowledge-based programs are good for those who recognize they need the knowledge and skills. Training is more effective if it's tailored to the skill level and needs and learning styles of the participant.
Evers, Brouwers, & Tomic (2006)	Given the popularity of coaching for leadership development, the authors examined the effectiveness of co-active coaching (a specific type of leadership coaching) on self-efficacy and outcome expectancies. They found that coaching has a positive effect on self-efficacy beliefs for setting one's own goals and for expecting to act in a more balanced (i.e., weighing alternatives and taking things in stride rather than trying to have or do it all now) as a result of coaching.	Some types of coaching help leaders feel more confident in their ability to set goals and achieve them, and to feel that they can make positive changes toward acting more stable or balanced (i.e., being socially minded and empathetic, not just focused on the achieving results).
Avolio, Reichard, Hannah, Walumbwa, & Chan (2009)	Meta-analytic results show a moderate to strong effect for leadership interventions on leadership development. Leader interventions in the form of role playing, challenging assignments, and other nontraditional (not classroom) development programs showed a higher influence on the success of development than training designed to increase leader's knowledge or skills. The authors also looked at return on investment and found that for the least effective development programs, the payoff only occurred with lower level managers. However, as you use more effective development programs, the return on investment goes up to 200% of the investment. Finally, the authors also found that leadership interventions had a bigger effect on lower vs. middle and higher level leaders.	Nontypical training is most effective and it does pay off in the organization if the training is a validated evidence-based program (like role-playing, assignments). It's not enough to just send the leader to a class. Remarkably, raising the leader's expectations of his or her followers actually changes how the leader sees him or herself, and this is quite effective in leader development, and should be considered a complement to other development interventions. Additionally, since interventions had the biggest effect on lower level leaders vs. middle or upper, organizations should invest early in leadership development, when their leaders are still new and moving up the organizational hierarchy—don't wait until they are at the top to invest.

TABLE 9.4   Review of Leadership Development Studies in Chronological Order *(continued)*

Authors	What did they find?	Implications of Findings?
Lester, Hannah, Harms, Vogelgesang, & Avolio (2011)	Using a longitudinal field study, they examined the effectiveness of mentoring on protégés' leader efficacy (belief in their ability to lead) and performance. Results showed statistically significant improvements. Even after being enrolled in a leader development program, those who also had a trusting mentor demonstrated higher levels of self-efficacy than those who didn't have a mentor. Additionally, those who sought negative or critical feedback from their mentors improved more than those who only sought positive feedback.	Leadership development is enhanced when combined with a formal mentoring program, wherein trusting relationships can be developed between mentor and protégé, and where the protégé seeks critical feedback to develop and correct weaknesses.
Harms, Spain, & Hannah (2011)	The results of their longitudinal study of Army officer cadets at West Point United States Military Academy, revealed that the cadets' personality traits played a role in their leadership development and in whether the effects of training lasted after completing the intense training program. Depending on the circumstances, some personality traits were positively associated with leadership development (e.g., dutiful, diligent), whereas others were negatively associated (e.g., skeptical).	Organizations should consider systematically assessing their potential leaders on personality traits, and not just the Big-5, before designing the training program. Depending on personality traits, the organization may have to tailor some programs to fit and adapt to potential leaders' needs.
De Rue, Nahrgang, Hollenbeck, & Workman (2012)	The authors examined the effectiveness of after-event reviews (AER; systematic analysis of your own behavior, and an evaluation of how that behavior contributed to your performance) and found that they did help participants "engage in more effective leader behaviors over time" (p. 1004). These results were stronger for participants who were conscientious and open to new experiences, as well as those who had experienced many developmental challenges in their careers (e.g., working across organizational boundaries, managing demographic and cultural diversity, facilitating novel change in the organization).	After-event reviews, or structured reflections, enhance experience-based leadership development, especially for those who are conscientious, open to new experiences, and who have had a rich and challenging career thus far. These AERs should be combined with other leadership development programs to enhance the learning experience, but perhaps only for those who will benefit—thus initial screening may be valuable.

Courtesy Zinta Byrne.

Developing Women Leaders

Much of the leader development research reviewed so far was studied using male participants, but whether it also unambiguously applies to women is unknown. Men predominantly occupy the leadership roles in the United States,

Europe, Asia, and India (Ely, Ibarra, & Kolb, 2011), although women are making progress in securing leadership positions, albeit at a slower pace than men (Carter & Silva, 2010). Part of the slow rate, argue Ely and colleagues (Ely et al., 2011), is that women's leadership identities are ill-formed and as an outcome, most employees (men and women) identify leadership with the male gender stereotype. Previous leadership models have proposed that a person's identity as a leader develops in a recursive and mutually reinforcing relationship between the leader-to-be and the environment. Thus, as individuals assert themselves taking actions that build leader experiences, the environment either reinforces these actions or puts them down. "As one's opportunities and capacity for exercising leadership grows, so too does the likelihood of receiving collective endorsement from the organization" (Ely et al., 2011, p. 476). This recognition and endorsement serves to build your identity as a leader. However, most people have been indoctrinated to perceive and identify leaders with being male (Bailyn, 2006; Dennis & Kunkel, 2004). Therefore, the reinforcement for women is simply not there. Hence, women fail to develop the same identity with being a leader as do their male counterparts. According to leadership researchers, leaders' identity serves a critical role in their purpose, and ability to espouse values, vision, and take action as needed (DeRue & Ashford, 2010; Ibarra, Carter, & Silva, 2010; van Knippenberg, van Knippenberg, De Cremer, & Hogg, 2004).

Members of the LGBTQ community may want to pay attention to opportunities like the International LGBTQ Leaders Conference for development workshops and networking..

How do we fix this problem and develop women or non-binary identified leaders who identify with being a leader? Ely and colleagues review a number of effective programs that include the use of 360-degree feedback; learning to network, negotiate, and lead change; and managing career transitions using case studies. 360-degree feedback, a type of feedback program, requires asking peers, subordinates, bosses, and clients for feedback on the leader, essentially creating a 360-degree perspective of how the leader behaves. Since women tend to receive less candid feedback than men (Heffernan, 2004), 360-degree feedback can provide the mirror that female leaders need to see how their behaviors and actions are being perceived. Because of the sometimes conflicting feedback obtained using 360-degree feedback (e.g., one review suggests you be more firm, the other says you're too firm), Ely and colleagues note the importance of using a coach and peers to make sense of the feedback, and to begin ongoing dialogue about your performance. Additionally, learning how to network is critical as you move up in the organization hierarchy (Day, 2001; Kanter, 1977). However, Ely et al. observed that women may not engage in networking as often or effectively as they should. This may be because they view networking as (a) using people, and (b) as having to participate in activities that are not in their areas of expertise (e.g., playing golf), or that they might interfere with personal home life (e.g., after hours drinks that conflict with home demands). Thus, addressing these roadblocks to networking is also important in leadership development programs designed for women (note that as of yet, programs identified specifically for developing LGBTQ leaders are scarce, though trends suggest this may be changing).

Contrary to the view that women don't ask their network for what they want or need (Babcock & Laschever, 2003), Ely and colleagues suggest that women do negotiate, but they have a ways to go in feeling legitimate or valued in terms of what they are negotiating for because often those needs oppose the organizational

Company Example 9.1   Fortune 500 Identifies 23 Female CEOs in 2018

Most Chief Executive Officers have been men. However, in 2018, out of the Fortune 500 companies, 23 reportedly have female CEOs. Of the 23, two are women of color, the rest are Caucasian. The CEOs and their companies are: Mary Barra at General Motors, Gail Boudreaux at Anthem, Ginni Rometty at IBM, Indra Nooyi at PepsiCo, Marillyn Hewson at Lockheed Martin, Safra Catz at Oracle, Phebe Novakovic at General Dynamics, Tricia Griffith at Progressive, Lynn Good at Duke Energy, Michelle Gass at Kohl's, Geisha Williams at PG&E Corp, Margaret Keane at Synchrony Financial, Deanna Mulligan at Guardian Life Insurance, Barbara Rentler at Ross Stores, Anna Manning at Reinsurance Group of America, Vicki Hollub at Occidental Petroleum, Kathryn Marinello at Hertz Global Holdings, Mary Laschinger at Veritiv, Michele Buck at Hershey, Joey Wat at Yum China, Patricia Poppe at CMS Energy, Kathy Mazzarella at Graybar Electric, and Beth Mooney at KeyCorp. For perspective with other minority groups, there are only three black CEOs heading up Fortune 500 companies. Asian CEOs are also scarce. Companies like Google, Microsoft, and Adobe are run by Asian American CEOs.

norms. For example, women are more likely than men to have to negotiate for flexible work schedules because women are still considered the primary caregivers, however, many organizations are structured such that the highest levels of the organization are either designed for men with stay-at-home partners or more accepting of men hiring care-takers versus women hiring care-takers. Accordingly, Ely and colleagues suggest that women must learn to view negotiation as an important process in getting what they need to be successful; to see themselves and their work as valuable; and understand how their goals align with the organization's goals and framing their negotiations to advance both. Finally, Ely and colleagues warn that women can get stuck in informal roles that use their strengths, but that ultimately derail them from transitioning to senior leadership positions. Therefore, they must learn to pass up on the informal roles that use their skills but have no advancement potential for formal roles that give them opportunity for growth and recognition.

Getting stuck in a role you don't want is not the same thing as being an ineffective leader or having an ineffective boss. Unfortunately, there are times when having a bad leader is the reason you don't get the best assignments, support, or developmental experiences you need to advance. Ineffective leaders come in many forms, the least of which is one who doesn't pay attention to your development needs.

What Happens if You Have an Ineffective Leader?

What happens if you have a really bad leader? Though critics have argued at times that it is difficult to attribute organizational success to leaders (e.g., Meindl & Ehrlich, 1987; Pandey, 1976; Pfeffer, 1977), others have provided evidence

A bad boss is a stressor (see Chapter 6 on Stress) that may not be manageable. What to do? Manage your stress as best as you can using tips in Chapter 6 and from stress management clinics. Talk to your Human Resource Manager, if you have one, to find out what options are available to you. Your conversations should be confidential and protected—demand that they are. Document every interaction with your boss—this documentation may be important later should charges be pressed against your boss or you. Seek legal counsel if the situation warrants; there are free services available in most communities. Some bad bosses leave on their own accord because people at higher levels find out about them and hold them accountable for their bad behavior. In the meantime, however, find support, help, and advice. Don't just ignore that the bad boss is negatively affecting your ability to be productive for the organization. The last outcome you need is to be let go for poor performance, which probably came about because of your bad boss.

that depending on which outcomes are considered, leaders have an effect (e.g., Day & Lord, 1988; Hargrove & Nelson, 1984; Lieberson & O'Connor, 1972; Mintzberg & Waters, 1982; Tucker, 1981). Therefore, a bad leader may have a negative effect on employees directly and indirectly on the organization.

A recent movie/comedy, called *Horrible Bosses*, depicts a variety of scenes wherein different bosses engage in very inappropriate behavior. Though the movie is meant to be a satire, taking inappropriateness to an extreme, a bad leader is no laughing matter and some of the bosses in the movie may not seem so fictional. Bad leadership contributes to employees quitting their jobs, suffering serious health problems, and experiencing ongoing unmanageable work stress (see Schaubroeck, Walumbwa, Ganster, & Kepes, 2007, for a review). Research on abusive supervision (Tepper, 2007) is a growing area of study. Abusive supervision refers to perceptions that supervisors are hostile, both verbally and nonverbally, but not necessarily physically aggressive (Tepper, 2007). Recent studies show those who are subjected to abusive supervision report higher levels of relationship tension at work that also spills over into home life (Carlson, Ferguson, Perrewe, & Whitten, 2011), low job performance and satisfaction (Aryee, Chen, Sun, & Debrah, 2007; Tepper, 2000), and reduced emotional health (Bowling & Beehr, 2006; Duffy, Ganster, & Pagon, 2002; Tepper, Moss, Lockhart, & Carr, 2007).

Research results also show that for employees with narrowly scoped jobs, who have limited ability to extend their job responsibilities or engage in a variety of job tasks, feel the effects of hostile and negative bosses more than those with high job enrichment who can perhaps escape the negative effects of bad bosses (Schaubroeck et al., 2007).

In an examination of cross-cultural effects, Kernan, Watson, Chen, and Kim (2011) found that cultures with high needs for social approval from boss and coworkers (e.g., South Korea) felt the impact of abusive supervision even more than cultures without high social approval needs.

This lack of impact in low social approval cultures, however, is not necessarily good for leadership or good for organizations, as a whole. In the last decade, the United States, a generally low social approval country, has experienced a number of large corporate scandals, all attributable to ineffective leadership. The two largest corporate financial scandals on record remain Enron, a large oil and gas company, and Worldcom, a large telecommunication firm. Hannah and Zatzick (2008) conducted a unique qualitative study on whether perceptions of leadership in the United States changed after these highly visible scandals. Surprisingly, their results showed that these landmark scandals had no effect on how ethical leaders are portrayed, even though subsequent to the scandals, considerable attention was placed on ethics in company boardrooms. Business press expects leaders to be entrepreneurial and to maximize firm profits, but they do not have explicit expectations for whether such goals are achieved ethically.

Chapter Summary

Leaders are responsible and sometimes held accountable for the success and failure of their organizations. To lead an organization means to set the strategy, to excite followers to follow your vision, and to bring on board the right people to help achieve the vision. Leadership is one of the most frequently studied topics in organizational psychology and behavior because of the public's fascination with what makes for a good (or bad) leader and why people follow. From hundreds of studies, we have accumulated theories and evidence to explain how leaders do what they do, what makes for good and bad leaders, and how good leaders are developed. The negative consequences of bad leadership are severe, yet there are many organizations with mediocre leaders who could be trained to be better and bad leaders who seem ignored. People are not born to be leaders—leaders are developed. The implications of research and study of leadership is that leaders can be made and good leaders need not be an anomaly.

Figure 9.18 provides a visual summary of the key concepts from Chapter 9. The visual summary shows the various categories of theories used to explain leadership. The path from start to finish, somewhat chronological/historical, the theories begin with trait theories of leadership, followed by the behavior theories including several dual axes theories such as consideration versus initiating. The contingency theories followed after behavioral theories, focusing instead on the importance of the situation, rather than just on the leader. New theories of leadership combine concepts from previous eras, incorporating the personality of the leader, the demands of the situation, and the behaviors that are required for leading in today's complex environments. The development of leaders is important

If you're wondering how it is that we vote for bad leaders, take a read of this interesting article in Scientific American Mind by Kevin Dutton (2016). The author reviews studies of U.S. presidents, World leaders, and the 2016 U.S. presidential candidates on their level of psychopathy.

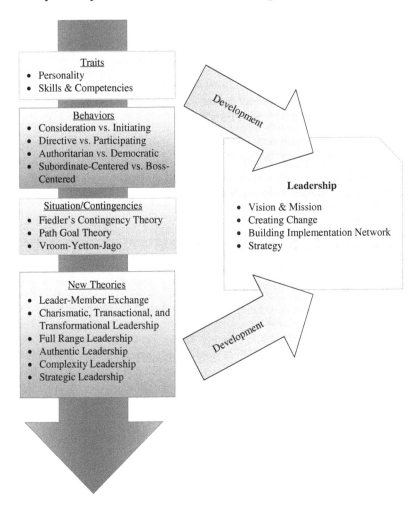

FIGURE 9.18   Visual Summary of Chapter 9

Courtesy Zinta Byrne.

because their primary role is to set the vision and mission of the organization, create and drive organizational change, support the organization in achieving its mission by establishing the strategy, and building important networks for implementing the strategy.

Discussion Questions

1. What makes a good leader? Is that different from a good manager? If so, how; if not, why not? Why might it be challenging to be both a good manager and a good leader? Under what circumstances can you be both easily?

2. The chapter reviewed a few traits of leaders that have withstood the test of time and are incorporated into the new leadership theories. Which other traits do you think are essential for leaders to have, that have not been discussed in this chapter? Why are these traits important?

3. What are your reactions to the literature reviewed in the chapter that discusses the impact of physical appearance on who is and is not considered a good or effective leader? What do you think we need to do to get away from how physical characteristics affect our perceptions of effective or good leaders?

4. What implicit biases do you have about leaders? In other words, what are your ideas of what a leader is, acts like, looks like, and talks like? What kind of leader would you follow?

5. Society makes a big deal about leaders—in fact, it does not matter where you go in the world, we are fascinated with leaders and want/need leaders. Why is that? Do you think we could do better without leaders? What would it look like if we were all leaders?

References

Albright, L., Kenny, D. A., & Malloy, T. E. (1988). Consensus in personality judgments at zero acquaintance. *Journal of Personality and Social Psychology, 55*(3), 387–395. doi:10.1037/0022-3514.55.3.387

Albright, L., Malloy, T. E., Dong, Q., Kenny, D. A., Fang, X., Winquist, L., & Yu, D. (1997). Cross-cultural consensus in personality judgments. *Journal of Personality and Social Psychology, 72*(3), 558–569. doi:10.1037/0022-3514.72.3.558

Antonakis, J., & Dalgas, O. (2009). Predicting elections: child's play!. *Science, 323*(5918), 1183.

Antonakis, J., Day, D. V., & Schyns, B. (2012, August). Leadership and individual differences: At the cusp of a renaissance. *Leadership Quarterly*. pp. 643–650. doi:10.1016/j.leaqua.2012.05.002

Arthur Jr., W., Bennett Jr., W., Edens, P. S., & Bell, S. T. (2003). Effectiveness of training in organizations: A meta-analysis of design and evaluation features. *Journal of Applied Psychology, 88*(2), 234–245. doi:10.1037/0021-9010.88.2.234

Aryee, S., Chen, Z., Sun, L., & Debrah, Y. A. (2007). Antecedents and outcomes of abusive supervision: Test of a trickle-down model. *Journal of Applied Psychology, 92*(1), 191–201. doi:10.1037/0021-9010.92.1.191

Avolio, B. J. (1999). *Full leadership development: Building the vital forces in organizations.* Thousand Oaks, CA: Sage.

Avolio, B. J., & Bass, B. M. (1991). *The full range leadership development programs: basic and advanced manuals.* Binghamton, NY: Bass, Avolio & Associates

Avolio, B. J., Gardner, W. L., Walumbwa, F. O., Luthans, F., & May, D. R. (2004). Unlocking the mask: A look at the process by which authentic leaders impact follower attitudes and behaviors. *The Leadership Quarterly, 15*(6), 801–823. doi:10.1016/j.leaqua.2004.09.003

Avolio, B. J., Reichard, R. J., Hannah, S. T., Walumbwa, F. O., & Chan, A. (2009). A meta-analytic review of leadership impact research: Experimental and quasi-experimental studies. *Leadership Quarterly, 20*(5), 764–784. doi:10.1016/j.leaqua.2009.06.006

Avolio, B. J., Waldman, D. A., & Yammarino, F. J. (1991). Leading in the 1990's: The four I's of transformational leadership. *Journal of European Industrial Training, 15*(4), 9–16.

Avolio, B. J., & Wernsing, T. S. (2008). Practicing authentic leadership. *Positive psychology: Exploring the best in people, 4,* 147–165.

Ayman, R., Chemers, M. M., & Fiedler, F. (1995). The contingency model of leadership effectiveness: Its level of analysis. *The Leadership Quarterly, 6*(2), 147–167. doi:10.1016/1048-9843(95)90032-2

Babcock, L., & Laschever, S. (2003). *Women don't ask: Negotiation and the gender divide.* Princeton, NJ: Princeton University Press.

Bailyn, L. (2006). *Breaking the mold: Redesigning work for productive and satisfying lives.* Ithaca, NY: Cornell University Press.

Bales, R. F. (1954). In conference. *Harvard Business Review, 32*(2), 44–50.

Bass, B. M. (1985). Leadership: Good, better, best. *Organizational Dynamics, 13*, 26–40. doi: 10.1016/0090-2616(85)90028-2

Bass, B. M. (1990). *Bass and Stogdill's handbook of leadership.* New York, NY: Free Press.

Bass, B. M. (1998). *Transformational leadership: Industrial, military, and educational impact.* Mahwah, NJ: Erlbaum.

Bass, B. M., & Avolio, B. J. (Eds.) (1994). *Improving organizational effectiveness through transformational leadership.* Thousand Oaks, CA: Sage.

Berlew, D. E., & Heller, D. (1983). Style flexibility—tools for successful leaders. *Legal Economics, 9*, 34–37.

Blake, R. R., Mouton, J. S., & Bidwell, A. C. (1962). Managerial grid. *Advanced Management - Office Executive, 1*(9), 12–15.

Blau, P. M. (1964). *Exchange and power in social life.* New York, NY: Wiley & Sons.

Bowling, N. A., & Beehr, T. A. (2006). Workplace harassment from the victim's perspective: A theoretical model and meta-analysis. *Journal of Applied Psychology, 91*(5), 998–1012. doi:10.1037/0021-9010.91.5.998

Bryman, A. (1992). *Charisma and leadership in organizations.* London, England: Sage.

Burke, M. J., & Day, R. R. (1986). A cumulative study of the effectiveness of managerial training. *Journal of Applied Psychology, 71*(2), 232–245.

Burns, J. M. (1978). *Leadership.* New York, NY: Harper and Row. doi: 10.1177/1745691610393980

Cangemi, J. P., & Pfohl, W. (2009). Sociopaths in high places. *Organization Development Journal, 27*(2), 85–96.

Carlson, D. S., Ferguson, M., Perrewé, P. L., & Whitten, D. (2011). The fallout from abusive supervision: An examination of subordinates and their partners. *Personnel Psychology, 64*(4), 937–961. doi:10.1111/j.1744-6570.2011.01232.x

Carlyle, T. (1907). *Heroes and hero worship.* Boston, MA: Adams (original work published in 1841).

Carré, J. M., McCormick, C. M., & Mondloch, C. J. (2009). Facial structure is a reliable cue of aggressive behavior. *Psychological Science, 20*(10), 1194–1198. doi:10.1111/j.1467-9280.2009.02423.x

Carter, N. M., & Silva, C. (2010). *Pipeline's broken promise.* http://www.catalyst.org/publication/372/pipelines-broken-promise

Chiaburu, D. S., Smith, T. A., Wang, J., & Zimmerman, R. D. (2014). Relative importance of leader influences for subordinates' proactive behaviors, prosocial behaviors, and task performance: A meta-analysis. *Journal of Personnel Psychology, 13*(2), 70–86. doi:10.1027/1866-5888/a000105

Chemers, M. M., Rice, R. W., Sundstrom, E., & Butler, W. M. (1975). Leader esteem for the least preferred co-worker score, training, and effectiveness: An experimental examination. *Journal of Personality and Social Psychology, 31*(3), 401–409. doi:10.1037/h0076473

Collins, D. B., & Holton, E. F. (2004). The effectiveness of managerial leadership development programs: A meta-analysis of studies from 1982 to 2001. *Human Resource Development Quarterly, 15*(2), 217–248.

Conger, J. A. (2013). Charismatic leadership. In M. G. Rumsey (Ed.), *The Oxford handbook of leadership* (pp. 376–391). New York, NY: Oxford University Press.

Conger, J. A., & Kanungo, R. N. (1987). Toward a behavioral theory of charismatic leadership in organizational settings. *Academy of Management Review, 12*(4), 637–647. doi:10.5465/AMR.1987.4306715

Daft, R. L. (1999). *Leadership: Theory and practice.* Orlando, FL: Dryden Press.

Dansereau, F., Cashman, J., & Graen, G. (1973). Instrumentality theory and equity theory as complementary approaches in predicting the relationship of leadership and turnover among managers. *Organizational Behavior & Human Performance, 10*(2), 184–200. doi:10.1016/0030-5073(73)90012-3

Dansereau, F., Graen, G., & Haga, W. J. (1975). A vertical dyad linkage approach to leadership within formal organizations: A longitudinal investigation of the role making process. *Organizational Behavior and Human Performance, 13,* 46–78. doi:10.1016/0030-5073(75)90005-7

Day, D. V. (2001). Assessment of leadership outcomes. In S. J. Zaccaro, R. J. Klimoski (Eds.), *The nature of organizational leadership: Understanding the performance imperatives confronting today's leaders* (pp. 384–410). San Francisco, CA: Jossey-Bass.

Day, D. V., & Lord, R. G. (1988). Executive leadership and organizational performance: Suggestions for a new theory and methodology. *Journal of Management, 14*(3), 453–464. doi:10.1177/014920638801400308

Dennis, M., & Kunkel, A. (2004). Perceptions of men, women, and CEOs: The effects of gender identity. *Social Behavior and Personality, 32*(2), 155–172. doi:10.2224/sbp.2004.32.2.155

DeRue, D., & Ashford, S. J. (2010). Who will lead and who will follow? A social process of leadership identity construction in organizations. *The Academy of Management Review, 35*(4), 627–647. doi:10.5465/AMR.2010.53503267

DeRue, D., Nahrgang, J. D., Hollenbeck, J. R., & Workman, K. (2012). A quasi-experimental study of after-event reviews and leadership development. *Journal of Applied Psychology, 97*(5), 997–1015. doi:10.1037/a0028244

Duffy, M. K., Ganster, D., & Pagon, M. (2002). Social undermining in the workplace. *Academy of Management Journal, 45*(2), 331–351. doi:10.2307/3069350

Dulebohn, J. H., Bommer, W. H., Liden, R. C., Brouer, R. L., & Ferris, G. R. (2012). A meta-analysis of antecedents and consequences of leader-member exchange: Integrating the past with an eye toward the future. *Journal of Management, 38*(6), 1715–1759. doi:10.1177/0149206311415280

Dutton, K. (2016). Would you vote for a psychopath? *Scientific American Mind,* 27(5), 50–55. doi: 10.1038/scientificamericanmind0916-50

Eagly, A. H., & Karau, S. J. (2002). Role congruity theory of prejudice toward female leaders. *Psychological Review, 109*(3), 573–598. doi:10.1037/0033-295X.109.3.573

Ehrhart, M. G. (2004). Leadership and procedural justice climate as antecedents of unit-level organizational citizenship behavior. *Personnel Psychology, 57*(1), 61–94.

Ely, R., Ibarra, H., & Kolb, D. M. (2011). Taking gender into account: Theory and design for women's leadership development program. *Academy of Management Learning & Education, 10*(3), 474–493. doi:10.5465/amle.2010.0046

Etcoff, N. L., Stock, S., Haley, L. E., Vickery, S. A., & House, D. M. (2011). Cosmetics as a feature of the extended human phenotype: Modulation of the perception of biologically important facial signals. *Plos ONE, 6*(10), 1–9. doi:10.1371/journal.pone.0025656

Evers, W. G., Brouwers, A., & Tomic, W. (2006). A quasi-experimental study on management coaching effectiveness. *Consulting Psychology Journal: Practice and Research, 58*(3), 174–182. doi:10.1037/1065-9293.58.3.174

Fiedler, F. E. (1962). Leader attitudes, group climate, and group creativity. *Journal of Abnormal and Social Psychology, 63*, 308–318.

Fiedler, F. E. (1964). A contingency model of leadership effectiveness. In L. Berkowitz (Ed.), *Advances in experimental social psychology.* (pp. 149–190). New York, NY: Academic Press.

Fiedler, F. E., (1967). *A theory of leadership effectiveness.* New York, NY: McGraw-Hill.

Field, R. G., & Andrews, J. P. (1998). Testing the incremental validity of the Vroom–Jago versus Vroom–Yetton models of participation in decision making. *Journal of Behavioral Decision Making, 11*(4), 251–261. doi:10.1002/(SICI)1099-0771(1998120)11:4<251::AID-BDM300>3.0.CO;2-2

Field, R. H., & House, R. J. (1990). A test of the Vroom-Yetton model using manager and subordinate reports. *Journal of Applied Psychology, 75*(3), 362–366. doi:10.1037/0021-9010.75.3.362

Fine, L. E. (2017). Gender and sexual minorities' practice and embodiment of authentic leadership: Challenges and opportunities. *Advances in Developing Human Resources, 19*(4), 378–392. doi:10.1177/1523422317728734

Fleishman, E. A. (1953a). The description of supervisory behavior. *Journal of Applied Psychology, 37*(1), 1–6. doi:10.1037/h0056314

Fleishman, E. A. (1953b). The measurement of leadership attitudes in industry. *Journal of Applied Psychology, 37*(3), 153–158. doi:10.1037/h0063436

Fleishman, E. A. (1995). Consideration and structure: Another look at their role in leadership research. In F. Dansereau & F. J. Yammarino (Eds.), *Leadership: The multiple-level approaches* (pp. 51–60). Stamford, CT: JAI Press.

Fodor, E. M., & Riordan, J. M. (1995). Leader power motive and group conflict as influences on leader behavior and group member self-affect. *Journal of Research In Personality, 29*(4), 418–431. doi:10.1006/jrpe.1995.1024

French, J. R., & Raven, B. (1959). The bases of social power. In D. Cartwright (Ed.), *Studeis in social power* (pp. 150–167). Oxford, England: University, Michigan.

Fromm, E. E. (1941). *Escape from freedom.* Oxford, England: Farrar & Rinehart.

Galton, F. (1869). *Hereditary genius: An inquiry into its laws and consequences.* London, England: Macmillan and Company.

Gardner, H. (1978). What we know (and don't know) about the two halves of the brain. *Journal of Aesthetic Education, 12*(1), 113–119. doi:10.2307/3331854

Gilmore, T. N. (1982). Leadership and boundary management. *Journal of Applied Behavioral Science, 18*(3), 343–356. doi:10.1177/002188638201800308

Gosling, S. (2008). *Snoop: What your stuff says about you.* New York, NY: Basic Books.

Gouldner, A. W. (1960). The norm of reciprocity: A preliminary statement. *American Sociological Review, 25,* 161–178.

Graen, G., & Schiemann, W. (1978). Leader–member agreement: A vertical dyad linkage approach. *Journal of Applied Psychology, 63*(2), 206–212. doi:10.1037/0021-9010.63.2.206

Graen, G. B., & Uhl-Bien, M. (1995). Relationship-based approach to leadership: Development of leader-member exchange (LMX) theory of leadership over 25 years: Applying a multi-level multi-domain perspective. *The Leadership Quarterly, 6*(2), 219–247. doi:10.1016/1048-9843(95)90036-5

Graham, J. W. (1991). Servant-leadership in organizations: Inspirational and moral. *The Leadership Quarterly, 2*(2), 105–119. doi:10.1016/1048-9843(91)90025-W

Greenleaf, R. K. (1970). *The servant as leader.* Newton Centre, MA: The Robert K. Greenleaf Center.

Halpin, A. W., & Winer, B. J. (1957). A factorial study of the leader behavior descriptions. In R. M. Stogdill & A. E. Coons (Eds.), *Leader behavior: Its description and measurement.* Columbus, Ohio: Ohio State University, Bureau of Business Research.

Hannah, D. R., & Zatzick, C. D. (2008). An examination of leader portrayals in the U. S. business press following the landmark scandals of the early 21st century. *Journal of Business Ethics, 79*(4), 361–377. doi:10.1007/s10551-007-9406-4

Hannah, S. T., Walumbwa, F. O., & Fry, L. W. (2011). Leadership in action teams: Team leader and members' authenticity, authenticity strength, and team outcomes. *Personnel Psychology, 64*(3), 771–802.

Hare, A., Hare, S. E., & Blumberg, H. H. (1998). Wishful thinking: Who has the least preferred coworker? *Small Group Research, 29*(4), 419–435. doi:10.1177/1046496498294001

Hargrove, E. C., & Nelson, M. (1984). *Presidents, politics, and policy.* Baltimore, MD: Johns Hopkins University Press.

Harms, P. D., Han, G., & Chen, H. (2012). Recognizing leadership at a distance: A study of leader effectiveness across cultures. *Journal of Leadership & Organizational Studies, 19*(2), 164–172. doi:10.1177/1548051812436812

Harms, P. D., Spain, S. M., & Hannah, S. T. (2011). Leader development and the dark side of personality. *Leadership Quarterly, 22*(3), 495–509. doi:10.1016/j.leaqua.2011.04.007

Hautala, T. (2008). TJ leaders as transformational leaders: Followers' and leaders' appraisals. *Journal of Psychological Type, 68*(9), 1–11.

Heckman, J. J., & Kautz, T. (2012). Hard evidence on soft skills. *Labour Economics, 19*(4), 451–464. doi: 10.1016/j.labeco.2012.05.014

Heffernan, M. A. (2004). *The naked truth: A working woman's manifesto on business and what really matters.* San Francisco, CA: Jossey-Bass

Heilman, M. E., & Okimoto, T. G. (2007). Why are women penalized for success at male tasks?: The implied communality deficit. *Journal of Applied Psychology, 92*(1), 81–92. doi:10.1037/0021-9010.92.1.81

Hemphill, J. K. (1950). *Leader behavior description.* Columbus, Ohio: Ohio State University, Personnel Research Board

Hoch, J. E., Bommer, W. H., Dulebohn, J. H., & Wu, D. (2016). Do ethical, authentic, and servant leadership explain variance above and beyond transformational leadership? A meta-analysis. *Journal of Management, 4*(2). 501–529. doi: 10.1177/0149206316665461

Hoffman, B. J., Woehr, D. J., Maldagen-Youngjohn, R., & Lyons, B. D. (2011). Great man or great myth? A quantitative review of the relationship between individual differences and leader effectiveness. *Journal of Occupational and Organizational Psychology, 84*(2), 347–381. doi:10.1348/096317909X485207

Hofstede, G. (1983). National cultures in four dimensions. *International Studies of Management & Organization, 13*(1/2), 46–74.

Hofstede, G. (1991). *Cultures and organizations: Software of the mind.* New York, NY: McGraw-Hill.

Hogan, J. C. (1978). Personological dynamics of leadership. *Journal of Research in Personality, 12*(4), 390–395. doi:10.1016/0092-6566(78)90065-X

Holder, A. M. B., Jackson, M. A., & Ponterotto, J. G. (2015). Racial microaggression experiences and coping strategies of Black women in corporate leadership. *Qualitative Psychology, 2*(2), 164–180. doi: 10.1037/qup0000024

House, R. J. (1971). A Path Goal Theory of leader effectiveness. *Administrative Science Quarterly, 16*(3), 321–339.

House, R. J. (1996). Path-goal theory of leadership: Lessons, legacy and a reformulated theory. *Leadership Quarterly, 7*(3), 323–352.

House, R. J., & Aditya, R. N. (1997). The social scientific study of leadership: Quo vadis?.*Journal of Management, 23*(3), 409–473. doi:10.1177/014920639702300306

House, R. J., & Baetz, M. L. (1979). Leadership: Some empirical generalizations and new research directions. *Research In Organizational Behavior, 1,* 341–425.

House, R. J., & Singh, J. V. (1987). Organizational behavior: Some new directions for I/O psychology. *Annual Review of Psychology, 38,* 669–718. doi:10.1146/annurev. ps.38.020187.003321

House, R. J., Woycke, J., & Fodor, E. M. (1988). Charismatic and noncharismatic leaders: Differences in behavior and effectiveness. In, *Charismatic leadership: The elusive factor in organizational effectiveness* (pp. 98–121). San Francisco, CA: Jossey-Bass.

Ibarra, H., Carter, N. M., & Silva, C. (2010). Why men still get more promotions than women. *Harvard Business Review, 88*(9), 80–126.

Ilies, R., Gerhardt, M. W., & Le, H. (2004). Individual differences in leadership emergence: Integrating meta-analytic findings and behavioral genetics estimates. *International Journal of Selection and Assessment, 12*(3), 207–219. doi:10.1111/ j.0965-075X.2004.00275.x

Ireland, R., & Hitt, M. A. (2005). Achieving and maintaining strategic competitiveness in the 21st century: The role of strategic leadership. *Academy of Management Executive, 19*(4), 63–77. doi:10.5465/AME.2005.19417908

Jackson, J. J., Hill, P. L., & Roberts, B. W. (2012, May). Misconceptions of traits continue to persist: A response to Bandura. *Journal of Management,* 745–752. doi:10.1177/0149206312438775.

Jago, A. G., Ettling, J. T., & Vroom, V. H. (1985). Validating a revision to the Vroom/ Yetton Model: First evidence. *Academy of Management Proceedings (00650668),* 220–223. doi:10.5465/AMBPP.1985.4979056

Javidan, M., Dorfman, P. W., de Luque, M., & House, R. J. (2006). In the Eye of the Beholder: Cross Cultural Lessons in Leadership from Project GLOBE. *The Academy of Management Perspectives, 20*(1), 67–90. doi:10.5465/AMP.2006.19873410

Jennings, H. (1943). *Leadership and Isolation.* Oxford, England: Longmans, Green.

Judge, T. A., Colbert, A. E., & Ilies, R. (2004). Intelligence and leadership: A quantitative review and test of theoretical propositions. *Journal of Applied Psychology, 89*(3), 542–552. doi:10.1037/0021-9010.89.3.542

Judge, T. A., Ilies, R., Bono, J. E., & Gerhardt, M. W. (2002). Personality and leadership: A qualitative and quantitative review. *Journal of Applied Psychology, 87*(4), 765–780.

Judge, T. A., Piccolo, R. F., & Ilies, R. (2004). The forgotten ones? The validity of consideration and initiating structure in leadership Research. *Journal of Applied Psychology, 89*(1), 36–51. doi:10.1037/0021-9010.89.1.36

Kanter, R. (1977). *Men and women of the corporation.* New York, NY: Basics Press.

Kattan, M.M., de Pablos Heredero, C., Montes Botella, J. L., & Margalina, V. M. (2016). Factors of successful women leadership in Saudi Arabia. Asian Social Science, 12(5), 94–107. doi: 10.5539/as.v12n5p94

Keene, A. (2000). Complexity theory: The changing role of leadership. *Industrial & Commercial Training, 32*(1), 15–18.

Kelloway, E., & Barling, J. (2000). What we have learned about developing transformational leaders. *Leadership & Organization Development Journal, 21*(7), 355–362. doi:10.1108/01437730010377908

Kennedy, J. K., Houston, J. M., Korsgaard, M., & Gallo, D. D. (1987). Construct space of the Least Preferred Co-worker (LPC) Scale. *Educational and Psychological Measurement, 47*(3), 807–814. doi:10.1177/001316448704700335

Kernan, M. C., Watson, S., Chen, F., & Kim, T. (2011). How cultural values affect the impact of abusive supervision on worker attitudes. *Cross Cultural Management, 18*(4), 464–484. doi:10.1108/13527601111179528

Kirkpatrick, S. A., & Locke, E. A. (1991). Leadership: Do traits matter? *Executive (19389779), 5*(2), 48–60. doi:10.5465/AME.1991.4274679

Kotter, J. P. (1988). The leadership factor. *Mckinsey Quarterly,* (2), 71–78.

Lacerenza, C., Reyes, D., Marlow, S., Joseph, D., Salas, E., & Chen, Gilad. (2017). Leadership training design, delivery, and implementation: A meta-analysis. *Journal of Applied Psychology,102*(12), 1686–1718.

Langlois, J. H., Kalakanis, L., Rubenstein, A. J., Larson, A., Hallam, M., & Smoot, M. (2000). Maxims or myths of beauty? A meta-analytic and theoretical review. *Psychological Bulletin, 126*(3), 390–423. doi:10.1037/0033-2909.126.3.390

Latu, I. M., Stewart, T. L., Myers, A. C., Lisco, C. G., Estes, S., & Donahue, D. K. (2011). What we "say" and what we "think" about female managers: Explicit versus implicit associations of women with success. *Psychology of Women Quarterly, 35*(2), 252–266. doi:10.1177/0361684310383811

Leong, L., & Fischer, R. (2011). Is transformational leadership universal? A meta-analytical investigation of multifactor leadership questionnaire means across cultures. *Journal of Leadership & Organizational Studies, 18*(2), 164–174. doi:10.1177/1548051810385003

Lester, P. B., Hannah, S. T., Harms, P. D., Vogelgesang, G. R., & Avolio, B. J. (2011). Mentoring impact on leader efficacy development: A field experiment. *Academy of Management Learning & Education, 10*(3), 409–429. doi:10.5465/amle.2010.0047

Leung, S., & Bozionelos, N. (2004). Five-factor model traits and the prototypical image of the effective leader in the Confucian culture. *Employee Relations, 26*(1), 62–71. doi:10.1108/01425450410506904

Lewin, K. K., & Lippitt, R. R. (1938). An experimental approach to the study of autocracy and democracy: A preliminary note. *Sociometry, 1292*–1300. doi:10.2307/2785585

Lieberson, S., & O'Connor, J. F. (1972). Leadership and organizational performance: A study of large corporations. *American Sociological Review, 37*(2), 117–130. doi:10.2307/2094020

Likert, R. (1961). *New patterns of management.* New York, NY: McGraw-Hill.

Lord, R. G., De Vader, C. l., & Alliger, G. M. (1986). A meta-analysis of the relation between personality traits and leadership perceptions: An application of validity generalization procedures. *Journal of Applied Psychology, 71*(3), 402–410.

Mann, R. D. (1959). A review of the relationships between personality and performance in small groups. *Psychological Bulletin, 56*(4), 241–270. doi:10.1037/h0044587

Marion, R., & Uhl-Bien, M. (2001). Leadership in complex organizations. *The Leadership Quarterly, 12*(4), 389–418.

McCrae, R. R., & Costa, P. R. (1997). Personality trait structure as a human universal. *American Psychologist, 52*(5), 509–516. doi:10.1037/0003-066X.52.5.509

McCrae, R. R., & John, O. P. (1992). An introduction to the five-factor model and its applications. *Journal of Personality, 60*(2), 175–215. doi:10.1111/j.1467-6494.1992.tb00970.x

McGregor, D. (1960). *The human side of enterprise.* New York, NY: McGraw-Hill.

Meindl, J. R., & Ehrlich, S. B. (1987). The romance of leadership and the evaluation of organizational performance. *Academy of Management Journal, 30*(1), 91–109. doi:10.2307/255897

Miao, C., Humphrey, R. H., & Qian, S. (2018). A cross-cultural meta-analysis of how leader emotional intelligence influences subordinate task performance and organizational citizenship behavior. *Journal of World Business, 53*(4), 463–474.

Mintzberg, H., & Waters, J. A. (1982). Tracking strategy in an entrepreneurial firm. *Academy of Management Journal, 25*(3), 465–499. doi:10.2307/256075

Morton, J. W. (2017). Think leader, think heterosexual male? The perceived leadership effectiveness of gay male leaders. *Canadian Journal of Administrative Sciences, 34*(2), 159–169. doi: 10.1002/cjas.1434

Montano, D., Reeske, A., Franke, F., & Hüffmeier, J. (2017). Leadership, followers' mental health and job performance in organizations: A comprehensive meta-analysis from an occupational health perspective. *Journal of Organizational Behavior, 38*(3), 327–350.

Naumann, L. P., Vazire, S., Rentfrow, P. J., & Gosling, S. D. (2009). Personality judgments based on physical appearance. *Personality and Social Psychology Bulletin, 35*(12), 1661–1671. doi:10.1177/0146167209346309

Newstetter, W. I., Feldstein, M. J., & Newcomb, T. M. (1938). *Group adjustment: A study in experimental sociology.* Oxford, England: School of Applied Sciences, Western.

Nieva, V. F., & Gutek, B. A. (1980). Sex effects on evaluation. *Academy of Management Review, 5*(2), 267–276. doi:10.5465/AMR.1980.4288749

Northouse, P. G. (1997). *Leadership: Theory and practice.* Thousand Oaks, CA: Sage.

O'Brien, G. E., & Harary, F. (1977). Measurement of the interactive effects of leadership style and group structure upon group performance. *Australian Journal of Psychology, 29*(1), 59–71. doi:10.1080/00049537708258727

Pandey, J. (1976). Effects of leadership style, personality characteristics and method of leader selection on members' and leaders' behavior. *European Journal of Social Psychology, 6*(4), 475–489. doi:10.1002/ejsp.2420060406

Parker, C. P. (1999). The impact of leaders' implicit theories of employee participation on tests of the Vroom-Yetton model. *Journal of Social Behavior & Personality, 14*(1), 45–61.

Parolini, J., Patterson, K., & Winston, B. (2009). Distinguishing between transformational and servant leadership. *Leadership & Organization Development Journal, 30*(3), 274–291. doi:10.1108/01437730910949544

Peterson, S. J., Walumbwa, F. O., Avolio, B. J., & Hannah, S. T. (2012). The relationship between authentic leadership and follower job performance: The mediating role of follower positivity in extreme contexts. *The Leadership Quarterly, 23*(3), 502–516. doi:10.1016/j.leaqua.2011.12.004

Peus, C., Wesche, J., Streicher, B., Braun, S., & Frey, D. (2012). Authentic leadership: An empirical test of its antecedents, consequences, and mediating mechanisms. *Journal of Business Ethics, 107*(3), 331–348. doi:10.1007/s10551-011-1042-3

Pfeffer, J. (1997). The ambiguity of leadership. In R. P. Vecchio (Ed.), *Leadership: Understanding the dynamics of power and influence in organizations* (pp. 54–68). Notre Dame, IN: University of Notre Dame Press.

Popper, M., Amit, K., Gal, R., Mishkal-Sinai, M., & Lisak, A. (2004). The capacity to lead: Major psychological differences between leaders and nonleaders. *Military Psychology, 16*(4), 245–263. doi:10.1207/s15327876mp1604_3

Rockstuhl, T., Dulebohn, J. H., Ang, S., & Shore, L. M. (2012). Leader–member exchange (LMX) and culture: A meta-analysis of correlates of LMX across 23 countries. *Journal of Applied Psychology, 97*(6), 1097–1130. doi:10.1037/a0029978

Rosenthal, S. A., & Pittinsky, T. L. (2006). Narcissistic leadership. *The Leadership Quarterly, 17*(6), 617–633. doi:10.1016/j.leaqua.2006.10.005

Rotter, J. B. (1966). Generalized expectancies for internal versus external control of reinforcement. *Psychological Monographs: General and Applied, 80*(1), 1–28. doi:10.1037/h0092976

Rule, N. O., & Ambady, N. (2009). She's got the look: Inferences from female chief executive officers' faces predict their success. *Sex Roles, 61*(9–10), 644-652. doi:10.1007/s11199-009-9658-9

Russ, T. L. (2013). The relationship between theory X/Y: Assumptions and communication apprehension. *Leadership & Organization Development Journal, 34*(3), 238–249. doi:10.1108/01437731311326675

Russell, R. F., & Stone, A. (2002). A review of servant leadership attributes: Developing a practical model. *Leadership & Organization Development Journal, 23*(3), 145–157. doi:10.1108/01437730210424

Sahin, F. (2012). The mediating effect of leader–member exchange on the relationship between Theory X and Y management styles and affective commitment: A multi-level analysis. *Journal of Management & Organization, 18*(2), 159–174. doi:10.5172/jmo.2012.18.2.159

Salovey, P., & Mayer, J. D. (1989). Emotional intelligence. *Imagination, Cognition and Personality, 9*(3), 185–211.

Schaubroeck, J., Walumbwa, F. O., Ganster, D. C., & Kepes, S. (2007). Destructive leader traits and the neutralizing influence of an 'enriched' job. *The Leadership Quarterly, 18*(3), 236–251. doi:10.1016/j.leaqua.2007.03.006

Schriesheim, C. A., Tepper, B. J., & Tetrault, L. A. (1994). Least preferred co-worker score, situational control, and leadership effectiveness: A meta-analysis of contingency model performance predictions. *Journal of Applied Psychology, 79*(4), 561–573. doi:10.1037/0021-9010.79.4.561

Sczesny, S., & Kühnen, U. (2004). Meta-cognition about biological sex and gender-stereotypic physical appearance: Consequences for the assessment of leadership competence. *Personality and Social Psychology Bulletin, 30*(1), 13–21. doi:10.1177/0146167203258831

Sczesny, S., Spreemann, S., & Stahlberg, D. (2006). Masculine = competent? Physical appearance and sex as sources of gender-stereotypic attributions. *Swiss Journal of Psychology/Schweizerische Zeitschrift Für Psychologie/Revue Suisse De Psychologie, 65*(1), 15–23. doi:10.1024/1421-0185.65.1.15

Shartle, C. L. (1950). Studies of leadership by interdisciplinary methods. In A. G. Grace (Ed.), *Leadership in American education.* Chicago, IL: University of Chicago Press.

Shaw, M. E., & Harkey, B. (1976). Some effects of congruency of member characteristics and group structure upon group behavior. *Journal of Personality and Social Psychology, 34*(3), 412–418. doi:10.1037/0022-3514.34.3.412

Shelton, S. H. (1990). Developing the construct of general self-efficacy. *Psychological Reports, 66*(3, Pt 1), 987–994.

Spielberger, C. D. (1972). Conceptual and methodological issues in anxiety research. In C. D. Spielberger (Ed.), *Anxiety: Current trends in theory and research* (Vol. 1, pp. 32–53). New York, NY: Academic Press.

Stirrat, M. M., & Perrett, D. I. (2010). Valid facial cues to cooperation and trust: Male facial width and trustworthiness. *Psychological Science, 21*(3), 349–354. doi:10.1177/0956797610362647

Stogdill, R. M. (1948). Personal factors associated with leadership; a survey of the literature. *Journal of Psychology: Interdisciplinary and Applied, 25,* 35–71.

Stone, A., Russell, R. F., & Patterson, K. (2004). Transformational versus servant leadership: A difference in leader focus. *Leadership & Organization Development Journal, 25*(4), 349–361. doi:10.1108/01437730410538671

Sue, D. W., Capodilupo, C. M., Torino, G. C., Bucceri, J. M., Holder, A. M. B., Nadal, K. L., & Esquilin, M. (2007). Racial Microaggressions in Everyday Life. *American Psychologist, 62*(4), 271–286. doi: 10.1037/0003-066X.62.4.271

Takahashi, K., Ishikawa, J., & Kanai, T. (2012). Qualitative and quantitative studies of leadership in multinational settings: Meta-analytic and cross-cultural reviews. *Journal of World Business, 47*(4), 530–538. doi:10.1016/j.jwb.2012.01.006

Tannenbaum, R., & Schmidt, W. H. (1958). How to choose a leadership pattern. *Harvard Business Review, 36*(2), 95–101.

Tepper, B. J. (2000). Consequences of abusive supervision. *Academy of Management Journal, 43*(2), 178–190. doi:10.2307/1556375

Tepper, B. J. (2007). Abusive supervision in work organizations: Review synthesis, and research agenda. *Journal of Management, 33*(3), 261–289. doi:10.1177/0149206307300812

Tepper, B. J., Moss, S. E., Lockhart, D. E., & Carr, J. C. (2007). Abusive supervision, upward maintenance communication, and subordinates' psychological distress. *Academy of Management Journal, 50*(5), 1169–1180. doi:10.2307/20159918

Trice, H. M., & Beyer, J. M. (1986). Charisma and its routinization in two social movement organizations. *Research In Organizational Behavior, 8,* 113–165.

Tucker, R. C. (1981). *Politics as leadership.* Columbia, Ohio: University of Missouri Press.

Tupes, E. C., & Christal, R. E. (1992). Recurrent personality factors based on trait ratings. *Journal of Personality, 60*(2), 225–251. doi:10.1111/j.1467–6494.1992.tb00973.x

Valla, J. M., Ceci, S. J., & Williams, W. M. (2011). The accuracy of inferences about criminality based on facial appearance. *The Journal of Social, Evolutionary, and Cultural Psychology, 5*(1), 66–91.

van Dierendonck, D. (2011). Servant leadership: A review and synthesis. *Journal of Management, 37*(4), 1228–1261. doi:10.1177/0149206310380462

van Knippenberg, D., van Knippenberg, B., De Cremer, D., & Hogg, M. A. (2004). Leadership, self, and identity: A review and research agenda. *The Leadership Quarterly, 15*(6), 825–856. doi:10.1016/j.leaqua.2004.09.002

Vroom, V. H., Yetton, P. W. (1973). *Leadership and decision-making.* Pittsburgh, PA: University of Pittsburgh Press.

Vroom, V. H., & Jago, A. G. (1974). Decision making as a social process: Normative and descriptive models of leader behavior. *Decision Sciences, 5*(4), 743–769.

Vroom, V. H., & Jago, A. G. (1988). Managing participation: A critical dimension of leadership. *Journal of Management Development, 7*(5), 32–42. doi:10.1108/eb051689

Wang, H., Sui, Y., Luthans, F., Wang, D., & Wu, Y. (2014). Impact of authentic leadership on performance: Role of followers' positive psychological capital and relational processes. *Journal of Organizational Behavior, 35*(1), 5–21. doi:10.1002/job.1850

Wofford, J. C., & Liska, L. Z. (1993). Path-goal theories of leadership: A meta-analysis. *Journal of Management, 19*(4), 857–876. doi:10.1016/0149-2063(93)90031-H

Wong, E. M., Ormiston, M. E., & Haselhuhn, M. P. (2011). A face only an investor could love: CEOs' facial structure predicts their firms' financial performance. *Psychological Science, 22*(12), 1478–1483. doi:10.1177/0956797611418838

Yukl, G. (1998). *Leadership in organizations.* Upper Saddle River, NJ: Prentice Hall.

Yukl, G., & Van Fleet, D. D. (1992). Theory and research on leadership in organizations. In M. D. Dunnette & L. M. Hough (Eds.) , *Handbook of industrial and organizational psychology* (2nd ed., Vol. 3, pp. 147–197). Palo Alto, CA: Consulting Psychologists Press.

Zaleznik, A. (1977). Managers and leaders: Are they different? *Harvard Business Review, 55*(3), 67–78.

Zebrowitz, L. A. (1997). *Reading faces: Window to the soul?* Boulder, CO: Westview.

Zebrowitz, L. A., & Montepare, J. M. (2005). Appearance DOES matter. *Science, 308*(5728), 1565–1566. doi:10.1126/science.1114170

Zhu, W., Zheng, X., He, H., Wang, G., & Zhang, X. (2017). Ethical leadership with both "moral person" and "moral manager" aspects: Scale development and cross-cultural validation. *Journal of Business Ethics,* 1–19. doi:10.1007s10551-017-3740-y

Disseminating Information:
Communication

Learning Outcomes

After studying this chapter you should be able to:

1. Explain how organizations use communication.

2. Choose appropriate communication methods or media given a specific organizational situation.

3. Describe nonverbal cues by offering examples and evaluating which media can convey these nonverbal cues, as well as explain why they matter in communication.

4. Explain how communication occurs in organizations.

5. Compare and contrast patterns of communication.

6. List best practices for communication within organizations.

Mini-Quiz: Communication

As an introduction to this chapter, please take the following mini-quiz (answers are in the back of the book). As you read the questions and consider the answers *before* diving into the chapter, you'll challenge yourself before you master the content, a process that helps facilitate learning for long-term retention. Some questions may have more than one correct answer. Don't worry if you cannot answer all questions correctly on your first try. By the time you read through the chapter and spend some of your own time thinking about these concepts, you should be able to determine the best answers. Try the quiz again after you finish reading the chapter.

1. Many employees say they prefer communicating face-to-face over e-mail or phone. What might be some of the reasons?

a. When talking face-to-face we can also receive nonverbal cues, which are essential for good communication
b. You can see if the other person is paying attention
c. If the person hasn't prepared what he or she wants to say, you can tell right away
d. Sharing information face-to-face means you know it was received, whereas with e-mail, people may not get the message or may not read it

2. What are the main benefits to communicating electronically?
a. You can more easily communicate with team members who are in a different location
b. Some people may be more willing to express their true opinions via e-mail rather than in-person
c. E-mails facilitate two-way, or synchronous, communication
d. There is a record of the communication, making misunderstanding about what was said less likely

3. Blogs have become more and more popular. How can organizations use blogging and make them effective for the company?
a. Let employees loose! They have the best picture of the organization and will capture the true culture all on their own
b. Make recommendations to employees about what type of language to use when blogging
c. Terminate any employee who posts negative comments about the organization in an internal or external blog
d. Encourage employees to share current events about the company as part of every blog entry

4. Written communication (e.g., letters) is used less frequently in many organizations. When might you want to use written communication rather than an e-mail or phone call?
a. When you have to communicate to a large number of people who need to know the information
b. When giving feedback
c. When providing a "thank you" note that needs to convey personal importance
d. When you want a record of the communication

5. When is communication especially important for organizations?
a. During times of conflict and conflict resolution
b. When going through large changes in the organization
c. When the organization has members from a variety of national cultures
d. When employees are sharing information informally among themselves

Overview

Imagine trying to get a class team project done without talking with your classmates—no face-to-face meetings, no e-mails or online chat apps, and no text messaging or phoning. It couldn't be done. Likewise, organizations cannot exist without communication. For example, employees spend most of their time talking with coworkers and supervisors, e-mailing, going to meetings and discussing projects, presenting results of projects, and sharing ideas. A study in Sweden showed that organizational leaders spend anywhere from 62% to 80% of their time directly communicating with other people in the organization (Tengblad, 2006). This includes phone calls, meetings, and touring the facility, but does not include non-face-to-face communications such as e-mailing, or corresponding via paper mail such as memos or letters to stakeholders (Tengblad, 2006). Thus, the percentage of overall time spent communicating is probably even higher than reported.

However, communication is not just talking or sharing printed materials; it must be effective to be useful and handled responsibly. Aside from whether spoken or written, there are many facets to communication that make it effective or not, or understood in the way it was originally intended. For instance, communication doesn't have to be formal, such as a newsletter, to have an effect. Often informal communications, such as gossip in the hallways or private off-the-record conversations with your manager have a bigger impact than formal communications.

Whether formal or informal, communication is a function of the environment, such that cultural factors play a role in the effectiveness of communication. For example, members of different countries with different assumptions regarding communication norms at work may not understand the content of the message just because of the style with which it was delivered and the choice of words or body language shared. Occasionally, however, what is *not* shared is the message. For instance, during large organizational changes, organizational charts are sometimes presented depicting the new organizational structure. The absence of names on the charts usually communicates who will be let go during the change event.

The effectiveness of your message may also be influenced by the medium you use, such as face-to-face or via the computer. For example, emotions cannot be as easily conveyed in written communications as they can in face-to-face conversations. Hence, explaining missing names on an organizational chart using face-to-face communication during a change intervention may be more effective than e-mailing the chart to employees and adding a written explanation in the message.

Given the amount of time spent communicating within organizations and the potential impact those messages have on the employees and organization as a whole, understanding methods and patterns of effective communication within organizations should be considered imperative for good management and leadership. One of the most important skills affecting the success of a leader is their communication skills.

Which Communication Methods Are Used in Organizations?

Communication in organization varies widely depending on how messages are shared (e.g., technology vs. face-to-face conversation), the frequency with which messages need to be shared, and who shares the message. The purpose of the message also makes a difference, as does the type of organization—global or local only. Unlike personal or social communication, business communication may have bigger consequences associated with it, like lifelong earning potential, making your mastery of the subtleties imperative!

In this section, these various aspects of how communication occurs in organizations are reviewed, and tips for good communication derived from the research literature are shared throughout.

Medium of Communication

The medium of communication refers to the transmission channel for the sharing of information; in plain English—it refers to *how* messages are shared. Are the messages conveyed via a face-to-face conversation, paper report, or electronic communication, which includes recorded messages, computer-mediated messages, or phone? A substantial amount has been written about various communication media; therefore, only a brief review is provided here (see also Byrne, Masterson, & Hurd, 2012, for more).

Face-to-Face Communication

Face-to-face communications include one-on-one meetings, group discussions, speeches, and informal communication that occur in the hallways as people pass one another. These communications are literally defined by one person facing or being next to another, although some include video communication as face-to-face since people can actually see each other.

Advantages of Face-to-Face Communication

Face-to-face communication (Figure 10.1) has the advantage of taking less time as compared to other media to when sharing complicated or emotionally laden information, allows for instant feedback on whether the message was understood, and provides the simultaneous opportunity to clarify the message if it appears to have been misunderstood. Additionally, face-to-face communication allows all nonverbal and verbal cues to be conveyed in a matter of seconds, if not less. **Paralanguage**, such as laughing, crying, and yawning, or vocal qualifiers such as rhythm, tone, and rate, as well as vocal segregates such as uh-uh, shh, oooh, or mmmh are communicated easily and instantly in a face-to-face conversation (Kahai & Cooper, 2003). Emotions are also easily conveyed in face-to-face communication through facial expressions, paralanguage, voice expressions such as pace and volume, touching, shrinking of physical distance between individuals, and stepping away to increase the distance.

FIGURE 10.1 Face-to-Face Communication

Nonverbal Cues   Four essential nonverbal cues are conveyed during face-to-face communication, making it a powerful medium: distance, eye contact, body orientation, and accessibility of body (Mehrabian, 1969).

FIGURE 10.2   Distance between Speaking Partners as a Nonverbal Cue

(1) © BlueSkyImage/Shutterstock, Inc.; (2) © Monkey Business Images/Shutterstock, Inc.; (3) © Blaj Gabriel/Shutterstock, Inc.; (4) © Gelpi JM/Shutterstock, Inc.

Distance between speakers refers to the norm for how close people should physically stand next to each other. When the norm for distance is violated, it leads to embarrassment, confusion over one another's intentions, possible rejection, and a perceived lack of responsiveness. When the norm is observed, people use that information as an indication of respect. Country culture, gender, and status in the organization can influence the norms for distance. For example, women are generally more comfortable with less space between themselves and other women, as compared to men with men or men with women.

Higher status individuals stand farther away from lower status individuals, unless attempting intimidation, which is achieved by standing closer (often uncomfortably) to the other person. Considering country culture, people from European and North American cultures tend to stand relatively far apart from each other when compared to Latin American, some Asian cultures, and Arab cultures, where communication partners may frequently touch one another (Steers, Sanchez-Runde, & Nardon, 2010). Pay attention to cultural norms because invading people's space (Figure 10.2) is one of the 10 worst body language blunders you can make, according to Forbes (see their article "10 Worst Body Language Mistakes" on their web site).

Eye contact conveys consent for people to start and stop their verbal exchanges, as well as express attitudes and emotions. In North American cultures, increasing or lengthening the amount of eye contact, but not staring, can communicate affiliation and intimacy, whereas avoiding eye contact can communicate dislike and disrespect (Mehrabian, 1969). In some Asian cultures, however, direct prolonged eye contact is a sign of disrespect.

Eye contact works with the third cue, *body orientation*, which refers to the angle of your shoulders and legs relative to the person with whom you're communicating.

The arrows in Figure 10.3 indicate the direction and angle of each communication partner, showing the explicit orientation of each person's body. The interpretation of body orientation varies by culture, but in general, direct face-to-face orientations (where arrows point directly at each other) tend to be perceived as the most formal and most confrontational, though leaning forward can reduce the formality or threat. Notice that most of the arrows in Figure 10.3 show people with arrows that are not directly facing one another. Be careful, however, because angling your body too far away from your partner can signal distrust and lack of interest!

FIGURE 10.3   Body Orientation as a Nonverbal Cue

(1) © Monkey Business Images/Shutterstock, Inc.; (2) © Monkey Business Images/Shutterstock, Inc.; (3) © Pressmaster/Shutterstock, Inc.; Bottom (4) © BlueSkyImage/Shutterstock, Inc.; (5) © Monkey Business Images/Shutterstock, Inc.; (6) © Monkey Business Images/Shutterstock, Inc.

Lastly, *accessibility of body*, such as openness of arms and legs (Figure 10.4), can communicate different messages, also dependent on culture. For example, open arms generally indicate a lack of defensiveness, whereas closed of folded

FIGURE 10.4   Accessibility of Body as a Nonverbal Cue

Left: © Minerva Studio/Shutterstock, Inc.; Right: © StockLite/Shutterstock, Inc.

arms can indicate disagreement, lack of acceptance, or readiness to defend position or point of view. Accessibility might also include a firm handshake that can signal confidence and authority. A weak or sweaty handshake, typically called the limp fish, is one of the worst body language mistakes you can make; alongside crossing your arms (see Forbes' "10 Worst Body Language Mistakes" on their web site).

These four critical nonverbal cues, distance, eye contact, body orientation, and accessibility of body, can easily be conveyed in face-to-face communications, but not so in non-face-to-face interactions. Although some eye contact, accessibility of body, and possibly body orientation may be shared via communication mechanisms that provide visual connection, such as webcam or televised communication, it can be difficult to see these cues if the person is not in focus on the camera or is too far from (or too close to) the camera. Additionally, one's body orientation is hard to infer without seeing the surrounding environment that provides perspective on the angle of the body.

Employees themselves believe face-to-face is more effective for some communications as compared to e-mail. In 2008, the Pew Research Center reported that out of 809 full-time and part-time employees surveyed, 65% indicated the most effective way to resolve work issues was via face-to-face conversation, with the percentage rising to 90 for resolving sensitive work issues (PEW, 2008). Some employees state that face-to-face, as opposed to electronic, communication is imperative when sharing sensitive, private, or confidential information (Kupritz & Cowell, 2011). Similarly, human resource professionals agree that communications involving performance appraisal, discipline, or situations with the potential for legal concern require in-person conversation, although managers may follow-up with written communication to ensure understanding and legality (Kupritz & Cowell, 2011). Some jobs, such as nurse, physician, social worker, teacher, or funeral home director require that one convey compassion—emotions—as part of the job. The work itself includes both positive and negative emotions (Miller, 2007), which are essential for effective performance. For example, in these work roles, employees must notice that compassion is necessary, feel emotionally connected to the other person, and behaving and communicating using compassion (which sometimes might require remaining neutral; Miller, 2007). One can argue that face to face communication is necessary for compassionate communication.

Face-to-face communication does allow for the conveyance of nonverbal cues, which serves as a great advantage; however, it also has disadvantages making other forms of communication preferred at times.

Disadvantages of Face-to-Face Communication

Disadvantages of face-to-face communication include that you must be in the same location as your listeners, which is becoming increasingly difficult as the workforce becomes more globally dispersed. Additionally, you can only be heard by a limited number of people unless your voice is amplified. When talking face-to-face, nonverbal cues, such as fidgeting with your face or hair may be distracting causing you and your listeners to lose track of your message. Another disadvantage of face-to-face conversation is that once something is said, it cannot be retracted. If the wrong words are shared at the wrong time or you say something you regret, you can't erase or stop your words from being heard by your listener.

Which do you think is more effective for resolving workplace issues: face-to-face conversation or electronic (e.g., e-mail) discussions? When would you use e-mail over face-to-face to resolve a work issue?

Gender (how we identify our sex) can be complicated to ascertain simply from visual characteristics. Ensuring your communication respects people who identify transgender, LBGTQ, or heterosexual can go a long way towards making the workplace welcome for all.

TABLE 10.1 Dos and Don'ts for Sharing Negative Feedback

Do This	Don't Do This
Focus on specific events as opposed to vague generalities.	Sugar coat negative news because it dilutes your message and the impact of your message.
Focus on "change" as the goal for the feedback. What needs to change to correct the behavior?	Put people on the defensive by making your message about their character or personality.
Tell it like it is; be straightforward and direct.	Don't sidestep the issue.
Give feedback immediately or at the earliest opportunity, so that corrective action can be taken quickly and to connect your feedback with the behavior that needs to change.	Exaggerate the frequency with which behavior occurs or doesn't occur. For example, terms like *always* and *never* feel extreme. Instead, provide the pattern of behavior "the last 10 times you clocked-in, you were 15 minutes late."
Describe what you see happening.	Avoid subjective opinions, but do share what the conclusion is when seeing specific behavior, even if your conclusion is subjective.
Share the consequences of their behavior. Connect their behavior with the outcomes or results of the behavior.	Use feedback as punishment
Recognize and acknowledge their attempts to act appropriately.	Expect perfection—it takes time to learn how to act differently.
Be clear about performance expectations.	Be vague about what good performance is.

Courtesy Zinta Byrne.

Face-to-face communication can be difficult, especially when it comes to sharing negative messages. For example, giving negative feedback or sharing potentially hurtful news (e.g., demotion or firing) can be hard to do because you may lack the skills in giving negative feedback (Larson, 1986) and you anticipate a negative reaction from your recipient, such as rejecting the feedback and defensiveness (Larson, 1984). Some managers end up withholding negative feedback, called the "mum effect" (Rosen & Tesser, 1970; Tesser, Rosen, & Tesser 1971), because of their fear of how their employees may react.

Since giving negative feedback to improve performance is a part of a manager's job, what is the best way to give negative feedback? In a 2013 *HR Specialist* article "The art of giving negative feedback: A 7-step approach," several "do this" and "don't do this" were shared for how to give negative feedback, shown in Table 10.1.

Although face-to-face communication may be the best method for discussing performance feedback, holding quick meetings, or sharing workplace gossip, many communications in the workplace are documented, such as the performance appraisal, and shared via paper or in an electronic written format.

Written Paper Communication

Written communication on paper still comprises a reasonable percentage of messaging in business. It is unclear just how much is still communicated via paper; however, it is becoming clear with efforts to eliminate paper waste and for efficiency and speed, that the favored communication media may be face-to-face and electronic.

Advantages of Paper Communication

Memos remain an effective method for sharing company policy changes and formal company-wide changes requiring enforcement. Company announcements are frequently made via paper messaging, in addition to other forms such as e-mail or web site, because paper messages seem to communicate an added level of authority or formality that sends a message in and of itself. Typically, company memos appear on company letterhead, making it clear who owns the message—the organization and not just the letter author. Paper messages are also helpful when a lot of information needs to be conveyed—they can be read and reread with little eye exhaustion and hopefully less interruption than on-screen messages that may compete with pop-up messages from chat rooms or blinking images on web sites.

Disadvantages of Paper Communication

Disadvantages of paper communication include how long it takes to produce and to be received by the intended party. Specifically, paper communication must be printed and then somehow delivered, and delivery does not always occur overnight. With recipients in different geographic locations, communications can be slow because of travel time, especially if overnight delivery is not possible. Even then, overnight may be too slow depending on the criticality of the message. Another disadvantage of paper communication is its distribution mechanism. When more than one person needs to receive the message, a lot of paper documents are produced and then distributed. To put this into perspective, the average office employee produces over two pounds of paper (about 250 pages) each day in the form of mistakes on the printer, bad copies, memos and reports, and journals, to name a few. That's about 1250 pages or nearly 3 reams of paper per week, which is about the same as two large African Elephants stacked on top of each other—26 feet of paper—per year! (Figure 10.5). The United States Environmental Protection Agency estimates that 90% of all office waste is paper.

26 Feet

FIGURE 10.5   Three Reams of Paper Wasted per Week

Like face-to-face communication, once a message is out there, in this case in print, it is hard, if not impossible, to retract or change. Unlike face-to-face communication, an erratum or correction can be released on paper, but one must ensure that the correction makes it to everyone who received or saw the first copy.

Electronic Communication

Electronic communication includes voice messaging, phones, video, and computer messaging systems such as e-mail. Electronic communication is essential for organizations needing to communicate across geographical and time boundaries. Even organizations within a single location take advantage of electronic communication in the form of meeting requests, e-mail messaging, and phone. It is not unusual for coworkers sitting a desk away from each other to use electronic chat functions or e-mails to communicate with one another. Organizations also communicate with external parties such as vendors or distributors via the Internet, webcam, and phone. Although some electronic communication is "written" (i.e., e-mail), electronic media carry different potential than paper, such as the ability to be distributed across the globe in seconds, animated, or transcribed into a verbal communication mechanism.

Some theories of media communication, such as media richness theory (Daft & Lengel, 1984), propose that communication media are characterized by their ability or capacity to convey nonverbal cues, such as facial expression, posture, and gestures, as well as pitch, tone, loudness, and pauses. Media richness theory suggests that face-to-face communication is the richest medium as it has the ability to send both verbal and nonverbal cues. Telephone-based communication is the next most rich because both verbal and nonverbal auditory cues (e.g., pitch, tone, loudness) can be conveyed. In both face-to-face and phone conversations, emotions can be shared. E-mail or text messaging is considered less rich than face-to-face or phone because it can only transmit verbal messages—nonverbal cues cannot be transmitted. Some people attempt to use emoticons such as a smiley face :-) or a wink ;-) to convey emotions; however, the effect is not the same (Rice & Love, 1987), and symbols vary by culture (e.g., a smiley face in Japan is depicted as ^-^). As noted previously, paralanguage cannot be shared easily in lean media (Kahai & Cooper, 2003). Though efforts to insert emotion and nonverbal cues into the message can sometimes be helpful, the communication lacks the multiplicity of cues available via face-to-face communication, rendering various communications faulty, negatively affecting the maintenance of relationships (Byrne, 1971, Short, Williams, & Christie, 1976).

Other theories such as channel expansion theory (Carlson & Zmud, 1999), an extension of media richness theory, suggest that comfort with the medium (also known as the channel) determines people's perception of the richness of the medium. People who are very comfortable with electronic communication are more likely to perceive more richness from it than those who are not comfortable. Regardless of comfort and ease of use, you cannot extract nonverbal cues from nonvisual electronic communication (see Byrne, Masterson, & Hurd, 2012, for more regarding computer-mediated communication).

With the focus on environmental sustainability increasing, do you think paper communication in organizations has a future? For which types of communication do you think an organization must continue using paper?

Advantages of Electronic Communication

Electronic media have several advantages over paper, some of which you are probably already familiar, but many of which you may not recognize. For instance, electronic communication is quick and can be transmitted at any time of day. Electronic messages are easily modified and may be resent as many times as needed. Electronic messages can be sent to many people at one time, making broad distributions across the organization very easy. Additionally, with new technology, electronic communication can be received just about anywhere, on any mobile device such as watch, phone, tablet, or laptop. Electronic media, specifically electronic mail, can include the original message along with a new one, providing a reminder of the initial communication. With e-mail, for instance, complete discussions are possible by including the original message along with the entire chain of back and forth replies. Electronic communication has few geographical boundaries; therefore, messages can be sent around the globe without hesitation.

Lastly, though some people may not consider this an advantage, research shows people are more willing to express honest opinions in online chat rooms as compared to face-to-face (Ho & McLeod, 2008), suggesting that you might get more honest feedback or replies using electronic media than face-to-face or paper. However, honesty in electronic communication is a two-edged sword.

Disadvantages of Electronic Communication

Because people may be more willing to be honest in electronic communication, they might also be more likely to share messages they later regret because honesty can sometimes be hurtful. We may share a white lie, a half-truth, or not share at all to save face or protect one another's egos. Thus, the "freedom" electronic media gives us for sharing more truthful statements may at times be a disadvantage; you may get feedback that you wish you hadn't or regret some that you gave.

Even though electronic messages may seem more truthful than would be expected in a face-to-face conversation, electronic communication might be considered somewhat more forgiving of communication mistakes than paper or face-to-face communication because a mistaken message, such as sharing incorrect information, could potentially be quickly retracted and reissued, sometimes before the incorrect version is ever seen. New applications for mobile devices allow for text messages that are automatically deleted after a few hours, leaving no clear trace of their existence. In contrast, some electronic communications are more permanent than paper, especially those posted to the Internet or accessible by many people. The electronic copy can reside in many locations, never fades, and cannot be easily destroyed. Mistaken communications face-to-face can easily be denied or changed in our memories over time, resulting in faulty recollections or arguments that the receiver simply misunderstood the message (whether true or not). Such accusations of misunderstandings are harder to make with electronic communication because the original message can frequently be used as evidence.

Anyone who has accidentally hit the "reply all" component of e-mail messaging or has been the recipient of a "forward" on a message that clearly was

What to do if you mess up and the consequence is hurtful to the recipient? Regardless of communication medium, if you make an honest mistake, fess up and offer a genuine and heartfelt apology. Even if you're not out to make this person your best friend, an apology for a hurtful mistake may the right thing to do. Of course, what is considered "right" depends on your country or national culture; however, most cultures value honesty and integrity.

not meant for forwarding can appreciate the downside of the ease of electronic messaging.

In addition, electronic messaging is a one-way communication; thus, messages are sent and received, and then responded to in a separate message. That is, only one person responds at a time (e.g., voicemail), taking turns and rendering the communication **asynchronous**. The main disadvantage of asynchronous messaging is that each person must wait their turn to communicate. Sometimes messages get out of order in the communication thread, making it harder to track and make sense of the conversation.

In contrast, **synchronous** communication allows for two-way conversation, such as during face-to-face dialogue, an active telephone call (i.e., not voicemail), or videoconferencing. In a face-to-face conversation, and to a degree phone or videoconferencing, your dialogue partner can simultaneously respond to you while you are talking, and you can hear or see his or her response while you are talking. The result of synchronous communication is increased potential for tracking the ordering of the conversation thread, and clarifying understanding midstream. With telephone or videoconferencing, the ability to communicate synchronously and smoothly is dependent on the quality of the technology. Think of a time when you and a friend were talking on your cell phones and you said something while your friend was talking. The conversation may have been broken or choppy at the moment you both tried to talk, resulting in neither of you having heard what the other said. The better the technology, the less likely this chopping up of conversation occurs, and the greater the potential for conversation thread tracking and conveying understanding.

Understanding is enhanced when nonverbal cues are conveyed along with verbal cues. Hence, another big disadvantage of electronic communication is its inability to transmit nonverbal cues. In addition to distance, eye contact, body orientation, and accessibility of body, the four nonverbal cues mentioned previously in this chapter, nonverbal communication includes body movement, facial expressions (Figure 10.6), and tone and intonations. Researchers have carefully distinguished nonverbal from verbal communication stating that nonverbal communication does not have language properties (Burgoon, Buerrero, & Manusov, 2011). This means that nonverbal communication must be interpreted as the thoughts it intends to share, as opposed to understood by words or message content. American Sign Language is a good example of nonverbal communication.

FIGURE 10.6   Facial Expressions as Nonverbal Cues

Think about communications where movements as subtle as shoulder shrugging, eye winking, or a raised eyebrow are used to send a message. The message may be "I understand," "I don't understand," "I'm not interested" or "are you sure?" Nonverbal cues, such as subtle movements, facial expressions, and intonations add depth and clarity to the message. We look to such cues during communication to determine if our message is being understood by the receiver and if our dialogue partner is still engaged. Without these cues, our ability to determine if our message is understood dramatically shrinks or becomes impossible, as does feedback that we are still in the conversation. Synchronous communication allows for the transmission of many nonverbal communication cues, whereas asynchronous communication is limited.

Lastly, a disadvantage of electronic communication that also affects understanding is communication delays. Failure to respond quickly to a somewhat sensitive message may instigate fears that the recipient misunderstood the message or is using the delay as a power tactic (e.g., unnecessary delays convey that the one delaying has the power to do so). The sender must wait for confirmation of understanding, confirmation of receipt, and hope that the delay is only due to time zone differences or a busy schedule, rather than a message in and of itself.

New Opportunities for Companies Engaging in Electronic Communication

With the explosion of electronic communication methods, disadvantages aside, organizations have several opportunities for using electronic communication methods strategically. For example, online communities are electronic "places" where employees can meet to share work-related issues, concerns, and questions. Online communities can be used for informal training or development efforts, fostering sharing of information and encouraging training through informal learning. The added benefit of online communities is that learning experiences are all recorded so others can refer to the information at a later time (Dolezalek, 2003).

Furthermore, online communities can boost interaction amongst employees, which can ultimately result in increased productivity (Dolezalek, 2003). However, implementing an online community for the organization is no easy feat. For easy adoption, the technology must be compatible with programs employees already use. Additionally, Dolezalek notes that online communities more readily form where existing communities of some kind already exist, which means if there is not an existing community of employees (e.g., like a learning or mentoring community), creating one online is that much more challenging.

Blogs are another electronic communication mechanism becoming more popular with organizations, even though they have been around since the 1990s (Dearstyne, 2005). A blog is short for "weblog" (i.e., World Wide Web log file), which is a web site on which the owner (called a blogger) publishes ideas and information in short, frequent messages (called posts), usually dated or tracked chronologically. A blog is typically focused on one topic, so that all posts in that blog are about the same general category or topic. The topic can be broad or narrow. Blogs are a simple, yet dynamic way of sharing information. They can include pictures, video, and links to other web sites. The information shared can be new ideas, opinions, or reviews of other people's work and comments. Because they are easy to use and people can comment on any blog posting (where all comments can be seen if the blog owner chooses), blogs encourage information sharing.

Dearstyne (2005) suggests organizations ask themselves the following 10 questions before implementing an internal blog:

1. Is hype or real applicability driving the need for a blog?

2. What are other successful blogs sharing and what makes them influential?

3. What criteria or measures will show the overall costs or gains of starting a blog?

4. What role, if any, will key management have in the blog?

5. Does the blog fit with the overall company strategy?

6. How can creativity be balanced with protecting the organization's interests?

7. How should employee blogs be categorized (official, personal)?

8. What policies (e.g., legal) need to be in place before blogging begins?

9. How will blogging records be managed?

10. Will the information technology of the organization be able to support blogging?

Because blogs can be internal or external to the organization (Cox, Martinez, & Quinlan, 2008), the organization should determine which type, if not both, is desired. The downside of an external blog is that shared information such as gripes about upcoming mergers may create problems for the organization, especially when the information is inaccurate and potentially damaging to company reputation.

To make blogs effective and control the release of inaccurate or harmful messages, organizations should implement policies governing the language and content of postings to protect professional and trade secrets. In addition, organizations should make clear statements about whether the blog is an official record for the company or not (has legal implications; Dearstyne, 2005).

Blogs also have their downsides. Sometimes blogs can present a bigger challenge than originally anticipated (Ebanks, 2005). How much and what kind of information is shared needs to be managed to a degree, to censure inappropriate postings or correct potentially harmful, inaccurate information. For example, if some employees comment on a merger, sharing that several groups are being let go and the information posted is inaccurate, it could result in many dissatisfied employees thinking they are losing their jobs when in fact they are not. In some cases, employees have been terminated for negative blogging about their organizations, inappropriately sharing personal information about patients or colleagues, breaching confidentiality, and engaging in insubordination (Sorensen, 2008). In one example, a personal-care worker started a personal blog about her patients and colleagues, writing negative information about them and the company for whom she worked. The employee was fired and appealed to the courts that she didn't understand the public nature of blogging. The courts sided with the company and the company's firing decision was upheld. Even though her blogging was done off company time, it still resulted in termination because of what she blogged. This particular blogging instance also had a negative effect on the company, as it faced negative publicity due to the comments that she posted. As Dearstyne (2005) recommends, company policies about blogging and general use

Why are blogs potentially beneficial to todays organizations?

of electronic communication are necessary for the protection of both employee and organization.

Twitter, another type of electronic communication, is a social networking global web site that transmits fast and short (280 characters or less) messages (called tweets). Using the "at" symbol, indicated by @ in a tweet (i.e., a message posting), directs the message specifically to someone, giving them an opportunity to reply. Hashtags, indicated by a # symbol, signify a message is related to a specific topic. For example, #vacation, #weekends, or #justsayin. Users "follow" or track each other's tweets, but following someone is not necessarily positive or negative—"follow" or "track" is just the word used for tracking specific people who are tweeting and whose tweets you'd like to read. Public messages can reach a wide range of people. Messages can be kept private by sending a direct message to someone who follows you. A key feature of Twitter is the ability to share relevant links in messages. Organizations can effectively use Twitter to share upcoming product information, connect with stakeholders and clients, and develop a presence with the online community (Lovejoy, Waters, & Saxton, 2012).

Exercise 10.1

Create a chart with the advantages and disadvantages of face-to-face, written, and electronic communications.

When to Use Which Medium?

Although in the review above of the various types of media and their uses, with so many options in communication media to choose from, it helps to consider in a comparative format the forms of media that organizations use. Table 10.2 provides a side-by-side review of media, their primary uses, and their advantages and disadvantages. They are listed in increasing order of ability to convey communication cues. You can use this chart to determine when to use which medium.

As technology advances and new techniques are developed, it would be easy to assume that the list in Table 10.2 will quickly become obsolete. However, although new forms of electronic communication are introduced, the basic forms noted in Table 10.2 remain quite stable over time. Thus, as

---

TABLE 10.2 Media and Their Advantages and Disadvantages

Medium	Use to Convey or Provide	Examples	Advantages	Disadvantages
Letter	A personal touch that does not require face to face or voice communication Formality or authority Detailed information Formal documentation	Thank you Promotion Grievance Pay increase	Permanent document Effective where Internet or electronic access is lacking Does not require recipient be simultaneously available	Slow Paper waste Easily lost Lacks nonverbal cues Lacks immediate feedback

(Continued)

TABLE 10.2   Media and Their Advantages and Disadvantages   (*Continued*)

Medium	Use to Convey or Provide	Examples	Advantages	Disadvantages
Email	Impersonal, brief, and casual message Exchange of information Sequenced chain of communication	Status update Quick question Referrals	Quick Easily mass distributed Easily forwarded Convenient— accessed from any electronic device Does not require recipient be simultaneously available Can be permanent	Easily forwarded No privacy Inaccessible if electricity fails or lack of access to Internet Lacks nonverbal cues Lacks immediate feedback (unless recipient is in e-mail)
Voicemail	Brief message Exchange of simple information Fast follow-up	Confirming appointment Sharing an appointment time	Quick Convenient Includes audio nonverbal cues Does not require recipient be simultaneously available Is semi-permanent	Inaccessible if phone battery dies Unless tied to an e-mail program, cannot be printed or forwarded Not permanent Lacks visual nonverbal cues Lacks immediate feedback
Telephone	Brief message Asking for clarification or understanding Fast turnaround Personal information	Clarifying confusing e-mail Clarifying potentially volatile message Sharing personal information	Quick Convenient Private unless tapped or on speaker setting Includes audio nonverbal cues Allows for immediate feedback Can be recorded	Cannot be forwarded Not permanent Inaccessible if phone line is disconnected Requires other person is available Lacks visual nonverbal cues
Videoconference	Dialogue between many people at one time Personal connection	Meeting of geographically dispersed team	Include multiple people simultaneously Includes audio and visual nonverbal cues Allows for immediate feedback Can be recorded	Lacks body orientation and accessibility of body nonverbal cues Technology may include delays if transmission must cross extreme geographic boundaries
Face-to-face	All nonverbal cues Personal connection and sensitivity Sensitive or emotionally charged messages Feedback	Performance appraisal Unwanted or difficult news such as being fired, laid off, or demoted Being promoted	Incorporates all nonverbal cues Can be quick and efficient Private (unless people repeat what was said)	Must be co-located Can be hard to give negative feedback in person

The medium you choose to communicate should match the type of message you want to convey.

new technologies are added, you can determine about where in the list the new technology belongs, and attribute advantages and disadvantages. For instance, face-to-face communication will always be the richest form of communication, unless humans eventually develop telepathic capability to feel one another's emotions and communicate nonverbals without the need for seeing and being physically present with one another.

Patterns of Communication

Specific media transmit messages, but *how* the information is transmitted in terms of directly from one person to another, or indirectly through multiple other people is referred to as patterns of communication. Research into how communication patterns affect group problem-solving has been active since the 1950s (e.g., Leavitt, 1951; Shaw, 1956), revealing that people use different patterns at different times depending on the type of problem being solved or type of decision that needs communicating. For example, Leavitt (1951) found, in a problem-solving task, that when people used a centralized pattern like that depicted on the left in Figure 10.7 (called a wheel), they were able to make decisions faster than in communication patterns such as the straight line depicted in the cell tower on the right of Figure 10.7 (called a chain: Leavitt, 1951).

Although several different patterns of communication are discussed int he next sections, they are not exclusive of one another. For example, vertical communication includes upward and downward at the same time.

In the straight-line pattern person A shares with person B, who then shares with person C, etc., but person A never shares directly with C or anyone else in the chain after sharing with person B. Not surprisingly, Leavitt (1951) found that more errors of communication were made in the chain than in the wheel. This research into different patterns of communication has led to categorizing communication into at least two specific configurations: centralized and decentralized. The patterns represented in Figure 10.7 are both centralized.

FIGURE 10.7 Centralized Communication Patterns

Left: © bluebay/Shutterstock, Inc.; Right: © maudanros/Shutterstock, Inc.

Centralized

A centralized pattern of communication refers to all information going through a pivotal person who then transmits the information to everyone else. Thus, communication between team members does not occur unless it first goes through the central person. The cell tower in Figure 10.7 illustrates the extreme idea of centralized communication. All cell phone communications must go through the cell tower to get to their intended destination, just like all members of a group or unit must go through a single person for their communication.

At work, a good example of a centralized communication is in the upper echelon of organizational authority. The most senior executive generally has more and better access to information than anyone else, and whether that information is passed along is up to that senior executive. The executive exercises the right to decide how the flow of information will proceed and when. Positions in organizations designated by the title "chief" generally operate using centralized communication patterns (e.g., chief of police, chief financial officer, and chief architect). Most leaders are in positions where they are the key decision-maker, which means the communication typically flows through them. Organizations with different units or divisions that are not colocated, such as different divisions spread throughout Europe, Asia, and the Americas, may require that those divisions cannot finalize product decisions until they have first communicated with the corporate office. This type of communication pattern, where each unit must share and obtain its information from the corporate office is centralized.

Advantages of centralized communication models include quality control. You have a better handle on the quality of information transmitted if it starts and stops with a single person. Sensitive information, such as urgent news (i.e., changes in the organization that are legally sensitive and may be regulated by law; Byrne & LeMay, 2006), can be managed carefully because it is not freely shared. Another advantage of centralized communication is that for simple problems (Shaw, 1964), a decision can be made quickly, especially if the central person managing communications is also the decision-maker. Additionally, having centralized communications can facilitate all divisions or units of an organization using the same approach and the same policies.

Disadvantages of centralized communication include that communication can be bottlenecked or held up with the one person or group who controls the message. When problems are complicated, a centralized communication pattern can delay decision-making and problem solving. Organizations with divisions in multiple countries may struggle with centralized communication patterns because each country may have its own laws or regulations and unless the corporate or central office is familiar with all country policies and nuances of culture, mistakes can be made or significant delays can occur.

Decentralized

Decentralized communication refers to a pattern of direct sharing of information between multiple people at the same time, without having to first go through a central individual (Figure 10.8).

Thus, in decentralized patterns all members can communicate directly with one another and also with the leader. An example of decentralized communication occurs in teams that are highly interdependent. The team members rely on one another to complete the various functions of their jobs, and as a result of their interdependence, they must be able to communicate freely with one another to keep making progress. A decentralized communication pattern facilitates the team effort by allowing information to flow freely from person to person, as needed.

An advantage of decentralized communication, therefore, is that information flows rapidly throughout the network of people. When a problem is complicated, more people can participate in the solution at one time because they're pulled in quickly and information is shared freely between all the people (Shaw, 1964). Early research conducted in the 1950s demonstrated that the decentralized pattern of communication as depicted in Figure 10.8 (called a comcon: Shaw, 1956) resulted in more shared messages between group members and faster problem solving than centralized communication patterns.

Disadvantages of decentralized communication include the challenges of quality control, ensuring that sensitive information is not distributed where it shouldn't be, and the inability to manage the timing of messages when timing may be an important factor, such as with urgent news. Urgent news, which is sensitive information to the organization, may need additional monitoring when it is released to the internal organization. For example, information that may affect stock prices is considered sensitive urgent news (Byrne & LeMay, 2006).

Other communication patterns, still referring to how information flows throughout the organization, indicate whether the flow is formalized by the organization or informal and may occur randomly or in unsanctioned directions throughout the organization.

Decentralized communication has the advantages of fast messaging and communicating with the exact people you need. Disadvantages include inability to control messaging for sensitivity.

FIGURE 10.8 Decentralized Communication Patterns

© violetkaipa/Shutterstock, Inc.

Formal Networks

Formal networks are represented by the organizational chart or the structure of the organization—who reports to whom and who has authority over whom. Communication that follows the formal network of the organization respects the paths of the organizational structure, as opposed to jumping diagonally across levels and groups. Thus, communication flows either vertically, up or down, or horizontally, as shown in Figure 10.9.

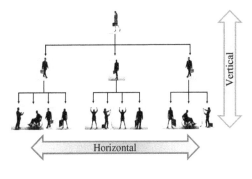

Vertical

Vertical communication denotes the sharing of information up or down within the organization's hierarchy. Examples include messages that go from manager to employee (down) and from employee to manager (up). With vertical communication, the pattern is only up or down and not lateral.

FIGURE 10.9   Formal Networks

Left: © aslysun/Shutterstock, Inc. ; Right: © Rawpixel/Shutterstock, Inc.

Downward   Communication initiated with the management team and targeted at employees is considered downward communication. Downward communication occurs with performance evaluations, feedback sessions outside of the performance appraisal meeting, company manuals that document policies, employee handbooks that document expectations for performance, company newsletters, and the company web site.

Challenges with downward communication are that information shared in this way may be filtered or modified by the manager. Thus, even if senior levels of the organization suggest that certain information should be shared, what is actually shared is determined by the management layers reporting to the higher levels. In some cases, by the time the message gets to the employee, it is generally not the same as when it started out and the amount shared is significantly reduced and not necessarily because of power plays or other politically motivated reasons.

Disadvantages of downward communication include that information needed to perform the job may be delayed, negatively affecting subordinate job performance. It may also be the case that the immediate manager does not have the necessary information, fails to remember all of the information that needs to be shared (e.g., all the details), or confuses aspects of complicated messages (Adler, 1989) causing further challenges for employees. Hence, the quality, timing, and effectiveness of downward communication rely on the communicator—in this case, the boss.

Upward   In contrast to downward communication patterns, upward communication refers to patterns where information starts at the lower levels of the organization such as the employee completing the job tasks, and is directed toward management at higher levels of the organizational hierarchy. For example, when the organization undergoes change, managers may hold group meetings to allow employees to ask about the change and voice their concerns or ideas about the change. These meetings are frequently called Town Hall meetings, a term coined in the early history of the United States of America, in which community members would meet in the actual town hall to develop policies for the town. The term has since been used to describe any meeting open to the public. The purpose of the company town hall meeting is to encourage upward communication; to provide feedback to the organizational leaders. The meetings also convey to employees that their voice is important and that management cares about their well-being and satisfaction at work (thus, providing a dual benefit to the organization in the form of upward *and* downward communication; e.g., Griffith-Cooper & King, 2007; Mion, Hazel, Cap, Fusilero, Podmore, & Szweda, 2006). At Google, the company co-founders hold weekly meetings with the entire company to share updates on products, welcome new hires, and conduct a question and answer session. These weekly meetings, call TGIF all-hands meetings, are a form of town hall meetings—they are open and anything goes.

Another form of upward communication is a suggestion box or e-mail address that allows employees to initiate ideas and communicate them upward to the executives, without a face-to-face meeting. Attitude surveys or opinions surveys fulfill a similar function, where they may be conducted regularly within the organization to obtain employees perceptions about their satisfaction, employee benefits, the work environment, or any other issue for which upper management seeks input.

Sharing information can be as simple as an employee discussing the status of the current project with his or her boss. These status reports can be shared either face-to-face or via e-mail communication, and may include feedback on how well downward messages were received and understood.

Typically, status reports, e-mails, suggestion boxes, and face-to-face discussions are mechanisms for sharing positive feedback and input between employees and supervisors. When negative feedback needs to be shared, grievance systems are used. These systems represent another form of upward communication, wherein individuals grieve (or complain) about a policy or procedure perceived as unfair, potentially causing some kind of harm to the employee.

Challenges with upward communication include establishing a trusting climate that encourages employees to believe there is low risk or reduced risk by sharing their concerns about decisions or policies. If the employees do not trust they can share their views without risk of retaliation or punishment, the upward communication mechanism fails—they will not share or if they do share, they may withhold the full truth. Coupled with concerns of trust, negative information, in general, is shared less frequently than positive because negative information may not be well received (Adler, 1989) and those sharing anticipate a negative reaction.

Horizontal

Horizontal or lateral communication refers to the pattern of sharing information between individuals who are considered peers. Thus, the individuals who are sharing information are not working at different levels of the organizational hierarchy. Lateral communication is used most often for coordination and problem solving, general information sharing, conflict resolution, and building rapport.

Challenges with lateral communication lie within the individual relationships themselves or physical barriers to the relationships. Relational issues include ingroup/out-group fighting, competition with others, or lack of motivation due to stress on the job. Physical barriers include geographical separation that incorporates large time zone differences.

Disadvantages with horizontal communication include inaccurate information, inability to manage or control the flow of information, and tendency toward gossip that may or may not be constructive.

Informal Networks

Informal networks are the communication paths that ignore the formal lines of authority. In Figure 10.10, the dashed red lines represent an example of informal communication paths. Note how they skip across levels and groups within the organizational hierarchy.

According to Krackhardt and Hanson (1993), three different forms of informal networks exist: advice network, trust network, and communication network. The advice network refers to who people go to for advice; the influential players whose recommendations or insight may end up influencing the direction of the organization. People in the advice network are most often the experts within the organization. They are not just technology experts. They may be experts in organizational politics, people relationships, or strategy. Trust networks refer to the people who are trusted when implementing major change events or handling big crises in the organization. These are the individuals who are reliable, dependable, and get the job done when asked, but who can also be trusted with sensitive information and tasks. Communication networks expose the in-groups (i.e., social groups to which you feel you belong), out-groups (i.e., social groups to which you are not considered a member), and subgroups. They represent the flow of information through the organization, sometimes essential for innovation and implementation of key decisions. Krackhardt and Hanson (1993) suggest that as long as the informal networks are not at odds with the goals of the organization, they are harmless.

The benefits of informal networks include that they can be faster in transmitting important information than formal networks because they can bypass and shrink the number of people through which information must travel. As a consequence of reducing the number of people required to transmit the information, the message itself tends to be more detailed and accurate (Adler, 1989). Informal networks can be used to confirm messages shared using the formal network or to clarify and expand on formal communications. The downside of informal networks is the potential for information to contradict the formal messages or circumvent official channels. Inaccurate information purposely shared throughout the informal network could result in the sabotaging of an organizational change process or decision that management is championing.

Because informal networks can provide many benefits to organizations, Adler (1989) suggests several ways you can develop your own informal network:

1. *Make friends with people whose work spans divisions and organizational levels.*
   Those exposed to a lot of information across the organization and across levels of the hierarchy may have insight into information and perspectives that their broad exposure gives them, beyond others who are limited to their own organizational unit. Examples include employees in accounting depart-

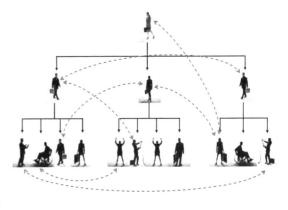

FIGURE 10.10   Informal Networks

Left: © aslysun/Shutterstock, Inc.; Right: © Rawpixel/Shutterstock, Inc.

ments, administrative assistants, and those who maintain the information technology systems.

2. *Be sure to respect and demonstrate genuine interest in everyone, regardless of their organizational position.*

   By demonstrating genuine interest and respect for everyone, including building and facilities maintenance, you may be surprised how your inclusivity leads to information that otherwise may not have been shared.

3. *Ask questions.*

   Simply asking for more information, an opinion, or for help may lead to a connection in your network that under other circumstances would not have been made. The question may also be "how can I help you?" By asking this question, you become a resource for someone who may later turn to you with valuable insights.

Contrary to what you might think, a form of informal gossip-like communication can be constructive and is typically called the office grapevine.

What Is the Office Grapevine?   Lateral communication includes the grapevine communication, which is distinct from gossip in that gossip focuses only on interpersonal information, whereas the grapevine is mostly about work-related information and may at times include only a little interpersonal information (Smith, 1996). The grapevine refers to work-related communication not controlled by management, believed to be reliable and in some cases can be more reliable than communication from top management, and is used by employees within the organization to share information considered pertinent to the employees themselves.

Grapevines, sometimes called rumor mills, develop when there is a lack of information or a lot of ambiguity around the available information. It is considered an informal and decentralized type of communication within organizations. Historically, the origins of the phrase "office grapevine" dates back to the civil war days of the United States when telegraph wires were hung from tree to tree, resembling grapevines in a wine vineyard (Baird, 1977). Communications transmitted via the grapevine tend to skip randomly and haphazardly from person to person. Hence, the image of wires traipsed throughout the vineyard captures the haphazard communication flow of office grapevine communications.

Leaders can take advantage of the speed and accuracy with which information flows along the grapevine to correct misinformation by providing alternative perspectives and offering honest information. When such information is conveyed via the grapevine as opposed to communicated directly in a group presentation, it can be considered more authentic and has a greater impact on employees. Some information is best heard from person to person (e.g., personal information), whereas other information is best heard through official channels. Leaders can manage the communication process by learning which type of message is helped by being spread through the grapevine, versus by a formal meeting.

Exercise 10.2

What are the different types of communication patterns—provide examples of each, using your own words.

What are the Best Communication Skills?

The most common communication skills identified in a review of 25 studies conducted over 10 years, include listening, writing, oral reporting, motivating/persuading, interpersonal skills such as getting along with others, informational interviewing, and small group problem solving (Di Salvo, 1980). With each of these skills comes the responsibility of handling the information-sharing process well, because the ramifications of poorly handled communications can be so high in organizations.

Whether common or not, one of the best communication skills consistently identified is active listening (Keyser, 2013), and anyone can learn active listening skills with attention and practice.

Active Listening

Active listening is not the same as just hearing what is said. Active listening means paying attention to what is said, interpreting what is said, and then effectively sharing what you understand through paraphrasing or summarizing. Active listening requires empathizing with the speaker to understand their point of view, which can increase your ability to understand the intent of the message and the actual content of the message. Active listening means accepting what is said without judging. Additionally, active listening means being a responsible partner in hearing the full message of the speaker, ensuring that judgment is withheld, and asking questions to fully understand the message. Active listening specifically incorporates open-ended questions, paraphrasing, listening first before speaking, and committing to the conversation, explained in Table 10.3 (Boyd, 1998; Brooks, 2010; Keyser, 2013).

Table 10.4 provides a few brief examples of how the four components of active listening may sound in conversation.

Active listening only applies to conversations face-to-face, via audio or video technology. Other common communication skills in the 25-study review included writing, which encompasses much of the electronic communication shared in organizations today. Even if you're a good writer, there are some tips for effective electronic communication.

> Why would you use informal over formal networks?

> Active listening is one of the most frequently mentioned best communication skills.

TABLE 10.3   Four Components of Active Listening

Component of Active Listening	What Does It Mean?
Ask open-ended questions.	Questions that can be answered with a single word, such as "yes" or "maybe" are not open-ended. Questions that invite an elaborated response such as those incorporating what, why, how, where, when, and who are considered open-ended (Eales-White, 1998).
Paraphrase to confirm understanding and demonstrate attention.	Paraphrase means to say in your own words what you believe your communication partner has just shared with you. Paraphrasing allows you to clarify what you heard. Paraphrasing requires that you listen not only to the spoken words, but the intonation, speed, and volume with which the words are said.

(Continued)

TABLE 10.3 Four Components of Active Listening *(Continued)*

Component of Active Listening	What Does It Mean?
Listen first before offering your viewpoint.	Active listening means listening! You can't listen if you're mentally assembling or rehearsing what you want to say. Your viewpoint only makes sense if it is in direct response to what your communication partner is saying or asks. Sometimes your best viewpoint is to ask more questions. By listening with an open mind, you avoid making judgments until after you have had a chance to fully understand what was said. Listening first before speaking also means that you need to avoid interrupting your communication partner.
Commit to the conversation	Avoid paying attention to noncritical distractions while you're listening to your communication partner. By focusing entirely on your communication partner, you convey both honest interest and respect, and avoid missing important words or emotions expressed by the other person. By paying attention to distractions, you're inadvertently communicating that you're not interested; that everything else around you is more interesting and deserves your attention more than the person with whom you're speaking. Listening with commitment means you can remember what your communication partner is saying, allowing you to make connections between the first part of the conversation and the later parts of the conversation.

Courtesy Zinta Byrne.

TABLE 10.4 Examples of Active Listening

Action	Examples
Asking open-ended questions.	<ul><li>What are your thoughts on that?</li><li>How do you feel about the merger?</li><li>What do you think about the change that was recently announced?</li></ul>
Paraphrase to confirm understanding and demonstrate attention.	<ul><li>I think what you're saying is...</li><li>Let me just check my understanding here, are you saying.</li><li>So you're saying (paraphrase here), is that right?</li></ul>
Listen first before offering your viewpoint.	<ul><li>I'd like to make sure I understand how you feel about this new policy. What else were you feeling at the time?</li><li>I'm happy to share my thoughts, but I want to first clarify what you said about that plan. Did you say [paraphrase]?</li></ul>
Commit to the conversation.	<ul><li>I heard you say X. Tell me what I missed.</li><li>I'm wondering if XYZ may also be true given what you said.</li><li>I'm sorry, when you mentioned the recent flood my mind immediately raced to the thoughts of the aftermath. Please tell me again what you just said about how the flood affected the design of the new building.</li><li>It sounds like the first thing you said earlier about the organization matches this new situation you're describing, but also ties into what you noted about the merger just a moment ago. Are all these situations connected to the new CEO?</li></ul>

Courtesy Zinta Byrne.

Electronic Communication Tips

The best skill for electronic communication is being a responsible communicator. That involves paying attention to privacy, broadcasting, emotions, viruses, and timing expectations. Personal responsibility in handling information electronically is absolutely critical and is emphasized in each section below. Because electronic communication is seductively easy and fast—the potential for failure of the communication is astronomical! With a single click, you can create a devastating domino effect of emotions and repercussions with severe personal and professional consequences that do not just affect you, but everyone in your communication chain.

So, you think you already know the best practices for communicating with technology? After all, you've been using technology all your life. Think again! You can be passed up for a job, fired, or arrested because of irresponsibility with handling of information in e-mails, much of it stemming from overconfidence. The problem is not *how* to communicate—the problem is *what* goes into the communication, and additionally *who* gets the communication. Take a read through these tips and reflect on how many times you passed up an opportunity to practice good e-mail etiquette.

Privacy

E-mail is not private and, therefore, what you send can be forwarded to others regardless of whether you mark it confidential or private. If you want to avoid having private information shared, assume that every e-mail message can be shared without your consent or knowledge. Most people treat e-mail as private and impermanent, but as mentioned, it can be broadcasted to thousands of people instantly and it typically remains on computer servers or backups for years.

As part of assuming e-mail is private, people generally also assume their own organization has no right to read or see their messages. However, all e-mail exchanges conducted using company property, such as your work computer, are owned by the organization. This means the organization has a legal right to read and monitor your e-mail if desired. Furthermore, under conditions of a lawsuit, these messages can be requested for evidence and displayed, shared, and discussed in court. One company, Buffer, decided to take an extreme approach to avoiding private versus non-private messages, by making all communications transparent and readable by everyone. This includes company financials, salaries, and emails. Thus, any employee can read any email message, since none are considered private.

Watch https://www.ted.com/talks/andy_yen_think_your_email_s_private_think_again for a thought provoking Ted Talk on privacy in electronic communication.

Broadcasting

One way to make mistakes with violating privacy is by broadcasting messages to many more people than necessary. This is easily done by using the *reply all* feature of e-mail. "Reply all" sends your response to everyone on the distribution list. However, some e-mail programs make it difficult to decipher who is on the distribution list, thus you can't be sure to whom your message is going. This confusion is particularly frequent in e-mail applications on mobile devices such as cell phones. Because of the size of the screen, they do not show the distribution list or the entire e-mail message unless you purposefully select a specific icon or pay careful attention. It's worth a few seconds to confirm who in addition to you received this message and who will receive your reply. If there's a distribution list, does everyone on the list need to receive your reply? Similarly, the *forward* function of e-mail programs allow you to send any message with its original attachments to whomever you wish. This feature, along with *reply all* makes broadcasting e-mail messages easy.

Why are informal networks sometimes more powerful than formal networks?

Emotions

Because e-mails are a quick way to share information, people attempt to use them to replace face-to-face conversation; especially when it seems meeting face-to-face is unnecessary or impractical (or maybe just inconvenient). However, as mentioned previously in this chapter, nonverbal cues cannot be conveyed in electronic communication, which means that the words of the e-mail must carry any emotion that should be expressed with the content. Adding all the necessary words to convey emotion makes for potentially long e-mails, and in the end, it may not work—attempts to express emotions without the nonverbal cues are easily misunderstood. Avoid reprimanding, expressing anger, conveying empathy, or other strong emotions via e-mail because the words expressed without the nonverbal cues can be easily misinterpreted by the receiver.

Viruses

To avoid putting private or emotionally laden text into e-mails, people may instead include an attachment, unaware that attachments are Internet security risks. For example, journal editors often include their decision letter about the researcher's article submission in an e-mail attachment. The letter may include a rejection decision with an attempt to empathize with the author on how frustrating it is to receive a rejection. Aside from the ease with which these messages can be broadcast and how hard it is to convey emotion in e-mail or any paper/electronic writing, the attachment presents a bigger concern.

Internet security has made us very aware that people can send viruses, without their knowledge, through e-mail attachments. It is now generally common knowledge that you should not open e-mail attachments regardless of the sender without first saving the file and running it through a virus-checking program. There are many virus-protection tools that allow you to save attachments and open them on your computer for viewing outside of the e-mail program. Those tools, however, cannot catch all the new viruses that are being developed daily. Be aware that computer viruses are not extinct! They do still exist and they are getting more and more sophisticated—some reside on your computer for years before being activated. You can easily be the sender or receiver of a virus without even knowing. Treat your colleagues with respect and make sure you have virus protection software on your computer to protect you and your colleagues, and practice safe electronic communication.

Timing Expectations

Sometimes messages are sent with attachments or inappropriately broadcasted because of occupational and organizational norms (i.e., established practices) that dictate how fast you should respond. For instance, if 1-hour response time is expected, you're more likely to rush to respond and make a mistake than you are if you have 1-day response time expectations. Timing expectations also factor into the sequence of conversation in e-mail. Since e-mail is asynchronous, conversation threads get out-of-sync or out-of-order if communication partners do not observe turn-taking. Taking turns in the conversation, where one person talks at a time, is especially important in audio conferences and videoconferences.

Audio Conferences and Videoconferences

Timing expectations affect audio conferences and videoconferences in a slightly different way than with e-mail, though there is overlap. Rather than rushed communications such as with e-mail, audio and video exchanges often incorporate a delay in transmission because of technology constraints or geographical distances. Audio conferencing involves having a group meeting using the phone, where each member has dialed or logged in to a shared line. Many phone companies provide audio conferencing capability. Videoconferencing is similar to audio conferencing except using technology that allows people to see each other via cameras at each conferenced location or on their computers rather than just hearing each other on the phone (Figure 10.11). Some examples of videoconferencing software includes Zoom, Skype, WebEx, or GoToMeeting, to name a few. People in a videoconference can see each other as well as hear each other. Because of transmission delays, best practices with audio conferencing and videoconferencing communication include recognizing that the transmission may be slightly delayed and allowing time for the message to be sent and received. Explicitly allowing for longer pauses before speaking can accommodate these slight delays.

Audio conferences and videoconferences not only share the problem that messages can be delayed, they may also confuse communication partners because some communication cues are present whereas others are not, which creates a mismatch of cues. Specifically, the presence and absence of different cues, such as audio but not visual in audio conferencing, causes the speaker and receiver to get out-of-sync with each other. Without the visual cues to signal when to join the conversation, both partners must rely on the audio cues to indicate how and when to participate in the conversation. Therefore, unless the audio conference leaders make it explicit when to join a conversation and whose turn it is to talk, people will interrupt each other, talk out of turn, or not join at all. A skilled audio conference leader is aware of the missing cues and tracks

FIGURE 10.11 Videoconferencing

© Andrey_Popov/Shutterstock.com

the conversation, the partners, and when to ask for verbal information that will convey the nonverbal cues (e.g., is anyone confused at this moment? How does everyone feel about this—Jerry, you first, then Samantha, and then Eduardo).

Why are emotions hard to convey or accurately interpret in email?

With videoconferencing, the delays in transmission occur with not only audio cues, but also visual cues, and they are not coordinated. Hence, you might hear words and then see mouths move, or vice-versa. Additionally, because the visual cues are not in 3D, distance and space cues vanish, as does your ability to see and recognize all body language cues. Thus, similar skills for facilitating a phone conference are necessary for videoconferencing to ensure proper turn taking and to avoid misunderstandings with body language. Having the ability to see everyone participating does make it easier to identify who wants to talk next (e.g., raise hands).

Regardless of audio or video communications, a good facilitator is constantly asking for confirmation, questions, tracking turn-taking, and stating what is happening so that everyone feels they are is in the same room as the tele- or video-conference facilitator. Ground rules for communicating in audio conferences and videoconferences can be very important and helpful in smoothing out communication concerns or issues. For example, ground rules may include:

1. Only one person can speak at a time

2. Restate the question that you are answering

3. State which slide or page you are looking at when referring to a slide or page

4. State your name every time you speak

5. Restate any decisions that are made

6. If on a videoconference, avoid small hand gestures or attempting to use facial expressions only to convey a point. Small gestures are hard to see.

Audio and teleconferencing are preferable to e-mail because of the audio and visual cues that can be conveyed.

7. If on a videoconference, do not assume everyone is looking at the screen at all times.

8. If on an audio conference, do not assume everyone is listening carefully enough to track every part of the multiple person conversation.

Exercise 10.3

List the best technics for electronic communication in organizations. What do you need to be most concerned about when using e-communication in organizational settings? Is that different from or similar to personal e-communication?

Best Practices for Crisis Communication

All the best communication practices reviewed so far should help you with most of the organizational messaging you'll encounter. However, crisis communication is a unique and specific type of messaging that has its own set of best practices. Crisis communication refers to messaging associated with public relations for organizations that occur because of a major organizational crisis. For example, the need to repair reputation damage that accompanies industrial accidents, financial abuse, or other types of events that harm people, environment, and the organization (Seeger, 2006). For example, recent crises include:

- Edward Snowden leaked U.S. government secrets to foreign countries
- A Bangladesh factory not built to code collapsed and killed over 1000 workers
- Horsemeat was secretly substituted for beef in Europe and somehow managed to bypass all European Union regulations
- GlaxoSmithKline suffered a 60% drop in sales due to alleged bribes to sell more pricey drugs than was appropriate
- The highly publicized Carnival cruise that was stranded for days with 4000 passengers and no working toilets (nicknamed—"the poop cruise"; Fry, 2013).

These are but a few examples of the many types of corporate crises that happen worldwide.

The best crisis communications include the following 10 best practices (Seeger, 2006):

1. The first best practice is combining planning and crisis avoidance, which means including communication during and after a crisis.

2. The second best practice is pre-event planning, which means identifying potential risks for crises before they occur and communicating these risks along with plans for how to mitigate them in the event they occur.

3. Partnership with the public is the third best practice, which refers to recognizing the right of the public to know what level of risk is involved and how the crisis is being handled. Including the public in the handling of the crisis and the communication of the crisis is important. Seeger (2006) notes that an impediment to good crisis communication is the assumption that if the public knows the true risk, they will panic. Such assumptions lead to withholding information. The best crisis communicators do not withhold information.

4. Seeger (2006) suggests the fourth best practice is to listen to the public and seek understanding. To manage risk and communicate appropriately, the organization must understand the public's concerns and what kind of audience is listening to the company communications. Developing positive relationships before a crisis helps when an actual crisis occurs; therefore, the recommendation is to not wait for a crisis to regularly interact with the public and maintain an open dialogue to hear their ongoing concerns or needs.

5. Being honest, candid, and open about potential risk prior and during the crisis is the next best practice because this builds credibility and trust, which are essential during a crisis. Seeger (2006) distinguishes honesty

from candor by defining honesty as not lying, and candor as sharing the entire truth even if the truth may be negative. Candor is desirable because honesty alone may not reveal all aspects of the situation, and people want to know everything that is happening. Openness involves being accessible and immediate.

6. Another best practice is collaborating and coordinating with credible sources before a crisis occurs, such as with subject-matter experts who can comment on the risk levels or potential harm, and fire and police departments if the risk is environmental or industrial. By establishing good communication partnerships before a crisis, organizations can hopefully avoid breakdowns in communication during a crisis, when stress levels are heightened.

7. The media can play a very important role, either positive or negative, in crisis communication. Thus, developing a good relationship with the media is essential. By engaging with the media, organizations can use the media as a resource to advance communication during the crisis. Seeger (2006) recommends that crisis spokespeople should have training in media communications before a crisis.

8. Recognizing that a crisis situation of any kind creates uncertainty and fear allows one to empathize with those potentially affected. Therefore, the eighth best practice in crisis communication is to communicate with compassion, empathy, and concern for those directly affected and potentially affected. Acknowledging concerns, listening, and demonstrating genuine compassion is essential.

9. Crisis situations are by nature uncertain and ambiguous, which means that one is never quite sure when to issue warnings, clarification messages, or public announcements. Therefore, because of the uncertainty, the ninth best practice is to admit the uncertainty upfront. Statements such as "the situation is constantly changing, this is what we know at this time … we'll update you as soon as we know more" can keep people informed and aware that the situation is ambiguous. Seeger (2006) warns, however, that hiding behind uncertainty as a strategy for avoiding sharing information will result in closing off communications as opposed to keeping the dialogue open, which is one of the previous best practices.

10. The last best practice is to help people understand what they can do to reduce the harm to them. By giving them specific information appropriate to the crisis, people can feel a sense of control and self-efficacy. Seeger (2006) suggests the messages explain the reasons behind the recommended action, along with the specifics of actions to take, so that people do not misunderstand why you are making those specific recommendations.

Crises communication refers to messaging associated with public relations for organizations, such as the need to repair reputation damage that accompanies industrial accidents, financial abuse, or other types of events that harm people, environment, and the organization. As a consequence, crises communication requires extra communication practices beyond other forms of communication.

Not only do crisis situations require specialized communications, so do change events. Because change is often ambiguous and creates uncertainty, employees may be reluctant to accept the change, resist it outright, or simply struggle trying to figure out what they are supposed to be doing. Communication can help reduce some of the ambiguity and feelings of fear in employees that crop up around big change events.

Best Practices for Communications during Change Events

Researchers interviewed senior executives at 10 firms that each underwent a large organizational change, and who were identified as having good communication throughout the transformation process. Results of the interviews revealed eight effective communication practices the executives used during their organizational changes (shown in Figure 10.12; Young & Post, 1993).

1. Chief Executive as Communications Champion
    - ❑ Attitude is conveyed from the top down, and the Chief Executive Officer (CEO) is essential in making communication a priority, setting the tone, and demonstrating a commitment to sharing information to eliminate uncertainty as best as possible. If the CEO isn't talking, it suggests a lack of commitment to the change.

2. The Match between Words and Actions
    - ❑ The implicit messages must match the official and explicit messages. Everyone needs to use the same language and behave consistently with what is said. If the organization says it values the employees, the organization and leaders need to honor policies and behaviors that demonstrate value for employees.

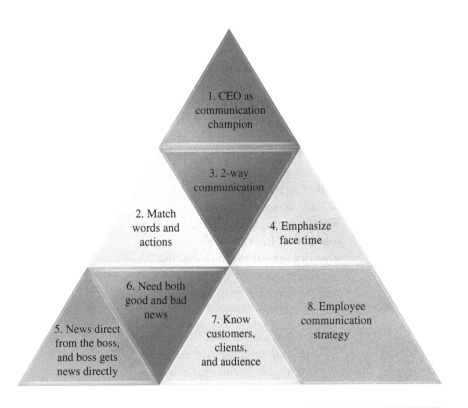

FIGURE 10.12   Eight Effective Communication Practices during Organizational Change

Courtesy Zinta Byrne.

3. Commitment to Two-Way Communication
   - ❏ Not only is it important to share information from higher levels of the organization to the lower levels (i.e., supervisor to employee), but also to encourage open conversation from lower levels to higher levels. Employees need a voice and assurance their voice will be heard. Asking for feedback and subsequently ignoring it or doing the exact opposite without explanation will result in distrust and resentment.

4. Emphasis on Face-to-Face Communication
   - ❏ Although electronic communication has many advantages, such as getting critical information to many people fast and simultaneously, important aspects of communication such as expressions of emotion and empathy are not conveyed. Face-to-face communication encourages and facilitates two-way communication.

5. Shared Responsibility for Employee Communications
   - ❏ Rather than leave all communications to the corporate or central office, during major change efforts communications need to be localized and owned by the immediate trusted management team, such as the direct supervisor. Communications must be accurate, not filtered or changed as they move up or down the organizational hierarchy, and they must provide an adequate explanation for decisions (important in managing perceptions of fairness).

6. The Bad News/Good News Ratio
   - ❏ In one of the highest performing organizations (in terms of performance and employee satisfaction) they studied, Young and Post (1993) found employees were held responsible for telling upper management about problems, and the organization's leaders shared an equal amount of good and bad news. Thus, communicating bad news became valued and supported at all levels, in that sharing important information, regardless of good or bad, was considered necessary for strategic advantage. Some organizations avoid sharing too much bad news for fear it will lower morale. However, compared to the other nine organizations they studied, Young and Post found the organization with the highest bad news/good news ratio was performing quite well and had satisfied employees—no low morale there!

7. Knowing Customers, Clients, and Audiences
   - ❏ Communications need to be tailored to the audience and that means knowing who your audience is—is it the customer, the client, or the next levels above you in the hierarchy? The answers provided in the communications are different depending on who is the targeted audience, and the best communications during change events are those serving the audience's needs.

8. The Employee Communication Strategy
   This practice includes several important points:

   ❏ Communicate what is happening, why, and how.
   ❏ Communicate what is happening, why it is happening, and how it is happening. When major change occurs in organizations, it creates uncertainty. Uncertainty creates disorganization and without answers, employees fill in the gaps with their own hypotheses about what is happening and why. Unfortunately, the stories they tell themselves are often misinformed and negative. Give them the stories so they don't have to make up their own.
   ❏ Be timely in communications.
   ❏ Share what you know when you know it, regardless of whether you know all the details yet or not. Share that you don't have all the answers, but here is what you do know. Young and Post (1993) note the consequence of waiting can be dissatisfaction, anger, and loss of trust.
   ❏ Be constant in communications.
   ❏ During major change, time takes on a different perspective and what would normally seem like a short time frame, such as a day or two, feels like a large gap in time. Keep information flowing frequently.
   ❏ Connect the bigger picture of the change event with how people are affected.
   ❏ Having perspective and knowing where and how you fit into the overall change event helps with understanding and sense-making. People want to make sense of the change, and knowing what their role in the change is helps them. Additionally, giving employees an idea of how changes in the economy, competitors, or clients affect the company enables employees to put into perspective why the change may be necessary.
   ❏ Avoid telling people how they should feel.
   ❏ Employees do not want to be told that the change is exciting and they should feel enthusiastic about the "opportunities" the change presents.

For example, when Federal Express (FedEx) acquired Flying Tiger Line, Inc., within 2 hours after the acquisition was announced the Chairman and CEO of FedEx gave an unscripted and unrehearsed speech over the company satellite television to over 35,000 employees in 800 locations to explain the acquisition as a merger. The word merger was chosen and emphasized several times in an effort to convey to the employees of Flying Tiger that they were being brought into the FedEx family, not over-taken, and to the FedEx employees that they were still essential. For several months after the announcement, two-way communication was encouraged, and face-to-face meetings were held regularly to answer questions.

The importance of face-to-face communication is made clear by the employees at FedEx who commented that they had a chance to see how the CEO would physically respond to questions, and that allowed them to see genuine concern and caring (Young & Post, 1993). At one of the other firms studied by Young

Think of a time when you were involved in a change, either at work or school, where you didn't have control of what was changing but also weren't given all the details about the change. What would you have liked the organization or school to communicate to make the change easier?

and Post, an executive shared that their organization spent money to send trained nonmanagement employees in groups of three or four people to each of their locations, to answer questions about their change efforts and share their personal concerns along with the answers they received for those concerns. They believed the expense was well justified in the long run.

> **Exercise 10.4**
>
> What is important to attend to in crisis communication?

Culture Sensitivity

Culture can present numerous unintended communication challenges. Specifically, different words, actions, and symbols mean different things in different languages. For instance, there are words in languages that are not easily translated, thus alternative words are used that may not directly translate to the concept that was initially desired. Furthermore, nonverbal cues in one culture might convey an entirely different message in another, and without advance preparation on the cultural context, you can blow a sales deal or anger an important manager.

Thus, communication is made up of its context; therefore, a barrier in cross-cultural communication may be due the lack of understanding of context. Some cultures, for example, are high-context cultures such as China, Korea, and Vietnam (Gudykunst & Nishida, 1986; Hall, 1976; Kim, Pan, & Park, 1998). High-context cultures are those in which people control their expressions and, therefore, the nonverbal and situational cues are absolutely necessary for understanding the actual content and meaning of the message (Hall, 1976).

Accordingly, what is *not* said and the situation in which the communication occurs may be more important for understanding meaning than the actual words themselves. For example, the status of the individual's or family's reputation may be more important than the actual content of the message. Family and group orientations are important in high-context cultures, and therefore, family relations or status in the community is an important social cue that adds meaning to message content. In contrast, Europeans and North Americans are in low-context cultures, where the words themselves convey the meaning and the nonverbal cues or situational cues are not as important, or not as central to understanding the message itself. In the low-context culture, titles must be spoken to communicate status. The implications of Hall's research is that in high-context cultures, it is crucial you learn as much personal information as you can about the person you are meeting, in addition to the standard information about their company. That personal information is just as important as what company is being represented. In a low-context culture, just learning about the company is sufficient.

FIGURE 10.13   Thumbs Up

© exopixel/Shutterstock, Inc.

Guidelines for Cross-Cultural Communication

Ways to improve communication with individuals from different countries or cultures include being aware of your own stereotypes and assumptions as you enter into the communication. Become more aware by learning what you can about your communication partner's culture. Are there norms for nonverbal communication that mean something different from what you would have expected based on your culture? For example, hand gestures are often misunderstood from culture to culture.

Hand Gestures

Be aware that hand gestures may hold different meanings in different cultures. For example, a "thumbs up" gesture (Figure 10.13) in North American countries means that everything is okay or "good luck." However, in Australia and Iran the same gesture is insulting (Archer, 1997).

Former Unites States President George Bush was unaware that when he greeted a large Australian audience using his hand to gesture a V (Figure 10.14) for Victory, by doing so with his palm facing his own face he was gesturing "screw you" (Archer, 1997).

The hand gesture in the United States used to convey "Okay" (Figure 10.15) means money in Japan, sex in Mexico, and homosexual in Ethiopia.

In addition to awareness of hand gestures, awareness of what and how you write, as well as how fast you speak factor into cultural sensitivity. Keeping your writing as simple and direct as possible can facilitate translation or communication with individuals for whom your language is a second language. Working with individuals who speak your language and the language of your communication partner can help you write your message so the intent is well received and the actual content is communicated accurately. When speaking, it helps to speak slowly and enunciate every word (Silverthorne, 2005), but be careful not to also assume you have to speak louder. Speaking slowly with clear word enunciation and pronunciation does not require an increase in volume.

Ethical Communication

Best communication skills include determining what the ethicality is of sharing or not sharing certain information. Whether the information can be shared at all, minimally shared, shared on a strict timeline, or shared with urgency involves ethical decision-making. Clampitt (2010) suggests leaders are faced with a number of communication situations that pose ethical dilemmas (see Table 10.5), and that a variety of questions need to be asked to determine how best to handle each situation.

In many cases, situations referred to in Table 10.5 may require consultation with the organization's legal counsel. Organizations sometimes form special committees or advisory teams to handle the situations, ask the questions, and recommend actions to the executive management team. Incorporated within many of the situations in Table 10.5, is conflict or disagreement, and conflict requires its own guidelines for effective handling.

Handling Conflict

No doubt, you've personally experienced a conflict of some kind. Conflict is a normal part of organizational communication. The word "conflict" suggests negative disagreement, but conflict can be positive. For instance, conflict can promote

FIGURE 10.14   Two Fingers Up

© inxti/Shutterstock, Inc.

There's a lot more to cross-cultural communication and sensitivity of cultural differences in communication than room to discuss here. Consider the many volumes of books and video programs available on best practices in cross-cultural communication. A good one is Steers, Sanchez-Runde, and Nardon's book "Management Across Cultures: Challenges and Strategies."

FIGURE 10.15   Thumb and Index Finger Joined

© Sergio Stakhnyk/Shutterstock, Inc.

TABLE 10.5 Situations Presenting Ethical Concerns

Situation	Concern	Questions to Ask
Dissent	Disagreement with policies or decisions.	Is the dissent an opportunity for healthy debate? Can the dissent be handled in a positive and transparent way? Can the feedback be received while maintaining an atmosphere of respect and trust?
Leaks	Anonymously releasing information to the public.	Can the information be verified? Is it imperative that the information is acted upon? Can additional confirming information be obtained from identifiable sources?
Lies	False information.	Can the accuracy or lack thereof be verified? What is the consequence of the lie? How extensive is the lie? Is the lie illegal, threatening, or harmful? Can the reason for the lie be determined?
Rumors	Information that may or may not be accurate and is shared via the informal communication networks.	Is the information accurate and/or can its accuracy be verified? Can similar information be obtained about all other employees? Is there a formal mechanism for obtaining the same information? Is the rumor harmful? Is there a threat that requires immediate action?
Secrecy	Intentional concealment	Is the concealment justified? Will revealing the information cause more harm than good? Is the concealment illegal?

Courtesy Zinta Byrne. Source: Clampitt (2010)

effective discussions, trigger important and necessary organizational or social changes in the work environment, and lead to problem solving. In contrast, conflict unbounded becomes unproductive and sometimes hurtful by leading to poor cooperation, aggressive competition, and distrust. Best practices in communication include the positive management of conflict in organizations.

Conflicts in organizations can occur because of organizational design, limited resources, or aspects of the organization's systems. For example, interdependence within teams, where team members cannot start or finish their work tasks without the input or output from other team members (i.e., interdependent teams, discussed in Chapter 7) can cause conflict. Incompatible group goals, such as the needs of manufacturing overlapping with the needs of production can create conflict over which goals take precedence. Organizational units that tap into the same resources, such as support staff or budget, are more likely to be in conflict when these resources are limited. Conflict can also result from differing beliefs or expectations, and power struggles over issues that relate to resources, support, or desires for control (Berryman-Fink & Fink, 1996).

Conflict can be managed through a series of steps that include diagnosis, intervention, dealing with the disagreements and emotions that conflict creates, and learning from the conflict to avoid repeating the same scenario again (Rahim, 2002). Diagnosis involves determining the source of the conflict and finding out what is the actual problem. Intervention involves determining the best resolution and answering the question "does the process need to change?" or "does the design of the organization need to change?"

TABLE 10.6 Quadrants of Diagnosis and Intervention

	Events (e.g., competitive threats)	Conditions (e.g., social pressure)
External (cause of conflict is outside of the parties)	Interaction management • May involve a third party referee to manage negotiations or interactions. • Since the conflict results from how the outside source behaves, the intervention must focus on that behavior.	Contextual modification • Focus on changing the external conditions such as changing who is responsible for what, budgets, or task assignments. • Change policies, change goals, mandate negotiations to compromise, institute higher level goals for both parties.
Internal (cause of behavior is within the parties)	Consciousness raising • Change the parties' perceptions, cognitions, and emotions about the conflict. • Persuasion and advocacy may be used to make each group more aware of the other and more appreciative of each position.	Selection and Training • Focus on making stable or lasting change by selecting people for specific positions. Recruit and hire/promote using screening for cooperative work style, and/or history of ethical negotiations. • Use job redesign strategies, training, and other programs (e.g., coaching) to facilitate change.

Courtesy Zinta Byrne. Source: Kilmann and Thomas, 1978.

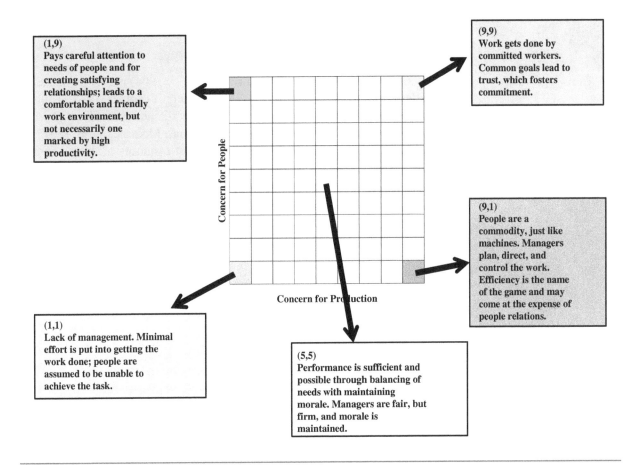

FIGURE 10.16 Managerial Grid

Courtesy Zinta Byrne. Source: Blake, Mouton, Barnes, and Greiner, 1964.

Different approaches to handling conflict have been recommended (e.g., Kilmann & Thomas, 1978; Shetach, 2009; Thomas, 1976). For example, Kilmann and Thomas (1978) suggested that conflict can be diagnosed along two axes: events versus conditions and external versus internal causes of behavior, resulting in four quadrants. Each quadrant requires its own intervention strategy (see Table 10.6).

Another approach to managing conflict was offered by Blake, Mouton, Barnes, and Greiner (1964) and depicted using a matrix that has two axes labeled: *concern for people* and *concern for production* (Figure 10.16; also discussed in Chapter 8). Blake et al. (1964) argued that managers' preferred behavior style for effective work relations varies depending on their concern for production (i.e., how much employees get done) versus their concern for the people (i.e., manager's concern for empowering and supporting the needs of their people). The goal behind the managerial grid was to help managers identify their style and then develop strategies to work toward behaving more like a 9,9 manager.

The Blake et al.'s (1964) grid, also discussed in Chapter 8, is a good tool for managers identifying a style (working toward 9,9) that gets the job done while conveying commitment to employees. The difficulty in using the grid for determining specifically how to handle conflict, however, is that it wasn't designed for conflict handling, not like Thomas and Kilmann's conflict taxonomy (the same two researchers who provided the diagnostic chart in Table 10.2).

Thomas and Kilmann Conflict-Handling Taxonomy

Depending on which style represented in Blake et al.'s (1964) matrix the manager prefers, different approaches to conflict resolution emerge (Thomas, 1976). Thomas and Kilmann (1978) proposed a taxonomy of conflict-handling modes that when mapped onto Blake and Mouton's grid produces Figure 10.17 (note: most instances of this taxonomy in publications show assertiveness on the Y-axis and cooperativeness on the X-axis. I've reversed them here just to show how the conflict-handling modes map onto the managerial grid).

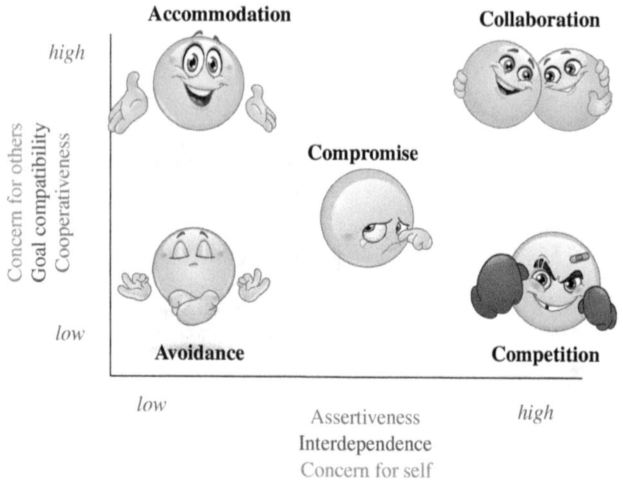

According to the model, conflict can be handled along two different axes: cooperativeness versus assertiveness. Cooperativeness is essentially the same as trying to satisfy a concern for others, whereas assertiveness is trying to satisfy one's own concerns or needs. Additionally, you need to remember that in this model, conflict is a function of group members relying on each other to complete tasks (i.e., interdependence) and the level of compatibility of individual goals (i.e., are our goals toward task completion aligned) provides another labeling of the axes: goal compatibility versus interdependence.

Competition refers to a high concern for the self and little concern for the needs of others, which results in a competitive conflict-handling

FIGURE 10.17 Conflict-Handling Taxonomy

Source: Adapted from Thomas and Kilmann (1978).

All images: ©Yayayoyo/Shutterstock, Inc.

style. The objective here is to win the conflict, which becomes more important that preserving the relationship.

Avoidance happens when you have nothing at stake and do not care whether others get their needs met, and you are likely to avoid the conflict all together; you're neither cooperative nor fighting for your own needs.

Accommodation, giving up your interests for others, is a great way to keep the peace; however, by being completely accommodating, you and your team lose out on meeting your goals or getting the job done.

Compromise, often called a win–win, is actually not the best conflict-handling mode because everyone has to give up something in a compromise. At some point, the conflict may pop up again because you had to give up getting some of your needs met in order to gain, which means there is still some leftover concern, need, or issue that was not addressed properly.

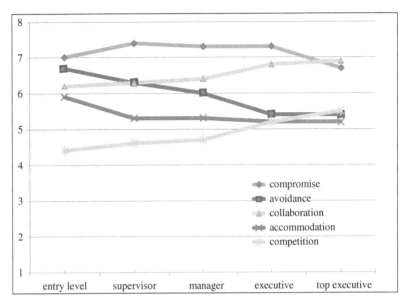

FIGURE 10.18   Adapted Illustration of Thomas et al.'s (2008) Results

Courtesy Zinta Byrne. Source: Thomas, Thomas, and Schaubhut, 2008.

Collaboration occurs when both sides of the conflict have important concerns that need to be met. By finding a new solution that can satisfy everyone, the conflict may be more easily resolved.

Although conflict can be handled using any of these approaches, Thomas, Thomas, and Schaubhut (2008) found that as you move up the management hierarchy in the organization, executives' preferred style of conflict handling is toward competition and collaboration, and less compromising, avoidance, or accommodation than at lower levels of the organization (see Figure 10.18). The researchers also found that at all levels of the organization, men tended to score higher than women did on competition.

Jeffrey Pfeffer (May 29, 2014) posted a blog entry in which he provided several rules for dealing with organizational conflict, rules distilled from his long career studying organizational behavior. A slightly modified version is provided here (see his original entry May 29, 2014, *Win at Workplace Conflict*, posted at Harvard Business Review's HBR Blog Network).

1. *Remain focused on essential objectives.*
    The issue with conflict is that you get side-tracked by the emotions and lose sight of the original goal. Try to avoid responding to the emotions of the situation; what is it that is really desired?

2. *Avoid fighting over things that don't matter or are inconsequential.*
    This means you have to identify what truly matters.

3. *Build an empathetic understanding of the other party's point of view.*
    Find out why there is a conflict without presuming negative intent of the

other party. It may be that the goals of each party are incompatible, and therefore finding a way to get alignment may be the better approach. You have to start first with understanding the other party's view.

4. *Keep your friends close, but your enemies closer.*
   The idea here is that those with whom you normally disagree (enemies) are more likely to be the ones with whom you're in conflict. Thus, knowing what your enemies think helps you during conflict resolution since you're more aware of their needs and for what they will argue. The way to know what they are thinking is to have frequent conversations; thus, this closeness should provide you with insight into what they are thinking and need.

5. *Use humor to defuse tough situations.*
   Appropriate humor helps, but inappropriate humor doesn't. Don't force or try hard to be funny by concocting a joke. If the moment offers an opportunity for light humor, it may be helpful to take the opportunity.

According to Pfeffer, conflict at work is unavoidable. Given that conflict is unavoidable in our personal lives, it's likely that Pfeffer is correct—we certainly can't avoid it at work either, no matter how hard we might try. Therefore, keeping perspective, keeping things simple, and keeping the above rules in mind may help with handling the conflict when it occurs.

Exercise 10.5

What is the best way to handle conflict in organizations?

Conflict across Cultures

Conflict is not a United States only construct, even though many studies seem to suggest it might be. For instance, in a study of 968 marketing managers in Japan, China (Hong Kong), the United States, and the United Kingdom, researchers (Song, Xie, & Dyer, 2000) found that goal incompatibility and the consequential conflict in all four samples was related to high levels of avoidance and low levels of collaboration. Specifically, in Japan and China, management support to integrate goals decreased avoidance and increased collaboration conflict-handling behaviors. This was not the case in the United States or United Kingdom. The authors explained these differences in study findings using Hofstede's (1980) supposition about power distance, which refers to the acceptance of inequity due to differing levels of authority in the organization, in each country.

Namely, the authors proposed that in a high power distance culture such as China (specifically Hong Kong) and Japan, where the power differential is accepted and expected, management support has a greater influence than in the United States and United Kingdom where the power distance is low. In low power distance cultures, employees do not accept inequity between the layers of the organizational hierarchy and they expect to take care of issues themselves. Low power cultures recognize responsibility differences in the hierarchy of the organization, but they expect to be treated as equals. The implications of Song et al.'s (2000) study are that in Japan and China, or high power distance cultures, managers should use management support to align goals and achieve higher collaborative conflict-handling behavior. In the United States and United Kingdom, or low power distance cultures, management needs to promote cross-functional integration through education to handle conflict appropriately.

For more information on how country cultures differ, Hofstede's (1980) works are recommended. A search of the Internet will also reveal an informative web site maintained by the Hofstede Centre that shows the latest research in cross-cultural differences (visit the interactive country comparison tool on Hofstede's website, https://www.hofstede-insights.com/product/compare-countries).

Chapter Summary

Communication in organizations serves many different purposes, such as managing behaviors, sharing direction, building and maintaining reputation, and essentially getting the job done, whatever that job may be. Communication can be informal, formal, quick, slow, written, face-to-face, or electronic. Not only is

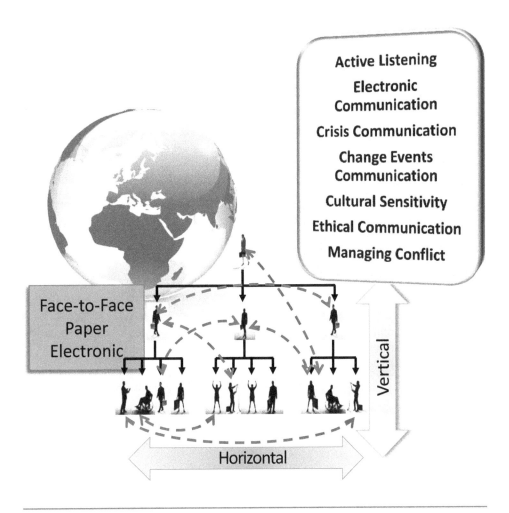

FIGURE 10.19   Visual Summary of Chapter 10

Globe image: © stockwerk.dk/Shutterstock, Inc.

Courtesy Zinta Byrne.

it shared via different routes, but how a message is communicated and which medium is used makes a big difference. In addition to choosing the best medium for conveying a message, you need good skills in communication to make it effective; skills that you can learn. Lastly, to communicate or not is an ethical decision and requires immense responsibility. Some information should not be shared, some shared within constraints, and some shared broadly without hesitation. That said, deciding which type of communication falls into which category is not always easy.

Poor organizational communication can wreak havoc on productivity, relations, and the organization itself. The consequences of ineffective communication are widespread and far-reaching. The best organizations make communication a part of their core strategy, training, and culture, and the best employees make mastering good communication a high priority. Be one of those best employees!

Figure 10.19 provides a visual summary of the key concepts from Chapter 10.

The visual summary provides a quick glance of what the key concepts are associated with organizational communication. The medium used, how communication flows through the organization, and what skills are essential for communication are captured in this visual summary. The modes of communication are different from the patterns of communication, which describe how communication flows through the organization. What is missing here, however, is what communication might look like in the future. With the advancement of technology and bandwidth, future communication might include more artificial intelligence, three dimensional communication, shorter—more brief communications, less privacy, more symbolic (all emojis?), more automation, constant never-ending communication, and simply more information.

Discussion Questions

1. The chapter clarifies the inherent differences between channels or modes of communication, but have you noticed the differences yourself? If so, what are the specific differences that YOU have noted/observed and how have those differences affected you? If you think communication modes are all the same, why do you think that and effectively disagree with the current literature? How have you made the modes of communication work effectively for you?

2. When you read in the chapter how communication is transmitted through the layers of hierarchy and through the various networks, what would you do differently in an organization to make communication more effective? What is missing in the current patterns of communication that you feel could make it that much more effective? Why is that?

3. Is there such a thing as privacy in communication within organizations?

4. Why do you think it was valuable to provide information on crisis communication and change events communication in the Chapter? What are your thoughts about how organizations communicate their crises situations today—should they? How transparent should an organization be?

References

Adler, R. B. (1989). Communicating at work: Principles and practices for business and the professions. New York, NY: Random House.

Archer, D. (1997). Unspoken diversity: Cultural differences in gestures. *Qualitative Sociology, 20*(1), 79–105.

Baird, J. E. (1977). *The dynamics of organizational communication.* New York, NY: Harper & Row.

Berryman-Fink, C., & Fink, C. B. (1996). Conflict management. In *The manager's desk reference* (2nd ed., pp. 45–51). New York, NY: American Management Association.

Blake, R. R., Mouton, J. S., Barnes, L. B., & Greiner, L. E. (1964). Breakthrough in organization development. *Harvard Business Review, 42*(6), 133–155.

Boyd, S. D. (1998). Using active listening. *Nursing Management, 29*(7), 55.

Brooks, B. (2010). The power of active listening. *American Salesman, 55*(12), 28–30.

Burgoon, J. K., Guerrero, L. K., & Manusov, V. 2011. Nonverbal signals. In M. L. Knapp & J. Daly (Eds.), *Handbook of interpersonal communication:* 239–280. Thousand Oaks, CA: Sage.

Byrne, D. (1971). *The attraction paradigm.* New York, NY: Academic Press.

Byrne, Z. S., & LeMay, E. (2006). Different media for organizational communication: Perceptions of quality and satisfaction. *Journal of Business and Psychology, 21,* 149–173. doi: 10.1007/s10869-006-9023-8

Byrne, Z. S., Masterson, S. S., & Hurd, B. M. (2012). Fairness in a virtual world: The implications of communication media on employees' justice and trust perceptions. In C. A. Schriesheim & L. L. Neider (Eds.), *Perspectives on justice and trust in organizations: Research in management* (Vol. 9, pp. 45–76). Charlotte, NC: Information Age Publishing.

Carlson, J. R., & Zmud, R. W. (1999). Channel expansion theory and the experiential nature of media richness perceptions. *Academy of Management Journal, 42,* 153–170.

Clampitt, P. G. (2010). *Communicating for managerial effectiveness: Problems, strategies, solutions.* Thousand Oaks, CA: Sage.

Cox, J. L., Martinez, E. R., & Quinlan, K. B. (2008). Blogs and the corporation: Managing the risk, reaping the benefits. *Journal of Business Strategy, 29*(3), 4–12. doi:10.1108/02756660810873164

Daft, R. L., & Lengel, R. H. (1984). Information richness: A new approach to managerial behavior and organization design. *Research in Organizational Behavior, 6,* 191–233.

Dearstyne, B. W. (2005). Blogs: The new information revolution? *Information Management Journal, 39*(5), 38–44.

Di Salvo, V. S. (1980). A summary of current research identifying communication skills in various organizational contexts. *Communication Education, 29*(3), 283.

Dolezalek, H. (2003). Collaborating in cyberspace. *Training, 40*(4), 32.

Eales-White, R. (1998). *Ask the right question!: How to get what you want every time and in any situation.* New York, NY: McGraw-hill.

Ebanks, K. (2005). Into the blogosphere: Managing the risks and rewards of employee blogging. *Computer & Internet Lawyer, 22*(10), 1–4.

Fry, E. (December 27, 2013). 11 most scandalous business events of 2013. Retrieved from Fortune Magazine, http://fortune.com/2013/12/27/11-most-scandalous-business-events-of-2013/

Griffith-Cooper, B., & King, K. (2007). The partnership between project management and organizational change: Integrating change management with change leadership. *Performance Improvement, 46*(1), 14–20. doi:10.1002/pfi

Gudykunst, W. B., & Nishida, T. (1986). Attributional confidence in low- and high-context cultures. *Human Communication Research, 15,* 525–549. doi:10.1111/j.1468-2958.1986.tb00090.x

Hall, E. T. (1976). *Beyond culture.* New York, NY: Anchor Press-Doubleday.

Ho, S. S., & McLeod, D. M. (2008). Social-psychological influences on opinion expression in face-to-face and computer-mediated communication. *Communication Research, 35*(2), 190–207.

Hofstede, G. (1980). *Culture's consequences: International differences in work-related values.* Beverly Hills, CA: Sage.

Kahai, S. S., & Cooper, R. B. (2003). Exploring the core concepts of media richness theory: The impact of cue multiplicity and feedback immediacy on decision quality. *Journal of Management Information Systems, 20,* 263–299.

Keyser, J. (2013). Active listening leads to business success. *T+D, 67*(7), 26–28.

Kilmann, R. H., & Thomas, K. W. (1978). Four perspectives on conflict management: An attributional framework for organizing descriptive and normative theory. *Academy of Management Review, 3*(1), 59–68. doi:10.5465/AMR.1978.4296368

Kim, D., Pan, Y., & Park, H. (1998). High- versus low-context culture: A comparison of Chinese, Korean, and American cultures. *Psychology & Marketing, 15*(6), 507–521. doi:10.1002/(SICI)1520-6793(199809)15:6<507::AID-MAR2>3.0.CO;2-A

Krackhardt, D., & Hanson, J. R. (1993). Informal networks: The company behind the charts. *Harvard Business Review, 71*(4), 104–111.

Kupritz, V. W., & Cowell, E. (2011). Productive management communication. *Journal of Business Communication, 48*(1), 54–82. doi:10.1177/0021943610385656

Larson, J. R. Jr. (1984). The performance feedback process: A preliminary model. *Organizational Behavior & Human Performance, 33*(1), 42–76.

Larson, J. R. (1986). Supervisors' performance feedback to subordinates: The impact of subordinate performance valence and outcome dependence. *Organizational Behavior and Human Decision Processes, 37*(3), 391–408. doi:10.1016/0749-5978(86)90037-3

Leavitt, H. J. (1951). Some effects of certain communication patterns on group performance. *The Journal of Abnormal and Social Psychology, 46*(1), 38–50. doi:10.1037/h0057189

Lovejoy, K., Waters, R. D., & Saxton, G. D. (2012). Engaging stakeholders through Twitter: How nonprofit organizations are getting more out of 140 characters or less. *Public Relations Review, 38*(2), 313–318. doi:10.1016/j.pubrev.2012.01.005

Mehrabian, A. (1969). Significance of posture and position in the communication of attitude and status relationships. *Psychological Bulletin, 71*(5), 359–372.

Miller, K. I. (2007). Compassionate communication in the workplace: Exploring processes of noticing, connecting, and responding. *Journal of Applied Communication Research, 35*(3), 223–245.

Mion, L. C., Hazel, C., Cap, M., Fusilero, J., Podmore, M. L., & Szweda, C. (2006). Retaining and recruiting mature experienced nurses: A multicomponent organizational strategy. *Journal of Nursing Administration, 36*(3), 148–154.

PEW (2008). Networked workers survey for the Pew Internet & American Life Project. Retrieved from www.pewinternet.org

Rahim, A. (2002). Toward theory of managing organizational conflict. *The International Journal of Conflict Management, 13*(3), 206–235.

Rice, R. E., & Love, G. (1987). Electronic emotions: Socioemotional content in a computer-mediated network. *Communication Research, 14,* 85–108.

Rosen, S., & Tesser, A. (1970). On reluctance to communicate undesirable information: The MUM effect. *Sociometry, 33*(3), 253–263. doi:10.2307/2786156

Seeger, M. W. (2006). Best practices in crisis communication: An expert panel process. *Journal of Applied Communication Research, 34*(3), 232–244. doi:10.1080/00909880600769944

Shaw, M. E. (1956). Random versus systematic distribution of information in communication nets. *Journal of Personality, 25*(1), 59. doi:10.1111/1467-6494.ep8930855

Shaw, M. E. (1964). Communication networks. *Advances in Experimental Social Psychology, 1,* 111–147

Short, J., Williams, E., & Christie, B. (1976). *The social psychology of telecommunications.* London: Wiley.

Silverthorne, C. P. (2005). *Organizational psychology in cross-cultural perspective.* New York, NY: New York University Press.

Smith, B. (1996). Care and feeding of the office grapevine. *Management Review, 85*(2), 6.

Song, S. M., Xie, J., & Dyer, B. (2000). Antecedents and consequences for marketing managers' conflict-handling behaviors. *Journal of Marketing, 64,* 50–66.

Sorensen, S. E. (2008). Employee blogging. *HR Professional, 25*(3), 16.

Steers, R. M., Sanchez-Runde, C. J., & Nardon, L. (2010). *Management across cultures: Challenges and strategies.* Cambridge, England: Cambridge University Press.

Tengblad, S. (2006). Is there a 'New Managerial Work'? A Comparison with Henry Mintzberg's Classic Study 30 Years Later. *Journal Of Management Studies, 43*(7), 1437–1461. doi:10.1111/j.1467-6486.2006.00651.x

Tesser, A., Rosen, S., & Tesser, M. (1971). On the reluctance to communicate undesirable messages (the MUM effect): A field study. *Psychological Reports, 29*(2), 651–654. doi:10.2466/pr0.1971.29.2.651

The art of giving negative feedback: A 7-step approach. (2013). *HR Specialist: Employment Law, 43*(4), 7.

Thomas, K. W. (1976). Conflict and conflict management. In M. Dunnette (Ed.), *Handbook of industrial and organizational psychology* (pp. 889–935). Chicago, IL: Rand McNally.

Thomas, K. W., & Kilmann, R. H. (1978). Comparison of four instruments measuring conflict behavior. *Psychological Reports, 42*(3, Pt 2), 1139–1145.

Thomas, K. W., Thomas, G., & Schaubhut, N. (2008). Conflict styles of men and women at six organization levels. *International Journal of Conflict Management (Emerald), 19*(2), 148–166. doi:10.1108/10444060810856085

Young, M. B., & Post, J. E. (1993). Managing to communicate, communicating to manage: How leading companies communicate with employees. *Organizational Dynamics, 22*(1), 31–43. doi:10.1016/0090-2616(93)90080-K

PART III

Designing and Changing the Organization Itself

Organizing the Organization: Structure

Learning Outcomes

After studying this chapter you should be able to:

1. Recognize and identify what structure is and what structure an organization has.

2. Describe the advantages and disadvantages of each type of structure.

3. Provide examples of different structures.

4. Explain why organizational structure is important to understand and identify.

Mini-Quiz: Organizational Structure

As an introduction to this chapter, please take the following mini-quiz (answers are in the back of the book). As you read the questions and consider the answers *before* diving into the chapter, you'll challenge yourself before you master the content, a process that helps facilitate learning for long-term retention. Some questions may have more than one correct answer. Don't worry if you cannot answer all questions correctly on your first try. By the time you read through the chapter and spend some of your own time thinking about these concepts, you should be able to determine the best answers. Try the quiz again after you finish reading the chapter.

1. What sorts of factors are relevant when talking about organizational "structure"?
   a. The size of the organization
   b. Organizational levels (i.e., who is the CEO, who are upper level managers, who are lower-level managers and nonadministrative workers)
   c. Who has the control in the organization
   d. How information is communicated in the organization

2. _____, _____, and _____ are considered the "essential dimensions" of structure and are the most commonly discussed when understanding an organization's structure.
   a. Technology, leadership, and organization size
   b. Leadership, decision-making, and organizational levels
   c. Centralization, formalization, and complexity
   d. Communication, number of subunits, and geographic location

3. Why is organizational structure so important?
   a. Different factors related to the structure can influence employee attitudes, like job satisfaction
   b. Factors related to organizational structure can actually impact employee performance
   c. Depending on the structure of the organization, employees may perceive it as a fairer or unfair workplace
   d. Organizational structure is directly tied to communication and information sharing

4. True or false? The structure of an organization may attract different kinds of employees.
   a. True! Some employees look for organizations with specific features and specific attributes
   b. False. When employees apply for jobs, they don't see or understand the inner workings of the organization

5. Some organizations have adopted flexible structures. Which of the following represents a more modern and flexible organizational structure?
   a. Virtual organizations
   b. Strategic alliances where one company joins another to temporarily solve a specific issue
   c. Boundaryless organizations that do not constrain themselves by size, or communication channels, etc.
   d. Organizations that adopt a particular division of labor so employees know who's doing what and how it fits into the bigger picture

Overview

When we talk with our friends about their jobs, we eventually find ourselves asking them to describe the structure of their organization/company. For example, we ask questions like "How many people are in your group? How big is the organization? Do you have one or more bosses? Is this the only location or are there others?" We ask these questions because the answers describe the context, the environment in which our friends work, and that helps us to understand what our friend deals with at work. Their answers reveal the structure of the organization. Specifically, the organizational structure describes how people's roles in organizations are related to each other, what level of authority (right to make decisions, give assignments, and expect them to be carried out) comes with those roles, how units/groups are distributed within the organization, and how communication is expected to flow through the organization. The arrangement of reporting relationships affects how work is completed, divided, communicated, and what kind of attitudes employees' develop that drives their behaviors.

In this chapter, we look at what structure is and how organizations structure themselves to achieve their mission/vision or goals. Different industries may impose their needs on the structure of the organization, and consequently, some organizational configurations are not entirely under the control of the leaders. In some cases, structure is not a pre-thought or developed by-design before work begins. Instead, it might be a by-product of how the organization starts out and continues to function, thus becoming an outcome rather than prescription.

What is Organizational Structure?

Organizational structure refers to the formal arrangement, the division of, and the relationships between different parts and positions within the organization (James & Jones, 1976; Porter & Lawler, 1965). Structure describes how activities are completed, decisions are made and communicated, and how

© fizkes/Shutterstock.com

people connect (or don't) in an organization. Organizational structure are the puzzle pieces of how an organization fits together. Structure concerns the division, coordination, and categorization of work tasks, job roles, groups, and components of the organization. Thus, the structure is designed to support achieving the organization's goals by delineating job roles. Because organizational structure determines to an extent how information travels through an organization, what role employees have within the organization, and the division of labor, it influences employees' (including leaders') behavior and attitudes.

In its simplest form, you can think of organizational structure a bit like driving on a road, where structure shows you the lines and guardrails are on the road. You stay on one side or the other, and between the guardrails. There are exceptions—just like driving on a road. Sometimes there are no lines and there is no guardrail. The lack of lines might tell you something about the road, such as how often it is traveled. Similarly, the lack of structure tells you something about the organization, such as informality of roles.

Only a few organizational structures are well known or commonly taught, such as the bureaucracy, mechanistic/organic, and the matrix, but a number of features or dimensions of structure exist that either make up these known models, or are used independently. All models and features of organizational structure are explained in the next sections.

The Bureaucracy

When you hear the term "bureaucracy", what comes to mind?

Organizational structure was originally described by Max Weber (Weber, 1946/1948) in his proposal of bureaucracy. Bureaucracy was an explanation for how public and lawful government was structured to ensure rule bound management.

Despite the current criticism and negative associations with the word "bureaucracy", bureaucratic organizations were considered superior to others because they were structured to maximize objectivity and clarity in decision-making through standardization that included:

1. Removing ambiguity about who reports to whom.

2. Eliminating ambiguity surrounding job position and scope.

3. Ensuring clarity around employment contract.

4. Taking away the perception of favorites by making salary tied to position description.

5. Removing conflicts of interest by disallowing employee ownership in the company.

6. Establishing rules for employees that eliminate unethical behavior (e.g., contracting oneself out to another organization, selling company secrets, hiring/selection based on specific criteria and placement test).

Accordingly, the structure of bureaucratic organizations was designed for role clarification and controlling the work environment so that work could be accomplished in an efficient and ethical manner.

Weber's bureaucracy possessed five key features (Table 11.1) that supported his idea of standardization:

1. Division of Labor.
    Similar to the foundation of scientific management discussed in Chapter 1, jobs are divided into their smallest parts. Manufacturing assembly lines may be the ideal example of division of labor—no single step is duplicated and each step is a small aspect of the entire production line. The advantages of division of labor include efficiency, specialized knowledge, and ability to hire less skilled and, therefore, less expensive workers. The disadvantages include those identified with scientific management: boredom, repetitive injuries, and low levels of responsibility that characterize highly specialized jobs. Another disadvantage is that people typically cannot see how they fit into the big picture (i.e., lack task significance), reducing their motivation on the job (see job characteristics theory in Chapter 3 on Motivation).

2. Decentralization.
    Decentralization spreads authority (ability to make decisions or command others to do work) across a number of individuals or units, giving each separate manager or person the power to make decisions and determine the future of that unit. Decentralization is the opposite of centralization

TABLE 11.1 Features of Weber's Bureaucracy

Feature	Definition
Division of labor	Extent to which jobs are divided into their specific tasks or specialties. High specialization means jobs are divided into their smallest parts, such that each job completes one task and/or function only. Low specialization means jobs incorporate many different tasks and/or functions.
Decentralization	Refers to the distribution of authority. Decentralization refers to spreading independent decision-making or authority across the organization, thus each group/unit has the authority to make its own decisions. Opposite of centralization, which is locating all decisions at one central unit or person.
Unity of command	Tied to authority, unity of command refers to having only one boss to whom you directly report and are accountable.
Departmentalization	An outcome of the degree of specialization. The grouping of jobs by their common functions or tasks.
Span of control	The number of employees under one manager's authority and responsibility.

Courtesy Zinta Byrne. Source: Weber, 1946/1948.

where a single person or group makes all decisions. As a consequence of each group making its own decisions, decentralization prevents one person or group from managing and controlling all decisions or ensuring consistency of choices. All groups can essentially do what they want. Decentralization has an advantage over centralization in the speed with which work is completed because each group determines its own fate. The decisions are made by the people who are most informed, have the knowledge, and can act without waiting for a central office to first learn the local policies. For example, many multinational organizations have human resource managers in each of their country locations. By doing so, they have people in the local region who understand the culture and the local laws. Bureaucracy favored centralization.

3. Unity of Command.
    With unity of command, people report to one person only. Hence, dual reporting relationships, reporting to two managers at a time (e.g., one at corporate and one in the field), do not exist. The simplicity of the structure removes ambiguity regarding who reports to whom, but introduces challenges when an individual's work spans functional boundaries.

4. Departmentalization.
    A product of division of labor is departmentalization because when jobs become specialized, they often need uniquely qualified managers to supervise them. They also tend to be housed in the same department for unity of command. Departmentalizing creates organization and structure, such that people doing the same job or working in the same location can work together. Thus, engineers, marketers, writers, or graphics designers can work in teams in departments designed for them. A good example is a university—departments are based on discipline, such as psychology, math or engineering.

5. Span of Control.
    The number of people one manager supervises makes up the span of control; the larger or wider the span of control, the fewer the levels of management necessary. However, the more people you have to manage, the harder the management task, in general. The size of the span of control depends on the types of jobs residing under that control, the goals of the organization, and the capabilities of the manager.

The original intent of the five features was to configure an organization so that it would function well, and in many cases, it worked. Unfortunately, initial failures of the model turned the term *bureaucracy* into a word associated with inefficiencies and unyielding layers of decision-making; failures that often still occur with organizations that use the bureaucratic structure.

One of the failures of bureaucracy is an overemphasis on the position title as opposed to the goal or objective of the job, which occurs because the job title rather than the employee holding the salary and responsibility becomes the focus. Thus, when unqualified people are placed in top jobs, rather than receive a salary based on performance, the employee is receiving a salary based on the job title.

Another failure is the tendency to apply too many restrictions around the selection of people into job roles. By overly restricting the qualifications required, filling jobs becomes next to impossible. Though role clarity generally results in positive outcomes, efforts to make every job role clear can bring about too much division of labor, making jobs too narrow in scope, and consequently tedious and boring.

In addition, failures in bureaucracy come about because of influences from external forces, such as competing markets or societal changes, come with expectations for changing quickly to accommodate those external forces, yet bureaucracies cannot change fast. With the organizational structure being rigid, it is hard to make fast adjustments.

Policies or procedures for decision-making that tend to be aligned with all those rigid roles have no room for adaptability in the bureaucracy. Changing the rules disrupts the careful controls designed to keep everything working smoothly and in its place. The general decision rule is that if a rule didn't exist to handle the situation, the situation cannot be handled.

Hence, Weber's original intent was for efficiency, and we can argue that a number of Weber's suppositions about organizational effectiveness and clarity are still valuable today (e.g., removing favoritism, preventing unethical decision-making). However, few, if any, would contend that Weber's bureaucracy is the best way to organize or structure businesses today because of its rigidity and excessive division of labor. That said, government agencies, banks, hospitals, large organizations, and those where standardization, rules, and specialization of jobs are essential, benefit from some of the principles of Weber's bureaucracy. Can you imagine a bank or hospital without clear rules and oversight?

> The bureaucracy as an organizational structure is recognized for standardization—controlling for efficiency and job clarity.

Company Example 11.1   Haier's End of Bureaucracy

Haier, a large appliance maker located in Qingdao, China, changed from a bureaucratic structure to a more competitive one. In Mamel and Zanini's (2018) article documenting the details of Haier's journey, the authors note seven key departures that Haier made ending their bureaucratic structure. These departures include (a) dividing into 4,000 microenterprises (MEs) each with groups of 10 to 15 employees only making them like mini-companies; (b) giving unique goals to each ME; (c) empowering each ME to purchase its own services as needed to achieve its goals; (d) organizing MEs along platforms (e.g., similar to products); (e) reenvisioning the overall company to be a hub within a larger network mimicking a boundaryless organization (discussed later in the chapter); (f) embracing fast innovation-like startups by having 50+ MEs that focus on incubating new ideas; and (g) granting all employees stock/ownership in the company to create commitment and personal accountability. Mamel and Zanini provide much more depth in their article about how Haier changed their structure; it is worth reading about how an established organization that was once bureaucratic is not anymore.

Mechanistic versus Organic Structure

Weber's work sparked researchers and scholars to propose alternative frameworks of structure. For example, Burns and Stalker (1961) determined that organizations may be best categorized along a continuum with one end represented by

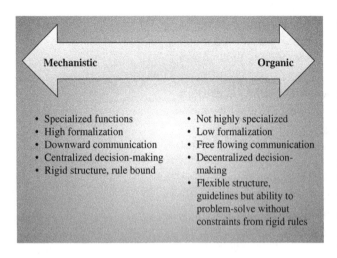

FIGURE 11.1 Mechanistic Versus Organic Organizational Structure

Courtesy Zinta Byrne.

A mechanistic organization is recognized by its rules, centralized communication and decision-making, and tall hierarchy of authority. A distinguishing characteristic of the organic organization is its flexibility, flat hierarchy, and decentralized informal communication patterns and decision-making.

the mechanistic structure (not all that different from Weber's bureaucracy) and the other end the organic structure (see Figure 11.1).

At the one extreme end of the continuum, mechanistic organizations are exemplified by substantial division of labor (very high specialization), formalized and centralized communication patterns (see Chapter 10), policies and rules for decision-making including resource allocation, and tall hierarchical structures that incorporate many levels of management that tend to embrace small spans of control. Roles tend to be clear and well-defined. The advantages of bureaucracy carry over to the mechanistic structure, including efficiency and role clarity. However, disadvantages include that in more mechanistic organizations, employees become less intrinsically motivated in their jobs (Sherman & Smith, 1984) and rate the fairness of decision-making low (Schminke, Ambrose, & Cropanzano, 2000), and managers feel unfulfilled by their jobs (Porter & Siegel, 1965).

The clear rules and formality of the mechanistic structure are well-suited for predictable or relatively stable industries such as energy and government, and unionized environments. Mechanistic organizations include the military, government agencies, and some health-care systems and hospitals that operate within strict boundaries. Health care in the United States, for example, must adhere to strict compliance with government health-care regulation, insurance, and safety stipulations. Many religious institutions favor rule bound structures, as do universities. Another example of a mechanistic organization is Dell Computer, which manufactures assembly-line made-to-order computers, and most fast food restaurants where consistency, safety, and procedural perfection is valued.

At the other extreme end of the continuum, organic organizations are characterized by flat hierarchies wherein few levels of management exist that typically incorporate large spans of control, low specialization (meaning fewer divisions of labor), informal and decentralized communication patterns, and flexibility to adjust quickly to external pressures. Roles are not well-defined, allowing employees to negotiate their responsibilities but also risking ambiguity. The flexibility and agility to adapt to changing external forces is a distinguishing characteristic of organic organizations and an advantage over mechanistic structures. These features make the organic structure desirable for fast changing or unpredictable industries and start-up or entrepreneurial companies where innovation is a core requirement (e.g., Pierce & Delbecq, 1977). For example, companies like Avaya, Inc. (business communication solutions), start-up companies like Lytro (makes a small camera that focuses after the picture has been taken), and Internet-based organizations like Zappos, Inc. (online shoe and clothing store) are all organically structured organizations. Other advantages of the organic structure include that the participative decision-making in flat structures is perceived as fair by employees (Schminke et al., 2000), leading to job satisfaction and commitment. Organizations can fall anywhere along the continuum, thus taking on a hybrid structure with characteristics of both types of organizational structures.

> **Exercise 11.1**
>
> Compare and contrast bureaucracy with mechanistic and organic organizational structures. When might each be the best structure for an organization? Give an example of a company that you know of or have heard of that fits each type of structure, not including those mentioned in the textbook.

Porter and Lawler's Seven Categories

Another way of understanding the structure of organizations was offered by Porter and Lawler (1965; Table 11.2), who proposed that organizations are structured along seven different categories.

Organizational level ties directly to the organization's hierarchy, where traversing up the hierarchy represents increasing levels of authority and responsibility within the organization. Thus, the structure dictates how authority and responsibility are dispersed among levels of management.

Line and staff hierarchy represents vertical division of labor, distinguishing managers from nonmanagers, or those with authority from those without. This category is not necessarily correlated with organizational level as one can be a staff member at a very high level of the organization (e.g., executive assistant to the Chief Executive Officer).

As mentioned previously, *span of control* represents the number of people a manager supervises or directs.

Consolidation or clustering of functions within their own groups results in organizational subunits. For example, work groups, such as accounting or marketing are subunits. The *size of subunit* has an effect on work within the organization as well as employee attitudes (see Chapter 4 on Attitudes and 7 on Teams). For example, morale, satisfaction, and productivity tend to be higher in small subunits

---

TABLE 11.2   Seven Categories of Porter and Lawler

Category	Description
Organizational level	Position of authority, amount of responsibility (e.g., manager vs. not manager)
Line and staff hierarchy	Administrative or advisory personnel (staff) vs. production line worker or manager who makes decisions about the work (line)
Span of control	Number of employees or units under a manager's supervision or control; lots of employees = wide span of control
Size of subunit	Number of people within a single unit or group
Size of entire organization	Total number of employees
Shape of entire organization	Number of levels of authority between decision-makers/leaders and lowest level of worker who is producing products; ratio of size of organization to the number of levels within the organization. A lot of levels or large ratio = tall vs. flat organization
Shape or design of communication	Centralized vs. decentralized

Courtesy Zinta Byrne. Source: Porter and Lawler, 1965.

than in large ones. Therefore, Porter and Lawler (1965) considered the size of subunit a key category of organizational structure.

The *size of the organization* refers to the total number of employees employed by that organization, including the chief executive officer or president, as opposed to the physical size of the buildings or campus containing the organizational members. Porter and Lawler suggested that the size of subunits relative to the size of the organization affects employee attitudes and behavior. For example, working in small subunits within a large organization masks the downsides of working for large organizations—you feel like you're in a small group even though the organization is big. Therefore, disadvantages of large organizations, such as lack of individual attention, are not perceived or experienced.

The *shape of the entire organization* indicates the hierarchy as either flat or tall, whereas the *shape or design of communication* denotes communication patterns: decentralized, and centralized, which have been explained in the previous section and in Chapter 10, Communication.

The categories are not exclusive of one another. For example, span of control is influenced by the shape of the organization. Taller organizations have small spans of control, whereas flat organizations have wide spans of control. The size of the subunit may be dictated by the size of the organization and the shape of the organization.

Porter and Lawler's understanding of structure sparked interest in developing models that reflected changes in industry. As new literature accumulated and scholarly calls for new models were made, review papers such as James and Jones' (1976) were published.

Why is a bureaucratic structure sometimes desirable?

James and Jones' Summary of Key Dimensions

In a review of the literature, James and Jones (1976) concluded that seven dimensions of structure are all you need to describe what organizations look like and how job roles are assigned. Even though their dimensions were strictly based on a literature review of pre-1976 studies (i.e., not empirically validated), the dimensions are still appropriate today. However, like other categorization systems for structure, the lack of information as to how the categories or dimensions relate to one another or relate to the success of the organization somewhat limits their overall utility and practical value. None-the-less, the seven dimensions include:

1. Total organization size
2. Centralization (locus of authority and decision-making)
3. Configuration (span of control, shape of hierarchy)
4. Formalization (rules and communications are written)
5. Specialization (division of labor by function, hierarchy, and task)
6. Standardization (procedures for decision-making across the organization)
7. Interdependence of organizational components (degree of task interdependence)

Similar to James and Jones' conclusion that many of the structural dimensions identified in early studies are still useful and can be retained, recent studies have shown the same (e.g., Huang, Rode, & Schroeder, 2011; Krasman, 2011).

Exercise 11.2

Create a chart with both Porter's and James & Jones' dimensions of structure—what are the similarities, what are the differences between their categories/dimensions?

Quick Summary of 'What is Structure'

In summary, over several decades a number of scholars have developed dimensions for describing how organizations are structured. Yet, grasping an understanding of what organizational structure simply doesn't seem to fall out of these dimensions. Your struggle may be particularly difficult if you're not an organizational leader trying to plan the structure or if you don't have access to the decision-making process, where structure may be highly relevant.

Hence, the next section may help clarify what structure is. Organizational structure may be more readily understood using a diagram, though be careful not to assume that structure is simply a diagram of who reports to whom!

What Does the Organizational Structure Look Like?

To facilitate the understanding of features or dimensions of structure, such as centralization or span of control, diagrams or illustrations are often used. Figure 11.2 provides a summary of the different features that can be used for structuring the organization.

Since the organizational structure cannot be physically seen, most frequent depictions use an organizational chart, much like that shown in Chapter 8, Figure 8.5 or here in Figure 11.2. In the sample shown in Figure 11.2, each box represents a formal position or job title within the organization.

This particular example is structured by function, product grouping, and geographical region. In the chart, the Executive Vice-Presidents directly report to the Chief Executive Officer (CEO) and President; thus, they are immediate or direct subordinates (also called direct reports) of the CEO. Employees performing job functions, such as manufacturing, marketing, and sales report to Associate Vice-Presidents responsible for those functions. The Associate Vice-Presidents are each accountable to an Executive Vice-President, one responsible for products and the other for clients. Individual Sales Managers report to their region's Sales Director. Therefore, Sales Managers in China report to Sales Directors in China, whereas Sales Managers in the United States are accountable to Sales Directors in the United States.

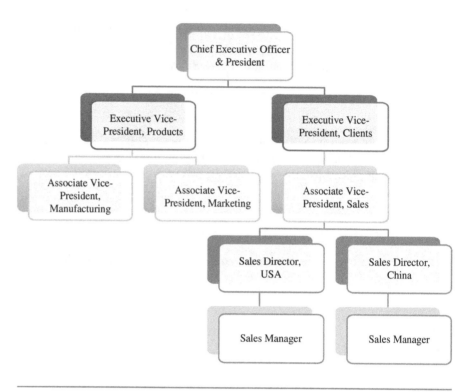

FIGURE 11.2 Hierarchical Chart

Courtesy Zinta Byrne.

If you currently work, what does your organization's chart look like? If you don't work, what does your university or college's organizational chart look like? The charts will tell you who has direct authority over whom.

The organizational chart represents the formal networks (see Chapter 10 on Communication) of the organization, indicating lines of authority that describe who reports to whom, or put another way who has authority over whom.

Having an organizational chart for your firm provides the advantage of communicating quickly where the lines of authority exist and where they do not. Not only does this convey responsibility to those outside the organization, but also to those inside the organization. Specifically, the chart can serve as a good reminder for those who may have a tendency to forget how they fit into the chain of command (the line of authority).

A potential downside of using the organizational chart is that the illustration of the structure *becomes* the structure without forethought as to whether that configuration is right for the organization in terms of size, location, and market. Moreover, it is easy to reconfigure lines on a diagram, but in reality, reconfiguring the organization's structure can be stress-inducing for employees (and organizational partners) and wasteful (especially in fast-paced markets).

That said, however, the value of diagrams cannot be understated! It helps, though, to keep in mind that you cannot design an organization's structure using pictures. The dimensions provided by Weber, Porter and Lawler, and James and Jones are what you need to design the organizational structure so that employees can achieve the goals set out by the company leaders. The diagram of your structure follows *after* you consider which dimensions fit your needs and your industry. Different industries may require different dimensions.

What Should You Consider When Choosing a Structure?

Based on previous works that delineated the dimensions of structure, Daft (2004) proposed that six factors should be considered when structuring an organization. Thus, Daft proposed that organizations be proactive in designing their structures, as opposed to discovering what their structure needs to be after the fact. The logic applied here is that industries require different configurations of firms in order for them to function effectively, and as such, the structure should be established and executed as people are added to the organization.

For example, hospitals may function best with a clear division of labor and departmentalization. In contrast, landscape companies may function best with little specialization. Instead, the more cross-trained their workforce, the more flexible they are to manage client demand and worker schedules. Thus, when designing the structure for your organization (see Burton, DeSanctis, & Obel, 2006 for a good resource), it's best to take time to determine where your organization falls on each of the six factors identified in Table 11.3. Additionally, the factors need not be exclusive; organizations can have a centralized corporate office with decentralized regional offices (e.g., Richardson, Vandenberg, Blum, & Roman, 2002). For example, multinational organizations, like IBM or Keysight Technologies, typically have a corporate office and regional offices that operate independently to accommodate local norms, culture, and legal requirements (Leung & Peterson, 2011).

Why is it useful to know what dimensions or categories there are for describing structure?

Effects of Features on Decision-Making

Incorporating many of the features from existing categorizing systems, such as those previously discussed, Fredrickson (1986) proposed three essential dimensions of structure frequently used to understand how the structure of the organization affects decision-making: centralization, formalization, and complexity. Centralization and formalization retain their definitions as described in the sections above. Complexity represents the number of parts that must be integrated in an organization (e.g., multinational organization engaging in many different lines of production. Think of organizations like Proctor & Gamble). High complexity can make coordinated strategic decision-making difficult.

Hypothesizing how these three dimensions of structure affect decision-making, Fredrickson (1986) suggested that

The impact of high centralization:

- Brings about delayed onset of decision-making processes
- Is likely to result in proactive decision making
- Creates focused goals (low centralization introduces conflicting goals for the organization)
- Generates more "major" strategic decisions (as opposed to incremental decisions only)

TABLE 11.3   Six Factors for Structuring Organizations

Factor	Description	Examples
Work specialization or division of labor	How separated, broken up, or divided the jobs are	Assembly line workers only work on one small part of the larger product. Healthcare systems – each doctor has a specialty and you see the doctor who best fits your problem (e.g., optometrist, radiologist, surgeon, cardiologist).
Departmentalization	How specialties or divisions of labor are sub-grouped; grouping similar functions or geographic locations; customers	Accountants all work in the Accounting Department. Product lines (e.g., Samsung produces phones, televisions, cameras, computers, lighting, home appliances). Geography: US, Asia-Pacific, Europe. Customers: consumers, corporate, small business
Chain of command	Line of authority between the lowest level worker to the highest level boss or supervisor for that person	Sales employee reports to Sales Manager, who reports to Sales Director, who reports to Sales Group Manager, who reports to Sales Division Manager, who reports to Sales Vice-President.
Span of control	Number of employees within a manager's control (positively related to the size of the organization)	Sales Group Manager may manage as many as 50 sales representatives (large or wide span), but the Sales Division Manager may only have five Sales Group Managers reporting to him or her (small span).
Centralization vs decentralization	Whether decision making rests with one person or one unit usually at the top of the organization (centralized); decision making is spread across the organization – push decision making down (decentralized)	Centralized: typically governments and government agencies such as the military; small businesses or family run shops. Decentralized: colleges and departments within higher education
Formalization	How much jobs are standardized, level of accountability, level of discretion one has over his or her own work	Low amount of formalization: college professors, book authors, to a degree doctors and surgeons. High amounts of formalization: administrative assistants, editorial positions, front desk clerk, many hospital jobs

Courtesy Zinta Byrne. Source: Daft, 2004.

The impact of intermediate to high formalization:

- Causes reactive decision-making. Highly formalized strategic planning systems are likely to discourage creativity and employees seeking new, idea-generating opportunities

- Creates specific rather than general goals that will primarily focus on achieving efficiency

- Is that the "means" (or the approach) tend to outweigh the outcomes

- Tends to generate incremental changes rather than drastic ones

- Is that planning systems will be well integrated

The impact of high complexity:

- Is increased division of labor requiring more strategic coordination

- Causes low or no decision initiation (because the problem may be detected at any place in the organization and those individuals may choose to respond or not)

- Generates varying goals across the organization

- Causes individuals to potentially hold individual goals in higher esteem (they might be more salient) than organizational goals

- Generates incremental changes more than major changes

- Creates lower integration of strategy across the organization

As a consequence of how structural features may affect decision-making, and based on specific business objectives and locations, organizations may choose alternative features and designs to all those discussed in the previous sections.

Alternative Organizational Configurations

Rather than being configured using traditional dimensions or factors such as the six offered by Daft (2004), or previous scholars such as Porter and Lawler (1965), organizations can configure themselves using departmentalization, shown in Table 11.4, which may facilitate decision-making to some degree. Departmentalization creates structural grouping by jobs that are performed in the same way or act on the same target (e.g., customer). Departmentalization creates manageable groups that are important for the organization.

TABLE 11.4   Alternative Organizational Structure Groupings

Structural Grouping	Description	Examples
Process	Processes executed. Similar to function but more specific.	Within Accounting: tax, compensation, billing. Within a publishing company: editing, proofing, images, indexing
Function	Broader than process, similar in that people are grouped by type of work they do or occupation.	Marketing, human resources, accounting, sales, research & development. At a university: academic units, administration, grants and research funding
Product	Outcome of the organization, either a service or consumer/industrial product.	PCs, desktops, monitors, printers, services.
Customer	Type of customer.	Consumer vs. commercial, men vs. women, distributor vs. reseller
Geography	Territory or region of the country.	Asia-Pacific, Europe; Local, regional, global. Domestic, International.
Matrix	Integrates one structural group within another.	Product within customer: PCs for consumer vs. commercial; Function within geography: Human resources in Asia-Pacific, Europe, Africa, and Americas

Courtesy Zinta Byrne.

The *process* dimension refers to organizing by the processes that must be followed, typically within a function or job type. This cluster represents an organizational structure with the highest division of labor, relative to all the others in the Table. Thus, in a hospital, all the lab technicians who test blood may be in the same group, whereas those who draw the blood from patients are divided into a different group. Even though both groups work with blood, testing it requires very different processes from working with patients to draw and label their blood samples.

Organizing by *function* is grouping by occupation, such as disciplines in an academic environment (e.g., management, psychology, engineering, chemistry), or collection of tasks and job types in an organization, such as accounting, marketing, and manufacturing. These groups or job types perform the same or similar purpose.

Product as a structural grouping makes sense with organizations that have several production lines, such as American Cast Iron Pipe Company (otherwise known as American Steel), 3M, Apple, or Proctor & Gamble. They create and sell more than one product. American Steel, for instance, has five product lines: iron pipes, valves and hydrants, spiral-welded steel pipe, ferrous castings, and electric resistance steel pipes. They are all cast-iron products, but they have several varieties that each has multiple types. Toyota, in contrast, has several automobile products, but in addition, the company has businesses in housing, IT systems, biotechnology and afforestation, financial services, and marine crafts and engines.

Organizations may be configured by *customer* type. For example, banks typically have different groups who handle business clients, investors, and consumers each separately. Thus, those who work with business accounts do not also work with the small family just opening a savings account. Similarly, organizations who sell directly to the public and also to distributers will have different groups dedicated to these customer bases.

Arranging by *geography* makes sense for large multinational organizations.

Lastly, a *matrix* organization is one where people are managed by both product and function forming a matrix of dual reporting relationships.

> Why are there so many different factors or dimensions for structuring an organization?

Matrix Organization

The matrix organization became a popular organizational structure in the late 1970s and early 1980s. Many organizations, such as Allianz Global Corporate & Specialty (AGCS) and Siemens, still use the matrix structure (Figure 11.3).

Matrix structures attempt to decentralize decision-making and encourage coordination across specialties. Employees in matrix structures have multiple bosses to whom they are accountable and must answer regarding their tasks, priorities, schedules, and progress. In Figure 11.3, employees would report to a product manager and a functional manager. For example, an employee whose job it is to sell smart phones might report to both a sales manager and the product development manager for smart phones. In this way the employee keeps the product manager informed of problems clients are having with the current upgrade to the phone, while also reporting to the sales manager about how the new upgrade is selling (or not). The employee, therefore, has two bosses—one who is primarily responsible for developing smart phones for the company, and the other primarily responsible for all sales for the company.

Advantages of the matrix organization include collaboration between potentially competing groups, effective use of experts, broad information exchange opening up communication channels between different parts of the organization, flexibility for the organization in how it uses its resources, and employees with more opportunities for relationship building across the organization (breaking down tight in-group/out-groups) and for working more autonomously.

		Product Development				
		PC	Laptop	Television	Smart Phone	Movie Theatre
Function	Manufacturing					
	Human Resources					
	Finance					
	Engineers					
	Technical Writing					
	Sales					
	Support					

FIGURE 11.3 Example of a Matrix Organization

Courtesy Zinta Byrne.

Disadvantages for employees include reporting to multiple bosses, ambiguity over work priorities, and struggles with competing demands. Matrix organizations were for many years considered novel and efficient, and several organizations still use the matrix configuration. Nonetheless, decision-making in the matrix can become complex fast and sometimes gridlocked by the competing lines of authority. Managers must have equal power to ensure they collaborate instead of competing with each other (Davis & Lawrence, 1978).

A potential consequence of the matrix is the question "who is in charge?" (Davis & Lawrence, 1978). This leads to employees in each group having more than one boss who each prioritizes their work as absolutely critical—whose work do you ensure is completed first if you cannot satisfy both managers at the same time? With dual reporting relationships, accountability may also become unclear.

Not only is it hard to figure out who is in charge or who gets priority, each employee who serves multiple product lines may experience high cognitive demand. That is, the employee not only has to track which manager wants what, but also track and manage the unique information associated with multiple products. In addition, employees most likely have to compete for shared resources while maintaining positive relations with the many people with whom they interact across both function and product teams.

Therefore, if you work in a matrix organization, be sure to ask questions about priorities, clarify your role with each boss, and communicate often with each to ensure they know what you're doing and why, as well as when. For the organization, make the lines of authority or responsibility for decision-making clear to avoid finger pointing.

Matrix organizations are recognized by their dual lines of authority, crossing two organizing features to create a literal matrix of authority, responsibility, and accountability.

Exercise 11.3

Before moving on, list the different elements of structure discussed thus far in the chapter, and summarize how these elements determine who work gets done and decision are made in organizations. Which components do you feel are MOST important in affecting how work gets done, people work together, and how decisions are made?

Putting it All Together

The features, factors, and categories introduced in the sections above were all offered by various scholars at different times, each either building on the previous or adding a new perspective, such as departmentalization or the matrix configuration. However, there does not seem to be a natural ordering or progression to the features or organizational designs except by when they were chronologically introduced. Figure 11.4 (not depicting statistically related paths) attempts to provide a summary of the features and categories proposed by Weber (1946/1948), Porter and Lawler (1957), James and Jones (1976), as well as departmentalization, and how they may determine or influence each other during the design of the organizational structure.

To make sense of Figure 11.4, start on the left with Formalization. Formalization determines to some degree the division of labor and the amount of decentralization. For instance, a more formal organization will typically have a high division of labor and be centralized rather than decentralized. Division of labor determines to a degree the organizational levels, extent of decentralization (the more specialized the groups, the more the tendency toward centralized structures), and the departmentalization of the organization (the more specialization, the more departments). Not all elements affect each other. For example, the size of the organization has a distinct effect on size of subunits and span of control, but you could configure the organization using just about any element from there. Since the figure does not depict any statistical relationships or summary research findings, the figure could have been drawn differently because each feature can have its benefits or downsides depending on the goals of the organization.

How would you draw Figure 11.4?

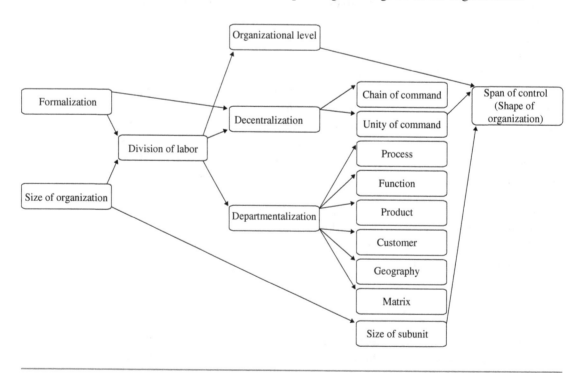

FIGURE 11.4 Summary of Structure Features, Factors, Categories, and Departmentalization

Courtesy Zinta Byrne.

What are the Advantages/Disadvantages with Different Structure Elements?

Each arrangement or factor can have advantages and disadvantages, depending on the nature of implementation or specific situation facing the organization. For example, when work becomes too specialized, it gets boring, and it becomes hard to see how what you do fits into the bigger vision of the organization. Consequently, your levels of satisfaction and motivation go down (remember the job characteristic theory from Chapter 3; Hackman & Oldham, 1976). Similarly, departmentalization can lead to over-segregation, which inhibits communication, ending up with less efficient decision-making. However, departmentalization may be necessary for efficiency of resources and people. For instance, centralizing all functions in one geographic region, such as placing the corporate office in London (see Figure 11.5 left image), may be more efficient than placing different functions in their own geographic locations. When placed in different locations, everyone must deal with time zone differences, local customs and laws, and the time and cost of exporting and transferring resources and supplies across customs so that functions across geographical regions can share (Figure 11.5 right image).

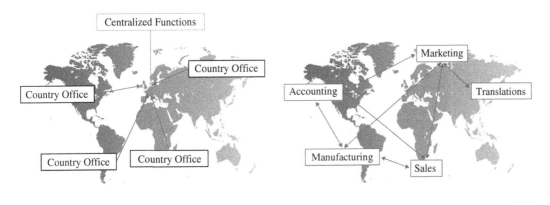

FIGURE 11.5   Geographic Placements of Departments

Left: © ildogesto/Shuttestock, Inc.; Right: © ildogesto/Shuttestock, Inc.

Thus, structuring based on geographical factors can not only result in some efficiencies (e.g., local groups know the customers and laws; some resources or supplies may be prohibitively expensive in one country, but very cheap in another offsetting shipping costs), but also brings about costs because of duplication (e.g., Asia Human Resources, Europe Human Resources).

Arranging for efficiency ties directly into span of control. Specifically, a wide span of control (Figure 11.6) offers benefits for many organizations because it translates into fewer layers of management to get to the decision-makers at the top. Figure 11.6 illustrates a wide span of control, especially for the four Vice-Presidents (VPs). The Chief Executive Officer (CEO) has a relatively narrow span of control. Nonetheless, a wide span of control has its downsides, in particular when managers ineffectively manage a large number of people. In contrast, narrow spans of control

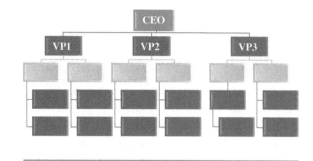

FIGURE 11.7 Narrow Span of Control

Courtesy Zinta Byrne.

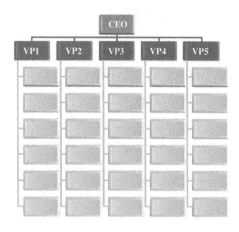

FIGURE 11.6 Wide Span of Control

Courtesy Zinta Byrne.

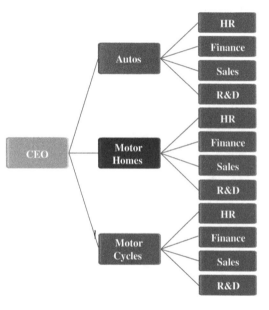

FIGURE 11.8 Grouping by Product

Courtesy Zinta Byrne.

allow for greater oversight, faster and more efficient communication, and ease of management. Figure 11.7 illustrates a narrow span of control for each management level. The downside of a narrow span of control is that you need more managers.

Hence, there is no ideal span of control—some functions are easier to manage than others, and some people are more independent than others and require less attention or supervision. The complexity of the jobs managed, the competency of the employees within those jobs, and the physical proximity of employees to supervisor (e.g., across regions) affect span of control.

The span of control may also be an outcome of a configuration arranged by product (Figure 11.8). State Farm Mutual Automobile Company is an example of an organization with several lines of business that are essentially run by different groups. Thus, each has its own organizational chart depicting span of control, chain of command, division of labor, and decision structure. For example, State Farm's products include insurance divided into property, life, and health, and banking, which is separate from investing. Each product has its own mini-company. Advantages of a product-based organizational structure include that all those with expertise in a particular product are working together, perhaps reporting to the same manager or management chain of command, thus minimizing conflicts. All activities needed for production are combined, resulting in a single semi-autonomous profit center. However, disadvantages include failure to learn and benefit from mistakes and innovations across product lines. Also, employees may become overcommitted to the success of their product, potentially creating failure in another product even though both are within the same overarching organization. Management at the highest levels may struggle with overseeing the various and sometimes competing groups. Like other arrangements, grouping by product leads to a duplication of functions (shown in Figure 11.8), which can have large financial implications for the organization. Similar disadvantages occur with organizing by customer groups.

No structure or feature is perfect; each has advantages and disadvantages. Each organization's leaders must determine for themselves which elements make sense given the organization's size, market, purpose, and life stage (e.g., entrepreneurial vs. mature). With such complexity in determining organizational design, many organizations turn to flexible structures; configurations that allow for rapid change while simultaneously reducing the impact of the change on employees.

Which elements of structure do you think are most important for an organization to consider?

Flexible Structures

Previously reviewed models and dimensions of structure tended toward configurations that could be established and held constant for some time. However, as business climates have changed and become more global and fast-paced, organizations have found they must adapt and modify their structures. Thus, the era of a fixed structure for the life of the organization no longer exists.

In recent years, organizations have been moving toward more flexible structures, ones that attempt to resolve conflicts and challenges associated with the traditional structures or combination of features reviewed in the previous sections. For example, the boundaryless structure, which epitomizes the flexible and changeable organizational configuration, comes in a variety of forms including a modular and virtual arrangement. Such flexible structures create efficiency, flexibility, cost savings, innovation, and globalization, as well as enable organizations to focus on what they do best, as opposed to trying to do everything, not so well.

Boundaryless Organizations

Boundaryless organizations, an idea launched by Jack Welch who was General Electric Company's former and most well-known chairman, describes the ideal organization as one not constrained by its chain of command, shape, structural groups, or boundaries to the organizations outside itself. You can think of boundaries as rules dictating who can talk to whom and when. Though chains of command and clear job descriptions remove ambiguity surrounding who should do what, adhering to these structure elements constrain people's ability to think and act outside of their job role. The boundaryless organization purposefully introduces ambiguity, forcing people to increase creativity and collaboration. Without communication restrictions, problem solving becomes faster because fewer levels of hierarchy stand in the way of approving changes or new advances. Thus, cross-hierarchical teams, participative management, matrixed project teams, and empowered teams make up the boundaryless organization. A good example of a boundarlyess organization is Gore, the maker of Gore-TEX. Gore has no organizational charts or formal titles, thus everyone can be a leader whenever a leader is needed.

Watch https://www.youtube.com/watch?v=xcTtQ0hiHbE for an example of how Apple, under the leadership of Steve Jobs, was (and may still be) like a boundaryless organization.

Boundaries to external suppliers and partners are also minimized in the boundaryless organization. Suppliers, regulators, customers, and other key external partners are included in the team, as new products are designed and developed. Welch's dream for the boundaryless organization was that it operates like a family-run grocery store, where barriers that separate employees within and outside the store are removed. Think of a typical family-run grocery store in which the store is highly dependent on suppliers, but also on customers to regularly shop

FIGURE 11.9   Two-Story House Interior

© TheBlackRhino/Shutterstock, Inc.

and help the store understand what they want and need. Section managers within the store, such as the manager for the meat counter or vegetables isles must work together to ensure the store is stocked, logically and esthetically flows from one unit to the next, is clean, and presents a unified look and feel to shoppers. Welch envisioned that the success of boundaryless organizations relies on mutual trust, sufficient skill levels so that excessive management is unnecessary, and employees who embrace a structure where power and authority in the hierarchical levels is not essential for their feelings of success. Thus, like a family-owned grocery store, you get the feeling that everyone is working together and has a mutual, invested interest in making the organization work. Employees are constantly learning new skills, changing jobs as needed to adjust to new market strategies, and shifting to new assignments (hard to do fast within a boundary or highly structured organization) or sometimes new locations as the organization innovates new solutions.

If the family-run grocery store does not present an image that clarifies the boundaryless organization for you, perhaps a more clear way of understanding boundaryless organizations is to visualize a two-story house as explained by Kerr, Chief Learning Officer at General Electric for a number of years (Hodgetts, 1996). Kerr described that boundaryless organizations are the opposite of your typical organization, which is a multiple story house (Figure 11.9).

In a multiple story house, you have floors, ceilings, and walls. Information does not travel well between the upstairs and downstairs because it must traverse the awkward stairs and go through doors and angles. In organizations, the lower level employees (on the first floor of the house) may not want to share their innovative ideas with the levels above them (managers on the second floor), because either their boss is a barrier or the norms of the hierarchy are that the boss comes up with the ideas and you on the lower level do not. Thus, the levels of the house are separated by strong floors and ceilings, and so are you from upper management in a traditional organization. The outside walls of the house keep you protected from the elements outside, but they also close you off to customers, suppliers, and key regulators. Insight and communication with the outside might help make your solutions more innovative, but because of the strong and thick walls, you are insulated from them. The boundaryless organization has none of these walls, floors, stairs, or ceilings.

Though Kerr did not go on to explain what the boundaryless house would look like, we can envision it in contrast to the traditional two-story house. Thus, the boundaryless organization may be more like a traditional Japanese tea house (Figure 11.10), where there are no upstairs floors and the walls move and open to the outside, so that the entire house allows air to freely flow from room to room. Rooms are changeable by the moveable walls, permitting multiple alternative room interior configurations.

With such flexibility and improvements in efficiency, the boundaryless organization became popular in an era when organizations were starting to face increasing challenges with global markets and worldwide competition leading to

FIGURE 11.10   Traditional Japanese Tea House

coordination that is more complicated. Yet, adopting the boundaryless organizational structure is not without challenges.

Ashkenas (1999) describes a number of challenges associated with adopting a boundaryless organizational configuration, several of which are reviewed here (the full article provides a variety of examples and more details). One of the first challenges is transferring information between units and giving everyone access to the same information that allows people to make fast decisions to address changing business needs. To use the information effectively, people need to demonstrate high levels of competence, which means they cannot possess a narrow set of skills or inability to integrate information. Thus, expectations for the competence and capability of employees goes up with boundaryless organizations; an expectation that may not be met with the current employees (this potential lack of skill or competence has implications for selection and team placement). Additionally, existing employees must be more capable of learning, growing, adapting, and integrating than may be the case with a traditionally structured organization. Consequently, boundaryless organizations emphasize training and development, potentially more so than organizations structured like a multi-story house.

Because there are no floors or ceilings in the boundaryless organization, decision-making is shared throughout the organization and located where the most informed and competent decision can be made. Another challenge, therefore, in adopting the boundaryless structure is handling these new decision-making expectations. To do so, employees must receive focused training in decision-making skills. Along with decision-making skill development, employees are also trained in communication skills because the increase in information flow requires greater ability in communication across organizational (and country) cultures and topic areas. Communication between units of traditional organizations can be challenging, as there are typically rules for who should hear the communication first and what is not supposed to be shared. However, in the boundaryless organization, information, and communication are free flowing and as such, there are no rules for how to communicate. You would think no rules should make sharing information easier, but without a template that tells you what to discuss or how to say it, communication may be a bit more challenging until you've learned how to judge for yourself what needs to be said, to whom, and when. Hence, the more employees embrace learning these new skills, the more effective they are (see Chapter 10 on Communication).

To encourage employees to embrace the training, new skills, and new model of the organization, rewards should match the new boundaryless organizational structure. Specifically, in the boundaryless organization, people are rewarded for expanding their skills, developing innovative and fast solutions, collaborating, and choosing to be effective doing any job that is needed at that time. In contrast, typical reward systems encourage people to pursue promotions, as bigger rewards are reserved for the upper echelons of the organization. Thus, when adopting the boundaryless structure, the organization must change its reward structure. For example, General Electric reduced the number of salary levels from 29 to 5, and increased the range of salaries within each level such that employees did not have to get a promotion just to get a raise (Hodgetts, 1996).

In addition to the emphasis on connection and communication internally within the organization, the boundaryless structure enables connection with external partners. In traditionally structured organizations, external partners and competitors are kept at bay to protect company trade secrets. In a boundaryless organization, the key to connecting with external partners lies in recognizing what kind of information must be kept separate from them, versus what can be shared that makes for better solutions. Thus, it may be that when competitors and external partners are brought into discussions about collaborative products or solutions, the initial discussions are broad and general. This allows everyone to share best practices and decide how to collaborate effectively, but when it is time to discuss specific details about the products or solutions, partners and competitors are no longer involved in the discussion (Hodgetts, 1996). Collaborative partners such as these may be called alliances, which the boundaryless organization makes possible through the reduction of constraints.

Examples of Boundaryless Organizations: Modular, Virtual, Strategic Alliance

The virtual organization is another approach to the boundaryless organization and can be referred to by many different names, such as modular, shamrock, spider webs, or starbursts (e.g., Handy, 1989; Lei, Hitt, & Goldhar, 1996; Sanchez & Mahoney, 1996). The modular or virtual organization outsources its major business functions (though not its core business) creating a temporary conglomerate of independent companies that are linked by information technology, sharing skills, costs, and market space (e.g., Achrol, 1997; Baldwin & Clark, 2000; Davidow & Malone, 1993). Thus, the companies, clients, and suppliers are all part of a large network. The key word of the day here is *temporary,* as the network disbands as soon as the objective or goal of the project has been achieved. A good example of virtual or modular organizations is large movie productions. Watch any movie today and you will see a number of different companies combining to create and produce the movie. For example, movies made within the last decade, such as *The Amazing Spider-Man*, *Brave*, or *Casino Royale* are made by a network of companies including Sony Pictures, Marvel, Columbia Pictures, Dolby Digital, Walt Disney, Pixar, and many others. It is unlikely that any movie these days is made and/or produced by only one company (Bates, 1998).

Corning, Inc. is another example of a company using the virtual or modular configuration, but on a larger scale called *strategic alliances* (Kogut, 1991). The strategic alliance is an organizational configuration where more than one separate company joins another to combine solutions, creating an entirely new product or market. Corning's alliances include Cormetech, Inc. a partnership between Corning and Mitsubishi; Dow Corning Corporation, which combines management teams from Corning and The Dow Chemical Company; Hemlock Semiconductor Corporation, which was created through a joint venture between Dow Corning and two Japanese companies Shin-Etsu Handotai Co, Ltd and Mitsubishi Materials Corporation; and Samsung Corning Prevision Materials, Co., Ltd., which is a joint company between Samsung and Corning based in Seoul, Korea to produce liquid crystal display glass (see Corning's web site for more information on its strategic alliances). Through these equal partner companies, Corning is able to jointly produce products and contribute to the production of other's products that they otherwise would not be able to create alone. By combining efforts, Samsung Corning Precision Materials is currently one of the only companies in the world to manufacture liquid crystal display glass for televisions, computers, cameras, mobile phones, and GPS navigation systems. Other examples of strategic alliances include Airbus Industries that consists of partnerships between European firms in France, Germany, Spain, and England; and Apple Inc., which partners with Foxconn, a Taiwanese company.

The organizational structure, whether flexible or rigid, affects how employees work, communicate, and feel. Whether they are one of many subordinates reporting to one or more bosses, required to address their colleagues formally or not, or work with others like them or fulfill a unique and lonely role in their unit, is determined by the organizational structure.

> Flexible organizational structures have advantages and disadvantages, just as traditional structures, such as bureaucracy and matrix organizational structures, do. Thus, rather than picking a design with a catchy name or what seems to be the latest trend, use careful thought and critical thinking to determine what your organization needs, what structure will support the organizational strategy, and answer the questions offered by numerous experts in organizational design. Most of those questions will revolve around the structural elements, your market, and your strategy.

Exercise 11.4

How does a flexible organizational structure differ from bureaucracy, mechanistic, and organic structures? What dimensions of Porter's or James & Jones' categorization schemes apply to flexible organizational structures?

How Does Structure Affect Organizational Members?

With so many possible design configurations to sort through, the impact of organizational structuring and restructuring on both the organization and employees is often overlooked. The structure of the organization can affect employees' attitudes, behavior, and stress levels (see Table 11.5 for a quick summary). For example, employees at higher levels within the organization tend to report greater satisfaction than those at lower levels of the structure (Herman & Hulin, 1973; Porter & Lawler, 1965; Smith, Kendall, & Hulin, 1969). Employees in small units or groups are happier, less likely to quit, and experience less conflict than those in large units (Porter & Lawler, 1965). Depending on the group they are in, such as their department, unit, division, or functional specialty, employees differ in their satisfaction levels and their perceptions of their supervisor's leader behavior (Adams, Laker, & Hulin, 1977). For instance, employees in functions that are structured and production-oriented generally report lower job satisfaction and perceive their bosses to be more job-centered than employees in less production-focused units (see Chapter 9 for production- or job-centered versus employee-centered management).

Employees working for employee-centered managers are probably in organizations whose structure may be considered decentralized and participatory. Such employees perceive higher levels of procedural justice (fairness of procedures and decision-making) than those in organizations that are more centralized (Schminke et al., 2000). In general, employees tend to report high levels of procedural justice when they perceive high levels of organizational support (Cohen-Charash & Spector, 2001), which would be more indicative of a decentralized structure with a narrow span of control. However, Ambrose and Schminke (2003) found that in organic organizations the relationship was less pronounced than in mechanistic organizations. Specifically, in their study of 506 employees from 98 departments in 64 organizations in the United States, employees in organic organizations reported less perceived support with high procedural justice levels than did those in mechanistic organizations. The contrast was present when procedural justice was low—those in mechanistic organizations reported lower perceptions of support than those in organic organizations when they perceived less fairness. The researchers concluded that employees at lower levels of the organization pay more attention to procedural fairness in organizations with a bureaucratic system with high formalization and little participation in decision-making, than do those in organic organizations.

TABLE 11.5 How Structure Affects Employees

Dimension/Factor of Structure	Attitudes/Behaviors Affected
Organizational level	Job satisfaction
Size of subunit	Satisfaction, retention
Specialization	Satisfaction
Decentralization	Justice (fairness perceptions), knowledge sharing
Bureaucratic, formal	Attention to fairness
Decentralized and informal	Self-managed teams more effective
Centralization and formalization	Empowerment (negative relationship)

Similar to Ambrose and Schminke's (2003) work examining organic versus mechanistic organizations, others have examined whether the nature of formalization and shape of the organization (e.g., levels of hierarchy) affects organizational performance. For instance, results from a study of manufacturing plants revealed that those with decentralized decision-making (few layers of hierarchy) outperformed those with centralized decision-making (Nahm, Vonderembse, & Koufteros, 2003). This lower performance might be explained by the negative relationship between centralization and empowerment (Rhee, Seog, Bozorov, & Dedhanov, 2017). Employees who do not feel empowered tend to demonstrate lower performance levels than their empowered peers. In contrast, researchers studying Chinese industrial state-owned enterprises found that decentralization was negatively related to performance (Xiaohua & Germain, 2003). Most likely, the difference in research findings may be partly attributed to the differences in cultural norms, expectations of leaders, and organizational practices.

Structure seems to affect knowledge-sharing practices in organizations, practices essential for organizational performance (Hsu, 2008). In a study examining the effects of structure on knowledge sharing, Chen and Huang (2007) found among Taiwanese firms that centralization was negatively related to trust, communication, and coordination (which may be considered proxies for performance). Formalization was also negatively related to trust and coordination. Integration, defined as how much subdivisions work collaboratively, was positively related to all three outcomes (trust, communication, coordination). Therefore, their results showed that employees in less formalized, decentralized, and highly integrated organizations exhibited the most knowledge sharing. In support of Chen and Huang's findings, a recent study demonstrated that centralization, via knowledge management, is also negatively related to effectiveness. Specifically, Zheng, Yang, and McLean (2010), studying 384 human resource professionals in organizations in the United States, showed that the relationship between organizational culture (i.e., the overriding expectations for behavior) and effectiveness was explained by knowledge management (i.e., knowledge sharing). The authors also found that the coordination and integration of knowledge across the organization (i.e., knowledge sharing) directly affects organizational effectiveness and is positively related to organizational structure.

Some researchers have hypothesized that the structure of the organization attracts certain kinds of employees and that the organization then hires those specific types of employees because of their fit with the structure. This attraction-hire process is called the "attraction-selection" framework (Oldham & Hackman, 1981) and has been used to explain the relationship between organizational structure and employees' reactions to work. The framework suggests that people with specific attributes are attracted to organizations with certain structures. Thus, certain types

© loreanto/Shutterstock.com

of people may be attracted to organizations with a narrow span of control, whereas other types of people are attracted to organizations with a wide span of control. Based on the attraction-selection model, the structure of an organization, therefore, influences who is drawn to work there, and employees' qualities, in turn, influence their reactions to work.

An alternative model to explaining the structure–employee relationship is the "job-modification" framework (Oldham & Hackman, 1981). This theory argues that the organization's structure influences how jobs may be altered and adapted, which influences employees' reactions to work. According to this model, the organizational structure determines the quality of core job dimensions from the job characteristic theory (e.g., task identity, challenge, autonomy) and as such, directly affects employees' reactions to work. Both models have received reasonable support (see Oldham & Hackman, 1981). In their study of 2960 employees in 428 jobs across 36 organizations in the United States and Canada, Oldham and Hackman examined which model would best explain the influence of organizational structure on employee attitudes. Structure was assessed using the organization's size, number of hierarchical levels, formalization, and centralization. Reactions to work were assessed using measures of employee motivation, growth satisfaction, general satisfaction, social satisfaction, supervisory satisfaction, security satisfaction, and pay satisfaction. To capture the attraction-selection framework, gender, age, and education were used as personal attributes. To evaluate the job modification framework, core job dimensions from the job characteristics theory (i.e., skill variety, task significance, task identity, autonomy, and feedback) were measured. Results of multiple regression analyses revealed little support for the attraction–selection framework, and reasonable support for the job-modification model. Specifically, the core job dimensions explained the structure–reactions relationships better than the attraction–selection variables. Although the authors' logic makes sense, given more advanced methodology and better choice of personal attribute variables (e.g., personality traits), the findings may differ. What is clear from their results is that structure can influence employee reactions to work.

Though their study shed light on how the structure of the organization could affect employees' reactions Oldham and Hackman, failed to consider the teams within which employees are organized. As it turns out, many organizations have adopted self-managed work teams (see Chapter 7), and yet these team arrangements are affected by the organization's structure. In self-managed teams, employees work collaboratively to make their own decisions, and this often increases team effectiveness because working interdependently increases felt responsibility of the team members.

Results of a recent study show that the structure of self-managed teams often mirrors the structure of their overarching organization (Tata & Prasad, 2004). In Tata and Prasad's study, self-managed teams were rated as more effective in organizations exhibiting low levels of formalization and centralization, as opposed to those with high levels of formalization and centralization (consistent with Chen & Huang, 2007, and Zheng et al., 2010 discussed previously). Tata and Prasad suggested that self-managed teams may operate better in decentralized organizations that typically do not promote strict rules and processes. The authors also suggested in highly centralized organizations, self-managed teams probably recognize that their "self-management" is only a label and decisions are not actually theirs to make. This perception of lack of real control or decision-making

The organizational structure affects how employees feel about work and how they behave on the job.

power, in turn, may prevent the teams from fully embracing the latitude they do have to make decisions.

The implications of the findings from Tata and Prasad's study are that before implementing a self-managed team, organizations should examine their structure for whether it can ensure adequate decision-making authority for the self-managed teams. Of course, the ultimate judgment as to whether self-managed teams are appropriate lies within the organizational strategy. Organizational structure and strategy are connected in a reciprocal relationship. Strategy is discussed in detail in Chapter 13, but for now, it is enough to know that strategy represents the vision or goals of the organization.

Exercise 11.5

Using the concepts from this chapter, describe your preferred/desired/ideal organizational structure—a structure in which you want to work. List all the dimensions, categories, and/or design elements from the chapter that can be used to clearly convey to a peer what your desired company/organization would look like. You should be detailed enough that someone else can take your description and recreate your ideal organization.

Chapter Summary

Organizations are structured to achieve their goals and as such, affect employee behavior. Through the division of responsibilities, scope, and labor, organizational structure can constrain behavior or direct it toward a specific path. For example, the more structured and defined an organization, the potential for less innovation and free creativity. There are exceptions. David Freedman, author of *Corps Business: The 30 Management Principles of the U.S. Marines,* found that the Marine Corps, though considered a traditional bureaucracy, is highly nimble, fast, effective, and dynamic. In some cases, one can argue the less ambiguity surrounding responsibilities, decision-making, and communications, the more free employees may be to innovate in their specific jobs. The structure one chooses for the organization depends on the type of work that must be achieved, and different structures have their advantages and disadvantages. Lastly, not only does the structure affect how employees behave, but employees affect the structure by pushing the boundaries, organizing into self-managed teams, and supporting or dissenting against the constraints of the structure.

FIGURE 11.11   Coloring Inside the Lines

©DmitriMaruta/Shutterstock, Inc.

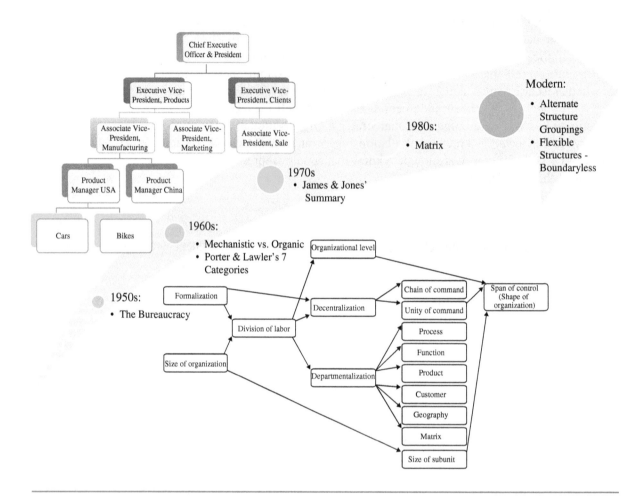

FIGURE 11.12   Visual Summary of Chapter 11

Courtesy Zinta Byrne.

Most of us are taught early in grade school to color inside the lines (Figure 11.11).

Structure creates the lines. The implications of the lines on organizations is that it defines how people function within the organization, how they communicate, and to what extent processes and decisions are compartmentalized or dispersed throughout the organization. Boundaryless organizations are not without lines—they are simply lines created by the artist rather than lines created by the coloring book publisher (Figure 11.12).

The visual summary of Chapter 11 provided in Figure 11.12 shows the progression of our understanding of structure starting with the early work in the 50s by Weber up to how we envision structure today as requiring the ability to be flexible and accommodate todays challenging work climate. Over the timeline from the early history of structure to modern conceptualizations, various elements of structure have been identified, which are captured in the map of what elements are related to each other. A sample organizational chart reminds us that structure includes a variety of factors such as span of control, line of authority, centralization versus decentralization, product version function, and so on, that are most often depicted in organizational hierarchy charts.

Discussion Questions

1. When you think of an organization's structure, what comes to mind first? Does this align with what is in the chapter? Why do you think your thoughts and the chapter align or do not align?

2. Given how the Gig economy works and how organizations are constantly changing, growing, or failing, do you think the structure of the organization is actually important, or is it an antiquated topic/concept at this point? What is it about structure that you think survives the times and what is it that is not important anymore?

3. How do you envision a boundaryless organization functioning? Do you think a Gig business is boundaryless? If not, what is? Do you think this concept—boundaryless—makes sense?

4. What do different types of flexible organizational structures (e.g., virtual, strategic alliance, boundaryless) have in common? What do they NOT have in common (i.e., how would you distinguish them from each other)?

5. What factors related to organizational structure can negatively impact employee performance?

6. What other organizational structures do you think we should be envisioning/considering that were not discussed in the chapter?

References

Achrol, R. S. (1997). Changes in the theory of interorganizational relations in marketing paradigm. *Journal of The Academy of Marketing Science, 25*(1), 56–71.

Adams, E. F., Laker, D. R., & Hulin, C. L. (1977). An investigation of the influence of job level and functional specialty on job attitudes and perceptions. *Journal of Applied Psychology, 62,* 335–343.

Ambrose, M. L., & Schminke, M. (2003). Organization structure as a moderator of the relationship between procedural justice, interactional justice, perceived organizational support, and supervisory trust. *Journal of Applied Psychology, 88*(2), 295–305. doi:10.1037/0021-9010.88.2.295

Ashkenas, R. (1999). Creating the boundaryless organization. *Business Horizons, 42*(5), 5.

Baldwin, C. Y., & Clark, K. B. (2000). *Design rules: The power of modularity* Vol. 1. Cambridge, MA: MIT Press.

Bates, J. (January 19, 1998). Making movies and moving on. *Los Angeles Times*, p. A1. Retrieved from http://articles.latimes.com/1998/jan/19/news/mn-9921

Burns, T. E., & Stalker, G. M. (1961). *The management of innovation.* London, UK: Tavistock.

Burton, R. M., DeSanctis, G., & Obel, B. (2006). *Organizational design: A step-by-step approach.* Cambridge, United Kingdom: Cambridge University Press.

Chen, C., & Huang, J. (2007). How organizational climate and structure affect knowledge management—The social interaction perspective. *International Journal of Information Management, 27*(2), 104–118. doi:10.1016/j.ijinfomgt.2006.11.001

Cohen-Charash, Y., & Spector, P. E. (2001). The role of justice in organizations: A meta-analysis. *Organizational Behavior and Human Decision Processes, 86*(2), 278–321. Doi:10.1006/obhd.2001.2958

Daft, R. L. (2004). *Organization Theory and Design* (8th Edition). Cincinnati, OH: Southwestern.

Davidow, W. H., & Malone, M. S. (1992). *The virtual corporation.* New York, NY: Harper Collins.

Davis, S. M., & Lawrence, P. R. (1978). Problems of matrix organizations. *Harvard Business Review, 56*(3), 131–142.

Fredrickson, J. W. (1986). The strategic decision process and organizational structure. *Academy of Management Review, 11*(2), 280–297. doi:10.5465/AMR.1986.4283101

Hackman, J., & Oldham, G. R. (1976). Motivation through the design of work: Test of a theory. *Organizational Behavior & Human Performance, 16*(2), 250–279.

Hamel, G., & Zanini, M. (2018). The end of bureaucracy: How a Chinese appliance maker is reinventing management for the digital age. *Harvard Business Review, 96*(6), 50–59.

Handy, C. (1989). The age of unreason. Boston, MA: Harvard University Press.

Herman, J. B., & Hulin, C. L. (1973). Managerial satisfactions and organizational roles: An investigation of Porter's Need Deficiency Scales. *Journal of Applied Psychology, 57*(2), 118–124. doi:10.1037/h0037127

Hodgetts, R. M. (1996). A conversation with Steve Kerr. *Organizational Dynamics, 24*(4), 68–79.

Hsu, I. (2008). Knowledge sharing practices as a facilitating factor for improving organizational performance through human capital: A preliminary test. *Expert Systems with Applications, 35*(3), 1316–1326. doi:10.1016/j.eswa.2007-08-012

Huang, X., Rode, J., & Schroeder, R. (2011). Organizational structure and continuous improvement and learning: Moderating effects of cultural endorsement of participative leadership. *Journal of International Business Studies, 42*(9), 1103–1120. doi:10.1057jibs.2011.33

James, L. R., & Jones, A. P. (1976). Organizational structure: A review of structural dimensions and their conceptual relationships with individual attitudes and behavior. *Organizational Behavior & Human Performance, 16*(1), 74–113.

Kogut, B. (1991). Joint ventures and the option to expand and acquire. *Management Science, 37*(1), 19–33.

Krasman, J. (2011). Taking feedback-seeking to the next 'level': Organizational structure and feedback-seeking behavior. *Journal of Managerial Issues, 23*(1), 9–30.

Lei, D., Hitt, M. A., & Goldhar, J. D. (1996). Advanced manufacturing technology: Organizational design and strategic flexibility. *Organization Studies, 17*(3), 501–524.

Leung, K., & Peterson, M. F. (2011). Managing a globally distributed workforce: Social and interpersonal issues. In S. Zedeck (ed.), *APA handbook of industrial and organizational psychology, Vol 3: Maintaining, expanding, and contracting the organization* (pp. 771–805). Washington, DC: American Psychological Association. doi:10.1037/12171-022

Nahm, A. Y., Vonderembse, M. A., & Koufteros, X. A. (2003). The impact of organizational structure on time-based manufacturing and plant performance. *Journal of Operations Management, 21*(3), 281. doi:10.1016/S0272-6963(02)00107-9

Oldham, G. R., & Hackman, J. (1981). Relationships between organizational structure and employee reactions: Comparing alternative frameworks. *Administrative Science Quarterly, 26*(1), 66–83. doi:10.2307/2392600

Pierce, J. L., & Delbecq, A. L. (1977). Organization structure, individual attitudes and innovation. *Academy of Management Review, 2*(1), 27–37. doi:10.5465/AMR.1977.4409154

Porter, L. W., & Lawler, E. E. (1965). Properties of organization structure in relation to job attitudes and job behavior. *Psychological Bulletin, 64*(1), 23–51. doi:10.1037/h0022166

Porter, L. W., & Siegel, J. (1965). Relationships of tall and flat organization structures to the satisfactions of foreign managers. *Personnel Psychology, 18*(4), 379–392.

Rhee, J., Seog, D. S., Bozorov, F. & Dedhanov, T. (2017). Organizational structure and employees' innovative behavior: the mediating role of empowerment. *Social Behavior and Personality, 45*(9). 1523–1536. https://doi.org/10.2224/sbp.6433

Richardson, H. A., Vandenberg, R. J., Blum, T. C., & Roman, P. M. (2002). Does decentralization make a difference for the organization? An examination of the boundary conditions circumscribing decentralized decision-making and organizational financial performance. *Journal of Management, 28*(2), 217–244.

Sanchez, R., & Mahoney, J. T. (1996). Modularity, flexibility, and knowledge management in product and organization design. *Strategic Management Journal,* 1763–1776.

Schminke, M., Ambrose, M. L., & Cropanzano, R. S. (2000). The effect of organizational structure on perceptions of procedural Fairness. *Journal of Applied Psychology, 85*(2), 294–304. doi:10.1037/0021-9010.85.2.294

Sherman, J., & Smith, H. L. (1984). The influence of organizational structure on intrinsic versus extrinsic motivation. *Academy of Management Journal, 27*(4), 877–885. doi:10.2307/255885

Smith, P. C., Kendall, L. M., & Hulin, C. L. (1969). *The measurement of satisfaction in work and retirement: A strategy for the study of attitudes.* Oxford, England: Rand McNally.

Tata, J., & Prasad, S. (2004). Team self-management, organizational structure, and judgments of team effectiveness. *Journal of Managerial Issues, 16*(2), 248–265.

Weber, M. (1921). *Theory of social and economic organization* (A. M. Henderson & T. Parsons Trans.). London, UK: Oxford University Press.

Weber, M. (1948). *From Max Weber: Essays in sociology* (H. H. Gerth & C. W. Mills Trans.). New York, NY: Oxford University Press

Xiaohua, L., & Germain, R. (2003). Organizational structure, context, customer orientation, and performance: Lessons from Chinese state-owned enterprises. *Strategic Management Journal, 24*(11), 1131–1151.

Zheng, W., Yang, B., & McLean, G. N. (2010). Linking organizational culture, structure, strategy, and organizational effectiveness: Mediating role of knowledge management. *Journal of Business Research, 63*(7), 763–771. doi:10.1016/j.jbusres.2009.06.005

CHAPTER 12

Organizational Culture and Climate: Transformation

Learning Outcomes

After studying this chapter you should be able to

1. Define organizational climate and culture.

2. Identify and clarify what to look for to assess the culture of an organization.

3. Explain several techniques for changing the culture of an organization.

4. Recognize potential roadblocks to organizational transformation.

Mini-Quiz: Organizational Change and Transformation

As an introduction to this chapter, please take the following mini-quiz (answers are in the back of the book). As you read the questions and consider the answers *before* diving into the chapter, you'll challenge yourself before you master the content, a process that helps facilitate learning for long-term retention. Some questions may have more than one correct answer. Don't worry if you cannot answer all questions correctly on your first try. By the time you read through the chapter and spend some of your own time thinking about these concepts, you should be able to determine the best answers. Try the quiz again after you finish reading the chapter.

1. If you are interested in applying to work at an organization, what would help you understand what the culture is like there?
   a. Reading through their policies and procedures
   b. Visiting the organization to see how peoples' offices and work spaces are arranged
   c. Looking at the company's mission and values statement
   d. Asking current employees about their benefits and other ways they are rewarded and recognized

2. Which of the following best represents organizational culture?

a.

b.

Courtesy Zinta Byrne.

c.

| Leaders: Decisions, Direction, Development |
| Managers: Rewards/Consequences, Rule Makers, Regulate |
| Employees: Operations, On-the-ready |

Courtesy Zinta Byrne.

3. Why do many organizations seem to have a story about them, like how a young couple took a bike trip through Belgium in 1988 and were inspired to launch New Belgium Brewing Company, how three University of San Francisco students started Starbucks, or how Louis Vuitton started in 1854 as a luggage maker building flat-topped trunks?
   a. Legends are a unique way to transmit culture to new employees
   b. They are fun to share and catch people's interest
   c. Leaders are more likely to get employees to act how they want if they tell stories
   d. Legends are based on true events, but are sometimes embellished to make information more memorable

4. What is the largest barrier to organizational change?
   a. Change isn't actually that hard; it's getting the change to stick, to make a lasting change, that is most difficult
   b. People do not like change, so they tend to resist it
   c. Norms that currently exist in the organization
   d. Leaders often don't know how to make changes and really can't be trained to be better in initiating change

5. Which of the following that we have learned about in previous chapters could also be an effective organizational change strategy?
   a. Structural changes
   b. Team building exercises
   c. Job redesign
   d. Performance feedback

Overview

Organizational culture is one of those aspects of organizations, businesses, or universities that just exists—everyone in the organization intuitively knows what it is and can, when asked, vaguely describe what they think organizational culture is. Yet, few employees bring it up on their own or can say what factors they look at that tell them what the culture is.

The goal of this chapter is to clarify what organizational culture is, how it is formed in organizations, and how to change it, if possible. Because organizational culture creates the psychological and, sometimes, physical experience of what it means to work in a particular organization, knowing how to recognize an organization's culture helps to determine (1) whether it is a place you want to work, and (2) how things get done—how decisions are made, how resources get distributed, who has decision and resource power, and who does not? Since organizational culture can be ingrained, changing culture may be difficult and take a longtime, like taking out an established tree with an invasive root system (e.g., Poplars, Cottonwoods, Aspens).

Despite the challenges, leaders of organizations want to change it or transform it to help move the organization in new directions or resolve old issues. External forces on the organization, such as changes in regulatory systems, competition, and adjustments in the world marketplace, cause organizations to adapt to survive, stay in the lead, or to get ahead (Porras & Silvers, 1991). As a consequence, internal forces such as attrition, promotions, group dynamics, and changes in resource allocations occur, which end up necessitating a shift in the organization's culture. For instance, Nelsons, one of the oldest natural health-care product manufacturers in Europe, was forced to change its culture to embrace globalization (Rickatson, 2013).

So, what exactly *is* organizational culture?

What Is Climate and Culture?

Organizational culture serves as an overarching guide for the behaviors, attitudes, and assumptions within organizations. Organizational culture specifically refers to how individuals in organizations experience and make sense of their work environment (Schneider, 2000) and what aspects of the workplace go into creating a shared organizational experience. Over time, employees come to share meaning, attitudes, traditions, and a common understanding of the psychological phenomena in their organization, and this shared experience makes up the notion of organizational culture (Ostroff, Kinicki, & Tamkins, 2003).

You might understand the concept of sharing of meaning, attitudes, or traditions by thinking about how groups of people in clubs, churches, or political affiliations refer to their views or attitudes. For example, members of religious organizations, regardless of where they are located, tend to value similar traditions that mark their religious holidays. They share their beliefs and traditions about their own religion. Similarly, people in organizations can tell comparable stories about how meetings are run, such as whether they start on time or have a rolling start time, that 8:07 a.m. is when everyone meets at the on-site coffee shop to share office gossip, or that no one works in the office on the weekends. These traditions and stories are shared among experienced and new members of the organization.

Thus, cultures perpetuate themselves—they continue a self-reinforcing cycle through a number of different practices. For instance, organizations select people to hire who are similar to those already in the workplace (see Schneider's 1987 Attraction-Selection-Attrition model; Schneider, Goldstein, & Smith, 1995). Once hired, they are socialized into the organization (Chapter 2), subjected to a variety of rituals (e.g., new-hire orientation games) and entrance ceremonies (e.g., welcoming meeting by the company president), and trained to act in ways that exemplify the culture (Schein, 1990). These employees quickly come to see themselves as part of the organization and identify with their peers and the values of the group. Employees who follow the norms and "fit in" are rewarded, whereas those who do not are either coerced to fit in or are ostracized and encouraged out of the organization.

Because it encompasses all aspects of work, organizational culture influences employees' attitudes, behaviors, and performance (Schneider, 2000; Ostroff et al., 2003). Schein (1990) referred to organizational culture as "(a) a pattern of basic assumptions, (b) invented, discovered, or developed by a given group, (c) as it learns to cope with its problems of external adaptation and internal integration, (d) that has worked well enough to be considered valid and, therefore (e) is to be taught to new members as the (f) correct way" (p.111). Employees' experience of organizational culture tells them what to believe within the organization, how they are allowed to and expected to behave while at work and even outside of work, how they are rewarded, what the organization values, and to what extent they come to feel connected to or identify with the organization (Jones & James, 1979; Rentsch, 1990; Schneider, 1990). Through an understanding of how and why things operate or function the way they do, employees make sense of their work environment and plan ahead as to how to approach solving organizational problems.

Organizational culture influences patterns of behavior and attitudes at a high level, over a range of time. Thus, you typically do not think about culture every day—it is just there. But your day-to-day reactions are not actually a part of culture. Many individuals outside of the research literature refer to organizational *culture* when they really mean to talk about organizational *climate*. Climate and culture are not necessarily one in the same, though they have often been used interchangeably (Denison, 1996a) since both refer to employees' shared meaning of their work environment. Climate specifically refers to those day-to-day procedures, policies, routines, and rewards that people experience regularly while working day in and day out (Jones & James, 1979; Rentsch, 1990; Schneider, 1990).

Climate refers to the work environment that is rooted in the organization's value system but presents a temporary state—that is, climate is subject to manipulation and change due to the composition of the immediate workforce and leadership. Climate focuses on the immediate experience and proximal situations of the organization, whereas culture is considered distal, fairly resistant to change, and an aggregate of daily experiences (Denison, 1996).

You can think of climate like walking into your organic chemistry class where the keyword of the day is "safety and precision," versus walking into your human sexuality psychology class, where the atmosphere is likely quite different. For graduate students, entering an undergraduate classroom as the teaching assistant may feel very different than walking into an advanced seminar as a student. The atmosphere of your classroom is like climate—it is temporary and changes with what happens in class from week to week. However, the classes are still offered within a single university and therefore, there are commonalities between the classes, originating from the university culture.

Consequently, climate develops from culture and can stem from the components of culture (Guion, 1973; Schein, 2000), but can also create culture by generating the feel of the organization (Schneider, Brief, & Guzzo, 1996). In fact, the concept of climate was first introduced in the 1950s (Lewin, 1951; Lewin, Lippitt, & White, 1939; Litwin & Stringer, 1968), thus preceding the introduction of culture as a concept. However, climate soon became a second cousin to the growing construct of culture (Denison, 1996b; Schein, 1990). Thus, climate and culture are connected in a symbiotic relationship, where one affects the other.

In addition to climates within cultures, cultures can have subcultures, which are like mini-cultures within a big culture.

Climate may be considered a manifestation of culture and is directly observable and measurable, whereas culture is not so observable or measurable.

Subcultures

Although organizations may have a single overarching culture, they might also possess subcultures—sublayers of culture operating within the overall organization's culture (Boisnier & Chatman, 2003; Jermier, Slocum, Fry, & Gaines, 1991; Morgan & Ogbonna, 2008). These sublayers of culture are similar to the overall organizational culture, but may differ slightly based on the core values of the group creating the subculture. Subcultures are like clubs within clubs, or mini-groups within big groups. For instance, subcultures may develop within departments or functional units, such as marketing versus product development versus sales. They may also form as professional identities within occupation domains (e.g., nurse vs. doctor: Hofstede, 1980; Degeling, Kennedy, & Hill, 1998). Subcultures can form around ethnicity, gender, geographic location (e.g., East coast vs. West coast, Europe vs. Asia), or organizational structure (Chapter 11; Horsburgh, Perkins, Coyle, & Degeling, 2006).

An example of cultures within cultures (subcultures), perhaps more recognizable to students in a college setting is walking into a Psychology Department versus a Management Department within a mid- to large-sized University. Both are housed within the overall culture of a university, which might emphasize research production (i.e., R1 or Research University/very high research activity: RU/VH;

Psychology   Management

FIGURE 12.1   Students from Psychology and Management Departments

Left: © BlueSkyImage/Shutterstock, Inc. Right: © Goodluz/Shutterstock, Inc.

"The Carnegie Classification of Institutions of Higher Education," 2005). Thus both departments are expected to produce scholarly publications. The visible difference between the departments lies within the Psychology department where you will probably find casually dressed faculty members, undergraduates, and graduate students, whereas in the Management department you will in all probability find faculty members and students dressed in either business casual attire or suits (Figure 12.1).

Subcultures have also been categorized as employee-centered, professional-centered, task-centered, and innovation-centered (see Palthe & Kossek, 2003). Though these subcultures may facilitate functional employee behavior, such as orienting around professionalism or tasks, they can also create challenges for the organization during efforts to change the culture. Challenges erupt because being a member of a subgroup naturally polarizes group members based on their beliefs (see Chapter 7), which may not align with the desired change, causing employees to resist change efforts. In contrast, the power and benefit of subcultures lies in their ability to generate pockets of high performance or excellence in areas, such as customer service, because of the tight values and beliefs of the group and the norms within the group to maintain the uniqueness of the subculture. Thus, subcultures can be aligned and consistent with the overall organizational culture, and when they are, they can facilitate organizational effectiveness by tapping into the power of groups.

Because organizational culture defines how we should behave and think within organizations, its impact on employees, in general, is fundamental—culture can make or break the organization. Forget whether you have a stellar leader or outstanding product, if the culture is dysfunctional, the organization will fail.

Exercise 12.1

Explain in your own words what organizational culture, subcultures, and climates are—how are they similar and different from each other?

Why Do We Care About Organizational Culture?

Cameron, Quinn, DeGraff, and Thakor (2006) argued that organizational culture is a powerful factor, the key ingredient in the success of organizations, and an organization's most important competitive advantage. In their research of the top five highest performing U.S. firms in the past 20 years, the only differentiator between those five organizations and all others was the organizational culture. Nothing else explained their success! After extensive review of the literature, the researchers concluded that a strong, unique culture reduced uncertainty by establishing social expectations and norms, thereby creating social order. Strong cultures also created continuity that maintained values and norms, established a collective identity and commitment among organizational members, and clarified and energized a vision of the future (Cameron et al., 2006; see also Kotter & Heskett, 1992; Trice & Beyer, 1993). Thus, a strong positive culture can have many benefits. A strong culture can also have disadvantages. Corrupt organizations have strong cultures that perhaps have gone a bit astray. For example, corrupt organizations consider themselves at war, where the end justifies the means in winning over the competition (Campbell & Göritz, 2013). The "at war" view inspires values and norms in the culture towards doing whatever it takes to get ahead. Results matter in these cultures and employees rationalize their approaches in the spirit of helping the organization win.

Benefits to Employees and Organizations

Employees working in positive, strong cultures tend to demonstrate high levels of morale, satisfaction, commitment, performance, and overall well-being (Kozlowski, Chao, Smith, & Hedlund, 1993; Xenikou & Simosi, 2006). Additionally, components of culture, such as fairness and opportunities for personal growth, have been shown to predict employees' levels of job satisfaction (Bellou, 2010). In contrast, when the culture is perceived as aggressive, employees report lower levels of job satisfaction. Bellou also found several gender differences in perceptions of the culture and levels of reported job satisfaction. Specifically, aspects of the culture that promoted personal growth, fostered the organization's reputation, and maintained open communication where information was free flowing, predicted males' satisfaction levels. In contrast, for women the cultural aspects of decisiveness and people-oriented promoted their job satisfaction. Bellou's study was conducted in three public hospitals in Greece, thus it is possible that the components of culture related to gender norms or job satisfaction may differ in other countries because organizations are influenced by country culture. When understanding organizational culture, you need to keep national culture and norms in mind.

Why is it important to understand the difference between cultures and climates?

How Do You Assess Culture as a Mechanism for Understanding It?

Schein's 3-Level View

A short 4 minute YouTube video that helps clarify what culture is using Schein's levels can be found at https://youtu.be/cjziCs-R2S4
Watch the video either before or after reading this section about Schein's 3-level view.

According to Schein (1990), three levels of culture determine how it is identified within organizations. These three levels include observable artifacts, values, and underlying assumptions.

Level 1—Observable Artifacts

Observable artifacts make up the first level, which include visible physical components of the work environment. These might include the type of furniture and equipment used by employees, picture and wall displays, and office arrangement such as cubicles, offices with or without windows or doors, and shared or individual desks as illustrated in Figure 12.2.

FIGURE 12.2 Schein's Level 1 Artifacts—Furniture, Lighting, Office Layout

Top left: © Baseileus/Shutterstock, Inc.; Top right © krsmanovic/Shutterstock, Inc.; Bottom left: © mariakraynova/Shutterstock, Inc.; Bottom right: © photowind/Shutterstock, Inc.

FIGURE 12.3   Schein's Level 1 Artifacts—Offices

Left: © Minerva Studio/Shutterstock, Inc.; Right: Courtesy Zinta Byrne.

Other examples include the books in offices, such as the wall-to-wall reference books frequently seen in law offices, or the many diplomas or certificates that sometimes cover the walls of a doctor's or university professor's office as illustrated in Figure 12.3.

Though the artifacts mentioned and illustrated thus far are physical components of the organization (e.g., chairs, walls), artifacts also include what can be seen and heard, such as what people say, the stories told about the organization or group, published lists of values such as those in employee handbooks, and rituals or ceremonies that are enacted. For example, uniforms or dress codes (Figure 12.4) convey beliefs or tenets, expressing the culture in terms of honoring heterogeneity (people can wear what they please) or homogeneity (everyone wearing suits of neutral colors; military uniforms). Uniforms convey occupational or rank distinctions, such as in the military where rank is conveyed by bars on the shoulders and stars on the collar (see Felten, 2008; Richardson, 2009). Uniforms can also signify gender boundaries, where women may be required to wear much more revealing clothing than men (Hayes, 2005). Lastly, uniforms may also be used to identify role status and identity (Pratt & Rafaeli, 1997). A significant challenge in todays business with either formal or informal (undocumented) dress codes is that they do not allow for expression of sexual identity. For example, individuals who identify as non-binary may feel restricted when required to wear what is considered a very feminine or very masculine attire (Baker & Lucas, 2017; Reddy-Best, 2018). People observe and use artifacts to describe what makes up an organizational culture and what makes it unique compared to other organizational cultures.

> You get an intuitive feel for culture by seeing physical aspects of the workplace, such as the chairs, walls, and how people dress.

Level 2—Values

Values make up Schein's second level of culture. Values refer to concepts and beliefs that employees internalize (Schein, 1990), that are not always the same as that which is communicated via the organization's strategy (Chapter 13). To get at values, you may have to interview and talk with employees. *Espoused values* are those that the managers or organizational leaders explicitly say they

FIGURE 12.4 Schein's Level 1 Artifacts—Uniforms

(1) © Andresr/Shutterstock, Inc.; (2) © CandyBox Images/Shutterstock, Inc.; (3) Courtesy Zinta Byrne.; (4) © Andrey_Popov/Shutterstock, Inc.; (5) © Kotin/Shutterstock, Inc.; (6) Courtesy Zinta Byrne.

endorse. For example, espoused values may be that "we value work-life balance" and various posters around the organization state in bold letters "WE BELIEVE IN THE FAMILY – BALANCE YOUR WORK AND LIFE FOR A HEALTHY OFFICE." However, as these managers tell their employees they value their work-life balance and encourage them to leave the office by 5:00 p.m. or 6:00 p.m., they may turn around and send them e-mails and phone messages all evening with work that is expected by the next morning. You may have experienced something similar with your research advisor who tells you to take your time working on the draft of a paper, but then sends e-mails asking you when you will be done. Thus, espoused values are those explicitly voiced, but not necessarily internalized.

In contrast to espoused values, *enacted values* comprise exhibited values. For instance, enacting the value for work-life balance would be a manager who actually leaves the office at 5:00 p.m. or 6:00 p.m. with his or her subordinates, and goes home to an evening of no work, no e-mail, and no phone calls. When espoused and enacted values contradict one another, they send employees mixed messages about how to behave.

The examples above illustrate how espoused and enacted values may sometimes contradict one another, but they may also be consistent with one another. For example, your manager might voice appreciation for work-life balance and

> Enacted values send a stronger message than the espoused values, very much like actions speak louder than words.

consistently leave work at the office. Espoused and enacted values need not be at odds; however, organizations must often work to realign them to ensure clarity of expectations of employees (Buch & Wetzel, 2001). Employees also infer expectations from underlying assumptions that contribute to culture.

Level 3—Underlying Assumptions

The third level of Schein's (1990) taxonomy of culture, or levels at which culture manifests itself, is called *basic underlying assumptions*, which refers to unobservable assumptions or underlying rules that employees follow. Basic assumptions are not espoused or openly expressed. They may include that the company is trustworthy, supportive, and rewards hard work. Basic assumptions may be determined from written material such as handbooks or personnel documents, but may be more easily understood and assessed by asking current or past employees of the organization.

A good example of a basic assumption present in many academic universities is that students are expected to refer to their teachers as "Dr. Jones" or "Professor Gupta," and never by their first names, unless the professor gives the student permission to do so. Such an expectation is not written down for students to read ahead of time—they learn by hearing how other students interact with the professor, or by suffering the misfortune of incorrectly calling a professor by her or his first name.

Within an organizational setting, a basic assumption may include that although the company has a policy that says you can start the workday at any time between 6:00 a.m. and 9:00 a.m. (called flextime), in your group it is understood that everyone arrives by 7:00 a.m. Basic underlying assumptions are like norms. Social norms are rules that govern or guide social behavior. They are formed and governed by the people within the social network and social situation; hence, they contribute to the organizational culture. Recall from Chapter 1 that in their attempt to study the relationship between lighting and efficiency, researchers studying the Western Electrical Company's Hawthorne Works Plant near Chicago, Illinois, found that employees monitored and regulated each other's productivity, providing the first example of group norms (Mayo, 1933, 1945; Roethlisberger & Dickson, 1939; Whitehead, 1935, 1938). We could even say that their finding of group norms was the first instance of what we have come to understand as organizational culture. Because norms are created within a social environment, such as an organization, they vary by environment.

Since the second and third levels of Schein's taxonomy of organizational culture are the most difficult to assess and often require time to evaluate, the best way to get a fast snapshot sense of the culture of an organization is to pay close attention to the observable artifacts.

Trice and Beyer's 4-Categories View

Although Schein's (1990) three-layer model is very popular for understanding organizational culture, Trice and Beyer (1993) suggest there are four categories of culture: *symbols* (e.g., physical setting), *organizational language* (e.g., jargon, slang, signs, jokes, rumors), *narratives* (i.e., stories, myths, or legends), and *practices* (e.g., rituals, ceremonies). For those struggling to understand Schein's layers, Trice and Beyer's categories may provide additional insight as to what culture is because the categories are a bit more visible than Schein's layers.

Symbols

Why are values considered different from underlying assumptions in Schein's framework?

Symbols are similar to Schein's (1990) observable artifacts and include furniture, office layout, wall décor, and building architecture. Company logos may be symbols or representations of that organization's culture. A quick search of the Internet will reveal many company logos, varying in color, size, shape, and structure (word vs. image). For example, compare the logos of Apple, Tencent, Eisai, and Mizuno. Although logos are sometimes representative of specific product lines, they also convey a bit about the organization's values.

Organizational Language

Organizational language refers to spoken and written words, nicknames, and company jargon. For instance, at Walt Disney, an amusement park in the United States, employees are called "cast members" and customers are called "guests." At New Belgium Brewing Company in Colorado, the corporate offices and main brewery are referred to as the "mother ship." At a health organization in the Midwestern regions of the United States, the administrative employees are referred to as "suits" working in the "West Wing." Indeed, the administrators are physically located in offices on the west side of the building. Employees do not call administrators "suits" to their face; this label represents the jargon or slang for those not working in administration (e.g., human resources, business services such as accounting, and the executive business leaders). Organizational language also includes referring to business challenges in military or sports metaphors, such as the corporate office as the "command center" or department as "taking one for the team," "passing the ball to the next player," and "making a sale that is out of this ball park." Physical symbols, such as dress and office design, can affect the language of the environment by clarifying status and identity within work relationships (Pratt & Rafaeli, 2001), which dictate what language is used. For instance, a larger office with a door when the rest of the offices are smaller with no door indicates someone in the organization who has authority occupies that office. This person may be referred to as sir, ma'am, or chief instead of by first name. More often, however, language is determined by narratives that are passed from person to person.

Narratives

Narratives include the stories organizational members share about their work and the people at work. These stories depict the culture, transmitting it to new hires and frequently to people outside of the organization. For example, at Starbucks

Coffee Company, employees are told the story of how Howard Schultz, the president and chief executive office, sought to make the Starbucks experience similar to visiting an Italian coffee house in rural Italy. Similarly, employees at New Belgium Brewing are told the story of how Jeff Lebesch and his wife Kim Jordan started brewing beer in their basement, creating the first beers that launched the brewery. The story of how Airbnb started is a legend like these others. The two original co-founders needed rent money in San Francisco, so they charged people to sleep on an air mattress on their apartment floor. A third friend joined to create the website to advertise the air mattress rental. Originally known as Air Bed and Breakfast, the three renamed the business years later after finally convincing the market that they had a good idea—people renting out a place in their house/apartment for someone to sleep. Thankfully, they relaxed the requirement that people had to sleep on blowup mattresses! Lastly, companies like Toyota have a well-shared narrative of the Toyoda (no, this is not a typo) family heritage: the founder, Sakichi Toyoda, grew up watching his mother work nights and days handweaving cloth. To make her life easier, he invented the automatic loom; the beginning of Toyota's long vision to make people's lives easier. Stories, such as these that occur in companies around the world, are based on true events, though they may exaggerate or embellish the truth a little to make the story more memorable or to transmit a stronger message.

The narratives convey the values of the organization. For example, Starbucks values creating the coffee shop experience and brewing good coffee drinks. In fact, if a Barista accidentally makes the wrong drink, they will quickly make the correct one for you and may give you a free drink card to apologize for the mistake. At New Belgium Brewing, the story of the founders communicates that even if the brewery is growing, it is still entrepreneurial and casual. Toyoda's life story suggests valuing family tradition. Narratives are not always stories about the founders; they sometimes include practices, such as hiring routines that are easily shared in a story-like manner.

Practices

Examples of *practices* include Japanese entrance (new-hire) ceremonies where every April, Japanese businesses welcome their newly hired university graduates. The City of Ventura, Los Angeles holds annual corporate games (team-building games such as Tug-O-War and sand castle building contests), which are team-building services for companies and businesses in the Ventura, Los Angeles, and Santa Barbara counties. New Belgium Brewing gives its employees a bicycle on their 1-year tenure anniversary with the organization. Lastly, in the 1980s, Hewlett-Packard (HP) Company was known for its "beer-busts," which were Friday afternoon gatherings on the company grounds and included free beer and food for all employees (Packard, 1995). The beer-busts are long over, but some HP employees still talk about them.

Rituals

Rituals, a specific type of practice, are further delineated into their own **typology** of six types of rites (Beyer & Trice, 1987; Trice & Beyer, 1984). These types

When joining an organization or even getting a promotion, listen to how your coworkers talk, see if you can recognize stories that keep coming up, and ask if there are any events that everyone experiences as a new person. By attending to the aspects of culture that Trice and Beyer (1993) proposed, you'll learn a lot about what behavior is expected of you, in a short amount of time.

include rites of passage (e.g., boot camp in the military; in an organization it might be reciting the department rules from memory), degradation (e.g., send a successful field officer back to a desk job; assign tedious paperwork), enhancement (e.g., award trips for top sales representatives), renewal (e.g., company or department off-site), conflict reduction (e.g., team building across groups, with accompanied negotiations), and integration (e.g., summer or fall company picnics).

Even though some components of culture may be more discernable than others, both Schein and Trice and Beyer note that artifacts, the most readily visible, might sometimes be difficult to decipher because their meaning to employees is hard to infer from observation alone. Hence, several different methods have been used for assessing culture, including Likert-type surveys. Likert-type surveys are those in which you answer questions using a response scale of 1–5. Each number in the response scale is assumed to represent a response that is equally distant in feeling or judgment from the other, though in reality that is rarely tested for measurement accuracy (Cooke & Rousseau, 1988; Jung, Scott, Davies, Bower, Whalley, McNally, & Mannion, 2009; Thumin & Thumin, 2011). Other methods include qualitative ethnographies (e.g., Spicer, 2011; Van Maanen, 1975), which are descriptions of culture based on observation (researcher becomes immersed in the day-to-day work). One-on-one interviews with organizational members are also used (Creswell, 1998).

Typologies of culture offered by Schein and Trice and Beyer, however, are not the only ways of looking at culture. Culture can be viewed from a more holistic perspective, as opposed to looking at its parts.

Exercise 12.2

Compare and contrast Schein's framework of culture with Trice and Breyer's. How are they similar/different from each other?

The Competing Values Model

Taking a different approach, Quinn and Spreitzer (1991) developed a multidimensional model to assess culture, but rather than focusing on what comprises culture, they concentrated on what makes an organization effective across a number of dimensions (similar to Cameron et al., 2006). Quinn and Spreitzer's efforts culminated in The Competing Values Model (Figure 12.5; Quinn, & Cameron, 2006; Quinn & Rohrbaugh, 1983), the outcome of an aggregation of Quinn's previous collaborations with several researchers. Because organizational leaders ultimately alter cultures to align with the strategy and improve organizational effectiveness, this model has good application appeal.

The model is organized into four quadrants, depicting four different cultures, expressed along two different axes. One axis ranges in effectiveness criteria from emphasizing flexibility and the ability to exercise independent discretion, to criteria that emphasize order, control, and stability (Quinn & Cameron, 2006). The other axis ranges from externally focused and differentiated to internally focused and integrated. The axes represent dimensions of criteria that differentiate organizations.

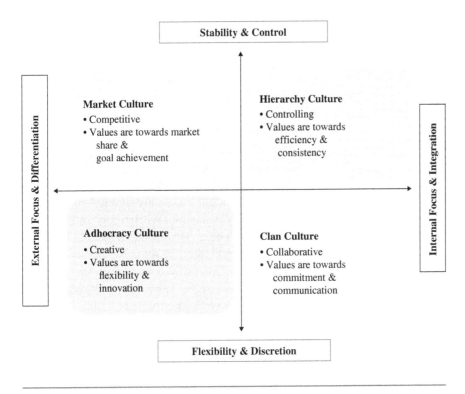

FIGURE 12.5   The Competing Values Model

Courtesy Zinta Byrne.

The organization culture types (each quadrant) are effective based on their unique mix. Thus, some organizations remain effective as long as they stay nimble, flexible, and are constantly adapting. For example, Apple, Inc. constantly changes its products, which requires high flexibility and innovation within the organization itself. Because of their high value for innovation and nimbleness, we might classify Apple as having an adhocracy culture. Google, Nike Corporation, and Genentech also possess cultures that are effective when they are constantly changing and innovating (Cameron & Quinn, 2006). Agilent Technologies, a technology instruments company spun off from HP in 1999, might have been considered a clan culture taking after HP's collaborate culture, until it recently split into two companies in September 2013. The "new" Agilent company (the half that kept the Agilent name) may retain its clan culture, but it is unclear what culture the new measurement business, Keysight Technologies, will create. The keywords for adhocracy cultures include temporary, flexibility, and constantly changing.

In contrast, some organizations remain effective as long as they remain stable, follow rules and procedures, and control their environment. Universities and governments tend to fall into this category. For instance, universities remain effective as long as they continue to produce successful graduates from traditional degree programs, in addition to any novel programs they might introduce. Although they do occasionally introduce new degree programs, Universities tend to value consistency and control, indicating they probably have hierarchy cultures. Conglomerate organizations, such as Boeing also fit into the stability culture. The hierarchy culture is similar to the bureaucratic organizational structure, discussed in Chapter 11.

Another example of companies that remain effective as long as they are stable, yet externally focused may be Philips Electronics, Xerox, or Starbucks. Starbucks customers expect the same quality, the same store look and feel, and the same friendly

FIGURE 12.6   Starbucks Coffee Shop in Moscow, Russia

Courtesy Zinta Byrne.

service from every Starbucks coffee shop they enter, regardless of country. That consistency forces the employees and procedures across the Starbucks stores to be consistent as well. For instance, Moscow, Russia, has Starbucks coffee shops that are easily recognizable (see Figure 12.6) even if you cannot speak or read a word of Russian.

The second axis of the model ranges in effectiveness criteria emphasizing an internal focus and collaboration within an external focus that is competitive and independent. Internally focused cultures are demonstrated by companies with strong "family-like" environments, where harmony and getting-along is what makes them effective. As noted previously, HP Company has traditionally been known for the "H-P Way," which reflected a value for employees and a conflict-avoidant work environment. Other examples of companies considered effective by having internal collaboration include New Belgium Brewing and Pixar. Organizations considered effective because of their competitive and external or global focus include Toyota and Honda. The focus of these organizations is on teamwork and commitment.

According to Quinn and colleagues, the four quadrants represent cultures identified by opposite or competing values, hence the name Competing Values Framework. A diagnostic tool based on this framework, called the Organizational Culture Assessment Instrument, assesses organizational cultures (see Quinn & Cameron, 2006, for full details).

What's important to note about Quinn and colleagues' approach to culture as compared to Schein's or Trice and Beyer's, is that the competing values framework focuses on what values make for an effective organization—thus, the model is not about what makes up culture, per se. It assumes culture is an attribute of the organization, a set of enduring values that reflect organizational members' sensemaking and interpretation of how things are (Quinn & Cameron, 2006).

The advantage of this approach is the availability of an instrument that can be used to examine the difference between how one sees the culture as it is now and what the desired culture is. The disadvantage of the approach is the criticism that aspects of culture, such as values and norms, cannot easily be captured using a Likert-type scale (Schein, 1990; Scott, Mannion, Davies, & Marshall, 2003), yet the Organizational Culture Assessment Instrument is a Likert-type survey. Regardless of the criticism of how the quadrants are assessed, the model is easy to remember and somewhat catchy.

Deal and Kennedy's Risk Versus Speed of Feedback

Another catchy model that also identifies four quadrants was proposed by Deal and Kennedy (1996). After studying hundreds of organizations, they concluded that most companies seemed to fall into four general categories or types, determined by two factors: degree of risk with company activities and speed at which companies get feedback that tells them their strategies are successful (Figure 12.7).

Tough-guy, Macho Culture

Shown in Figure 12.7, Deal and Kennedy proposed that *Tough-guy, Macho* cultures tend to be young and do not necessarily last long. Their focus is on immediate wins and if the win is not big and does not happen fast, the CEO is replaced with another who will make things happen. The intense pace and pressure exhausts people quickly, making for a generally younger employee staff and one where the older individuals are found in management or training positions. The big value is on risk-taking, and the feedback comes quickly as to whether the risk pays off. People who survive this type of culture best are those who like to gamble or take chances and need instant feedback. They tend to be individualists who seek reward and fame.

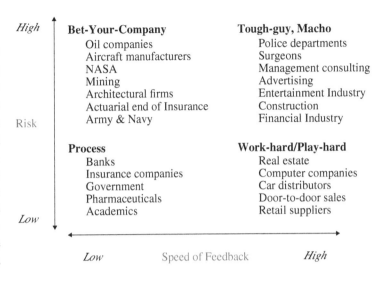

FIGURE 12.7   Deal and Kennedy's Risk Versus Speed of Feedback Model

Courtesy Zinta Byrne. Source: Deal and Kennedy, 1996.

Deal and Kennedy argued that although the culture is named tough-"guy", it is the least biased of all the four cultures against women; "after all, a star is a star" (p. 91). In this type of culture, rituals become a form of a security blanket. That is, rituals create procedures, and as long as you can say you followed a procedure (even if it is experimental), you're protected if the risk fails. The biggest weakness of this culture is its strength—the emphasis on quick feedback; quick wins take resources away from the long-term strategy required for survival. There is no opportunity to learn from mistakes because failure is hidden by having followed the procedure. Additionally, the emphasis on stars breeds prima-donna behavior (i.e., temperamental, unpredictable, self-focused and overinflated importance), tantrums and all, creating a management nightmare. High turnover is common of this type of culture, which means building strong, cohesive cultures can be difficult.

Work-Hard/Play-Hard Culture

The *Work-hard/Play-hard* culture is characterized by small risks, such that if they do not pan out, one can quickly recover by pursuing another lead or going back to the customer to try again. The culture centers on the customers and their needs. Action or activity is valued, though the activity does not necessarily convey risk. That is, the real estate agent will show you multiple properties and list many different properties. The car distributor will try to show as many cars as possible every day. The work-hard/play-hard culture creates rituals that inspire activities, such as games for top sales person, contests for best door-to-door technique, and conventions for real estate agents or retail suppliers. Deal and Kennedy suggested the strength of this culture is in getting a lot done. Highly active, energetic people who thrive on quick and tangible feedback do well in this culture; though they may prefer to take too many risks to make things happen. These companies have a short-term view of the future because of the speed with which they get feedback. Employees tend to be young, like the tough-guy culture; the high level of activity is attractive and suggests success, regardless of whether it is there or not.

Bet-Your-Company Culture

Bet-Your-Company cultures are those characterized by making big investments now for the possibility of a large future gain. The risk is high and the feedback on whether taking that risk was worth it, is slow. For example, oil companies such as Exxon or Statoil spend billions of dollars and euros exploring regions for the potential for oil, without knowing for years whether that prospect will pay off. Aircraft manufacturers spend millions in research to explore whether a new type of metal will work, only to find out after years of testing that the metal is not strong enough to withstand the pressure of take-offs and landings. Like manufacturing or product-driven organizations that spend a lot of money that does not result in any tangible outcome, Deal and Kennedy include the military in this culture. Their rationale is that the military (doesn't matter what branch) spends large portions of the country budget preparing for the war that most hope never actually happens.

The attention in this culture is on making the right decision, and if that means taking a time-out for a few weeks to explore other possible consequences or contingencies, then so be it. Employees in this culture tend to be mature, appreciative and respectful of authority, seek mentors, and appreciate the developmental cycle of promotions. The greatest strengths of this culture are in the high-quality inventions and scientific breakthroughs resulting from the careful research and decision-making. The weaknesses of this culture are that they become vulnerable to short-term market and economic risks while they wait for their long-term investments to pay off.

Process Culture

Lastly, the *Process* culture is characterized by organizations typically slow to change. Generally, those in heavily regulated markets, such as health care, tend to fit into this category. Others that fit into this culture include universities. There is little feedback except when something goes wrong. Little action is taken within the organization because there is little feedback to say what the right direction is. Deal and Kennedy argued the lack of feedback results in employees focusing on how they conduct their work, rather than on what exactly it is that they do. Small events, therefore, take on importance, and people tend to protect themselves against blame. The culture values perfection, removing risk and defending every decision.

Organizations categorized as having a process culture do not adjust or respond to every fad or fashion and, as a result, withstand brief bursts of excited change. People who do well in this culture are those who protect the integrity of the system, attend to detail, and "survive on their memories" (Deal & Kennedy, 1996, p. 99). They follow procedures without questioning, whether they really make sense or not. They create rituals out of long unnecessary meetings, retirement ceremonies, and honoring the hierarchy. Hierarchy is visible in the symbols—furniture, size of office, and ability to create privacy. The greatest strength of this culture is its predictability; some work requires predictability and stability. Its weaknesses lie in the slow movement and difficulty of getting any real work accomplished. Law firms might fit into this category.

The appeal of Deal and Kennedy's framework is high—it is easy to talk about (and kind of fun), the labels instantly convey what the culture is about, and the axes make intuitive business sense. Thus, unlike several other ways of understanding and assessing culture that focus on the parts of culture, the Risk Versus Speed of Feedback Model, and the Competing Values Model focus on providing

What kind of culture do you work in? Tough-guy, Macho? Work-hard/Play-hard? Bet-Your-Company? Or are you in a Process culture? Do you fit into this culture or do you seem like you should be in one of the other cultures, just based on the descriptions provided?

a more holistic picture. You might think of a comparison this way: one model is a large puzzle with all the pieces scattered on the table (Schein, and Trice & Beyer), versus the other model that is the completed puzzle with all the pieces connected (Competing Values, Risk versus Speed of Feedback).

Exercise 12.3

Before moving on, describe how the Competing Values Framework and the Deal and Kennedy model are different from Schein's and Trice & Beyer's approaches. When are the different frameworks useful and not useful in understanding and/or describing an organization?

How Do Managers Use Assessing Culture Models in the Workplace?

Deal and Kennedy's (1996) taxonomy of cultures provides an understanding of what kind of behavior is necessary given the level of strategic risk and speed with which the organization gets feedback on its strategy. Its utility is in identifying the right approach given the nature of the organization (P-O fit theories may serve as an underlying foundation; Chapter 2). Thus, their model differs from the Competing Values Framework, which focuses on the structure of the organization that influences its culture. This model attempts to convey that competing values are not necessarily bad; the conflict between values can enhance opportunities for creativity and innovation by pursuing multiple perspectives and avoiding tunnel vision. Both Deal and Kennedy's, and Quinn and colleagues' models focus on the whole rather than the parts. They integrate various aspects of behavior, values, and leadership approaches within organizations to describe an overall profile or image of what culture is and how it is evaluated.

In contrast, both Schein's (1990) and Trice and Beyer's (1993) frameworks emphasize the parts that make up the whole. They describe what makes up culture and in doing so provide more direction toward the organizational components that may need modification to change an organization's culture. Consequently, the utility of these models is in their specificity, which facilitates identifying the culture and pinpointing how to change the culture.

Another mechanism for identifying culture and determining if culture change is necessary is the organizational culture profile (OCP), which is an instrument for assessing person-organization fit (O'Reilly, Chatman, & Caldwell, 1991). The OCP can be used to identify the degree to which employees feel they fit into the culture and whether the culture is one they prefer. Using 54 items (e.g., adaptibility, decisiveness, working long hours, being highly organized), employees are asked to sort the items into nine piles, from most to least preferred or most to least reflective of the culture, such that the piles have the following number of items: 2, 4, 6, 9, 12, 9, 6, 4, 2. This creates a distribution of the items, such that most and least characteristic or preferred items are in the smaller piles. Those familiar with the organization's culture and not part of the assessment are asked to do the same, but instead sort based on how the current culture appears. O'Reilly and colleagues' analyses of the OCP showed it describes culture using eight factors: innovative, detail oriented, results oriented, aggressive/competitive, supportive, growth focused, team oriented, and decisive. Congruence between individual preference and current culture has been shown to predict employee job satisfaction and retention; thus, if it appears a gap in congruency exists, managers may want to explore in more detail where and why the gap exists and how to work with employees to create positive (and appropriate) culture change.

How Do We Change the Organization's Culture?

Though many leaders attempt to change their organization's culture through their decisions, actions, and design of the organizational structure, changing the culture requires much more. In fact, an entire field of study and large consulting firms are dedicated to culture change—thus, it is not a simple tweak of the organizational chart or hiring a new manager.

"What if we don't change at all ... and something magical just happens?"

Changing an organization's culture typically falls under the heading of Organizational Development (OD), or organizational change and development (OCD). OD is an interdisciplinary field, focusing on planned change. Stemming from a history of applied work in organizations, where the emphasis has been on the betterment of individuals and the organization as a whole, OD as a discipline originated in organizations, as opposed to having been developed in a research or academic laboratory first and then implemented/tested in organizations.

OD efforts tend to be organization-wide, typically sponsored by top management, with the aim of improving organizational processes and performance (Beckhard, 1969; Beer & Walton, 1987; Margulies & Raia, 1978). A system-level approach, OD interventions (i.e., organized set of actions) are planned efforts that affect the overall system (Beckhard, 1969; Huse & Cummings, 1985), are process oriented (Beckhard, 1969; French & Bell, 1999; Huse & Cummings, 1985), and action research oriented (recall from Chapter 1; Beer & Walton, 1987; French & Bell, 1999; Margulies & Raia, 1978). This means that change efforts focus on big changes and collaborative efforts between OD specialists and organizational leaders.

A hallmark of OD is that people at all levels of the organization collaborate and participate in decision-making and problem solving, alongside the OD specialist. This approach, therefore, is too broad for laboratory work in a research setting. As a consequence of its deep roots in the field versus the lab, OD is recognized as being a field-driven area, and one that normally starts with a focus on the organization overall.

Organizational transformation, a concept used to discuss organizational change, has been described in terms of first-order change and second-order change (Levy & Merry, 1986). First-order refers to incremental adjustments that do not alter the core of the organization, tend not to be system-wide changes, and might occur naturally during the lifecycle of the organization. Such modification does not affect the organizational culture, but may affect climate or subcultures. For example, as organizations grow and add more people, procedures and more structure in decision-making is necessary to coordinate across groups and provide consistent and fair treatment of employees. This represents a first-order change. It is incremental and follows naturally with the organization's development. As the organization continues to grow or is already large, bigger modifications may be required.

Second-order change involves system-wide alterations, fundamental adjustments to the organizational structure, and may be considered transformational. Levy and Merry (1986) state that "second-order change (organization transformation) is a multi-dimensional, multi-level qualitative, discontinuous, radical organizational change involving a paradigmatic shift" (p.5). Such alteration is designed to, and inevitably does affect the organizational culture. Consequently, we should see shifts in the elements of culture identified by Schein (1990), and Trice and Beyer (1993). Thus, we might conclude that to transform the culture, the basic assumptions, artifacts, espoused and enacted values, languages, and practices must change. Though transformation can be achieved, doing so is easier said than done, and not without overcoming multiple challenges (Higgins & McAllaster, 2004; see the case study of Crummer Graduate School of Business by Higgins, McAllaster, Certo, & Gilbert, 2006).

OD as an Outgrowth of its Historical Roots

To understand some of the challenges involved with changing an organization's culture, it helps to have some perspective on how OD as a field developed. Its history, tied directly to the history of the fields of organizational psychology and organizational behavior, reviewed in Chapter 1, provides insight into what makes culture change exciting, yet also so challenging.

Historical factors that, to an extent, drove the need for OD include scientific management. Taylor is credited with developing the principles of scientific management (Taylor, 1911), which emphasized scientific methods to improve productivity and efficiency (see Halpern, Osofsky, & Peskin, 1989 for a more detailed review). He focused on the interaction of human characteristics, social environment, task, and physical capacity, speed, and cost with the goal of eliminating human variability. As a result of the application of scientific management in organizations, productivity increased dramatically. New departments within organizations were created to focus on the efficiency of work and human action in specific job tasks such as industrial engineering, personnel, and quality control. Additional layers of middle management were formed as planning became separated from operations. Within internal processes, rules replaced trial and error, and management became formalized, with a focus on efficiency.

Though Taylor's work within organizations caused alterations to organizations and their structure, which created large gains for organizations overall,

Why do organizations need to change their cultures?

there was resistance to what was becoming knowing as Taylorism (Halpern et al., 1989; Taylor, 1911). For instance, older, more established managers were resistant to their jobs being boiled down to the results of a time and motion study, rather than the result of the talents of the manager. Likewise, workers were resistant to what some considered the dehumanization or mechanization of work (Shotter, 1987). The addition of new layers and departments to the organization appeared to create added bureaucracy that slowed decision-making, dispersed power across a larger number of people, and signaled change. People often struggle with change and, consequently, dealing with and anticipating resistance is now a step in nearly every change process (Ford, Ford, & D'Amelio, 2008).

Probably, the most well cited historical event credited with the launch of the human relations movement and the development of OD is the Hawthorne experiments conducted in the 1920s and 1930s (Chapter 1; also see Roethlisberger & Dickson, 1939 for the full account). The temporary change in employees' behavior at the onset of a novel treatment (being watched by researchers) has been coined the Hawthorne Effect; however, the Hawthorne Effect should really be attributed to a variety of findings from the many studies at the Hawthorne plant and not just the illumination studies (Brannigan & Zwerman, 2001). Several of the findings included the power of social norms, **subject reactivity**, management style, and small group dynamics (Roethlisberger & Dickson, 1939; Mayo, 1933). Though recent work has criticized whether the Hawthorne studies should be credited with starting the human relations movement (see Bruce & Nyland, 2011), the conclusions from the studies are still relevant for the field of OD when considering changing organizational culture. The particularly relevant conclusions from the Hawthorne studies include

a. existence of informal employee groups and their effect on production (group norms)
b. (importance of employee attitudes about their work
c. value of a sympathetic and understanding boss
d. need to treat people as people—not simply as human capital

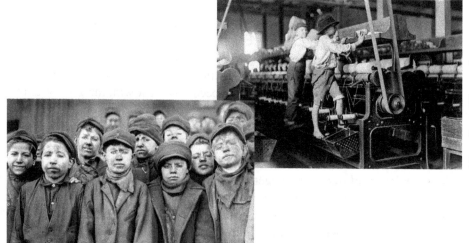

Thus, OD rose in reaction to the hardships and abuse of the industrial revolution, including exploitation of children, and began focusing on how individuals in groups behave and interact within organizations (Bakke, 1950; Halpern et al., 1989; Tredgold, 1959). The primary goal of OD is on improving the organization and effecting positive changes for the employees within. When attempting to modify organizational culture, the historical roots of OD give us a number of important components to consider:

1. Change is not always perceived as positive by all, even if it is intended to help employees

2. Employees fear uncertainty, the unknown of what the new organizational state brings for them personally and for their employees (in the case of a manager)

3. Group norms are powerful and can prevent modification from lasting

4. The novelty of change may invoke a temporary initial modification in behavior, but this can fade once the novelty wears off

5. Just altering the components of the job without focusing on the overall work environment or climate may lead to efficiencies for the organization but fail to consider important motivational factors for the employee

The learning gains from Taylorism and the Hawthorne studies lead to the conclusions that to change an organizational culture, we may have to reconfigure the organizational structure along with modifying the elements within it (e.g., artifacts, symbols, language). There have been many models of change discussed in the literature; however, the models evolved over time as researchers and OD specialists learned what works, what does not work, and what factors cannot be ignored. The following section reviews a few of the well-known models that incorporate the majority of factors researchers have identified as critical to organizational transformation.

Change Models

A number of organizational change models have been proposed over the years, with most becoming more sophisticated over time. Most frameworks are unable to adequately specify all the aspects of the organization that must change; therefore, they tend to focus on specific aspects such as the role of the leader (e.g., Katz & Miller, 1996), how employees cognitively recognize change (e.g., alpha, beta, gamma; Golembiewski, Billingsley, & Yeager, 1975), and how to handle resistance (e.g., Erwin & Garman, 2010; Kotter & Schlesinger, 2008).

To create a customized change model, the practitioner or organizational leader with knowledge and insight can draw from the different frameworks presented here. Each model provides a slightly different view of how transformation in organizations occurs. Hence, every approach offers value and perspective-they are not exclusive of each other, but rather overlap and complement one another.

Perhaps the best place to start in the review of transformation approaches is Kurt Lewin's 3-step model of change, potentially considered the formative paradigm of organizational change.

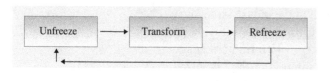

FIGURE 12.8   Lewin's Model of Change

Courtesy Zinta Byrne. Source: Lewin 1947.

Unfreeze-Transform-Refreeze

Probably the most well-known approach to organizational transformation is Lewin's (1947) 3-step model of change: unfreeze–transformation–refreeze (shown in Figure 12.8). A distinguishing feature of this model is its simplicity.

Unfreeze

In the *unfreeze* stage, the managers and leaders of the organization recognize that something needs to change. Here we see that the leaders realize change may be tough. Unfreezing refers to the process of getting the organization ready for modification, by relaxing policies, norms, and habits that support the status quo. Management prepares employees for the change (e.g., Choi & Ruona, 2011) and helps neutralize their anticipated resistance (see resistance below) through education, communication, and getting employees involved (i.e., identification or internalization of change objectives; Kelman, 1961). Once employees have also recognized the need for transformation, the leaders and OD specialists can move into the transform stage.

Transform

In the *transform* stage of change, the organizational members alter the way they operate. This is the change event (often called an intervention), when the actual transformation is taking place. We can recognize this stage because popular press discussions of transformations always talk about the "transform" but fail to share the readying process or what follows the change event.

The transform stage can be very long, as it was for Nelsons mentioned in the introduction. The length of this stage depends on the complexity of the modifications required and sometimes on the size of the organization. At some point, the organizational leaders or practitioners determine the change event and all its steps are complete. The organization is at a somewhat vulnerable point because the required steps are complete and the organization appears to have transformed into the new objective, yet it is easy for employees to fall back into their old habits. To make the change permanent, the organization must refreeze into the new state.

Refreeze

Lewin's unfreeze–transform–refreeze paradigm of organizational transformation is simple, conveying the overarching goal. The model is too simple, however, to effectively design all the components of organizational change, such as the social aspects, which can make or break a change attempt.

Hence, to solidify the modifications and make them permanent, we must go through the *refreeze* stage. Here, organizational leaders follow up on complaints, unanticipated consequences, and any lingering resistance. Communication (Chapter 10) plays a big role in keeping the new organizational structure and processes in place.

The important take-home message from Lewin's model is that it's one of the first; many frameworks that follow build on the basic concept of shaking up the current organizational system, transforming it, and then solidifying the changes. The model is simple, making it easy to remember. However, the model is too simple to describe organizational change effectively. For example, an aspect of unfreezing an organization is readying it for transformation, yet such detail is missing from Lewin's model.

Readying the Organization for Change

Armenakis, Harris, and Field (2001) proposed that communication is critical to readying the organization for change, which is a process that takes place in the unfreeze stage. These authors offer five messages that must be conveyed as part of the communication plan:

1. the discrepancy between the current and desired states (i.e., the need for change)

2. the efficacy of the transformation (i.e., how likely the organization is to successfully implement the change)

3. the valence of the transformation (i.e., the benefits of changing)

4. its appropriateness (i.e., why the proposed modifications are right for the organization)

5. who is providing the principal support (i.e., who in the leadership team is committed to the success of the effort).

Through persuasive oral and written communication, the organization can transmit the five messages of readiness to the organization to prepare its members for change. Mechanisms for effectively transmitting the message include active participation, which involves participative decision-making and vicarious learning experiences. Managing external sources of information is essential to avoid competing messages. To distribute the communication plan and gain buy-in at multiple levels, it helps to have change agents. Change agents are people in the organization identified as leaders of the transformation, and/or individuals who are helping to influence processes or other members to alter their behavior.

Preparing organizational members for change can proactively address some of the issues that cause resistance (e.g., lack of understanding about the need for transforming; Self & Schraeder, 2009). Other approaches to readying the organization can be found in Walinga (2008).

Unfortunately, the need to ready the organization for change is undervalued, and many organizations rush through this step or skip it altogether. Even though Lewin included the idea of readying the organization within the unfreeze stage, this process does not appear in most models. Effective organizational transformation involves taking time to prepare employees for the alterations that are required in the organizational structure and of them.

Action Research

Similar to his 3-step change approach, Lewin (1951) introduced a high-level model, called Action Research, used to explain the general process of organizational change. Action Research refers to a cyclical process of problem identification, hypothesizing the cause of the problem, collecting data to test the hypothesis, and then testing the determined cause in a collaborative relationship between researcher and organization.

The organization must first recognize and identify a problem exists that requires change. The problem could be externally or internally driven requirements that the organization must now implement. For example, externally driven requirements compel hospitals to meet new medical legislation, and manufacturing plants must meet new environmental protection standards. Internally driven changes may be addressing the constant failures in communication between marketing and product development that is creating backlogs, unmet customer expectations, and products that are not fulfilling marketing projections.

Oftentimes the organizational leaders and/or its members have a hunch as to what the cause of the problem might be, or the collaborating consultant/researcher may form a hypothesis of cause based on prior work with the organization.

Based on the hypothesis, data are collected (often in the form of organizational surveys, focus groups, and observations) to test the hypothesized cause. Once the data have been collected and analyzed, the researcher and organization interpret the results in light of the organizational context. Decisions are made about what to do next and how to solve the problem.

This model should look familiar to students of science in that it essentially depicts how empirical research is conducted: identify problem, develop a hypothesis (or many hypotheses), collect data to test hypothesis, determine if hypothesis is supported or not, interpret findings and design next study to test a follow up hypothesis. The biggest difference here is that the work is all conducted with the collaboration of the organization and in a synergistic relationship between science and practice. That is, practice and the specifics of the organization inform each stage, and the results are immediately implemented back into the organization for testing (Figure 12.9).

Why is Lewin's unfreeze-change-freeze model useful?

Practitioner
Management is demanding higher performance and we've been giving incentives, but it's not working. What can we do to increase performance?

Scientist
Hypothesis: Expectancy theory suggests people value incentives differently; Hierarchy of Needs says some people are at lower needs level than others.
Data collection to test hypothesis that employees vary in their needs and that this affects their performance.
Analyze data and provide interpretation to the practitioner.

Practitioner
We modified incentives, but performance went back to normal. We need permanent performance change.

Scientist
Hypothesis: Job Characteristics Theory suggests improvements with core job dimensions should increase motivation, which should increase performance.
Data collection to test hypothesis that employees may need improvements in core job dimensions.
Analyze data and provide interpretation to the practitioner.

FIGURE 12.9   Action Research or the Scientist–Practitioner Model

Courtesy Zinta Byrne.

Some organizations value the Action Research model to the extent they repeat the cycle over again, evaluating the new solutions to ensure appropriate change was taken. They also value the insight the cyclical process provides of needing to attack other ongoing problems that are indirectly triggering challenges elsewhere in the system.

Lewin's Action Research paradigm is a general framework effective for large (system-wide) or small scale (unit or department-wide) change. However, like the unfreeze–transform–freeze model, information about what within an organization needs changing is vague without conducting a full diagnosis. Two good resources for learning about and doing Action Research include Coghlan and Brannick's (2014) *Doing Action Research in Your Own Organization*, and specifically for students, Herr and Anderson's (2014) *The Action Research Dissertation: A Guide for Students and Faculty.*

The cyclical nature of the paradigm, specifically that change is a process, provided the foundation for several approaches succeeding it, including Burke's theory of change.

Burke and Litwin's Model of Organizational Change

Burke's (1994; Burke & Litwin, 1992) theory of organizational change provides a general explanation of the organizational transformation process. Burke and Litwin's model depicts change as driven by interrelated factors, such as external environmental factors and internal organizational factors, such as leadership, that affect organizational and individual performance. These factors directly affect organizational culture and the stated mission and strategy of the organization.

Leaders modify the mission and strategy to mold the organizational culture. Changes to the strategy and culture affect the work unit climates, and employees' jobs and behavior, which in turn affect individual and organizational performance. How the organization performs influences how the organization is viewed by external partners and consumers.

Thus, each factor reciprocally affects another and feeds back into informing both the organization and its partners.

Researchers have demonstrated that change initiated within the organization, as shown in the model depicted in Figure 12.10, has implications for employee acceptance, depending on who starts the effort (Griffin, Rafferty, & Mason, 2004). For example, Griffin and colleagues found that changes initiated outside of the immediate group led employees to report negative perceptions about their own group leader. When their own group leader initiated the changes, however, employees reported positive perceptions. These findings could be interpreted as supporting Burke and Litwin's framework, in that changes need to occur within the organizational units to be most accepted and effective, since such modifications would be perceived as initiated within the group, even if their initial trigger lies outside of the group.

Similar to Burke's (1994; Burke & Litwin, 1992) interrelated model of change (Figure 12.10) is Porras and Robertson's (1992) paradigm of the transformation process. No surprise, the Porras and Robertson model reviewed in the next section looks remarkably like Burke and Litwin's. However, Porras and Robertson extended the model by capturing both alterations to the work setting and employee behavioral change required for a successful transformation.

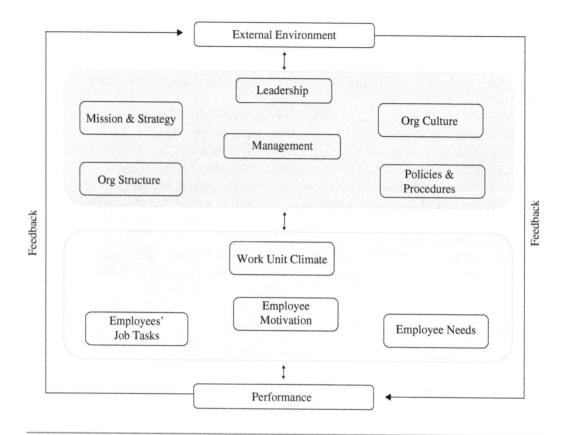

FIGURE 12.10 Model of Change

Courtesy Zinta Byrne. Source: Burke & Litwin, 1992.

Porras and Robertson's Model of Planned Change

After an extensive review of successful organization transformation efforts, Porras and Hoffer (1986) identified specific behaviors required at the management level and the employee level for successful organizational change. Porras and Robertson (1992) developed their theoretical model of change based on this previous work (see Figure 12.11). They proposed that all planned change efforts require behavioral modification at the individual level to be successful. Hence, employees must change their behavior on the job for a transformation effort to work. They also argued that if all else changes around the employee, yet the employee continues to behave in the same way as prior to the intervention, there can be no long-lasting organizational transformation.

In addition to the employees, management also had to enact specific behaviors for change to be successful. More important than the specific list of what behaviors should be enacted with the greatest frequency to ensure successful change was Porras and Robertson's assertion that for successful long-lasting transformation, organizations must achieve individual behavioral modification system-wide. Individual employee behavior change is influenced by the setting within which the employee behaves; therefore, changing the work environment will ultimately lead to the necessary culture and organization changes required for improved performance.

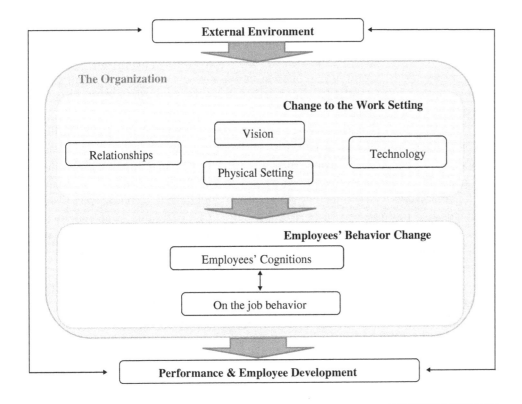

FIGURE 12.11   Model of Planned Change

Courtesy Zinta Byrne. Source: Porras & Robertson, 1992.

Few general, high-level, all-encompassing models like Burke and Litwin's, or Porras and Robertson's exist because of the complexity of describing and testing change that affects the entire organization. Because of their comprehensiveness, they are unique and valuable in the OD literature, regardless of how old they might seem to newcomers to the field. Some other scholars have provided comprehensive reviews of the literature, discussing process theories of organizational change (e.g., Quinn & Cameron, 1983; Van de Ven & Poole, 1995). Others include process theories with their review of implementation theories (theories that explain how it works or why the model should work, vs. what must actually be done to effect organizational change; e.g., Austin & Bartunek, 2003; Van de Ven & Sun, 2011). Hence, these comprehensive models are unique, and most models that have followed Burke and Litwin's or Porras and Robertson's (with a few exceptions) models tend to be more narrowly focused on a single component of the transformation process.

Exercise 12.4

Compare and contrast Burke and Litwin's model with Porras and Robertson's.

Weick and Quinn's Typology

Even though preceding models suggested change was a continuous process, many researchers attempted to sort out organizational transformation in terms of when change actually starts to take place and the pattern with which modifications occur. For example, in an attempt to characterize how transformations happen, Weick and Quinn (1999) developed a typology describing exactly how change takes place in organizations, proposing that it is either episodic (discontinuous, intermittent) patterned after Lewin's unfreeze–transform–refreeze model, or continuous (evolving, incremental), characterized by ongoing activities.

Modifications in personnel, technology, or other short but impactful alterations in the organizational structure or environment can be considered episodic. For example, hospitals have been moving to electronic patient tracking systems—so, paper files with patient records are converted to electronic and all interactions with patients are noted in the computer system and instead of on paper. Episodic changes like this may occur periodically, might be dramatic when they occur, and are designed to achieve a specific goal. Episodic changes might occur within one of Lewin's stages, but they do not describe modifications that happen across stages or that take more than one stage to achieve.

In comparison, continuous change in Weick and Quinn's typology refers to a pattern of modifications that require a longer period to achieve, may be cyclical without a clear end state in mind, and might operate across Lewin's stages. Continuous change events include ongoing efforts to increase communication by loosening up overly rigid formal communication practices that have inhibited exposing failing processes or violations of safety rules.

Weick and Quinn's (1999) typology has been quite popular, used to conceptualize and delineate organizational transformation (e.g., Plowman, Baker, Beck, Kulkarni, Solansky, & Travis, 2007). The model is simple in terms of suggesting change is either quick and short or long and evolving, but lacks detail on exactly how change occurs. Perhaps in response to many of the previous prescriptive models is Kotter's (1995), another very popular model, but one focused on how to execute the organizational transformation rather than on what the components of change are within the organizational structure.

Kotter's 8-Step Model of Change

Kotter's (1995) 8-steps to organizational change has become a popular model of transformation, more so in the practice literature than in the research literature. Its popularity is likely due to its practical and simple structure that summarizes much of the previous research on change in eight simple steps. Kotter developed his paradigm of 8-steps for successful organizational transformation based on learning from the failures of over 100 organizations attempting to change. Though most failed, some were successful providing insight for a framework for successful transformation. The steps include

1. establish a sense of urgency

2. form a powerful guiding coalition

3. create a vision

4. communicate the vision

5. empower others to act on the vision

6. plan for and create short-term wins

Watch https://www.youtube.com/watch?v=p8loc2DBVQw to see Kotter's change model using SpaceX as the case study.

7. consolidate improvements and produce more change

8. institutionalize new approaches

His framework can be loosely transposed onto Lewin's (1947) 3-step model of change, unfreeze–transform–refreeze, where Kotter's steps 1–4 could be thought of as unfreezing the organization, steps 5–7 as transforming the organization to the new changed state, and step 8 as refreezing the organization into its new state.

Research has shown the 8-step model works. For example, Wright, Roche, and Khoury (2010) applied Kotter's 8-steps to transforming an academic pediatric hospital's operating rooms. Though the problem solved was very specific, to improve the hospital's ability to start surgeries on time, the changes were extensive, affecting clinical and support personnel. Other researchers have used and supported the model in higher education (Borrego & Henderson, 2014; Uys, 2010) and action research (Pollack & Pollack, 2015).

Not unlike the comprehensive frameworks reviewed in this section previously, few, if any, rigorous empirical studies exist evaluating pre- and post-change states to determine actual effectiveness of the model. Substantial anecdotal evidence from practice suggests it works and Kotter provides considerable evidence of his own for the effectiveness of the model. The biggest values of the model may be its clear plan for how to make successful change happen, now matter what the organization is or focuses on, and that many of the steps are grounded in empirical evidence, even if the entire model itself lacks significant rigorous scientific pre-post testing. Another model that was also derived directly from organizations undergoing change is McKinsey's 7-S model.

McKinsey's 7-S Model

Another popular framework used in the field is McKinsey's 7-S model (Figure 12.12), developed by Peters and Waterman (1982) during their time as consultants for the McKinsey Consulting firm. This model has no publicly published empirical evidence or theoretical framework supporting its construction, though McKinsey has used it worldwide for many years, suggesting it has some value.

The 7-S model suggests organizations comprise seven key dimensions, all of whose names begin with the letter 'S'. The seven dimensions include structure, strategy, systems, shared values, skills, staff, and style. The framework is generally used for assessing misalignment between dimensions and then applying interventions to align the seven dimensions. The ultimate goal in using this model is to achieve high levels of organizational performance. An example of alignment occurs when the company *strategy* includes aggressively pursuing new markets and the sales *staff* has the skills to do so. An example of misalignment

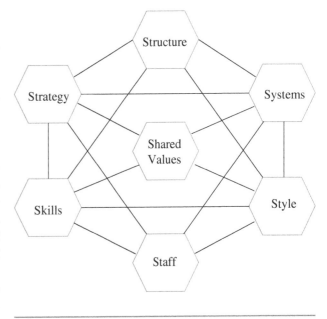

FIGURE 12.12   McKinsey's 7-S Model

Courtesy Zinta Byrne. Source: Peters and Waterman, 1982.

might be that the organizational *structure* has too many layers that do not facilitate aggressive and quick sales, making it difficult to pursue new markets quickly, which is part of the *strategy*.

Higgins Eight S's of Strategy Execution

Higgins (2005) recently extended the 7-S model to the Eight S's of Strategy Execution (see Figure 12.13). His framework was based on the McKinsey 7-S model with a few specific differences.

First, the skills dimension was replaced with a resource dimension. Resources such as money, information, and technology are essential for executing a successful strategy. Higgins incorporated skills into strategy since strategy includes core competencies and capabilities.

Second, Higgins wanted the model to illustrate alignment and misalignment by showing arrows pointing either in the same direction to signify alignment or in different directions to signify misalignment (Figure 12.14).

Third, since the alignment of the components is to achieve strategic performance, he included this factor into the model as the eighth element.

The McKinsey 7-S model was quite popular, to which Higgins' created his extension. McKinsey's and Higgins' models may be considered macro level frameworks. However, with very little specification of how to align the components of the organization (probably since the models are proprietary), the framework offers little value without the accompanying diagnostic tools that McKinsey and Higgins provide. If lacking the consulting from McKinsey or others offering these models as their strategy for organizational change, managers could use the models to convey that alignment between aspects/components of the organization are essential for overall effectiveness. Using a different tool, or many tools, you could then assess misalignment and implement your own strategies to get aligned. Thus, the figure could have utility even if the consulting is not readily available.

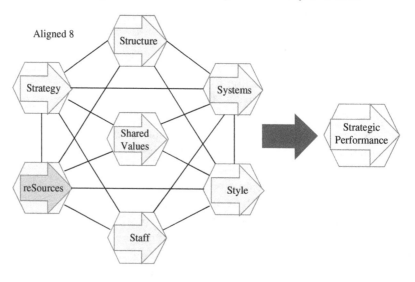

FIGURE 12.13   Eight S's of Strategy Execution (Aligned Components)

Courtesy Zinta Byrne. Source: Higgins, 2005.

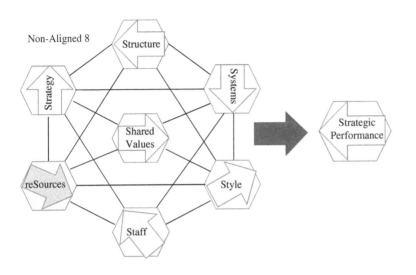

FIGURE 12.14   Eight S's of Strategy Execution (Misaligned Components)

Courtesy Zinta Byrne. Source: Higgins, 2005.

Because comprehensive models and patterned models don't offer results in every situation, still other models have been created. Taking an entirely different approach, Armenakis and colleagues (2001) suggested that successful transformation required the alteration of employees' cognitive paradigm about work.

Other models of change from practice include Prosci's ADKAR model (awareness, desire, knowledge, ability, reinforcement) and Mindtools' Change Curve (status quo, disruption, exploration, rebuilding)—just to name a few. Look these up on the Internet to see more about change management.

Armenakis et al.'s Paradigm Change Model

Armenakis et al. (2001) emphasized that for change to be successful, organizational leaders must alter individuals' paradigms of the current culture. Paradigms are theories and views that we hold to help us make sense of our world. Paradigms also guide our behavior and interpretations; therefore, changing them to fit the new organization is critical. Armenakis and colleagues suggested we must make paradigm shifts to experience successful permanent change. Thus, we must think and act differently than before the transformation.

This cognitive shift captures a similar idea to Porras and Robertson's individual behavior modification, though it is unique in that it focuses on our thinking rather than on our behavior. The model is also vaguely similar to Kotter's (1995) in that Kotter recommended adopting a new vision for the organization, which we could argue might lead to a paradigm shift.

Armenakis et al. additionally proposed that organizations must make **alpha, beta, and gamma changes** (see Golembiewski et al., 1975). Alpha changes were defined as incremental alterations in our knowledge and skills that move us closer to how we need to behave in the new organization. Beta or gamma changes (Armenakis et al. tie these together under "fundamental change", p. 632) affect the content of the paradigms, such that we modify (a) what we consider valuable, (b) how to do our jobs, (c) what events mean to us, and (d) how we should react to change. In addition, two models were proposed: readiness and institutionalization, in which Armenakis et al. focused on how paradigms must be changed to facilitate and solidify organizational transformation. Armenakis and colleagues offer relatively complete descriptions of factors involved in the paradigm shifts.

The appealing aspect of Armenakis et al.'s model is the acknowledgement that accepting the permanent change in the organization requires a shift in our thinking about what the organization means to us and how we fit into it in terms of the meaningfulness of our work and how we do our job. Therefore, this change model makes for a great companion to any one of the previous models that address structure changes or behavior modification. Another valuable aspect of the model is in recognizing that if change is occurring, people alter their views, which means the measure of change must modify as the change itself occurs (i.e., the bar moves, so you can't measure to the same bar/level).

Exercise 12.5

Before moving on, describe the similarities and differences between Kotter's 8-steps, McKinsey's 7-S, and the Paradigm Change Model.

How do Managers Use the Models of Organizational Change in the Workplace?

In the previous section, a number of models of change were reviewed, and yet there are still many more that could have been included. The ones reviewed are some of the most well-known and still cited in the practice and research literature. Accordingly, if you are conducting literature reviews to determine which paradigm to rely on for organizational change, these frameworks offer a good place to start.

Unfortunately, none of models reviewed cover all of what needs to happen in an organization to change the culture. A single comprehensive model is probably not possible, given all the complexities within organizations and their employees. Hence, the work of Burke and Litwin (1992) and Porras and Robertson (1992) has been valuable because their work is more comprehensive than most. These two models provide a general idea of the interconnectedness of culture change, illustrating that aspects of several layers of the organization must be tweaked for effective and lasting culture change. Kotter's (1995) 8-step plan provides operational details that can be used in conjunction with Armenakis et al.'s (2001) paradigm shift. The McKinsey and Higgins' frameworks are less immediately useful because little published empirical evidence exists to support that aligning all the aspects of the organization makes for culture change, and they lack readily available detail necessary to apply them without first having to purchase consultation from the firms.

Typically, an organizational diagnosis is conducted to assess issues within the organization and to identify which parts of the culture may need to be attacked first. Many organizations bring in industrial and organizational psychologists, management consultants, or organizational behaviorists from the outside to assess their culture. The disadvantage for the insider is that by being part of the system it can be difficult to identify problems with that system. Because the system is new to them, outsiders can more readily spot the problems with the system. Their diagnosis of the organization may be accompanied by interventions using

A nice example of an organization that applied a combination of the various models reviewed here is Aetna, explained by Katzenbach, Steffen, and Kronley in the Harvard Business Review 2012.

an Action Research approach or a scientist–practitioner model. However, not all organizations can afford an external diagnosis, some have their own internal consultants who specialize in OD, and there are organizational leaders unaware that the assessment of problems that require culture adjustment should be conducted before change is instigated. Thus, without such diagnostic work, organizational leaders may end up applying several approaches to transformation and find that none work. External assessors have the disadvantage of not understand underlying meanings attributed to different aspects of the organization and hence, may have to rely on internal people to conduct a thorough diagnosis.

There is nothing wrong with combining frameworks, based on what they target, to attack the areas of your organization that appear most influential and potentially misguided (e.g., in terms of the strategy). Caution in making such changes is required as an ill-planned or botched intervention can create much more harm than good, leading to even bigger problems. Another downside is that modifications to the organization do impact employees and their productivity while they wrestle with the changes. None of this includes the challenges with changing a culture, discussed in the next section.

Challenges in Changing a Culture

Just as changing ingrained habits is really hard, so is changing a culture. Attempts to change the organization's culture do not necessarily work even after years of effort. For example, change efforts at Avinor, a Norwegian airport management and air navigation services provider failed after a 3-year attempt (Lofquist, 2011). The researchers who studied the failed culture change attributed the lack of success to challenges arising from a mismatch between the original culture, the implementation strategy, and subcultures.

There are a number of challenges to changing an organizational culture identified in the research literature. Challenges can be categorized into four groups: content, process, contextual, and organizational (e.g., Armenakis & Bedeian, 1999).

Content challenges refer to the substance of the organizational transformation effort, such as the strategy for modification or focus of change (i.e., the goal). Process challenges are related to change management, which includes handling resistance, addressing existing group norms, communicating the change, and readying the organization for culture change. Contextual challenges comprise the social, environmental, industry, or societal conditions under which the organization operates that may influence how the culture is molded and how receptive employees might be to the desired change. For example, contextual challenges might include regulatory compliance policies proposed by an outside governmental agency that require the organization to change in response (e.g., worker safety and health, environmental pollution). Additionally, contextual challenges include stakeholders, such as clients who inform the company of what they like and do not like, which shapes the culture (e.g., Apple's culture reflects internal as well as external values for creativity and utility). Lastly, organizational challenges refer to features of the organization itself, such as structure (i.e., layers of management, board of executives, founder) or history.

Many authors suggest the greatest challenge in changing culture is that it differs from organization to organization. Each must be treated independently. Furthermore, how the culture develops is based on deep-seated values and norms,

Another example of the challenges in changing culture can be seen at World Bank, an organization working on changing its culture for about 50 years. Denning (2011) reviews the change history at World Bank—an interesting example, for sure.

passed from group to group, and organizational generation to generation. As a consequence of these deep-seated values and norms, employees frequently display resistance to change, just like we display resistance to forming new habits (even when we know they are good for us).

Why is Porras and Robertson's model potentially more useful than Kotter's?

Resistance

Changing a culture can invoke resistance (Bovey & Hede, 2001; Erwin & Garman, 2010; Kotter, 1995; Kotter & Schlesinger, 2008; van Dam, Oreg, & Schyns, 2008). Lack of buy-in, push-back, criticism for the new state, reluctance to take necessary actions when they are needed and other actions that indicate a less-than-favorable attitude toward change characterize resistance (Ford & Ford, 2010). Resistance may stem from a fear of the unknown, new structure of the organization (uncertainty), which challenges our work identity (van Dijk & van Dick, 2009). The fear of change may also touch on ingrained norms that are hard to identify but if left unchanged will support the old way of being (Kotter, 1995; Lewin, 1951; Schein, 1990).

Resistance may be either passive or active. Passive resistance takes the form of procrastination, withholding information, or simply failing to implement aspects of the transformation. Active resistance is characterized by direct sabotage, deliberately spreading rumors, and arguing in public forums about the change (Hultman, 1998; Petrini & Hultman, 1995).

Resistance is often cited as a challenge of culture change, yet some authors suggest that resistance may facilitate organizational modifications (e.g., Ford & Ford, 2010; Mabin, Forgeson, & Green, 2001; Msweli-Mbanga & Potwana, 2006; Oreg, 2006). For example, Ford and Ford (2010) proposed that resistance may function as a mechanism for keeping change efforts in focus by keeping people talking about the change initiative. Discussions and thorough conversations raised in the spirit of resistance might improve solutions and get more people involved in the change than otherwise would be. Ongoing conversation provides more opportunity for managers to clarify the adjustments associated with the transformation, and more opportunity for employees to make sense of the change (Ford & Ford, 2010). Objections may be effective at pointing out flaws in the change initiative that with further conversation serve to bring about a better solution. Ford and Ford offer examples of change events where those most resistant to the variations were often those who cared the most about the transformation, or were close enough to the inner workings of the system to identify the holes in the plan. Thus, by engaging the resisters, leaders can demonstrate a true interest in getting the change right, give employees voice and opportunity to make sense of the change, and engage them in becoming part of the solution by owning how to make the change event work.

For additional reading, several approaches have been studied for dealing with resistance to change. See Furst and Cable (2008), and Van Dam, Shaul, and Birgit (2008).

Hence, even though resistance is typically considered a challenge, it is possible to use employees' opposition to make for a better solution. Resistance to change frequently exposes the norms that people are reluctant to let go of because those norms make the job easier and automatic.

Norms

Change efforts must be made with an understanding of the current group norms, as well as overall organizational and societal norms (e.g., Danisman, 2010). No matter what is done to change the organization, if group norms that are no longer desirable (almost like old ingrained habits that are so automatic you don't realize they are just habits) are left untouched, they may steer the organization back to its former course (Axelrod, 1986; Jaffe, Scott, & Tobe, 1994; Kotter, 1995). For example, some groups might have norms about who can work together and when, which contradicts a new matrix structure (see Chapter 11) where flexibility of group formation is required. Thus, if the organization is attempting to move to increase team collaboration, this norm will become destructive to the organizational change. Hence, organizations need to consider ensuring that the optimal conditions for change are in place before moving forward.

Optimal Conditions

A challenge with changing the culture is ensuring the optimal conditions are in place for bringing forth modifications and moving through the change process. Change takes effort, people, and affects many individuals in the organization—some in good ways, some in ways that hurts the organization's productivity. A way to create optimal conditions for successful transformation is to secure top management support and accountability. Most change efforts fail without top management support (Kotter, 1995).

Sometimes organizations hire an outside consultant to guide the transformation. In this case, the success of the transformation relies on the quality of the consultant. Avoid skimping on this key component; hire a qualified and experienced consultant. A botched change in the organization is far more expensive and impactful than a high-quality consultant hired at the start of the effort.

Company Example 12.1   How Traeger's CEO Built a New Culture

Sometimes, optimal conditions do not initially seem so optimal and have to be created, like for the CEO of Traeger, an outdoor cooking company based in the United States. When employees set one of their shipping trucks on fire to prevent outsourcing to United Parcel Services, the CEO knew the culture was toxic and had to change (Andrus, 2019). As he put it "I knew we needed to dismantle the existing corporate culture and build a new one from scratch" (p. 34). He was the eighth CEO, thus employees did not expect him to last long. They disrespected him, refused to meet his requests for company data, and even refused to make time to meet with him (even though he was the boss!). He described the culture as fear-based, created by one of the senior executives who owned a lot of the company stock. The CEO initially brought in some of his own executives thinking that would help, but it made things worse—we versus them kind of situation. Thus, though you might not consider the situation optimal for culture change—it was—the CEO had to do something for the company to survive. His first step was to remove the fear-creating majority owner, which he did by buying him out. The next step involved giving a culture survey to assess how ready people were to change. This was followed by the development of a new missing and value statements (see Chapter 13 for mission, vision, strategy). The next step was to relocate the corporate office to where the CEO had a stronger network and could leave behind employees who were sabotaging culture change. His rationale for physically relocating the offices was that transforming the firmly rooted legacy culture was nearly impossible with the group of employees who were deeply committed to the existing location and culture. They were preventing

(Continued)

the culture change. Each employee was assessed on potential for moving and fitting into the new culture. "We needed to be certain we didn't bring anyone who could infect the new culture we were trying to create" (p. 37). The CEO and new executive team worked with architects to create a working environment that reflected the desired culture, which includes areas and space to cook and eat together. The 450 person organization now has breakfast together every Monday and they cook lunch together Tuesday through Friday. The CEO attributes their growth in sales from $70 million to $400 million in 5 years to the culture overhaul.

Assuming all challenges to change have been resolved or identified and an action plan is in place for resolving them, the next step is to actually change the culture. The following section reviews a number of techniques for changing culture, techniques that you might use or see used in your organization.

Exercise 12.6

What are the key challenges with changing organizational culture?

How Do Managers Apply Theory to Change Climate and Culture

A number of methods derived from several of the theories and models reviewed in the previous sections and chapters are available to change agents or managers for modifying the climate, with the long-term intent of changing the culture. Though changing climate and culture tend not to be as simple as applying a few techniques, there are a few methods of altering aspects of climate and culture that need not be overwhelming and that possess a theoretical foundation. Techniques targeted at various levels of the organization including organization-wide, group level, and at the individual level exist. Generally, culture change requires interventions at all three levels.

Organization-Wide

Action Research

Action Research, reviewed earlier in the chapter, serves as a diagnostic tool and mechanism for making change, one step at a time, with the aim of problem solving. Advantages of this approach include that it always has a focus (we are solving a problem the organization has) and we work closely with organizational leaders motivated to solve the problem. Hence, securing optimal conditions for change may be facilitated, though not always.

Appreciative Inquiry

Rather than focus on the problems within an organization, appreciative inquiry is an approach to OD that lies in emphasizing the unique qualities and strengths of an organization. Appreciative inquiry involves working with organizational leaders to determine how to use core competencies and strengths to improve the organization further (Cooperrider & Whitney, 2005; see Bright, Cooperrider, & Galloway, 2006 for an example of an implementation of appreciative inquiry). Based on Action Research, Appreciative Inquiry developed out of the researcher's role in appreciating, without judgment, the client's problem or being predisposed to a particular solution before the problem is identified (Stowell, 2013). This approach relies on the idea that we make more progress capitalizing on our strengths than on always focusing on our weaknesses.

Learning Organization

Learning organizations refer to companies wherein employees become skilled at developing, acquiring, and transferring knowledge. The organization embraces a culture of tolerance, open discussion, and thinking at a system level. Senge (1990) is most well-known for the learning organization due to his book "The Fifth Discipline"; however, this work was stimulated by earlier writings of Argyris in the 1970s and 1980s (Argyris, 1989, 1990; Argyris & Shon, 1976). This approach uses systems theory as its foundation. System-level thinking refers to considering how all components of a process or system (such as an organization) are intertwined (Katz & Kahn, 1966). Thus, solving one problem means looking at all the intended and unintended consequences, and what other problems may be contributing to this one that will eventually prevent permanent change.

The purpose of becoming a learning organization is to adapt quickly to external pressures and market challenges because the organization and its members can quickly learn what is necessary for changes to be successful (see Garvin, Edmondson, & Gino, 2008, for a business perspective of becoming a learning organization). Innovative organizations and start-ups are often learning organizations, as are organizations focused on environmental sustainability.

Process Consulting

Process consulting refers to a form of consulting where the consultant facilitates change by advising and guiding organizational members or change agents through the process of transformation. The process consultant does not implement the change—rather facilitates the effort and keeps its ownership within the organization. Process consulting can take the form of evaluating how the modification efforts are going and facilitating discussion and brainstorming sessions on how to improve those efforts. The process consultant may also provide direct feedback, helping the organizational change agents identify what is and is not working. Process consultants believe the organization's managers and change agents understand their own work environment better than they do, and consequently, are in the best position to make alterations and keep them going long after the consultant's work is done. Theories forming the foundation of process consulting include self-determination theory (Ryan & Deci, 2000, see Chapter 3).

Two good reference books on process consulting include Block's (2011) "Flawless Consulting," the first edition was published in 1978, but this is a good revision to that, and Schein's (1988) "Process consultation: Its role in organization development, Volume 1."

Survey Feedback

Organizations may conduct a company-wide survey to obtain feedback and insight into how employees perceive the organization and its leaders, as well as give employees an opportunity to voice their opinion about the organization in general. Sometimes just the act of asking for feedback starts the ball rolling on the change process (Byrne, Palmer, Smith, & Weidert, 2011). The survey makes them aware the organization is seeking information and will make a change. Thus, people ready themselves for taking action. The survey makes them aware that the organization is seeking information and will make a change.

Unfortunately, surveys are frequently haphazardly designed because it appears easy to create a survey, and they are sometimes given with no follow-up. Asking questions and not taking subsequent action generally affects the organization far more negatively than if the survey was not conducted at all. The power of the survey as a technique for feedback and/or change should not be underestimated. Unfortunately, it is easily misused because of poor planning, poor design, and lack of follow through.

Why is appreciative inquiry useful?

Total Quality Management

© arka38/Shutterstock.com

Total quality management (TQM) was made popular in the 1980s when Japanese manufacturing embraced the concepts of Deming and others in process improvement. TQM refers to an approach whereby interventions systematically focus on quality improvement to save costs and increase efficiency in production. TQM involves everyone within the organization, collaboratively working together to continuously improve the processes, decisions, and work environment that will result in high customer satisfaction. TQM is a system-wide effort to create a work climate and culture for continuous improvement in employees' abilities, knowledge, and capability of developing and creating products that satisfy customers. Karuppusami and Gandhinathan (2006) provide a nice review of the TQM success factors and literature.

Structural Changes

Both the McKinsey 7-S and Higgins' 8-S imply that structural changes may be needed to align various aspects of the organization that are out of alignment with the strategy. Structural changes to the organization, such as reshuffling functional areas, reassigning entire divisions, closing or opening new business, and changing the management structure, result in change efforts that ultimately affect every employee. Such modifications are frequently implemented with the intent of satisfying stakeholders, resolving major problems in the organization that threaten its survival, or responding to a major change in either ownership or board membership. Structural modifications are difficult to implement in large organizations, and the results are often not seen for years after the change has long been implemented.

Visioning or Strategic Planning

Visioning and Strategic Planning refer to interventions that help the organization look to the future (Peters, 1988). The success of Visioning and Strategic Planning lies in gap analysis, where organizational leaders develop a map of what they want the organization to look like (the ideal), where they are currently, and what has to be done to cross this gap. After identifying the gap, organizational members develop action plans for closing the gap. These gaps may take years to close and involve hundreds of actions. For organizations to successfully implement their new vision, they must develop and share the vision to the point that all levels of the organization buy-into and own the vision.

Sometimes organizational-level modifications do not get at the specific issues that negatively affect subcultures, and therefore, group-level methods may also be necessary.

Group Level

Team Building

The most frequently implemented group-level change is team building and team structuring. Regardless of the specific team building intervention, all are designed with the goal of increasing communication, collaboration, and group cohesiveness (see Chapter 7). The long-term outcome of team-building change programs is for teams to identify and solve their own problems. Team-building activities are sometimes undertaken to bring a newly formed team to high-functioning levels quickly, or to resolve old conflicts. Group-level interventions include ropes courses and the use of the Myers–Briggs Type Indicator®. Ropes courses, also known as challenge courses, refer to a group of interventions that involve outdoor activities (not necessarily just ropes) that require team members to place themselves in stressful situations where relying on other team members is the only way out. An outcome of the ropes course includes members learning about themselves and their teammates.

The Myers–Briggs Type Indicator®, a psychological test, provides an alternative method for members to learn about themselves and their peers. The test identifies individuals' preferences for situations and then categorizes the individual along four quadrants. Through sharing their preferred approach to work, employees break down communication barriers and learn how to work effectively with others in their group who prefer or are more comfortable with a different approach (see the Myers & Briggs Foundation for more information on the MBTI®).

As noted by several researchers, such as Burke and Litwin (1992), and Porras and Robertson (1992), individual behavior must also change along with group and organizational-level systems for change to be effective and potentially long-lasting.

Think about the process you use for figuring out how to complete a class project. You determine how far along you are at this point, what the product has to look like and when it's due, and then you evaluate how far you have to go to get to that end point. You then set goals for what to do and by when to get the project done. Guess what? You've just done a gap analysis! Gap analysis may be bigger and more complex in an organization, but the concept is the same—figure out where you are now, where you need to go, and how to get there.

Individual Level

Job Redesign

Recall from Chapter 3, job redesign is an intervention focused on changing aspects of the employee's job to trigger motivational states that lead to higher job satisfaction and performance. In practice, job redesign can be challenging because changing aspects of one job can require modifying others. Occasionally, structural aspects of the organization also change, which can become costly. However, some changes may ultimately save the organization money. For example, using technology to facilitate virtual work and working from home can save travel costs and improve morale. Job redesign is a good technique for focusing on the job-level issues and demonstrating to employees they are valued (the attention and focus is on them).

Performance Management (Also Considered Organization Level)

Through joint goal setting with employees, rewards, and performance feedback, managers can move employees toward actions valued by the organization. Performance management techniques use behavioral observation, reinforcement schedules and techniques (Skinner, 1972), and feedback to guide employee motivation in the direction required. For example, Aubrey Daniels International is a consulting firm that sells performance management systems that rely on operant conditioning—the reinforcement techniques of B. F. Skinner—to manage performance. Numerous other techniques and approaches have been proposed for performance management, too many to review here; hence, there is no shortage of options for organizations. Organizational leaders or change agents should also consider the latest information on performance management as some recent practitioner publications suggest predetermined tools may not be the right solution (e.g., Pulakos, Mueller-Hanson, O'Leary, & Meyrowitz, 2012).

Leadership Development (Also Considered Organization-Wide)

Why is team-building a good change effort?

Developing leaders in organizations is typically conducted via executive coaching, mentoring, or formal development programs designed for upper levels of management. These development options may be offered internally to the organization (such as offered within Cisco Systems) using internal trainers or coaches. They may also be offered externally using a consulting firm hired for this purpose. Firms such as Personnel Decisions International (now part of Korn Ferry), The Center for Creative Leadership, and Data Dimensions International offer executive development that includes coaching, mentoring, and formal training programs. The focus of these development programs is typically on helping the leader to identify behaviors that are derailing his or her career. Career derailment refers to leadership patterns of behavior that cause an otherwise promising leader to side track as a consequence of his or her flaws or inhibiting behaviors.

Increasing Emotional Intelligence

Emotional intelligence is defined as "the ability to perceive and express emotion, assimilate emotion in thought, understand and reason with emotion, and regulate emotion in the self and others" (Mayer, Salovey, & Caruso, 2004, p. 396). Increasing emotional intelligence, considered a relatively new intervention, involves modeling, role-playing, receiving feedback, reinforcement, and training on handling interpersonal aspects on the job (see Druskat & Wolff, 2001).

Techniques reviewed in this section should be used together—they are not exclusive of one another (see for example, Byrne, Palmer, Smith, & Weidert, 2011). Perhaps the best approach to deciding which one to use within each level may be to evaluate whether the focus of the specific intervention gets at the problem or part of the climate or culture that needs to be changed first. For example, if performance does not seem to be an issue at this moment, focusing energy on designing a performance-management solution may not be the best intervention to select first. It is possible that after several aspects of the organization have been changed, leaders or the OD specialists will have to come back and change the performance management system. For now, the best course of action is to focus on the overarching issues at each level, first.

> **Various readily available techniques for changing organizational climate range from simple to complex, and their effect on the organization, group, or individual also ranges from temporary to long-lasting. Unfortunately, there is no easy guide for which one is best.**

Exercise 12.7

Describe how managers engage in organizational change—what are the different efforts/approaches they can use?

Chapter Summary

Organizational culture describes how employees experience their work environment. Many components of the work environment play a role in determining how we experience culture, including furniture, expectations, values, and communication, such as stories. Because culture is expressed in our language, actions, and norms, it can be somewhat hard to describe. However, culture is not so hard to experience. Changing culture is difficult because organizational culture is ingrained in how people think about their work, their habits, and their accepted norms for behavior. Even if change is good, it frequently does not feel right at first; just like forming any new habit. There are a number of techniques for attempting to change the culture, including organizational transformation. There are several techniques for change that target different levels of the organization where culture manifests itself, such as organization-wide, in the teams, and within individuals. As a consequence of how pervasive organizational culture is and how challenging it might be to modify, our role in understanding it, understanding how it is maintained, and what we can do to make even incremental changes is essential for working in and managing an organization.

Figure 12.15 provides a visual summary of the key concepts from Chapter 12. The visual summary shows that culture is a high-level overarching concept, like the atmosphere, that subsumes subcultures and climate, which lie within the atmosphere. The stars represent aspects of the culture that we tend to try to connect to tell a story—like making sense out of the shapes/constellations (e.g., big dipper)—aspects that have taken years to form and also do not easily change or go away. The moving clouds show how subcultures can form and change shape but remain clouds—they are still within the overarching culture.

FIGURE 12.15 Visual Summary of Chapter 12.

© Maksim Shmeljov/Shutterstock, Inc.

The image shows that 1st-order change affects lower levels of the organization, whereas 2nd-order change is bigger and more impactful, like the gravity pull or heat of the sun on the planet. Climate is at the lower level—the ocean that was formed by the atmosphere, clouds, sun, but that flows and changes as things are added to or taken away from it (e.g., chemical spills change the makeup of the oceans over time).

Discussion Questions

1. Using your own words, define organizational culture? What is it? Why is it important to understand and talk about?

2. Of the different models of organizational culture described in the chapter, which one do you like the most and why? What differentiates the model you like from the others in the chapter?

3. Many employees who identify lesbian, bisexual, gay, transgender, or queer (LBGTQ) find the culture of established organizations uninviting and/or not welcoming. What do you think it is about the culture in particular (thinking back on models like Schein's or Trice and Beyer's) that would make it seem unfriendly to those of the LBGTQ community?

4. Using the ideas of the previous question, which model of organizational change do you think would work to make/change the aspects of culture that you identified in Question 3 more friendly to those identifying as LBGT or Q?

5. What role do you think organizational culture plays in the Gig economy? Is there a role for organizational culture in the future economy, where independent contractors might be the norm rather than the minority of business associates?

References

Andrus, J. (2019). How I did it: Traeger's CEO on cleaning up a toxic culture. *Harvard Business Review, 97*(2), 33–37

Argyris, C. (1989). Strategy implementation: An experience in learning. *Organizational Dynamics, 18*(2), 5–16.

Argyris, C. (1990). *Overcoming organizational defenses: Facilitating organizational learning.* Needham Heights, MA: Allyn & Bacon.

Argyris, C., & Shon, D. (1976). *Organizational learning.* Reading, MA: Addison Wesley.

Armenakis, A. A., & Bedeian, A. G. (1999). Organizational change: A review of theory and research in the 1990s. *Journal of Management, 25*(3), 293–315. doi:10.1177/014920639902500303

Armenakis, A., Harris, S., & Feild, H. (2001). Paradigms in organizational change: Change agent and change target perspectives. In R. T. Golembiewski (Ed.), *Handbook of organizational behavior* (pp. 631–658). New York, NY: Marcel Dekker.

Austin, J. R., & Bartunek, J. M. (2003). Theories and practices of organizational development. In W. C. Borman, D. R. Ilgen, & R. J. Klimoski (Eds.), *Handbook of psychology: Industrial and organizational psychology* (Vol. 12, pp. 309–332). Hoboken, NJ: Wiley.

Axelrod, R. (2006). An evolutionary approach to norms. *American Political Science Review, 100*(4), 682–683.

Baker, S. J., & Lucas, K. (2017). Is it safe to bring myself to work? Understanding LGBTQ experiences of workplace dignity. *Canadian Journal of Administrative Sciences, 34*(2), 133–148.

Bakke, E. (1950). *Bonds of organization; an appraisal of corporate human relations.* Oxford, England: Harper.

Beckhard, R. (1969). *Organization development: Strategies and models.* Reading, MA: Addison-Wesley.

Beer, M., & Walton, A. E. (1987). Organizational change and development. *Annual Review of Psychology, 38*, 339–367. doi:10.1146/annurev.ps.38.020187.002011

Bellou, V. (2010). Organizational culture as a predictor of job satisfaction: The role of gender and age. *The Career Development International, 15*(1), 4–19. doi:10.1108/13620431011020862

Beyer, J. M., & Trice, H. M. (1987). How an organization's rites reveal its culture. *Organizational Dynamics, 15*(4), 5–24. doi:10.1016/0090-2616(87)90041-6

Block, P. (2011). *Flawless consulting: A guide to getting your expertise used* (3rd ed.). San Francisco, CA: Pfeiffer.

Boisnier, A., & Chatman, J. A. (2003). The role of subcultures in agile organizations. In R. S. Peterson, E. A. Mannix (Eds.), *Leading and managing people in the dynamic organization* (pp. 87–112). Mahwah, NJ: Lawrence Erlbaum Associates Publishers.

Borrego, M., & Henderson, C. (2014). Increasing the use of evidence-based teaching in STEM higher education: A comparison of eight change strategies. *Journal of Engineering Education, 103*(2), 220–252.

Bovey, W. H., & Hede, A. (2001). Resistance to organizational change: The role of cognitive and affective processes. *Leadership & Organization Development Journal, 22*(8), 372–382. doi:10.1108/01437730110410099

Brannigan, A., & Zwerman, W. (2001). The real "Hawthorne effect." *Society, 38*(2), 55–60.

Bright, D. S., Cooperrider, D. L., & Galloway, W. B. (2006). Appreciative inquiry in the office of research and development. *Public Performance & Management Review, 29*(3), 285–306.

Bruce, K., & Nyland, C. (2011). Elton Mayo and the deification of human relations. *Organization Studies, 32*(3), 383–405. doi:10.1177/0170840610397478

Buch, K., & Wetzel, D. K. (2001). Analyzing and realigning organizational culture. *Leadership & Organization Development Journal, 22*(1), 40–43. doi:10.1108/01437730110380219

Burke, W. (1994). Diagnostic models for organization development. In, *Diagnosis for organizational change: Methods and models* (pp. 53–84). New York, NY: Guilford Press.

Burke, W., & Litwin, G. H. (1992). A causal model of organizational performance and change. *Journal of Management, 18*(3), 523–545. doi:10.1177/014920639201800306

Byrne, Z. S., Palmer, C. E., Smith, C. L., & Weidert, J. M. (2011). The engaged employee face of organizations. In M. A. Sarlak (Ed.), *The new faces of organizations in the 21st century* (Vol. 1, pp. 93–135). Canada: NAISIT Publishers.

Cameron, K. S., Quinn, R. E., DeGraff, J., & Thakor, A. V. (2006). *Competing values leadership: Creating value in organizations.* Northampton, MA: Edward Elgar Publishing.

Campbell, J., & Göritz, A. S. (2013). Culture corrupts! A qualitative study of organizational culture in corrupt organizations. *Journal of Business Ethics, 120*(3), 291–311. doi:10.1007/s10551-013-1665-7

Choi, M., & Ruona, W. A. (2011). Individual readiness for organizational change and its implications for human resource and organization development. *Human Resource Development Review, 10*(1), 46–73. doi:10.1177/1534484310384957

Coghlan, D., & Brannick, T. (2014). *Doing action research in your own organization.* Thousand Oaks, CA: Sage.

Cooke, R. A., & Rousseau, D. M. (1988). Behavioral norms and expectations: A quantitative approach to the assessment of organizational culture. *Group & Organization Studies, 13*(3), 245–273. doi:10.1177/105960118801300302

Cooperrider, D. L., & Whitney, D. (2005). Appreciative inquiry: A positive revolution in change. San Francisco, CA: Berrett-Koehler Publishers.

Creswell, J. W. (1998). *Qualitative inquiry and research design: Choosing among five traditions.* Thousand Oaks, CA: SAGE.

Danışman, A. (2010). Good intentions and failed implementations: Understanding culture-based resistance to organizational change. *European Journal of Work and Organizational Psychology, 19*(2), 200–220. doi:10.1080/13594320902850541

Deal, T., & Kennedy, A. (1996). Corporate tribes: Identifying the cultures. In J. Billsberry (Ed.), *The effective manager: Perspectives and illustrations* (pp. 88–100). Thousand Oaks, CA: Sage.

Degeling, P., Kennedy, J., & Hill, M. (1998). Do professional subcultures set the limits of hospital reform? *Clinician in Management, 7,* 89–98.

Denison, D. R. (1996a). What is the difference between organizational culture and organizational climate? A native's point of view on a decade of paradigm wars. *Academy Of Management Review, 21*(3), 619–654. doi:10.2307/258997

Denison, D. R. (1996b). *Corporate culture and organizational effectiveness.* New York, NY: Wiley.

Denning, S. (July 23, 2011). How do you change an organizational culture? Retrieved from https://www.forbes.com/sites/stevedenning/2011/07/23/how-do-you-change-an-organizational-culture/#10692fa39dc5

Druskat, V. U., & Wolff, S. B. (2001). Building the emotional intelligence of groups. *Harvard Business Review, 79(3)*, 80–90.

Erwin, D. G., & Garman, A. N. (2010). Resistance to organizational change: Linking research and practice. *Leadership & Organization Development Journal, 31*(1), 39–56. doi:10.1108/01437731011010371

Felten, E. (2008, November 7). Dressed for Duty. *Wall Street Journal - Eastern Edition.* p. W11.

Ford, J. D., & Ford, L. W. (2010). Stop blaming resistance to change and start using it. *Organizational Dynamics, 39*(1), 24–36. doi:10.1016/j.orgdyn.2009.10.002

Ford, J. D., Ford, L. W., & D'Amelio, A. (2008). Resistance to change: The rest of the story. *The Academy of Management Review, 33*(2), 362–377. doi:10.2307/20159402

French, W. L., & Bell, C. H. Jr. (1999). *Organization development: Behavioral science interventions for organization improvement* (6th ed.). Upper Saddle River, NJ: Prentice-Hall.

Furst, S. A., & Cable, D. M. (2008). Employee resistance to organizational change: Managerial influence tactics and leader-member exchange. *Journal Of Applied Psychology, 93*(2), 453–462. doi:10.1037/0021-9010.93.2.453

Garvin, D. A., Edmondson, A. C., & Gino, F. (2008). Is yours a learning organization? *Harvard Business Review, 86*(3), 109–116.

Golembiewski, R. T., Billingsley, K., & Yeager, S. (1975). Measuring change and persistence in human affairs: Types of change generated by OD designs. *Journal Of Applied Behavioral Science, 12*(2), 133–157. doi:10.1177/002188637601200201

Griffin, M. A., Rafferty, A. E., & Mason, C. M. (2004). Who started this? Investigating different sources of organizational change. *Journal of Business and Psychology, 18*(4), 555–570. doi:10.1023/B:JOBU.0000028451.22685.a4

Guion, R. M. (1973). A note on organizational climate. *Organizational Behavior and Human Performance, 9,* 120–125.

Halpern, D., Osofsky, S., & Peskin, M. I. (1989). Taylorism revisited and revisited for the 1990s. *Industrial Management, 31*(1), 20.

Hayes, J. (2005). WingHouse soars to victory in lawsuit with Hooters. *Nation's Restaurant News, 39*(1), 1–79.

Herr, K., & Anderson, G. L. (2014). *The action research dissertation: A guide for students and faculty.* Thousand Oaks, CA: Sage.

Higgins, J. M. (2005). The eight 'S's of successful strategy execution. *Journal of Change Management, 5*(1), 3–13. doi:10.1080/14697010500036064

Higgins, J. M., & McAllaster, C. (2004). If you want strategic change, don't forget to change your cultural artifacts. *Journal of Change Management, 4*(1), 63–73. doi:10.1080/1469701032000154926

Higgins, J. M., Mcallaster, C., Certo, S. C., & Gilbert, J. P. (2006). Using cultural artifacts to change and perpetuate strategy. *Journal of Change Management, 6*(4), 397–415. doi:10.1080/14697010601087057

Hofstede, G. (1980). *Culture's consequences: International differences in work-related values.* Beverly Hills, CA: Sage.

Horsburgh, M., Perkins, R., Coyle, B., & Degeling, P. (2006). The professional subcultures of students entering medicine, nursing and pharmacy programmes. *Journal Of Interprofessional Care, 20*(4), 425–431. doi:10.1080/13561820600805233

Hultman, K. (1998). *Making change irresistible: Overcoming resistance to change in your organization.* Palo Alto, CA: Davies-Black Publishing.

Huse, E. F., & Cummings, T. G. (1985). *Organization development and change* (3rd ed.). St. Paul, MN: West.

Jaffe, D. T., Scott, C. D., & Tobe, G. R. (1994). *Rekindling commitment: How to revitalize yourself, your work, and your organization.* San Francisco, CA: Jossey-Bass.

Jermier, J. M., Slocum, J. W., Fry, L. W., & Gaines, J. (1991). Organizational subcultures in a soft bureaucracy: Resistance behind the myth and facade of an official culture. *Organization Science, 2*(2), 170–194. doi:10.1287/orsc.2.2.170

Jones, A. P., & James, L. R. (1979). Psychological climate: Dimensions and relationships of individual and aggregated work environment perceptions. *Organizational Behavior and Human Performance, 23,* 201–250.

Jung, T., Scott, T., Davies, H. O., Bower, P., Whalley, D., McNally, R., & Mannion, R. (2009). Instruments for exploring organizational culture: A review of the literature. *Public Administration Review, 69*(6), 1087–1096. doi:10.1111/j.1540-6210.2009.02066.x

Karuppusami, G., & Gandhinathan, R. (2006). Pareto analysis of critical success factors of total quality management: A literature review and analysis. *TQM Magazine, 18*(4), 372–385.

Katz, D., & Kahn, R. L. (1966). *The social psychology of organizations.* Oxford, England: Wiley.

Katz, J. H., & Miller, F. A. (1996). Coaching leaders through culture change. *Consulting Psychology Journal: Practice and Research, 48*(2), 104–114. doi:10.1037/1061-4087.48.2.104

Katzenbach, J. R., Steffen, I., & Kronley, C. (2012). Cultural change that sticks. *Harvard Business Review, 90*(7/8), 110–117.

Kelman, H. C. (1961). Processes of opinion change. *Public Opinion Quarterly, 25*(1), 57–78. doi:10.1086/266996

Kotter, J. P. (1995). Leading change: Why transformation efforts fail. *Harvard Business Review, 73,* 59–67.

Kotter, J. P., Heskett, J. L. (1992). *Corporate culture and performance.* New York, NY: Free Press.

Kotter, J. P., & Schlesinger, L. A. (2008). Choosing Strategies for Change. *Harvard Business Review, 86*(7/8), 130–139.

Kozlowski, S. W. J., Chao, G. T., Smith, E. M., & Hedlund, J. (1993). Organizational downsizing: Strategies, interventions, and research implications. In C. L. Cooper & I. T. Robertson (Eds.), *International review of industrial and organizational psychology* (pp. 263–332). New York, NY: Wiley.

Levy, A., & Merry, U. (1986). Organizational transformation: Approaches, strategies, and theories. New York, NY: Praeger Publishers.

Lewin, K. (1947). Group decision and social change. In T. M. Newcomb & E. L. Hartley (Eds.), *Readings in social psychology* (pp. 340–344). New York, NY: Holt, Rinehart, & Winston.

Lewin, K. (1951). *Field theory in social science: Selected theoretical papers.* In D. Cartwright (Ed.). Oxford, England: Harpers.

Lewin, K. K., Lippitt, R. R., & White, R. K. (1939). Patterns of aggressive behavior in experimentally created "social climates". *The Journal of Social Psychology, 10,* 271–299.

Litwin, G. H., & Stringer, R. R. (1968). *Motivation and organizational climate.* Oxford, England: Harvard U., Graduate School of Business.

Lofquist, E. (2011). Doomed to fail: A case study of change implementation collapse in the norwegian civil aviation industry. *Journal of Change Management, 11*(2), 223–243. doi:10.1080/14697017.2010.527853

Mabin, V. J., Forgeson, S., & Green, L. (2001). Harnessing resistance: using the theory of constraints to assist change management. *Journal of European Industrial Training, 25*(2–4), 168.

Margulies, N., & Raia, A. P. (1978). *Conceptual foundations of organizational development.* New York, NY: McGraw-Hill.

Mayer, J. D., Salovey, P., & Caruso, D. R. (2004). Emotional intelligence: Theory, findings, and implications. *Psychological Inquiry, 15*(3), 197–215.

Mayo, E. (1933). *The human problems of an industrial civilization.* New York, NY: The Macmillan Company.

Mayo, E. (1945). *The social problems of an industrial civilization.* Boston: Harvard University.

Morgan, P. I., & Ogbonna, E. (2008). Subcultural dynamics in transformation: A multi-perspective study of healthcare professionals. *Human Relations, 61*(1), 39–65. doi:10.1177/0018726707085945

Msweli-Mbanga, P. P., & Potwana, N. N. (2006). Modelling participation, resistance to change, and organisational citizenship behaviour: A South African case. *South African Journal Of Business Management, 37*(1), 21–29.

O'Reilly, C. A., Chatman, J., & Caldwell, D. F. (1991). People and organizational culture: A profile comparison approach to assessing person-organization fit. *Academy of Management Journal, 34*(3), 487–516.

Oreg, S. (2006). Personality, context, and resistance to organizational change. *European Journal of Work and Organizational Psychology, 15*(1), 73–101. doi:10.1080/13594320500451247

Ostroff, C., Kinicki, A. J., & Tarmkins, M. M. (2003). Organizational culture and climate. In W. C. Borman, D. R. Ilgen, & R. J. Klimoski (Eds.), *Handbook of psychology: Industrial and organizational psychology* (Vol.12, pp.565–593).

Packard, D. (1995). *The HP way: How Bill Hewlett and I built our company.* New York, NY: HarperBusiness.

Palthe, J., & Kossek, E. (2003). Subcultures and employment modes: Translating HR strategy into practice. *Journal of Organizational Change Management, 16*(3), 287–308. doi:10.1108/09534810310475532

Peters, T. (1988). *Thriving on chaos: Handbook for a management revolution.* New York, NY: Harper.

Peters, T. J., & Waterman, R. H. Jr. (1982). How the best-run companies turn so-so performers into big winners. *Management Review, 71*(11), 8–17

Petrini, C., & Hultman, K. E. (1995). Scaling the wall of resistance. *Training & Development, 49*(10), 15.

Plowman, D., Baker, L. T., Beck, T. E., Kulkarni, M., Solansky, S., & Travis, D. (2007). Radical change accidentally: The emergence and amplification of small change. *Academy of Management Journal, 50*(3), 515–543. doi:10.5465/AMJ.2007.25525647

Pollack, J., & Pollack, R. (2015). Using Kotter's eight stage process to manage an organisational change program: Presentation and practice. *Systemic Practice & Action Research, 28*(1), 51–66.

Porras, J. I., & Hoffer, S. J. (1986). Common behavior changes in successful organization development efforts. *Journal of Applied Behavioral Science, 22*(4), 477–494. doi:10.1177/002188638602200409

Porras, J. I., & Silvers, R. C. (1991). Organization development and transformation. *Annual Review of Psychology, 42,* 51–78. doi:10.1146/annurev.ps.42.020191.000411

Porras, J. I., & Robertson, P. J. (1992). Organizational development: Theory, practice, and research. In M. D. Dunnette, L. M. Hough (Eds.), *Handbook of industrial and organizational psychology, Vol. 3 (2nd ed.)* (pp. 719–822). Palo Alto, CA: Consulting Psychologists Press.

Pratt, M. G., & Rafaeli, A. (1997). Organizational dress as a symbol of multi-layered social identities. *Academy of Management Journal, 40*(4), 862–898. doi:10.2307/256951

Pratt, M. G., & Rafaeli, A. (2001). Symbols as a language of organizational relationships. *Research In Organizational Behavior,* 2393.

Pulakos, E. D., Mueller-Hanson, R. A., O'Leary, R. S., & Meyrowitz, M. M. (2012). *Building a high-performance culture: A fresh look at performance management.* SHRM Foundation Publication.

Quinn, R. E., & Cameron, K. (1983). Organizational life cycles and shifting criteria of effectiveness: Some preliminary evidence. *Management Science, 29*(1), 33.

Quinn, R. E., & Cameron, K. S. (2006). *Diagnosing and changing organizational culture: Based on the Competing Values Framework* (revised edition). San Francisco, CA: Jossey-Bass.

Quinn, R. E., & Rohrbaugh, J. (1983). A spatial model of effectiveness criteria: Toward a competing values approach to organizational analysis. *Management Science, 29,* 363–377.

Quinn, R. E., & Spreitzer, G. M. (1991). The psychometrics of the competing values culture instrument and an analysis of the impact of organizational culture on quality of life. In R. W. Woodman & W. A. Pasmore (Eds.), *Research in organizational change and development,* (Vol. 5, pp. 115–142). Greenwich, CT: JAI Press.

Reddy-Best, K. L. (2018). LGBTQ women, appearance negotiations, and workplace dress codes. *Journal of Homosexuality, 65*(5), 615–639.

Rentsch, J. R. (1990). Climate and culture: Interaction and qualitative differences in organizational meanings. *Journal of Applied Psychology, 75,* 668–681.

Richardson, A. (2009). Get in line. *Design Week, 24*(2), 32.

Rickatson, S. (2013). Culture change enables ambitious growth at Nelsons. *Strategic HR Review, 12*(5), 241–244. doi:10.1108/SHR-03-2013-0031

Roethlisberger, F. J., & Dickson, W. J. (1939). *Management and the worker: An account of a research program conducted by the Western Electric Company, Hawthorne Works, Chicago.* Cambridge, MA: Harvard University Press.

Ryan, R. M., & Deci, E. L. (2000). Self-determination theory and the facilitation of intrinsic motivation, social development, and well-being. *American Psychologist, 55,* 68–78. doi: 10.1037//0003-066X.55.1.68

Schein, E. H. (1988). *Process consultation: Its role in organization development (Vol. 1).* Boston, MA: Addison-Wesley.

Schein, E. H. (1990). Organizational culture. *American Psychologist, 45,* 109–119.

Schein, E. H. (2000). Sense and nonsense about culture and climate. In N. M. Ashkanasy, C. P. M. Wilderom, & M. F. Peterson (Eds.), *Handbook of organizational culture & climate* (pp. xxiii-xxx). Thousand Oaks, CA: Sage.

Schneider, B. (1987). The people make the place. *Personnel Psychology, 40*(3), 437–453. doi:10.1111/j.1744-6570.1987.tb00609.x

Schneider, B. (1990). The climate for service: An application of the climate construct. In B. Schneider (Ed.), *Organizational climate and culture* (pp. 383–412). San Francisco, CA: Jossey-Bass.

Schneider, B. (2000). The psychological life of organizations. In N. M. Ashkanasy, C. P. M. Wilderom, & M. F. Peterson (Eds.), *Handbook of organizational culture & climate* (pp. xvii-xxi). Thousand Oaks, CA: Sage.

Schneider, B., Brief, A. P., & Guzzo, R. A. (1996). Creating a climate and culture for sustainable organizational change. *Organizational Dynamics, 24*(4), 7–19. doi: 10.1016/S0090-2616(96)90010-8

Schneider, B., Goldstein, H. W., & Smith, D. (1995). The ASA framework: An update. *Personnel Psychology, 48*(4), 747–773. doi:10.1111/j.1744-6570.1995.tb01780.x

Scott, T., Mannion, R., Davies, H., & Marshall, M. (2003). The quantitative measurement of organizational culture in health care: A review of the available instruments. *Health Services Research, 38*(3), 923–945. doi:10.1111/1475-6773.00154

Self, D. R., & Schraeder, M. (2009). Enhancing the success of organizational change: Matching readiness strategies with sources of resistance. *Leadership & Organization Development Journal, 30*(2), 167–182. doi:10.1108/01437730910935765

Senge, P. M. (1990). *The fifth discipline: The art and practice of the learning organization.* New York, NY: Doubleday/Currency.

Shotter, J. (1987). Cognitive psychology, 'Taylorism', and the manufacture of unemployment. In A. Costall, A. Still (Eds.), *Cognitive psychology in question* (pp. 44–52). New York, NY: St Martin's Press.

Skinner, B. F. (1972). *Cumulative record: A selection of papers (3rd ed.).* East Norwalk, CT: Appleton-Century-Crofts.

Spicer, D. P. (2011). Changing culture: A case study of a merger using cognitive mapping. *Journal of Change Management, 11*(2), 245–264. doi:10.1080/14697017.2010.550266

Stowell, F. (2013). The Appreciative inquiry method – A suitable candidate for action research? *Systems Research and Behavioral Science, 30,* 15–30. doi:10.1002/sres.2117

Taylor, F. (1911). *The principles of scientific management.* New York, NY: Harper and Brothers.

Thumin, F. J., & Thumin, L. J. (2011). The measurement and interpretation of organizational climate. *Journal of Psychology: Interdisciplinary and Applied, 145*(2), 93–109. doi:10.1080/00223980.2010.538754

Tredgold, R. F. (1959). Human relations in industry. *International Social Science Journal, 11*(1), 34–43.

Trice, H. M., & Beyer, J. M. (1984). Studying organizational cultures through rites and ceremonials. *The Academy of Management Review, 9*(4), 653–669. doi:10.2307/258488

Trice, H. M., & Beyer, J. M. (1993). *The cultures of work organizations.* Englewood Cliffs, NJ: Prentice Hall.

Uys, P. M. (2010). Implementing an Open Source Learning Management System: A Critical Analysis of Change Strategies. *Australasian Journal of Educational Technology, 26*(7), 980–995.

van Dam, K., Oreg, S., & Schyns, B. (2008). Daily work contexts and resistance to organisational change: The role of leader-member exchange, development climate, and change process characteristics. *Applied Psychology: An International Review, 57*(2), 313–334. doi:10.1111/j.1464-0597.2007.00311.x

Van De Ven, A. H., & Poole, M. (1995). Explaining development and change in organizations. *Academy of Management Review, 20*(3), 510–540. doi:10.5465/AMR.1995.9508080329

Van de Ven, A. H., & Sun, K. (2011). Breakdowns in implementing models of organization change. *The Academy of Management Perspectives, 25*(3), 58–74. doi:10.5465/AMP.2011.63886530

van Dijk, R., & van Dick, R. (2009). Navigating organizational change: Change leaders, employee resistance and work-based identities. *Journal of Change Management, 9*(2), 143–163. doi:10.1080/14697010902879087

Van Maanen, J. (1975). Police organization: A longitudinal examination of job attitudes in an urban police department. *Administrative Science Quarterly, 20*(2), 207–228. doi:10.2307/2391695

Walinga, J. (2008). Toward a theory of change readiness: The roles of appraisal, focus, and perceived control. *Journal Of Applied Behavioral Science, 44*(3), 315–347. doi:10.1177/0021886308318967

Weick, K. E., & Quinn, R. E. (1999). Organizational change and development. *Annual Review Of Psychology, 50,* 361–386. doi:10.1146/annurev.psych.50.1.361

Whitehead, T. N. (1935). Social relationships in the factory: A study of an industrial group. *Human Factors (London), 9*381–9382.

Whitehead, T. N. (1938). *The industrial worker.* Cambridge, MA: Harvard University Press.

Wright, J. G., Roche, A., & Khoury, A. E. (2010). Improving on-time surgical starts in an operating room. *Canadian Journal of Surgery, 53*(3), 167–170

Xenikou, A., & Simosi, M. (2006). Organizational culture and transformational leadership as predictors of business unit performance. *Journal of Managerial Psychology, 21*(6), 566–579. doi:10.1108/02683940610684409

CHAPTER 13

The Future and How to Get There: Strategy

Learning Outcomes

After studying this chapter, you should be able to:

1. Define organizational strategy.

2. Identify external and internal factors that drive an organization's strategy.

3. Identify stakeholders and critique their investments in strategy.

4. Explain the role of the leader in developing and changing strategy

Mini-Quiz: Organizational Strategy

As an introduction to this chapter, please take the following mini-quiz (answers are in the back of the book). As you read the questions and consider the answers *before* diving into the chapter, you'll challenge yourself before you master the content, a process that helps facilitate learning for long-term retention. Some questions may have more than one correct answer. Don't worry if you cannot answer all questions correctly on your first try. By the time you read through the chapter and spend some of your own time thinking about these concepts, you should be able to determine the best answers. Try the quiz again after you finish reading the chapter.

1. Fill in the blanks to complete this diagram:

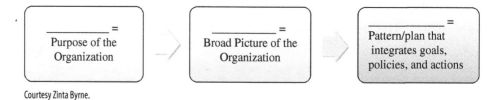

Courtesy Zinta Byrne.

2. In the 1980s, organizational strategists began to focus on processes like decision-making, biases, heuristics, and attribution errors. This movement added what focus to organizational strategy that still predominates today?
   a. Transactional leadership
   b. Cognitive perspective
   c. Organizational structure
   d. Organizational change

3. Developing organizational strategy is an internal effort, but there are important *external* factors to consider. Which of these external factors should be considered, as it will shape the organization's strategy?
   a. Technology
   b. Allocation of resources
   c. Politics
   d. Core Competencies

4. Who is likely to be invested in the organization's strategy?
   a. Customers
   b. Suppliers and distributors

c. Frontline workers

d. The company leadership team

5. "Strategic leadership" is a term often used to describe what?
   a. Ability to anticipate the future
   b. Empowering of others in the organization
   c. Focusing on the tasks that must be accomplished for organizational success
   d. Maintaining current status to secure market share

Overview

Successful companies know who their customers are. These companies consistently meet and exceed their clients' wants and desires, most often because they have a well-developed strategy that achieves the organization's vision (dream for the future).

Strategy, a discipline steeped in the tradition and literature of business, guides the direction of the organization toward effectively using its core competencies (e.g., resources and capabilities) in a way that helps the organization exceed customer expectations.

Strategy:

1. informs the structure of the organization (Chapter 11)

2. informs the types of leaders the organization should have (Chapter 9)

3. informs how organizational change is implemented (Chapter 12)

4. establishes whether teams are appropriate for achieving the organization's goals (Chapter 7)

Because of how strategy guides the direction of the organization, "Structure follows strategy" (Bartlett & Ghoshal, 1994, p.79). However, organizational culture is critical to the implementation of strategy and effectively captured by the phrase "Culture eats strategy for breakfast," a phrase attributed to Peter Drucker, a well-known management expert in the United States. The statement essentially means that your strategy is worthless if you do not have a culture that supports it and if your organizations' employees cannot implement the strategy.

Given the overarching and integrative role of strategy, it is fitting that the topic occupies the last chapter of this textbook. Note that the language of Strategy is oriented toward management and leadership; hence, much of the terminology comes from business.

If you haven't yet been exposed to management or business classes or readings, you might need to look up a few words as you read this chapter.

What Is Organizational Strategy?

Strategy (Figure 13.1), a statement with a goal and a series of actions/plans to get to that goal, determines product and service offerings, the allocation of resources, and influences in which industries or countries the organization

FIGURE 13.1 What Is Strategy?

© UMI Studio/Shutterstock.com

operates. Goals can include organizational performance or financial return to shareholders.

Defining organizational strategy may be harder than just a simple statement about a plan to achieve a goal because it has many different definitions and uses in organizational language. For example, strategy can be defined as the organization's market *position*, the kind of products and markets the organization pursues for competitive advantage (i.e., inimitable value). Thus, as a position, strategy refers to where the organization places itself within the environment (Mintzberg, 1987). For instance, Apple, Inc. positions itself more within the consumer market than the commercial market, whereas IBM Corporation positions itself more within the commercial or industrial market than the consumer market.

Probably the most commonly understood definition of strategy is that it is a *plan*. When we think of the word strategy, we think of intent (Mintzberg, 1987), or a preconceived path to achieve a particular goal. A good strategy states the end-goal and the necessary means, tactics, or schemes to achieve that goal. The goal could be to dominate a specific market or segment of the market, thereby incorporating the idea of position into strategy as a plan. Harvard University provides a good example of a strategy as "plan" (Table 13.1), with a well-developed (75 pages worth!) strategy for student, research, and overall school success.

TABLE 13.1 Sample Strategies of Organizations

Companies	Notes About the Strategy	Strategy (Taken verbatim from the company websites, June, 2014)
FedEx Corporation FedEx provides worldwide transportation, e-commerce, and business services, and is based in the United States.	Their strategy fits best under the ploy definition.	The unique FedEx operating strategy works seamlessly—and simultaneously—on three levels. • *Compete collectively* by standing as one brand worldwide and speaking with one voice. • *Operate independently* by focusing on our independent networks to meet distinct customer needs. • *Manage collaboratively* by working together to sustain loyal relationships with our workforce, customers, and investors.

(Continued)

TABLE 13.1 Sample Strategies of Organizations (*Continued*)

Companies	Notes About the Strategy	Strategy (Taken verbatim from the company websites, June, 2014)
Harvard University Harvard University is in the United States of America.	The strategy was approved in 2001 and designed to shape the school for 10–20 years in the future. The strategy document is 75 pages long; thus, the statement on the right is the short version. Their strategy fits best under the plan definition.	Dramatically shrink first-year class sizes, increase financial aid, strengthen connections to the legal practice, expand research and teaching in international law, and improve the School's infrastructure.
IBM IBM is an international information technology and consulting company headquartered in the United States of America.	IBM has several business strategies that are listed on their website. Their strategy fits best under the ploy and position definitions.	We are making a new future for our clients, our industry and our company. This is how: (a) we are making markets by transforming industries and professions with data; (b) we are remaking enterprise IT for the era of cloud; (c) we are enabling systems of engagement for enterprises. And we are leading by example.
Sanergy Sanergy provides hygienic sustainable sanitation systems to Kenya's urban communities and is headquartered in Kenya. Sanergy is considered one of the top 10 innovative companies in Africa in 2014, according to *Fast Company Magazine*	Their strategy fits best under the perspective definition.	Sanergy builds healthy, prosperous communities by making hygienic sanitation affordable and accessible throughout Africa's informal settlements.
Sanofi Sanofi is a global healthcare company and pharmaceuticals developer (including vaccines for people and animals), headquartered in France.	Under each of the strategy priorities (bulleted list in the column on the right), a full paragraph explains their priority and direction. The full paragraph can be found on their website. Their strategy fits best under the position and plan definition.	• Be a global healthcare leader with synergistic platforms. • Bring innovative products to the market. • Seize value-enhancing growth opportunities. • Adapt structure for future challenges and opportunities.
Equinor (used to be Statoil) Equinor is an international energy company headquartered in Norway.	The strategy shows up on their website. Their strategy fits best under the position definition.	(from their website): We're looking for new ways to utilize our expertise in the energy industry, exploring opportunities in new energy as well as driving innovation in oil and gas around the world. We know that the future has to be low carbon. Our ambition is to be the world's most carbon-efficient oil and gas producer, as well as driving innovation in offshore wind and renewables.

Courtesy Zinta Byrne.

You don't have to be a fan of Starbucks Coffee to notice how many of them there are within a square block radius in big U.S. cities like Seattle, Washington, San Francisco or New York.

In the educational space, Harvard's plan for student, research, and school success might also be a means for beating the competition—schools against which Harvard rivals for top quality students (e.g., Stanford University). When the goal is to outmaneuver the competition, the strategy is considered a *ploy* (Mintzberg, 1987). Strategy as a ploy may be illustrated by a retailer opening a store location on every major street corner so the competitor cannot easily occupy that same space. We might conclude that Starbucks Coffee Company uses this strategy because of their multiple locations in a single community, many times within a one-mile radius of one another. With such location saturation, competing coffee shops have a tough time setting up shop in that same area and attracting customers, unless they have something unique to offer that Starbucks cannot.

As a consequence of Starbucks's actions of opening many coffee shops in a single community, they have established a pattern of capitalizing on principles of familiarity (i.e., mere exposure, just being exposed to something a number of times increases your comfort with it; Zajonc, 1968) and ease of access. Thus, strategy can also be a *pattern* of behavior or notable repetition of actions that an organization takes (Mintzberg, 1987) indicating a particular direction, even if that direction was not originally stated as a plan. When an organization makes decisions that end up looking consistent with previous decisions, the pattern of choices becomes the perceived organizational strategy. The consequence is that the stated strategy could look different from what people perceive the strategy to be, which can create conflict when the two are at odds with one another. This may have been the case for Walmart.

An example of a pattern of behavior creating perceived strategy may be how Walmart Stores, a large U.S.-based multinational retail corporation, became known as a ruthless employer partly because of the its low wages and lack of health-care offerings to employees. In the early 2000s, the retailer was heavily criticized for exploiting workers, ruining suppliers, and destroying communities (Foley, 2008). Consequently, Walmart's strategy was strongly associated with cutting costs at the expense of its employees (Mattera, 2013), as opposed to what Walmart stated: being a discount store that achieves low costs through expert market negotiations (their statements of strategy conveyed on their website). In response to the damage to its reputation, Walmart made many changes to the extent that "fewer Americans might now sign up to the notion that Wal-Mart is evil; a handful might even sign up to a notion that Wal-Mart could be part of the solution to many of the problems facing the US and the planet" (Foley, 2008, p. 46). Wal-Mart and Walmart are the same—the company was originally named "Wal-Mart Stores" but later just adopted the "Walmart" name.

Walmart Stores also serves as a good example of strategy as a position because their strategy places them as the largest low-cost leader, the biggest discount store. They are known for having prices that undercut all others, making them a fierce competitor in every community where they locate a store (Mattera, 2013).

In contrast to strategy defined as a position, plan, ploy, or pattern, when strategy is defined as a *perspective* it is considered a way of perceiving the world and operating based on that perception (Mintzberg, 1987). For example, organizations may adopt a focus on technology, engineering, or on customer service (e.g., being "the" premiere service provider). The strategy is a way of being or thinking about the "personality" or predominant culture of the organization. For example,

Sanergy (Table 13.1) perceives that hygiene is essential for quality of life and can be achieved while honoring environmental sustainability. In comparison, a company such as Sanofi (Table 13.1) has a strategy defined as a position. They are a leading provider of pharmaceutical drugs and vaccines.

In summary, organizational strategy is the plan that integrates an organization's goals, policies, and actions toward a particular goal, in a cohesive and consistent manner (Mintzberg, 1987). A well-formed strategy gives the organization direction for how it should allocate its resources, how it should consider internal and external drivers (discussed below), and how it should position itself against the competition. To provide comprehensive direction, strategies can exist at different levels of the organization, such as at the business unit, corporate, and global levels. Furthermore, statements of strategy usually cover the entire organization, with sections providing individual strategy statements about each component of the business or level.

Some examples of strategy statements, shown in Table 13.1, may help clarify what strategy is.

With such variety in how strategy statements are phrased and their breadth (or narrowness) of focus, designing an effective strategy may be a challenge; however, there are a few guidelines that may help.

> A strategy for an organization is similar to your plan for achieving a goal, such as college or graduate degree completion. The strategy, like your plan, establishes how you go from point A to point B, and what resources (you either have or need) are required to get there.

Exercise 13.1

Explain in your own words what organizational strategy is?

What Makes an Effective or Competitive Strategy?

An effective strategy includes the most important goal the organization should achieve, the policies that guide or limit actions toward that goal, and the major programs that will help accomplish the goal (Porter, 1996). Remember from Chapter 3 on Motivation that setting well-defined goals motivates you as an individual to take action. Similarly, with organizational strategy, goal development and articulation is an integral part of developing an effective strategy. Just as an individual goal moves you in a new direction, so does the organizational strategy move the organization toward a desired state. Hence, an effective strategy is not about what the organization already knows it can achieve or has already accomplished. Strategies are about what is unknown and where the organization wants to go; therefore, an effective strategy tackles the unpredictable and the unknowable. For example, in the strategy statements noted in Table 13.1, each organization makes a statement about its future success—an unpredictable and unknowable outcome. Usually, the future success incorporates some competitiveness, since business survival generally relies on differentiating oneself from the competition.

A sustainable competitive strategy defines how the organization is different from the opposition, and different in a way that others cannot duplicate (Barney, 1991). Actions must be taken to ensure distinctiveness from what the competition is doing, usually by exploiting a unique internal strength. For example, a potential source of competitive advantage for an organization is its non-inimitable

Why is strategy essential for organizations?

(i.e., valuable but cannot be copied) resources (Barney, 1991), such as how it combines distribution mechanisms to achieve world-class delivery faster than anyone else (e.g., Federal Express). Another competitive advantage may be unique location that creates some capability none others can easily duplicate (e.g., mining). Google, Inc. is known for its one of a kind organizational culture that gives it an advantage over similar organizations when it comes to hiring the brightest, most innovative employees. Thus, competitive advantage can be achieved through a variety of means that are generally connected to the strategy.

In addition to focusing on what makes for unique advantage, strategy helps determine what *not* to do, what trade-offs to make, and helps guide the effective use of the organization's resources. For example, if part of the organization's goal is to be sustainable (i.e., ensuring long-term survival), which involves knowing or understanding the competition's strengths and planning ahead to outlast the competition, the strategy must guide the organization away from succumbing to its internal weaknesses. Competitive advantage is achieved and maintained by having a strategy that not only capitalizes on the organization's core strengths (e.g., reacting to opportunities), but also minimizes external threats and internal weaknesses (Barney, 1991). Organizations want a strategy that helps them be successful for tomorrow, as the economy and market changes (see Equinor for a good example of a company that adjusted its strategy to address market change).

Most effective and competitive strategies, therefore, are designed with a horizon that fits within their goals and industry. For example, larger companies may have a 5–10-year horizon (though this has been shrinking to 2–5), whereas start-up or small entrepreneurial companies may have a 1–2-year horizon. Mining companies that require up to 7–10 years just to develop the mine, or companies entering a country with a high barrier of entry and slow development for profitable local presence (e.g., Japan, India, China) may have 15–20 year, or more, horizons. A high barrier of entry is a market that is difficult to get started in for numerous reasons, including fitting in with the local customs and norms that ban outsiders (Bain, 1956).

Good strategies set a plan for an organization's horizon but are not rigid about how to get there. Good strategies challenge preconceived notions of what is achievable and what is not (Porter, 1996). A good strategy pushes the organization beyond where people think it can go, yet incorporates the understanding that it will do so using the existing or obtainable resources and acquiring new strengths. New strengths are obtained either through growing people or by merging and buying other organizations of people with core competencies necessary to achieve the strategy. A good strategy helps organizations align their activities to achieve success by identifying what should be measured and tracked. For example, in project-based organizations, where the income is based on completing projects (e.g., consulting firm) and not on a product per se (e.g., appliance), it is essential for the strategy to include how organizational processes and people combine to achieve successful project execution (see Cound & Meyer, 2015, for an example). Brandenburger (2019) argues that a good strategy needs creativity, which means jarring your thinking to create a breakthrough strategy. The author outlines four paths for strategy development: contrast (challenge assumptions), combination (connect things that are in conflict), constraint (using constraints as strengths), and context (find how your problem was solved in a different context). A good strategy, therefore,

Take a look at https://www.ted.com/talks/martin_reeves_your_strategy_needs_a_strategy to get a different and somewhat humorous perspective on strategy.

crafts a novel approach (See Brandenburger, 2019 for clear details on using the four paths). Examples of companies mastering the different paths as taken from Brandenburger's article include: contrast - PayPal, Netflix, and DonorsChoose.org; combination - WeChat, BMW Daimler, Nike + iPod Sport Kit, Nest's Intelligent Home Thermostat uses Amazon's Alexa, and machine text analysis or machine learning; constraint - Tesla, Bonobos, farm to table restaurants, and Audi's racing team; context - Velcro, Intel, Teflon, HAX, and extreme sports.

Because strategy includes the ideas of futures and plans, it is not unusual for organizations to confuse vision, mission, and strategy in their statements of how they will achieve their future success. In many cases, organizations combine vision and mission; however, the concepts are considered distinct.

How Is Strategy Different from Vision and Mission

Vision refers to the organization's long-range goals. Mission is the purpose of the organization. Strategy says how the organization will achieve the Vision.

Vision refers to a very broad picture of the future, what the organization intends to become (Middleton & Gorzynski, 2006). Vision provides the long-range goals for the organization (de Kluyver & Pearce, 2009). A few examples of vision statements include Mental Health Partners' (MHP), a nonprofit mental health-care provider in Colorado, USA, says "healthy minds, healthy communities." Amazon.com's (online retailer based in Washington, USA) vision is "Amazon strives to be Earth's most customer-centric company where people can find and discover virtually anything they want to buy online. Toyota Corporation's (automotive manufacturer based in Tokyo, Japan) vision statement is "Toyota will lead the way to the future of mobility, enriching lives around the world with the safest and most responsible ways of moving people. Through our commitment to quality, constant innovation, and respect for the planet, we aim to exceed expectations and be rewarded with a smile. We will meet our challenging goals by engaging the talent and passion of people, who believe there is always a better way."

In contrast to the long-range goals expressed in a vision statement, *mission* refers to the purpose of the organization (de Kluyver & Pearce, 2009). The purpose is typically consistent with the organization's values and stakeholder expectations (e.g., profitability). For example, MHP's mission is "partnering to improve quality of life as a non-profit organization dedicated to mental health and wellness." Thus, MHP's purpose is to promote mental health and it does so by collaborating with other organizations such as the court system, local aging clinics, and shelters for the homeless, who all interact with and help individuals with mental illness and their families. Thus, the mission statement clarifies how the organization achieves its vision. In comparison, strategy says how the organization achieves its mission and/or vision (Figure 13.2).

FIGURE 13.2   Vision, Mission, Strategy

© arka38/Shutterstock, Inc.

Not all organizations have all three: vision, mission, strategy, nor have them all as distinct concepts.

Toyota may be an example of an organization that intermixes the concepts. Toyota Company's mission statement, which is based on seven guiding principles (i.e., values), is the same as their vision statement. Toyota's vision, which also serves as its strategy, comprises components depicted as part of a tree with roots (the values) as shown in Figure 13.3.

As described on the Toyota website, the tree metaphor represents a living, sustainable symbol of Toyota's natural strength. The 12 tenets make up the vision—the "fruit" of the tree. The tree is grounded by its roots—the values. The tree and roots metaphor, it turns out, is popular in strategic management (Mintzberg & Lampel, 1999).

Toyota's mission, vision, global strategy (the website shows strategy by region), and values appear intermixed, making it challenging to identify what each is, exactly. Given that Toyota was founded in 1938, the lack of clear delineations between vision, mission, and strategy may be a carryover from the history of how strategy as a concept has been understood and changed over time. It is probable that many other companies' strategies were designed such that they reflect how the concept of strategy was understood at that time in history.

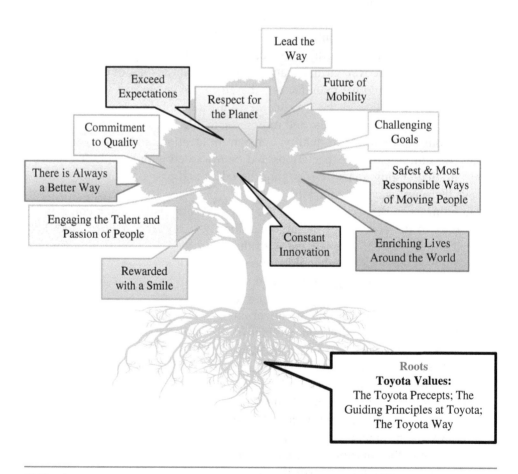

FIGURE 13.3 Toyota Motor Company's Global Vision (Adapted by Zinta Byrne from their website)

> **Exercise 13.2**
>
> Compare and contrast strategy, vision, and mission.

How Strategy Has Been Understood

Given that the concept of strategy has morphed over time, to understand some companies' strategies, it is helpful to have an overview of the historical development of strategy as a business construct.

In the 1950s, strategy was considered the ideal fit between the strengths and weaknesses within the organization, and the external opportunities and challenges confronting the organization. Consistent with attention to an organization's focus on business survival, another perspective on the early start of strategy is that it evolved out of the economic and business climate of the day (Daniell, 2004). The business climate in the 1950s was for companies to drastically cut their costs and expenses, as well as redefine their markets, in response to increasing external industry pressures. Daniell (2004) suggests the strategy adopted by organizations during the 1950s was oriented toward establishing the boundaries for each business unit to closely manage costs, customers, and competitors (called the 3C's model).

Just managing the business is not enough, however; consequently, the 1960s and 1970s defined strategy as a planning process marked by formal, distinct steps with checklists and techniques (Mintzberg & Lampel, 1999). The planning process was designed to answer the following types of questions: "Where are we now?," "Where are we going?," and "How do we get there?" (gap analysis as described in Chapter 12; de Kluyver & Pearce, 2009). Answering each question involved assessment, evaluation, and critical analysis.

As the concept of strategy developed further, scholars defined it more precisely and with greater attention to the many factors involved with creating an organizational strategy. Hence, during the 1980s, strategy was considered the positioning of the organization within the competitive market, an entrepreneurial agenda, and a series of cognitive models or frameworks. Porter's best-selling book *Competitive Strategy* (Porter, 1980) excited the "strategy as position" perspective. Porter (1980, 2008) outlined five Forces that drive strategy:

1. Entry of new competitors into the market

2. Threat of substitutes (e.g., generic for brand name products; videoconferencing for travel)

3. Bargaining power of buyers (e.g., Walmart is known for having buying power just because of its size)

4. Bargaining power of suppliers (i.e., they can charge more for their material than it's worth)

5. Rivalry among existing competitors (e.g., can force prices artificially high or low).

Through analyzing each force, the business could position itself to succeed by formulating a comprehensive strategy.

An example of a model developed to maximize competitive strategy is the "8 Strategic Laws of Gravity" shown in Table 13.2 (Daniell, 2004).

During the same timeframe as the 5 Forces, another perspective of strategy called the *entrepreneurial view* emerged, wherein strategy was centered on the Chief Executive Officer (CEO) and their entrepreneurial focus (e.g., start-up, niche market, turnaround, or privatization; Mintzberg & Lampel, 1999). Instead of developing a strategy based on an analytical approach to existing markets or cost considerations, strategies developed under an entrepreneurial perspective were entirely oriented toward where the CEO wanted to go with the company and/or its products. If Apple's early strategy was made public, it is possible we might see an early version with direct ties to Steve Job's (founder and former CEO) product innovations, just as we might see the same for Microsoft's Bill Gates (founder and former CEO).

Why is vision important to an organization's success?

Also in the 1980s, and continuing through today (though not a dominant trend), strategy has been described by some academicians using a cognitive lens (March & Simon, 1958). Models, maps, and schemas or mental processes characterize the cognitive perspective (Mintzberg & Lampel, 1999). The attention here is on recognizing cognitive biases (or errors) in decision-making. Such biases include recency effects (i.e., remembering the most recent event better than prior events), availability heuristic (i.e., relying on only those ideas most readily available in memory), anchoring (i.e., current state is compared to and influenced by another state that was introduced first), attribution errors

TABLE 13.2 The 8 Strategic Laws of Gravity

Laws	Definition
Correct business definition	Current and future boundaries of the organization
Market control and leadership	Market-leading position driving shareholder value
Incremental share to the leader	Value incremental share gain because it reinforces leader position, builds profit, and extends ability to differentiate in the market
Relative competitive position, performance, and investment	Relative market share (e.g., 30% vs. 70%) possesses strength when the value of the market share has strategic and financial leverage; it can determine financial return
Declining costs and prices	With accumulated experience, one gains economic insight from the predictable decline in unit costs and prices
Discouraging competitive investment	The cost of discouraging the competition is usually much less than the cost of direct competition
Industry value chain and profit pool	Profits across industry or business solutions determine the profit pool (e.g., the potential accumulation of profits), which one must understand to develop an effective strategy
Organization investment	One must invest in the people (e.g., reward innovation, individual and team performance), structure (e.g., policies, support systems), and functioning or operation of the organization to get the most out of the preceding laws

Courtesy Zinta Byrne. Source: Daniell, 2004.

(i.e., misattributing the cause of an event to internal vs. external causes), and illusory correlations (i.e., assuming things that look related to one another are correlated when there is no evidence to indicate they are related). The emphasis of this approach to strategy is objective versus subjective, with an emphasis on mapping the current reality of the business direction as opposed to mapping the future.

Consistent with the emphasis on cognition, strategy can also be understood as an emergent process that results from learning (Mintzberg & Lampel, 1999). Leaders of the organization learn from their mistakes and develop an emergent strategy based on lessons learned. Through experimentation and struggles with ambiguity, mistakes are made and consequently, organizational leaders change the strategy, constantly adapting. In this view of strategy, the direction in which the organization should go (vision) is blended with how the strategy is achieved. Toyota again provides a good example. Toyota modified its strategy in 2011 as a consequence of learnings from a 2008 to 2009 financial crisis in the business due to series of quality-related problems (e.g., sticking accelerator pedal problems). Toyota's strategy illustrates the blend of vision with strategy achieved through learning from mistakes.

Not necessarily associated with any particular era, other models of strategy adopted at various times include the 7-S model (as discussed in Chapter 12), associated with McKinsey and Company (a management consulting firm; Daniell, 2009). The 7-S framework is depicted on McKinsey & Company's website in a figure similar to Figure 13.4. The framework was designed to represent the organizing configuration of the best-run companies in the United States that the McKinsey firm studied in the 1970s. It was not a framework for strategy, per se, but the framework has frequently been incorporated in chapters describing the evolution of strategy (e.g., Daniell, 2009) because it guides analytical thinking during organizational design and strategy development. Its primary purpose is for analyzing strengths and weaknesses of the key aspects of the organization, its style, skills, systems, shared values, strategy, staff, and structure.

Figure 13.4 illustrates the interrelations of the various components, which cannot be stressed enough in the framework. The seven individual variables were meant to be considered together because of how interdependent they are within the organization. Each S includes several components as noted in Table 13.3.

Examples of companies that McKinsey identified in the 1970s as exemplars of the 7-S include International Business Machines Corporation (IBM), Hewlett-Packard (H-P), Johnson & Johnson, Delta Airlines, McDonald's, Boeing, and Proctor & Gamble (P&G; Peters & Waterman, 1982). Although some of these organizations may not be performing as well as they did in the 1970s, they provided supportive evidence for McKinsey's model that identified how coordination across the S's could result in organizational effectiveness.

Recent developments in strategy blend and integrate the phases and perspectives, thus changing approaches across the lifetime of a business. Organizations may start out with an entrepreneurial strategy, change to a learning/emergent strategy, and then move to a position strategy. What is most evident of the evolution of the field of strategy is that it has become complex over time, more closely reflecting the many forces that shape and influence strategy.

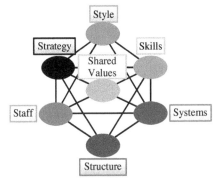

FIGURE 13.4   The 7-S Framework

Courtesy Zinta Byrne.
Source: McKinsey & Company website.

TABLE 13.3 7-S Framework Components

7-S	Definition	Focus
Shared values	Implicit and explicit values and goals that are shared internally through the culture and norms	Alignment with the Vision and Mission
Skills	Capabilities of the employees within the organization and their collective capacity for accomplishing desired goals	Ensuring employees have the necessary skills to do the jobs and to grow into new jobs as demands for know-how increase
Staff	People who make up the organization	Hiring, training, motivation, and reward systems designed to retain top talent and encourage high levels of performance
Strategy	Decisions and actions that create competitive advantage and customer relations	Direction, goals, intent of the business. Does it include the mission and vision?
Structure	The structure of the organization that defines responsibilities and roles	The dimensions that make up the configuration of the organization, such as centralized vs decentralized, span of control, division of labor, etc. (from Chapter 11)
Style	Leadership, including decisions, priorities, behaviors, and symbols of the organizational culture that determine the norms (i.e., way of behaving) within the organization	Culture and climate of the organization, which includes the artifacts, values, and assumptions
Systems	Procedures, policies, processes, and mechanism by which employees get their work done on a daily basis	Includes information systems such as technology or computers and software used to get work done, the organization of information or data, and human resource management

Courtesy Zinta Byrne.

Exercise 13.3

Before moving on, describe how strategy has been understood.

What Shapes Strategy?

Forces or drivers that shape strategy are both external and internal to the organization.

External Drivers

External influences on an organization's strategy include changing demographics and their market influence, economic conditions, political landscape, social and cultural factors (i.e., sociocultural), and advances in technology.

Demographics

Demographic influences on organizational strategy include the size of the population served by the organization, the age of the population, the ethnic diversity or mix of the target population, and income statistics (i.e., does the target population have limited funds or spending capacity?). According to the United Nations, Department of Economic and Social Affairs, Population Division (UNPD), wealthier nations are aging and shrinking in population, whereas poorer countries are expanding (Fisher, 2013). Africa and Asia are expected to grow in population the most over the next 90 years, whereas the United States, Europe, and South America are expected to stay the same or shrink slightly. The UNPD predicts that Nigeria will experience the most rapid population growth in the next 50–100 years. South Africa is expected to remain roughly the same in population size, whereas Egypt, Tanzania, and Ethiopia are all expected to increase (see Figure 13.5). These changing demographics are just a few that may affect several multinational organizations.

Why is it valuable to have both a vision and strategy?

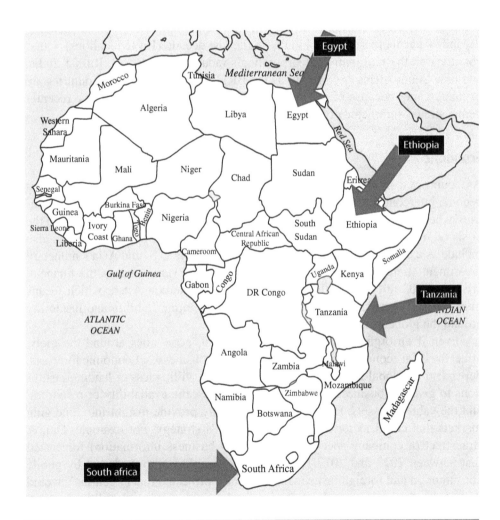

FIGURE 13.5   Map of Africa with Egypt, Ethiopia, Tanzania, and South Africa Indicated by Arrows

© pavalena/Shutterstock, Inc.

The changing demographics noted above refer to the influences of expected increases in population sizes around the world on organizational strategy. When considering the opposite demographic trend, large reductions in populations are unlikely as life expectancy is also on the rise across the globe (Fisher, 2013).

As workers live longer, organizations also need to consider to which age group their solutions are best targeted. They also need to incorporate that workers will not retire at 65 years of age because they are expecting to live until 90 or 100. In addition, the increased life expectancy around the globe affects organizations' strategies in another way. Strategies with a 10-year-horizon may not reflect these anticipated demographic changes over the next 50 years or more. It is possible that the "next" strategy can take these figures and changes into consideration; however, it may be necessary to modify a few current strategies.

Though organizations cannot control demographic characteristics, they must consider the demographics of the population to which they predominately advertise, sell, and hire. For example, in addition to the changes in Africa, global companies need to consider the growing Chinese population, whose spending capability has increased substantially in the last decade (United Nations). Other countries on the multinational corporation's radar include Brazil, Russia, India, and now South Africa (referred to as the BRICS countries). These countries are of interest, not because of growing populations, but because they have recently demonstrated significant economic development.

What demographic factors do you think an organization should account for in its strategy?

Economic

As countries continue to export, import, and collaborate globally, economies become interconnected and dependent on one another. For instance, many countries experienced a financial crisis in 2008. Most reports blamed (and still do) the crisis on major U.S. banks and the U.S. financial system, but other reports also include as a cause Europe's heavy borrowing from the U.S. and Asia's monetary investment strategies (Origins, 2013; Figure 13.6). Events such as the financial crisis of 2008 tell us that the world economy is interconnected, which means multinational organizations must consider the economic stability and instability around the globe as they construct their strategy.

Even if an organization is not multinational, economies around the globe affect the local economy, directly impacting local businesses. Economic forecasts, dependent on global financial markets, project the willingness of lending institutions to give out business loans and at what rates, the availability of resources, and the value of assets. Economic forecasts may provide insight into emerging markets that could factor into an organization's strategy. For example, Dun & Bradstreet (a company specializing in global business information) forecasted that between 2013 and 2017 Brazil's market would improve, driven by public consumption and foreign investment. They also projected that Argentina's would deteriorate driven by a lack of foreign investment, continued political unrest, and poor trade relations. Thus, if the company strategy relies on business from Argentina, the organizational leaders may need to plan ahead and shift investments into the Brazilian capability instead. Such planning also requires consideration of political forces as economic and political factors tend to accompany one another. In addition to direct economic impacts of governments and global

FIGURE 13.6   World Financial Crisis

market trends, consumers themselves can influence strategy. For example, the green movement pushed Chinese manufacturing companies to develop proactive environmental strategies (Dai, Chan, & Yee, 2018).

Political

Politics influences the strategic direction of an organization, whether desired or not. Businesses may operate under the oversight of government and/or legal institutions that set the boundary conditions for legal operation. Some countries have more oversight than others do, and some have more political interests than others. These oversights do not just affect local holdings. For example, European Union antitrust officials prevented General Electric (GE) from acquiring Honeywell in 2001 (*CNN Money*, July 3, 2001), even though both GE and Honeywell are based in the United States. It was their operations in Europe, however, that drew the attention of local European Union officials. Organizational leaders developing their company strategy must, therefore, consider interest groups competing for resources, oversight, or market influence, regardless of where the organization is headquartered.

Business policies may change under different political regimes or administrations, which all affect the organization's strategy. Some organizations attempt to influence these political changes or debates, such as those focused on environmental concerns, trade issues, or workforce laws. As each new administration is appointed or comes to power, laws may become more restrictive or more lenient, which affect organizations' short and long-term strategies. Thus, even if you hate politics, as a business leader developing the company strategy, you cannot ignore the governments and decisions of other countries and political systems.

Lest you think that **e-commerce** is immune to politics and regulations since it does not reside in any particular country, you'd be wrong. E-commerce (i.e., business on the Internet) has become a growing area of regulation within the United States, with many lobbying for fraud and privacy of information protection, taxation, and general regulation (Hitt, Ireland, & Hoskisson, 2003). Organizations with e-commerce interests (e.g., online retailers) or an online presence have to monitor progress continuously to determine the impact on their current and future business plans. For example, the Court of Justice of the European Union ruled on May 13, 2014 that individuals have "the right to be forgotten"—under certain conditions (thus on a case-by-case basis), people have the right to ask search engines (like Google) to remove links with personal information about them. Though the ruling is in Europe, it had an impact on organizations like Google, who not only operates in Europe but whose strategy is to make all information available at the click of a mouse. The ruling is currently only applicable to European countries; hence, Google is not held to the same law in the United States. Similarly, laws regarding drugs, exports, and environmental concerns (e.g., pollution) change as political groups gain and lose power. Companies like Pfizer, Johnson & Johnson, and Sanofi pay close attention to political changes surrounding drug approval.

The economic and political climate affects perspectives within countries, which are influenced by general attitudes within those countries and by cultural values. Thus, like nearly every other aspect of organizational psychology and behavior discussed in previous chapters, strategy is also influenced by sociocultural factors.

Sociocultural

Sociocultural influences on strategy encompass society's attitudes and cultural values. These include attitudes about health care, retirement, family care, and education. For instance, whether a culture values one gender over another in leadership or family roles affects workforce planning and business unit strategies. In the Arab culture, for example, the extended family is the most important entity in society, influencing economic and political choices (Ambah, 2006). Within the family, gender roles, elders' roles, and decision-making are strongly governed by the cultural values. Seniority and older adults are considered wise and have considerable authority over decisions that affect the family. As a patriarchal society following traditional gender roles, men are the family providers, managers, decision makers, and business leaders (Steers, Sanchez-Runde, & Nardon,

© Thinglass/Shutterstock.com

2010). Thus, a business strategy established within an Arab culture will be heavily influenced by these cultural values and look different from a strategy established in Great Britain, for instance, where the cultural values are for gender and age equality and substantial independence in decision-making.

According to Hofstede's (1980, 2001) cultural classification, the United Kingdom scores low on uncertainty avoidance, which means the society is comfortable with ambiguity and lack of planning or with plans that frequently change. Accordingly, strategic plans in the United Kingdom will have shorter forecast ranges and incorporate opportunity for flexibility. In contrast, Egypt (an Arab culture) scores very high on uncertainty avoidance, which means the society prefers careful planning and rigid codes of behavior. Strategy in Egyptian business may, therefore, be comprehensive and detailed with little room for vagueness or flexibility. These are, however, generalities based on Hofstede's work on cultures. It may be that organizations within these countries challenge the cultural norms with the justification that they must conduct business worldwide.

Regardless of where else it does business, a company has to operate within the cultural forces of the country within which it is located. Attempts to go against ingrained value systems will probably present predictable challenges and could fail as a consequence. Companies such as Toyota Motor Corporation explicitly state in the code of conduct that the company will respect the culture, customs, and history of each country within which it operates, recognizing that cultures and norms differ and local customs need to be honored for the organization to achieve success. To add more challenge, boundaries between countries and cultures become less distinct as technology enables businesses to operate seamlessly around the globe.

Technology

The influence of technology has dramatically changed businesses and organizations around the globe. Clear impact can be seen in the transformation of retail stores—where once streets and shopping malls may have been filled with retail outlets, their presence is now seen on the Internet more than in local communities. For example, retailers like The Gap, Staples, and bookseller Barnes & Noble (Figure 13.7) who had a significant presence in malls and brick-and-mortar stores, now also conduct business online (McIntyre & Hess, 2014).

Retailers are not the only firms whose strategies change because of advancing technology. Health-care providers are changing how they provide medicine as a result of technology systems that more effectively track a patient's drug use, hospital visits, and length of stay (Topol, 2013). The near future may see a change in Google's strategy spurred on by their recent technological advances, such as the intelligent car that drives itself (Robinson, 2014).

What other external factors do you think influence the strategy?

Internal Drivers

Strategy is not only influenced by external environmental factors, but also by internal factors within the organization, such as resources, core competencies, and outsourcing. Conducting an internal analysis to assess (a) available and potential future resources, (b) existing and future core competencies, and (c) the need for outsourcing, is essential for developing a good strategy. Such a

FIGURE 13.7   Barnes & Noble Store

© Ken Wolter/Shutterstock, Inc.

strategy can adequately account for where the organization sits today relative to the competition, where it needs to go, and *ideally* where it *should go* in the future.

Resources

Resources available to an organization include labor, finances, assets, processes, information and knowledge, capabilities, firm attributes (e.g., physical, human, and organizational resources, such as structure) and raw materials, to name a few (Barney, 1991).

By staying agile and innovative, organizations can effectively use existing resources and acquire new ones (Drucker, 2002; Verona, 1999). For example, 3M, a multinational technology company, changed its competitive advantage in the mid-1980s by changing how management supervised employees. The company changed its emphasis away from control over its labor force to considering its labor force as a resource. Accordingly, rather than seeing employees as those who needed controlling, managers treated employees as individual entrepreneurs, encouraging them to develop new ideas (Bartlett & Ghoshal, 1995). Senior managers changed their focus to strategy and delegated responsibility for management and decisions to the lowest levels possible. As a consequence, 3M remains a competitive and successful multinational corporation producing over 55,000 products including cleaners, adhesives, electronics (e.g., communication technology, data centers), displays (e.g., optical systems), and aircraft sealant and paint removal (see 3M's website). Their ability to use their existing labor more effectively became an important component of their new strategy. Labor is just one of many resources, however. Financial resources are critical to an organization's ability to hire and acquire necessary equipment and knowledge.

Financial resources refer to the organization's borrowing and purchasing power. Without the ability to borrow money, many firms cannot hire enough labor, buy know-how, or purchase the raw materials needed to build their products. The organization's strategy has to accommodate the borrowing and purchasing capability of the company. For instance, in the last 10 years, Hewlett-Packard Company (H-P) has acquired ArcSight, 3PAR, Stratavia, Trulogica, Tabblo, Autonomy, LeftHand Networks, Hiflex, Fortify Software, Snapfish, Vertica, PIXACO, Colubris Networks, Silverwire, SPI Dynamics, Logoworks, Tower Software, IBRIX, 3Com, Palm, EDS, Opsware Inc., EYP, AppIQ, Scitex, NUR Macroprinters Ltd., CGNZ Ltd., Exstream Software, Technology Partners SpA, Printelligent, and MacDermid ColorSpan Inc., just to name a few (see Hewlett-Packard Company's website). To achieve its strategy in the various business units in which these acquisitions occurred, H-P had to have the financial capital to do so. If the number of acquisitions is an indicator of borrowing and/or purchasing power, H-P appears to have (or at least had) a lot. Whereas some companies affect strategy by using financial resources to acquire smaller companies and employees, others use technological resources as an internal driver for refining strategy.

> Why are sociocultural values critical to company strategy?

Resources include *technological* elements such as patents, trademarks, copyrights, and trade secrets. Most technology firms have substantial technological resources, which enable them to control a market or sector of the market and keep competitors at arm's length. For example, pharmaceutical companies have patents on their specialty drugs, enabling them to be the sole provider for a set number of years (typically 8–10). This patent gives them the rights to market the drug and to protect the ingredient list. Once the patent term ends, other drug manufacturers can produce generic versions, which have the same ingredients as the brand name (though not necessarily identical or in the same relative percentages). Generic versions are highly marketable because of their reduced price relative to the original. Similar examples exist for memory chip manufacturers such as Intel Corporation and X2Y Attenuators, LLC. The benefits of the patent protection period to the original manufacturer are large, in terms of market control, profitability, and opportunity for developing newer versions before the competition. Thus, technological resources are not just electronics, and differ substantially from labor or physical resources in that they may only appear on paper in the form of patents.

© cgstock/Shutterstock.com

In contrast to technological resources that may be knowledge based, *physical* resources include tangible items, such as buildings or equipment. For example, pharmaceutical laboratories have substantial investments in equipment necessary for drug manufacturing and testing. Another example includes the physical property and equipment used in diamond mining. Mines in Angola, Botswana, South Africa, and Russia must all have the right equipment, such

© Dmitry Kalinovsky/Shutterstock.com

as drilling machines and bits, air suppliers, and diamond jiggers that separate minerals from one another based on gravity. Similarly, construction firms may have heavy machinery, such as backhoe loaders, excavators, cranes, and other equipment, such as trailers and portable facilities, necessary for their projects.

Regardless of the type of resources that organizations have, the organizational strategy includes a consideration for what existing resources can do now and what resources are necessary for competitive advantage and long-term sustainability of the organization as a whole. Some resources are relatively easy to exchange as the strategy changes, but others, such as physical resources or people, are not so transformable. In some cases, resources may be combined, which allows the organization to create a new resource or capability.

Capabilities refers to what the organization is capable of doing with the resources it has and when given additional resources. For example, capability may include innovation, speed, and quality processes. These capabilities typically develop over time, as employees gain more knowledge and skill from problem-solving. Hitt et al. (2003) suggest that employees are essential for an organization's capability and a firm committed to developing employees' competencies will enjoy increasing capabilities. Because of the value of capabilities, organizations have created the Chief Learning Officer (CLO) position to oversee the training employees need and to secure growth and development opportunities for them. The CLO might also work to promote a culture that supports ongoing learning.

With advanced knowledge and skill, employees can combine resources to create new ones, called *dynamic capabilities*. Dynamic capabilities refers to the ability to combine various resources in new ways, such as identifying potential opportunities, determining ways to gain from those opportunities, and how to make changes to the organization to take advantage of new opportunities. A good example of a company that has combined resources (dynamic capability) to achieve competitive advantage is Amazon.com (Hitt et al., 2003). Amazon combined service with product distribution, enabling the company to partner with hundreds of businesses using their distribution facilities. As an outcome of the partnership, Amazon offers extended services beyond just the purchase of books—you can buy just about anything on Amazon.com. The ability to acquire product and distribute fast is one of Amazon's core competencies.

Company Example 13.1   DTE Energy's Purpose-Driven Organization

DTE employees were not engaged and the CEO Gerry Anderson knew he had a bigger problem—with employees unable to feel creative and committed to performing, recovering from the 2008 economic recession in the United States was not going to be possible. To spark his employees, Anderson created a video to show how DTE employees could strive for a higher purpose—something beyond just financial gain for DTE—a purpose statement "We serve with our energy, the lifeblood of communities and the engine or progress" (Quinn & Thakor, 2008, p. 80). The video had DTE employees from all over, including truck drivers, plant operators, corporate leaders, and more sharing how their jobs impacted the community that relies on DTE energy. The video sparked the engagement of company leaders to support and affirm their purpose statement in every aspect of business: training, socialization, meetings, and other company events. Slowly, employees picked up on their passion and internalization of the purpose—leading to a transformation in the company. Consequently, not only did engagement improve but so did performance to the tune of tripling their stock price in less than 10 years after the 2008 recession. Giving employees a true and genuine higher purpose provided them a sense of meaningfulness, a reason to do better, and to do more than just be at work. They were inspired to bring commitment, personal growth, and energized enthusiasm to achieving the company purpose/goal—provide for the communities they support.

Core Competencies

Core competencies refer to the key strengths of the organization that enable it to provide key benefits to its customers. For example, one might consider innovation as a core competency of Apple and Google. Toyota might include quality and reliability. Southwest airlines might have customer service as a core competency. And Honda's core competencies might include engine and propulsion systems. Competencies serve as a source of competitive advantage (Hamel & Prahalad, 1994; Prahalad & Hamel, 1990). Strategy is, therefore, influenced by core competencies. Specifically, the strategy must be based on what the organization can achieve, which puts competencies and capabilities within the strategy. For example, Amazon.com's core competencies include helping people find what they want online, enabling them to buy it online, and getting it to them fast.

Check out https://www. thebalancesmb.com/ core-competency-in-business-2948314 to learn more about core competencies in business. This article provides several examples.

Though Amazon.com's corporate strategy could not be found on their website, their mission statement is "To be Earth's most customer-centric company where people can find and discover anything they want to buy online" (taken from Amazon's website). By providing third-party sellers, such as Zappos, MyHabit, AbeBooks, and Yoyo.com, the ability to connect to shoppers as part of the Amazon.com (Figure 13.8) experience (consistent with their core competencies), Amazon achieves its goal.

If the competencies for achieving the "ideal" future organization defined in the strategy do not currently exist within the organization, the company must obtain them through financial acquisitions or by developing them (Bowman, 2001). An example of a company that advertises its core competencies (they have a link to "core strengths") on its website is Proctor & Gamble, or P&G. Though P&G notes many internal resources, other organizations must outsource to obtain theirs.

Outsourcing

Outsourcing refers to purchasing or obtaining solutions or resources from an external supplier (Murray & Kotabe, 1999). Companies outsource because they are unable to possess all the necessary resources and capabilities for excellence in every area of their business. By staying focused on the core competencies and outsourcing functions in which there is no strategic need for competence (e.g., human resources), the organization can fully concentrate on value creation. Functions such as human resource management, accounting, janitorial, landscaping, security, and information technology to name a few, can be and often are

FIGURE 13.8 Shopping Online at Amazon.com

© Annette Shaff/Shutterstock, Inc.

outsourced. The strategy, therefore, takes into account what will or can be outsourced (Insinga & Werle, 2000).

In summary, the forces that shape strategy come from the external and internal environment of the organization. A good strategy takes these forces into account and recognizes which play a critical role for the success of the organization and its ability to achieve its vision or mission. This consideration is essential because there are various people, entities, and groups all with a vested interest in the organizational strategy.

Exercise 13.4

Compare and contrast internal and external drivers of strategy.

Who Has a Stake in the Strategy?

Those who have a stake in the strategy include employees, customers, partners, investors, shareholders, suppliers, sellers or distributors, leaders, and society—essentially anyone associated with the organization has an "investment" in the strategy. Though many types of stakeholders exist, Freeman and McVea (2001) proposed three groups of key stakeholders: capital market, product market, and organizational. Capital market stakeholders refer to major suppliers (i.e., equipment, raw material, banks) who have a financial share in the company. Product market stakeholders include primary customers, host communities, and unions. These stakeholders benefit from lower priced products, long-term employment, and tax revenues. Unhappy customers can create significant challenges for organizations because the customers withdraw their business and go elsewhere. Lastly, organizational stakeholders include all employees. They expect the organization to provide a positive work environment, job security, good pay, and benefits. Regardless of how you classify stakeholders, people are at the center.

People, the stakeholders, believe in the organization based on its strategy, the stated direction the organization wants to go. Any deviation from that strategy signals either a lack of commitment or lack of ability to achieve the strategy (unless the change is purposeful and incorporated into the strategy as part of learning). However, stakeholders who influence the strategy have differing objectives (Frooman, 1999; Frooman & Murrell, 2005). For example, the organization's strategy affects employees in a different way than it does the investors of the organization, whose interests lie in the stock price and value of the company. Shareholders have the same objective—maximizing the return on their investment in the organization. Maximizing return on investment sometimes comes at the expense of employee relations or investments in employees, by drawing investments away from employee development or benefits. Thus, these two stakeholder groups, shareholders and employees, may be at odds with one another. Those creating and implementing strategy must struggle with the challenge of satisfying as many groups as possible, or making the trade-off of who to displease and when. Typically, the one responsible for making that trade-off is the organizational leader.

> What other stakeholders to you think are at odds with each other based on their objective for the organization? How do you think the organization can incorporate all those competing objectives in their strategy?

Company Example 13.2   How United Way Engaged Donors in Their Strategy

United Way, 130-years old, began in the rural towns of Colorado, United States. To help folks who were moving out of cities into the towns, local employers set up a pool of employee contributions, which were shared among local charities. Donors were kept secret—thus United Way would receive many donations, including in later years automatic payroll deductions, but never knew who the actual donors were. In the 1990s, however, they changed the model and aimed for one-on-one relationships with large donors in and effort to increase contributions. However, the biggest shift in United Way's strategy came when the now CEO—back then head of marketing in Atlanta, Georgia—involved donors by asking them what their biggest concerns were that they felt funds should be aimed at solving. They received 186,000 responses to a paper survey just in Atlanta alone (Gallagher, 2018). By involving people—giving them voice in the strategy—United Way dramatically increased donor contributions. Hence, began the start of a new strategy—regularly involving and engaging people through digital surveys, online web access, and phone apps that allow donors to contribute online, allocate their donations to specific causes, and provide feedback/input on what issues are critical to support. The strategy, therefore, is reliant on donor input and engagement, and on the return of information back to the donors in terms of their collective voice in determining the priority for where funds should go.

What Is the Role of the Leader in Strategy?

In most organizations, the leader, or group of top executives of the organization, develop the strategy. The leader defines the reality for the organization through establishing a shared vision, mission, and strategy. The company leaders also play a critical role in communicating and executing the strategy. Hitt et al. (2003) defined strategic leadership as the "ability to anticipate, envision, maintain flexibility, and empower others to create strategic change as necessary" (p. 386). Hence, the leader is vital in setting and executing on the strategy.

In addition, organizations expect the leader to challenge existing thinking and assumptions that hinder the firm's ability to establish a far-reaching strategy or to achieve the strategy. Leaders must dare organizational members to think beyond their current capabilities and envision the possibility of a bigger and better future for the organization. Through systems thinking, which involves paying attention to all the processes and functions of the organization, leaders define necessary interrelationships or partnerships. They additionally determine what needs to change in the culture to support the strategy (Mintzberg, Lampel, Quinn, & Ghoshal, 2003). Consequently, effective strategic leadership is a necessity. Effective strategic leadership (Hitt et al., 2003) includes

1. determining the strategic direction of the organization (long-term vision)

2. using, growing, and maintaining the core competencies of the organization (competitive advantage in terms of resources and functional skills)

3. developing the knowledge and skills of the organization's employees (often referred to as human capital in strategy or business books) including hiring and developing leadership talent

4. sustaining an effective organizational culture, which often involves infusing an entrepreneurial spirit

5. focusing on and adhering to ethical practices

6. establishing organizational procedures that are essential to the organization's strategy; namely controls on the financials and a balance of risky and safe decisions.

Watch https://www.ted.com/talks/elon_musk_the_future_we_re_building_and_boring to hear about a vision for solving traffic problems in Los Angeles. In the interview, Elon Musk, the leader of this vision talks about strategy as well.

Thus, as noted in Chapter 9, and again here, being the leader is demanding, but essential to the organization's success.

Chapter Summary

The organizational strategy determines the plan for the organization, the charted course that is necessary for achieving the organization's goals—the vision. "Structure follows strategy" (Bartlett & Ghoshal, 1994, p.79), "culture eats strategy for breakfast," and leaders play a key role in creating strategy after considering the external and internal drivers that affect the strategy. Strategy is absolutely central to an organization's success, yet it can be complex and hard to define and create.

You can consider strategy as the culmination of all chapters in this book. The strategy sets the direction for how the organization may change or transform itself over time, what structure is necessary to support the strategy, how communications must work to achieve the strategy and align with the structure, and the role that leadership plays in setting the strategy. Once the strategy is established, managers supervise the work necessary to accomplish the strategy as conveyed to them by the leaders. Teams are developed to put into action the plan of the strategy, and their stress levels must be managed to offset reductions in performance. With the right strategy, employees develop positive attitudes about the organization and its future, which is shared during socialization. Hence, everything is connected, and strategy starts the ball rolling.

Figure 13.9 provides a visual summary of the key concepts from Chapter 13.

In this visual, we see that culture eats strategy for breakfast, and that structure helps achieve the strategy. The organizational vision is the overall idea that culture, strategy, and structure achieve and support. Internal and external forces lean on the ability to achieve the strategy. Hence, the visual shows how culture, strategy, structure, vision, and overall objectives of the organization are interrelated and combine.

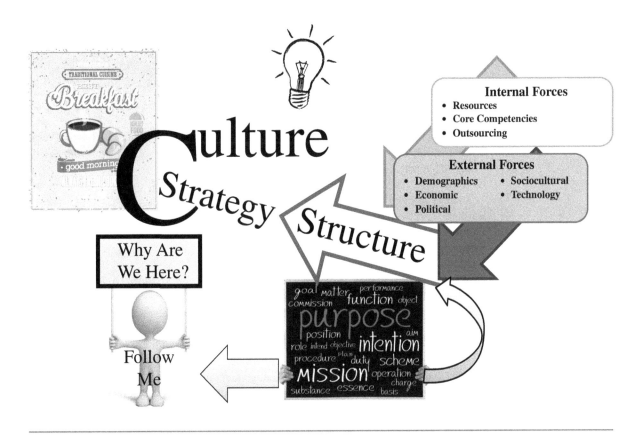

FIGURE 13.9 Visual Summary of Chapter 13

© avian/Shutterstock, Inc.; © UKRID/Shutterstock, Inc.; © Alexander Maslennikov/Shutterstock, Inc.; © teeranop/Shutterstock, Inc.

Discussion Questions

1. Of the different strategy examples offered in the chapter, including those in the text outside of Table 13.1, which one appealed to you the most? Why? What was it about the strategy that you found most clear, defining, and future oriented? Which one did you think was the least helpful?

2. Do you think a strategy is necessary for every organization? Why or why not? What does a strategy do for an organization?

3. Pick one to two different companies you want to work for in the future. Find their strategy statement online. What defines their strategy—is it a position, a plan, a pattern, or a competitive ploy? What is the vision their strategy is attempting to achieve? What organizational structure do they have in place and how does that structure fulfill/support meeting the strategy? How hard or easy was it to find this information?

4. Referring back to earlier chapters on socialization, motivation, attitudes, teams, leadership, and communication, explain how strategy determines to a large extent how these other concepts operate and fit together. That is, how does strategy define socialization in an organization—what effect would strategy have on socialization? How does strategy affect employees' attitudes? In what way does strategy define what kind of leader(s) the organization should have?

References

Ambah, F. S. (June 1, 2006). Saudi women rise in defense of the veil. *The Washington Post*, p. A12.

Bain, J. (1956). *Barriers to new competition.* Cambridge, MA: Harvard University Press.

Barney, J. (1991). Firm resources and sustained competitive advantage. *Journal of Management, 17*(1), 99–121.

Bartlett, C. A., & Ghoshal, S. (1994). Changing the role of top management: Beyond strategy to purpose. *Harvard Business Review, 72*(6), 79–88.

Bartlett, C. A., & Ghoshal, S. (1995). Changing the role of top management: Beyond systems to people. *Harvard Business Review, 73*(3), 132–142.

Bowman, C. (2001). "Value" in the resource-based view of the firm. *Academy of Management Review, 26,* 501–502.

Brandenburger, A. (2019). Strategy needs creativity. *Harvard Business Review, 97*(2), 58–65.

CNN Money (July 3, 2001). EU Kills GE-Honeywell. Retrieved June 14, 2014 from http://money.cnn.com/2001/07/03/europe/ge_eu/

Cound, R. J., & Meyer, J. (2015). Aligning project success with organizational strategy within a project-based organization. *PM World Journal, 4*(10), 1–20.

Dai, J., Chan, H., & Yee, R. (2018). Examining moderating effect of organizational culture on the relationship between market pressure and corporate environmental strategy. *Industrial Marketing Management, 74,* 227–236.

Daniell, M. (2004). Strategy: A step-by-step approach to the development and presentation of world class business strategy. New York, NY: Palgrave McMillan.

De Kluyver, C. A., Pearce, J. A. (2009). *Strategy: A view from the top (an executive perspective)* (3rd ed.). Upper Saddle River, NJ: Pearson/Prentice Hall.

Drucker, P. (2002). They're not employees, they're people. *Harvard Business Review, 80*(2), 70–77.

Fisher, M. (July 16, 2013). The amazing, surprising, Africa-driven demographic future of the Earth, in 9 charts. Retrieved June 14, 2014, from http://www.washingtonpost.com/blogs/worldviews/wp/2013/07/16/the-amazing-surprising-africa-driven-demographic-future-of-the-earth-in-9-charts/

Foley, S. (June 6, 2008). From Zero to Hero? For years, Wal-Mart was attacked for exploiting its staff and suppliers. But now the world's biggest retailer has stopped fighting its critics and started listening. *The Independent* (London), p. 46. Retrieved from www.lexisnexis.com/hottopics/lnacademic

Freeman, R. E., & McVea, J. (2001). A stakeholder approach to strategic management. In M. A. Hitt, R. E. Freeman, & J. S. Harrison (Eds.), *The Blackwell handbook of strategic management* (pp. 189–207). Oxford, England: Blackwell Business.

Frooman, J. (1999). Stakeholder influence strategies. *The Academy of Management Review, 24*(2), 191–205. doi:10.2307/259074

Frooman, J., & Murrell, A. J. (2005). Stakeholder influence strategies: The roles of structural and demographic determinants. *Business & Society, 44*(1), 3–31. doi:10.1177/0007650304273434

Gallagher, B. (2018). United Way's CEO on shifting a century-old business model. *Harvard Business Review, 96*(5), 38–44.

Hamel, G., & Prahalad, C. K. (1994). Competing for the future. *Harvard Business Review, 72*(4), 122.

Hitt, M. A., Ireland, R. D., & Hoskisson, R. E. (2003). *Strategic management: Competitiveness and globalization* (5th ed). Mason, OH: Thomson South-Western.

Hofstede, G. (1980). Motivation, leadership, and organization: Do American theories apply abroad? *Organizational Dynamics*, 42–63. doi: 0090-2616/80/0014-0042

Hofstede, G. (2001). *Culture's consequences: Comparing values, behaviors, institutions, and organizations across nations* (2nd ed). Thousand Oaks, CA: Sage.

Insinga, R. C., & Werle, M. J. (2000). Linking outsourcing to business strategy. *Academy of Management Executive, 14*(4), 58–70. doi:10.5465/AME.2000.3979816

March, J. G., & Simon, H. A. (1958). *Organizations.* New York, NY: Wiley.

Mattera, P. (2013). Challenging Wal-Mart's freeloading ways. *Social Policy, 43*(4), 60.

McIntyre, D. A., & Hess, A. E. M. (March 12, 2014). Nine retailers closing the most stores. (see USA Today) Retrieved July 6, 2014 from http://www.usatoday.com/story/money/business/2014/03/12/retailers-store-closings/6333865/

Middleton, J., & Gorzynski, B. (2006). *Strategy express.* West Sussex, England: Capstone Publishing, Ltd.

Mintzberg, H. (1987). The strategy concept I: Five Ps for strategy. *California Management Review, 30*(1), 11–24.

Mintzberg, H., & Lampel, J. (1999). Reflecting on the Strategy Process. *Sloan Management Review, 40*(3), 21–30.

Mintzberg, H., Lampel, J., Quinn, J. B., & Ghoshal, S. (2003). *The strategy process: Concepts, context, cases* (4th ed.). Upper Saddle River, NJ: Prentice Hall.

Murray, J. Y., & Kotabe, M. (1999). Sourcing strategies of U.S. service companies: A modified transaction-cost analysis. *Strategic Management Journal, 20*(9), 791–809.

Origins of the financial crisis, Crash Course (September 7, 2013). Retrieved June 14, 2014 from http://www.economist.com/news/schoolsbrief/21584534-effects-financial-crisis-are-still-being-felt-five-years-article

Peters, T. J., & Waterman, R. H. Jr. (1982). *In search of excellence: Lessons from America's best-run companies.* New York, NY: Warner Books.

Porter, M. E. (1980). *Competitive strategy: Techniques for analyzing industries and competitors.* New York, NY: Free Press

Porter, M. E. (1996). What is strategy? *Harvard Business Review, 74*(6), 61–78.

Porter, M. E. (2008). The five competitive forces that shape strategy. *Harvard Business Review, 86*(1), 78–93.

Prahalad, C. K., & Hamel, G. (1990). The core competence of the corporation. *Harvard Business Review, 68*(3), 79–91.

Quinn, R. E., & Thakor, A. V. (2018). Creating a purpose-driven organization. *Harvard Business Review, 96*(4), 78–85

Robinson, B. (July 2, 2014). Intelligent cars draw investors to tech stocks. Retrieved July 6, 2014, from http://www.reuters.com/article/2014/07/02/us-tech-autos-stocks-idUSKBN0F70H320140702

Steers, R. M., Sanchez-Runde, C. J., & Nardon, L. (2010). *Management across cultures: Challenges and strategies*. Cambridge, UK: Cambridge University Press.

Topol, E. (July 12, 2013). How technology is transforming health care. (see U.S. News & World Report). Retrieved July 6, 2014, from http://health.usnews.com/health-news/hospital-of-tomorrow/articles/2013/07/12/how-technology-is-transforming-health-care

United Nations, Department of Economic and Social Affairs (*n.d.*). http://esa.un.org/wpp/unpp/panel_population.htm

Verona, G. (1999). A resource-based view of product development. *Academy of Management Review, 24,* 132–142.

Zajonc, R. B. (1968). Attitudinal effects of mere exposure. *Journal of Personality and Social Psychology, 9*(2, Pt.2), 1–27. doi:10.1037/h0025848

APPENDIX

Mini-Quiz Answers

Chapter 2 Mini-Quiz: Socialization

1. When first becoming part of an organization, socialization most likely involves:
   a. Picking up social cues from other employees
   b. Attending after work parties
   c. Reading company materials or exploring internal databases and employee profiles
   d. Individualized processes, such as being assigned a mentor

   > Socialization may involve a, c, or d, but not b. There is no single way to socialize employees and messages about what is accepted (or unacceptable) may come from a variety of sources, formal and informal. Typically, however, socialization does not include after work parties, unless the job specifically includes such parties as part of the actual job tasks (like wedding planners or caterers).

2. True or False: Socialization happens when an employee joins the organization.

   > FALSE: Contrary to what many may think (and what some organizations practice), socialization is an ongoing process. Anticipatory socialization begins even when recruiting and selecting employees. Organizations often have socialization programs for new hires, but the organization is always changing, even if very slowly, and so employees continually receive messages about the acceptable norms and values of the organization.

3. If a manager elected to "onboard" a new employee, they are likely:
   a. Picking up an employee from the airport
   b. Securing the employee's agreement in regards to standard policies and procedures
   c. Introducing the employee to their new team
   d. Facilitating a team building exercise for the group of new hires

   > The best answer for this question is "b". Onboarding is a relatively new term that is sometimes used interchangeably with socialization, but the two processes are different and have different goals. While socialization focuses on "psychological investment" of new employees (such as in answers "c" and "d"), onboarding focuses on the logistical and physical aspects of bringing an employee into the organization (such as office, phone, badge, and paper work for human resources).

4. If an organization doesn't adequately socialize its employees:
    a. New hires may be more likely to quit
    b. Employees may feel less attached to the company
    c. New employees may experience less stress because they can dive right into their work and not have to mingle
    d. It may not recruit the right kinds of employees

> Answers "a", "b", and "d" could be the result of poor socialization processes. Answer "c" is incorrect because proper socialization can actually help employees feel less anxiety and uncertainty in their new roles.

5. Which of the following is/are true about socialization methods?
    a. When recruiting employees, more information is better
    b. People who are socialized with informal methods tend to stay at the organization longer than employees who only receive formal socialization
    c. Having current employees help socialize the new employees is not very beneficial
    d. Processes that focus on employees' first experiences (e.g., first mistake in the new role) do not work because first impressions don't stick with employees very long

> Answers "a" and "b" are correct. Contrary to answer "c", current or existing employees can be very helpful because they help new employees feel connected with the organization. Answer "d" is also incorrect. According to Gustafson's (2005) Guiding Principles, first impression are actually quite lasting. Also, the Chapter discusses why addressing the "first experiences" can be very effective when socializing employees.

Chapter 3: Mini-Quiz: Motivation

1. Which of the following factors has the longest impact on employee motivation?
    a. Providing more challenging work.
    b. Presenting an "employee of the month" award.
    c. Offering the possibility of a promotion.
    d. A raise.
    e. Purchasing new, updated equipment.
    f. Better benefits.
    g. Providing an opportunity for employee feedback.
    h. Dedicate a time for employees to socialize.

> It is hard to say which of these factors might have the longest lasting impact on motivation, but we know from the theories in Chapter 3 that changing aspects of work that lead to meaningfulness at work will be more effective than single efforts that increase satisfaction, at least for the moment (e.g., raise, award).

2. You were brought into an organization to improve employee motivation by redesigning jobs. You began by assessing core dimensions of several jobs, which helped identify areas for improvement. Now, a year later, you surveyed employees and found that your efforts were wildly successful. Not only are employees more motivated, they also reported higher job satisfaction and fewer intentions to quit. What explains why changing core dimensions of the job increases satisfaction and reduces intentions to quit?
   a. Extrinsic motivation
   b. Felt responsibility
   c. Meaningfulness
   d. Knowledge of results

   > Based on job characteristics theory, changing parts of the jobs may have resulted in "b", "c", or "d" which then led to the positive outcomes.

3. How do organizations typically measure their employees' level of motivation?
   a. Observation
   b. Employee Performance
   c. Asking employees
   d. Organizations only care about performance and don't typically assess motivation

   > Organizations almost always use surveys to understand employee motivation, such as with the Job Diagnostic Survey (i.e., answer "c"). Motivation can be hard to observe because it is internal. There is evidence that higher motivation translates to better employee performance, but the two are not one in the same. Measuring employee motivation and attitudes can help understand the current state of the organization.

4. Does goal setting actually help employees achieve better performance?
   a. YES! Employees can take ownership of goals, which makes them personal
   b. NO! Goals are just assigned by managers because they have to
   c. Yes, because setting goals helps employees think through the strategies which may lead to successful performance
   d. Yes, because working towards a goal presents the opportunity to receive feedback

   > Answers "a", "c", and "d" are all correct. Goal setting theory is one of the most well-supported theories in Organizational Psychology and goals are one of the most effective ways to motive employees (given that the goals are set appropriately). Answer "b" can also be true; if managers dictate goals and employees don't actually buy into them, the goals will likely be unsuccessful.

5. According to some theories in psychology, people are driven by certain needs. True or False: People cannot be motivated by higher level needs (e.g., belonging) until their basic needs (e.g., having food and shelter) are met.

> False. This question is referring to Maslow's theory, which suggests that needs are hierarchical, or build on one another. While this theory is quite popular, it is largely unsupported by empirical studies. People can have multiple needs, which are not always met in a linear fashion. See Existence, Relatedness, Growth (ERG) Theory for an updated and more well-supported theory.

Chapter 4: Mini-Quiz: Attitudes

1. Which of the following diagrams best represents attitudes?
   a. A
   b. B
   c. C

   > Behavior is represented as an *outcome* of attitudes, rather than a component, making answer "b" the best choice. Answer "a" represents the tripartite view of attitudes, which was initially used to illustrate the components of attitudes, but has since been replaced with "b". More recently, Answer "c" is incorrect because it leaves out the cognitive component, which is an important part of attitudes.

2. Attitudes can be formed by:
   a. Looking around and seeing what's acceptable to other people
   b. Thinking about what our friends would do and think
   c. Looking back on our own behavior and thinking about why we might have done what we did
   d. Our own past experiences

   > All of these answers could be correct, depending on the theory or perspective you're using to explain attitudes. Self-perception theory explains answer "c" and social information processing theory explains answers "a" and "b". For answer "d", as the chapter says, often we must experience something before having an attitude about it.

3. Attitudes lead to
   a. Other work attitudes.
   b. Employees' behavior.
   c. Nothing; they are an end in themselves.
   d. Important outcomes of socialization.

   > All of the above can be true at some time. Attitudes can lead to other attitudes, employee behavior, and outcomes of socialization. They can also just be an end in themselves, though they typically are connected over time to other attitudes and behaviors.

4. (Choose one of the following): Job satisfaction, Commitment, Turnover _____ is the most widely and commonly studied job attitude and the one most often assessed in organizations.

Job satisfaction! Although the other attitudes are studied, satisfaction with one's job has been the most heavily studied attitude over time.

5. If you are a manager and you want to change your employees' attitudes about their jobs, you are going to be more successful if you:
   a. Focus on something that the employees care about, and use strong arguments and logical reasoning to explain why their jobs are so important
   b. Highlight how the employees' attitudes are inconsistent with how they want to act on the job (e.g., employees feel fatigued and dissatisfied, yet want to be highly energetic and productive sales people)
   c. Conduct an employee satisfaction survey
   d. Unfortunately, the attitudes are unlikely to change no matter what you do

Answer "a" (based on Elaboration Likelihood Model) or "b" (based on cognitive dissonance) may be a good route to take. As for answer "c"—sometimes asking the questions actually can change attitudes, but it depends on too many other factors that may be outside your control. Just asking about attitudes is not the most successful way to change attitudes. Answer "d" is not the best answer because there is empirical research showing that attitudes can be changed. It may be true, however, that some attitudes are firmly locked into a person's value system, making those attitudes particularly resistant to change.

Chapter 5: Mini-Quiz: Performance

1. Which of the following are correct about this statement: When we think about employee "performance", it includes only what a person is expected to do and that they do it well.
   a. True! We can only monitor and consider what employees are expected to do based on the descriptions of their jobs
   b. Not always—"performance" can also include voluntary and extra tasks that are outside of a person's normal job
   c. False. There are many different ways to view performance, such as adaptability, completing specific tasks, and broad skills like communication
   d. Performance is not only tasks. We can understand performance better when we split it into *utility, efficiency, and productivity*.

All answers except "a" are correct. There are many ways to think about how an employee performs, such as the examples provided in answers "b", "c", and "d".

2. You manage an employee who is known for taking particularly long breaks. This person can get rather chatty with other workers and often distracts them from what they are supposed to be doing. You have spoken with your employee about this, but the situation doesn't seem to be improving. This troublesome employee is best described as:

a. Having low motivation
b. Being unethical
c. Engaging in counterproductive behavior
d. Using "extra-role" behaviors

> Answers "b" and "c" could be true, but it is very hard to tell simply based on this employee's behavior. This employee is best described as engaging in counterproductive behavior ("c"), which is any behavior counter to the organization's goals or that prevents others from successfully working towards achieving the organization's goals. "d" is incorrect, as extra-role behaviors tend to be helpful. These include behaviors, such as showing respect and courtesy to others.

3. As a leader in your organization, how can you help manage employee performance?
   a. Performance appraisals
   b. Consistent punishment
   c. Giving feedback
   d. Setting goals

> All of these answers are correct; leaders can help manage performance with any of these strategies, although some may be more effective than others depending on the situation. For example, punishment is rarely effective over the long run but can change some behaviors in the immediate moment.

4. You are a manager at a local grocery store and it is that time of year to have meetings with employees to talk about their performance—annual performance appraisal time! What can you do to make these meetings more successful?
   a. Clearly identify which behaviors were considered and rated when making the feedback report
   b. Have employees reflect on their own performance and evaluate their own performance
   c. Give the employee one, overall score. This is easier to understand and talk about
   d. Go through training yourself to better understand biases and common errors that people make when evaluating others

> Answer "a" can be quite helpful—creating behaviorally anchored ratings scales clarify what "good" versus "needs improvement" looks like in terms of concrete behaviors. Although self-ratings and ratings made by others can differ, answer "b" can be helpful because it sparks useful conversation between a manager and employee. Answer "d" is also correct; training has shown to reduce errors in manager ratings of performance. Answer "c" is rarely a good strategy. Many organizations do this, but it doesn't pinpoint what the employee is doing well and/or not doing well and provides no examples or information to support the rating. If the single score is accompanied by information and more detailed specifics about how the single score was obtained, it "could" be effective.

5. How can you help employees improve their performance?
    a. Focus on changing employees' personalities
    b. Provide opportunities to get more experience
    c. Pay people more money
    d. Do whatever it takes to make employees happy (i.e., have high satisfaction)

> Personality is often difficult to change, making "a" an unwise strategy. More experience is related to increased job knowledge, which often leads to higher performance ("b" is the correct answer). For answer "c", although money can be motivating, performance is not only about motivation but also knowledge of *how to* do a job. Plus, based on the chapter about motivation, money is not the only thing people care about. As for answer "d", satisfaction is positively related to performance, but again, being happy is not the only factor in improving performance.

Chapter 6: Mini-Quiz: Occupational Stress

1. Which of the following *best* characterizes how people generally talk about "stress" at work?
    a. Having a headache from balancing too many projects at work
    b. Struggling with an ongoing conflict with a coworker
    c. Feeling like you just cannot live up to your boss's expectations while working on a project
    d. Lifting heavy boxes all day as the main part of your job

> Answer "c" is probably the most common response people give when talking about stress at work. Answer "a" is better described as a strain, an outcome of the stress process. Answers "b" and "d" are characterized as stressors, things that lead to strains.

2. What sorts of factors affect how we experience stress?
    a. Personality
    b. Individual coping mechanisms
    c. Continued exposure to stressful events
    d. Having support from others

> All of these answers are correct. Different models and theories of stress explain how these components play into individuals' experiences of stress.

3. True or false: Stress can actually be good for employee performance.
    a. True! Eustress can create a positive energy for accomplishing work goals.
    b. It depends—some level of eustress is good for people, but distress most often leads to negative consequences.
    c. True, although eustress is rare and hardly ever discussed.
    d. False, stress feels negative and inhibits performance.

Answer "a" is true, although answer "b" is the better choice. We often talk about stress in the form of either positive or negative stress. *Eustress* is a term used to describe positive responses to stress, whereas distress is the term we use for describing negative stress. Answer "c" is incorrect—eustress is discussed in the literature; though probably not discussed in common conversation. Answer "d" is also correct, but fails to acknowledge that we can experience positive stress that can energize our performance. Thus, answer "b" is the best one.

4. Why should organizations care about stress?
    a. Stress is related to many job attitudes, such as job satisfaction and turnover intentions.
    b. While stress has negative individual outcomes, it doesn't typically impact employee performance, so organizations really shouldn't be too concerned.
    c. When employees are stressed, they are more likely to cause accidents so for safety reasons, organizations should care about stress.
    d. Organizations incur higher health care costs due to stress-related injuries and illnesses.

Answers "a", "c", and "d" are good choices because each of these can be the case for organizations that have "stressed" employees. Contrary to answer "b", stress can affect performance, giving organizations another reason to consider the impact of stress on employees.

5. Stress is not only about physiological responses but about a/an _____ the situation.
    a. Appraisal of
    b. Biological response to
    c. Instantaneous reaction to
    d. The cause of responses to

Answer "a" is correct—the appraisal of a situation is VERY important to understanding stress and how people will react to stressful situations. Answer "b" is similar to the question stem—physiological responses include our biological response. Answer "c" is sometimes correct—stress is not always instantaneous. Answer "d" is also true—as we talk about stress as a cycle and process, what causes our responses plays an important role.

Chapter 7: Mini-Quiz: Teams

1. Which of the following can be classified as a "team"?
    a. Two people who are working on a project together.
    b. Three coworkers who have been emailing each other to resolve a problem with one of the company policies.
    c. The finance department.
    d. A manager and the employees the manager supervises.

> Teams come in a variety of shapes and forms, have many combinations of people, and may perform any number of tasks. All of these groups can be considered a team.

2. True or false: Diversity in teams is highly desirable.
   a. False. Diverse teams often experience higher levels of conflict than non-diverse teams, which is not desirable for organizations.
   b. True. Having a variety of personalities, backgrounds, and skills can lead to greater team effectiveness.

   > This question is a bit of a tricky one. Most of the time, it depends on what kind of team you have, what task the team needs to accomplish, and what type of "diversity" you're referring to (ethnicity, skills, personality, etc.). At times, both of these answers may be correct. In general, diverse but complementary team members can increase the effectiveness of a team. However, teams made up of diverse members can lead experience significant conflict as well, that can reduce the team's effectiveness—at least until the team members learn how to work together.

3. What makes for an effective self-managed team?
   a. Teams need some sort of leader; if they are 'self-managed' they will fail.
   b. Clarifying the processes in the team, such as how to make decisions.
   c. Selecting team members who are experts and can work independently.
   d. Selecting team members who all have similar skills so they can work closely together to complete a given task.

   > Answer "a" is not correct; there are self-managed teams in organizations and they can be successful. Answers "b" and "c" are correct—both could help contribute to effectiveness for self-managed teams. Answer "d" is not correct because distributed leadership, where each member has a slightly different skill set to offer, can help the team be effective.

4. What special challenges do virtual teams face?
   a. Because communication can be so much easier and quicker virtually, teams can be very large, making it more difficult to keep up with everyone.
   b. Having a strong leader.
   c. Training employees to deal with conflict.
   d. Not having the ability to put "a face" to the people with whom you interact and work.

   > Answer "a" is the best choice here. Having a strong leader is actually one of the 'best practices' for virtual teams, making "b" the incorrect answer. Additionally, training may not be any more or less challenging for virtual teams, but may be more important to help members learn how to deal with conflict or establish good group processes. Not all virtual teams are completely virtual; teams that have any kind of interaction with virtual technology can be called "virtual" and so you may be able to have some face-to-face contact with your team members, yet still be considered a virtual team.

5. _____ are social guidelines for how to act in a particular group and when violated, may result in the group rejecting that particular team member.

> Norms!

Chapter 8: Mini-Quiz: Management

1. You are the manager of a regional hospital. Which of the following would be among your primary responsibilities?
   a. Helping teams of nurses set and achieve organizational level goals
   b. Working with others on the administrative team to create a mission and value statement for the organization
   c. Hiring and training new staff
   d. Developing new processes that contribute to a positive work environment at the hospital

   > Although managers can "lead" and leaders can "manage", the responsibilities listed in "a", "b", and "d" are more likely to fall under a leader's role. Therefore, answer "c" is the best choice here.

2. Leaders and managers can differ in:
   a. Personality
   b. Work tasks
   c. They aren't really different
   d. Focusing on people versus tasks

   > There is evidence that leaders and managers can differ in personality, day-to-day tasks, and what their focus is (tasks or people). Some people also suggest that answer "c" is correct and that there are more similarities than differences between managers and leaders. Hence, all of the above can be correct depending on the people themselves and the organization.

3. As a manager, you want to help your team members perform their jobs well. Giving feedback is an essential part of accomplishing this goal. What do we know about feedback that can help you advise your employees?
   a. Written feedback and defining negative consequences for poor performance are most effective
   b. Incorporating simple goals for improvement is important
   c. You should meet frequently with employees, rather than just once a year to do an annual review
   d. When working with a team, individual goals (rather than team goals) are most important for performance

Answer "a" could be improved by pairing verbal feedback with training and reinforcement (reinforcement affects behavior more consistently than punishment). As for "b", setting goals is a good idea, but unless there is training for *how* to accomplish the goals, employees may not be successful. Answer "d" is not the best answer here, as setting team goals is important when talking about *team* performance rather than individual performance. Thus, answer "c" is the best given the other alternative choices.

4. When giving feedback and helping develop employees, focusing on _____ will be more effective than focusing only on how to overcome weaknesses.

Strengths AND areas for improvement! Strengths-based approaches have shown to be very effective when developing employees, thus focusing on how building existing strengths AND using strengths to develop/improve areas where one is a little less capable is most effective.

5. How have management practices changed since the early 1900s when we started studying how to manage people?
   a. Management currently operates much like the military, using a "command and control" mentality
   b. Management today focuses on stability and highly structured systems
   c. Management today tries to embrace flexibility
   d. Management today is most concerned with the end result, or "management by objective"

Answers "a" and "b" refer more to early management practices and while they may still be approaches used today, modern management often tries to embrace flexibility, as in answer "c". Answer "d" describes transactional management approaches, which are only effective some of the time; thus shouldn't be used exclusively. Hence, flexibility in approach is again the best answer (c).

Chapter 9: Mini-Quiz: Leadership

1. As a leader of an organization, it is your job to influence people, attaining their buy-in for the organization's goals and direction. What technique is going to be most effective when gaining employee buy-in to your vision and mission?
   a. Coerce them—if people know there are negative consequences, they will fall in line and do what they are supposed to do for the organization.
   b. Reward them—if you give bonuses and other rewards, employees will like you and help drive organizational goals.
   c. Make it known you are the leader—if you use the "because I am the leader and I say so" mentality, employees will know who's boss and will complete tasks that you ask them to do.

d. Consistently share information—when you share information that employees want and need, they will accept you as a leader and will more readily follow you.

> "d" is the best answer here, though it does depend on the consistency of providing important information. Coercing and rewarding are not very effective for influencing people; they only help create compliance and depend on the consequence being severe enough or the reward being valued enough. Answer "c" refers to *legitimate* or *professional* power, which is also not very effective over the long-run.

2. True or false: Leaders are born, not made.
    a. False. The "trait" approach to leadership is not supported as a solo explanation for leadership; we can definitely train people to be better leaders.
    b. True. Personality is the most important factor for being a good leader.

> Answer "a" is correct—traits are not the be-all-end-all when it comes to leadership. People can learn to be better leaders. Research shows that personality can sometimes predict effective leadership behaviors, but more consistently predicts who will *become* a leader naturally.

3. What will help you be a better leader?
    a. Being intelligent
    b. Focusing on tasks rather than people/relationships
    c. Asking for input and involving your employees when making decisions
    d. Act in ways that are consistent with your own values

> Intelligence is related to effective leadership, which makes answer "a" a good choice. Answers "b" and "c" are also possible answers here because effective leadership can depend on the situation, which is a theme of this leadership. Answer "d" refers to *authentic leadership*, which has shown positive results so far, though more research is needed; thus, it is not clear yet how and to what extent leaders are considered better when acting consistent with their values, as opposed to the other response options for this question.

4. If you were going to train a group of management-level employees to be better leaders, what would you do:
    a. Select the employees of the managers and have them help explain what leadership they need
    b. Use traditional learning, such as reading books on leadership and having classes that employees can sign up for
    c. Pair employees with a mentor
    d. Provide opportunities after the training to follow-up with leaders and have them reflect on how they have changed

> Answer "c" or "d" is going to help make your leadership training more effective. Answer "a" is not an effective or advised approach, thus this answer is incorrect. Contrary to answer "b", traditional styles of training, such as taking formal classes, training is typically more effective for lower-level than managerial-level employees.

5. What might your organization face if it has a somewhat abusive or dictatorial leader?
   a. High turnover and people leaving the organization
   b. High prevalence of employee health problems
   c. Employees experiencing unusually high levels of stress at home as well as at work
   d. Employees performing better on the job

> All answers but "d" could be correct. *Abusive leadership* has recently been studied and we have come to understand some of the negative consequences of bad leaders.

Chapter 10: Mini-Quiz: Communication

1. Many employees say they prefer communicating face-to-face over email or phone. What might be some of the reasons?
   a. When talking face-to-face we can also receive nonverbal cues, which are essential for good communication
   b. You can see if the other person is paying attention
   c. If the person hasn't prepared what he or she wants to say, you can tell right away
   d. Sharing information face-to-face means you know it was received, whereas with email, people may not get the message or may not read it

> Answers "a" "b" and "d" are correct. With answer "c" you may not always know if someone wasn't prepared—he or she might be good at coming up with something to say, in the moment.

2. What are the main benefits to communicating electronically?
   a. You can more easily communicate with team members who are in a different location
   b. Some people may be more willing to express their true opinions via email rather than in-person
   c. Emails facilitate two-way, or synchronous, communication
   d. There is a record of the communication, making misunderstanding about what was said less likely

> All answers except "c" can be true. Contrary to answer "c", emails are "asynchronous" because only one person can respond at a time, instead of both talking at the same time and understanding each other, like in person.

3. Blogs have become more and more popular. How can organizations use blogging and make them effective for the company?
   a. Let employees loose! They have the best picture of the organization and will capture the true culture all on their own
   b. Make recommendations to employees about what type of language to use when blogging

c.　Terminate any employee who posts negative comments about the organization in an internal or external blog

d.　Encourage employees to share current events about the company as part of every blog entry

> The most important aspect of using blogging for organizations is to establish clear policies and procedures, making "a" an unwise choice. With careful planning and generating good policies, "b" or "d" could work out well for the organization. While there was a case where an organization terminated an employee for blogging personal and confidential information about patients, repercussions of blogging should be clearly outlined for employees before any actions are taken to avoid suggest extreme negative consequences.

4.　Written communication (e.g., letters) is used less frequently in many organizations. When might you want to use written communication rather than an email or phone call?

a.　When you have to communicate to a large number of people who need to know the information

b.　When giving feedback

c.　When providing a "thank you" that needs to convey personal importance

d.　When you want a record of the communication

> Answer "c" is the best here since a personally written thank you note conveys you took time, rather than an email that seems fast, easy, and less personal. Written communication is not advantageous when you want to reach a large group; email may be better in that case since it is cheaper, supports green conservation, and is faster. When giving feedback, it should be done in person, though sometimes you may want to write-up what was discussed so both parties have a record. Answer "d" is not the best because there are other ways than writing to create a record of communication (e.g., emails or phone recordings work too).

5.　When is communication especially important for organizations?

a.　During times of conflict and conflict resolution

b.　When going through large changes in the organization

c.　When the organization has members from a variety of national cultures

d.　When employees are sharing information informally among themselves

> Communication is pretty much *always* important! This chapter will give more information about communication in times of conflict and change and about how it can be utilized to convey cultural sensitivity.

Chapter 11: Mini-Quiz: Structure

1. What sorts of factors are relevant when talking about organizational "structure"?
   a. The size of the organization
   b. Organizational levels (i.e., who is the CEO, who are upper level managers, who are lower-level managers and non-administrative workers)
   c. Who has the control in the organization
   d. How information is communicated in the organization

   > Organizational "structure" may sound most similar to answer "b" but all of these factors come into the conversation when talking about structure.

2. _____, _____, and _____ are considered the "essential dimensions" of structure and are the most commonly discussed when understanding an organization's structure.
   a. Technology, leadership, and organization size
   b. Leadership, decision-making, and organizational levels
   c. Centralization, formalization, and complexity
   d. Communication, number of subunits, and geographic location

   > "c" is the best answer here. Structure can have many dimensions, but centralization, formalization, and complexity are key. This chapter provides information about these important parts of structure.

3. Why is organizational structure so important?
   a. Different factors related to the structure can influence employee attitudes, like job satisfaction
   b. Factors related to organizational structure can actually impact employee performance
   c. Depending on the structure of the organization, employees may perceive it as a fairer or less fair workplace
   d. Organizational structure is directly tied to communication and information sharing

   > All of these answers can be true! Organization structure influences many parts of an organization.

4. True or false? The structure of an organization may attract different kinds of employees.
   a. True! Some employees look for organizations with specific features and specific attributes
   b. False. When employees apply for jobs, they don't see or understand the inner workings of the organization

> Answer "a" is correct. Various dimensions of structure can be identified easily from company websites or news articles about the company. Thus, prospective employees can see what kind of structure the company has (to a degree) and decide if they want to apply to the company to learn more.

5. Some organizations have adopted flexible structures. Which of the following represents a more modern and flexible organizational structure?
    a. Virtual organizations
    b. Strategic alliances where one company joins another to temporarily solve a specific issue
    c. Boundaryless organizations that do not constrain themselves by size, or communication channels, etc.
    d. Organizations that adopt a particular division of labor so employees know who's doing what and how it fits into the bigger picture

> All answers except "d" are correct. "d" reflects a more traditional structure such as in bureaucratic organizations.

Chapter 12: Mini-Quiz: Organizational Change

1. If you are interested in applying to work at an organization, what would help you understand what the culture is like there?
    a. Reading through their policies and procedures
    b. Visiting the organization to see how peoples' offices and work spaces are arranged
    c. Looking at the company's mission and values statement
    d. Asking current employees about their benefits and other ways they are rewarded and recognized

> Answer "a" would give you clues about the organizational *climate*, which is related to, but different from the organization's overall culture. However, each of these could give you good insight into how the organization operates and what it's like to work there.

2. Which of the following best represents organizational culture?

> Answer "b" represents Schein's 3-level view of culture. Other factors like leadership and communication are important and related to culture, but "b" is your best answer here because it captures the layers of norms, values, and how culture is solidified.

3. Why do many organizations seem to have a story about them, like how a young couple took a bike trip through Belgium in 1988 and were inspired to launch New Belgium Brewing Company, how three University of San Francisco students started Starbucks, or how Louis Vuitton started in 1854 as a luggage maker building flat-topped trunks?

a. Legends are a unique way to transmit culture to new employees
b. They are fun to share and catch people's interest
c. Leaders are more likely to get employees to act how they want if they tell stories
d. Legends are based on true events, but are sometimes embellished to make information more memorable

> Answers "a" and "d" are correct. *Narratives*, or stories, are one category of organizational culture according to Trice & Beyer's view. Answers "b" and "c" may be true but are not relevant to why many organizations continue to share the "legend" about how they were formed.

4. What is the largest barrier to organizational change?
   a. Change isn't actually that hard; it's getting the change to stick, to make a lasting change, that is most difficult
   b. People do not like change, so they tend to resist it
   c. Norms that currently exist in the organization
   d. Leaders often don't know how to make changes and really can't be trained to be better in initiating change

> Answer "d" is not correct because as discussed in chapter 9, leaders can be trained in many skills. Answers "a" and "b" are true, but norms ("c") are especially difficult to change and are a significant barrier to organizational change efforts.

5. Which of the following that we have learned about in previous chapters could also be an effective organizational change strategy?
   a. Structural changes
   b. Team building exercises
   c. Job redesign
   d. Performance feedback

> Depending on the organization and the desired change, all of these could facilitate organizational change!

Chapter 13: Mini-Quiz: Organizational Strategy

Fill in the blanks to complete this diagram:

> Mission, Vision, Strategy

1. In the 1980s, organizational strategists began to focus on processes like decision-making, biases, heuristics, and attribution errors. This movement added what focus to organizational strategy that still predominates today?
   a. Transactional leadership
   b. Cognitive perspective
   c. Organizational structure
   d. Organizational change

> The correct answer here is "b"—cognitive psychology was growing rapidly in the 1980s and its influence impacted our understanding of organizational strategy.

2. Developing organizational strategy is an internal effort, but there are important *external* factors to consider. Which of these external factors should be considered, as it will shape the organization's strategy?
   a. Technology
   b. Allocation of resources
   c. Politics
   d. Core Competencies

> Answers "a" and "c" are correct. Answers "b" and "d" are important *internal* factors to consider.

3. Who is likely to be invested in the organization's strategy?
   a. Customers
   b. Suppliers and distributors
   c. Front-line workers
   d. The company leadership team

> While all of these people/groups may not actively be invested in the organization's strategy, they sure should be! Anyone who is associated with the organization can be affected by the strategy and so may have investment in it.

4. "Strategic leadership" is a term often used to describe what?
   a. Ability to anticipate the future
   b. Empowering of others in the organization
   c. Focusing on the tasks that must be accomplished for organizational success
   d. Maintaining current status to secure market share

> Answers "a" and "b" are correct, as they are part of the definition for strategic leadership. Answer "c" is most similar to *transactional leadership*, and so is not the best answer here. Answer "d" is not strategic leadership, but is one example of a strategy; a leader may decide to focus on 'maintaining' or may take a different strategy that requires growth and expansion.

GLOSSARY

360-degree feedback Feedback process that entails asking peers, subordinates, bosses, and clients for feedback on the leader, essentially creating a 360-degree perspective of how the person being rated is perceived.

Academy of Management A professional association dedicated to the study of management, which represents management and organizational scholars worldwide.

Action research An approach, credited to Kurt Lewin, where organizations and researchers collaborate on studying specific problems within the organization and then apply the results to solve those organizational problems. Refers to a partnership between an organization and researcher collaborating in the cyclical process of problem identification, hypothesizing the cause of a problem, collecting data to test the hypothesis, and then testing to determine the cause.

Affiliation Relationship with another person or group. Usually referred to in Maslow's Hierarchy of Needs as a component of social needs, in communicating a form of relationship, or association with political group who shares similar views.

Affirmative action Policy that rectifies imbalances related to race, gender, or ethnicity.

Alpha, beta, gamma change Alpha change involves process changes and arguably the only real form of change that can be assessed in organizations. Alpha change is noted when a group scores higher on a scale than it did previously, but there is no examination of the actual rating instrument or how people perceive the rating instrument. Thus, a group of people can be asked to rate their perception of the culture on a scale of 1 to 5, and if their previous score averaged a 2 and their current score now averages a 4, we would say that we have an alpha change.

Beta change refers to the change in people's perceptions of how they are being assessed—thus, the markers or events they used previously to determine if something has changed, take on a different meaning than they did previously. Using the example above, we note the change in average score, but now when you're asked to use that same rating scale, it turns out

that you don't view the numbers the same way. You've recalibrated what a 5 means from the previous time you thought what a 5 meant. Thus, a beta change is a recalibration of the measurement tool, rather than an actual change in behavior or perceptions. In this case, the culture didn't change—your cognition of what a 5 means is what change.

Gamma change refers to a change in the understanding of the construct. As a consequence of an OD intervention, people may view the organization differently, but it may not necessarily reflect that the organization itself changed. It might just be a redefinition of what was being changed. For example, efforts to change the culture from one that doesn't care about employee safety to one that does may result in people describing the culture as aggressive and focused on creating the best products. The concept of creating safety may have been redefined in terms of creating better products and perhaps one way to do so is in being safer. However, the measurement of safety is no longer appropriate given the new definition of what the culture is. It is typically a gamma change that is sought in OD interventions.

American Psychological Association The APA is an association dedicated to the scientific and professional study and practice of psychology and represents psychologists in the United States.

Antecedents (predictors) Predictors are constructs used to determine when another variable will occur—they come before the variable of interest, and are therefore called antecedents.

Anticipatory socialization Communication and information gathering that occurs just before an employee actually enters as a new hire into an organization. It is a step in the socialization process before the actual socialization within the organization occurs.

Asynchronous Refers to communication that does not occur linearly. The transmission of data that does not happen at regular intervals, but instead takes place outside of any logical order.

Attitudes Attitudes are summary evaluations of a psychological object, such as a person, people, place, or event. These evaluations are based on beliefs, feelings, and/or on past behavior, either ours' or others'.

Autonomy   Refers to how much freedom, independence, control, or discretion the employee has to perform their work, and when to schedule the work.

Benchmarks   Benchmarking specifically refers to the process of comparing results from business to business; the standard results to which each business is compared is called the benchmark.

Bureaucracy   Refers to a type of organizational structure that Weber proposed would make the organization more efficient.

C-suite   The level of an organization at which executives hold positions that are titled or labeled beginning with Chief, such as Chief Executive Officer, Chief Operating Officer, and Chief Technology Officer.

Cafeteria-style benefits   Type of approach to offering employee benefits, where employees can choose between several options, tailoring their benefits to match their needs. The array of options are lined up like a buffet, hence the name cafeteria-style.

Carbon footprint   The amount of greenhouse emissions created by the use or burning of environmental resources, such as coal, trees, or minerals by an organization. For example, air travel has a very large carbon footprint—airplanes burn a tremendous amount of fuel that leaves a very large carbon trail.

Carpal tunnel syndrome   A compression of the median nerve in the carpal tunnel where the nerve passes through the wrist into the hand. Occurs as a result of repetitive motion.

Case study   A report based on a single organization, person, or phenomenon.

Citizenship behaviors   Performance behaviors that are not formally expected within a job role but that when displayed tend to advance the functioning of the organization. Sometimes referred to as "going above and beyond" the job expectations, helping behaviors, extra-role performance, and contextual performance.

Collectivistic   Refers to a cultural emphasis on fitting in, belonging, connections with others, and distinguishing between in-groups and out-groups. The expectation is that the in-group (e.g., relatives, organization) looks after each other and is loyal to one another at the expense of the self. The value is for the group decision and what helps or benefits the group, as opposed to the self.

Common method bias   Also known as common method variance. Refers to spurious variance that

is attributed to having collected all the data using a single method, such as one survey, rather than to actual variance that explains true relationships between variables. It is a biasing that occurs when measuring focal variables using the same method and then assessing their relationship to one another.

Commitment   Also referred to as organizational commitment. Refers to an emotional attachment or identification with the organization and its values. Employees who are committed to the organization report feeling like family, like they belong.

Competency   In this textbook, it refers to the knowledge, skill, and ability requirements of an employee given a particular job role or organization. An organization's core competency could be speed of product delivery. The competencies required for a job are the skills, knowledge, and ability categories required to do that job (e.g., decision-making, programming)

Computer-mediated communication   Communication that occurs via the computer—such as the Internet (e.g., Skype), chat rooms, or virtual communication tools.

Conscientiousness   A personality trait characterized by attention to detail, structure, planning, efficiency, dependability, self-discipline, and follow through.

Consequences (outcomes)   The dependent variable in an experiment; what the predictor predicts. The variables that an organization is trying to change or understanding, such as employee attitudes or performance.

Constituencies   Interested parties; body of individuals most interested in a particular outcome. A group of supporters.

Contextual performance   Also referred to as citizenship behaviors, extra-role behaviors. Other activities that do not fall under task performance but are still important for organizational effectiveness. Includes volunteering, extra enthusiasm or effort to complete tasks successfully, helping, following organizational rules, and endorsing, supporting, or defending organizational objectives.

Contingency planning   Anticipating issues and readying a plan to address them.

Counterproductive work behaviors   Negative action, such as taking excessively long breaks or negative gossiping, which harm the organization or its members. The actions are not always intended to be harmful. Examples of counterproductive work behaviors include avoiding work, incorrectly performing tasks, aggression, verbal abuse such as being rude and insulting, theft, sexual harassment, rumor spreading, sabotage, and disruptive behavior.

Criminality Refers to being a criminal or illegal, forbidden behaviors.

Cross-functional Refers to a type of team that takes advantage of the diversity of skills among team members. Such teams are made up of employees from various functional areas across the organization, such as marketing, technical writing, customer service, production, design, and manufacturing. Most often the employees work at the same organizational hierarchical level; hence, they are peers, but not within the same team.

Cross-training Learning a few new skills or processes that allow you to fill in for others in their job roles when needed. Those job roles are still within your job family, so you're not learning an entirely new job—just new skills that allow you to fulfill more roles than just the current one. For example, working as a barista but cross-trained at the register as well.

Dissonance An unpleasant tension that drives or motivates the person to reduce the unpleasant state.

Distress Negative stress, such as anxiety.

E-commerce Business conducted on the Internet, such as online stores (e.g., Amazon.com engages in e-commerce).

Employee assistance programs Programs established by human resource departments to provide short-term counseling or related assistance providing referrals to counseling professionals, or encouraging time off from work.

Employee engagement A psychological state of motivation at work, where we are physically, cognitively, and emotionally absorbed and focused on the work. Also defined as feeling dedicated, vigorous, and absorbed at work.

Environmental sustainability Making decisions and taking actions that support protecting the planet and ensuring its survivability. Actions that preserve the ability to continue life on the planet, which promote new growth and not just maintenance.

European Association of Work and Organizational Psychology EAWOP is an association dedicated to the development and application of work and organizational psychology in Europe.

Eustress Positive stress, such as a challenge.

Expectancy Belief that actions and efforts will actually influence levels of performance.

Extra-role performance behaviors Actions employees take that contribute to the overall functioning of the organization and potentially the organization's goals, but that generally fall outside of the specific job requirements or defined job role.

Extraversion Being outgoing and social, and needing or thriving on interactions with others.

Extrinsic motivation About people doing things because those things are externally rewarded (e.g., pay, incentive, recognition from others). You are motivated because something external to you is reinforcing your behavior—you are not motivated by an internal drive.

Force The motivating potential resulting from the multiplicative power of valence, instrumentality, and expectancy.

Fortune 500 The top 500 companies ranked by Fortune Magazine, in terms of their financial performance. Generally a list of America's largest and most financially profitable companies.

Fossil fuels Fuels formed as a consequence of normal planet activity—examples include coal, oil, and natural gas. They are hydrocarbons formed from dead plants and animals that have decayed and been exposed to heat and pressure in the earth for millions of years. Fossil fuels are nonrenewable sources of energy.

Framework Model, theoretical structure, or abstract scaffolding that holds different thoughts together and forms the basis on which other thoughts can be built or explained.

Frustration regression Movement back down the needs hierarchy to focus on lower-order needs. A feature of ERG theory.

Fundamental attribution error A bias that occurs when we attribute our successes to internal factors and failures to external factors, but attribute others' successes to external factors and failures to internal factors.

Gantt chart A planning tool named after Henry Gantt in the early 1900s.

Globalization The interconnectivity of the world's cultures, economies, and political systems.

Group norms Unspoken or informal rules or guidelines that group members hold or value, which govern their behaviors as part of the group.

Hawthorne effect The workers increased their performance with the introduction of novel treatment, after which their performance returned to normal. This change in behavior following the onset of novel treatment (in this case, being a part of an important study) was termed the *Hawthorne Effect*.

Hawthorne studies   Series of experiments between 1924 and 1933 at Western Electrical Company's Hawthorne Works Plant near Chicago, Illinois.

Hierarchy   A classification or arrangement that follows a ranking where one concept is ranked or given more power than a concept below it in the rank-order.

High potentials   Employees identified as having a high potential for success, typically in some kind of leader role.

Homeostasis   State in which the system, in this case human, is stable, even-keeled, and relatively in balance.

Homeostatic physiological mechanisms   People seek or are driven to balance or resolve dissonance (discomfort), preferring a state of homeostasis or equilibrium. Control theory is an example of general theory of regulation that is based on homeostatic physiological mechanisms, such as internal body chemistry or motivational drive.

Human capital   An economic view of employees, where in the cost and value are assigned based on knowledge, skills, and other social attributes of employees.

Human relations movement   A period of history characterized by researchers interested in motivation theories and the emotional world of workers. The human relations movement emphasized people as individuals with specific and unique needs, and as people with desires for creativity.

Hygiene factors   Dissatisfiers in Herzberg's two-factor theory. These are factors of the job, such as pay or working conditions, which prevent dissatisfaction but do not cause satisfaction.

Individualistic   Refers to a cultural emphasis on individuals making their own decisions that benefit or focus on their own needs rather than the group's needs. The individual is valued about the group. The United States is considered a very individualistic society.

Industrial psychology   A subfield of psychology that complements the study of organizational psychology, with its intense focus on the individual in organizations. Industrial psychology focuses on the design and practice of exposing how individuals differ from one another, to facilitate creating a workplace that distinguishes where and how they fit.

Interdependence   Refers to how much team members must rely on each other to complete their job tasks. The mutual dependence may be emotional, task-based, or economical.

Instrumentality   The belief that actions and efforts taken to achieve or obtain the outcome will be rewarded.

Inter-rater agreement   The amount of agreement between two raters rating the same task or assessment of someone. Agreement of ratings between multiple peers, usually in peer performance assessments.

Intervention   An intervention in an organization is a planned event or action that is designed to change the culture or climate, or change specific variables of interest such as behavior in a particular unit. It is generally a solution to a problem and takes various forms such as a workshop, coaching, new forms or policies, changes to staffing or organizational structure, a job redesign, and other actions that create change.

Intrinsic motivation   Motivation driven by internal sources. People doing things because those things are interesting and satisfying; they are self-rewarding.

Job boards   Website that posts job advertisements or job listings for multiple jobs from various different companies. Central location for job ads.

job insecurity   The real or perceived threat of losing your job.

Job involvement   The centrality of work in your life and to how important work is to your self-identity and self-image.

Job performance   The collection of behaviors or actions taken on the job to complete the expectations or requirements.

Job redesign   Approaches to changing aspects of the job that lead to increased motivation. Job redesign includes approaches, such as job rotation, job enrichment, and job enlargement.

Job swapping   Changing jobs with someone else in order to increase skill and/or task variety and to encourage cross-training. Temporarily changing jobs with someone else.

Leader emergence   The process by which a person is recognized as a leader by others in the group or surrounding organization.

Leaderless team   Self-managed teams; groups without an officially designated leader or manager.

Leader-member exchange Describes the relationship between leaders and individual group members; a relationship wherein the follower is either in the "in-group" enjoying the benefits of a close relationship with the leader in exchange for giving performance or information that the leader might otherwise struggle to obtain, or in the "out-group" wherein the follower is excluded from receiving special support and insider status with the leader.

Leadership Primary emphasis in leadership is on influencing people to focus on achieving organizational goals while achieving their own goals, as well as on creating a supportive work climate where people want to accomplish the work at hand.

Management Primary objective of management is to accomplish the task or project. Management is a term for the group of people whose jobs are to accomplish the organizational goals using all resources efficiently.

Management by Objectives or MBO To manage by defining objectives for achieving organizational goals and then manage employees, through mutual agreements, to achieve those objectives. Both employees and managers agree on and understand the objectives.

Manifests Display, show, demonstrate, indicate, or presents.

Mastery-goal orientation An approach to goal-setting that is based on the desired to master knowledge, skills, and ability. An orientation toward achievement, which suggests that the focus is on learning, improving, and becoming an expert.

Market share Percentage of total sales in a particular industry or product line.

Mediating Intervening; explanatory mechanism that says why X relates to Y. The effects of X are transmitted on Y via the mediating variable—the variable in the middle between X and Y.

Meta-analysis Statistical technique for combining the results of many different studies to identify patterns in findings. The technique takes into account different sample sizes, effect sizes of findings, and methodological differences in how studies were conducted.

Mission A proclamation or statement that the organizational leaders write, which states what the goal of the organization is or what it is striving to accomplish. The statements tend to be very comprehensive and espouse values, as well.

Moderating A variable that changes the effects of X on Y, by either increasing or decreasing the effect.

Motivation A psychological concept developed to explain why people get involved in, engage in, take action toward, do, or get excited about things. Discretionary—energy, arousal, or effort a person chooses to devote to a task or action. Results from within a person.

Motivators Factors in the work environment that cause satisfaction, according to Herzberg's two-factor theory. Elements of work such as how meaningful it is, or how much recognition a person gets can make people feel satisfied with their jobs. Meaningfulness and recognition are considered motivators.

Multisource rating systems An evaluation system that relies on ratings from many different sources, such as one's boss, subordinates, peers, customers, or friends. The ratings are combined and examined to determine how people see you and whether your self-perception is different from their perception of you. Helps you to determine how others see you.

Narcissism Overwhelming or excessive self-admiration and self-interest. Self-centered and excessive preoccupation with personal adequacy and prestige or power.

Norms Norms are social rules for what behavior is accepted and expected—they prescribe how one should behave. They are formed and governed by the people within the social network and social situation.

Neurological and/or physiological arousal Neurological arousal is an active state or heightened awareness in the brain—excited nervous system that is ready for attention and responsiveness. Physiological arousal is an active state or heightened awareness of one's physiology or body. The body is alert or excited.

O*NET Occupational Information Network. An online resource of detailed job descriptions or occupational information. A database of hundreds of standardized occupation-specific descriptors.

Occupational health psychology A discipline dedicated to the study of health, well-being, and safety in the workplace (e.g., offices, agricultural settings, manufacturing), and stress is just one of the major topics of focus within this discipline.

Occupational stress Specifically refers to the process whereby work or job-related stress responses are triggered by factors at work that may be situational, contextual/environmental, or psychological/social, and that force employees to deviate from their normal feelings or behaviors.

Onboarding   Refers to the process of form completion, equipment assignment, personnel records, issues regarding regulatory compliance, and the physical aspect of introducing new employees to the organization. Onboarding may also include sending the employee documents sharing the company history, but the primary focus of onboarding is the form completion, equipment allocation, and other human resource functions.

Organizational behavior (OB)   Multidisciplinary field of study, extracting knowledge from areas such as economics, sociology, anthropology, and political science, as well as psychology.

Organizational citizenship behaviors   Also called contextual performance. Helping behaviors that support performance in the organization. Often considered voluntary or extrarole behaviors.

Organizational climate   Refers to how individuals in organizations experience and make sense of their work environment. It refers to the day-to-day procedures, policies, routines, and rewards that people experience regularly while working every day.

Organizational culture   Organizational culture refers to how individuals in organizations experience and make sense of their work environment, and what components go into creating a shared organizational experience.

Organizational development   Organizational climate refers to the day-to-day procedures, policies, routines, and rewards that people experience regularly while working day in and day out.

Organizational psychology   A distinct subfield within psychology that draws from other subfields of psychology such as social psychology and cognitive psychology. The lens of organizational psychology incorporates both the individual and group.

Organizational strategy   The outlook and goals for the organization. Can be the market position, plan, or ploy for achieving a goal or vision.

Organization   Organized or coordinated bodies of people, people who come together to achieve a common goal; is an entity made up of many people, with policies and rules for interaction, and with policies.

Paradigm   Model, framework (e.g., prototype, or pattern).

Paralanguage   Vocal expressions that contribute to the understanding of messages in communication.

Performance appraisal   An evaluation of an employee's performance. The appraisal is typically a report or feedback session in which the evaluation of how well the employee has fulfilled his or her job role and expectations is shared.

Performance management   Refers to how organizations use appraisals and feedback to make performance-based decisions and improve employee performance. Performance management refers to a "systematic, data-oriented approach to managing people at work that relies on positive reinforcement as the major way to maximizing performance."

Performance-goal orientation   A mindset driven by achieving a goal, accomplishing an outcome, regardless of whether any learning occurred along the way. The focus is on getting the task done.

Person–environment fit   P–E fit theory suggests strains are experienced when a lack of congruency between the person and his or her environment exists in the form of demands in excess of and incongruent with what a person can handle, or in the form of an incongruence between a person's needs and what the environment supplies.

Person–organization fit   Refers to how well and individual's values match those of the organization. A congruence or incongruence between the person's needs and values with those of the organization.

PERT chart   Program Evaluation and Review Technique Chart—a planning tool that tracks amount of time activities take.

Power distance   Describes the degree to which the society accepts power differences in organizations or institutions. A high power distance culture accepts that power is distributed unevenly. In organizations, lower levels within the organization accept and respect that higher levels in the organization have more power and authority.

Predictor   Predictors are constructs use to determine when another variable will occur—they come before the variable of interest. Also known as antecedents.

Proactive personality   Tendency to seek out and act on opportunities to create change.

Program managers   A program manager is responsible for managing the production of a solution or product that has many associated projects. A program manager engages in project management on a large scale, coordinating several different projects that are all interconnected.

Project management   Project management is the effort and application of techniques to ensure the execution of the plan from start to finish.

Project plan   A project plan maps out the tasks, resources, and timeline required to achieve a particular goal, which is usually a product, service, or other outcome that is desired.

Psychological capital   A construct that represents a psychological state comprising self-efficacy, hope, optimism, and resilience.

Psychological contracts   A concept that represents the unspoken and unwritten obligations that employees expect of the organization and that the organization expects of the employees.

Psychological withdrawal   Pulling back of oneself, mentally, from the work environment. Mentally checking out on the job.

Quality circles   Temporary groups of diverse members across the organization established to focus on a quality issue, such as obtaining and maintaining zero defects.

Quasi-experimental study   A study in which participants cannot be randomly assigned or the independent variable cannot be manipulated. Quasi-experiments typically occur in the field as opposed to the laboratory.

Recruitment   Process an organization undertakes to encourage job applicants to apply to the organization's job openings.

Renewable resources   Resources that are self-sustaining or can be regrown or replaced. Naturally replenishing resources, typically regenerating as fast as they are used. Examples include sunlight or wind.

Role Ambiguity   Refers to unclear expectations about your role at work. That means the objectives or purpose of your role is unclear, and therefore, you do not know if your performance will meet expected levels.

Role Conflict   Incompatible or competing sets of expectations about the job or tasks associated with the job.

Scientific management   Also known as Taylorism. Emphasized scientific methods to improve productivity and efficiency.

Self-actualization   Refers to the desires for fulfilling one's maximum potential; the top of Maslow's Hierarchy of Needs.

Self-efficacy   Belief in one's ability to perform a specific task or achieve a goal.

Self-managed teams   Teams that have no formal leader or manager. The team members manage themselves.

Self-regulatory or self-regulation   Ability to self-manage internal systems to achieve homeostasis.

Shareholders   Shareholders include people or groups with a financial investment in the organization, whose focus rests entirely on the financial value of the organization.

Social cognitive theory   A learning theory that says we learn by interacting in our social context, such as learning by observing others.

Social–emotional intelligence   Form of intelligence or awareness that is tied to self-awareness, self-management, and social awareness of others and our relationship with others.

Socialization   Refers to the ongoing process of sharing the values, beliefs, and norms of the organizational culture with new employees. It is how newcomers (whether new to the entire organization or just new to a particular team) learn what is expected of them and not allowed in the group.

Socialization tactics   Actions taken to bring people into the organization and influence their behavior.

Society for Human Resource Management, SHRM   Organization that represents human resource professionals worldwide.

Sociopathic personality   Also called antisocial personality, characterized by a lack of remorse or shame, disregard for the feelings of others, lack of empathy, and manipulative behavior displayed to achieve one's own goals. Can be very creative and charming until you are no longer useful in achieving the goal. Very good at telling lies. May be very bright and can be very hurtful.

Staffing plan   Staffing plans identify who works on the project, at what point in time, and for how long, coordinating parts so that everything is done at the right time and when needed.

Stakeholders   Person, group, or business with a vested interest in the organization. Can influence or affect the organization because of their support and direct influence.

Strain   Response or reaction to the stressor

Strategy   The outlook and goals for the organization. Can be the market position, plan, or ploy for achieving a goal or vision.

Status reports A report that subordinates usually provide to their managers to update them on their progress on their work tasks or on a particular project. Reports can take various forms from one page to multiple pages depending on the job and project. Due dates are set by the manager or lead.

Stressors Used to describe the various stimuli that evoke a response indicative of stress.

Subject reactivity Participants or subjects in a research study reacting to their awareness of those observing them or the study manipulations.

Synchronous Refers to communication that occurs in real-time and allows for simultaneous conversations—one can speak over another—and both parties can hear the other. When one person talks, it does not cut off the other partner's ability to talk. It is usually compared to asynchronous communication.

Task forces A group pulled together to work on a specific task. Temporary groups established to solve a particular problem, like how to assign shared space and equipment or develop a plan for distributing grant funds.

Taxonomy A categorization or classification system.

Taylorism Also known as scientific management.

Teams A group comprised two or more people working together to accomplish a common set of goals.

Teleconferencing Meetings conducted by phone or other telecommunication devices to ensure participation from individuals at different locations.

Trait A characteristic or quality of a person that is usually a stable attribute. A personality trait is a pattern of behavior that characterizes some aspect of someone's personality, such as conscientiousness or extraversion.

Transformation Refers to a dramatic or large change.

Turnover Quitting or leaving the job or organization.

Typology A classification system ordered by type, such as type of job or type of leadership.

Valence The value given to a particular outcome.

Virtual teams Teams whose members work in different locations from one another and must use computer-mediated communication to work together. A geographically dispersed group of people, who work across time and location.

Vision Refers to a very broad picture of the future, what the organization intends to become; provides the long-range goals for the organization.

Voice Usually associated with "giving employees' voice," which means giving employees an opportunity to share their opinion, input, or feedback.

Voting power Ability to vote on a decision an organization makes, where the decision is influential and not just "interesting input." Where the vote makes a difference.

INSTRUCTOR RESOURCE

Sample reflection questions for each Chapter

Chapter 1

1. What is the relationship between organizational psychology and organizational behavior? Using your own words, explain how they are similar and/or different from each other (and do not say money or salary)?
2. In your own words, describe the scientist–practitioner model, its benefits, and potential drawbacks.
3. Although several important events are mentioned in Chapter 1, one significant historical event, in particular, marked the beginning of organizational psychology. Briefly say what you believe that event was and explain in your own words why this event was so important to the development of organizational psychology. Describe how you have seen this same process, the one described in this major event, unfold in one of your classes.

Chapter 2

1. Your job is to identify motivational practices that will work best for the employees of a particular organization. Out of the methods in Chapter 2, explain which you would use for data collection. Using your own words, describe the advantages of the method you picked and the disadvantages of the methods you did not pick?
2. Explain what multiple regression can tell you that a plain correlation cannot. In your answer, describe the advantages of using multiple regression.
3. Why is it important to consider statistical power in research? If you were conducting research in an organization, when and how would you take steps to improve statistical power for your study?

Chapter 4

1. The readings refer to at least two taxonomies of job performance, Campbell's and Murphy's. In your own words, compare and contrast the two models—what are the features of each that make them similar to one another, and those that make them unique? (Do not repeat the information provided in the Tables). Why would you use one over the other?
2. The readings referred to two other forms of job performance, OCBs, and innovation. How are they similar to and different from one another? How does an organization promote OCBs and innovation, and why would an organization want to promote both?
3. Based on the readings, what would you recommend a manager do to measure his/her employees' job performance? What method(s) would you use, and what are its advantages? What are some potential problems the manager would face when measuring performance?

(Continued)

(Continued)

Chapter 5	1. An organization would like to examine its employees' job satisfaction. From the reading, which measure should the organization use? What information would they obtain from the measure? What are the advantages of the measure you recommend over the others?
	2. Using previous research findings reviewed in the readings to make your case, how would you convince the organization that increasing satisfaction and commitment would benefit them?
	3. The reading briefly reviews other job attitudes. From these attitudes, select two that you believe organizations should be concerned about. Explain why they should matter to organizations—what do these attitudes tell them about their employees that job satisfaction and commitment do not?
Chapter 6	1. Managers and coworkers often make the fundamental attribution error when assessing the causes of employee/coworker counterproductive behavior. Provide an example of this error from your own experiences and then explain what other possible causes for counterproductive might exist (provide at least two and explain them).
	2. Compare and contrast Mobley's model of turnover from Chapter 5 with Lee and Mitchell's Unfolding Model in Chapter 6. Because the book offers how they are similar to each other, focus on the main differences.
	3. Substance use and sexual harassment are listed as less common forms of counterproductive work behaviors (CWB) in the reading. Because these CWBs may not occur often or may not be reported, should organizations be concerned about their effect on their employees? Explain your answer using information from the reading and using your own words.
Chapter 7	1. Consider the different types of workplace stressors described in the reading. Certainly, you have experienced these types of stressors from your schoolwork and/or job. Give us some examples of your perceived stressors, and use the language/labels from the reading to identify the types of stressors and strains you have experienced.
	2. The reading gives an overview of theoretical models that have been used to understand how employees experience and respond to stress in the workplace. Taking a broad look across the models, what are some differences between the models? Which model best explains the stressors you perceive at work or school and your reactions (strains) to them?
Chapter 8	1. We can generally surmise that people motivate themselves—you cannot motivate someone to do something they do not want to do. How do the need-based, job-based, and cognitive-based theories of motivation help us in organizational psychology? (Do not just give the practical value as provided in the reading) Why are we spending so much time and effort learning these theories if we cannot motivate people—they have to motivate themselves?
	2. Consider the job-based theories presented in the reading. Does the given explanation match how you consider yourself motivated in your job or at school? Why? Why not?

(Continued)

(Continued)

Chapter 9	Management has made you aware of performance problems in your department and has asked you to develop a solution. You determined that motivation is the problem and that job redesign is the solution to motivate the employees (i.e., the clerical/janitorial examples from the reading are NOT appropriate here; think of engineers, lawyers, nurses, doctors, or technicians and pick one type of employee for your answers). 1. Which approach (from the reading) will you use to motivate the employees (tell us which employee type you are motivating)? 2. Justify the redesign's cost and time commitments to upper management—here is where you are convincing them that your approach is worth the cost. 3. If you were to use a reward system to motivate employees in this job, what reward would you use? What differences in motivation would you expect when using tangible versus intangible reward?
Chapter 10	1. The chapter refers to three different approaches to leadership: trait, behavioral, and contingency. Compare and contrast these three approaches (how are they similar and how are they different from each other). 2. Given your personal job/work situation, which of the contingency leader theories best describes your current boss' style, or best describes the style your current boss *should* have if he/she were to be more effective. If you do not currently work in a job outside of school, then use one of your professors as the boss (no names please). Give enough details so that we can understand why that leadership theory fits your situation, and so that it is clear that you understand that theory. 3. Consider the types of power presented in the reading. Using three of the bases of power, provide examples of how they are used by leaders in organizations.
Chapter 11	1. Talk about a group in which you are currently or have previously been a member. What is/was the structure of the group (norms, values, your individual role, etc.)? Which model, referred to in the reading, would you use to describe the process of the development of the group you just identified? Use examples to illustrate why this model best describes your group. 2. Identify and describe conflicts you experienced while working in a team. Explain the cause of the conflicts. Was the cause covered in the chapter? What steps from the chapter did/could the group take to resolve the conflict?
Chapter 12	1. Critique and evaluate whether Gladstein's model is better than Hackman's model for understanding team effectiveness; provide a clear and succinct explanation for your evaluation. Remember: a critique and evaluation is a judgment about the model—it is not a "list the missing parts" or "list the different components of the model" question. 2. Now critique and evaluate your winner (either Gladstein's or Hackman's model) from the question above against Campion's model, and explain which is the best in understanding team/group effectiveness.

(Continued)

(Continued)

	3. In your experience working in teams, which determinants of team effectiveness from the reading have had the greatest impact on your teams' performance? Describe how they impacted performance. If you were to create a team now, what would you do to ensure future success? What types of reward (individual or team level) would you use and why?
Chapter 14	Imagine you are a researcher interested in studying organizational culture and a local organization has agreed to let you study their culture. Use the information presented in the book to answer these questions:

1. Why would you be interested in studying organizational culture? In your own words, what will you learn from studying the organization's culture?
2. Which method will you use to measure the organizational culture? Why is this the best method for your study? (i.e., compare and contrast your selected method with the other possibilities)
3. Who or what will you consult to obtain information about the culture? (e.g., managers, employees, organizational records, etc.). Why are these the best sources of information about the organizational culture?

Two Questions we Ask Every Time:

In your own words, what are the top three most important concepts you learned from this module?

What specifically, if anything, did you find confusing or do you wish was covered in more detail? **[Do not just list major section headings in the book]**

INDEX